Anti-social Behaviour Orders

Special Bulletin

Fourth Edition

Anesh Pema and Sharon Heels

JORDANS

Published by
Jordan Publishing Limited
21 St Thomas Street
Bristol BS1 6JS

British Library Cataloguing-in-Publication Data

A catalogue record for this book is available from the British Library.

ISBN 978 1 84661 099 8

Typeset by Letterpart Ltd, Reigate, Surrey

Printed and bound in Great Britain by CPI Antony Rowe, Chippenham, Wiltshire

Anti-so

Special B

Fourth Editic

About the Authors

Anesh Pema is a barrister at Zenith Chambers, Leeds, with extensive experience of representing and advising in anti-social behaviour applications. He has appeared in a number of the important decisions in the field and has conducted the largest multiple ASBO application in the country on behalf of Leeds City Council. He can be contacted at Zenith Chambers, 10 Park Square, Leeds LS1 2LH, DX Leeds 26412, telephone 0113 245 5438, fax 0113 242 3515 or by email (apema@zenithchambers.co.uk).

Sharon Heels is a senior housing management solicitor with Accent Housing Group Ltd and a Deputy District Judge. Specialising in nuisance, anti-social behaviour and housing law, she has considerable expertise in these matters and runs training and workshops in these areas. Sharon can be contacted by email (sharontraining@yahoo.co.uk).

Preface

Since the first edition of this *Special Bulletin*, law and practice in ASBO applications has moved on significantly and so consequentially has the length of this *Bulletin* now in its 4th edition. For the first time we have included commentary on the new Drinking Banning Orders which have been described as mini-ASBOs and also upon the powers of the local authority to create Designated Public Place Orders. The former has only just come into force and it remains to be seen what use or value they will have in practice.

As ever the law does not stand still however we have endeavoured to include all the changes up to October 2009.

Anesh would like to thank Justin Crossley and Nicola Phillipson at Zenith Chambers for their invaluable assistance in checking the text, and his wife, Louise McCallum, for her patience and support with another edition of this ever expanding *Bulletin*. Special thanks also are due to Adrian Phillips of Barnsley District Council for his assistance with the early research and development of the new edition.

Sharon echoes the thanks to the contributors named by Anesh. She also acknowledges and thanks all the colleagues and friends she has been fortunate to meet and make at Leeds City Council, Kirklees Council and now Accent Group. They have all taught her many things in the field of anti-social behaviour, the most important being flexibility, humanity and a sense of perspective of what really matters.

Finally we would like to thank Tony Hawitt of Jordans for the patience and assistance he has shown us through the four editions of this *Bulletin*.

Anesh Pema
Sharon Heels
October 2009

Foreword to the Third Edition

In the introduction to the Respect Action Plan (January 2006), Tony Blair says:

> 'I am pleased that an ASBO is now a household expression – synonymous with tackling anti-social behaviour . . . There is good work being done by local communities to apply this approach to tackle unacceptable behaviour. 6,500 ASBOs . . . have been issued.'

Anti-social Behaviour Orders (ASBOs) come from the Crime and Disorder Act 1998 and have been amended by the Police Reform Act 2002 and the Anti-social Behaviour Act 2003. Their part in changing the agenda from tolerating to tackling anti-social behaviour is becoming clear.

The Social Landlords Crime and Nuisance Group (SLCNG) has always supported them – not as a panacea but more as another option. ASBOs are injunctive tools – they say 'STOP! This is what you must not do'. Originally some thought them a clumsy tool. We have become better – though there is still some way to go – in partnership working. Interim orders are enabling urgent action to be taken to protect people from the behaviour of others. We welcomed the provision that enabled Registered Social Landlords and the British Transport Police to apply for ASBOs.

Mr Blair also stated that 'Anti-social behaviour by both adults and children creates havoc for the communities around them'.

This perhaps is our only gripe about ASBOs. In concept, when the embryonic SLCNG walked Jack Straw around an estate in Coventry they were known as 'community safety orders', which is exactly what they do. They are designed to protect the community from the behaviour of others.

As the Home Affairs Select Committee report on Anti-Social Behaviour said in April 2005:

> 'We welcome the introduction of new powers to tackle ASB . . . [which] can provide much needed relief for communities suffering from the impact of nuisance behaviour . . . ASBOs are commonly seen as the central element of the response to ASB.'

The Respect Action Plan refers to improving ASBOs – a new Guidance is likely this year, a one-year review for young people and for enabling the Environment Agency to apply.

ASBOs have been challenged by some, but never by the witnesses or victims of ASB, for example, like Ms G admitted:

> 'There were drugs and drink parties and motorbikes at all hours. They were burning cars. Now the atmosphere has changed completely. ASBOs are great.'

Tim Winter
SLCNG co-ordinator
January 2006

CONTENTS

About the Authors   v

Preface   vii

Foreword to the Third Edition   ix

Table of Cases   xxi

Table of Statutes   xxv

Table of Statutory Instruments   xxxi

Table of European Material   xxxiii

List of Abbreviations   xxxv

Chapter 1

Anti-social Behaviour in the Community   1

A definition of 'anti-social behaviour'?   1

Non-legal remedies to combat anti-social behaviour   2

Remedies in court   3

    Possession proceedings   3

    Injunctions   4

    Criminal proceedings   5

Solutions offered by the Crime and Disorder Act 1998   5

    Sex offender orders   6

    Parenting orders   6

    Parental compensation orders   7

    Child curfew schemes   8

    Child safety orders   8

Acceptable behaviour contracts   9

Advantages of ASBOs   9

Disadvantages of ASBOs   10

    Cost   10

    Bureaucracy   10

    Criminalisation of anti-social behaviour   10

Choosing the appropriate solution   10

Home Office Guidance   11

The Anti-social Behaviour Act 2003 – the main changes   11

Chapter 2

The Problem-Solving Group and Consultation   15

Introduction   15

Consultation   15

    Statutory requirements   15

Consultation with other agencies 18

Home Office recommendations 19

Protocols 19

Data protection and information exchange protocols 20

Accessing 'personal data' 20

Information exchange 21

Relations with other bodies 22

Crown Prosecution Service 22

The courts 23

The defendant 23

Chapter 3

Applications for Anti-social Behaviour Orders 25

Where can an application be made? 25

When can an application be made? 25

'Relevant authority' – who can apply? 25

Who can be the subject of an application? 26

'Has acted in an anti-social manner ...' 27

'Caused or was likely to cause harassment, alarm or distress to one or more persons ...' 31

'Not of the same household as himself . . .' 34

Aggregation 34

'... necessary to protect relevant persons from further anti-social acts by him' 36

Burden and standards of proof 37

'Necessity' for ASBO after interim order 39

Defences and disregards 40

Mental health problems 41

Summary 43

Chapter 4

Evidence 45

Home Office Guidance 45

Sources of evidence 46

Documentary evidence 46

(i) Housing services 46

(ii) Social services 46

(iii) Environmental services 47

(iv) Education/school records 47

(v) Police 47

Disclosure 47

Previous convictions 48

Lay witnesses 49

Professional witnesses 50

Covert surveillance	50
Videos and CCTV	50
General	50
Using video footage	51
Using CCTV footage	51
RIPA 2000 considerations	52
Hearsay evidence	53
Use of hearsay evidence	53
Adducing hearsay evidence before the court	54
Hearsay notices	54
Case-law	57

Chapter 5
Applications to the Magistrates' Court

Applications to the Magistrates' Court	61
Court forms	61
Service of court forms and evidence	62

Chapter 6
Anti-social Behaviour Orders in the County Court and on Criminal Conviction

Anti-social Behaviour Orders in the County Court and on Criminal Conviction	65
County court	65
ASB Act 2003	65
Practice and procedure	66
Application to join a non-party	67
Interim orders	68
Service	68
Orders on criminal conviction	68
Test	69
Practice and procedure	69
Hearsay evidence	71
Variation and discharge	72
Practice and procedure	73
Civil or criminal proceedings?	74
Case-law – R (C) v Sunderland Youth Court	75
Comment	76
R v P	77
Discussion	78
Case-law post R v P	79
R v Scott Parkinson	79
R v Werner	79
R v Paul Rush	80
R v Vittles	80
R v Jamie Paul McGrath	80
R v Michael Hinton	81

Guidelines for fairness in post-conviction order applications   81

Chapter 7

First Court Appearances   83

Magistrates' courts   83

   Directions on adjournments   84

   Reporting restrictions   85

Chapter 8

Interim Orders   87

Interim orders without notice   87

Practice   92

Publicity   93

Summary   93

County court   93

Criminal courts   94

Chapter 9

Hearing of the Main Application   95

Magistrates' court   95

Special measures for witnesses   97

Application   97

Measures   99

   Eligibility   99

Procedure for applications   100

Opposing an application   100

Special measures directions   101

Special measures for child witnesses   102

   Available measures   102

     Screens   102

     Live link   103

     Evidence to be given in private   103

     Removal of wigs and gowns   103

     Video-recorded evidence-in-chief   104

     Video-recorded cross-examination or re-examination   104

     Examination of a witness through an intermediary   104

     Aids to communication   104

     Status of evidence   104

     Restrictions on reporting directions under Chapter I   105

County court   105

   Vulnerable witnesses in the county court   105

On criminal conviction   106

Publicity and reporting restrictions   106
   Stanley v London Borough of Brent   108
      Defendants' case   108
      Respondents' arguments   109
      Court of Appeal ruling   109
Costs   110
   Magistrates' court   110
   County court   111
   Crown Court   111
   Enforcement of costs orders   112

Chapter 10
Terms and Duration of an Order   113
Terms of the order   113
Criminal offences as terms   114
Boness   119
R v Lamb   120
R v Stevens   121
Discussion   122
Improper terms   122
   Specific terms and considerations   124
   Exclusion zones   124
   Non-association   125
   Curfew   126
   Clothing   126
General prohibition as to anti-social behaviour   127
   Drunkenness   128
Practical considerations for applicants   129
Practical considerations for defendants   129
   Grounds for challenging the order   129
   Negotiating and bargaining   130
   Appeals   130
   Variation and discharge   130
Duration of the order   130

Chapter 11
Post-Order Procedure and Ancillary Orders   133
Service of the order on the defendant   133
Service of an ASBO on the police and witnesses   134
   Applicants' considerations   134
   Defence considerations   135
Effective monitoring   135
   Applicants' considerations   135

Defendants' considerations   136
Monitoring and recording information relating to ASBOs   136
Variation and discharge of order   137
  Practice and case-law   137
Variation and extension   138
Magistrates' courts in their civil capacity   140
Post-conviction orders   141
County court orders   141
Ancillary orders   141
  Intervention orders   141
    When?   141
    Relevant conditions   142
    Procedure   142
    Breach   142
    Variation and discharge   143
  Parenting orders   143
    When?   143
    Variation or discharge   144
    Breach   144
    Appeals   144
  Individual support orders   145
    Breach   146

Chapter 12
Appeals Against Anti-social Behaviour Orders   149
Appeals by the defendant   149
  Magistrates' courts' decisions   149
  Notice of appeal and time-limits   150
  Format of Crown Court appeal hearing   150
  Case stated   151
  Appeal from the Crown Court   151
Appropriate venue of appeal   152
Appeals by the applicant body   153
  Appeals from the county court   154
  Appeal from post-conviction orders   154
Appeals from variation of orders   155
Rectification of mistakes   155

Chapter 13
Breach of an Anti-social Behaviour Order   157
General principles   157
Challenging the order in breach proceedings   158
Proving the order   159

Defence of reasonable excuse 160

Breach of interim orders 160

    Breaches by young people 161

    Who can prosecute? 162

Sentencing 163

    Sentencing starting points 166

    Youths 166

Sentencing case-law 167

    Consecutive or concurrent 170

Chapter 14

Anti-social Behaviour Orders and Young People 171

Assessment of young people's needs and circumstances 171

    What form should the assessment take? 174

Applications against children in the care of the local authority 175

Service of court forms 177

Court procedure 177

Which court? 178

Review of ASBOs imposed against young persons 178

    Review periods 179

    Nature of the review 180

    Who does the review? 180

Sentencing 180

Other available orders 181

Conclusion 181

Chapter 15

Drinking Banning Orders 183

What are they? 183

When can they be made? 183

Vulnerable individuals 183

Who can apply? 184

What can be ordered? 184

Duration 185

Approved courses and completion certificates 186

Applications to the magistrates' court 187

County court 188

Procedure 188

Applications on criminal conviction 189

Publicity 190

Variation or discharge of DBOs 190

Interim orders 191

Appeal 192

Breach   192

Chapter 16
Designated Public Place Orders   193
What are they?   193
Who can make one?   193
Designating a DPPO   193
Consultation   194
Publicity   195
Signs   196
Notification to the Government   196
Extension and revocation of a DPPO   196
Enforcement   197

Appendix 1
Statutory Material   199
Crime and Disorder Act 1998   199
Civil Evidence Act 1995   230
Youth Justice and Criminal Evidence Act 1999   236
Magistrates' Courts (Hearsay Evidence in Civil Proceedings) Rules 1999, SI 1999/681   252
Magistrates' Courts (Anti-social Behaviour Orders) Rules 2002, SI 2002/2784   255
Civil Procedure Rules 1998, SI 1998/3132   260
Criminal Procedure Rules 2005, SI 2005/384   271

Appendix 2
Precedents   291
Draft ASBO application   291
Draft ASBO   293
Application for interim Anti-social Behaviour Order   295
Interim Anti-social Behaviour Order   297
Orders on conviction   299
County Court Anti-social Behaviour Order (Form N113)   301
Hearsay Notice   303

Appendix 3
A Guide to Anti-social Behaviour Orders 307

Appendix 4
**A Guide to Reviewing Anti-social Behaviour Orders Given to Young People and
Individual Support Orders** 375

Appendix 5
Breach of an Anti-social Behaviour Order 393

Appendix 6
Working Together Guidance on Publicising Anti-social Behaviour Orders 407

Appendix 7
**Home Office Guidance on Drinking Banning Orders on Application for Local
Authorities, Police Forces, Magistrates and Course Providers within England and
Wales** 415

Appendix 8
Useful Contacts 449

Index 451

TABLE OF CASES

References are to paragraph numbers.

Anderson v UK [1998] EHRR 218   10.43

Associated Provincial Picture Houses v Wednesbury Corporation [1948] 1 KB
223; [1947] 2 All ER 680   2.14, 12.10

B v Chief Constable of Avon and Somerset Constabulary [2001] 1 WLR 340   6.46

Birmingham City Council v Dixon [2009] EWHC 761 (Admin)   3.23

Boddington v British Transport Police [1999] 2 AC 143   13.6

Carl Wareham v Purbeck District Council, *Times Law Reports*, 28 March 2005   2.38

Chief Constable of Lancashire v Potter [2003] EWHC 2272 (Admin); [2003] All
ER (D) 199; [2003] 42 LS Gaz R 31   3.28, 3.35, 3.39, 3.51, 3.52

Chief Constable of West Midlands Police v Birmingham Justices [2002] EWHC
1087 (Admin)   2.7

City of Bradford MDC v Booth (2000) 164 JP 485   9.54

CPS v T [2006] EWHC 728 (Admin)   10.52, 13.7–13.9

Delcourt v Belgium (1970) 1 EHRR 355   11.36

DPP v Hall [2005] EWHC 2621 (Admin)   11.28–11.31

Fairweather v Commissioner of Police for the Metropolis [2008] EWHC 3073
(Admin)   3.65

Gough v Chief Constable of the Derbyshire Constabulary [2002] QB 459   6.46

Harrow London Borough Council v G (a child) [2004] EWHC 17 (QB)   1.17

Heron v Plymouth City Council [2009] All ER (D) 149 (Nov)   10.58

Hills v Chief Constable of Essex [2006] EWHC 2633 (Admin), (2006) 171 JP 14   10.30, 10.44

Hussain v Lancaster City Council [2001] QB1   1.8

Keating v Knowsley Metropolitan Borough Council (unreported) 22 July 2004,
Lawtel AC90600602   7.8, 8.20

Kingsnorth & Kenny v DPP [2003] EWHC Admin 786   13.15

KL and LK v DPP [2001] EWHC 1112 (Admin), (2002) 166 JP 369   9.29

Leeds City Council v Harte (1999) Current Law Cases 4069   4.66

Leeds City Council v RG (2007) 1 WLR 3025; (2007) 4 All ER 652, (2007) *The
Times*, 11 September   11.27–11.31

Lonergan (Ashley) v (1) Lewes Crown Court (2) Brighton & Hove City Council
& Secretary of State for the Home Department (Interested Party) [2005]
EWHC 457 (Admin); [2005] 1 WLR 2570; [2005] 2 All ER 362; (2005) *The
Times*, April 25   3.47, 10.2, 10.47, 10.48

M (Care Proceedings: Disclosure: Human Rights), Re [2001] 2 FLR 1316   4.8

M v DPP [2007] EWHC 1032 (Admin)   4.67–4.70

Manchester City Council v Muir & Another [2006] EWCA Civ 423   2.12

McClarty & McClarty v Wigan MBC (Unreported) 30 October 2003   2.8, 2.15

McVittie v Rennison [1941] 1 KB 96   3.16
Mote v Secretary of State for Work and Pensions [2007] EWCA Civ 1324   3.25
Mowan v London Borough of Wandsworth [2001] LGR 228   1.8

N v DPP [2007] EWHC 833 (Admin)   10.46
Nottingham City Council v Zain [2001] EWCA Civ 1248; [2001] 1 WLR 607   1.15

Parker v DPP [2005] EWHC 1485 (Admin)   8.3, 13.19

R (on the application of A) v Leeds Magistrates' Court and Leeds City Council
        [2004] EWHC 544 (Admin); (2004) *The Times*, March 31   8.17, 8.19, 12.12, 14.6, 14.10
R (on the application of AB and SB) v Nottingham City Council [2001] EWHC
        Admin 235, [2001] 3 FCR 350   4.7, 14.9
R (on the application of B) v Greenwich Magistrates' Court v The
        Commissioner of Police of the Metropolis [2008] EWHC 2882 (Admin)   10.49
R (on the application of C (by his mother and litigation friend, C)) v
        Sunderland Youth Court, Northumbria Police and Crown Prosecution
        Service [2003] EWHC 2385 (Admin), [2004] Crim LR 75   6.48, 6.56, 12.11, 13.11
R (on the application of Chief Constable of West Mercia Constabulary) v
        Boorman [2005] EWHC 2559 (Admin)   3.17
R (on the application of Cooke) v Director of Public Prosecutions [2008]
        EWHC 2703 (Admin)   3.61, 3.64
R (on the application of D) v Camberwell Green Youth Court; R (on the
        application of the DPP) v Camberwell Green Youth Court [2005] UKHL
        4, [2005] 1 WLR 393   9.15
R (on the application of Delaney) v Calderdale Magistrates' Court,
        (unreported) 25 August 2009   10.37
R (on the application of G) v Barnet London Borough Council [2003] 3 WLR
        1194   14.10
R (on the application of Gosport Borough Council) v Fareham Magistrates
        [2007] 1 WLR 634   3.32
R (on the application of Kenny) v Leeds Magistrates' Court; R (on the
        application of M) v Secretary of State for Constitutional Affairs and
        another [2003] EWHC 2963 (Admin); [2004] 1 All ER 1333   8.10, 8.18, 12.12, 14.6, 14.10
R (on the application of Langley) v Preston Crown Court [2008] All ER (D) 300
        (Oct), [2008] EWHC 2623 (Admin)   11.32–11.36
R (on the application of M (a child)) v Sheffield Magistrates' Court [2004]
        EWHC 1830 (Admin)   10.2, 14.14
R (on the application of M) v Secretary of State for Constitutional Affairs and
        another [2004] 2 All ER 531   8.10, 8.16
R (on the application of Manchester City Council) v Manchester Magistrates'
        Court [2005] EWHC 253   8.4
R (on the application of McCann) v Crown Court at Manchester; Clingham v
        Kensington and Chelsea Royal Borough Council [2003] UKHL 39, [2002]
        3 WLR 1313, [2002] 4 All ER 593, HL   3.35, 3.47, 3.49, 3.51, 4.62–4.65, 6.43, 6.45, 8.9, 8.10,
                                                                                          8.14, 9.12
R (on the application of Mills) v Birmingham Magistrates' Court [2005] All ER
        (D) 94   3.31
R (on the application of Perisamy Mathialagan) v London Borough of
        Southwark [2004] EWCA Civ 1689   12.21
R (on the application of Rabess and another) v the Commissioner of Police for
        the Metropolis [2007] EWHC 208 (Admin)   3.37
R (on the application of T) v Manchester Crown Court [2005] EWHC 1396
        (Admin); [2005] All ER (D) 03 (Jun)   12.2

R (on the application of T) v St Albans Crown Court; Chief Constable of
    Surrey v JHG and DHG [2002] EWHC 1129 (Admin)   9.46, 9.47
R (on the application of the Howard League for Penal Reform) v Secretary of
    State for the Home Department [2002] EWHC 2497 (Admin); [2002] All
    ER (D) (Nov)   14.6
R (on the application of W) v (1) Commissioner of Police for the Metropolis (2)
    Richmond-upon-Thames LBC (Defendants) Secretary of State for the
    Home Department (Interested Party) [2005] EWHC 1586 (Admin)   1.57
R (on the application of W) v Acton Youth Court [2005] All ER (D) 284   3.49, 4.65, 6.43, 12.22
R v Anthony [2005] EWCA Crim 2055   13.46
R v Boness (Dean) and 10 others [2005] EWCA Crim 2395; [2005] All ER (D)
    153; 169 JP 621; (2005) *The Times*, October 24   6.21, 6.58, 10.3, 10.19, 10.21, 10.23, 10.25,
    10.29, 10.31, 10.33, 10.35, 10.36, 10.42, 10.48
R v Braxton (Curtis) (aka Kamorudeen Owodunni) [2004] EWCA Crim 1374;
    [2005] 1 Cr App R (S) 167   10.19, 10.20, 10.27, 10.29, 10.31, 13.40, 13.41, 13.43, 13.47, 13.55
R v Brighton Magistrates' Court [1986] 1 FLR 426; [1086] Fam Law 134   11.2
R v Chuck Charles [2009] EWCA Crim 1570   13.16
R v Craig Lawson [2006] EWCA Crim 2674   13.54, 13.55
R v Cyril Stevens [2007] EWCA Crim 1128   10.26, 13.50
R v English [2005] EWCA Crim 2690; [2005] All ER (D) 115 (Oct)   13.11, 13.13
R v H Stevens and Lovegrove [2006] EWCA Crim 255, 2 Cr App R (S) 68,
    (2006) *The Times*, February 24   13.53
R v Hall [2004] EWCA Crim 2671; [2004] All ER (D) 377; [2005] 1 Cr App R (S)
    671; [2005] Crim LR 152   10.9, 10.14, 10.18
R v Harriman [2007] EWCA Crim 1185   10.37
R v Harris [2006] EWCA Crim 1864   13.52
R v HM Coroner for Newcastle upon Tyne ex parte P A (1998) 162 JP 387   9.28
R v Israilov [2004] EWCA Crim 2931   3.31
R v Jones & others [2006] EWCA Crim 2942   3.26
R v Kearns [2005] EWCA Crim 2038   13.45
R v Kirby [2005] EWCA Crim 1228; [2005] Crim LR 732   3.47, 10.11, 10.18
R v Lamb [2005] EWCA Crim 2487; [2005] All ER (D) 132 (Nov); (2005) *The
    Times*, December 1   10.27–10.29, 10.31, 13.2, 13.42, 13.43, 13.47
R v Manchester Crown Court ex parte McCann [2001] EWCA Civ 281; [2001] 1
    WLR 1084   3.16, 3.49, 4.44, 4.63
R v McGrath (Jamie Paul) [2005] EWCA 353; [2005] All ER (D) 81; [2005] 2 Cr
    App R (S) 525; [2005] NLJ 826   3.47, 6.67–6.69, 10.32
R v Michael Hinton [2006] EWCA Crim 1115   6.69, 6.71, 6.72
R v Morrison [2005] EWCA Crim 2237   10.15, 10.18, 10.19, 10.27–10.29, 10.31, 13.47
R v Nicholson [2006] 1 WLR 2857, [2006] EWCA Crim 1518   3.57
R v P [2004] EWCA Crim 287, (2004) *The Times*, February 19, alternatively
    known as R v Parkin   6.54–6.59, 6.63, 6.73, 10.4, 10.10, 12.19, 13.11
R v Parkinson (Scott) [2004] EWCA Crim 2757   6.59
R v Pedder [2005] EWCA Crim 3163   10.31
R v Richards 163 JP 246, CA   9.30
R v Rush (Paul) [2005] EWCA Crim 1316   6.64, 6.65
R v Secretary of State for Social Services ex parte Association of Metropolitan
    Authorities [1986] 1 WLR 1   2.9
R v Stevens [2006] All ER (D) 23; Lawtel AC9300667   10.28, 10.29, 10.31, 13.47
R v Swain [2007[EWCA Crim 1621   13.48
R v Tripp [2005] EWCA Crim 2253   10.20, 10.31
R v Vittles [2005] 1 Cr App R (S) 8   6.66
R v Waltham Forest Youth Court [2004] EWHC 715 (Admin); [2004] 2 Cr App
    R 21   9.15
R v Ward [2005] EWCA Crim 2713   13.45

R v Werner [2004] EWCA Crim 2931   6.61–6.63
R v Williams [2005] EWCA Crim 1796; [2005] All ER (D) 03; [2005] Crim LR
    872; 169 JP 588   10.13, 10.15, 10.18, 10.19, 10.31
R v Winchester Crown Court ex parte B [1999] 1 WLR 788; [2000] 1 Cr App R
    11   9.46
R v X, Y and X (1990) 91 Cr App R 36   9.28
Rall v Hume [2001] 3 All ER 248   4.31
Rowland v Bock [2002] EWHC 692 (QB)   9.41

S v Poole Borough Council [2002] EWHC 244 (Admin)   3.53, 3.55, 4.18, 6.34
Samuda v Birmingham Magistrates' Court [2008] EWHC 205 (Admin)   11.23–11.26, 12.21
Stanley v London Borough of Brent [2004] EWHC 2229 (Admin); [2005] EMLR
    3; [2005] UKHRR 115; [2005] HLR 8; [2005] ACD 13; (2004) *The Times*,
    October 22   7.8, 9.48, 9.53, 11.12, 11.16, 12.6
Stevens v South East Surrey Magistrates' Court [2004] EWHC 1456 (Admin)   3.15, 3.18, 4.66

W v DPP [2005] EWCA Civ 1333   13.5, 13.7, 13.12
W v DPP [2006] EWHC 1211 (Admin)   13.14, 13.15
W, F v Regina [2006] EWCA Crim 686   4.53
Walking v DPP [2003] All ER (D) 57 (Dec)   11.2

TABLE OF STATUTES

References are to paragraph numbers.

Anti-social Behaviour Act 2003   1.14, 1.26,
        1.32, 1.41, 1.48, 1.51, 1.62, 1.64, 3.1,
                3.4, 6.17, 6.31, 13.22, 14.25
   ss 1–11   1.58
   s 12   1.49
   ss 12–13   1.51
   ss 14–17   1.50
   ss 18–22   1.56
   ss 18–29   1.56
   s 23   1.57
   ss 25–29   1.56
   s 30   1.57
   ss 30–36   1.57
   ss 37–39   1.59
   ss 65–84   1.60
   s 85(1)   3.4, 6.3, 13.22
   s 85(2)(a), (c)   3.4
   s 85(4)   13.22
   s 85(5)   6.3
   s 85(6)   6.3
   s 86(3)   13.23
   s 91   1.53, 3.9
   Sch 1   1.50

British Transport Commission Act 1949
   s 53   3.4

Children Act 1989   1.37
   s 17   14.2, 14.9, 14.10
   s 22   14.18
   s 22(4)   14.18–14.20
   s 33   14.39
   s 47(1)(a)(iii)   1.32
   s 17   14.34
Children Act 2004
   s 18   11.53
Children and Young Persons Act 1933
   s 39   7.8, 9.46, 13.20
   s 44   9.46
   s 47   13.22
   s 49   13.20
   s 107   14.22
   s 39   15.37
   s 47(2)   15.54
   s 49   15.37, 15.54
Children and Young Persons Act 1969
   s 12   14.39

Civil Evidence Act 1995   4.47, 4.63
   s 1   4.63
   s 1(1)   4.63
   s 1(4)   4.45
   s 2(4)   4.48
   s 4(2)   4.48
   s 2(4)   4.68
Clean Neighbourhoods and
   Environment Act 2005   1.61
   s 1   1.21
Courts and Legal Services Act 1990
   s 71   13.25
Crime and Disorder Act 1998   1.20, 3.1, 3.4,
                4.21, 6.22, 9.14, 9.17, 9.40, 9.44,
                9.53, 10.6, 10.25, 10.48, 13.11
   s 1   3.13, 3.50, 13.22
   s 1(1)   3.8, 3.17, 3.38, 3.57, 6.5, 6.8, 6.63,
                                        10.1, 14.7
   s 1(1)(a)   1.2, 3.3, 3.11, 3.25, 3.32, 3.34, 3.40,
                        3.41, 3.51, 3.66, 6.19, 6.34
   s 1(1)(b)   1.2, 3.3, 3.15, 3.21, 3.42, 3.50, 3.51
   s 1(1)A(d)   3.4
   s 1(1A)   3.4
   s 1(1A)(aa)   3.4
   s 1(4)   3.51, 10.1
   s 1(5)   3.57
   s 1(9)   11.1, 11.2
   s 1(10)   6.42, 13.22, 13.23, 13.26
   s 1(10A)   13.23
   s 1(10C)   13.13
   s 1(10E)   13.20
   s 1(11)   13.21, 13.26
   s 1(12)   3.5
   s 1A(1), (2)   3.4
   s 1AA   11.60
   s 1AA(1)   11.60
   s 1AA(2)(a), (b)   11.63
   s 1AA(3)(a)–(c)   11.60
   s 1AA(4)   11.60
   s 1AA(9)   11.62
   s 1AB(1)   11.65
   s 1AB(3)   11.67
   s 1AB(6), (7)   11.65
   s 1B   3.42, 6.1, 9.40, 11.44, 11.46, 11.50
   s 1B(3A)   6.9
   s 1B(3A)–(3C)   6.3
   s 1B(3B)   6.9

Crime and Disorder Act 1998—*continued*

s 1B(4)	6.5
s 1B(5)	6.3, 6.5, 11.41
s 1B(6)	10.63, 11.1, 11.41
s 1B(7)	6.5, 13.23
s 1C	6.16, 6.37, 6.52, 6.67, 9.11, 11.66
s 1C(2)	9.44
s 1C(2)(b)	6.18
s 1C(3), (3A), (3B)	6.17
s 1C(3A)	6.31
s 1C(3B)	6.31
s 1C(6)–(8)	6.36
s 1C(8)	11.1
s 1C(9)	6.42, 13.23
s 1C(9A)	13.23
s 1CA	6.36, 6.37, 11.40
s 1CA(1)	6.37
s 1CA(1)(4)(b)	6.38
s 1CA(1)(5)	6.38
s 1CA(2)	6.37
s 1CA(3), (4)	6.38
s 1CA(4)(a)	6.38
s 1CA(7)(a)	6.37
s 1CA(7)(b)	6.38
s 1D	6.36, 8.1, 9.11
s 1D(1)	8.15
s 1D(1)(b)	6.5
s 1D(1)(c), (d)	6.22, 9.44
s 1D(2)	8.2, 8.15
s 1D(4)	8.3, 8.7
s 1D(4)(b)	8.10
s 1D(4A–C)	6.22, 9.44
s 1D(4A)	6.22, 9.44
s 1D(4B)	6.22, 9.44
s 1D(4C)	6.22, 9.44
s 1D(5)	6.35, 8.2
s 1D(9A)–(9C)	13.23
s 1E	2.3, 2.11, 2.13, 5.8
s 1E(1)(b)	6.5
s 1E(2)	2.3
s 1E(3)	2.3, 2.4
s 1E(4)	2.3
s 1F	3.7
s 1F(1)	3.7
s 1F(5)(a), (b)	3.7
s 1F(6)	3.7
s 1G	11.42
s 1G(1)	11.44
s 1G(1)(b), (c)	11.44
s 1G(3)	11.46
s 1G(4)(a), (b)	11.47
s 1G(4)(c), (d)	11.47
s 1G(5)(a), (b)	11.43
s 1G(6)(a), (b)	11.43
s 1G(7)	11.43

Crime and Disorder Act 1998—*continued*

s 1G(8)	11.49
s 1H	11.42
s 1H(1)	11.48
s 1H(1)(b), (c)	11.48
s 1H(3)	11.49
s 1H(4)	11.50
s 1H(5), (6)	11.50
s 1H(7)	11.50
s 1K(2)(a)	11.66
s 1K(2)(b)	11.66
s 1L	9.9, 9.10
s 1L(1)	9.11
s 2	1.24
s 4	9.12, 12.1
s 4(1)	8.10
ss 5–6	1.21
s 8	1.25, 14.39
s 8(4)	11.51
s 8(7A)	11.51
s 8(7A) (a), (b)	11.51
s 8(8)	11.53
s 9(1)(a)	11.55
s 9(1B)(a), (b)	11.55
s 9(2)	11.54
s 9(4)	11.52
s 9(5)(a), (b)	11.56
s 9(6)	11.56
s 9(7)	11.57
s 9(a), (b)	11.55
s 10	13.22
s 10(1)(a), (b)	11.58
s 10(4), (5)	11.58
s 10A	13.22
s 10B	13.22
s 10C	11.1
s 10D	13.20
s 11	14.39
ss 11–13	1.35
s 13A–E	1.27
s 13A(1)	1.27
s 13A(1)(b)	1.27
s 13A(2)(a), (b)	1.27
s 13A(3), (4)	1.27
s 13A(6)	1.29
s 13B(1)(a)–(f)	1.28
s 13B(2)(a), (b)	1.28
s 13B(7)	1.27
s 13D(1)	1.30
s 13D(5)	1.30
s 13E	1.30
s 14	14.39
ss 14–15	1.32
s 14(1)	1.33
s 16	1.22

Crime and Disorder Act 1998—*continued*

s 17	1.23, 2.9, 2.29, 3.6
s 37	14.11
s 39	8.20
s 115	2.27, 2.29–2.31
s 115(2)(d)(a)	2.28
s 1(8)	11.29
s 1(10)	13.18
s 1AA(1A)	14.31
s 1AA(6), (7), (8)	11.64
s 1B(8)	11.60
s 1B(9)	11.60
s 1C(9AA)	11.60
s 1D(1)(c) and (d)	8.23
s 1D(4)	11.28
s 1J(1)	14.28
s 1J(2)(a)	14.28
s 1J(2)(b)	14.28
s 1J(3)(a)(ii)	14.30
s 1J(3)(b)(i)	14.30
s 1J(3)(b)(iI)	14.30
s 1J(3)(i)	14.30
s 1J(4)	14.31
s 1K(1)	14.35, 14.36
s 1K(2)(a)	14.35
s 1K(2)(b)	14.35
s 1K(3) and (4)	14.36
s 1K(5)	14.36
s 4	11.32, 11.33

Criminal Appeal Act 1968

s 9(1)	12.19
s 50(1)	12.19

Criminal Justice Act 2003

s 322	11.60, 11.65
s 174(2)(a)	13.34

Criminal Justice and Immigration Act
2008 — 11.66

s 123	14.28, 14.29

Criminal Justice and Police Act 2001 — 16.1

ss 39–41	1.18, 5.2
s 48	1.33
s 12(1)	16.18
s 12(2)	16.18
s 12(3)	16.18
s 12(4)	16.18
s 12(5)	16.18
s 13	16.1
s 13(2)(a)	16.4
s 13(2)(b)	16.4
s 13(3)	16.16, 16.17
s 14(1)(a)	16.8
s 14(1)(aa)	16.8
s 14(1)(b)	16.8
s 14(1)(c)	16.8
s 14(1)(e)	16.8

Criminal Justice and Police Act
2001—*continued*

s 15(2) and (3)	16.2
s 16(1)	16.5

Criminal Procedure and Investigations
Act 1996 — 4.15, 13.3

Data Protection Act 1998 — 2.22, 2.26

s 1	2.22

Drugs Act 2005 — 11.42

Family Law Reform Act 1987

s 3	14.22

Housing Act 1985

s 121A	1.13
Sch 3, Ground 2	1.55
Sch 3, Ground 2A	1.13

Housing Act 1988

Sch 2, Ground 14	1.55

Housing Act 1996 — 1.51, 1.54, 1.55, 3.4

Pt 1	1.50
s 1	3.4
s 125A, B	1.10
s 153A	1.15, 3.10

Housing Act 2004

s 179	1.10
s 191	1.13
s 192	1.13
s 194	2.33
s 219	2.28

Human Rights Act 1998 — 2.19, 4.63, 9.44

Sch 1	8.8

Local Government Act 1972

s 222	1.15, 1.53, 3.9, 13.24

Magistrates' Courts Act 1980 — 7.1, 9.2, 15.22

ss 54–57	14.23
s 55(1), (2), (3)	7.1
s 64(1)	9.54
s 64(2), (3)	9.55
s 96(1)	9.55
s 98	9.3, 14.23
s 108	12.19, 13.12
s 111	12.9, 12.16
s 111(2)	12.16
s 111(4)	12.9
s 111(6)	12.16
s 127	3.13, 3.16
s 142	11.2
s 1(1)(a)	9.2
s 127	15.22
s 142	12.21, 12.22

Mental Health Act 1983 — 9.15

National Health Service and
    Community Care Act 1990   15.5
    s 47   15.5

Police and Criminal Evidence Act 1984   13.3
Police Reform Act 2002   1.24, 2.19, 3.1, 3.4,
    3.42, 6.1, 6.17, 6.36, 10.63
    s 61(1), (2)   3.4
    s 63   6.1
    s 64   6.16, 6.20
    s 65(1)   8.1
    s 66   2.3
    s 75   1.22
Powers of Criminal Courts (Sentencing)
    Act 2000
    s 137(3)   11.67
    s 100   13.37
Prevention of Crime Act 1953   10.8, 10.23
Prosecution of Offences Act 1985
    s 3(2)   13.22
    s 5(1)   13.25
    s 6(1), (2)   13.24
Protection from Harassment Act 1997   1.18,
    11.28
Public Order Act 1986   10.8, 10.23
    s 4   10.19, 10.26, 10.55
    s 5   3.11, 10.25, 10.55

Regulation of Investigatory Powers Act
    2000   4.37, 4.42
    s 26(8)   4.39
    s 27(1)   4.41
    s 48   4.38
Rehabilitation of Offenders Act 1974   4.20
    s 4(1)   4.20
    s 4(1)(b)   4.20
    s 5(1)   4.20
    s 7(3)   4.20

Serious Organised Crime and Police Act
    2005   1.27, 3.1, 3.4, 4.21, 6.22, 9.9, 11.1,
    13.11, 13.13
    s 139(1)   6.22, 9.44
    s 139(3)   3.4
    s 139(4)(a)   6.22, 9.44
    s 140(1), (4)   6.36
    s 141   13.20
    s 142   3.7
Sexual Offences Act 2003
    ss 104–113   1.24
Supreme Court Act 1981
    s 28   12.10
    s 28(1)   12.10
    s 29(3)   12.10
    s 79(3)   12.6

Violent Crime Reduction Act 2006   15.1, 16.1
    s 1(2)   15.4, 15.10, 15.11
    s 1(4)(a)   15.13
    s 1(4)(b)   15.13
    s 1(4)(c)   15.13
    s 1(4)(d)   15.13
    s 2(1)   15.14
    s 2(2)   15.14
    s 2(3)   15.15
    s 2(4)   15.15
    s 2(5)   15.15
    s 2(6)   15.16
    s 2(7)   15.16
    s 3(2)(a)   15.6
    s 3(2)(b)   15.6
    s 3(3)   15.22
    s 3(4)   15.23
    s 3(6)   15.22
    s 4(2)   15.25
    s 4(3)   15.25
    s 4(4)   15.26
    s 4(5)   15.26
    s 4(7)   15.28
    s 5(5)   15.39
    s 5(6)   15.40
    s 6(1)   15.32
    s 6(2)   15.32
    s 6(4)   15.32
    s 6(5)   15.32
    s 7(3)   15.35
    s 7(4)   15.35
    s 7(5)   15.35
    s 7(6)   15.35
    s 7(7)   15.36
    s 7(11)   15.33
    s 8(2)   15.41
    s 8(3)   15.41
    s 8(5)   15.42
    s 8(6)   15.42
    s 9(1)   15.43
    s 9(2)   15.43
    s 9(3)   15.44
    s 9(4)(b)   15.45
    s 9(5)   15.45
    s 9(6)(a)   15.47
    s 9(6)(b)   15.47
    s 9(7)   15.47, 15.48
    s 9(8)   15.49
    s 9(9)   15.49
    s 10(1)   15.50
    s 10(2)   15.50
    s 10(3)   15.50
    s 11(2)   15.51
    s 11(3)   15.51
    s 11(6)   15.53

Violent Crime Reduction Act 2006—*continued*

s 12(1)	15.19
s 12(4)(a)	15.19
s 12(4)(b)	15.19
s 12(5)	15.17
s 12(8)	15.18
s 13(1)(a)	15.20
s 13(1)(b)	15.21
s 13(2)	15.20
s 13(3)	15.20
s 14	16.1
s 14(1)	15.9, 15.23

Youth Justice and Criminal Evidence

Act 1999	9.12, 9.17, 9.40
Pt 2, Ch 1	9.10, 9.15
s 16	9.15, 9.19, 9.22, 9.24
ss 16–33	9.15
s 16(1)	9.15
s 16(1)(b)	9.15
s 16(2)(a)(i), (ii)	9.15
s 16(2)(b)	9.15
s 16(5)	9.15
s 17	9.16, 9.19, 9.22, 9.24
s 17(1)	9.16
s 17(2)(a)–(d)	9.16
s 17(3)	9.16
s 18	9.22
s 19	9.23, 9.38
s 19(1)(a), (b)	9.23
s 19(2)(b)	9.24
s 19(4)	9.25
s 20	9.14

Youth Justice and Criminal Evidence Act
1999—*continued*

s 20(1)	9.12
s 20(2)	9.25
s 20(2)(a)	9.25
s 20(3)(a), (b)	9.26
s 20(5)	9.25
s 21	9.24
s 21(2)(a), (b)	9.24
s 21(4)	9.26
ss 23–28	9.22
ss 23–30	9.22
s 23(1), (2), (3)	9.28
s 24	9.26
s 24(2)	9.30, 9.31
s 24(3)	9.30, 9.31
s 24(5)	9.31
s 24(8)	9.30
s 26	9.32
s 27	9.20, 9.26, 9.33
s 27(3)	9.33
s 27(5)	9.33
s 28	9.34
s 29	9.35
s 30	9.36
s 31(2)	9.37
s 31(4)	9.37
s 45	13.20, 14.23
s 45(6)	13.20
s 47	9.38
s 49	9.38
s 51	9.38
s 55(2)	14.23

TABLE OF STATUTORY INSTRUMENTS

References are to paragraph numbers.

Civil Procedure Rules 1998
 (SI 1998/3132) 4.15, 4.16, 7.4, 15.29,
             15.31
Pt 1 4.15
Pt 19 6.10
r 19.1 6.9
r 19.2 6.9
r 19.4 6.9, 15.31
Pt 23 9.43, 11.41
Pt 25 6.13, 8.22
r 25.3(1) 6.13
PD 25, para.2.2 6.14
r 31 4.15
r 32.1 4.31
r 32.1(6) 4.31
r 32.2(4) 9.42
r 32.3 9.41
Pts 43–48 9.57
Pt 52 12.17
r 52.3(1), (2) 12.17
r 52.4 12.17
r 52.11 12.18
PD 52, para 2A.2 12.17
PD 52, para 4.6 12.17
Pt 55 12.17
Pt 65 6.6, 9.39, 12.17
r 65.22(1)(a), (b) 6.6
r 65.22(2) 6.7
r 65.22(3) 6.7
r 65.23(1), (2), (3) 6.9
r 65.25 6.8
r 65.26 8.22
r 65.26(2)(b) 6.13
r 65.32(1)(a) 15.29
r 65.32(1)(b) 15.29
r 65.32(2) 15.29
r 65.32(3) 15.30
r 65.33(1)(a) 15.31
r 65.33(1)(b) 15.31
r 65.33(2) 15.31
r 65.34(1) 15.31
r 65.34(2) 15.31
r 65.35 15.29
r 65.36(1) 15.43
r 65.36(2) 15.43
r 65.36(3) 15.46
PD 65, para 13.1 6.15, 8.22, 11.3

Civil Procedure Rules 1998
 (SI 1998/3132)—*continued*
Pt 72 9.59
Pt 73 9.59
para 2.4 6.14
r 25.3(3) 6.13
Sch 2, CCR Ord 26 9.59
Sch 2, CCR Ord 27 9.59
Criminal Defence Service (General) (No
 2) Regulations 2001 (SI 2001/1437)
reg 3(2)(b) 9.55
Criminal Procedure Rules 2005
 (SI 2005/384) 6.22, 6.40, 8.23
Pt 29 9.18
r 29.1 9.18
r 29.1(1), (2), (3) 9.18
r 29.1(4)(b) 9.18
r 29.1(5), (6) 9.19
r 29.1(8) 9.19
r 29.1(9)(a), (b) 9.21
r 29.1(10) 9.18, 9.21
r 29.2(3), (4) 9.18
r 29.3(2) 9.18
r 29.7(7) 9.20
r 50 6.22
r 50.2 6.23
r 50.2(1) 6.23
r 50.2(2) 6.23
r 50.2(3) 6.23
r 50.3 8.23, 12.23
r 50.3(2) 6.24
r 50.3(2)(a) 6.24
r 50.3(2)(b) 6.24
r 50.3(3) 6.24, 6.25
r 50.3(4) 6.26
r 50.3(5) 6.28
r 50.3(8) 8.23
r 50.4 6.29
r 50.4(2) 6.29
r 50.5(2) 6.40
r 50.5(3) 6.40
r 50.5(4) 6.41
r 50.5(5)(a) 6.41
r 50.5(5)(b) 6.41
r 50.5(6)(a) 6.40
r 50.5(6)(b) 6.41
r 50.6(1)(a) 4.54

Criminal Procedure Rules 2005
    (SI 2005/384)—*continued*
  r 50.6(1)(b)   4.54
  r 50.6(2)   4.55
  r 50.7(1)   4.56
  r 50.7(2)(a)   4.56
  r 50.7(3)   4.57
  r 50.7(4)(a)   4.57
  r 50.7(4)(b)   4.57
  r 50.8(2)   4.60
  r 50.8(b)   4.59
  r 50.9(a)   4.61
  r 50.9(b)   4.61
Crown Court Rules 1982 (SI 1982/1109)
  rr 6–11   12.1
  r 7(3)   12.5
  r 7(5), (6), (7)   12.5
  r 26   12.10

Family Proceedings Rules 1991
    (SI 1991/1247)
  r 4.23   4.8, 4.10

Local Authorities (Alcohol
    Consumption in Designated
    Public Places) Regulations 2007   16.3,
                           16.7, 16.16
  reg 3(1)(a)–(d)   16.6
  reg 3(3)(a)   16.8
  reg 5   16.10
  reg 6   16.10
  reg 8(1)   16.13
  reg 8(2)   16.13
  reg 9   16.15

Magistrates' Courts (Anti-social
    Behaviour Orders) Rules 2002
    (SI 2002/2784)   5.1, 5.5, 5.8, 6.39, 8.11,
                           8.12, 12.23
  r 4(1)   5.1
  r 4(4)   6.47
  r 4(5)   5.1, 8.2
  r 5   8.8, 8.9
  r 5(1)   8.4
  r 5(2)   8.4
  r 5(3)   8.7
  r 5(4)   8.7, 8.10
  r 5(5)   8.7, 8.10
  r 5(6)   8.3
  r 5(8)   8.7, 8.10
  r 6   8.16, 11.38, 11.39
  r 7(1)   5.5, 11.3
  r 7(2)   5.8

Magistrates' Courts (Anti-social Behaviour
    Orders) Rules 2002
    (SI 2002/2784)—*continued*
  r 6(4)   6.39
  r 7   6.39
  Sch 1   11.39
  Sch 4   6.52, 6.53
  Sch 5   8.2
Magistrates' Courts (Hearsay Evidence
    in Civil Proceedings) Rules 1999
    (SI 1999/681)   4.45, 4.47, 4.53, 4.63
  r 3(1)   4.48
  r 3(2)   4.48
  r 3(3)   4.48
  r 3(4)   4.49
  r 4   4.64
  r 2(3)   4.53
  r 4(3)(a)(ii)   4.58
  r 5(2)   4.51
  r 5(3)   4.51
  r 5(4)   4.51
  r 6(1)(a)   4.52
  r 6(1)(b)   4.52
  r 6(3)   4.52
  r 6(3)(a)   4.52
Magistrates' Courts (Miscellaneous
    Amendment) Rules 2003
    (SI 2003/1236)   6.47
  r 88   6.52
  r 89(2)   6.52
Magistrates' Courts Rules 1981
    (SI 1981/552)   9.2
  r 14   9.2
  r 14(2)   9.6
  r 14(3)   7.6
  r 14(5), (6)   9.7
  r 74   12.1
  r 75   12.1

Serious Organised Crime and Police Act
    2005 (Commencement No 1,
    Transitional and Transitory
    Provisions) Order (SI 2005/1521)   1.64

Violent Crime Reduction Act 2006
    (Commencement No 7) Order
    2009   15.1
Violent Crime Reduction Act 2006
    (Drinking Banning Orders)
    (Approved Courses) Regulations
    2009 (SI 2009/1839)   15.17, 15.19
  r 4   15.17

TABLE OF EUROPEAN MATERIAL

References are to paragraph numbers.

European Convention for the Protection of Human Rights and Fundamental Freedoms   4.16, 4.63, 7.6, 8.8, 8.9, 8.11, 8.12, 8.16, 9.15, 10.43

Art 6	2.38, 2.39, 3.16, 11.32, 11.36
Art 6(1)	8.10, 8.12, 8.21, 9.44
Art 6(2)	9.18
Art 8	2.39, 9.48–9.50
Art 8(2)	4.40
Art 10	9.50
Art 11	9.50
Art 17	9.50

List of Abbreviations

1999 Rules	Magistrates' Courts (Hearing Evidence in Civil Proceedings) Rules 1999
2002 Rules	Magistrates' Courts (Anti-social Behaviour Orders) Rules 2002
ABC	acceptable behaviour contract
ADHD	attention deficit hyperactivity disorder
ALMO	arm's length management organisation
ASB Act 2003	Anti-social Behaviour Act 2003
ASBO	Anti-social Behaviour Order
BTP	British Transport Police
CDA 1998	Crime and Disorder Act 1998
CDRP	Crime and Disorder Reduction Partnership
CJPA 2001	Criminal Justice and Police Act 2001
CPR	Civil Procedure Rules 1998
CPR 2005	Criminal Procedure Rules 2005
CPS	Crown Prosecution Service
DA 2005	Drugs Act 2005
DBO	Drinking Banning Order
DPA 1998	Data Protection Act 1998
DPP	director of public prosecutions
DPPO	Designated Public Place Order
ECHR	European Convention on Human Rights
FPR 1991	Family Procedure Rules 1991
HRA 1998	Human Rights Act 1998
ISO	individual support order
ISSP	intensive supervision and surveillance programme
LEA	local education authority
MCA 1980	Magistrates' Courts Act 1980
MCR 1981	Magistrates' Courts Rules 1981
MIB	Motorist Insurers' Bureau
PNC	Police National Computer
PJB	Police and Justice Bill
POA 1986	Public Order Act 1986
PRA 2002	Police Reform Act 2002
RIPA 2000	Regulation of Investigatory Powers Act 2000
RSL	registered social landlord
SOCPA 2005	Serious Organised Crime and Police Act 2005

VCRA 2006   Violent Crime Reduction Act 2006

YOT   Youth Offending Team

YJCEA 1999   Youth Justice and Criminal Evidence Act 1999

CHAPTER 1

ANTI-SOCIAL BEHAVIOUR IN THE COMMUNITY

1.1   This chapter looks at what is meant by the term 'anti-social behaviour' and examines the various methods of dealing with such behaviour which should be considered before applying for an anti-social behaviour order (ASBO).

A DEFINITION OF 'ANTI-SOCIAL BEHAVIOUR'?

1.2   Before an ASBO is chosen as the appropriate solution, an applicant must be satisfied that the alleged conduct is in fact 'anti-social behaviour'. However, anti-social behaviour is *not* defined in the current Home Office Guidance beyond repeating the statutory definition.[1] Examples of the types of behaviour which would appropriately trigger an application for an ASBO are, however, given. These include:

- verbal abuse;

- harassment;

- assault;

- graffiti;

- excessive noise;

- drunk and disorderly conduct;

- throwing missiles;

- vehicle crime; and

- prostitution.

Further examples of the types of behaviour that should be dealt with using ASBOs and acceptable behaviour contracts (ABCs) are given in the current Home Office Guidance.

1.3   Other sources of assistance in classifying what is or is not anti-social include nuisance clauses in tenancy agreements, and definitions or examples in case-law or statute.

1.4   The Home Office consultative document of 2002 'Tackling Anti-Social Tenants' considered whether there should be a statutory definition of what is anti-social behaviour. However, no definition has been brought into being and some practitioners believe a valuable opportunity to regulate or clarify this area has been lost. Unless and until that occurs, applicants should satisfy themselves that the allegations in the complaints constitute anti-social behaviour and not just an

---

[1]   See Crime and Disorder Act 1998 (CDA 1998), s 1(1)(a), (b).

example of conflicting lifestyles. A distinction needs to be drawn between petty, low-level nuisance and persistent and serious misconduct.

1.5   A recent article from the Institute for Public Policy Research[2] highlighted the lack of an overall definition and what problems that can cause:

> 'The very elasticity of the term anti-social behaviour adds to the problem. In covering everything from dropping litter to serious criminal activity it implies that the jump from illegally parked cars (a problem experienced in most neighbourhoods) to crack dens (a problem experienced in far fewer) is a short one. The "I know it when I see it" approach is not terribly helpful in trying to disentangle what we mean by these very different – and admittedly anti-social behaviours.'

However, it is unlikely to happen in the short term. The Government welcomed the opinion of the House of Commons Homes Affairs Select Committee whose views in this area were as follows:

> 'We have listened carefully to criticisms of the current legal definitions of anti-social behaviour as too wide. We are convinced, however, that it would be a mistake to try and make them more specific. This is for three main reasons; first, the definitions work well from an enforcement point of view and no significant practical problems seem to have been encountered; second, exhaustive lists of behaviour considered anti-social by central government would be unworkable; third, anti-social behaviour is inherently a local problem and falls to be defined at a local level. It is a major strength of the current statutory definitions of anti-social behaviour that they are flexible enough to accommodate this. We would argue also that the definitions are helpful in backing an approach that stands with the victims of anti-social behaviour and their experience rather than narrowly[3] focusing on the behaviour of the perpetrators.'

NON-LEGAL REMEDIES TO COMBAT ANTI-SOCIAL BEHAVIOUR

1.6   The reasons, causes and remedies for anti-social conduct are complex and diverse. The most appropriate solution is not always court action. Other options can be equally or more effective. The key principle is for the lead agency to engage with other relevant agencies as soon as possible to contain, tackle and solve the problem. The following agencies may be called upon:

- social services can assist with challenging behaviour from young people in a number of ways – by supporting parents, or providing lessons in parenting skills, or seeking court proceedings for care or supervision orders;

- the council's housing department (or other similar social housing providers) can assist by enforcing nuisance clauses in tenancy agreements against unruly tenants and, to reduce the opportunities for conflict, by enforcing a sensible allocations policy and other planned housing strategies;

- schools can assist with issues of discipline, control and truancy; they can also provide focused teaching and strategies to identify and address learning difficulties, failure to deal with which can, in some instances, lead to anti-social conduct;

- the youth offending team (YOT) can help young people within and outside the youth criminal justice system by engaging formally and informally with them to change their

---

[2]   'Anti-social behaviour, perception or reality' by Miranda Lewis, Senior Research Fellow, People and Policy article in *Inside Housing*, 2 September 2005.

[3]   Paragraph 44 of the House of Commons Home Affairs Committee 5th Report of Session 2004–05 on anti-social behaviour.

behaviour from what is perceived as anti-social – this can include diversionary schemes (eg such as organised sports activities or supervising court sentences);

- the health authority can assist with health or behavioural problems;

- the council's environmental health department can help with noise or public safety issues;

- the council's planning department can help with breaches of planning control.

REMEDIES IN COURT

Possession proceedings

1.7 Any landlord can seek to evict a tenant for breach of the terms of a tenancy agreement or seek a demotion of a secure tenancy to the level of an introductory one. For registered social landlords (RSLs), there is greater expectation to use nuisance clauses in tenancy agreements to control anti-social tenants. Tenancy agreements can be varied to tighten nuisance clauses.

1.8 Although current law does not allow those affected by tenants' behaviour to sue the landlord for failing to control them,[4] this developing area of law may one day impose a duty of care.

1.9 For possession proceedings to succeed there must be grounds for possession (breach of tenancy agreement, or a statutory possession ground) but the court also has a wide-ranging discretion to decide if it is reasonable to grant possession in each case.

1.10 Another option for RSLs is to grant introductory or starter tenancies to new tenants. If there is a breach of tenancy in the first year, the landlord can take steps to end the tenancy. Court possession proceedings must be brought in the normal way but the court has limited discretion. Provided the landlord has followed internal procedures correctly (including acceding to a tenant's request for review of the decision to regain possession), the court *must* grant a possession order. Recent changes in legislation now enable local authorities to extend the 12-month period of new introductory tenancies by an additional 6 months where the landlord has continuing concerns about the behaviour of a tenant. Safeguards exist in that the landlord must first serve a notice of extension of the trial period on the tenant at least 8 weeks before the original introductory tenancy expiry date. Secondly, either the tenant must not have requested a review of that decision or the decision to extend was upheld following a review.[5]

1.11 In a consultation exercise, alternative means of strengthening the response to nuisance tenants were explored. The options included allowing the landlord to decide on the issue of possession; demoting tenancies by turning a secure tenancy into an introductory tenancy; and allowing the courts to grant possession for serious, persistent anti-social behaviour when injunctions are sought. The Government's response in the shape of new legislation is set out at **1.50** onwards.

1.12 Possession proceedings are more drastic, and potentially less effective in dealing with anti-social behaviour. Possession proceedings can displace households for the behaviour of an individual, and affect only certain premises for a limited time, which ends when possession is regained. There are many examples of evicted households moving to new accommodation within the area, exposing the same community to the behaviour that initially gave rise to the

---

[4] See *Hussain v Lancaster City Council* [2001] QB 1, and *Mowan v London Borough of Wandsworth* [2001] LGR 228.

[5] Housing Act 2004, s 179, inserting ss 125A and 125B of the Housing Act 1996. This came into force on 6 June 2005.

eviction. ASBOs provide the means for targeted control of individuals with terms tailored to deal with specific misconduct. Importantly, an ASBO does not affect the family home, only the perpetrator of the anti-social behaviour.

1.13 Social housing tenants enjoy the right to seek mutual exchange of their properties with other social housing tenants and to seek to buy their homes. Recent changes in legislation can suspend these rights in the event of anti-social behaviour. A ground is added to which a landlord can withhold consent to a mutual exchange if a possession order based on statutory nuisance, a demotion order, certain injunctions or an ASBO is in force or pending.[6] Social landlords can also ask the court to suspend a tenant's right to buy their home where a resident or visitor has engaged or threatened to engage in anti-social behaviour or used the premises for unlawful purposes and the court is satisfied it is reasonable to make an order.[7]

Injunctions

1.14 Injunctions are a discretionary remedy in the county court, which can be used to control a person's behaviour. They can be an effective tool against those aged 18 or over and for those with the mental capacity to understand what they are doing and how to change their behaviour. Breach of an injunction can result in a prison sentence of up to 2 years and/or an unlimited fine for contempt of court. This law has been modified by the Anti-social Behaviour Act 2003 (ASB Act 2003) and the principle changes are discussed at **1.48–1.64**.

1.15 A cause of action is required to bring proceedings. In respect of anti-social behaviour, the following causes of action will be relevant:

- breach of tenancy agreement;

- trespass to land;

- trespass or assault to the person;

- preventing criminal activity;[8]

- a Housing Act 1996, s 153A injunction with or without powers of arrest (a specific injunction available to the local housing authority to restrain anti-social conduct, threats and violence on or near its housing stock): see **1.51**.

1.16 Interim injunctions are also available. They provide protection to those in need in the period before a trial is heard. The evidential burden to obtain an interim injunction is not as great as that required for the main hearing. Interim ASBOs were clearly styled on the tried and tested remedy of interim injunctions.

1.17 ASBOs may be applied for in a greater number of situations, for a longer period of time and over a wider geographical area. However, injunctions can provide a quick, simple, but short-lived remedy. Breach of an injunction will not result in imprisonment for those under 18 years of age[9] and therefore, apart from the threat of a fine, injunctions are a relatively toothless remedy for young persons. Practitioners are being encouraged to make greater use of injunctions. This area is under government review (eg injunctions against minors) and it remains to be seen what changes may be made and how that may affect ASBOs.

---

[6] Housing Act 2004, s 191, inserting Ground 2A in Sch 3 to the Housing Act 1985. This came into force on 6 June 2005.
[7] Housing Act 2004, s 192, inserting s 121A of the Housing Act 1985. This, too, came into force on 6 June 2005.
[8] See *Nottingham City Council v Zain* [2001] EWCA Civ 1248, [2001] 1 WLR 607; and Local Government Act 1972, s 222.
[9] See *Harrow London Borough Council v G (a child)* [2004] EWHC 17 (QB).

Criminal proceedings

1.18 The criminal law remains an option for more serious complaints of misconduct. The following is a non-exhaustive list of crimes relevant to this area:

- assault (including common assault, assault occasioning actual bodily harm and aggravated assault);

- grievous bodily harm; wounding;

- intimidating or harassing a witness in civil proceedings (Criminal Justice and Police Act 2001, ss 39–41) – similar provisions apply for witness intimidation in the criminal courts;

- Protection from Harassment Act 1997 prosecutions;

- public disorder and breach of the peace offences;

- violent disorder; affray;

- taking a vehicle without consent and associated criminal vehicle-related activities;

- criminal damage;

- theft, robbery and burglary;

- possession of an offensive weapon;

- drunk and disorderly behaviour;

- drugs offences.

1.19 ASBOs were introduced in part to tackle the perceived gap in the criminal law to deal with the full range of anti-social conduct. ASBOs were initially viewed as easier to pursue than criminal prosecutions, as the standard of proof often applied was the civil standard (ie on the balance of probabilities). Now that the standard of proof for ASBOs is the criminal standard (see chapter 3), criminal sanctions should not be discounted in favour of ASBOs without due consideration. Bail conditions, which apply to criminal charges, can be imposed for the protection of witnesses and the community, although obviously the bail conditions will lapse on sentence (or acquittal).

SOLUTIONS OFFERED BY THE CRIME AND DISORDER ACT 1998

1.20 The Crime and Disorder Act 1998 (CDA 1998) introduced new remedies and wide-reaching changes to the criminal law. This included the removal of the presumption of lack of criminal intent for children aged 10 and over, and more varied sentencing options such as detention and training orders and reparation orders.

1.21 Sections 5–6 of the CDA 1998 identify those who are responsible for formulating crime reduction strategies. These are local authorities, the police and, from a date to be appointed, will include the fire authority and primary care trusts or health authorities. These bodies set local priorities for the reduction of crime and disorder after consultation with the local community. They must also co-operate with other bodies, such as the probation service and RSLs, when formulating strategies. In addition, s 1 of the Clean Neighbourhoods and Environment Act 2005 introduces the requirement to consider anti-social and other behaviour adversely affecting the local community when formulating crime reduction strategies.[10] Greater public accountability in this area may be introduced with an extended role of local authority overview and scrutiny committees.

1.22 CDA 1998, s 16 gives the police power to remove truants to designated premises. It was used with success by North Yorkshire Police in York city centre, where town centre shoplifting was reduced by 30% by targeted use of this power during one school term. Other targeted initiatives achieve similar success. This power has been extended by s 75 of the Police Reform Act 2002 (PRA 2002) to include the British Transport Police (BTP).

1.23 CDA 1998, s 17 imposes a statutory duty on the police and local authority to exercise their various functions with due regard to the likely effect of them and to do all that they reasonably can to prevent crime and disorder in their area.

Sex offender orders

1.24 CDA 1998, s 2 gives the police the power to apply for sex offender orders. Sex offender orders can be made where a person is a sex offender and the police have reasonable cause to believe an order is necessary to protect the public from serious harm. Sex offenders' conduct can be regulated by orders similar in terms to an ASBO (eg non-association and exclusion zones). The PRA 2002 introduced a new interim sex offender order. The Sexual Offences Act 2003[11] introduced the sexual offences prevention order, which allows the court to impose or the police to apply for an order prohibiting a defendant from specified acts for a minimum period of 5 years where it is necessary to protect the public from serious sexual harm. Interim orders are also available.

Parenting orders

1.25 CDA 1998, s 8 introduced parenting orders. Designed to impose compulsory parenting classes and, in some cases, conditions for parental supervision (eg ensuring the child attends school), they are triggered by a number of matters such as a criminal conviction against a young person, or the imposition of an ASBO. Breach is prosecutable and punishable by a fine of, currently, up to £1,000.

1.26 Experience from the pilot schemes shows the greatest success has been with parents who are willing to learn and change; it gives them access to resources which may not otherwise have been available. In addition, it emphasises the need for parents and guardians to take responsibility for their children. Parenting orders are viewed by the Home Office Guidance as a complementary tool to help the conditions of the ASBO be met and so reduce the chances of breach. These orders are supervised by a 'responsible officer', who can be from social services, education, YOT or probation. The Home Office Guidance encourages the responsible officer to work closely with the parent in the event of breach to improve compliance before prosecution steps are taken. This has been extended by the ASB Act 2003, and is discussed at **1.56**. For further details about parenting orders see chapter 11 (Post Order Procedure and Ancillary Orders).

---

[10]   This came into force on 7 April 2005.
[11]   Sections 104–113.

Parental compensation orders

1.27 Inserted into the CDA 1998 as s 13A–E by the Serious Organised Crime and Police Act 2005, parental compensation orders (PCOs) have only been brought into force in certain specified areas.[12] A PCO is an order which requires a specified parent or guardian of a child aged 9 or less to pay compensation of not more than £5,000 to a specified person.[13] The order can be made on the application of a local authority if the court is satisfied on a balance of probabilities[14] that:

(a) the child has taken, caused loss to, or damaged property in the course of committing an act which would have been a criminal offence if the child was aged 10 years or more[15] *or* acting in a manner which caused, or was likely to cause, harassment, alarm or distress to a person not of the same household as himself;[16] *and*

(b) it was desirable to make the order in the interests of preventing a repetition of the behaviour in question.[17]

An application arising from damage or loss can be made within the earlier of either 2 years of the commission of the date of offence or within 6 months of its first discovery by the local authority.[18] Before a court can make a PCO it has to obtain and consider information about the child's family circumstances and the likely effect of the order on those circumstances. The court shall before making an order explain to the parent or guardian in ordinary language the effect of the order and the consequences of a failure to comply with its requirements.

1.28 In assessing the compensation the court is required to take into account various factors including whether any reparation has already been made and whether there was any lack of care on the part of the victim which meant that it was easier for the child to take or damage the property![19] If property is taken and recovered before compensation is ordered to be paid no compensation[20] shall be paid if it is not damaged; however, strangely, if it is damaged then any damage is treated as being caused by the child regardless of how it was caused or by whom.[21] Therefore if the 'victim' in recovering it drops it or otherwise acts without care in damaging it then the parent remains liable.

1.29 The court will specify in the order how and by when the compensation is to be paid and can require the parent or guardian to provide a statement of financial circumstances. Failure without reasonable excuse to provide such a statement, if required, makes the parent liable to criminal conviction and a fine not exceeding level 3. Failure to comply with the terms of the PCO can result in a variation by adding to the terms of the order. For the purposes of collection and enforcement a PCO is to be treated as if it were a sum to be paid on conviction in the magistrates' court.[22]

---

12 Serious Organised Crime and Police Act 2005 (Commencement) (No. 7) Order 2006 (SI 2006/1871).
13 CDA 1998, s 13A(3) and (4).
14 CDA 1998, s 13A(1).
15 CDA 1998, s 13A(2)(a).
16 CDA 1998, s 13A(2)(b).
17 CDA 1998, s 13A(1)(b).
18 CDA 1998, s 13B(7).
19 CDA 1998, s 13B(1)(a)–(f).
20 CDA 1998, s 13B(2)(a).
21 CDA 1998, s 13B(2)(b).
22 CDA 1998, s 13A(6).

1.30 There is a right of appeal to the Crown Court by a parent against the making of a PCO[23] and the victim cannot receive compensation until the time for appeal has lapsed.[24] Any sum in a PCO has to be deducted from any damages awarded in civil proceedings in respect of the same loss or damage.[25]

1.31 It is hard to see PCOs being used very often by local authorities. The cost of these applications will not be small and the need for reports into family circumstances is also not likely to be without cost. It is unlikely that any parent or guardian who is likely to be the subject of an application will be able to pay more than a very small sum per week in any event. Perhaps by visiting the consequences of the child's anti-social behaviour on the parent in a financial consequence it is hoped that better control will be exercised by the parent. This remains to be seen, however, it is most notable that the imposition of a PCO permits the court to make a parenting order which may be the most productive consequence of the new subsections.

Child curfew schemes

1.32 Local child curfew schemes were introduced by CDA 1998, ss 14–15. Local authorities were given the power, after due consultation with the police and those specified in the scheme, and for the sole purpose of maintaining order, to ban children under 10 years of age from specified places for limited periods (not exceeding 90 days) unless accompanied by a responsible adult. Breach of an order permits the police to take the child home unless there is reasonable belief that the child would suffer significant harm there. Breach imposes a duty on the police to notify the local authority. Under s 47(1)(a)(iii) of the Children Act 1989, the local authorities have a duty to make 'such enquiries as they consider necessary to enable them to decide whether they should take any action to safeguard or promote the child's welfare'. Because of this, the police will have new powers to disperse groups in the ASB Act 2003 (see **1.57**).

1.33 There was a very limited initial take-up of child curfew schemes by local authorities because of practical problems such as identifying those under 10 years of age, and establishing whether or not accompanying adults are responsible for the child. In 2001, the scheme was extended to those under 16, and gave the police (in addition to the local authority) power to impose a ban under CDA 1998, s 14(1).[26] However, such practical problems persist and the remedy has been rarely used, although such schemes as have been implemented have had a high profile, and the police and local authorities have reported successful results, eg in Seaford.

1.34 To address the problem of youth 'gangs' that instil fear in some elements of the community, other methods such as greater visible use of CCTV, youth diversionary schemes or community-based activities which bring the youths and those who fear them together to promote a greater understanding of each other may be more effective.

Child safety orders

1.35 Child safety orders are available against those under 10 years old and were introduced by CDA 1998, ss 11–13. The local authority can apply to the family proceedings section of the magistrates' court which can make an order if it is desirable. Triggers for this application include anti-social behaviour or conduct which would amount to a criminal offence had the child been of prosecutable age. If a child safety order is made, the young person comes under the

---

23   CDA 1998, s 13D(1).
24   CDA 1998, s 13D(5).
25   CDA 1998, s 13E.
26   Inserted by Criminal Justice and Police Act 2001, s 48.

supervision of a social worker of a member of a YOT. Some have already discounted this remedy as adding little to existing child protection measures such as supervision orders or care orders.

ACCEPTABLE BEHAVIOUR CONTRACTS

1.36 First introduced in Islington in North London, acceptable behaviour contracts (ABCs) are seen as an alternative to ASBOs. They are essentially a contract of good behaviour between the police and/or members of the local authority, other partner agencies and the person who has been involved in anti-social behaviour.

1.37 ABCs can be made with anyone aged 10 and over, although they were designed specifically to deal with young persons under the age of 18. For children under 10, the parents of the child should be asked to sign up to a parental responsibility contract. Parental responsibility contracts (not to be confused with parental responsibility agreements under the Children Act 1989) are based on the same principles as ABCs.

1.38 ABCs often contain the same or very similar terms to those found in an ASBO application. They are a voluntary recognition by alleged perpetrators of their misconduct, and a set of agreed terms to help stop it. The ABC, where appropriate, should come with the offer of support to enhance its prospects of successfully abating the anti-social behaviour.

1.39 ABCs have no legal effect or sanctions for breach. They may, however, be cited in a later ASBO application. Where an ABC has been breached an ASBO may often be the only remaining solution. The ABC usually lasts for one year, although this can be shortened or extended, depending on the circumstances. It is good practice to post a clear warning on the face of the document that breach of the contract may ultimately result in the relevant agency seeking an ASBO. For young people, ABCs are most effective when couched in terms they can understand.

1.40 The current Home Office Guidance contains extensive information on the ABC process.[27] The Guidance deals with the relationship between ASBOs and ABCs, and emphasises that ASBOs and ABCs are *not* in competition with each other.[28]

1.41 The experience of many local authorities has shown that ABCs can address anti-social behaviour in certain people. For the perpetrator of repeated and serious anti-social behaviour however, nothing short of an ASBO from the outset may be appropriate. The use of ABCs has been extended by the ASB Act 2003 in the context of contracts with parents (see **1.56**). Practical experience continues to extend the use of ABCs to encompass group, family and even community ABCs. More information on this area can be obtained from the 'useful links' section.

ADVANTAGES OF ASBOS

1.42 Alternatives to ASBOs have been explored earlier in this chapter. The following is a checklist of the principal advantages of ASBOs:

- they do not depend on the status of a defendant as tenant to apply;

- they are not locality-specific – other remedies (eg some injunctions) are tied to certain locations or their vicinity, whereas ASBOs can apply throughout England and Wales;

---

[27] See current Home Office Guidance reproduced in Appendix 3.
[28] See current Home Office Guidance reproduced in Appendix 3.

- they can have a long duration and a wide-ranging application – ASBOs last for a minimum of 2 years and may last indefinitely;

- they can apply to anyone aged 10 and over.

DISADVANTAGES OF ASBOS

Cost

1.43 A common criticism of ASBOs is that they are expensive to obtain compared to other remedies. As well as legal costs, there are the hidden costs of the time of the officers involved in the process.

Bureaucracy

1.44 To satisfy the necessity test and requirements to consult partner agencies, some discount ASBOs as too slow and complex. Although there can be more work in the ASBO process, systems should be streamlined instead of discarding ASBOs altogether. Properly prepared ASBO applications can provide a speedy and lasting remedy to the problem of anti-social behaviour.

Criminalisation of anti-social behaviour

1.45 Some view ASBOs as fundamentally wrong in that criminal penalties flow from acts which in themselves do not amount to criminal behaviour, for example, being in breach of an exclusion zone. This can be addressed by having proper safeguards in place to justify the imposition of an ASBO in each case. Safeguards can include representation from all quarters on the ASBO decision panel (eg YOT when young people are ASBO candidates). This ensures that the correct balance and thought processes precede each application and the terms sought.

CHOOSING THE APPROPRIATE SOLUTION

1.46 The most effective key to combating anti-social conduct is to choose the right solution from all available options as quickly as possible. The following are useful pointers in choosing the appropriate solution:

- early intervention can prevent a problem developing or worsening;

- if court action is inevitable, injunctions are available as a 'short, sharp shock';

- possession proceedings can be used for serious or persistent or multi-faceted household problems where the only practical solution is for one party to leave;

- ASBOs are available for persistent or serious misconduct to target specific terms against a specific defendant over a potentially wide area for a potentially long time;

- the criminal law is available as well as or instead of other remedies to punish and rehabilitate;

- a recognition that the three-pronged approach of preventative, enforcement and rehabilitatory remedies is required to find a long-lasting, holistic solution to anti-social behaviour.

HOME OFFICE GUIDANCE

1.47 To help practitioners with ASBOs, the Home Office has issued written Guidance. The first was issued in March 1999; the second came out in June 2000. The third and latest was published on 12 November 2002 and the most recent one came in August 2006 and replaces the earlier three. It is a considerable improvement on its forerunners, and is more practical. The Guidance does not have the force of law. However, the court may have regard to it when interpreting law on ASBOs. Any public body, such as the police or local authority, must take proper and reasonable notice of any Guidance or their decisions can be challenged by judicial review. The full text of the current Guidance is reproduced in Appendix 3. The Home Office has also recently announced that the Guidance on ASBOs will be updated again but at the time of writing no further details are available.[29]

THE ANTI-SOCIAL BEHAVIOUR ACT 2003 – THE MAIN CHANGES

1.48 The ASB Act 2003 introduced changes to remedies for dealing with anti-social behaviour, covering a range of matters from noise and graffiti to high hedges, the closure of premises used for drugs, and nuisance behaviour.

1.49 Social landlords have had to prepare, publish and review policies and procedures for tackling anti-social behaviour. A summary must be available free of charge. The full policy document must be available for inspection at the landlord's main office or on request for a fee. Whether an actionable duty will be created if a landlord does not follow its own policies and procedures remains to be seen.[30]

1.50 From 30 June 2004 RSLs, as defined in Part I of the Housing Act 1996, can apply to the county court for a demoted tenancy order in respect of assured and secure tenancies. Where there is evidence of anti-social conduct by a tenant and/or a resident or visitor to a tenant's home and it is reasonable to make an order, the court can create a demoted tenancy for a period of one year. Existing terms, for example, rent, remain the same. If a landlord during that year applies to the court for possession of a demoted tenancy for *any breach of tenancy*, the scheme operates in a similar way to the introductory tenancy regime. The court *must* grant possession provided proper internal procedures for taking and reviewing the decision to take possession have been followed.[31]

1.51 The ASB Act 2003 replaced the current anti-social behaviour injunction provisions of the Housing Act 1996 from 30 June 2004. The changes allow *all* RSLs to take out this form of injunction where there is evidence of anti-social conduct, which is defined as conduct capable of causing nuisance or annoyance to any person and which directly or indirectly relates to or affects the housing management function of a relevant landlord. Other provisions prevent the unlawful use of premises and breach of tenancy agreement also by injunction.[32] It is also possible to exclude tenants from their homes.

---

[29] Home Office Press release dated 20 December 2005, quoting Home Office Minister Hazel Blears.
[30] See ASB Act 2003, s 12.
[31] ASB Act 2003, ss 14–17 and Sch 1.
[32] ASB Act 2003, ss 12–13.

1.52 Powers of arrest can be attached if the conduct includes the use or threat of violence or there is a significant risk of harm to the relevant category of person, depending which injunction is being applied for.

1.53 Powers of arrest are also available for an injunction brought under s 222 of the Local Government Act 1972 where there is the threat of or actual violence.[33] However following the case of *Birmingham City Council v Shafi*[34] it would seem that where the local authority seeks an injunction in circumstances in which an ASBO would be available the court should not, save in an exceptional case, grant an injunction under s 222 but leave the local authority to seek an ASBO so that the detailed checks and balances developed by Parliament and in the decided cases should apply. The Court of Appeal also considered that even if the application for an injunction was considered the burden and standard of proof should be as in an ASBO, ie on the applicant authority to show beyond reasonable doubt that the defendant had acted in an anti-social manner.

1.54 The changes to the injunction provisions were introduced to overcome problems in case-law that arose under the Housing Act 1996 regime which demanded a nexus between the conduct complained of, the persons the injunction was designed to protect and the correct application of Housing Act legislation to protect others. A new test of 'conduct which directly or indirectly relates to or affects the housing management functions of a landlord' was introduced to remedy these problems. This term itself is imprecise and is likely to lead to similar satellite litigation as to its meaning.

1.55 The courts must have regard to the past, present and future effect on the community of anti-social behaviour when exercising discretion in possession proceedings brought under Ground 2 of the Housing Act 1985 (as amended by the Housing Act 1996) and Ground 14 of the Housing Act 1988 (the statutory grounds for nuisance possession for secure and assured tenancies respectively).[35]

1.56 The concept of parenting orders and contracts has been extended. Local education authorities (LEAs) and schools can enter into parenting contracts with parents of pupils excluded on disciplinary grounds. YOTs can enter into parenting contracts with parents of young people displaying anti-social or criminal-like behaviour. LEAs, schools and YOTs can also apply to the magistrates' court for a free-standing parenting order now.[36] A court must make a parenting order where it makes an ASBO against a person under 16, or give reasons for not doing so in open court.[37] This area may also be extended in more planned government initiatives.

1.57 The police can disperse groups of two or more persons where there has been evidence of anti-social behaviour. Believed by some to be mainly used to tackle youth nuisance, other provisions against those under the age of 16 include fixed penalty notices for unruly children or for parents of truants,[38] and power to return children of under 16 who are out in a public place after 9 pm to their home or to a place of safety if not accompanied by a responsible adult over the age of 18.[39] This latter power has been clarified in case-law.[40] There, W applied for judicial review of the authorisation given to the police to remove persons under 16 from dispersal areas in town centres. W had been given a piece of paper including a map of the dispersal area. W was

---

[33] ASB Act 2003, s 91.
[34] [2008] EWCA Civ 1186.
[35] From 30 June 2004.
[36] See ASB Act 2003, ss 18–22 and 25–29.
[37] ASB Act 2003, ss 18–29.
[38] ASB Act 2003, ss 23 and 30.
[39] ASB Act 2003, ss 30–36.
[40] *R (on the application of W) v (1) Commissioner of Police for the Metropolis (2) Richmond-Upon-Thames LBC (Defendants) Secretary of State for the Home Department (Interested Party)* [2005] EWHC 1586 (Admin).

concerned the police might use their power to use reasonable force to remove him to his home from a dispersal area against his will at any time. He objected to how that fear would constrain his life, especially as he lived in one of the dispersal areas. The Divisional Court decided the power to 'remove' in s 30(6) was permissive not coercive. It did not confer a power on the police or community support officer to interfere with the movements of someone under the age of 16 conducting himself lawfully within a dispersal area between the stated hours. It only gave the police power to use police resources to take a person home if he was willing to be taken home.

1.58 Other provisions give powers to the police and the magistrates' courts to close premises associated with class A drugs and serious public nuisance for a maximum period of 6 months.[41]

1.59 Changes to firearms legislation make it generally illegal for imitation firearms to be carried in a public place. The age limit for owning a firearm has also been increased to 17.[42]

1.60 The local authority has extended powers to close noisy licensed premises for up to 24 hours and can serve fixed penalty notices for fly tipping and graffiti. Graffiti remedial notices to tackle property defaced by offensive or detrimental images can also be served; a local authority scheme to deal with high hedges where local neighbours cannot resolve their differences is also introduced.[43]

1.61 Further powers[44] have been given to the local authority. These include the power to increase the scope of fixed penalty notices, to remove abandoned cars immediately and to provide for new offences of nuisance parking and car repair businesses. Powers to control litter have also been extended. Dropping litter is now an offence on *all* land; councils can now make businesses and people alike clear up litter from their land under litter clearing notices.

1.62 Street litter control notices strengthen powers to make local businesses clean up the litter they generate. Councils can now restrict the distribution of flyers, handouts and pamphlets that can end up as litter. Cigarette butts and discarded chewing gum are now regarded as litter. Graffiti, flyposting and waste management powers introduced by the ASB Act 2003 have been strengthened.

1.63 There is a simplified system for dealing with nuisance caused by dogs such as fouling and stray dogs. Noise nuisance powers in relation to burglar alarms and licensed premises have been strengthened.

Gating orders also allow local authorities to restrict public access/rights of way over land affected by crime or anti-social behaviour.

1.64 The ASB Act 2003 introduced individual support orders (ISOs), which are discussed in detail at **11.46** et seq.

---

[41] ASB Act 2003, ss 1–11.
[42] ASB Act 2003, ss 37–39.
[43] ASB Act 2003, ss 65–84.
[44] These are contained in the Clean Neighbourhoods and Environment Act 2005; they came into force on 7 April 2005.

CHAPTER 2

THE PROBLEM-SOLVING GROUP
AND CONSULTATION

INTRODUCTION

2.1   The framework for dealing with ASBOs has been in place since 1999, when the first Home Office Guidance was published. Many problem-solving groups are now well established. For authorities yet to form such groups, it will not be sufficient to adopt the structure of existing groups without tailoring them to local practices and procedures. The experience of established groups shows that it is essential to monitor practices and procedures and be prepared to review, refine and, if necessary, rewrite operational systems in the light of experience. For the defendant, it is important to understand not just the legal framework in which ASBOs operate, but also how the local decision-making process works, and to examine whether the group is operating within its own defined policies and procedures.

2.2   This chapter looks at the consultation requirements placed on anti-social behaviour problem-solving groups, protocols for partnership working, data protection issues that arise from handling sensitive personal data, and relationships between the anti-social behaviour problem-solving groups and other bodies such as the courts.

CONSULTATION

Statutory requirements

2.3   Before a summons for an application for an ASBO can be issued, CDA 1998, s 1E[1] requires there to be consultation between the 'relevant authorities'. The statutory consultation requirements can be summarised as follows:[2]

(a)   the council must consult with the chief officer of police for the area;[3]

(b)   the chief officer of police must consult with the council;[4] and

(c)   RSLs, the BTP, Housing Action Trusts and county councils must consult with *both* the police and the council for the area.[5]

2.4   The relevant council for consultation is the one which has responsibility for the address at which the defendant lives or would appear to reside.[6] It is intended that every local authority and police force should have a designated person who can be consulted, which appears to have been largely carried out in practice.

---

1   Police Reform Act 2002 (PRA 2002), s 66.
2   CDA 1998, s 1E, inserted by PRA 2002, s 66.
3   CDA 1998, s 1E(2).
4   CDA 1998, s 1E(3).
5   CDA 1998, s 1E(4).
6   CDA 1998, s 1E(3).

2.5   Consultation should not be confused with consent. The purpose of consultation is to inform other agencies of intended applications and to exchange information. There is no requirement to have the consent of the other relevant agencies – only that they should have had the opportunity to comment. However, in reality, if there is a lack of agreement, the application would have to be very carefully reconsidered before proceeding to a hearing.

2.6   The only document that should be filed with the court is a signed document of consultation. There is no need to indicate whether or not an agreement was reached or otherwise. There may be a temptation to file notes from case conferences together with the information and comment forms which many local authorities send to the various interested professional bodies. This is unnecessary and should not be done. Similarly, the case conference notes should not be filed or disclosed. These are prepared at a meeting in the anticipation and contemplation of the application and need not be disclosed. If support from other agencies or authorities is forthcoming and thought necessary, statements can be provided.

2.7   The wording of the statute clearly states that consultation with the police shall be with the chief officer of the police force. In practice, this never happens, and a subordinate officer, usually an inspector or lower rank, takes on the duties of consultation on behalf of the police. The notice of consultation is, therefore, not generally signed by a Chief Constable and this led to challenges to the validity of consultation certificates, and, thus, the entire applications. The case of *The Chief Constable of West Midlands Police v Birmingham Justices*[7] deals decisively with this argument. A district judge (crime) had held that the delegation by the Chief Constable of his or her powers to consult for ASBOs to persons of rank lower than a superintendent by internal memorandum was incapable of satisfying the requirements of the Act. In quashing the decision of the district judge, Sedley LJ held that:

(a)   all but the most important powers of the Chief Constable could be delegated;

(b)   the power could be delegated to an officer for whom he or she is answerable;

(c)   it was not necessary to rely on implied delegation; and

(d)   it was not for the courts to say that the Chief Constable's choice of the level or person to whom the power was delegated was right or wrong, unless that choice was irrational or otherwise beyond his or her powers.

2.8   In this case, it was not determined whether or not the sergeant involved had actual authorisation to act. Therefore, this remains a point which the defendant can legitimately seek to challenge. Conversely, the applicant should ensure that this issue has been properly addressed before the application is made. The Divisional Court did not consider the consequences of failing to consult. Whilst it could be argued that the omission was not fatal to the application, the use of the word 'shall' in the Act would seem to be a condition precedent and render the application void. However, in the unreported case of *McClarty & McClarty v Wigan MBC*,[8] the High Court considered the meaning of consultation in more depth. In this case, two applications for ASBOs were made, with the lead being taken by the housing management company, which was wholly owned by the council but was set up as an arm's length management organisation (ALMO). Before the circuit judge there was evidence of consultation by a tenancy relations manager of the ALMO with a council employee duly authorised by the council to consult on ASBO applications. That person then consulted with a duly authorised person at the police. An appeal was lodged on the previously unargued point that the circuit judge did not have jurisdiction to grant an ASBO, as consultation had not been properly complied with. By the hearing before Mr Justice

---

[7]   [2002] EWHC 1087 (Admin).
[8]   (Unreported) 30 October 2003, Mr Justice Beatson.

Beatson, evidence had been filed showing that many months prior to the applications being made, the defendants had been referred to a Positive Action Team, where officers from both the council and the police (and both duly authorised to consult) were present. The group met fortnightly and discussed the defendants' case every 10 weeks. The group attempted but failed to solve the problem and an application was to be approved. However, before the meeting to authorise formally an application for an ASBO, a chance to issue such an application arose during a hearing in the principal proceedings and was taken. On the day of the application (and not as previously told to the circuit judge), the tenancy relations manager called both the police and council officers 'as a courtesy to senior officers in both organisations' and they agreed to seek the orders. In fact, whilst an interim order was to have been requested, final orders were made.

2.9 Mr Justice Beatson noted that, notwithstanding the Home Office Guidance, there was no certificate of consultation produced or filed. The appellants argued that consultation required a genuine invitation to give advice and a genuine consideration of that advice with sufficient time to achieve both.[9] The appellants argued that there was no adequate consultation in this case: calls by the ALMO to the council and police could not constitute consultation between the police and council. The referral to the Positive Action Team could not constitute consultation, as there was no proposal to seek ASBOs at that time. They also argued that there was a failure to seek comments from the YOT or notify the social services department to obtain a s 17 assessment.

2.10 The judge was highly critical of the manner in which consultation had been arranged by the tenancy relations manager of the ALMO and made clear that they had no locus to bring ASBO proceedings. He also was critical of the lack of recording, note or minute-taking at the Positive Action Team meetings and the council's seeming lack of awareness of the Home Office Guidance. He highlighted the lack of structure in the consultation process and noted that where an authority could not show that there had been co-ordination between the specified agencies, it may find that the court could not be satisfied that the order was necessary. He advised the council to review its procedures and consider their adequacy, given that the ALMO was not part of the council, but a separate company.

2.11 The court also found that the telephone call by the tenancy relations manager could not constitute consultation, because, first, this was done, in his words, as a 'courtesy' and, secondly, he was not employed by the council and could not consult with anyone for the purposes of the Act's requirements. On the issue of whether consultation was a condition precedent, however, the judge held:

> 'I have concluded that in the context of the 1998 Act as amended, the requirement in section 1E to consult is fulfilled by substantial compliance even though there may not have been strict compliance. This is because the purpose of section 1E or one of the purposes is to ensure co-ordination between agencies which have authority to institute proceedings in particular before the institution of court proceedings. Such co-ordination may be achieved in a number of ways. The Home Office Guidance indicates that one of these is by partnership working arrangement such as the Positive Action Team.
>
> ... the obligation to consult is not to consult those who would be primarily affected by an order but it is to consult other public bodies with authority to institute proceedings for Anti-social behaviour orders. Nothing before me suggests that the police, the party to be consulted in these proceedings which were to be launched by a local authority consider that there has been no or inadequate consultation.'

The court held that the participation of the authorised police and local authority representatives at the Positive Action Team meetings when the defendants' position was considered over many

---

9   See *R v Secretary of State for Social Services ex parte Association of Metropolitan Authorities* [1986] 1 WLR 1, per Webster J at p 4.

months (albeit every 10 weeks) substantially complied with the obligation to consult. This, however, should not be encouraged, as the meaning of substantial compliance is not clear and is open to construction and argument. A recognised system of authorisation to consult and proper panel meetings is preferable. Producing a certification of consultation should not be difficult and should be in a simple form, capable of proof.

2.12 In *Manchester City Council v Muir & Another*[10] the Court of Appeal held that 'a judge hearing an application for an interim order under s 1D not only has jurisdiction to decide whether there has been sufficient consultation, but is obliged to do so if the issue is raise'. If the point is then taken by the defendant and ruled on it could be raised again at the hearing of the final order. Further Lord Justice May observed that whilst a certificate of consultation was mentioned in the Home Office Guidance, such a certificate was not a statutory requirement. All that was required was evidence that the council had consulted the chief officer of police. The court noted that in the instance case there was unchallenged witness statement evidence of a case management conference with all relevant agencies and a certificate of consultation signed on behalf of the chief constable and on behalf of the city council. The appropriate consultation requirement had therefore been substantially satisfied.

Consultation with other agencies

2.13 A case-by-case decision should be made as to which agencies, other than those defined in s 1E of the CDA 1998, should contribute to the decision-making process. Appropriate bodies can be asked to make contributions, either in writing or in person. Such bodies may include:

- the Probation Service;

- an RSL (if not the main applicant);

- the health authority;

- Community Action Groups;

- social services or the YOT (essential where the defendant is a minor);

- housing departments (where the defendant is a council tenant); and

- other council departments (eg environmental services).

2.14 The group needs to be able to discuss and, if appropriate, put into action alternative remedies. This is more likely to occur if all relevant bodies are present at meetings. If alternative remedies are not discussed and considered, it can be argued that the decision-making process was flawed and that it was not a reasonable or proportionate decision to apply for an ASBO. The decision-making of a public body can also be subject to judicial review on the grounds that its actions are 'unreasonable'.[11]

2.15 Alternatively, the defence may argue that the court should not make an order because it was not 'necessary', as there were other means to protect the public which were more appropriate and were not considered before the ASBO application was made. Whilst the legal advice that a group receives will be privileged, minutes or a written record of the decisions of

---

[10] [2006] EWCA Civ 423.
[11] For a definition of 'unreasonable', see *Associated Provincial Picture Houses v Wednesbury Corporation* [1948] 1 KB 223, [1947] 2 All ER 680.

the group and the resulting action plan should be kept in each case. The failure to keep such records has been the subject of judicial criticism.[12] Examination of the decision summary is an essential part of the defence preparation.

Home Office recommendations

2.16 The current Home Office Guidance makes the following recommendations with respect to consultation and group dynamics:

- a fully co-ordinated approach is essential – 'effective defence of communities' rests with all agencies working together;

- one specific person in the lead agency should take overall responsibility and manage and co-ordinate the case, and liaise with other agencies to take necessary actions within set time-scales;

- a suggested protocol for partnership working is provided (see **2.16**);

- the consultation process ensures that relevant information about a possible defendant is obtained from all partner agencies;

- the purpose of consultation is not to secure agreement between all partner agencies but to give all parties an opportunity to comment in order to reduce conflicting actions being taken by different agencies in a case;

- no one agency has the right to veto another's application; and

- case conferences are meant to allow reservations and any alternative proposals to be 'discussed carefully', but with the overriding need to bring the anti-social behaviour to an end quickly.

PROTOCOLS

2.17 The Coventry Crime and Disorder Reduction Partnership (CDRP) is used as a role model of partnership working in the current Home Office Guidance. Essential features of this scheme include:

- a wide-ranging membership, comprising most agencies suggested at **2.13**, but also the courts and the Crown Prosecution Service (CPS);

- defined protocols that also allow for the receipt of views from outside the main group;

- the use of case conferences to facilitate information exchange and discussion – these can be requested by any agency – which should be held within 2 weeks of a case referral, and should end with an action plan recorded by the lead officer; and

- the appointment of one lead officer to manage all aspects of the case.

2.18 It is not necessary for problem-solving groups to set up elaborate or complicated protocols before they become operational. Protocols should set out the framework in which the group

---

[12] *McClarty & McClarty v Wigan MBC* (unreported) 30 October 2003, Mr Justice Beatson – see further **2.8**.

should operate. If available to the general public, and it is recommended that they should be, such protocols will be essential reading for the defence. The defence should examine whether the group is working within its protocols when reaching decisions. The second set of Home Office Guidance of June 2000 contained extensive guidance on how to set up local protocols. However, the current Guidance does not include such advice, but sets out the Coventry CDRP as a model to follow.

2.19 Protocols should be revised regularly to take account of best practice and new legislation, (eg the Human Rights Act 1998 (HRA 1998) and the PRA 2002). They should be flexible enough to take proper account of the views of the defendant and the interested parties.

2.20 If a defendant requests an opportunity to be heard prior to a final decision being made, this request should ordinarily be granted. Failure to give the request and any subsequent submissions serious consideration could potentially result in an application for judicial review.

DATA PROTECTION AND INFORMATION EXCHANGE PROTOCOLS

2.21 As evidence is gathered by the ASBO problem-solving group, this will almost inevitably raise issues of the proper use of the defendant's personal information by other agencies. A proper balance must be achieved between the two, often conflicting, principles of a person's right to privacy and the need to protect the public.

Accessing 'personal data'

2.22 The Data Protection Act 1998 (DPA 1998) provides an individual with the right to access his or her 'personal data' held by another. 'Personal data' means data which relate to a living individual who can be identified:

'(a)   from those data, or
(b)   from those data and other information which is in the possession of, or is likely to come into the possession of, the data controller,

and includes any expression of opinion about the individual and any indication of the intentions of the data controller or any other person in respect of the individual.'[13]

2.23 On payment of a fee – currently, £10 – a request by a person to access his or her personal data must be processed within 40 days, provided it has been properly made. This is defined as when it is accompanied by the correct fee, the material required to be disclosed has been properly identified and the person whom the data is about is either making the request or has given consent to do so to another.

2.24 It is good practice for the defence to consider making such a request to the local authority and the police. It may only reveal what will be disclosed as part of the applicant's evidence; however, it may also reveal information that can be used to support an argument that an ASBO was not necessary, or to establish a 'disregard' defence. For example, it may reveal that the defendant has had a difficult upbringing, with no support from social services, despite parental requests for assistance.

---

[13]   Extract from Data Protection Act 1998, s 1.

2.25 A defendant will often receive advance warning that he is being considered for an ASBO, either because he receives a warning letter from the anti-social behaviour problem-solving group, or because he is approached by the YOT to conduct an assessment of needs. Potentially, therefore, the defendant has an opportunity to influence the decision-making process by giving reasons for his or her behaviour or providing acceptable assurances as to his or her future conduct. However, if the group proceeds with an application for an ASBO and refuses to hear the defendant, this may provide grounds for attacking the process as a whole.

2.26 The defendant may complain to the Information Commissioner if he or she believes that the provisions of the DPA 1998 have been breached. The Commissioner can now award compensation for breach and non-compliance can result in criminal sanctions. For more details, refer to the Information Commissioner's website (www.dataprotection.gov.uk).

Information exchange

2.27 CDA 1998, s 115 states:

'Any person who, apart from this sub-section, would not have power to disclose information –

(a)   to a relevant authority, or
(b)   to a person acting on behalf of such an authority,

shall have *power* to do so in any case where the disclosure is necessary or expedient for the purposes of any provision of this Act.'

'Relevant authority' is defined as the chief police officer, a local authority, a police authority, a local probation board in England and Wales and a health authority/primary care trust.

2.28 RSLs have recently been added to the list of 'relevant authorities' to enable them to receive information to sit with extended powers for dealing with anti-social behaviour themselves in the field of injunctions, demoted tenancies and ASBOs. (See chapters 1 and 3 for further information.)[14]

2.29 Section 115 gives a power, not a duty, to give disclosure. The decision on what and how to disclose remains with the person holding the data. The 'purposes in the Act' are any of the provisions in the CDA 1998 and can include local crime audits, YOT work, ASBOs, sex offender orders and parenting orders. When coupled with the general statutory provision of s 17, this creates the potential for far-reaching disclosure.

2.30 Information sharing is addressed in part by the Home Office Guidance. Where a body is an agent of a relevant authority for the purposes of s 115, the 'body so acting' must have consented to act and had authority to do so. Authority can be implied, be in writing or given orally and can be general or case-specific. The Guidance also suggests that information-sharing protocols should be negotiated in advance, and provides helpful website addresses. Queries should be directed to the Information Commissioner. Anti-social behaviour working group protocols should be freely available to the public.

2.31 In order to carry out disclosure lawfully, the principles of data protection principles must be followed. These include processing information fairly and lawfully, keeping information only for as long as is necessary, and ensuring that it is secure. This will only cause problems in the processing of personal data for particular cases, as opposed to depersonalised data for use in crime statistics. Unless consent has been given by a possible defendant to disclose his or her

---

[14]   Housing Act 2004, s 219, inserting s 115(2)(d)(a), CDA 1998. This came into force on 18 January 2005.

personal information to others, the best advice to applicants is to consider carefully how much personal information is needed in each case and if it can be justified under s 115 or the data protection exemptions for the prevention of crime. If in doubt, seek expert advice or consult the Information Commissioner, with a request for advice within a certain timescale so as not to delay the ASBO process.

2.32 The defendant and his or her legal advisers will wish to ensure that the defendant's rights to privacy in general are preserved and also that evidence has been obtained properly and fairly for the purposes of an ASBO application. If material has been released or obtained in an unauthorised way, it may be argued that this evidence should not be used in court.

2.33 RSLs have also been given greater powers to receive information from any person relevant to deciding whether they should exercise powers to withhold consent to a mutual exchange where an order is in force or pending in relation to anti-social behaviour or to apply to court to suspend a tenant's right to buy. See **1.13** for further details.[15]

RELATIONS WITH OTHER BODIES

Crown Prosecution Service

2.34 The CPS is responsible for the prosecution of alleged breaches of an ASBO (although local authorities are also authorised to bring a prosecution since 31 March 2004).[16] They also may have a greater part to play in obtaining ASBOs with the introduction of the post-conviction ASBO. However, applicant authorities may find it helpful to consider the following practices in relations with the CPS:

- Agree a procedure with the CPS as to what information should be provided and to whom, which should include the precise nature of the information to be provided to the CPS when it is prosecuting the breach of an ASBO.

- Invite the CPS to all ASBO problem-solving group meetings. If CPS attendance is not practicable, send minutes or case action plans. The CPS should be asked to advise where it has concerns about the prosecution of particular terms of an ASBO, and may also be given information about forthcoming cases.

- Inform the CPS of any case which relies upon an incident of anti-social behaviour which is also being prosecuted as a criminal offence. This ensures that the CPS gives particular attention to the matter, rather than offering a bind-over or agreeing not to proceed in exchange for a guilty plea on another, more serious, charge unrelated to anti-social behaviour.

- Develop named liaison officers and contacts between the CPS and the problem-solving group. The co-location of CPS officers in police stations may assist here.

- Utilise the designated anti-social behaviour expert prosecutors.

---

[15] Housing Act 2004, s 194. This came into force on 6 June 2005.
[16] See **13.14**.

The courts

2.35 The procedures for presenting applications and appeals are dealt with in later chapters. However, meetings with court officials to agree standard procedures to deal with ASBO applications are advised. The offer of training by applicants to magistrates and their clerks on ASBO matters is usually well received.

2.36 If an agreement has been made, it should be available on request to the defence, so that they have the opportunity to consider the agreement and to argue against the application on any of the points set out in the agreement. Constructive criticisms made by defendants' solicitors should be given equal consideration in any review of a service level agreement.

The defendant

2.37 It should not be forgotten by either the authorities making the application or by the defendant or his or her legal advisers that preventative work with the defendant remains an option throughout the whole ASBO process. Before an application is made, other methods of dealing with anti-social behaviour should be considered and rejected as less appropriate. If a defendant accepts an offer of help, it would be difficult to satisfy the necessity test unless the defendant continues to behave in an anti-social manner. Depending on how the defendant responds to the voluntary work with agencies such as social services or the YOT, the applicant must decide whether to proceed with the ASBO application or to withdraw it, provided some acceptable guarantees as to future conduct and/or continued participation with agencies are given. This can often be achieved by entering into a carefully worded ABC. If the defendant fails to respond, then it is likely to be necessary to proceed with an application, although the applicant should remain open to any genuine and sustained change in the defendant's behaviour and/or willingness to work with the agencies.

2.38 There is, however, no absolute right of the defendant to attend or address a case conference. This point was considered in *Carl Wareham v Purbeck District Council*.[17] In this case the council had written to the defendant saying that they intended to have a conference to decide whether to apply for an ASBO. The letter said that he would be told what was decided but did not invite him to attend or comment. He did neither in any event. The council decided to apply for an ASBO and did so. The defendant argued that as he had not been consulted in the decision-making process as to whether to apply for an order his rights under Art 6 and 8 had been infringed and sought relief accordingly from the administrative court.

2.39 A strong administrative court held that the decision to apply did not constitute an infringement with the right as the defendant had the right to be represented at the main hearing and to argue against the order and/or the terms. The defendant's analogy with care orders was not an appropriate one. Further it was not a breach of Art 6 to not invite the defendant to comment. Whilst 'in some, perhaps many, cases' the defendant could be involved before a decision was taken, this was for the decision-making group to decide. The point should therefore be addressed by the conference. It is suggested that it would be rare indeed for the defendant to be allowed to attend, however, there is no reason why they cannot be asked to commit any comments they wish to make into writing. The minutes should of course record that they were considered.

---

[17]　*The Times Law Reports*, 28 March 2005.

CHAPTER 3

APPLICATIONS FOR
ANTI-SOCIAL BEHAVIOUR ORDERS

3.1 The CDA 1998 has been amended significantly[1] in several important ways; however, the legal basis under which applications are made is unchanged.

WHERE CAN AN APPLICATION BE MADE?

3.2 An application for an ASBO may be made:

(a) to the magistrates' court sitting in its civil jurisdiction; or

(b) to a county court in appropriate cases; or[2]

(c) to criminal courts (both magistrates' and crown courts) on criminal conviction.

WHEN CAN AN APPLICATION BE MADE?

3.3 An application may be made by a relevant authority if it appears to that authority that:

(a) the person has acted, since the commencement date,[3] in an anti-social manner – that is to say, in a manner that caused or was likely to cause harassment, alarm or distress to one or more persons not of the same household as himself; and

(b) such an order is necessary to protect relevant persons from further anti-social acts by him.[4]

'RELEVANT AUTHORITY' – WHO CAN APPLY?

3.4 An application for an ASBO may only be made by a 'relevant authority'. Whereas under the original wording of the 1998 Act, an application could only be brought by a local authority or the chief officer of police for an area, the PRA 2002 amended the CDA 1998[5] to expand the definition of relevant authority to allow applications by the Chief Constable of the BTP[6] and any RSL.[7] The amendments contained in the ASB Act 2003 have resulted in the addition to those permitted to bring ASBO proceedings of county councils for England[8] and housing action

---

[1] PRA 2002, ASB Act 2003 and SOCPA 2005.
[2] See chapter 6.
[3] 1 April 1999.
[4] CDA 1998, s 1(1)(a) and (b).
[5] CDA 1998, s 1(1A), as inserted by PRA 2002, s 61(1) and (2); see Appendix 1(A).
[6] The force of constables appointed under s 53 of the British Transport Commission Act 1949.
[7] Defined by CDA 1998, s 1(1A)(d) as any person registered under s 1 of the Housing Act 1996 as a social landlord who provides or manages any houses or hostels in a local government area.
[8] CDA 1998, s 1(1A)(aa), inserted by ASB Act 2003, s 85(1) and (2)(a).

trusts.[9] The Secretary of State may, following further amendments inserted by the SOCPA 2005, add to the list of relevant authorities by order.[10] Currently, the Environment Agency is the only body set to be added to the list to deal with enviro-crime issues such as vandalism. No further details were available at the time of writing.[11]

3.5   The local authority for the purposes of ASBO applications is the council for the local government area, which includes a district or London borough, the City of London, the Isle of Wight and the Isles of Scilly in relation to England, and a county or county borough for Wales.[12]

3.6   The ever-increasing trend towards stock transfer of housing by local authorities has led to a need to expand the range of bodies which may apply for ASBOs. A number of local authorities no longer have any housing stock, and it was perceived that their inclination to take out ASBOs would be limited by this. The Home Office Guidance is at pains to state that the extension of those capable of bringing applications does not compel RSLs or the BTP to do so. It goes on to make clear that the police and local authority remain jointly responsible under s 17 of the CDA 1998 to develop and implement strategies for tackling anti-social behaviour and disorder in the local area.[13] It would seem that this is highlighted to disabuse those local authorities who have transferred their housing stock from the view that anti-social behaviour caused by social housing tenants or on such estates is no longer their concern. The addition of housing action trusts is welcome and recognises the recent trend in social housing. In practice the majority of ASBOs are mostly still applied for by local authorities albeit with full consultation and input from the RSL or housing action trusts who often provide the evidence for the local authority's legal teams.

3.7   In further accepting that local authorities may wish to delegate the power to bring ASBOs where they no longer hold direct responsibility for housing stock, s 1F has been added to the CDA 1998 by the SOCPA 2005.[14] The section will allow a local authority to contract out its functions in applications for ASBOs to specified persons.[15] This, however, will only occur if the Secretary of State makes an order permitting the contracting out and he must not make such an order unless he first consults the National Assembly in Wales for Welsh authorities[16] and such representatives of local government as he thinks appropriate.[17] The Secretary of State's order may restrict the circumstances in which specified bodies are able to discharge contracted-out ASBO functions or may restrict the persons or bodies to which it could be contracted out to. Even if the local authority contracts out their functions they may still exercise them independently.[18]

WHO CAN BE THE SUBJECT OF AN APPLICATION?

3.8   One of the significant advantages of an ASBO is the wide range of its application. An ASBO may be obtained against any person who is aged 10 or over,[19] provided certain statutory criteria are satisfied (see **3.2** et seq). In the original Guidance issued by the Home Office, it was stated that it would be rare for an order to be made against a child aged either 10 or 11. This caveat is not included in the most recent Guidance and perhaps reflects the use of ASBOs since

---

[9]   CDA 1998, s 1(1A)(aa), inserted by ASB Act 2003, s 85(1) and (2)(c).
[10]   CDA 1998, s 1A(1) and (2), inserted by SOCPA 2005, s 139(3).
[11]   Home Office press release dated 20 December 2005, quoting Home Office Minister Hazel Blears.
[12]   CDA 1998, s 1(12).
[13]   See current Home Office Guidance, reproduced in Appendix 3.
[14]   SOCPA 2005, s 142.
[15]   CDA 1998, s 1F(1).
[16]   CDA 1998, s 1F(5)(a).
[17]   CDA 1998, s 1F(5)(b).
[18]   CDA 1998, s 1F(6).
[19]   CDA 1998, s 1(1).

the commencement of the Act. Whilst the courts were initially reluctant to make orders in respect of 10- and 11-year-olds, as applications became more common, it became apparent that children of that age were often being considered for orders by panels. The first order in respect of a child of 10 was in Leeds in 2000 and, thereafter, there have been a number of others. It seems unlikely, however, that the absence of the proviso in the Guidance will lead to a sudden increase in applications against 10- and 11-year-olds. The limitations on punishment alone would militate against them. Further in *Manchester City Council v Muir & Another*[20] the Court of Appeal noted that HHJ Armitage QC had held that allegations of conduct before a person was aged 10 cannot support a case for an ASBO and there was no appeal before them.

3.9 An ASBO is not dependent on the defendant being a tenant, whether of social or private housing. It is available against any person, whether house owner or hostel inhabitant. The defendant may not have a home at all. For instance, there are a number of ASBOs which have been obtained by local authorities against beggars who seek money in an aggressive or harassing way. A different course was taken by Manchester City Council, which used its powers under s 222 of the Local Government Act 1972 to bring an injunction against a beggar to ban him from the city centre. The use of s 222 against 'non-aggressive' beggars may be more prevalent now that the ASB Act 2003 has strengthened the injunction's effect by allowing the court to make a power of arrest when making injunctions which prohibit actions which are capable of causing nuisance or annoyance.[21]

3.10 The application for an ASBO is not limited by any notion of locality or nexus between the defendant's home and the scenes of his or her anti-social behaviour. Indeed, the current Home Office Guidance refers to ASBOs as being highly relevant to misconduct in public spaces, such as parks, shopping centres, transport hubs, etc. The lack of a need to show a connection between the defendant's behaviour and his or her home or a housing management function of the landlord is a significant attraction of an ASBO over remedies such as injunctions (eg Housing Act 1996, s 153A) (see **1.44**). ASBOs are, therefore, widely available against almost any person and experience has shown that the courts have been willing to make applications in very wide circumstances. The presumed boundaries of ASBOs may have been extended somewhat, however, in a case brought by Camden Borough Council which sought ASBOs against music advertising executives of Sony UK to prevent fly posting, which the council believed the company to be condoning. At the final hearing, however, the company gave a pledge to stop the practice, which the council accepted, withdrawing the proceedings.

'Has acted in an anti-social manner ...'

3.11 The definition in s 1(1)(a) bears some relation to s 5 of the Public Order Act 1986. However, an important difference should be noted. There is no need for the anti-social behaviour to have *actually* caused any person harassment, alarm or distress. The only stipulation is that the conduct was likely to cause harassment, alarm or distress. There is no need to prove that the defendant *intended* his or her conduct to cause harassment, alarm or distress – only that it did or was likely to do so. The presence of someone who was caused or was likely to have been caused harassment, alarm or distress is now however seemingly necessary (see **3.29**). There is little doubt however that the definition has been widely drawn to ensure that orders are available in the greatest variety of cases.

3.12 As there is no need for evidence from the persons who were caused harassment, alarm or distress, orders can still be obtained with the use of the professionals as witnesses. In this case, the behaviour would be proved by hearsay evidence or by live evidence from professionals, such as police or housing officers. The current Home Office Guidance goes so far as to say that

---

[20] [2006] EWCA Civ 423.
[21] Section 91 of the ASB Act 2003.

this was a specific intention of the draftsman.[22] The Home Office Guidance provides examples of behaviour which it considers can be the subject of an order and they include behaviour which one might not have associated with the strong measure which an application for an ASBO is often seen to represent. The examples include writing graffiti, begging, prostitution, vehicle crime, fouling the street with litter and drunken behaviour in the street.

3.13 Whilst the Act itself only refers to the relevant authority having to prove that the acts complained of occurred after the commencement date of s 1, there is, however, a time bar which applies at least to applications in the magistrates' courts. In considering an application for an ASBO, the magistrates' court is acting in its civil capacity and a complaint must be laid before it within 6 months from when the acts relied on occurred.[23] Provided a complaint is laid within the 6-month period, there is no impediment to serving the defendant outside that period or of having a hearing after it. It is, therefore, imperative that when an application is being considered, one of the first steps to undertake is to draw up a chronology of events so that from the outset incidents likely to be cited in the application will not become time-barred. This is particularly important when criminal proceedings have been taken in relation to one or more of the incidents.

3.14 Many ASBO applications are delayed due to pending or coexistent criminal proceedings. Although this matter is not dealt with in the current Home Office Guidance, it must be right that the view expressed in the original Guidance that an ASBO application should not include evidence which is due to be heard in the course of criminal proceedings remains valid. To do otherwise would be to prejudice the defendant in the criminal hearing and risk a breach of his or her right to a fair trial. It is important, however, to ensure that applications are not unduly delayed whilst awaiting the outcome of criminal proceedings. Consideration should be given to proceeding with the application without those allegations or, alternatively, to issuing an application to remove any concerns about time-limits and applying for an interim order[24] until the criminal trial is concluded. In appropriate cases, it may also be advisable to reach an agreement with the CPS for them to withdraw the criminal matter so that it can be dealt with in the ASBO application. This is often appropriate where the offence to be tried in the criminal courts is a minor one, for which the punishment is unlikely to be significant. However, the effect of its proof at the ASBO application would be likely to result in an order being made. Care must, however, be taken that the CPS are advised to inform the defendant that whilst the criminal charge is being withdrawn, the conduct in question will be included as grounds for an ASBO application.

3.15 There is no minimum number of incidents which has to be proved to obtain an order. However, it is likely that unless the incident is a serious one, a single incident will not be sufficient. Incidents which fall outside the 6-month period can, it would seem, be relied on to support an application based on limited incidents within that period. The original Home Office Guidance suggested that a 'pattern of behaviour' had to be shown. The phrase is reproduced in the current Home Office Guidance, with reference to the use of earlier incidents to establish such a pattern.[25] In *Stevens v South East Surrey Magistrates' Court*[26] the applicant had relied on documentary hearsay of 30 alleged incidents for their application. Eight of the incidents were within the 6 months and the remaining 22 outside with the oldest 3 years previously. The evidence was in the form of a witness statement from a police officer who had collated police incident reports, crime reports and victim statements. He had interviewed victims about

---

[22]   See current Home Office Guidance, reproduced in Appendix 3.
[23]   Magistrates' Courts Act 1980, s 127.
[24]   See chapter 7.
[25]   See current Home Office Guidance, reproduced in Appendix 3.
[26]   [2004] EWHC 1456 (Admin).

incidents and gave evidence that many were unwilling to attend court for fear of reprisals. The police did not argue that the incidents were similar fact only that they went to establishing that an order was necessary pursuant to s 1(1)(b).

3.16 Lord Justice Auld in giving the judgment of the Divisional Court commenced by setting out three basic propositions 'by way of clearing the legal thicket'. First, he stated that s 127 was concerned with jurisdiction and not admissibility of evidence. Once there was jurisdiction to hear the application (here eight incidents were within time) it could not be used to exclude evidence. Secondly, where the matter is of a continuing nature, s 127 operated differently depending on whether the proceedings were commenced by information or complaint. If by information, time ran from the date of each offence taken separately. Where by complaint, as here, time does not run until the matter is complete in every way (eg *McVittie v Rennison*).[27] For an ASBO there were two constituents, namely harassment and necessity to make an order. Only if the magistrates were satisfied that the total course of ASB proved showed such necessity could the basis for an order be complete. Thirdly, *McCann* was conclusive authority that an application for an ASBO was civil not criminal proceedings for the purposes of Art 6 and that hearsay evidence was not only admissible but depending on its legal probativeness may be sufficient to prove that a defendant had acted in an anti-social manner to the criminal standard.

3.17 The conclusion of the judgment is actually rather confusing in that Lord Justice Auld at paragraph 17 concludes that it would not be 'intellectually sound' to conclude that the pre-6 months incidents only went to necessity and in paragraph 21 notes that it would curious if s 127 prevented reliance on incidents outside the 6-months limit given that no such restriction existed in the county or Crown Court equivalents. Having made the above points Lord Justice Auld, however, went on to conclude:

> 'In the circumstances of this case, I am of the view that the magistrates were entitled to admit the documentary hearsay evidence of the "out of time" incidents for the purpose of considering the necessity to make an order despite the age of many of them. They reveal a fairly regular and consistent pattern of "out of time" anti-social behaviour, continuing seamlessly into the 8 courses of conduct "within-time" incidents.'

Further, when considering the weight to be attached to the 'out of time' incidents, he said:

> 'If they are very old and amount to only a single or very few incidents they may have little relevance or weight however reliable the evidence of them may be, looking at each incident on its own. On the other hand, if, as here, they indicate a solid and consistent line of anti-social behaviour beginning possibly well out-of-time and ending within-time they would usually be highly relevant to the decision whether an order is, in the circumstances, necessary and to what form it should take.'

This would seem to be inconsistent with the earlier comments which would seem logically to have led to 'out-of-time' incidents being able to be relied on for both parts of s 1(1). The court, however, stopped short of finding this although it did confirm that they could be used as 'similar fact' to prove incidents within-time. More recently the High Court in *R (on the application of Chief Constable of West Mercia Constabulary) v Boorman*[28] reconsidered the issue in answering four questions of a stated case. They were:

(1) Should evidence of events that took place more than 6 months before the application only go to the issue of whether an order was necessary?

(2) Is there a requirement of proof of an incident within the 6 months which was objectively anti-social?

---

[27] [1941] 1 KB 96.

[28] 2 November 2005, at [2005] EWHC 2559 (Admin).

(3)   Were they correct in refusing to admit evidence from outside the 6 months which might have assisted in proving that the behaviour alleged within the period was in fact anti-social?

(4)   In giving reasons, did the court have to make findings of fact as to the defendant's actual behaviour and whether that behaviour was likely to cause harassment, alarm and distress or was it enough to simply state that they were not satisfied beyond reasonable doubt the defendant had acted in a manner likely to cause harassment, alarm or distress?

3.18 Mr Justice Calvert-Smith cited *Stevens* including the passages above and concluded that in answering the first and third questions:

> '… in principle, any evidence which may be relevant to either limb of section 1 should be admitted during the hearing of the application. Therefore, by mirror image, in the generality of cases, it is wrong to exclude as far as question 3 is concerned, pre-period evidence merely because it is pre-period evidence.'

3.19 In respect of the second question Mr Justice Calvert-Smith considered that the test was an objective one in the sense that the court had to make up its mind as to whether the conduct complained of was such as to cause, or likely to cause, harassment, alarm or distress. It was objective in the context of the defendant's mens rea, he could not escape responsibility by saying that he was too drunk or that he was only having a laugh. Similarly, that a member of the public said that they had been caused harassment, alarm or distress was not enough of itself; a reasonable view had to be taken.

3.20 Finally, in answering the fourth question, Mr Justice Calvert-Smith held that as ASBO proceedings were civil proceedings the court should give reasons if the application were refused. If granted he considered that the reasons would be clear from the terms of the order granted. He found no fault with the magistrates' reasons which had stated that they were not satisfied beyond reasonable doubt that the defendant had acted in a manner likely to cause harassment, alarm or distress.

3.21 The 'settled' position would appear to be that whilst a court can and should hear all evidence in relation to out-of-time incidents, unless they are relied on as similar-fact evidence to within-time incidents they will only be relevant in relation to the court's consideration of s 1(1)(b), ie necessity. Whilst there remains this rather strange position that generally incidents outside 6 months are inadmissible in magistrates' court applications but can be relied on in the county or crown courts, it is perhaps not as significant as it may first seem. This is because if there are no incidents within the 6 months which can be established to a criminal standard then it is highly unlikely that there will be a necessity for an order to prevent further anti-social behaviour. The only situation in which the applicant would be significantly disadvantaged would be if there was a serious incident just outside the 6 months which resulted in a conviction and there were only hearsay incidents thereafter. This situation is, however, one which the applicant can avoid by the simple expedient of issuing earlier even if the criminal prosecution is ongoing.

3.22 In practice, it is suggested that an applicant should provide the court with a second schedule of those incidents which are capable of proof, whether by hearsay evidence or otherwise, but which occurred outside the 6-month period. This ensures that the court has a convenient and clear list of the incidents which the relevant authority alleges the defendant has committed and when. Usually, those incidents include the previous convictions of the defendant, although it is good practice to also provide an up-to-date antecedent history within the bundle of evidence supplied to the court. If any of the convictions are within the 6-month period, it is important to provide the court with the statements which gave rise to the conviction (if available) and any basis of plea which was accepted by the court. For convictions outside the

6-month period, where the incidents are public order offences or offences against the person, the court may well wish to know about the facts giving rise to the conviction, as this may assist in determining whether an order is necessary.

3.23 A further point of principle regarding alleged conduct which was not within the original complaint arose in the case of *Birmingham City Council v Dixon*.[29] The defendant was the subject of an application for an ASBO which was not heard for some time due to various reasons. He was however subject to an interim order pending the trial at which the council sought to rely on alleged further acts of ASB since the application had been made. Some of those would have been in breach of the interim ASBO but for unspecified reasons had not been tried. The council alleged that the incidents were of a similar nature to those in the complaint itself.

3.24 The district judge in the magistrates' court ruled that whilst it may have been relevant as to whether an order was necessary the evidence was inadmissible as to the first question for the court as to whether there had been acts of anti-social behaviour. He considered that the incidents could be the subject of outstanding criminal proceedings with possible prejudice to the defendant, that the conduct was not in the contemplation of the authority when it had applied and that the incidents could be relied on in any application for an order on conviction.

3.25 The administrative court hearing the council's application for case stated held that it was settled law that pending criminal proceedings would not prevent a defendant from answering a civil complaint based on the same facts.[30] Further evidence of later conduct could in principle be relevant to whether the defendant had previously acted in an anti-social manner both as to factual matters of actions or as evidence of propensity to so act. Lord Justice Richards was however at pains to point out that the applicant still had to prove allegations within the complaint in order to obtain the order. If post-complaint behaviour was to be relied on as conduct establishing the test in s 1(1)(a) then there had to be an amendment of the complaint. This is an important point for practitioners to be aware of. Applicants must ensure that they amend the complaint to include the new matters post application and defence representatives should be alive to the possibility that the applicant will fail to prove s 1(1)(a) is satisfied in the absence of any application to amend.

'Caused or was likely to cause harassment, alarm or distress to one or more persons ...'

3.26 There is limited case-law on the meaning of harassment, alarm or distress in the context of ASBOs. However, in *R v Jones & others*[31] the Court of Appeal held that there was distinction between activity which qualified and that which merely caused 'frustration, disappointment, anger or annoyance'.[32] The court held that the section was aimed at activities likely to cause what might be globally described as 'fear for one's own safety'. If it is to be asserted that the defendant's actions actually caused harassment, alarm or distress to a person, then that needs to be proved by evidence. This would ordinarily be done by way of direct evidence from the person or persons who were affected or by hearsay evidence from a professional witness who can show the reaction of the person affected and/or speak to that person about it.

3.27 If, however, the allegation against the defendant is that his or her conduct was *likely* to cause harassment, alarm or distress, then, clearly, a direct witness of the effect cannot be called. Rather, the court will hear evidence of the conduct of the defendant and then be asked to

---

29 [2009] EWHC 761 (Admin).
30 See *Mote v Secretary of State for Work and Pensions* [2007] EWCA Civ 1324, paras 20–32.
31 [2006] EWCA Crim 2942.
32 [2006] EWCA Crim 2942, para 45.

conclude that this conduct was likely to cause harassment, alarm or distress. The question then arises – what must the applicant show to the court to establish such a likelihood?

3.28 The issue was examined in detail in the case of *The Chief Constable of Lancashire v Potter*.[33] The administrative court was asked to consider an appeal by way of case stated against the decision of the deputy district judge, who had refused to make an ASBO against Potter. The Chief Constable had brought the application against Potter, alleging that she had acted as a prostitute in an area of Preston. He called evidence which was almost exclusively hearsay evidence from two police officers that there was a problem with prostitution in the area, of which residents and visitors had complained. Potter had convictions for prostitution outside the 6-month period and had been seen regularly in the area, and, on occasion, had been seen to step forward and look into moving motor cars to attract attention. Potter did not appear and so the evidence was uncontroverted. The district judge, however, noted that there was no evidence that she had actually caused harassment, alarm or distress, or any direct evidence from local residents (the evidence was hearsay evidence from anonymous sources). Having applied his mind to the weight to be applied to hearsay evidence, he decided that he could not be sure that anyone had actually been caused harassment, alarm or distress and that he did not feel it fair, in the absence of real examples, to find that simply being a prostitute was likely to cause harassment, alarm or distress.

3.29 Lord Justice Auld considered various permutations, including that which has been used in the family law jurisdiction for findings of facts in child abuse cases, but discounted them and came to the conclusion that:

> '[32] Accordingly, as to the meaning of "likely" in this context, my view is that a higher threshold of likelihood is called for than, for example, that of "a real possibility" arising in the context of the safety of children under the Children Act 1989. It is true that the making of an anti-social behaviour order is not a criminal sentence, and serves only to prohibit in specified ways further anti-social behaviour of the sort giving rise to it. However, breach of such an order is a serious matter and can lead to a substantial term of imprisonment or fine. I would give "likely" the meaning in this context of "more probable than not". That meaning, it seems to me, is much the same as that of the Divisional Court in *Parkin v Norman* [1983] QB 92, [1982] 2 All ER 583, [1982] 3 WLR 523, which concerned a charge of insulting behaviour "likely" to occasion a breach of the peace. McCullough J, giving the judgment of the court consisting of Donaldson LJ and himself, emphasised that the test was whether the conduct in question was "likely", not "liable", to have that effect.'

Lord Justice Auld went on to emphasise the need for the court not to confuse incidents which actually caused and those likely to cause harassment, alarm or distress:

> 'The case demonstrates the importance for a court when dealing with the issue of likelihood in this context of avoiding at least two pitfalls critical to its final decision. The first is not to confuse the second and third constituents of the s 1(1)(a) condition so as to require proof to the criminal standard that a defendant's conduct has actually caused someone harassment, alarm or distress when considering the alternative, whether it is likely to have caused that result. It is in that respect, it seems to me, that the Deputy District Judge, in the passages from his paras 6(Q) and (R) of the statement of case that I have set out and emphasised in para 19 above, fell into error. The thrust of those passages is that he rejected the likelihood alternative because the evidence was wanting as to any instances of actual harassment, alarm or distress ....'

3.30 The second pitfall concerns the standard of proof to be applied and is considered later in this chapter. However, the effect of the above seems to mean that the court will require the applicant to prove (to the appropriate standard) that the defendant's conduct could more

---

[33] [2003] EWHC 2272 (Admin), [2003] 42 LS Gaz R 31, [2003] All ER (D) 199 (Oct).

probably than not have caused harassment, alarm or distress. To do this, the applicant does not need to provide evidence of any actual persons who may have been subjected to the same – only that the conduct of the defendant could do so.

3.31 In *R v Israilov*[34] the court of appeal found that burglary of an unoccupied dwelling house did not cause harassment or alarm but that it did cause distress. It is, however, strange that they did not consider whether it was *likely* to do those things. In *R (on the application of Mills) v Birmingham Magistrates' Court*[35] the defendant had been seen by a plain clothes police officer taking three pairs of gloves without paying. The officer followed her outside the shop and arrested her. She was co-operative and in no way abusive. The Divisional Court held that whilst some thefts might cause harassment, alarm or distress this did not mean that all would. In this case there was no evidence of anti-social behaviour by the claimant, the theft was unbeknown to the shop employees and therefore the actions were not likely to have caused them any harassment.

3.32 The definition in s 1(1)(a) had been given a more narrow interpretation by Mr Justice Bean in *R (Gosport Borough Council) v Fareham Magistrates*.[36] Here the council had sought an ASBO against a defendant who owned a jet ski and had on 3 occasions ridden in what was described as a 'grossly excessive speed' circling buoys and riding in the wake of a ferry. The district judge refused to make an ASBO and the matter was brought before the Divisional Court by way of judicial review as he also refused to state a case.

3.33 Mr Justice Bean noted that the court had filed a witness statement in which he had said that whilst he had found that the defendant was riding dangerously there was no evidence to prove that there was in fact a swimmer in the area whilst he was riding in that fashion. He went on to hold that the incidents showed that the defendant had acted in an 'irresponsible manner in speeding in the harbour and that this would have caused harassment, alarm or distress to any swimmers had there been any there'.

3.34 The judge however went on to find that whilst the 'or was likely to cause' must add something to the word 'caused' in s 1(1)(a) this was not sufficient in this case.

> 'In order to show that the behaviour "caused" harassment, alarm or distress it would probably be necessary to have evidence from one of the harassed, alarmed or distressed victims; whereas the alternative formulation "or was likely to cause" enables police witnesses to demonstrate that there were potential victims present who it was likely were caused harassment, alarm or distress.'

3.35 As the council was not able to prove that there had been anyone in the water at the time of the incidents the Divisional Court rejected the council's application. This is a narrow construction of the definition which is not it is submitted borne out by the wide construction applied by House of Lords in *McCann* or the Divisional Court in *Potter*, nor is it really in accordance with the plain words of the statute. The statute only requires proof that the defendant's conduct caused or was likely to have caused harassment, alarm or distress not that anyone was there to witness it. Strangely the judge went on to give an example which emphasises why we would submit his construction is an unnecessarily narrow one:

> '… if a man is swaggering around in a public place brandishing a knife, but he is the only person in the area, his behaviour is observed on CCTV and police arrive in a police car and arrest him, I doubt very much whether that behaviour would be sufficient to found an ASBO. It would be quite different if the CCTV showed one or more members of the public in the vicinity.'

---

[34] [2004] EWCA Crim 2931.
[35] [2005] All ER (D) 94.
[36] [2007] 1 WLR 634.

'Not of the same household as himself . . .'

3.36 This limitation was presumably included to prevent conduct which occurred within a family from being used to support an application for an ASBO. The question of what constitutes 'household' has not been the subject of any case-law as yet however it is seems likely that it would be given its ordinary meaning of someone living in the same house as the defendant. This must presumably be taken at the time of application so that if the person leaves the household and continues to cause anti-social behaviour towards his former household then it can be used.

3.37 There is however no doubt that even though the anti-social behaviour may have been 'aimed' at someone of the same household as themselves, if it also effects others outside the household it can be used in an application. In *R (on the application of Rabess and another) v the Commissioner of Police for the Metropolis*[37] the court had found that the defendant had been in a volatile and abusive relationship. There had been frequent arguments involving shouting and abusive language. They had called the police about each other on numerous occasions. Whilst most of the arguments had been in private they had also spilt out into the public domain and carried on in the street. There was evidence before the court that neighbours had been prevented from sleeping for fear of something happening to one of them. There were also incidents at a family centre were supervised contact was taking place.

3.38 The defendants argued that 'household' in s 1(1) precluded the making of ASBOs in domestic circumstances as allegations concerning the defendant and his partner should be discounted by the court. Mrs Justice Dobbs found that the conduct having caused distress and alarm to others not of the same household meant that an ASBO could be made. The court was concerned only about the effect of the behaviour on the neighbours and other members of the public, and not as between the defendant and his partner.

AGGREGATION

3.39 *Potter* is also the only higher court authority on whether the defendant's conduct has to be taken alone or whether it can be aggregated with others. In *Potter*, the applicant called evidence of prostitution, as a whole, causing problems for the residents. There was evidence that used condoms were left in the area and that some prostitutes were getting into cars of single men and refusing to leave until given money. Neither of these 'aggravated conducts' could be proved against the defendant. The defendant was not, in any real sense, acting in concert with the other prostitutes frequenting the area. The deputy district judge accepted that the presence of the defendant would contribute to the problem of kerb-crawling, etc, to a small degree and that the activities, as a whole, of the prostitutes represented a problem to the residents; however, by the nature of the activity, prostitutes tended to congregate in an area but not to operate in concert. He therefore discounted the effect of the prostitutes as a whole and any 'aggravated conduct', as this could not be proved to have been caused by the defendant.

3.40 Lord Justice Auld observed, in agreement with the deputy district judge, that:

> 'Street prostitution in residential areas, whatever the extremes of behaviour by individual prostitutes, is clearly capable, when considered as a whole and depending on the circumstances, including the number, regularity and degree of concentration of activity, of causing or being likely to cause harassment, alarm or distress to others in the area. It is a question of fact whether any individual prostitute, by her contribution to that activity and its overall effect, has caused a "problem" which is

---

[37] [2007] EWHC 208 (Admin).

caught by s 1(1)(a). Proof of such a fact need not depend on the attribution to her of proved "aggravated conduct" of other prostitutes that might, considered on its own, constitute harassment, alarm or distress.'

What Lord Justice Auld, however, also stated was that having found that the actions of the defendant had caused or had been likely to cause the problems arising from prostitution in the area in the sense of her contribution to it, it was inconsistent of the judge to then not find that she had caused, in the same sense, harassment, alarm or distress, as the 'aggravated behaviour' had not been proved to her own actions. He disapproved of the concept of 'aggravated conduct', considering that the only test was whether it was proved that there was conduct, whether committed individually or with others, that had caused or been likely to cause harassment, alarm or distress. He went on, crucially, to state:

'Section 1(1)(a) does not require proof of intent to cause any such effects, or, where the conduct of a number of persons is involved that a sole defendant was acting in concert with them. Nor, where harassment, alarm or distress are caused by the conduct of a number of people, including the defendant, does it require proof that the defendant's conduct on its own should have been of a sufficiently aggravated nature to cause harassment, alarm or distress or, if not, that she should have in some way shared responsibility with the others for their aggravated conduct. Section 1(1)(a) is concerned simply with a defendant's conduct and its effect, whether looked at on its own or with the conduct of others.'

3.41 The first part of the above quote affirms the statutory wording that the intention of the defendant in his or her actions is irrelevant to determining its effect. Where the decision goes further is that, whilst given in the context of a case involving prostitution and its effects, it has implications for the wider application of aggregation of conduct in ASBO proceedings. Lord Justice Auld specifically states that proving the first part of the statutory test does not require proof of joint enterprise but, further, that if the conduct of many people is causing the harassment, alarm or distress, then the defendant's conduct alone does not need to cause harassment, alarm or distress. Broader application, however, comes when the defendant is not a prostitute but a member of a group whose actions, as a whole, cause harassment, alarm or distress. Often, it is hard to say which person did what or even to prove that the defendant who can be proved to be present did any specific act. The most common examples are where a witness can give evidence that he or she was verbally abused by a group which included the defendant but cannot say what, if anything, he said, or where the witness has been subjected to stone-throwing which came from a group of youths but the thrower is unidentifiable. The decision would seem to mean that the defendant's conduct, in being part of the group which verbally abused the witness or threw stones, will be sufficient to establish s 1(1)(a). The only caveat must, of course, be that the defendant's conduct has always to be considered individually as well. So, for instance, where the defendant walked away from the gang which performed the above actions, it could properly be argued that he had distanced himself from them and their conduct. Where, however, the defendant simply rejoins the group and continues, this would be harder to argue. Aggregation of a defendant's conduct with that of others must be considered very carefully, however, and care must be taken by the court to ensure that only where the group's actions as a whole cause (or are likely to cause) harassment, alarm or distress are they taken into account. Similarly, as Lord Justice Auld stated, the court must then concern itself with the defendant's conduct and its effect, taken on its own and/or with the conduct of the others in the group. The judgment remains, however, a very useful examination of what the court is permitted to consider when assessing whether the statutory test is made out and will undoubtedly make it easier to prove anti-social behaviour where gangs or groups of offenders are involved.

'... necessary to protect relevant persons from further anti-social acts by him'

3.42   Even if it has been proved that the defendant has acted in an anti-social manner, the court *must* go on to consider whether an order is necessary to protect relevant persons from further anti-social acts. This test found in s 1(1)(b) was amended by the PRA 2002, which also added a definition of 'relevant persons' which is found in s 1B of the CDA 1998. For an application by a local authority, relevant persons are those falling within the local government area of that council and, similarly, within a police area for an application by a chief constable or a county council.

3.43   Where the application is by the BTP, 'relevant persons' means:

(1)   persons on or likely to be on policed premises in a local government area; *or*

(2)   persons in the vicinity of or likely to be in the vicinity of such premises.

3.44   Where the application is by an RSL or housing action trust, 'relevant persons' are:

(1)   persons who are residing in or who are otherwise on or likely to be on premises provided or managed by that authority; or

(2)   persons who are in the vicinity of or likely to be in the vicinity of such premises.

3.45   It would seem unlikely that any application which either a BTP, RSL or housing action trust would wish to bring would fail for inability to show that relevant persons needed to be protected. The only potential problem may be for an application by an RSL to a housing action trust where the defendant's conduct was aimed at a particular person or family who have since left the area. In those circumstances, unless it could be shown that other persons were likely to become victims of similar behaviour, there would not be a relevant person to protect. In practice, however, it would be highly unlikely that an ASBO would be sought, as, where the anti-social behaviour was so focused on one person or family, an injunction may well be a better solution. If, however, the actions of the defendant affected persons not proximate to his or her home but the affected persons were RSL or housing act trust tenants, there is no bar to an application. It would, however, be important to provide the court with either a statement or a plan, showing the properties in the affected area which were provided or managed by the RSL or housing act trust. This plan will also have some significance if an exclusion zone is sought.

3.46   In seeking to show that an order is necessary, we have seen above[38] that there are no time-limits as to the evidence which may be relied upon. Incidents which have occurred over a period of time are extremely relevant in establishing that an order is necessary. Clearly, the longer the period over which the conduct has continued, the more likely it is that an order is necessary. Evidence from residents or victims, often in the form of hearsay evidence, about the effect of the conduct on them and their fears if no action is taken, is particularly effective in showing to the court that an order is needed, with the difference in the standard of proof to establish necessity (see below). The statements of the professionals in the case should always contain details of statements given to them by residents or members of the public about the defendant's conduct. Where the information is available the professional should state why the victims of the anti-social behaviour do not wish to give a statement or live evidence. They should also provide details of relevant statistics (eg the number of applications for transfer of housing that cite anti-social behaviour as the reason for applying or the number of vacant, un-let properties in the area). This type of evidence was used to very good effect in a series of

---

[38]   See **3.15–3.22**.

applications by Leeds city council to show the extent of the problems in a particular area. The evidence provided to the court included the cost of cleaning graffiti, repairing vandalism damage, attending malicious fires, and collection and disposal of drug users' hypodermic needles.

3.47 The need for the court to consider the necessity for an order has been re-iterated in the case-law on numerous occasions, eg *R v McGrath*[39] and *R v Kirby*.[40] An ASBO is not to be imposed to punish an offender,[41] it must be necessary to protect the public from further acts. The purpose of ASBOs was to prevent future ASB and consequential suffering. If the order was not capable of having that effect, its effect could only be to increase the sentence that would be available to a court, should he commit a further offence.[42] This was not an appropriate use of ASBOs. Ultimately whether it is, is an exercise of judgment by the court as decided by the House of Lords in *Clingham*. It should be remembered, however, that considerations of necessity will inevitably also be at the forefront of the court's mind at a later stage when considering the prohibitions. It should be noted, however, that when considering what terms are necessary the court is not limited to protecting relevant persons but can impose them to protect persons elsewhere in England and Wales from anti-social behaviour.[43] This is further considered in chapter 10.

BURDEN AND STANDARDS OF PROOF

3.48 The burden of proof, both evidentially and legally, is on the applicant, save where the defendant seeks to show that his or her alleged anti-social conduct was reasonable in the circumstances. In such a situation, it is suggested that the defendant bears an evidential burden to adduce evidence in support of his or her contention, but not a legal one to prove it to any standard. Whether the applicant then bears the burden of disproving it (eg self-defence in criminal trials) remains unresolved.

3.49 The standard of proof to which the applicant must establish the case has caused a number of problems which have now been resolved and are settled law. It is now clear, beyond doubt, that ASBO proceedings are civil proceedings[44] and, therefore, all the civil rules on the admissibility of evidence (including hearsay) apply. However, the standard of proof to which the applicant must prove that the defendant has acted in an anti-social manner is a criminal standard (ie beyond a reasonable doubt). This is the ruling of the House of Lords, as given by Lord Steyn[45] in October 2002. The reason for the higher standard of proof is one of pragmatism. The Court of Appeal in the *McCann* case[46] had suggested that, whilst there was a sliding scale in respect of the standard of proof in civil cases, it would be advisable for magistrates to apply the criminal standard for uniformity. This view was approved by Lord Steyn.

3.50 Lord Steyn also went on to make clear that the standard of proof to be applied to proving the first part of the statutory criteria in s 1 has *no* application to the second part of the test (ie whether an order was necessary). He said:

---

[39] [2005] EWCA 353.
[40] [2005] EWCA Crim 1228.
[41] *Lonergan (Ashley) v (1) Lewes Crown Court (2) Brighton & Hove City Council & Secretary of State for the Home Department (Interested Party)* [2005] EWHC 457 (Admin), [2005] 1 WLR 2570, [2005] 2 All ER 362, (2005) *The Times*, April 25.
[42] *R v Jones & Others* [2006] EWCA Crim 2942.
[43] CDA 1998, s 1(1B)(6).
[44] See *R (on the application McCann and others) v Crown Court at Manchester; Clingham v Kensington and Chelsea Royal Borough Council* [2002] UKHL 39, [2002] 3 WLR 1313, [2002] 4 All ER 593, and *R (on the application of W) v Acton Youth Court* [2005] All ER (D) 284, at [4].
[45] *R (on the application McCann and others) v Crown Court at Manchester; Clingham v Kensington and Chelsea Royal Borough Council* [2002] UKHL 39, [2002] 3 WLR 1313, [2002] 4 All ER 593.
[46] *R v Manchester Crown Court ex parte McCann* [2001] EWCA Civ 281, [2001] 1 WLR 1084.

'The inquiry under section 1(1)(b), namely that such an order is necessary to protect persons from further anti-social acts by him, does not involve a standard of proof: it is an exercise of judgement or evaluation.'

This was a welcome clarification of the legal test to be applied, as there had been a rising number of cases in which argument had been raised about whether it was actually possible to prove beyond a reasonable doubt that an order was necessary. The court, in deciding whether an order is necessary, should therefore take into consideration all the evidence presented to it and reach a *reasoned* decision as to the need for an order. It is important to note that the applicant is not required to show that all other steps and possible methods to regulate the defendant's behaviour have been tried. It is sufficient to show that other means have been considered and that an ASBO has been decided as the most suitable. This 'message' is repeated in the current Home Office Guidance on a number of occasions.

3.51 Whilst it is clear from *McCann* that where the applicant alleges that the defendant has committed acts which have actually caused harassment, alarm or distress, he or she must do so to the criminal standard, ie so that the court is sure, the question arose in *Potter* as to what should be the standard of proof where the allegation was only that the actions of the defendant *were likely to cause* harassment, alarm or distress. Lord Justice Auld considered the meaning of the word 'likely' in the statute. He discounted any notion that he could distinguish *McCann* to impose a lower standard of proof, stating:

> '[28]   It might be open to this court to focus in a way that the House of Lords did not in *McCann*, on the possibility of a lower than criminal standard of proof of the likelihood of a defendant's conduct having caused harassment, alarm or distress. However, in my view, it would be a futile exercise. "Proof", to whatever standard, of a likelihood is necessarily a different mental exercise from that of proving a fact in the sense that something has actually happened. It might be described as an evaluative exercise of a similar kind to that in s 1(1)(b), notwithstanding that s 1(4) requires *proof* of it, as well as the condition in s 1(1)(a). Or it might, true to that requirement, be characterised as proof of a speculative outcome.'

And, further, that:

> '[33]   As to the standard of proof required, probably the fairest and simplest solution is to say that a court, in conducting what is necessarily an evaluative exercise on this issue as well as that under s 1(1)(b), must, on the evidence before it, be sure to the criminal standard, that a defendant's conduct has caused the likelihood in the sense I have indicated. It seems to me that, whether that is a matter of proof and/or of evaluation, is no more a matter for philosophical analysis or agonising by courts than, say, a magistrate or a jury having to decide to the criminal standard whether an accused's conduct was dishonest or intentional or reckless. As I have said, determining whether conduct had a likely effect is a frequent demand made on lay and professional decision-makers in our courts in all sorts of criminal offences.'

3.52 The practical application of the two aspects of *Potter* is that the court must (where considering an allegation that the defendant's actions were likely to cause harassment, alarm or distress) be sure that the conduct would more probably than not cause harassment, alarm and distress. The court has, therefore, to be careful when doing so not to confuse the likelihood of harassment, alarm or distress being caused by the defendant's conduct ('more probable than not') with the standard of proof required to establish that likelihood ('sure'). In practice, as Lord Justice Auld observed, courts are well used to determining such issues and do so in the context of other jurisdictions. In the majority of cases, this should not prove difficult, as conduct such as violent behaviour, abusive language and dangerous driving will almost inevitably be likely to cause harassment, alarm or distress. The more difficult areas concern the effects of prostitution, begging and other less directly 'offensive' conduct on the part of the defendant. The deputy district judge in *Potter* applied too strict a test and should have considered the lower test, described above. The case was remitted for him to apply the proper test.

3.53 The issue of whether it was necessary to make an order where the conduct complained of had stopped prior to the application was considered in the case of *S v Poole Borough Council*.[47] The court also rejected any possible argument by the defendant of 'double jeopardy' by the use of the incidents for which there had been a previous criminal conviction.[48] In *S v Poole Borough Council*, the defendant, a youth aged about 15, was alleged to have been involved in anti-social behaviour for about 18 months, running up to just prior to the application for an ASBO. The hearing in the magistrates' court had not occurred until 5 months had passed and a further 7½ months went by before the Crown Court hearing. There were no alleged incidents in that time, and the defendant's representatives argued that there was no necessity for an order, as there had been no anti-social behaviour for over a year. The Crown Court upheld the making of an order and the defendant appealed by way of case stated. Lord Justice Stephen Brown, in rejecting the argument in the Divisional Court, said:

> 'With the best will in the world, that is to my mind a hopeless argument. It must be expected that, once an application of this sort has been made, still more obviously once an ASBO has been made, its effect will be to deter future misconduct. That, indeed, is the justification for such orders in the first place. It would be a remarkable situation were a defendant, against whom an order has rightly been made, then able, on appeal to the Crown Court, to achieve its quashing because in the interim he has not disobeyed it; rather the very effectiveness of such an order would to my mind justify its continuance. The conduct on which the magistrates and in turn the Crown Court should concentrate on determining whether an order is necessary is that which underlay the authority's application for the order in the first place ...'

3.54 It therefore follows that, with the introduction of interim orders, it will be almost impossible for a defendant to argue that the making of an ASBO is not necessary by arguing that he or she has not acted in an anti-social manner since the application was made. The period of time between the last incident of anti-social behaviour and the making of the application remains relevant, however, and the defence may raise a reasonable argument, especially if there is a sizeable gap. Of course, the need to avoid potential issues such as this makes it important for the applicant to bring an application as soon as possible.

'NECESSITY' FOR ASBO AFTER INTERIM ORDER

3.55 An extension of the point in *S v Poole* occurs where it is argued that, where interim orders are made in terms which are less than the full orders applied for at the main application, the additional final order terms are not necessary, as the interim order terms have not been breached. The argument is, therefore, that the interim terms are all that is necessary to protect relevant persons from further acts of anti-social behaviour. Whilst this can be an attractive argument in some cases, where the additional terms sought are minor and do not add anything, it would seem hard to justify this argument when the statutory model and case-law are considered. First, an interim order is one which is made because there is an urgent need to protect relevant persons. It is made without any detailed consideration of the strength of the applicant's case and no findings of fact are made. Interim orders are very often made in very limited terms, with reduced exclusion zones or without non-association clauses, so that the minimal appropriate restrictions are placed on the defendant, pending his or her full trial. That is the statutory model as supported by the Home Office Guidance. To argue at the full hearing that the interim order has not been breached and, therefore, is enough to prevent further acts would fly in the face of the reasoning in *S v Poole*. The fact that an order has been made and the defendant complied with it cannot be grounds for concluding that only those terms would be necessary. If correct, the applicant would be entitled to ask for the same terms on an interim basis as a final order to prevent this argument. Further, a defendant, by complying with a limited

---

[47] [2002] EWHC 244 (Admin), (unreported) February 2002.
[48] See further **4.18**.

interim order for a short period, could defeat the applicant's full order terms in every case. The defendant who complies with an interim order is in no better a position than S when he complied with the original order pending his appeal. The court should consider the necessity of the order *and* the terms as of the time of the application – not the hearing.

3.56 The introduction of interim orders has led to a further point when necessity is considered, namely whether a breach of an interim order can go towards establishing whether a final order is necessary. If the breach is one which amounts to anti-social behaviour, eg verbal abuse or violent conduct, there can be little doubt of its relevance. Indeed, it would be likely to make an order hard to resist in many cases. If, however, the breach is one which contravenes the interim order but is not anti-social per se, eg entering an exclusion zone, can it be argued that this should be considered by the court as to necessity? There are reported cases on this issue, however, where it has been argued at first instance and the courts have taken the view that the breach of the interim order shows the defendant's attitude to the orders and failure to accept responsibility for his or her actions, even at that late stage. Therefore, the courts' approach seems to be that any breach of an interim order, however minor, is relevant. This approach is borne out by the attitude of the sentencing courts in respect of breaches of interim orders. Custodial penalties are not uncommon, even for minor first breaches, with the view being taken that failure to comply with exclusion zones, for instance, is more serious than the actual acts of the defendant due to the history of anti-social behaviour which resulted in the interim order being made. It is also likely that there is a deterrent element to the sentencing, including the fact that the order being breached is a court-made order. Stronger punishment than would be the case for the actual act giving rise to the breach is necessary to maintain the court's authority and integrity.

DEFENCES AND DISREGARDS

3.57 Neither the statute nor the Home Office Guidance provides any specific defences for a defendant to rely upon. Therefore, in order to defeat an application, a defendant will have to counter the applicant's evidence in relation to either the first or second limb of the test in s 1(1) of CDA 1998. With respect to the alleged anti-social conduct, CDA 1998, s 1(5) states that the court must disregard any conduct which was reasonable in the circumstances. The burden of proof is on the defendant to establish on a balance of probabilities that his conduct was reasonable. In *R v Nicholson*[49] the defendant, an animal rights campaigner, had been made subject to an ASBO which prevented her from going within 500 metres of a number of named premises. She attended a demonstration which had been sanctioned by the High Court which was within 500 metres of one of those premises. She said that she had not checked the terms of the order and in particular the inclusion of premises which were not connected to the main object of her activities, Huntingdon Life Sciences. She asserted that she had a reasonable excuse to breach the order as she had no recollection of every having heard before, or at the demonstration of any reference to the premises and mistakenly believed she was entitled to attend the demonstration. The prosecution asserted that ignorance of the law was no excuse and that an ASBO created legal obligations particular to a defendant which they had to follow. The Crown Court was asked to determine whether her account could amount to a defence in law.

3.58 The judge of the Crown Court ruled that the offence was one of 'strict liability' and that qualifications of 'without reasonable excuse' should be narrowly construed so as to exclude ignorance, forgetfulness or misunderstanding of clear terms. The defendant then changed her plea, was sentenced to 4 months and then appealed to the Court of Appeal.

---

[49]   [2006] 1 WLR 2857; [2006] EWCA Crim 1518.

3.59 The Court of Appeal noted that it was not helpful to consider breach of an ASBO as one of strict liability merely because the crown did not have to prove mens rea. Lord Justice Auld held:[50]

> 'It seems to us artificial to characterise a claim of reasonable excuse based on ignorance, whether by reason of forgetfulness or misunderstanding of the terms of an anti-social behaviour order, as an impermissible reliance on an error of law because the order imposes particular legal restrictions on its subject. It is the fact of such ignorance, whether because of forgetfulness or misunderstanding as to the application of the particular terms of the order, combined with appreciation or lack of it as to where the subject was at the material time, and also a value judgment as to its reasonableness in the circumstances, which are in play, not the subject's knowledge or memory at the material time of the law. Such matters, depending on the reasons advanced in support of a defence of reasonable excuse, may be capable of constituting such a defence. Where that is so, the issue of fact, if any, and the value judgment as to reasonableness of the excuse, are ones for a jury, not for the judge.
>
> In our view (and without expressing any view as to the proper outcome), the circumstances here were such, coupled with the fact that the defence had not been articulated with precision in evidence, that the judge should have left the matter to a jury-certainly at that stage. He should not have deprived Miss Nicholson of her entitlement to present her defence of ignorance by reason of forgetfulness or misunderstanding of the terms of the order.
>
> In so concluding we have not disregarded Mr Stillwell's important reminder to the court of the policy consideration touched on by the court in *R v Densu* [1998] 1 Cr App R 400 , as to the ease with which defendants claiming ignorance or forgetfulness might seek to frustrate the effective application and enforcement of the law as to anti-social behaviour orders. But the fact is, as the court indicated in *R v Quayle* [2005] 1 WLR 3642, in *R v Wang* [2005] 1 WLR 661 and also in *R v Evans* [2005] 1 WLR 1435, there is a line to be drawn in the particular circumstances of any case. The issue raised is often likely to be highly fact-sensitive-one which it is eminently desirable should be resolved by a jury where it is the fact-finder. Of course there may be cases which are so clear, where, whether before or in the course of trial, the judge can so rule. But, as we have indicated, we do not consider this to be one of them.'

3.60 In essence therefore unless the issue is simply without possible argument it should be left to the jury to determine whether the defendant had reasonable excuse for the alleged conduct.

Mental health problems

3.61 The issue of whether orders can be made against persons with mental health problems has been one of real debate but without any higher court authority. Recently however two cases have come to the attention of the court by way of case stated. In *R (on the application of Cooke) v Director of Public Prosecutions*[51] the defendant was a habitual beggar. He was convicted under s 5 of the PHA 1997 and after a 3 day hearing a post conviction order was made on the finding that he was an aggressive beggar, had been aggressive to police officers and had self harmed. The defendant admitted the conduct but submitted that an ASBO was not necessary as it would not protect persons from further ASB since his mental state was such that he would be unable to comply with the order and secondly that it would be unjust to make one. The defendant argued that the only effect would be to 'criminalise the defendant's mental health problems'.

3.62 The defendant called a psychiatric nurse who gave evidence that the defendant had been diagnosed as having an emotionally unstable personal disorder, evidence of PTSD with a possible diagnosis of Asperger's syndrome. He gave evidence that his behaviour could be construed as deliberately antagonistic but this was consequential to his mental health problems.

---

[50]   [2006] 1 WLR 2857; [2006] EWCA Crim 1518, para 15 at 2862.
[51]   [2008] EWHC 2703 (Admin).

He recommended mental health treatment and that his behaviour could not be prevented without it. He was not capable of complying with an ASBO and would repeatedly breach an order.

3.63 The magistrates held that the defendant did know right from wrong and had demonstrated that he was capable of choice. He had chosen not to engage with mental health services. The magistrates made an order for 3 years. In the case stated they found that he had understanding when he was well but could be irrational when unwell. The magistrates recognised that the defendant needed treatment, but this had to be weighed against protection of the public. They considered that the order would not prevent him obtaining treatment nor that he would inevitably breach the order. They did not accept the evidence of the psychiatric nurse was correct as to the absence of risk to the public. The administrative court was asked to consider whether an ASBO should be made against a person whose ASB was caused by or consequently of, a mental health disorder.

3.64 The defendant argued that if it was impossible for a person to obey an order there was no point in making it and therefore it was not necessary. Alternatively it was unjust and a wrongful exercise of the discretion to make an ASBO. Lord Justice Dyson held:

> '...if the justices had concluded that the appellant's mental state was such that he was truly incapable of complying with the conditions of any ASBO that they were minded to make, they would have been wrong in law to make the order. If by reason of mental incapacity an offender is incapable of complying with an order, then an order is incapable of protecting the public and cannot therefore be said to be necessary to protect the public.'[52]

This was qualified by the judge later when he stated:[53]

> 'The justices should not refuse to make an ASBO on such grounds unless the defendant does not have the mental capacity to understand the meaning of the order, or to comply with it. Such an incapacity being a medical matter, evidence should normally be given by a psychiatrist and not by a psychologist or a psychiatric nurse.
>
> A defendant who suffers from a personality disorder may on that account be liable to disobey an ASBO. In my judgment, however, that is not a sufficient reason for holding that an order, which is otherwise necessary to protect the public from a defendant's anti-social behaviour, is not necessary for that purpose, or that the court should not exercise its discretion to make an order.'

3.65 The court held that on the evidence before the magistrates' court the defendant did have the mental capacity to understand the order. In answer to the questions the court held that it would be wrong to make an ASBO if the defendant did not have the mental capacity to understand or comply with the order however the fact that he would be likely to breach the order because he suffered from a personality disorder was not of itself a good reason for not making the order. The above reasoning was approved in the case of *Fairweather v Commissioner of Police for the Metropolis*.[54]

---

[52]   [2008] EWHC 2703 (Admin), para 10.
[53]   [2008] EWHC 2703 (Admin), para 12.
[54]   [2008] EWHC 3073 (Admin).

SUMMARY

3.66 In summary:

- ASBOs can be brought by the police, the local authority, an RSL, the BTP, a housing action trust or a county council.

- ASBOs can be brought against defendants aged 10 years or over.

- There is a two-stage test: (i) have acts caused or are they likely to cause harassment, alarm or distress; and (ii) is an order necessary?

- The applicant must prove that someone present was caused harassment, alarm or distress or that conduct was likely to cause the same.

- Stage (i) has to be proved to the criminal standard of proof.

- Stage (ii) is an exercise of judgment and discretion and not a standard of proof.

- Hearsay evidence may be relied on at all stages.

- Applications in the magistrates' court are limited to incidents within 6 months of the summons to establish s 1(1)(a) and out-of-time incidents can be used if similar fact or to show necessity.

- The defendant's individual conduct may be aggregated with that of others in certain situations.

- Criminal convictions may be used to prove either stage.

- Acts after the issue of proceedings can be used to support both limbs of the test.

- The defendant must have the mental capacity to understand an ASBO.

CHAPTER 4

EVIDENCE

4.1   As with all court proceedings, evidence is the key to a successful outcome. This chapter will cover the general techniques of evidence-gathering, which are particularly important to ASBO applications. Whether the reader seeks to secure an ASBO or defeat one, persuasive and comprehensive evidence is of crucial importance.

HOME OFFICE GUIDANCE

4.2   Applicants are encouraged not to produce over-elaborate or excessively voluminous court files. Instead, they are asked to select their material to 'strike a balance and focus on what is most relevant and necessary to provide sufficient evidence for the court to arrive at a clear understanding of the matter'. This is something which is easier for the Home Office to state than to comply with. Whilst bringing less material to court saves money, the burden of proof is a criminal one and the order often perceived as draconian. Achieving the balance is a difficult process and it is far better to lean towards more evidence than less.

4.3   A list of available sources of evidence is provided, including:

- breach of an ABC;

- witness statements of officers attending incidents or those affected by the behaviour;

- evidence of complaints recorded by the police, housing providers or other agencies;

- statements from professional witnesses (eg council or truancy officers or health visitors);

- video or CCTV evidence (effective where resolution is high; alternatively, high-quality still images can be used);

- supporting statements or reports from other agencies (eg probation reports);

- previous successful relevant civil proceedings (eg eviction for similar behaviour);

- previous relevant convictions;

- copies of custody records of previous relevant arrests; and

- information from witness diaries.

In this chapter we shall examine sources of evidence, covert surveillance and hearsay evidence.

SOURCES OF EVIDENCE

Documentary evidence

4.4 Applicants *and* defendants should be fully aware of all relevant documents. Chapter 2 deals more fully with effective information exchange between agencies and how the defendant may access various records. However, the following section should provide a useful checklist of what documents may be available from various agencies.

(i) Housing services

4.5 The files of the housing department should contain comprehensive information in respect of each tenancy, including allegations of nuisance made by or against the defendant. Further, the file should record housing management matters, such as copies of warning letters sent to the defendant and notices before possession proceedings are issued. Interviews with the defendant should also be recorded, detailing the allegations and responses.

4.6 For the applicant, the file can provide useful background information if past nuisance has been recorded. This can establish a pattern of anti-social behaviour and previous, unheeded warnings. For the defence, if there has been a lack of proper housing management, it can be argued that an ASBO is not necessary, as the defendant has not been given the opportunity to change his or her behaviour, or it may provide mitigating circumstances.

(ii) Social services

4.7 The social services department encompasses a wide variety of services, including work with young people, mental health and, in some authorities, the YOT. Documentation from their files can be used in support of or against an application. For the applicant, it can prove, for example, that, despite work having been done with a child, anti-social behaviour continues. For the defendant, the file may show that parental requests for support from the department have been ignored. Failure to provide such support can lead to awkward internal questions, especially if the local authority is also the statutory parent. In appropriate cases, a defendant's representative may successfully argue that an ASBO is not necessary if he or she can demonstrate that other, more appropriate actions should have been taken.[1]

4.8 A request for the production of social services files is often met with resistance. In relation to a child, if care proceedings have begun, permission of the court is needed before documentation can be used.[2] The case of *Re M (Care Proceedings: Disclosure: Human Rights)*[3] contains useful observations on the application of the rules in practice. In other circumstances, disclosure should, in theory, be relatively straightforward.

4.9 Applicants need to appreciate the background against which social services operate. Often, they work with Area Child Protection Committees, in which there is a culture of free and frank disclosure of information, and case discussions are held with parents or alleged perpetrators. More guidance on how these committees work in partnership with other agencies is contained in the Home Office document, 'Working Together to Safeguard Children'. The child protection process may be undermined if that information is subsequently used against a person as part of a court case. Therefore, a framework must be established for departments to come to a

---

[1] See *R (on the application of AB and SB) v Nottingham City Council* [2001] EWHC Admin 235, [2001] 3 FCR 350.
[2] FPR 1991, r 4.23.
[3] [2001] 2 FLR 1316.

workable solution so as not to compromise either party's position. In the event of a lack of internal agreement, there should be a protocol for resolving internal difficulties.

4.10 Defendants and their legal advisers should consider requesting access to files or documents, provided that the request does not constitute 'a fishing expedition'. Defendants might seek access to minutes of meetings about the child, action plans to address the child's needs and any special issues concerning the child which can provide support for arguments that alternatives that are short of an ASBO should be pursued. Often, those involved in social services conferences are given access to minutes of meetings or action plans where they have been present, provided this does not contravene the Family Proceedings Rules 1991 (FPR 1991), r 4.23.

(iii) Environmental services

4.11 Evidence of previous convictions or successful applications for seizure of equipment can assist in building a case against a defendant. Similarly, in eviction cases, especially those cases concerning noise complaints, such records may reveal useful information for the defence. If a complaint has been investigated, what have those investigations shown? For instance, the records may show that the use of monitoring equipment failed to prove a statutory nuisance. Such evidence might deliver a blow to the credibility of the complaints.

(iv) Education/school records

4.12 Documentation from educational sources can potentially help both applicant and defendant. The applicant may be assisted by information which establishes a pattern of misconduct throughout a defendant's schooling. Conversely, the records may reveal a system that has failed the defendant, eg by not exploring the possibility of specialist units, pupil referral or home tutoring, in order to try and address the defendant's conduct. The defendant may be able successfully to contend that such avenues should have been explored before recourse to the courts.

(v) Police

4.13 Documentary evidence from the police can include previous convictions (see **4.17–4.20**), as well as police information which is not normally disclosed. Pocketbook entries of police officers can stand as evidence and printouts of calls made to the police can provide corroborative evidence of complaints, but these are of limited use if they do not identify the perpetrator or nuisance in detail. Where individuals, other than the defendant, are referred to in evidence, the defence may claim that it is discriminatory to take action against one individual and not others.

4.14 The police can also provide analyses of crime patterns. Such information can provide an indication of crime hotspots involving a particular defendant. A detailed plan can be produced to demonstrate the complaints made to the police and to highlight the areas in which the anti-social behaviour has taken place. These plans are often very useful in showing to the court the extent of a defendant's behaviour.

DISCLOSURE

4.15 While the applicant should know the evidence available in the files, it is necessarily more difficult for the defence to identify and obtain the relevant documents. The checklists given earlier in this chapter can assist in identifying sources of evidence but obtaining them can be difficult. In ASBO proceedings, magistrates have the ultimate power to regulate their own procedure. There are no specific rules for disclosure of documents in civil proceedings in the magistrates' court. The Criminal Investigations and Procedures Act 1996, with its detailed provisions for disclosure, does not apply to ASBO proceedings, which are civil in nature. Unfortunately, the Civil Procedure Rules 1998 (CPR 1998), which govern civil actions, do not apply to the magistrates' courts. Disclosure is mentioned in the current Home Office Guidance.[4] It recommends that checks on witness support and intimidation should be made by agencies before any evidence in a case is disclosed. It states that the witness's express permission should be given before any evidence is disclosed, but evidence not disclosed cannot be relied on. The magistrates' courts should, however, be encouraged to adopt the CPR 1998 as far as possible. Direct application of the CPR 1998 will follow in any application for an ASBO in the county court. CPR 1998, r 31 places an obligation on both parties to disclose relevant documents on which they rely and those which adversely affect their own case or support the case of the opposition. Only a reasonable search need be made for such documents. In dealing with disclosure, the parties should bear in mind the overriding objective of dealing with cases fairly, justly, reasonably, proportionately and efficiently (CPR 1998, Part 1).

4.16 Currently, the best way for the defence to obtain access to undisclosed documents is to request them. If the applicant does not accede to the request, an application should be made to the relevant court for disclosure of the documents, relying on the procedures in the CPR 1998 and Art 6 of the European Convention for the Protection of Human Rights and Fundamental Freedoms (ECHR), in that the defendant would be denied a fair trial if refused access to the relevant documents. The applicant may argue that some or all of the information is privileged if prepared in the contemplation of actual or pending litigation. How far the arguments will go or which will prevail is as yet untested in the magistrates' courts. Although it was hoped that when the county court obtained the power to grant ASBOs there would follow a standardisation of procedure between both courts, it does not seem that there have been sufficient proceedings in the county court (probably due to the need for principal proceedings) for this to have occurred. It would seem, however, inappropriate not to utilise the clear rules on disclosure and other procedural steps set out in the CPR 1998. Again it is surprising that there has not been legislative change or Guidance to make this clear.

Previous convictions

4.17 Evidence of previous convictions can be invaluable to applicants because no witnesses are required to prove the incident. As a matter of course, checks should be made for relevant convictions for use in an ASBO application. Proof of convictions can be introduced in court in one of two ways – either by exhibiting police records of convictions to a statement from a police officer or by requesting certificates of conviction from the appropriate magistrates' court or Crown Court. It is, however, very important for an applicant to file the statements of the complaints in the criminal conviction, or at least a summary of the facts. Otherwise, the bare fact of the conviction may not tell the whole story.

4.18 The use of criminal convictions was challenged in the case of *S v Poole Borough Council*.[5] The defendant sought to argue that facts which were used to found a criminal conviction should not be used to obtain an ASBO. Lord Justice Simon Brown, giving the judgment of the Divisional Court on a case stated from the Crown Court, disagreed, and stated:

> 'It seems to me to be perfectly proper to use the same material to base a criminal conviction and then, in civil proceedings, to support an order that was akin to an injunction. Indeed it would seem to me to

---

4   See current Home Office Guidance, reproduced in Appendix 3.
5   [2002] EWHC 244 (Admin), (unreported) February 2002.

be positively eccentric to omit reference to part of the conduct which undoubtedly contributed to the public mischief when it came to seeking to deter it in the future.'[6]

4.19   The court clearly approved the use of previous convictions as evidence in related nuisance proceedings. Previous convictions can, therefore, be used by applicants to establish the first limb of an ASBO (ie harassment, alarm or distress, if they involve offences of this nature). Experience shows that, faced with numerous relevant (and recent) previous convictions (eg assault, burglary and theft), the defence's ability to argue against all parts of the application is seriously undermined. A practical approach to these problems may well be for the defence to make limited concessions and seek to negotiate. For example, in exchange for such concessions, the defendant could attempt to negotiate with the applicant not to proceed with some of the allegations or to relax the terms of the ASBO. Alternatively, the first limb of the test could be conceded and the issue of necessity contested alone.

4.20   Consideration should also be given to the provisions of the Rehabilitation of Offenders Act 1974. If a conviction has become 'spent' under the provisions of this Act the defendant shall be treated for all purposes in law as a person who has not committed the offence.[7] A conviction is spent if the period appropriate to that form of sentence has expired.[8] Once it has, a person cannot be asked questions which may indicate that that person has committed that offence.[9] It follows that a person may not have to answer questions in cross-examination that would lead to the disclosure of spent convictions. Whilst the defendant may seek to rely on these provisions in relation to his or her own previous convictions, there is an exception under s 7(3). If a court is satisfied, in the light of any considerations which appear to it to be relevant, that justice cannot be done in the case except by admitting or requiring evidence relating to a person's spent convictions, that authority may admit or, as the case may be, require the evidence in question. It seems likely that a very strong argument can be made by the applicant that previous convictions showing anti-social behaviour by the defendant *are* necessary to do justice in an ASBO application. The point has yet, however, to be tested.

Lay witnesses

4.21   Witnesses who suffer nuisance can provide documentary evidence in the form of diary sheets or log sheets, or letters of complaint. They can also provide compelling evidence of harassment, alarm or distress, in the form of witness statements and, better still, live evidence. Lay witnesses are, however, often reluctant to give evidence for a variety of reasons, including fear of reprisals or intimidation after the court process. Support, encouragement and protection by the police or through injunctions are very important in securing lay witnesses' co-operation and attendance. As a consequence of the SOCPA 2005 amendments have been made to the CDA 1998 to provide witnesses with special measures to protect them as they give evidence. Full consideration is given to these provisions in chapter 9 at **9.9** onwards.

4.22   The points that have been made in relation to the applicant's lay witnesses apply equally to the defence witnesses, although perhaps naturally, much of the focus of court intimidation and process concerns the applicant's witnesses.

---

6   [2002] EWHC 244 (Admin), (unreported) February 2002, at [16].
7   Rehabilitation of Offenders Act 1974, s 4(1).
8   Rehabilitation of Offenders Act 1974, s 5(1).
9   Rehabilitation of Offenders Act 1974, s 4(1)(b).

Professional witnesses

4.23 Professional witnesses are increasingly used in the context of ASBOs. These can range from council officers, police officers, health authority employees or professional surveillance personnel. Professional witnesses may themselves have been harassed, alarmed or distressed by the defendant, and they may provide information about the defendant's past conduct in order to establish the necessity test.

4.24 The current Home Office Guidance encourages the use of anonymous statements as evidence. The courts, however, do not seem to accord such statements very much weight. Therefore, professional witnesses will often be used in order to spare lay witnesses the ordeal of court attendance, whilst permitting the voice of the local community to be heard in the proceedings. This is achieved by the professional witnesses' referring in their statements to the comments made by local residents. Such comments will, of course, be hearsay (hearsay provisions are dealt with at **4.43–4.61**).

4.25 Professional surveillance firms may be used for such purposes. However, as they can be expensive and results cannot be guaranteed, they should be given very specific tasks, to ensure value for money and effective results in court.

4.26 Professional witnesses can also be used by the defence but, for reasons of finance, often are not. However, access to the same information or statements may be available, using the same tactics explored in the disclosure of documents. The defence can ask if any professional surveillance firms have been engaged and, if so, what the results were. If their findings are adverse to the applicant's and helpful to the defendant's case, they should be disclosed. As this is still an untried concept, it is not known how far the court will go in ordering disclosure for reasons of trial fairness when balanced against arguments of privilege.

4.27 There is nothing to prevent the defence from approaching council employees (or similar), eg the family social worker, a YOT worker, a teacher, etc, for witness statements to support their case. The response to such a request may differ from authority to authority. A typical reaction is often to refuse the request so as not to compromise the applicant's case. If the defence feels that the person approached would be likely to assist the case but feels compelled to refuse to give a statement, a witness summons can be served, to require that person's attendance. However, there is a risk that, in such circumstances, the witness may not give helpful evidence at trial. This risk can be reduced, but not removed, by interviewing the witness outside the court, prior to calling him or her.

COVERT SURVEILLANCE

4.28 Covert surveillance can often reveal the truth of the situation or at least provide dispassionate, independent, corroborative evidence of nuisance.

Videos and CCTV

General

4.29 Video or CCTV footage can provide compelling evidence in court. Indeed, it is specifically mentioned in the Home Office Guidance as an example of what evidence can be included in a case. It notes that such evidence is effective where resolution is high, and that high-quality still images can be used. In one of the first ASBO applications taken by Liverpool city council, such evidence was adduced of a defendant's jumping up and down on cars, which proved incontrovertible evidence of harassment, alarm or distress. CCTV footage has now been used to significant effect in the multiple-defendant ASBOs obtained in Leeds and by many other applicants. On a practical note, it is important to provide the court with statements from people identifying defendants on the video. This is often best done by using a still taken from the video, so that the court can readily follow the identified person as he or she appears in the video.

4.30 More and more lay witnesses have access to home video cameras. The use of such equipment should be encouraged, as neighbours are able to monitor the area over a far longer period than could be done by professional witnesses. However, the defendant can also use home video footage to undermine the case against him or her. If the allegations centre on the intimidating behaviour of the defendant, and footage shows the local community happily interacting with him or her, that will undermine the case. Also, if the defendant captures footage of the applicant's witnesses engaging in similar exploits to those levelled against the defendant, this can be raised as explaining the defendant's conduct as reasonable or, in relation to the necessity test, that the claimant's witnesses did not require protection from the defendant, but the converse.

Using video footage

4.31 If video footage is to be used, the other party should be notified as soon as is practicable, and given the opportunity to view it, to avoid any unnecessary court adjournments. Whoever is adducing video evidence should provide the other side with a copy, or should arrange for private viewing facilities at their office. If the receiving party insists on viewing the original or it is not possible to obtain copies, it should be released only on the solicitor's undertaking to hold it to order, return it on demand and keep it safely. There are no rules in the magistrates' court that deal with the presentation of video evidence in civil proceedings. Applicant authorities and defendants are, therefore, left with the general powers by which the magistrates control their own procedure. In the county court, the position is governed by CPR 1998, r 32.1. This states that the court may control evidence as it sees fit. It can regulate the nature and way in which evidence is presented, and can even exclude evidence that is normally admissible. It can require a party to give evidence by videotape. However, under CPR 1998, r 32.1(6), the court should not let any party hold back evidence to ambush a witness. Video evidence undermining a claimant's case should be disclosed at an early stage. However, following *Rall v Hume*,[10] the fact that video evidence is disclosed late in the day is not always sufficient to justify its exclusion.

4.32 It is important to notify the court as soon as possible, to ensure that the correct equipment is available at court. No assumption should be made about the nature of the technical facilities available at court. Tapes should be wound to the relevant place to save court time. A chronology may assist in identifying individuals or events, unless self-evident.

4.33 As ASBO applications are civil proceedings, there is no strict need to preserve the chain of evidence, as in criminal proceedings. Often, rightly, there is little point in challenging the continuity of evidence but it is useful for the applicant body to be able to prove, if called upon, that the equipment was in good working order and in whose possession the video was before being used in evidence in court.

Using CCTV footage

4.34 In practice, CCTV footage is only available to the police or local authority. The quality of the tapes is generally very clear and, thus, may avoid the additional financial outlay of using professional surveillance firms. Where this is available, still pictures can be taken from the tapes and often provide telling pieces of evidence.

---

[10] [2001] 3 All ER 248.

4.35　The defence should be given the opportunity to view the tapes. The operation of CCTV is heavily regulated by codes of practice issued by the Information Commissioner to ensure fairness and compliance with data protection and human rights legislation. A detailed examination of these codes is beyond the scope of this book, but more information about them can be obtained from the Information Commissioner's website.[11] The defence should check to see if these operating guidelines have been followed, to ensure that evidence obtained cannot be challenged or undermined by operational irregularities.

4.36　Effective planning and gathering of evidence by applicants can reduce or remove the necessity for witness evidence. For example, ASBOs targeted at controlling conduct in areas covered by CCTV, such as city centres or train stations, can benefit from such planning if the operatives are tasked with targeting and recording anti-social conduct.

RIPA 2000 considerations

4.37　The Regulation of Investigatory Powers Act 2000 (RIPA 2000) provides a framework for the effective authorisation and conduct of 'directed surveillance' by local authorities and the police. This is defined as surveillance which is 'covert but not intrusive', and is part of a planned operation which is likely to result in the acquisition of private information, which is not an 'immediate response to events or circumstances', and where it is not reasonably practicable to obtain prior authorisation.

4.38　Surveillance is defined in s 48 of RIPA 2000 as including monitoring, observing or listening to persons, their movements, their conversations or various other activities or communication. Communication is, itself, widely defined to cover anything comprising speech, music, sounds, visual images or data of any description. An example of directed surveillance in an ASBO context is where evidence is covertly gathered by installing secret cameras, trained on a person's home, to obtain evidence of nuisance allegations in and around his or her home and estate as part of a planned investigation.

4.39　The RIPA 2000 also impacts on local authorities and the police when they permit the use of what s 26(8) refers to as a 'covert human intelligence source'. This is where a personal or other relationship is established or maintained for the covert purpose of using that relationship to obtain or provide access to any information to another, or covertly disclosing information obtained because of that relationship to another (eg where professional surveillance firms pose as local neighbours and befriend an alleged perpetrator to gather evidence of anti-social conduct or nuisance in the community).

4.40　Appropriate officers within the police and local authority can authorise others within their related public bodies to carry out surveillance operations for planned aims and for set periods of time. The request for authorisation must persuade the authorising officers that it is necessary on one or more specific grounds, such as national security or for the prevention or detection of crime. Considerations of proportionality are also built in. Similar grounds are, of course, available in Art 8(2) of the ECHR to reconcile interference by a public body with interference in a person's right to respect for his or her private and family life, home and correspondence.

4.41　If covert surveillance is carried out relying on a RIPA 2000 authorisation, according to s 27(1), it makes conduct pursuant to it 'lawful for all purposes'. The exact application of this is unclear, as there is little defining case-law in this area. Applicant authorities can rely on RIPA 2000 authorisations to meet any challenge to the fairness of evidence gathered and relied on as part of the application. The defence may, however, attempt to challenge the parameters of

---

[11]　www.dataprotection.co.uk.

'lawful for all purposes' or seek to challenge whether the authorisation was proportionate and necessary or whether the conduct carried out went beyond the bounds of that which was authorised. The prospects of success of such an application are doubtful. It remains unclear whether this would lead to exclusion of the evidence.

4.42 The police have wider powers to intercept communications contained in RIPA 2000 by the use of interception warrants, and can obtain access to communications data about a subject. For example, lists of email subscribers can be obtained and also the key to encrypted electronic data using other provisions of RIPA 2000. Since 5 January 2004, local authorities also have limited powers to access certain types of communications data. The issues in relation to these matters are varied and beyond the scope of this book, and unlikely to be directly relevant to ASBOs.

HEARSAY EVIDENCE

Use of hearsay evidence

4.43 The court system in England and Wales is adversarial and the rules of evidence are dictated by this doctrine. Persons who have directly witnessed the events giving rise to the application normally give evidence of those events. Their evidence is then tested and challenged through cross-examination by the opposing party. The court then adjudicates on where the truth lies.

4.44 Hearsay evidence is the term given to evidence that the court is asked to accept when the person who directly witnessed events is not giving evidence. The evidence, therefore, cannot be tested in the same way as when a live witness is available to be cross-examined. Hearsay falls into two categories: first-hand or multiple hearsay. Hearsay is not generally admissible in criminal proceedings, but, as has been confirmed by the House of Lords in *McCann*,[12] ASBOs are civil proceedings. Therefore, hearsay evidence is generally admissible.

4.45 *W, F v Regina*.[13] The admissibility of hearsay evidence in civil proceedings is governed primarily by s 1(4) of the Civil Evidence Act 1995,[14] which states that evidence shall not be excluded purely on the grounds that it is hearsay. Those provisions apply to magistrates' courts and, therefore, ASBOs by virtue of the Magistrates' Courts (Hearsay Evidence in Civil Proceedings) Rules 1999.[15] In *W, F v Regina* however, a lacuna in the procedural rules became apparent when the issue of hearsay evidence in a post conviction application before the Crown Court was raised. The court noted that the above 1999 Hearsay Rules could not apply in an application to the Crown Court. The result was an urgent review of the criminal procedure rules and several amendments later there are a set of procedural rules[16] for all post conviction orders. They apply to both magistrates and Crown Courts and openly states that they draw heavily from the 1999 Hearsay Rules.

---

[12] *R v Manchester Crown Court ex parte McCann* [2001] EWCA Civ 281, [2001] 1 WLR 1084.
[13] [2006] EWCA Crim 686.
[14] See Appendix 1(B).
[15] SI 1999/681 (L3), set out at Appendix 1(D).
[16] Criminal Procedure Rules 2005.

Adducing hearsay evidence before the court

4.46   There are several types of hearsay evidence. These may be summarised as follows:

- a statement identifying the witness, signed and dated by him or her, giving a direct account of events – this is the best form of hearsay, especially if accompanied by a statement that the witness is too afraid to attend court;

- an anonymous statement in which the witness states the reasons for not attending;

- direct evidence from a professional witness, telling the court what an identified (or even anonymous) witness has told him or her and why that witness will not attend court.

Hearsay notices

4.47   These are the means used to put the other side on notice of the intention to adduce hearsay evidence and can be used as a tactic to give greater weight to hearsay evidence. If hearsay evidence is to be used, notice should be given to the other party. The requirements under the Civil Evidence Act 1995 are less onerous than those under the 1999 Hearsay Rules, and seem difficult to reconcile. The procedure under the Criminal Procedural Rules is more akin to the 1999 Hearsay Rules but as will be seen below by no means the same.

4.48   Under the 1999 Hearsay Rules,[17] a party wishing to rely on hearsay evidence must give the other party 21 days' written notice by serving a hearsay notice. This notice must also be filed with the court. The court may, however, reduce or increase the period of notice required either on application by a party[18] or its own motion.[19] Applicants should avoid delay, and should, therefore, make such an application when the papers are issued. The court clerks will need to have proper reasons if they are to shorten deadlines (eg the witnesses are suffering current nuisance and there is a real risk that some witnesses will become too afraid to give evidence if the matter is delayed in coming to court). It should, however, be noted that, by virtue of s 2(4) of the Civil Evidence Act 1995, failure to comply with notice requirements will not affect the actual admissibility of the hearsay evidence but will adversely affect the weight to be attached to it. In considering weight, the court will have regard to the various points at s 4(2) in particular. These include whether it would have been reasonable and practical to produce the maker of the hearsay evidence, whether the statement was made contemporaneously with the events described, and whether the person involved had any motive to conceal or misrepresent matters.

4.49   Under the 1999 Rules, a hearsay notice must:

'(a)   state that it is a hearsay notice;
(b)   identify the proceedings in which the hearsay evidence is to be given;
(c)   state that the party proposes to adduce hearsay evidence;
(d)   identify the hearsay evidence;
(e)   identify the person who made the statement which is to be given in evidence; and
(f)   state why that person will not be called to give oral evidence.'[20]

4.50   A single hearsay notice may, however, deal with the hearsay evidence of more than one witness. A sample hearsay notice also appears at Appendix 2(H).

---

[17]   SI 1999/681 (L3), r 3(1).
[18]   SI 1999/681 (L3), r 3(2).
[19]   SI 1999/681 (L3), r 3(3).
[20]   Magistrates' Courts (Hearsay Evidence in Civil Proceedings) Rules 1999, r 3(4).

4.51 Where a party seeks to attack the credibility of the maker of a hearsay statement or seek to assert that their evidence is inconsistent with a previous statement they must notify the other party of that intention[21] within 7 days of service of the hearsay notice unless the court orders otherwise.[22] If the party seeking to rely on the hearsay statement then seeks to call the witness they must give notice to the court and the other party[23] within 7 days of the above of their intention to call them.[24]

4.52 All documents relating to hearsay evidence which need to be served on a party can be served on the solicitor acting for the party by post, DX or fax[25] and is deemed served (unless the contrary is proved) on the second business day after posting, leaving with DX and the day of receipt prior to 4 pm, respectively.[26] If the party is known not to have a solicitor then it must be served personally or sent by first class post.[27] In the case of the latter it is deemed served on the second business day after posting.[28]

4.53 The above rules govern applications for ASBOs by the court in the magistrates' court. The Criminal Procedural Rules specifically state that they apply to all applications for a post conviction order. The real difficulty is that, as will be seen below, they are similar but are by no means the same and some conflict remains. Whilst *W & F* was undoubtedly correct that the 1999 Hearsay Rules[29] could not apply to post conviction Crown Court applications they clearly do apply to all post conviction applications in the magistrates' court. It is settled law that these applications are civil hearings and the Regulations specifically apply to all civil proceedings in the magistrates' court.[30] The result is that both sets of rules in theory apply and therefore arguably a party wishing to rely on hearsay evidence has to comply with both. Indeed the notes to the 2005 Rules indicate at various points that there are time limits in the 1999 Hearsay Rules but does not say if they are to be complied with or not. Another difference is that the 1999 Hearsay Rules require the party seeking to rely on the hearsay evidence to file with the court and then serve certified copies as endorsed by the court with the time and date of a hearing. The 2005 Rules require simple filing and service. Which is to be followed in the case of a post conviction order application in the magistrates' court? In practice it is suggested that applicants for post conviction orders should aim to comply with the Criminal Procedural Rules unless there are specific time limits in one or the other in which case those should be followed.

4.54 Under the Criminal Procedural Rules any party who wishes to introduce hearsay evidence must serve a written notice on the court officer and the other part(ies).[31] The notice must:[32]

(i)   explain that it is a notice of hearsay evidence;

(ii)   identify that evidence;

(iii) identify the person who made the statement which is hearsay, or explain why if that person is not identified; and

(iv)   explain why that person will not be called to give oral evidence.

---

[21] Magistrates' Courts (Hearsay Evidence in Civil Proceedings) Rules 1999, r 5(1).
[22] Magistrates' Courts (Hearsay Evidence in Civil Proceedings) Rules 1999, r 5(2).
[23] Magistrates' Courts (Hearsay Evidence in Civil Proceedings) Rules 1999, r 5(3).
[24] Magistrates' Courts (Hearsay Evidence in Civil Proceedings) Rules 1999, r 5(4).
[25] Magistrates' Courts (Hearsay Evidence in Civil Proceedings) Rules 1999, r 6(1)(b).
[26] Magistrates' Courts (Hearsay Evidence in Civil Proceedings) Rules 1999, r 6(3).
[27] Magistrates' Courts (Hearsay Evidence in Civil Proceedings) Rules 1999, r 6(1)(a).
[28] Magistrates' Courts (Hearsay Evidence in Civil Proceedings) Rules 1999, r 6(3)(a).
[29] Magistrates' Courts (Hearsay Evidence in Civil Proceedings) Rules 1999.
[30] Magistrates' Courts (Hearsay Evidence in Civil Proceedings) Rules 1999, r 2(3).
[31] Criminal Procedure Rules 1999 (as amended), r 50.6(1)(a).
[32] Criminal Procedure Rules 1999 (as amended), r 50.6(1)(b).

4.55 One notice can deal with hearsay in more than one statement and can cover more than one witness.[33] There is no specified time limit in the 2005 Rules for the service of the hearsay notice save that any evidence to be relied on in an application, which presumably includes hearsay evidence, must be served 'as soon as practicable (without waiting for the verdict)'.[34] This is in contrast to the 1999 Rules which require service of the notice not less than 21 days before the hearing (see **4.48** above). Therefore there is a theoretically more onerous duty on an applicant in a magistrates' post conviction hearing than in a Crown Court one. In practice however unless it is a very short period from charge to trial there should be more than sufficient time and 'as soon as practicable' will be at least 21 days.

4.56 If a party wishes to cross-examine a person who made a statement which another party wants to introduce as hearsay then they must ask for the court's permission[35] by written application with reasons.[36] The application has to be made not more than 7 days after service of the hearsay notice and must be served on the court officer and the other parties.

4.57 The court could determine the application without a hearing[37] however it cannot dismiss it unless the applicant[38] has been allowed to make oral representations[39] nor can it allow one unless everyone served has been 7 days in which to make representations about the application including whether there should be a hearing.[40]

4.58 In essence therefore under the 2005 Rules if an application is made by a party to call a 'hearsay witness' there must be an oral hearing unless it is being rejected. Conversely the court can require a witness to be called without hearing oral representations if it so chooses. This is in contrast with the 1999 Hearsay Rules under which there must be an inter parties hearing[41] to determine this issue unless it is in the interests of justice to hear it ex parte. This seems to put the party seeking to rely on hearsay evidence in a worse position under the 1999 Hearsay Rules. Further the applicant is strangely in a worse position under the 2005 Rules in that they are required (potentially even before the verdict) to serve the witness evidence on which they wish to rely. Under the 1999 Hearsay Rules the applicant can wait until verdict or other direction of the court.

4.59 Where a party wishes to challenge the credibility or consistency of a witness who made a statement which the party wants to introduce as hearsay, they must serve a notice on the court office and the other party. Such notice must be not more than 7 days after the hearsay notice was served. Further and in contrast with the requirements in the 1999 Hearsay Rules the notice must identify any statement or other material on which the party relies.[42] Therefore the party seeking to rely on the hearsay statement gains an advantage by knowing the defendant's evidence/arguments in a post conviction application which the party applying in the magistrates' court for an ASBO would not.

4.60 If such a notice as above is served the party who served the hearsay notice can call that person to give oral evidence instead but must serve a notice on the court and the other party within 7 days of the above notice.[43]

---

[33] Criminal Procedure Rules 2005 (as amended), r 50.6(2).
[34] Criminal Procedure Rules 2005 (as amended), r 50.3(4)(a).
[35] Criminal Procedure Rules 2005 (as amended), r 50.7(1).
[36] Criminal Procedure Rules 2005 (as amended), r 50.7(2)(a).
[37] Criminal Procedure Rules 2005 (as amended), r 50.7(3).
[38] The applicant need not attend personally.
[39] Criminal Procedure Rules 2005 (as amended), r 50.7(4)(a).
[40] Criminal Procedure Rules 2005 (as amended), r 50.7(4)(b).
[41] Magistrates' Courts (Hearsay Evidence in Civil Proceedings) Rules 1999, r 4(3)(a)(ii).
[42] Criminal Procedure Rules 2005 (as amended), r 50.8(b).
[43] Criminal Procedure Rules 2005 (as amended), r 50.8(2).

4.61 The court retains a general power to shorten or extend a period for compliance with the above rules even if the time has passed.[44] Further the court can waive the requirement to use a prescribed form or allow the notice or application to be presented orally.[45]

Case-law

4.62 The first (and ultimately the authoritative) case to consider the question of admissibility of hearsay evidence in ASBO proceedings was *Clingham v Kensington and Chelsea Royal Borough Council*.[46] In this case, the defendant appealed by way of case stated against the decision of the district judge in the magistrates' court to admit evidence of complaints of anti-social behaviour when the witnesses to the acts complained of were not being called. This comprised police officers giving live evidence of what they had seen *and* also what others had told them the defendant had done. The district judge had initially ordered proper hearsay notices to be served but, at the hearing, decided that the evidence was not hearsay evidence at all and admitted it as of right without any notices being required. The defendants appealed the decision.

4.63 Schiemann LJ, giving the judgment of the Divisional Court,[47] referred first to the Civil Evidence Act 1995 and then to the 1999 Hearsay Rules. He held that the evidence was hearsay and, therefore, both the Act and the Rules applied. The primary consequence of failing to serve the notice was that this had to be considered in assessing the weight to be attached to it. The judge, however, left open whether there would be other consequences. What is clear is that the court accepted that hearsay evidence was admissible and should not be excluded simply because it may have little or negligible weight. It was a matter for the court to determine whether the weight was sufficient to make an order, having regard to all the circumstances. This view was reinforced in the House of Lords' decision in the conjoined appeals of *Clingham* and *McCann*, which confirmed that hearsay evidence is admissible in ASBO applications. Lord Steyn, giving the judgment of the House, said:

> 'Having concluded that the proceedings in question are civil under domestic law and Article 6, it follows that the machinery of the Civil Evidence Act 1995 and the Magistrates' Courts (Hearsay Evidence in Civil Proceedings) Rules 1999, SI 1999/681, allow the introduction of such evidence under the first part of section 1. The weight of such evidence might be limited. On the other hand, in its cumulative effect it could be cogent. It all depends on the particular facts ....'[48]

> '... use of the Civil Evidence Act 1995 and the rules in cases under the first part of s 1 are not in any way incompatible with the HRA ....'[49]

> '... hearsay evidence will often be of crucial importance. For my part, hearsay evidence depending on its logical probativeness is quite capable of satisfying the requirements of s 1(1).'[50]

4.64 The 'other consequences' which the Court of Appeal in *Clingham* referred to may well be a reference to an application by the defence to require hearsay witnesses to be called.[51] When acting for the defendant, it is essential that hearsay evidence is challenged immediately and the

---

44 Criminal Procedure Rules 2005 (as amended), r 50.9(a).

45 Criminal Procedure Rules 2005 (as amended), r 50.9(b).

46 *R (on the application McCann and others) v Crown Court at Manchester; Clingham v Kensington and Chelsea Royal Borough Council* [2002] UKHL 39, [2002] 3 WLR 1313, [2002] 4 All ER 593, HL.

47 (2001) *The Times*, February 20, DC.

48 *R (on the application McCann and others) v Crown Court at Manchester; Clingham v Kensington and Chelsea Royal Borough Council* [2002] UKHL 39, [2002] 3 WLR 1313, per Lord Steyn at [35].

49 *R (on the application McCann and others) v Crown Court at Manchester; Clingham v Kensington and Chelsea Royal Borough Council* [2002] UKHL 39, [2002] 3 WLR 1313, per Lord Steyn at [36].

50 *R (on the application McCann and others) v Crown Court at Manchester; Clingham v Kensington and Chelsea Royal Borough Council* [2002] UKHL 39, [2002] 3 WLR 1313, per Lord Steyn at [37].

51 Magistrates' Courts (Hearsay Evidence in Civil Proceedings) Rules 1999, r 4 – on 7 days' notice.

court is asked for permission to require the witness's attendance. If this is not possible or it is refused, submissions should be made to the court that the evidence should carry little or no weight, as there has been no opportunity to challenge the witness. Further, it can demonstrate that there was direct evidence available to the applicant which it has failed to adduce. The defence can also take issue with the applicant body's proffered reasons for the evidence being hearsay. Ultimately, however, it is for the court to decide whether the reasons are genuine and what weight to give to the evidence.

4.65 If there was any doubt after *Clingham* that applications for ASBOs were civil in nature whether free-standing or post-conviction applications, this has been conclusively determined by the administrative court in *R (on the application of W) v Acton Youth Court*.[52] See further **6.43–6.46**.

4.66 There are cases in the county courts where immediate possession orders have been made, relying on the direct evidence of previous convictions and the hearsay evidence of a housing officer alone.[53] How far the court will apply this to ASBO proceedings, where the consequences are potentially more draconian, is open to real dispute. The most likely result is that, unless there are previous convictions (which are incontrovertible and do not therefore require proof), hearsay evidence alone is unlikely to be sufficient in the vast majority of ASBO applications. This, however, cannot be an absolute rule and, with the right evidence, an application based solely on hearsay may well succeed. In *Stevens*[54] the application seems to have been made and granted based on hearsay evidence alone, however, a careful consideration of the judgment would seem to show that CCTV footage was available which presumably showed the defendant acting in an anti-social manner. Whilst the taker of the footage was not present at court and therefore the date, time and location of the incidents would be proved by hearsay evidence, the evidence would have significant weight nonetheless provided the defendant could be easily identified. If not, or no incidents were shown, its relevance would seem to be questionable. Aside from the above the most likely way in which hearsay evidence alone would be enough is where a police officer takes several statements from people about the same incident and that the accounts corroborated each other and were perhaps supported by a police crime report. The suspicion, however, would remain that the interviewees had an axe to grind against the defendant and had 'got together' to fabricate the incident. Certainly a defendant could make this point and as he was unaware of the identity of the alleged victims he cannot say what reason they would have to lie. A court may have some difficulty in such a case finding a case proved beyond reasonable doubt although the quality of the defendant's evidence would probably also be crucial.

4.67 In *M v DPP*[55] the defendant pleaded guilty to possession of cannabis and the CPS applied for a post conviction order. Evidence was served by the applicant 1 month before the hearing of the application. This evidence was anonymous hearsay evidence but no notice was ever served. The magistrates' court were asked to exclude the evidence for that reason. The magistrates' court held that as the defendant was fully aware of the nature of the evidence more than 21 days before the hearing the failure to serve a notice was procedural and the interests of justice would not be served by an adjournment. They admitted the hearsay saying there was no prejudice to the defendant. The defendant appealed by way of case stated.

4.68 The administrative court was asked to consider whether it was an error of law to have imposed an ASBO based on hearsay evidence in the form of statements and public record where they had been no notice to adduce pursuant to the 1999 Regulations. The court noted that s 2(4) of the Civil Evidence Act 1995 specifically stated a failure to serve a notice did not affect the admissibility of the evidence but could be taken into account by the court as to weight to be given to the evidence. The appellant argued not against admissibility but instead that it was an

---

[52] [2005] All ER (D) 284.
[53] *Leeds City Council v Harte* (1999) *Current Law Cases* 4069.
[54] See **3.15**.
[55] [2007] EWHC 1032 (Admin).

error of law to impose any ASBO when the rules had not been complied with. The appellant argued that because of the failure to comply with the rules no consideration had been given as to why the unidentified witnesses were unwilling to come and give evidence. No consideration had been given to special measures for witness protection and no consideration to weight. The procedural error had led, they argued, to substantive errors.

4.69 Mr Justice Gross giving the decision of the court stated that whilst they wished to make it plain that they did not say that the rules were mere technicalities because the evidence had been served 1 month before the hearing there was no error of law in proceeding with the hearing and making an ASBO. The justices were not faced with arguments relating to possible special measures nor were they addressed as to how they should weight such evidence. In those circumstances they could not be said to have erred in law.

4.70 The court made it clear that they were not considering the more difficult question as to whether it was appropriate to make an ASBO when the evidence came only from anonymous witnesses. They noted that the answer to the question may not be straightforward and would need to be considered by the higher courts in due course. That was however not the subject of the case stated before them in this case.

4.71 The current Home Office Guidance expressly refers to hearsay evidence. It classifies such evidence as 'vital' to protect those in the community who are fearful of reprisals. It refers to the different forms of hearsay covered at **4.46** and offers the advice that hearsay evidence must be relevant, and include specific details of dates, places, times and actions. This advice is simple and obvious, but remains true when deciding what evidence to submit in an application.

CHAPTER 5

APPLICATIONS TO THE MAGISTRATES' COURT

COURT FORMS

5.1 The Magistrates' Courts (Anti-social Behaviour Orders) Rules 2002 (the 2002 Rules) previously dictated that any application for an ASBO or interim order had to be in the form which is at Sch 1 to the Rules; however, this was amended in June 2003 so that the application 'may' be in such form.[1] The Rules also previously provided mandatory forms for the summons, ASBO and interim ASBO order. This requirement was removed by amendment to the 2002 Rules at the same time. Whilst there is no requirement to follow set forms, many courts have approved formats for such forms, and it is suggested that it is appropriate to follow these unless there are good reasons not to do so. A sample draft ASBO application is set out in Appendix 2.1, a sample draft ASBO in Appendix 2.2, and a sample draft interim order application at Appendix 2.3.

5.2 When laying the complaint, the applicant body should ensure that the following documents are filed with the court and served on the defendant:

- summons;

- ASBO application;

- draft order;

- certificate of consultation;

- list of previous convictions;

- information to the defendant on how to obtain legal advice;

- hearsay notices;

- evidence in support;

- case summary; and

- a clear warning to the defendant that it is an offence to pervert the course of justice and that witness intimidation in civil proceedings is a criminal offence[2] and can lead to prosecution.

5.3 In order to keep delays to the minimum, in practice, it is advisable for the applicant body to give the defendant a letter in which not only is he or she told of the right to legal advice and representation but which also includes addresses and telephone numbers of the Citizens Advice Bureau, local law centre and advice where legal representation can be obtained (eg the Law Society). The letter should finish with a large typeface warning that the defendant must seek

---

[1]   The 2002 Rules, SI 2002/2784, r 4(1) and (5), as amended by SI 2003/1236. The 2002 Rules are set out at Appendix 1(E).

[2]   Criminal Justice and Police Act 2001, ss 39–41 (note that the Home Office Guidance citation is wrong).

legal advice immediately and that failure to do so may result in the hearing proceeding without his or her having legal representation. This letter can be of real importance when opposing an application to adjourn by the defendant. Where the letter has been personally served (there is no reason why it cannot be served with the papers) and includes the above warning, it would be hard to argue for an adjournment if there has been delay by the defendant.

5.4 Whilst it is usual to serve the evidence which the applicant body relies upon with the summons, it is not always appropriate to serve all the available evidence at this time. On occasions, where it is feared that the defendant may intimidate a witness or there is a reasonable prospect that he or she will accept an order being made, statements from lay persons can be withheld. It may, however, be that if all the evidence is served the defendant will concede the making of the order and save the witnesses giving evidence in any event. If the defendant seeks to contest the application, that evidence can be served at that time. If not, the defendant need never know that there were other witnesses willing to come forward, thus protecting them from possible reprisals.

SERVICE OF COURT FORMS AND EVIDENCE

5.5 Save in the case of service of interim ASBOs, the 2002 Rules provide that any summons, or copy of an order or application required to be sent under the Rules, can be served either:

- in person; or

- by post to the last known address.[3]

If sent by the latter method, it is deemed to have been received unless the defendant proves otherwise. In practice, however, it is unlikely that a court would reject a defendant's assertion that he or she had not received notice unless there was good reason to disbelieve the defendant. As a matter of pragmatism, it is suggested that service, certainly of the initial summons and documents, should always be effected by personal service, unless impracticable to do so. A certificate of service can then be lodged with the court. New evidence or documents can then be sent by post if personal service is not straightforward.

5.6 If possible, when serving the original summons, it would be wise to serve an indexed and paginated trial bundle on the defendant and on the court. It should be remembered that four copies may be needed for the court and a further one brought to the hearing for any witnesses. Whilst many magistrates' courts have now had experience in ASBO applications, it is unfortunately rare that lay magistrates, at least, have read much, if anything, of the bundle before the trial. It is therefore important for the applicant to send a letter with the trial bundles, reminding the clerk that, as the magistrates are sitting in their civil capacity, they should be given the bundle to read prior to the hearing – preferably the day before. If they can read the papers in advance, valuable time will be saved at the hearing, as witnesses' evidence-in-chief will be significantly shorter, as can be the opening.

5.7 If the defendant is under 18 years of age, a person with parental responsibility or the defendant's guardian must also be served with at least the summons. If the child is being 'looked after' by the local authority or there is a care order in place, the local authority social services social worker may be served instead of the parent.

5.8 By virtue of r 7(2) of the 2002 Rules, the summons, order, applications, etc, shall also be sent by the justices' chief executive to the applicant body and to any relevant authority whom

---

[3] Rule 7(1).

the applicant body was required by s 1E of CDA 1998 to consult with. Rather oddly, r 7(2) then goes on to state that, where appropriate, these authorities shall be invited to make observations and be advised of their right to be heard at the hearing. It would seem most unusual that, having filed a certificate of consultation, which the Guidance says should not indicate whether they consent, the court should be able to ask these authorities to comment on the application. Still stranger is the notion that they have the right to be heard at the application hearing. Where the power for this right to be heard arises is not clear, and it is hard to see why that right should exist. Finally, there is no assistance as to when the court may think it appropriate to invite observations or advise authorities of this right to be heard. The strong likelihood is that the court will do it in all cases, to ensure uniformity, until some guidance is given either by case-law or amended guidance. What can be said for the moment is that if the magistrates' courts are to routinely ask relevant authorities for comments, it would be a brave applicant who applied without the support of all.

CHAPTER 6

ANTI-SOCIAL BEHAVIOUR ORDERS IN THE COUNTY COURT AND ON CRIMINAL CONVICTION

COUNTY COURT

6.1   Following the amendments brought about by the PRA 2002, an application for an order akin to an ASBO could be commenced in the county court.[1] Whilst not strictly an ASBO, the criteria and punishments are the same and therefore are referred to as ASBOs in this book. The circumstances in which such orders could be brought were, however, far too restrictive and of very limited practical use. Essentially, an application for an ASBO could only be brought by a relevant authority[2] and only in two instances:

(1)   where the relevant authority was already a party to the principal proceedings to which the intended defendant was a party;

(2)   where the relevant authority was not a party to the principal proceedings but considered that it would be reasonable to make an application against a party to them.

6.2   The use of the section was therefore limited to cases where a person was already being proceeded against (eg for possession) and it was thought appropriate to obtain an ASBO to regulate that person's behaviour beyond those possession proceedings. Applications could not be brought under this section against a child unless he or she had a tenancy and was the subject of the proceedings. This meant that, where possession proceedings were brought against a person as a result of, or in part due to, the behaviour of a partner or child who was not a tenant, there was no power for the court to join the partner or child or make an ASBO against them. This led to the expensive and potentially embarrassing position whereby ASBO proceedings against the partner or child were commenced in the magistrates' court and ran alongside the county court possession proceedings. This could have led to inconsistent findings of fact and was certainly an unwelcome complication.

ASB ACT 2003

6.3   In response to the criticism raised as a result of the above problems, a number of changes were introduced by the ASB Act 2003.[3] Now, where the relevant authority is a party to the principal proceedings and considers:

(a)   that a person who is not a party to the proceedings has acted in an anti-social manner; and

(b)   that the person's anti-social acts are material in relation to the principal proceedings,

---

[1]   CDA 1998, s 1B is added by PRA 2002, s 63.
[2]   See chapter 3 for definition.
[3]   Section 85(1), (5), (6) of the ASB Act 2003, inserting s 1B(3A)–(3C) into the CDA 1998 and amending s 1B(5) of that Act.

it may apply to join that person to the principal proceedings and apply for an ASBO (or then apply to join another person to defend such an application). However, a person may not be joined unless the anti-social acts complained of are material to the principal proceedings. This prevents applications where only one incident is material to the possession proceedings and the remaining allegations have no bearing on them but the relevant authority wishes to obtain an order. The current Home Office Guidance suggests that the county court will be able to make an order only where the principal proceedings involve evidence of anti-social behaviour and, indeed, its use will predominantly, if not exclusively, be in association with possession proceedings. This amendment will have most effect when it is feared that, if a possession order is made, the defendant will simply move into privately rented accommodation, close by, without abating the alleged anti-social behaviour. By the use of this section, in appropriate circumstances, it would be possible to apply for an ASBO in general terms but, more particularly, perhaps, to prevent the defendant from returning to live within a particular area or estate and/or harassing named persons (eg witnesses in the possession proceedings).

6.4   In relation to adult defendants, the above amendments came into force on 31 March 2004.[4] However, the power to join defendants who are under 18 years of age came into force on 1 October 2004. It was being piloted in 11 county courts[5] for an 18-month period, the outcome of that pilot was inconclusive and it seems has been extended. It is vital that practitioners make enquiries of their local court as to whether the court has power to bring such claims against minors.

6.5   In considering an application, the court has to be satisfied that the conditions in s 1(1) are fulfilled.[6] Formal consultation must be established before making any application for an order in the county court.[7] Interim orders can be applied for,[8] and the order must be for a minimum of 2 years, cannot be discharged in that period without the consent of the applicant and carries on breach the same punishment as an ASBO.[9] Either party may apply to the court for the order to be varied or discharged.[10]

PRACTICE AND PROCEDURE

6.6   The procedure is governed by CPR Part 65 and the Practice Direction which accompanies it. The rules state that where the application for an ASBO is being made by the party who is the claimant in the main proceedings, the application *must* be made in the claim form.[11] Where the applicant is the defendant in the main proceedings the application notice must be filed with the defence.[12] This may well occur where a claim for disrepair is initiated and the council seeks possession of the property.

6.7   If an application for an ASBO is not raised in the claim form, and the applicant becomes aware of circumstances which lead it to apply for one, this application must be made as soon as possible by an application notice.[13] Any such application should normally be on notice.[14]

---

[4]   SI 2004/690, art 2(b)(ii).
[5]   Bristol, Central London, Clerkenwell, Dewsbury, Huddersfield, Leicester, Manchester, Oxford, Tameside, Wigan and Wrexham.
[6]   CDA 1998, s 1B(4).
[7]   CDA 1998, s 1E(1)(b).
[8]   CDA 1998, s 1D(1)(b).
[9]   CDA 1998, s 1B(7).
[10]   CDA 1998, s 1B(5).
[11]   CPR, r 65.22(1)(a).
[12]   CPR, r 65.22(1)(b).
[13]   CPR, r 65.22(2).
[14]   CPR, r 65.22(3).

6.8 Any application for an ASBO in the county court must be accompanied by written evidence and *must* include evidence that consultation has been complied with.[15] It is also important that both applications to join and applications for ASBOs should be accompanied by evidence showing the connection between the principal proceedings and the application to join/for an ASBO. ASBOs made in the county court should be made on Form N113.[16] This form is for final orders only, but the initial paragraph referring to the test in s 1(1) can be deleted, and wording that the court found it 'just to make an interim order pending the hearing of the main application' can be inserted. Further, the sentence which begins 'Unless both parties consent …', just over halfway through the order, should be deleted, as this applies only to full orders. It is hoped that a practice form will be available shortly, with these or similar amendments included.

APPLICATION TO JOIN A NON-PARTY

6.9 To use the powers granted under s 1B(3B) of the amended CDA 1998 to join a party to the principal proceedings to obtain an ASBO against them, application must[17] be made:

- at the same time as and in the same application notice in which the ASBO application is made out;

- in accordance with CPR, r 19.1;

- as soon as the applicant considers that the criteria in s 1B(3A) are made out.[18]

This means that the application has to be brought complying with CPR, rr 19.2 and 19.4, ie that permission of the court is required and that the order joining the person must be served on all relevant parties. The application notice must contain the applicant's reasons for claiming that the person's acts are material to the principal proceedings and details of the acts alleged.[19] This would be necessary in any event as CPR, r 19.2(2) requires the court to be satisfied that it is desirable to add the party to resolve all matters in dispute or that there is a connection issue which the court should resolve. Applications to join non-parties can be made without notice but should normally be made on notice.[20] Unless there was a very urgent need for an interim order without notice it is hard to foresee circumstances when notice would not be given.

6.10 Where the relevant authority is not a party to the principal proceedings, e g if an ALMO is bringing a possession claim , but wishes to apply for an ASBO, it must apply in same way as above, but must apply to become a party in accordance with CPR Part 19. Again, applications should be made as soon as the authority becomes aware of the principal proceedings and should normally be made on notice and with evidence of why the authority needs to be joined to the action.

6.11 In *Manchester City Council v Muir & Another*[21] the council issued proceedings for an injunction against Mrs Muir, a tenant of theirs. They also sought to join her son to the proceedings and to seek an ASBO against him. The county court made an interim ASBO against him and accepted an undertaking from Mrs Muir for 6 months with a further term that if no application was made within that period to restore the injunction application it would stand dismissed. This period passed without application but the proceedings for an ASBO against her

---

[15] CPR, r 65.25.
[16] See Appendix 2(F).
[17] See CPR, r 65.23(1).
[18] See **6.3**.
[19] CPR, r 65.23(2).
[20] CPR, r 65.23(3).
[21] [2006] EWCA Civ 423.

son continued. The matter reached the Court of Appeal on other issues but they were also asked to dismiss the proceedings against the son on the basis that as the principal proceedings against his mother had been dismissed the joined proceedings could not continue.

6.12 Lord Justice May giving the judgment of the court rejected this argument entirely stating that it was 'simply wrong'[22] in that once a person was properly joined to principal proceedings that person was a party to those proceedings and the continuation or otherwise of the initial proceedings was irrelevant. The court did however state that it would not be a proper use of the statutory procedure to issue county court proceedings against a principal defendant only for the sham purpose of joining another person. However in this case there was no evidence of this and indeed the mother had given a substantive undertaking.

INTERIM ORDERS

6.13 Applications for interim ASBOs in the county court must be made in accordance with CPR Part 25, which provides that any application must be made with supporting evidence in witness statements, and that if it is made without notice (applications should normally be made on notice),[23] then the statements should explain why notice has not been given.[24] The court may grant an interim order without notice if it appears to it that there are good reasons for not giving notice.[25]

6.14 Where the application is made on notice then the notice and evidence in support must be served as soon as practicable after issue and in any event not less than 3 days before the hearing of the application.[26] The applicant is responsible for filing a draft order and bringing to the court a copy of the order on a computer disk.[27]

SERVICE

6.15 Unlike ASBO orders granted in the magistrates' courts, orders granted by the county court, whether interim or full, must be served on the defendant personally.[28]

ORDERS ON CRIMINAL CONVICTION

6.16 Any criminal court, on conviction of a person of a relevant offence, can make an order to prohibit the defendant from doing anything specified in the order.[29] The order, whilst made by the criminal court, has the same effect as an ASBO. The order may be made by the magistrates' court, youth court or Crown Court. Again, for convenience, these orders will generally be referred to as ASBOs.

6.17 ASBOs on conviction were introduced by the PRA 2002 but have proved to be a difficult vehicle by which to make an application. The ASB Act 2003 brought a complete change to the legislation with the introduction from 31 March 2004 of new s 1C(3), (3A) and (3B). Now the

---

[22] [2006] EWCA Civ 423 at [26].
[23] CPR, r 65.26(2)(b).
[24] CPR, r 25.3(3).
[25] CPR, r 25.3(1).
[26] CPR, PD 25, para 2.2.
[27] CPR, para 2.4.
[28] CPR, PD 65, para 13.1.
[29] CDA 1998, s 1C, as added by PRA 2002, s 64.

court may make an order only if the prosecutor asks it do so or if the court thinks it appropriate. This would seem to remove any role for the local authority, county council or other relevant authority in making applications or submissions unless they are the prosecuting authority, for instance, for breach of a noise abatement notice. The Home Office has stated that local agreement and protocols with the court can allow relevant authorities to ask for an order themselves. However, this would seem to be contrary to the statute, which refers to a prosecutor. Although the hearing as to whether to make a post-conviction order is a civil one, a relevant authority cannot in any way be described as a prosecutor in those circumstances. It would seem strange if an agreement between the court and the applicant could override a statute if the defendant (not party to the agreement) objected and referred to the statutory wording as regards *locus standi*.

Test

6.18   To make an order the court has to be satisfied that:

(1)   the offender has acted in an anti-social manner (ie has acted in a manner which caused or was likely to cause harassment, alarm or distress to one or more persons not of the same household as the offender);[30] *and*

(2)   an order is necessary to protect persons in any place in England and Wales from further anti-social acts by him.[31]

6.19   The first part of the test mirrors CDA 1998, s 1(1)(a), but the second part is far wider as there is no need to show that the order is necessary to protect 'relevant persons' rather than simply 'persons in England and Wales'.

6.20   The court may only make an order if it sentences the offender in respect of the relevant offence or conditionally discharges him or her. A relevant offence is one which is *committed* after the coming into force of PRA 2002, s 64 (ie 2 December 2002).[32] There is, however, no bar to the court considering incidents which pre-date the Act in consideration of the second part of the test (see **3.14–3.22**).

Practice and procedure

6.21   The decision as to whether an order should be made follows the sentencing hearing for the criminal offence. The Court of Appeal has made it clear in *R v Boness*[33] that a court should decide the appropriate sentence for the criminal matter before moving on to consider whether an ASBO should be made so as to not influence the court in determining the proper sentence for the crime. The court raised this point as some defendant's representatives had, during the plea in mitigation, been arguing that the court could avoid making a custodial sentence in otherwise inevitable cases by making an ASBO.

6.22   Following further amendments to the CDA 1998 introduced by the SOCPA 2005,[34] the criminal courts have the power to adjourn any application for a post-conviction order even after sentencing the offender.[35] There does not appear to be any power to remand. However, the court

---

[30]   CDA 1998, s 1C(2)(b).
[31]   CDA 1998, s 1C(2)(b).
[32]   SI 2002/2750, art 2(a)(vii).
[33]   [2005] EWCA Crim 2395, 169 JP 621, (2005) *The Times*, October 24, [2005] All ER (D) 153 (Oct) at para 30.
[34]   CDA 1998, s 1D(4A–4C) inserted by SOCPA 2005, s 139(1), 4(a), in force 1 July 2005, SI 2005/1521, art 3(1)(s).
[35]   CDA 1998, s 1D(4A).

does have the power to make an interim order pending such an adjourned hearing.[36] If the defendant does not attend the adjourned proceedings then the court may further adjourn the proceedings or may issue a warrant for his arrest,[37] but only if it is satisfied that the defendant has had adequate notice of the time and place of the adjourned proceedings.[38] The procedure to be followed in post conviction orders is now set out in the Criminal Procedural Rules 2005 (as amended), in particular r 50.

6.23 By virtue of r 50.2 a court must not make any post conviction order unless the defendant has had the opportunity to consider the order (and presumably terms) sought and to make representations at a hearing.[39] There is an exception for interim orders.[40] However the Rules unnecessarily repeat the legislation to state that an interim order is not effective unless the defendant is present or served personally within 7 days of making.[41]

6.24 In order for a prosecutor to seek a post conviction order they must serve a notice of intention to apply for such an order on the court officer and the defendant.[42] In fact the Rule refers to 'any person on whom the order would be likely to have a significant adverse effect' which opens argument to whether members of a family might be so affected. The notice must be in the prescribed form in the Practice Direction[43] and be served as soon as practicable and without waiting for the verdict.[44]

6.25 The notice of intention to seek an order must include:[45]

(a)   a summary of the relevant facts;

(b)   an identification of the evidence on which the prosecutor relies on in support;

(c)   written statements which had not been already served; and

(d)   specify the order sought.

To this we would add that a schedule of the alleged acts of anti-social behaviour must be included. Prior to the inception of the above Rule the Court of Appeal had been repeating the need for every court to make detailed findings of fact on each alleged act or behaviour. It seems strange that this was ignored in the drafting of the Rule. It is suggested that as the defendant is entitled to know the case against him and must state whether they agree or disagree to each of the allegations, a schedule setting them out is a pre-requisite for any application.

6.26 After the above has been done the defendant must serve written notice of any evidence on which he wishes to rely.[46] Again this must be done without waiting for any verdict and must include any written statement which had not already been served.[47]

6.27 It would seem that a defendant facing a post conviction order application is under more onerous duties of disclosure than one facing a free standing application. The defendant is

---

[36]   CDA 1998, s 1D(1)(c) and (d).
[37]   CDA 1998, s 1D(4B).
[38]   CDA 1998, s 1D(4C).
[39]   CPR 2005, r 50.2(1).
[40]   CPR 2005, r 50.2(2).
[41]   CPR 2005, r 50.2(3).
[42]   CPR 2005, r 50.3(2)(a) & (b) respectively.
[43]   CPR 2005, r 50.3(3) – see further Appendix 1G.
[44]   CPR 2005, r 50.3(2).
[45]   CPR 2005, r 50.3(3).
[46]   CPR 2005, r 50.3(4).
[47]   CPR 2005, r 50.3(4).

obliged to serve a statement in accordance with the Rules. Further the evidence has to be filed before the outcome of the criminal case. In practice it is most unlikely that any defendant or their legal representatives will focus energy on this element of the case which may require substantial investment of time to obtain evidence. This is particularly so as the work would be 'wasted' if the defendant was acquitted. The more likely practical situation will be that a defendant will file their supplemental evidence after conviction before the adjourned hearing to consider the post conviction order. A court may however be unsympathetic to such an approach given the stark requirements in the Rule.

6.28   It should be noted that the Rule expressly states that the above requirements do not apply to applications for interim ASBOs.[48] This is strange in that if the requirement is that a prosecutor must serve an intention to seek an order and file evidence 'as soon as practicable and without waiting for the verdict' and an interim order is only available after conviction (verdict) then how can the Rule exempt interim order applications? The only possibility is that the Rule drafter envisaged situations where the prosecutor had not got the evidence together before the defendant pleaded guilty. It would seem to us that a prosecutor would be well advised to serve a notice of intention as soon as possible even if all the evidence is not complete. The notice should expressly record that fact and identify, if possible, the additional evidence to be served and timescales for the same. This would prevent arguments of breach of the Rule by the defendant in the above situation.

6.29   Finally the Rules provide for a situation where the court indicates that it may make a post conviction order on its own initiative.[49] If this occurs then any party who wishes the court to consider any particular evidence must serve a written notice on the court officer and the other parties together with witness statements on which it is sought to rely. The Rules state that this notice and evidence should be served as soon as practicable and without waiting for the verdict.[50] Again this seems to be strange drafting as it is inconceivable that a tribunal would express on possible punishments whilst trying the case. To do so would give the impression of bias and would be avoided by most, if not all, judges and magistrates.

Hearsay evidence

6.30   If any of the evidence on which a party wishes to rely includes hearsay evidence they must comply with further requirements in the Rules and statutory regulations. A detailed consideration of those requirements is contained in chapter 4 at paras **4.43–4.71.**

6.31   A post-conviction ASBO application is based on the evidence which was heard in the criminal proceedings, but also on any additional evidence which is presented by the prosecution and defence. CDA 1998, s 1C(3A) was inserted by the ASB Act 2003 to make this point clear, as it appeared that, notwithstanding the Home Office guidance, many courts refused to consider any matters outside the offence before them. To further clarify this point, s 1C(3B) provides that it is immaterial whether the evidence which the prosecution wishes to adduce would have been admissible in the proceedings in which the defendant was convicted. Again this should have been an obvious matter not requiring statutory force, as the decision as to whether to impose an order is a civil hearing entirely distinct from the criminal proceedings.

6.32   It would seem sensible for relevant authorities to work closely with the police and CPS, as it may well be that valuable time could be saved if an application for an order could be made following the defendant's conviction in the criminal courts. It is submitted, however, that it will be very difficult to prove that an order is necessary unless the relevant authority is in a position

---

[48]   CPR 2005, r 50.3(5).
[49]   CPR 2005, r 50.4.
[50]   CPR 2005, r 50.4(2).

to provide the court with evidence to establish the second criteria. Whilst the changes to the primary legislation now make it plain that the courts must consider the evidence put before them, there continue to be problems with applying for orders in this way. Pilot schemes and protocols now in place in many areas allow a relevant authority to work with the CPS to present the appropriate evidence. If, however, the defendant denies the allegations in the further evidence he must be permitted to test it and have a contested hearing. Therefore a full hearing is required, making it no different from that which would have occurred if a free-standing application had been made. However, there is likely to be reluctance on the part of busy criminal courts to embark on lengthy consideration of contested evidence in relation to other incidents of anti-social behaviour which have not been the subject of the criminal proceedings.

6.33 The applicant authority may be disadvantaged in waiting and supporting this application in that it will not be able to give direct instructions to the prosecutor, who is unlikely to be an expert in the field of ASBOs or civil procedure and evidence. The Government has promoted a scheme to have designated anti-social behaviour prosecutors. The scheme was rather ineffectual in its commencement with poor training and numbers being the initial problems, however, these difficulties seem to have been lessened. There are now some regions where there are good relations between local authorities and prosecutors and many applications are done by them. There are other areas where the experience has not been as good and local authorities continue to take on applications themselves for the greater part. Whilst it is to be hoped that the new procedures will lead to smoother processes and to the making of post-conviction ASBOs, where appropriate, there seem to be more reasons why the prudent relevant authority would be better advised to pursue the application itself in the civil courts.

6.34 In any event, it may not be wise for a relevant authority to simply wait for a criminal conviction in order to request an order. This could prove to be a significant problem if the person was not convicted (or was convicted of a more minor offence), or the court refused to make an order, as the evidence of this incident (and/or others) was more than 6 months old. The suggested best practice is for a relevant authority to proceed to make its own free-standing application but to seize the opportunity of shortening the process if the defendant is convicted prior to the application being made in the normal way. The prospects of obtaining an order will be far greater if the criminal conviction related to significant anti-social behaviour which could satisfy the criteria at s 1(1)(a). However, another option is to seek the order at the time of charging. This has the advantage of reducing the costs but has the risks discussed above. Further, if no application has been made, the defendant could properly argue that there is no need for an order if there have been no incidents since the criminal offence took place. This argument would not be open to him or her if an application had already been made.[51]

6.35 Any order which is made will come into force on the day on which it is made. However, the court may state that some (and presumably all) of the requirements of the order will be suspended until the defendant is released from custody.[52]

Variation and discharge

6.36 An order made under CDA 1998, s 1D must be made for a minimum of 2 years and as originally legislated in PRA 2002 gave no provisions for variation by a relevant authority. This meant that a post-conviction order could be made with limited terms and then there was no mechanism for a local authority to vary those terms unless there were other relevant criminal offences. This meant that an additional stand-alone application had to be made with the other post-conviction order running in the background. Clearly this was highly unsatisfactory and should have been foreseen by the draftsman. This rather poor drafting has therefore required yet

---

[51] See *S v Poole Borough Council* [2002] EWHC 244 (Admin), (unreported) February 2002.
[52] CDA 1998, s 1D(5).

another substantive amendment to the CDA 1998. The SOCPA 2005, s 140(1) and (4) repeals s 1C(6)–(8) and adds yet another section, namely s 1CA which came into force on 1 July 2005.[53]

6.37   Section 1CA provides that a defendant can apply to the court which made the order for variation or discharge.[54] However a written notice of the application has to be sent by him or her to the DPP.[55] No order made under s 1C can be discharged before the expiry of 2 years from the date it was made unless the DPP consents.[56]

6.38   Both the DPP[57] and the relevant authority[58] may apply to the court which made the order for either variation or discharge, however, a relevant authority can only apply if either it considers that 'the protection of relevant persons from anti-social acts by the person subject to the order would be more appropriately effected by a variation of the order'[59] or it is no longer necessary to protect relevant persons.[60] Any application for variation or discharge by the DPP or a relevant authority has also to be sent in writing to the defendant.[61] Any application for discharge by the relevant authority or DPP within 2 years can only be granted if the defendant agrees![62] It is impossible to imagine circumstances in which the defendant would not agree and this seems to be a pointless requirement. Any application to vary an order of the magistrates' court should be made in accordance with the magistrates' court (Anti-Social Behaviour Orders) Rules 2002.[63] Applications are required to be in writing addressed to the magistrates' court which made the order and must specify the reason why the application should be granted. If the court considers that there are grounds on which it might conclude that the order should be varied or discharged then a summons is issued giving the other party no less than 14-days' notice of the hearing date[64] and enclosing the application notice. Service can be personal or to his last known address by post and is deemed to have been received unless proved otherwise.[65]

PRACTICE AND PROCEDURE

6.39   The Magistrates' Court (Anti-social Behaviour Orders) Rules 2002[66] contain specific requirements for the procedure to be adopted in relation to orders made. Applications are required to be in writing addressed to the magistrates' court which made the order and must specify the reason why the application should be granted. If the court considers that there are grounds on which it might conclude that the order should be varied or discharged then a summons is issued giving the other party no less than 14 days notice of the hearing date[67] and enclosing the application notice. Service can be personal or to his last known address by post and is deemed to have been received unless proved otherwise.[68]

6.40   The Criminal Procedure Rules 2005 as amended contain further provisions as to the procedural and evidential requirements for an application to revoke or vary a post conviction

---

53   SI 2005/1521, art 3(1)(s).
54   CDA 1998, s 1CA(1).
55   CDA 1998, s 1CA(2).
56   CDA 1998, s 1CA(7)(a).
57   CDA 1998, s 1CA(3).
58   CDA 1998, s 1CA(4).
59   CDA 1998, s 1CA(4)(a).
60   CDA 1998, s 1CA(1)(4)(b).
61   CDA 1998, s 1CA(1)(5).
62   CDA 1998, s 1CA(7)(b).
63   Magistrates' Court (Anti-Social Behaviour Orders) Rules 2002, r 6, see Appendix 1(E).
64   Magistrates' Court (Anti-Social Behaviour Orders) Rules 2002, r 6(4).
65   Magistrates' Court (Anti-Social Behaviour Orders) Rules 2002, r 7.
66   Section 6, see Appendix 1E.
67   Magistrates' Court (Anti-social Behaviour Orders) Rules 2002 (SI 2002/2784), s 6(4).
68   Magistrates' Court (Anti-social Behaviour Orders) Rules 2002 (SI 2002/2784), s 7.

order. It is not clear why they needed to be made given the detailed rules above. In any event the 2005 Rules state that the application is by complaint[69] and the applicant must apply in writing as soon as practicable after becoming aware of the grounds for the application and explain why the order should be varied or revoked.[70] The application must be served on the other parties (and the DPP in appropriate circumstances). If any party wishes the court to consider evidence it must serve a written notice on the court officer and other parties identifying the evidence and attaching written statements.[71]

6.41 The court has the power to determine the application without a hearing[72] but cannot dismiss the application without an oral hearing[73] nor allow it without giving parties at least 14 days to make representations including whether there should be a hearing.[74] If there is to be a hearing the court office must give notice by summons.[75] The reality is that unless the 'respondent' to an application does not wish a hearing or it is an overwhelming unarguable case for variation (eg cannot attend hospital for treatment) the court will have to order an oral hearing.

6.42 Breach of a post-conviction order carries the same punishment on breach as the breach of an ASBO, ie up to 5 years' imprisonment on conviction on indictment.[76]

Civil or criminal proceedings?

6.43 The application for an ASBO in these circumstances comes after conviction of a criminal offence and with the court obviously sitting in its criminal jurisdiction. The issue is therefore what is the nature of the proceedings in which an order is applied for? *Clingham* had of course determined that stand-alone ASBO proceedings in the magistrates' courts were civil in nature, however, the decision pre-dated the introduction of post-conviction orders. Whilst it has been assumed that post-conviction orders would similarly be civil proceedings the point was not tested until *R (on the application of W) v Acton Youth Court.*[77] W applied for judicial review of the making of an ASBO against him after a conviction for taking a vehicle without consent and driving without insurance or licence. After sentence the CPS invited the magistrates to make an ASBO and relied on a statement from a police officer. The statement had been produced that morning to the defendant's solicitor. The statement set out 32 incidents based mostly on hearsay from local residents who were unwilling to give evidence and some from other police officers. Five of the incidents were, however, directly witnessed by the officer giving evidence. Two of those incidents had resulted in convictions in any event, the last for harassment when a restraining order had been made for 5 years together with a 2-month curfew order, tagging order and supervision order for 12 months.

6.44 The defendant's representative asked for and was given a short adjournment and then argued that the statement should not be admitted and in any event the order was unnecessary and excessive given the sentence for the last incident. The magistrates retired and made an order without giving reasons. At the judicial review hearing the defendant argued that the proceedings were criminal not civil and that hearsay evidence was therefore inadmissible.

---

[69]   CPR 2005, r 50.5(6)(a).
[70]   CPR 2005, r 50.5(2).
[71]   CPR 2005, r 50.5(3).
[72]   CPR 2005, r 50.5(4).
[73]   CPR 2005, r 50.5(5)(a).
[74]   CPR 2005, r 50.5(5)(b).
[75]   CPR 2005, r 50.5(6)(b).
[76]   CDA 1998, s 1C(9) applying CDA 1998 s 1(10).
[77]   [2005] All ER (D) 284.

6.45 Mr Justice Pitchers sitting with Lord Justice Sedley in the administrative court concluded that the reasoning in *Clingham* was not restricted to stand-alone applications, he cited with approval the following passage from Lord Steyn's judgment:

'18. There is no doubt that Parliament intended to adopt the model of a civil remedy of an injunction, backed up by criminal penalties, when it enacted section 1 of the Crime and Disorder Act 1998. The view was taken that the proceedings for an anti-social behaviour order would be civil and would not attract the rigour of the inflexible and sometimes absurdly technical hearsay rule which applies in criminal cases.'[78]

6.46 Mr Justice Pitchers noted that when Lord Steyn considered similar types of orders to ASBOs such as disqualification of company directors, he had not distinguished between those orders which could only be imposed following a conviction and those triggered by one. Further, he noted that the courts had concluded that those similar types of orders were civil in nature, eg football banning orders, in *Gough v Chief Constable of the Derbyshire Constabulary*[79] and sex offenders orders in *B v Chief Constable of Avon and Somerset Constabulary*.[80] Taking all those matters into account Mr Justice Pitchers concluded that post-conviction order applications were clearly civil proceedings. The consequence of this was that the hearsay evidence in the police officer's statement was admissible but the justices had to still consider the weight to be attached to it.

6.47 In relation to lack of reasons the court found that whilst there was no longer a requirement to give written reasons[81] it was still necessary for the justices to give reasons in some form. These could be given orally at the time of making the order but:

'They should be sufficient to enable the person who is the subject of the order to understand why it has been made and to indicate to all that the justices have applied their minds to the correct issues.'

The court however found that there was nothing before then to suggest that the magistrates had applied the wrong standard of proof.

Case-law – R (C) v Sunderland Youth Court

6.48 There are a number of important cases to be considered in relation to post-conviction ASBOs. In *R (on the application of C (by his mother and litigation friend, C)) v Sunderland Youth Court*[82] the defendant appeared before the youth court after being convicted of number of offences and having a very poor criminal record. Having given notice of his intention to do so, the CPS prosecutor expressly reminded the sentencing court of its power to impose an ASBO. The Bench declined to do so, imposing community penalties and a parenting order. The defendant was subsequently convicted of one charge, and pleaded guilty to another. Both the offences pre-dated the previous sentencing date. After the above convictions, the CPS invited the court again to consider making a post-conviction order. There was a further report from the Sunderland Youth Offending Service, which indicated that the defendant was complying fully with his Intensive Supervision and Surveillance Programme (ISSP) (positive comments were made) and a recommendation for a reparation order was made.

6.49 The magistrates returned from their deliberations and stated that they were making an order, and the chairman indicated that his wing member had been able to give more detail about

---

[78] [2005] All ER (D) 284, para 17.
[79] [2002] QB 459.
[80] [2001] 1 WLR 340.
[81] Magistrates' Courts (Miscellaneous Amendment) Rules 2003, SI 2003/1236 repealing r 4(4) of the Magistrates' Courts (Anti-Social Behaviour Orders) Rules 2002, SI 2002/2784.
[82] [2003] EWHC 2385 (Admin), (2004) Crim LR 75.

one of the offences than the prosecutor had (it is assumed that the wing member was, coincidentally, on the Bench that heard the trial). The exact nature of this detail was never specified. The order that was made was vague and contained no geographical restrictions, and was served on the defendant's parents, in a format that was consistent with a s 1 ASBO and not a post-conviction order.

6.50   Mr Justice Sullivan held that the court had failed to act fairly in its procedure, both in relation to its reasons and in relation to the terms of the order purportedly made:

> 'Whatever may be the extent of the general duty upon magistrates to give reasons for their decisions, in the particular circumstances of this case, fairness to the claimant required the court to give him an explanation, however brief, as to why it was now considered appropriate to make an order under section 1C. Consistency in the exercise of discretionary powers is an important aspect of fairness. If, having had the matter fully explained to them on 8 May, the magistrates decided not to make a section 1C order, then absent any further evidence justifying the making of such an order, it would not be prima facie reasonable to make one on 12 June. The only change of circumstances since 8 May was the two matters for which the claimant was being sentenced on 12 June.' (at [27])

6.51   Further, the absence of a formal application meant that a court had to have greater regard to fairness to the defendant in its procedure:

> '… if no application is made to the magistrates for an order, there is a danger that the defendant may suffer unfairness because he will not be in a position to know the case that he has to meet under section 1C. The nature of the case may be obvious from the surrounding context, eg where the defendant has just been convicted, and is about to be sentenced, for a string of anti-social offences. But that was not the case here, particularly having regard to the decision on 8 May. Elementary fairness requires a court, if it proposes to make an order of its own motion, to indicate the basis on which it provisionally considers an order may be appropriate, and the material on which it proposes to rely so that the person potentially liable can make meaningful submissions as to why the order should not be made at all or should not be made in the form provisionally proposed by the court. That did not happen in the present case.' (at [31])

6.52   The judge went on to criticise the seeming reliance on 'detail' provided by the wing member which was never explained and the lack of any record of the details of the order made by the court. He observed that it was an unfortunate lacuna in the statutory scheme that there was no requirement for service of an order made under s 1C. Further, the absence of any geographical restriction to the prohibitions without any reasons was also criticised. Lord Justice Brooke re-emphasised the need for a fair procedure, but both he and all counsel (including Treasury Counsel for the Home Office) in the case seemed to be surprisingly unaware of the standard form for post-conviction orders which appeared at Sch 4 to the 2002 Rules.[83]

Comment

6.53   The case of *C* is a good example of the potential problems which can arise in post-conviction orders unless care is taken. The adherence to the requirements in the Criminal Procedure Rules as to notice and evidence will assist. However, it is imperative that the prosecutor and court clerk are alive to the potential problems which can arise. It is important to ensure that the defendant is given the opportunity to respond to all the matters which the prosecutor wishes to rely upon and, if an order is made, the court record should be checked by both legal representatives before the hearing is concluded. The terms should also be read out to the defendant and the consequences of breach explained. Whilst not strictly necessary, it is suggested that it would be prudent for a court and prosecutor to serve on a defendant a formal

---

[83]   Now repealed by Magistrates' Courts (Miscellaneous Amendments) Rules 2003, SI 2003/1236, rr 88, 89(2), with effect from 20 June 2003.

note of the order before he leaves the court. There can be no good reason why a post-conviction order cannot be served on the defendant. The requirement to use the form which previously appeared at Sch 4 to the 2002 Rules has been removed; however, the form itself with suitable amendments is still a useful precedent.[84]

R v P

6.54   The second case to be considered is that of *R v P*.[85] The facts bear careful consideration in order to place the judgment in context. On first blush, it would appear to present serious difficulty to most post-conviction order applications and even, potentially, to free-standing applications.

6.55   In *P*, the defendant was 15 when he committed 12 offences over a 6-day period. The offences were mostly theft and robbery of mobile phones from people in public places. The defendant acted alone and, whilst serious threats were made, no actual violence was used. The judge at the crown court imposed a 4-year custodial sentence and also a 2-year post-conviction order, suspended until his release. The defendant appealed to the Court of Appeal against both matters.

6.56   The Court of Appeal first of all reduced the sentence to one of 3 years, to take into account his guilty pleas and troubled youth. Turning to the imposition of the post-conviction order, Mr Justice Henriques, giving the unanimous decision of the court, held that the judge was empowered to make the order he did and to suspend it until his release from custody. He cited with approval the comments of Mr Justice Sullivan as to fairness of procedure in the case of *R (C) v Sunderland Youth Court*, as discussed above. He then went on to consider that:

> '... the principal question for our consideration is whether in the particular circumstances of this case, assuming proper procedure, the judge was satisfied in making such an order having regard in particular to the fact that aged 16 this appellant would remain in custody until he was 18. Thereafter, he would remain on licence for a further year if he was convicted of any imprisonable offence committed within 2 years of his release from custody or 18 months on the reduced sentence which we are minded to substitute.'

Mr Justice Henriques then pointed out that this defendant was not a hopeless case who would not succeed in amending his behaviour. He noted the contents of the pre-sentence report and a psychiatric report which recommended psychological intervention for chronic depression and detailed the defendant's difficult childhood, which included not seeing his mother since he was 5 and being brought up by a father with acute psychiatric problems. He accepted that imposing geographical restraints may well properly supplement licence conditions and that there was public confidence in ASBOs; however, each case depended on its particular facts. On the facts of this case, it was not possible to say that an order would be necessary in the future, as custody may well prove effective and the deterrence of a return to custody for breach of licence was sufficient.

6.57   In a later passage, which is probably *obiter dicta*, Mr Justice Henriques noted that it was likely that the conduct primarily envisaged as triggering applications for orders consisted of less grave offences than street robbery. However, he expressly drew back from saying that orders would be necessarily inappropriate in cases with characteristics such as these. However, the judge observed that, where custodial sentences in excess of a few months were passed and offenders were liable to be released on licence, the circumstances in which necessity could be

---

[84]   See Appendix 2.5.
[85]   [2004] EWCA Crim 287, (2004) *The Times*, February 19, alternatively known as *R v Parkin*.

shown were likely to be limited, although he did endorse the suggestion that there still would be cases were geographical restraints may properly supplement the licence conditions.

Discussion

6.58   The case of *R v P* and subsequently the judgment in *R v Boness* has resulted in a number of hearings where it was argued that, in free-standing applications for ASBOs, as the defendant had been sentenced to a term of custody of more than a few months, an order was not necessary. Initially this argument was mostly unsuccessful and, in the majority of cases, it is submitted, correctly so. P committed 12 offences in 6 days, had no previous convictions for robbery (he had one for assault and five for theft) and had never served a period in custody. He had had a tragic childhood and chronic depression for which there was proposed treatment, with prospects of success. If the offences had not been so serious that it was impossible to do other than impose a custodial penalty, it is likely that he would have been given a supervision order, with a condition of attendance for treatment. This is to be contrasted with the vast majority of applications for ASBOs. Often, there will have been a long period of anti-social behaviour, with a variety of types of offending. Whilst there may be a more serious matter which has been prosecuted in the criminal courts, often, the majority of incidents are either borderline or sub-criminal. It is submitted that this is not the type of case which the Court of Appeal envisaged when the comments about custody and necessity were made. As the court observed, each case must depend on its own particular facts and a properly brought, free-standing application is not likely to depend solely on a number of serious offences over a 6-day period. Had there been proper evidence before the court in *P* of other anti-social behaviour, aside from the robberies, carried out over a longer period, it is submitted that the Court of Appeal may well have considered the geographical constraints suitable, notwithstanding other matters. If the judge's dicta were to have general application beyond post-conviction orders, this could easily result in some unjust outcomes. For instance, an application could be made, alleging 2 years of anti-social behaviour over a wide area but the trial delayed for 5 months due to unavailability of witnesses, length of trial or pending criminal trials. If the defendant, in the meantime, was charged with social security fraud, pleaded guilty and was sentenced to 6 months' custody, he could avoid an ASBO being made and, by the time he was released, all the previous incidents would be lost to the time bar if a further application was made because the behaviour had started again. This says nothing of the loss in public confidence for all those witnesses who would then have no protection from any order and the expense incurred in bringing the proceedings in the first place. Therefore, it is only in cases where the evidence is wholly or almost entirely limited to serious criminal offences without any history of a pattern of anti-social behaviour that the court will normally consider that necessity will be hard to establish. There are however a growing number of ASBOs which have been overturned on appeal by the Court of Appeal Criminal Division all citing the principles in *R v P* and *Boness*. The approach seems to be that if the application is based on the actual offence before the court and that alone then if a sentence of imprisonment is imposed then the period of licence is sufficient deterrent to obviate the need for an ASBO.[86] This is not a particularly happy position given the well known lack of any focused terms of licence however it is clearly the Court of Appeal's approach post-*Boness*. Any applicant authority has to be aware of this and provide evidence of a pattern of ASB not limited to the offence and evidence of a need to protect the public beyond that which the licence provisions and term may do. This, of course, assumes also that the defendant has not previously had terms of imprisonment so that he can still argue that the first custodial sentence will, when linked with the threat of recall under licence conditions, have a deterrent effect. Where the defendant has been to prison and continued to offend, it is suggested that this would be a difficult argument for the defence to advance.

---

[86]   Cf *R v JR, DW, Connor* [2006] EWCA Crim 3287; *R v Burrows* [2006] EWCA Crim 2241.

Case-law post R v P

6.59 *R v P* has been considered in a number of cases in the context of post-conviction applications for ASBOs.

R v Scott Parkinson[87]

6.60 The defendant was sentenced to 3 years' imprisonment for an offence of robbery of a person at night and given a 2-year ASBO. The defendant appealed against the making of the ASBO to the Court of Appeal. The Court of Appeal noted that the defendant, aged 19, had unlike P a very considerable previous criminal record. He had spent time in custody for short periods and also had community penalties imposed over the course of several years. Further, the sentencing judge had details of those previous convictions setting out the location and also evidence from another officer as to the problems which the defendant had caused in the community over a period of years which had resulted in eviction 6 months before the offence. The Court of Appeal concluded that the judge had been right to impose the order but referred to it as 'one of those exceptional cases' where an order was necessary even though there was a 3-year term of imprisonment:

> 'It is to be hoped that his time in custody will improve his behaviour. It is to be hoped that he is not a lost cause. In addition to protecting the public it is perhaps significant that this order may in fact protect him from succumbing to the temptation of resorting to his old ways.'[88]

R v Werner[89]

6.61 The defendant had been released from prison for a few days when she broke into several hotel rooms stealing credit cards and property. She also made use of the credit cards. She was sentenced to 18 months' imprisonment with a further 6 months of recalled licence and made subject to a post-conviction order for 7 years from her release which prevented her from entering any guesthouse, hotel, etc in the Greater London area. It was from this order that the defendant appealed.

6.62 The defendant was 33 years of age and begun offending in 2001 and had received other punishments including a suspended sentence taking into account previous pre-sentence reports which identified a possible psychiatric condition. These were also before the sentencing court reports from a psychiatrist indicating a diagnosis of schizophrenia which was being treated and if treated would diminish or completely remove her risk of re-offending.

6.63 The Court of Appeal noted that the offences of burglary (the occupants being absent) did not cause harassment or alarm in the sense used in s 1(1) of the CDA 1998 but they did cause distress. The court considered that whilst the possibility of rehabilitation through custody that was indicated in *R v Parkin* was not perhaps relevant here with an adult defendant, the presence of the psychiatric condition meant that there was reason to believe that the order was not necessary. The court declined to consider the other more fundamental points of whether burglary, dishonesty, etc were appropriate offences for ASBO applications.

---

[87] [2004] EWCA Crim 2757.
[88] Per Mr Justice Royce at para 8 [2004] EWCA Crim 2757.
[89] [2004] EWCA Crim 2931.

R v Paul Rush[90]

6.64 The appellant appealed against a sentence of 30 months' imprisonment and a 10-year ASBO following a plea of guilty to burglary. R, who had been ejected from his parents' home 3 years previously, had returned and caused a disturbance. He asked for cigarettes and when his father refused he pushed into the house and took some from a cupboard. R had a history of previous offending which was almost entirely targeted at his parents. The ASBO was imposed to protect R's parents from his offending. R argued that the sentence was manifestly excessive.

6.65 Whilst a prison sentence was inevitable, the burglary was at the lowest end of the scale and, taking into account the plea of guilty, the sentence was too long for the particular offence. Whatever the aggravating surrounding circumstances and background the sentence was too long for the activity, particularly when passed with the ASBO. The sentence was reduced to 12 months' imprisonment. The test for the use of the power to impose an ASBO was one of necessity to protect the public. Making an ASBO should not be a normal part of the sentencing process especially if the crime did not involve harassment or intimidation. Imposing an ASBO was a course to be taken in particular circumstances. The instant case had involved a persistent course of conduct of harassment of R's parents but whilst R's parents were entitled to the protection of the ASBO the duration was excessive and was reduced to 5 years.

R v Vittles[91]

6.66 The appellant was sentenced to a total of 3 years 10 months' imprisonment for numerous thefts from motorcars belonging to American servicemen. The defendant had a long history of criminal offending mostly for offences of dishonesty. An ASBO was imposed for an indefinite period banning the defendant from entering the entire district council area. The Court of Appeal considered that the transient, vulnerable nature of the American population which had been specifically targeted by the defendant meant that it was appropriate to make an ASBO. They were not convinced that there was a lesser exclusion area that could practically be imposed and affirmed the order but only for a 5-year period.

R v Jamie Paul McGrath[92]

6.67 The appellant appealed against the imposition of an ASBO for a 2-year period which formed part of his sentence following his conviction for theft. M had broken into a car in a car park and had stolen compact discs. He had a long history of offending. At the time of sentencing, M was found by the sentencing judge to have turned over a new leaf. In sentencing, the judge took into account M's conduct prior to the commencement of CDA 1998, s 1C.

6.68 M submitted that:

(1) the judge had not been entitled to take into account M's behaviour prior to the commencement of the CDA 1998;

(2) the extent to which ASBOs could be applied to offences of dishonesty was questionable; and

(3) an ASBO was not necessary given that M had reformed his behaviour.

---

90   [2005] EWCA Crim 1316, 12 May 2005.
91   [2005] 1 Cr App R (S) 8.
92   [2005] EWCA Crim 353S, 10 February 2005.

6.69 The court held that the court could take into account matters pre-CDA 1998 once a qualifying offence had been established (and this was accepted as being one as it caused people distress). There was nothing wrong in making an ASBO post conviction following vehicle crime. ASBOs should be approached with a 'proper degree of caution and circumspection. They are not cure-alls. They are not lightly to be imposed.'

R v Michael Hinton[93]

6.70 The defendant had committed three offences of theft, one of handling, two of obtaining property by deception and being in breach of a drug treatment and testing order for similar offences. The court sentenced him to three and a half years imprisonment and made an ASBO for three years post release prohibiting him from using trains from a number of mainline stations. He appealed arguing that in accordance with *Boness* there was nothing exceptional about the circumstances of this defendant's offending and therefore an ASBO should not have been made.

6.71 The Court of Appeal, which included Lord Justice Hooper who gave the judgment in *Boness* noted that the defendant's offences all followed a very similar pattern in that he would steal from passengers on the trains whilst at Paddington or Kings Cross stations. He had a large number of previous convictions mostly for theft and many committed in the same way. He had previously had a 30 month sentence of imprisonment and had a Drug Treatment and Testing Order. They noted that the defendant had previously received very substantial terms of imprisonment for identical offences, and having been released from custody he recommenced his offending. In those circumstances an ASBO particularly one which did not affect his right to travel on public transport, but merely provided precautionary protection for the public was both desirable and necessary. They amended the term so that he could not enter or remain on a train at various mainline stations without a valid ticket for travel.

6.72 It will be noted that the principle that an order could be made was not limited in this case however the term was, with respect to the Court of Appeal, a very weak one. All the defendant had to do to avoid breach of the ASBO was to buy the cheapest single fare for the train he had targeted. It would seem to us that the original term was far more useful as a prohibition.

GUIDELINES FOR FAIRNESS IN POST-CONVICTION ORDER APPLICATIONS

6.73 It is also important to note that the court in *R v P* set out clear general principles of fairness and procedure which the court must follow, particularly when considering whether to make post-conviction orders. The Court of Appeal stated that these principles were:[94]

(a) the test for making an order is one of necessity, to protect the public from further anti-social acts by the offender;

(b) the terms of the order must be precise and capable of being understood by the offender;

(c) the findings of fact giving rise to the making of the order must be recorded;

(d) the order must be explained to the offender; and

---

[93] [2006] EWCA Crim 1115.
[94] [2004] EWCA Crim 287, (2004) *The Times*, February 19, at [34].

(e)   the exact terms of the order must be pronounced in open court and the written order must accurately reflect the order as pronounced.

Mr Justice Henriques also made it clear that the Court of Appeal disapproved strongly of submissions or comments being made in the defendant's absence and that it was plainly the duty of the court making any order to identify the matters relied on by the party seeking the order, to give the defendant an opportunity to dispute the allegation, and to record the findings of fact in the order.[95]

6.74 It therefore follows that the defendant's representatives must be alive to any breaches of the above principles in the procedure adopted by the court. Any breach should be highlighted at the time to ensure that no adverse comment is made of the representative if an appeal is required. Similarly it is incumbent on the prosecution to ensure that all the above matters are adhered to by the court and to ensure that the presentation of evidence and drafting of any order complies with those principles. It should be remembered that there is no power in the magistrates' court which allows drafting slips to be corrected in civil hearings save by further formal applications to amend.

---

[95]   [2004] EWCA Crim 287, (2004) *The Times*, February 19, at [32].

CHAPTER 7

FIRST COURT APPEARANCES

MAGISTRATES' COURTS

7.1   The application, having been made by complaint, is heard by the magistrates in their civil capacity, as determined by the Magistrates' Courts Act 1980 (MCA 1980). The defendant is obliged to attend and the court has the power to proceed in his or her absence,[1] or may compel attendance at an adjourned hearing by issuing a warrant for his or her arrest.[2] If either course is to be adopted, the court may not do so unless it is proved, on oath or otherwise, that the defendant has been served within a reasonable time before the hearing date or has appeared in the matter before.[3] Whilst the current Home Office Guidance[4] encourages the court to continue and hear matters in the defendant's absence and suggests that adjournments should be avoided unless absolutely necessary, in practice, it has not been common for courts to proceed to make an order on the first non-attendance of the defendant. The prospects of persuading the court to do so are enhanced if there has been personal service and a clear information letter to the defendant as to the likely consequence of his or her non-attendance. Similarly, the courts are reluctant to refuse a defendant an adjournment if he or she attends on the first occasion, requesting legal representation, even if he or she has failed to make real efforts to do so prior to the hearing.

7.2   As a consequence of the difficulties related above, especially with having lay witnesses attend court unnecessarily, it is now accepted that the best practice is to request the court to list the application as soon as possible after service for a preliminary hearing, to last for no more than 2 hours. At this hearing, no lay witnesses should be asked to attend but proof of service should be available to provide to the court, and at least one professional witness to relevant incidents should be present. This approach is made even more sensible in the light of the availability of interim ASBOs (see chapter 8). It would seem appropriate, therefore, to issue an application for an interim order to be heard at the same time, unless the interim order is to be sought without notice to the defendant.

7.3   If the defendant does not attend the initial hearing, the court can be asked to hear the application in the defendant's absence. Live evidence can be called and the remainder submitted as hearsay evidence (notices should be served with summons). Subject to satisfying the relevant test (see **8.2** et seq), an interim order will be granted. However, with regard to the final order, the defendant may well be given a further chance to attend, or a warrant for his or her arrest is made and the matter can be adjourned to a fixed date. If the defendant does attend, it can then be ascertained whether he or she objects to the making of the interim and/or final order. It may well be that if the defendant has legal representation an order can be agreed at that stage. This saves the lay witnesses attending and saves the substantial costs of a trial. If the defendant does oppose the making of the order, the application for the interim order can proceed and the case can be listed for trial of the main issue with appropriate directions.

---

[1]   MCA 1980, s 55(1).
[2]   MCA 1980, s 55(2).
[3]   MCA 1980, s 55(3).
[4]   See current Home Office Guidance, reproduced in Appendix 3.

Directions on adjournments

7.4   If there is to be an adjournment, it is important to ensure that the court makes full and clear directions. Whilst the CPR 1998 do not strictly apply to magistrates' courts, the court has the power to control the procedure of the hearings before it, and it is widely accepted, in practice, that the substance and spirit of the CPR 1998 should apply to ASBO applications. A number of local authorities and magistrates' courts have entered into discussions about the appropriate procedure to be followed in applications for ASBOs and have prepared agreed service level agreements.

7.5   The most important directions to be sought are:

- requirement for defence to serve a defence statement;

- time period for the service of further evidence by the applicant;

- time-limit for the service of evidence from the defendant;

- all statements of witnesses to stand as their evidence-in-chief;

- reporting restrictions relating to any juveniles until the conclusion of the proceedings; and

- special measures for witnesses provisions. (See **9.18** et seq for procedure.)

Written statements of witnesses should be regarded as their primary evidence for the application, which is in accordance with the CPR 1998 and also a matter of time management. The amount of information/evidence in many statements is large and it would significantly extend the length of a hearing if professional witnesses such as housing officers had to go through each document. In any event, the statements will have already been seen and read by the magistrates prior to the hearing. It must also be noted that it would be almost impossible for witnesses to recall hearsay evidence which was taken from a file or from complaints from residents. Given the clear parliamentary intention to be able to rely on such evidence, it would seem impossible to argue that the criminal rules should apply. It would be strange if witnesses were forced to recall the whole of their evidence in one forum and not another, especially now that proceedings can be brought in the county court.

7.6   The requirement that defendants must serve witness evidence on which they rely is a matter on which there should be more debate. Whilst it is ultimately an issue for the court to determine, it would again seem odd if the county court should order disclosure of statements in proceedings for an ASBO before it but the magistrates do not. It is unlikely, however, that a court would prevent a defendant from giving evidence at a subsequent hearing if he or she has failed to comply with the direction. It may, however, take a different view if the defendant seeks to call evidence from a number of witnesses. Whilst the applicant is allowed to call evidence to rebut the evidence called by the defendant,[5] it may be that permission to call the evidence would be refused or an adjournment granted. Defendants' representatives should challenge any such finding strongly, as Art 6 of the ECHR may weigh heavily in such an argument. The availability of interim orders also means that there would be little prejudice, save that of costs and potentially witness unavailability (or reluctance) in an adjournment.

7.7   If there is to be a full hearing then this is the appropriate time to deal with special measures for witnesses. Doing so ensures that the court has a record of the need to facilitate the same at the next hearing and also so that any objections by the defendant can be addressed well

---

[5]   Magistrates' Courts Rules 1981, SI 1981/552, r 14(3).

before such a hearing. Given the consequences for the witnesses or need for adjournment it is very important that the applicant ensures that the court has recorded the orders made in relation to the special measures and that a letter is sent to the court reiterating the need for any special facilities or equipment at least 10 days before the trial date. The procedure and time limits for applications for special measures are set out and discussed in **9.18–9.20**.

Reporting restrictions

7.8   The issue of whether any reporting restrictions should apply after the making of an ASBO is very much open to argument and is considered fully at **9.45** et seq. Until the final hearing it would seem to us to be impossible to argue against making an order preventing publicity of an application against a minor pursuant to s 39 of the Children and Young Persons Act 1933. It would seem to be contrary to principle and good sense if the child's details were able to be published in a newspaper, pending the hearing of an application where the council may fail to obtain an order. If, however, an interim order is made pending the final hearing, the issue is open to debate. There is an argument that, for the interim order to be effective, the terms need to be disseminated to the community at large. This point was considered by the High Court[6] where Mr Justice Harrison held that it should *not* be the standard practice to make a s 39 order. Each case was to be considered on its own particular facts and that involved a balancing exercise between the public interest in disclosure and the welfare of the person against whom the application was made. The fact that the order was an interim one was a factor to be put into the balance. The fact that the allegations were unproven, and the defendant had not had the opportunity to put his case were weighty matters, but the nature of the allegations did reinforce the public interest in disclosure. It is submitted that it is likely, however, that in most cases the balance of public interest as against the interests of the child weighs against publicity by way of media coverage or leaflet distribution at the interim stage. The Home Office Guidance on publicity[7] which followed *Stanley* (see further **9.48**) makes it clear that it would only be in exceptional cases where publicity would follow an interim order. There is, of course, no reason why only the witnesses concerned cannot be personally told of the interim order (and its terms) which has been obtained partly for their benefit.

---

[6]   *Keating v Knowsley Metropolitan Borough Council* (unreported) 22 July 2004, Lawtel AC90600602.
[7]   'Working Together Guidance on Publicising Anti-Social Behaviour Orders' published in October 2005. To view this Guidance see Appendix 6.

CHAPTER 8

INTERIM ORDERS

8.1   Introduced by the PRA 2002,[1] interim orders are available in all applications for ASBOs save for post-conviction orders, interim orders have become a much used and valuable tool for applicants and, indeed, are applied for more often than not. Their use has also become more common where a local authority seeks ASBOs against multiple defendants from one area. These applications have always involved obtaining interim ASBOs, some without notice.

8.2   Interim orders may be made where the court considers it to be 'just' to make an order pending the determination of the main ASBO application.[2] An application for an interim order may be made in the form given by Sch 5 to the 2002 Rules.[3] The court must be satisfied that the requirements of consultation and necessity have been satisfied before making such an order and, once made, breach of an interim order carries the same penalties as breach of a full order. The right to apply, vary, discharge and appeal also applies in exactly the same way as on the making of a full order.[4] There is no definition given in the statute or Home Office Guidance as to the meaning of 'just' or what the standard of proof is; however, as discussed below, this has been ruled on determinatively by the courts.

8.3   Any interim order which is made will cease to have effect on the determination of the main application, including where that application is withdrawn.[5] It should also be noted that even if the determination of the main application results in different provisions to that in the interim order, breach of a 'discontinued' term of the interim order will still be a criminal offence.[6]

INTERIM ORDERS WITHOUT NOTICE

8.4   Interim orders may be sought without notice by leave of the justices' clerk,[7] but leave should only be granted if the clerk is satisfied that it is necessary to do so.[8] In *R (on the application of Manchester CC) v Manchester City Magistrates' Court*[9] the Divisional Court had to consider the appropriate procedure for commencing without-notice hearings and in so doing also gave some valuable guidance as to the role of the clerk and the contents of the application. The council had applied to the justices' clerk for permission to bring a without-notice ASBO. The clerk refused leave stating that he did not consider that it would be just to make a without-notice order. The council sought to state a case.

---

[1]   CDA 1998, s 1D was added by PRA 2002, s 65(1).
[2]   CDA 1998, s 1D(2).
[3]   2002 Rules, r 4(5).
[4]   CDA 1998, s 1D(5).
[5]   CDA 1998, s 1D(4), and 2002 Rules, r 5(6).
[6]   *Parker v DPP* [2005] EWHC 1485 (Admin).
[7]   2002 Rules, r 5(1).
[8]   2002 Rules, r 5(2).
[9]   [2005] EWHC 253.

8.5   The Divisional Court found that the clerk had applied the wrong test and exceeded his powers. The test for him was whether it was necessary for the applicant to bring the application for an interim ASBO without notice. The question of whether it was just to make an interim order was for the magistrates alone.

8.6   The court went on to give some general guidance to be considered when deciding if the application was urgent enough, namely:

(i)   the likely response of the defendant if given notice of the application;

(ii)   whether such response was likely to prejudice the applicant given the vulnerability of the witnesses;

(iii) the gravity of the conduct within the scope of conduct tackled by ASBOs in general as compared to this case;

(iv)   the urgency of the matter;

(v)   the nature of the prohibitions sought;

(vi)   the right of the defendant to know about proceedings;

(vii) protections for defendant's rights of a limited period of order, right to apply to vary/discharge and ineffectiveness until served.

8.7   If the interim order is granted, both the order and a summons giving a date for the defendant to attend court must be served on the defendant personally, as soon as possible.[10] Any interim order is only effective on service[11] and, if not served within 7 days, ceases to have any effect.[12] If the defendant applies to have the interim order discharged or varied, the court *must* hear his or her oral application.[13] As interim orders must be for a fixed period but may be renewed,[14] it is suggested that every order which is made without notice should have a return date as soon as possible for the defendant to either challenge or accept the interim order. There is merit in having the first hearing in the main application at the same time as the return date for the interim order, as this saves both time and costs.

8.8   The lawfulness of the interim order regime came under challenge when without-notice ASBOs were made in Leeds Magistrates' Court in 2003. The local authority made applications for interim without-notice ASBOs against 66 individuals who they claimed were responsible for anti-social behaviour in a particular area of Leeds. The main allegations related to drug dealing but also associated anti-social behaviour, including abusive behaviour, car crime, robbery, burglary and intimidation. The clerk to the justices gave permission for the application to be made without notice, and the district judge granted the orders without notice. The orders were confirmed at an on notice hearing of the interim orders, and the defendants issued an application for judicial review, asserting that r 5 of the 2002 Rules, which introduced the without-notice procedure, was incompatible with Art 6 of the ECHR (as set out in Sch 1 to the HRA 1998). Further, they contended that the test applied by the court was too low and should have required proof to a heightened civil standard and that without-notice orders should only be made in exceptional circumstances, which were not met here.

---

[10]   2002 Rules, r 5(3).
[11]   2002 Rules, r 5(4).
[12]   2002 Rules, r 5(5).
[13]   2002 Rules, r 5(8).
[14]   CDA 1998, s 1D(4).

8.9   The defendants argued:

(a)   that Art 6 was engaged at every stage of the ASBO proceedings, including at the without-notice hearing, and that the without-notice procedure was incompatible with this requirement of scrupulous fairness. This was on the basis that an interim order could be made for the same terms as a final order and carried the same punishment;

(b)   that the procedure in r 5 meant that the defendant was denied the right to oppose the making of the interim order by representations, etc;

(c)   that the procedural safeguards were not effective, as there was no prescribed requirement for a return date, that an application to vary or discharge required 14 days' notice and that, at the application to discharge or vary, the burden would be unfairly on the defendant to prove that the order was not just;

(d)   that the test to be applied by the court should have been whether there was an extremely strong prima facie case, and that without-notice ASBOs should only be granted in exceptional circumstances where there was compelling urgency; and

(e)   that there should be a heightened civil standard of proof, to be applied when the court considered the application, as in *McCann*.[15]

8.10   Mr Justice Owen[16] concluded that whilst Art 6(1) was engaged, this was not the situation with which the House of Lords was concerned with in *McCann*, as this was an interim order without notice. Whilst this was a hearing which necessarily did not comply with the requirements under Art 6(1) as to a fair hearing, that did not make the procedure incompatible with the Convention. He stated that:

> '[28]   … There is nothing inherently unlawful in interim injunctions made without notice. The power to make such orders is a necessary weapon in the judicial armour, enabling the court to do justice in circumstances where it is necessary to act urgently to protect the interests of a party, or where it is necessary to act without notice to a prospective defendant in order to ensure that the order of the court is effective.'

He went on to say:

> '[25]   Furthermore the 2002 Rules provide important safeguards for the protection of a defendant, namely that an order does not take effect until served on the defendant (rule 5(4)), if not served within 7 days of being made the order will cease to have effect (rule 5(5)), it is open to a defendant to apply for the discharge or variation of an order (section 1D(4)(b)), and on such an application the defendant has the right to make oral representations (rule 5(8)), and finally that a defendant has a right of appeal to the Crown Court (section 4(1) as amended).'

8.11   This is an important point, as the safeguards under the 2002 Rules are what go towards making the without-notice procedure lawful, notwithstanding the failure to comply with Art 6. Mr Justice Owen, however, went further and concluded that an interim ASBO was not, in any event, a determination of the defendant's rights within the meaning of Art 6. Determination of civil rights involved three things: (a) a decision as to whether Convention rights are engaged, (b) a decision as to whether there has been an interference with Convention rights, and (c) a decision as to whether any interference with Convention rights is lawful (ie whether it is in accordance with law, necessary in a democratic society, in pursuit of a legitimate aim and

---

15   *R (on the application McCann and others) v Crown Court at Manchester; Clingham v Kensington and Chelsea Royal Borough Council* [2002] UKHL 39, [2002] 3 WLR 1313, [2002] 4 All ER 593, HL.

16   *R (on the application of Kenny) v Leeds Magistrates' Court; R (on the application of M) v Secretary of State for Constitutional Affairs and another* [2004] 1 All ER 1333.

proportionate). Whilst a without-notice order engaged the defendant's rights, the remaining matters could not be resolved on a without-notice hearing and, therefore, there was no determination of civil rights.

8.12 Further, Art 6 was concerned with procedural fairness in that procedure which leads ultimately to a determination. The interim order was, by its very nature, temporary, and regulated behaviour pending a full hearing. He cited, with approval, a passage from Clayton and Tomlinson *The Law of Human Rights* (2000), at p 623, para 11.157:

> 'Determination or "decisiveness" in relation to civil rights and obligations refers to the decision on the merits of a case and its finality. Proceedings which are not determinative are not subject to Article 6 guarantees. It has been held that the following are not "determinative": applications for interim relief'
> ...'

In essence, his conclusion was that, whilst there may be a determination at an application to vary or discharge the without-notice order, the procedural safeguards in the 2002 Rules had already had effect and satisfied the requirements of Art 6(1) at that stage.

8.13 Mr Justice Owen then turned to consider the test to be applied by the court and the standard of proof. He rejected any attempt to 'put a gloss' on the wording of the statute, holding that the test was whether it was just and that there could be no requirement to prove compelling urgency or exceptional circumstances. He concluded that:

> 'Consideration of whether it is just to make an order without notice is necessarily a balancing exercise. The court must balance the need to protect the public against the impact that the order sought will have upon the defendant. It will need to consider the seriousness of the behaviour in issue, the urgency with which it is necessary to take steps to control such behaviour, and whether it is necessary for orders to be made without notice in order for them to be effective. On the other side of the equation it will consider the degree to which the order will impede the defendant's rights as a free citizen to go where he pleases and to associate with whosoever he pleases.'

8.14 On the issue of what standard of proof was to be applied, Mr Justice Owen declined to apply the heightened civil standard of proof settled in *McCann* (ie the criminal standard) and further emphasised the balancing act for the court, which was an exercise of judgment or discretion, as was suggested in the first edition of this *Bulletin*. He said:

> 'But as I have already observed, the House of Lords was not considering the position with regard to an application for interim relief in *McCann*. Secondly the balancing exercise involved in consideration of whether it is just to make an interim order, is an exercise of judgment or evaluation. As Lord Steyn said in *McCann*:
>
> > "The inquiry under section 1(b), namely that such an order is necessary to protect persons from further anti-social acts by him, does not involve a standard proof; it is an exercise of judgment or evaluation. This approach should facilitate correct decision making and should ensure consistency and predictability in this corner of the law. In coming to this conclusion I bear in mind that the use of hearsay evidence will often be of crucial importance."'

8.15 The judge went on to cite, with approval, the Home Office Guidance in relation to ASBOs and, as this and the above test was cited to the judge, the correct test had been applied. He went on to consider the individual facts of the two defendants' cases before him, approving one but quashing another, which related to incidents only outside the relevant area, one of which, by the on notice hearing, had been shown to be a case of mistaken identity. As an important final note, he provided assistance to magistrates' courts which heard applications to discharge or vary without notice (and, presumably, on notice) interim orders:

> '[61] I do not consider that the effect of the Rules is to shift the burden to the defendant to demonstrate why an interim order made without notice should be varied or discharged. The test to be

applied on such an application will be that set out in s 1D(1), (2), namely whether *"… it is just to make an order under this section pending the determination of that application (the main application)"*. In applying that test the court will necessarily consider the material relied upon by the party seeking the interim order, and will obviously take account of any evidence adduced by and/or submissions made on behalf of the defendant. The burden remains on the party seeking the order to demonstrate that it is just for there to be an interim order until the hearing of the main application.'

8.16 The defendant, M, appealed against the decision of the administrative court on the issues of compatibility with the ECHR and the correct test. A strong Court of Appeal of three Lord Justices, including the Master of the Rolls, heard the appeal. The unanimous judgment of the court[17] was given by Kennedy LJ, who gave succinct conclusions at [39], namely that:

(1) whilst unusual for courts to make orders without notice, they could be made where necessary and with proper safeguards. There was nothing intrinsically objectionable about the power to grant an interim ASBO without notice;

(2) the more intrusive the order, the more the court will require proof that any order is necessary and that it is necessary in the form applied for;

(3) the safeguard that the without-notice order was ineffective until served was an important one, as was the fact that there was an early on notice return date or final hearing. The former was preferable (here, it was 13 days, after which the court would have power to vary or discharge the order),[18] unless the final hearing was at a very early date. At that return date, it would be open to the court to reconsider the order, either to vary or to discharge it;

(4) the defendant could apply to have the without-notice order varied or discharged, and the requirement that the justices' chief executive give not less than 14 days' notice of the hearing of the application was judged a sensible and realistic procedural requirement, which did not undermine the right of the person affected to seek rapid relief. It was not a breach of Art 6 that, under r 6, it is for the defendant to seek discharge rather than a requirement on the court to list for an on notice hearing;

(5) as a without-notice order could only be made when the justices' clerk was satisfied that it was necessary for the application to be made without notice, and because the order could only be made for a limited period, and when the court considers that it is just to make it, and in circumstances where it can be reviewed or discharged, as indicated above, it was impossible to say that it determined civil rights. For a time, it restricted certain freedoms, and the restriction could be enforced by sanctions, but that is the nature of any interim order, and, therefore, Art 6 of the Convention would not be engaged (at either the without-notice hearing or at any application to discharge or vary);

(6) although Art 6 is not engaged, the procedure must be fair, but there was no apparent unfairness in the procedure;

(7) even if Art 6 were engaged, it would be appropriate to look at the process as a whole, bearing in mind that the application for an ASBO is a civil procedure to which an application for an interim order is ancillary, and if that approach were adopted, no contravention of the requirements of Art 6 could be discerned;

---

[17] *R (on the application of M) v Secretary of State for Constitutional Affairs and Lord Chancellor and another* [2004] 2 All ER 531.

[18] Ibid, per Kennedy LJ at [29].

(8)   the test to be adopted by a magistrates' court when deciding whether or not to make an interim order must be the statutory test: whether it is just to make the order. That involved consideration of all relevant circumstances, including, in a case such as this, the fact that the application has been made without notice. Obviously, the court must consider whether the application for the final order has been properly made, but there is no justification for requiring the magistrates' court, when considering whether to make an interim order, to decide whether the evidence in support of the full order discloses an extremely strong prima facie case;

(9)   the correct test having been used in the present case, there was ample evidence to support the conclusion of the judge that it was just for an interim order to be made. The fact that no vulnerable witnesses were identified by name was of no significance when the available evidence and information were considered as a whole.

8.17   One final matter which should be borne in mind when making submissions to the court about the appropriate test to be applied is that, whilst made in the context of considering the interests of young persons at interim order applications (see, further, chapter 14), it is clear that whilst the interests of a child are a primary consideration for the court, the interests of the public are also a primary consideration when it considers the making of an order.[19]

PRACTICE

8.18   The test to be applied when an applicant seeks an interim order is, therefore, not a high test and, indeed, the guidance, which was approved by Mr Justice Owen in the Leeds case, is at pains to say that the court, when considering an application, should be aware that the full extent of the evidence may not have been obtained. The court is directed instead to consider whether the application for a full order has been properly made and whether there is sufficient evidence of an urgent need to protect the community. The Guidance suggests that an order will be appropriate where the applicant feels that persons need to be protected from the threat of further anti-social behaviour before the main hearing. To this can be added that an application would seem appropriate where there are vulnerable witnesses and there is a real risk that they will be intimidated by the defendant (and/or subjected to anti-social behaviour) before the main application is heard. Following the Leeds cases, a without-notice order can also be appropriate where there is a significant problem in an area for which interim orders were urgently required to provide some regulation of the anti-social behaviour,[20] or where without-notice orders are required to make them efficacious.

8.19   When commencing an application for an interim order, it will be important for the applicant to file detailed statements providing evidence of the urgent need for an order. Hearsay evidence is likely to be more prominent in such statements and will carry more weight at the interim order application stage than may be appropriate at the final hearing. Such statements should ordinarily be compiled by the housing officers and can include matters within their own knowledge and those obtained from other sources. If exclusion areas are sought it is helpful to provide a plan showing the location of the incidents alleged in relation to those areas, and it is important to produce a statement which explains the need and extent of the exclusion area. The prudent applicant for a without-notice ASBO will of course address each of the guidance points in **8.6**. Careful consideration should also be given to the terms which are requested at the interim application stage, taking into account the fact that the allegations have not been proved. The

---

[19]   *R (on the application of A) v Leeds Magistrates' Court and Leeds City Council* [2004] EWHC 554 (Admin), (2004) *The Times*, March 31.

[20]   *R (on the application of Kenny) v Leeds Magistrates' Court; R (on the application of M) v Secretary of State for Constitutional Affairs and another* [2004] 1 All ER 1333.

stronger and more serious the evidence, the easier it will be to persuade a court to make more restrictive terms. Any defence submission that the terms are not in a child's best interests will have to be positively stated and supported by evidence[21] (see further **14.6**).

PUBLICITY

8.20 The correct approach as to whether to make an order pursuant to s 39, imposing reporting restrictions on the making of an interim order, has been considered in the case of *Keating v Knowsley Metropolitan Borough Council*.[22] Mr Justice Harrison considered that the making of such an order was not automatic, however, the fact that the ASBO was an interim one was a factor to be put into the balance. That the allegations were unproven and the defendant had not had the opportunity to put his case forward were weighty matters, but the nature of the allegations did reinforce the public interest in disclosure. It is submitted that, as made clear in the Home Office Guidance on publicity in ASBOs, it is likely that in most cases the interests of the child weighs against publicity by way of media coverage or leaflet distribution at the interim stage save in the most exceptional cases. There is, of course, no reason why only the witnesses concerned cannot be personally told of the interim order (and its terms) which has been obtained partly for their benefit.

SUMMARY

8.21 We would suggest that the following principles can be discerned from the statutes and case-law which now exists on interim orders.

(a) The test to be applied is only whether it is just to make an order.

(b) 'Just' requires consideration of all the relevant circumstances, including whether the order is applied for without notice, the behaviour complained of, the terms applied for and the age of the defendant.

(c) Article 6(1) is not engaged by the making of a without-notice interim order or at an application to discharge or vary.

(d) The needs of a child may be a primary consideration for the court, but so are the needs of the community.

COUNTY COURT

8.22 The procedure for applications for ASBOs in the county court is dealt with in more detail in chapter 6. Applications for interim orders may also be made in county court proceedings but should be made as soon as possible within those proceedings (ie within the claim form if the applicant is the claimant or in the application notice in all other cases). The application must be made in accordance with CPR Part 25 and normally on notice.[23] This would seem to accept that without-notice orders can in appropriate circumstances be made. We would suggest that the Court of Appeal's approach in *M* can properly be applied to all such applications. Similarly it would be advisable that any statement in support of the application should be full and frank as

---

[21] *R (on the Application of A) v Leeds Magistrates' Court v Leeds City Council* [2004] EWHC 554 (Admin), (2004) *The Times*, March 31.

[22] (Unreported) 22 July 2004, Lawtel AC90600602.

[23] CPR, r 65.26: see Appendix 1.6.

to the evidence which the court is being asked to consider in support and also deal with the points at **8.6**. Service of an interim order (and final orders) in the county court must be personally effected.[24]

CRIMINAL COURTS

8.23 As noted above, interim orders are available in post conviction ASBOs whether on application by the prosecution or of the court's own initiative.[25] The power can be exercised before the determination of the main hearing and before adjourning the matter for a full hearing of that issue. The Criminal Procedural Rules 2005 specifically state that the rules relating to the service by the prosecution of a notice of intention to seek a post conviction order and evidence[26] do not apply to applications for interim orders.[27] This begs the question how the remainder of the requirements can be enforced when the requirements in the section require the evidence to be served without waiting for the verdict. It can only be assumed that it is a catch-all provision to cover failures of the CPS to comply with r 50.3. In theory the evidence which would support the need for an ASBO has already been served. The only potential situation where this exception may be needed is where there had been new evidence on which the CPS wish to rely which had not been served at the early stage.

---

[24] CPR, PD 65, para 13.1: see Appendix 1(F).
[25] CDA 1998, s 1D(1)(c) and (d) respectively.
[26] CPR, r 50.3.
[27] CPR, r 50.3(8).

CHAPTER 9

HEARING OF THE MAIN APPLICATION

9.1   Prior to the hearing of the main application, it is the responsibility of the applicant body to ensure that all parties have an agreed paginated bundle[1] and that the court has sufficient copies of that bundle.[2]

MAGISTRATES' COURT

9.2   Proceedings are governed by the court's powers under the Magistrates' Courts Act 1980 (MCA 1980) and the Magistrates' Courts Rules 1981[3] (MCR 1981). Rule 14 of MCR 1981 provides that before calling any evidence the applicant may address the court. It is important when opening the case to the magistrates to give a clear picture of what the applicant body alleges has happened, exactly what findings of fact the court is being asked to make and the evidence on which the authority will be relying. This is also an opportunity to ensure that the court is aware of the correct legal tests to be applied and also the duration and terms of the order being sought. For obvious reasons, it is worthwhile seeing if agreement as to the law and issues can be reached between the applicant body and the defendant's representatives prior to the commencement of the hearing. In any case where there is likely to be substantial dispute, it would be prudent for the applicant to have a skeleton argument to ensure that their case is put clearly for early consideration by the magistrates. It has the added benefit that there is a record of the test which the court is being asked to apply in case of dispute on appeal. Whilst the schedule of incidents relied on will be in the bundle with the application notice, it is good practice to have one (updated if there are incidents post issue but note the need to apply to amend if those incidents are needed to satisfy s 1(1)(a)) separate from the bundle, perhaps attached to the skeleton argument for the use of the magistrates' as they hear the evidence.

9.3   When the applicant body comes to call its witnesses, that evidence is given on oath.[4] If the written statement is to be the witness's evidence-in-chief, it is usual for the witness to confirm that he or she has read the statement and to verify the truth of its contents. Whilst it may be sufficient to leave the witness to be cross-examined, it is often far better to ask for permission to ask a few supplementary questions. This allows for the expansion of key parts of the witness's evidence and also gives the opportunity to deal with any incidents which may have occurred since the statement was made. Importantly, it also allows a lay witness to become more comfortable with the process of giving evidence in court prior to what may well be hostile cross-examination.

9.4   Cross-examination of witnesses by the defendant's representatives is often a delicate process. Whilst the points which the defendant wishes to have made need to be put to each witness, the manner in which this is done may have a decisive effect on the impression which each witness gives. It should be borne in mind that most lay witnesses will not wish to give

---

[1]   See Home Office Guidance, reproduced in Appendix 3.
[2]   Four copies if being heard by lay magistrates and two if being heard in the county court or by a district judge (crime).
[3]   SI 1981/552.
[4]   MCA 1980, s 98.

evidence and are often vulnerable individuals. Unless there is a good reason to do so, courts are generally not positively influenced by attacking the characters of witnesses. Of course, if the witness has a criminal record, especially for dishonesty, or has an ulterior motive for giving evidence, the whole application may fall on the defendant establishing the same. It is often the case that a witness will report an incident but, on cross-examination, it transpires that he or she did not actually hear or see the defendant do anything and are giving hearsay evidence for which there has been no notice. As there are usually a number of incidents which the authority will be relying on, it is important to challenge each and every incident cited in the application notice. Failure to do so will mean that the evidence is unchallenged and should be found as a fact. It will also pose problems if the defendant later asserts something about an incident or witness which is not put to that witness.

9.5   When cross-examining the professional witnesses, one tactic is to seek to undermine the process by which the application came to be made against the defendant. If doubt can be thrown on the steps that the applicant body took before applying for the order, it may be possible to persuade a court that the order is not necessary. Another line of inquiry is to seek information from the witness about the action taken against similar other persons whom the defendant may identify as being involved in the incidents. If there is a disparity in the level of action, it may again provide support for a submission that an order is not necessary. Clearly, when representing a juvenile, there is more scope to ask questions relating to the measures taken by the local authority to provide assistance and services and to discharge the various duties imposed by statute.

9.6   After the evidence for the applicant has been heard, the defendant has the right to address the court, whether or not he or she later gives evidence.[5] It is unusual for this right to be taken up unless the evidence from the applicant body has been so poor as to justify a dismissal of the case at that stage or there has been a serious procedural or evidential irregularity (eg failure to prove consultation which may defeat the application). In any event, the defendant may choose to give evidence or not. It is unlikely, however, if he or she decides not to give evidence, that any issues of fact will be found in his or her favour. Whilst the test on the first criteria is a criminal one, the presence of 'one-sided' evidence coupled with supporting hearsay evidence is likely to be sufficient to pass that hurdle unless it was inherently unbelievable. The issue of whether the court should make an order at all, however, may be easily argued against in the absence of evidence from the defendant. In many cases, the sole argument before the court is whether an order is necessary, as the defendant concedes some or all of the allegations made in the application notice. This is often a more successful method of resisting the making of an ASBO than for a defendant to deny various incidents and to be found to be untruthful by the court. After such findings, it is often hard to submit to the court that the defendant is unlikely to repeat such behaviour and can be believed in such assurances given that he has denied he did it.

9.7   It is open to the applicant to call evidence in rebuttal of the defendant's case; however, this is rarely done. Thereafter, the defendant has the right to a closing speech, but the court may grant leave for both parties to have a second speech. If one side is allowed a second speech, so must the other. However, if the applicant has a second speech, it must be the last to be heard.[6] This leads to the situation where, unless the defendant's representative addresses the court after the applicant's evidence, there is no second speech for the defendant's representative to make and the applicant cannot have a closing speech. In practice, this is not adopted and a more sensible approach is taken to mirror the practice in the county courts where the applicant opens the case and has a closing speech as well. As ASBO proceedings are heard in the civil jurisdiction, it would seem appropriate to follow the same procedure. The only difference

---

[5]   MCR 1981, r 14(2).
[6]   MCR 1981, r 14(5) and (6).

perhaps is that in a civil trial, if the defendant calls no evidence then the claimant gives his speech first. It is not likely that this would be appropriate in ASBO hearings.

9.8   It is suggested that it is important when making submissions for both applicant and defendant to clearly divide their arguments into sections. The first would be to make those points which can be made as to the law, the second as to the evidence in support of the allegations of anti-social behaviour which are sought, the third as to the issue of necessity, bearing in mind those matters proved and adduced outside the 6-month period, the terms of any order if the court were minded to make one and, finally, the duration of the same. If followed, it is likely that the magistrates will also be able to produce reasons which mirror that progression of required findings.

SPECIAL MEASURES FOR WITNESSES

9.9   One of the particular problems for local authorities in combating anti-social behaviour and applications for ASBOs is persuading lay witnesses to give evidence at court. Many witnesses are afraid of being seen at court by the defendants and are also afraid of reprisals. Whilst in almost every case a lay witness should be protected by a term in the interim (and final) ASBO, little could be done to make the experience of giving evidence less stressful. With this in mind the special measures for witnesses in the SOCPA 2005 have been incorporated into the CDA 1998 by the insertion of a new section.[7]

APPLICATION

9.10   Section 1L ostensibly operates by applying the provisions of Ch I of Part II of the Youth Justice and Criminal Evidence Act 1999[8] (YJCEA 1999) save for some subsections and 'any other necessary modifications' to specified ASBO proceedings. The subsections which are excluded are those which apply only to criminal proceedings; no further explanation is given as to what might constitute necessary modifications.

9.11   The proceedings to which s 1L makes the special measures for witnesses available are:[9]

(a)   proceedings in a magistrates' court on an application for an ASBO; and

(b)   any proceedings in a magistrates' court or the Crown Court insofar as it relates to the issue of making an order under s 1C; and

(c)   any proceedings in a magistrates' court relating to a s 1D order application.

This means that special measures are available in proceedings for standalone applications in the magistrates' court including interim orders and post-conviction applications in magistrates' and Crown Courts. There are two omissions from this list, one seemingly intentional the other clearly not. The seemingly intentional omission is that the provisions are not available to applications for interim orders in the Crown Court. This is strange given that whilst evidence is not often called in interim order applications, why exclude Crown Court hearings?

---

[7]   CDA 1998, s 1L.
[8]   Chapter 1 of Part 2 of the YJCEA 1999 (special measures directions in the case of vulnerable and intimidated witnesses).
[9]   CDA 1998, s 1L(1).

9.12   The second omission is clearly not intentional and is potentially much more serious. The above list of proceedings includes standalone applications in the magistrates' courts and post-conviction order applications in the Crown Court, however, it does not include the appeal hearings from the standalone applications. Those proceedings (see **12.1**) are heard by the Crown Court. The Crown Court is sitting in its civil capacity as an appellate authority and is not covered by any of the three categories above. There is no solution either to the problem directly from the YJCEA 1999 as this Act applies only to criminal proceedings. The appeal hearings must be civil proceedings otherwise *Clingham* would have to be ignored and hearsay evidence would not be admissible. Only one possible saving argument exists and that is to be taken from s 20(1) of the YJCEA 1999 which states that a special measures direction has binding effect from the time it is made until the proceedings for the purposes of which it is made are either determined by acquittal, conviction or 'otherwise' or if abandoned. It could therefore be argued that the direction runs through to the appeal hearing as it is an 'otherwise' determination. The problem, however, would seem that there is a conviction in the magistrates' court proceedings which has determined the proceedings and therefore the direction ends. 'Otherwise' seems in reality to refer to outcomes in the criminal courts which are not acquittals, convictions or abandonment, e g left to lie on court file, not to appeals. Some support could be gained by relying on this being a 'necessary modification' referred to in s 1L, however, this would really be an addition rather than a modification. In any event this remains an arguable point and one where the court would very much wish to find in the applicant's favour if possible, however, would seem to require a significant deviation from the statutory wording. Even if the above could be used to get around that problem another one remains. Consider the situation where witnesses give evidence in the magistrates' court in the normal way but feel so intimidated that they say they will only give evidence in the Crown Court if they can have screens or video link. There would seem to be no power for the Crown Court on appeal to make a special measures direction for them. Section 4 of the CDA 1998 does not assist as it refers to consequential orders and orders to give effect to its determination of the appeal. Similarly if new witnesses were found before the appeal and were deserving of protection they could not be protected. Neither is a desirable state of affairs.

9.13   The implications of the above omission are potentially very serious. When hearing the standalone application in the magistrates' court a witness could have been provided with effective special measures to protect them and given compelling evidence which convinced a court to make an ASBO. The defendant having an automatic right of appeal can appeal to the Crown Court where the hearing is a complete re-hearing but where the witnesses would have no protection.

9.14   The omission is unfortunately yet another example of poor drafting in the CDA 1998. The need for so many amendments to the CDA 1998 (three substantive ones) is testament to this and the Home Office when this omission was raised has stated that it is seeking legislative time to correct the above omission (which would indicate that the above potential argument using s 20 is not one which they believe is viable). Until then there remains the issue of what to do about special measures in appeal hearings. If the argument utilising s 20 failed then aside from agreement by the defendant, there are no means to give the witness special measures at the appeal hearing. The only way which we can see to deal with this problem is to use their evidence as hearsay evidence. The hearsay notice should cite that the witness having given evidence in the court below is afraid to give live evidence without the special measures which were available in the magistrates' court and that the defendant will not agree to them for the appeal hearing. Unfortunately, the magistrates' court is not a court of record and therefore there is no way in which a transcript of the witnesses' evidence could be put before the Crown Court. The less satisfactory alternative is the magistrates' court clerk's notes of evidence. The fact that the defendant will not agree to special measures will of course make it more difficult for him to argue that the witness is not believable. Hopefully the legislative omission will be corrected sooner rather than later.

MEASURES

Eligibility

9.15 The relevant parts of Ch I of Part II of the YJCEA 1999 runs from ss 16 to 33. Section 16 states that a witness (other than the defendant)[10] is eligible for special measures if they are 16 years of age or less[11] or if they suffer from a mental disorder within the meaning of the Mental Health Act 1983[12] or have significant impairment of intelligence or social functioning[13] or physical disability or disorder[14] *and* the court considered that the quality of their evidence would be likely to be diminished by this.[15] It is hard to understand what condition could be a physical disorder which is not also a disability. 'Quality of evidence' is said to be in terms of its completeness, coherence and accuracy. Coherence relates to the witnesses' ability to give answers to the questions put.[16]

9.16 Section 17 applies where the court considers that the quality of *any* witness' evidence (not the defendant) was likely to be diminished by reason of fear or distress in connection with testifying in the proceedings.[17] In determining whether a witness falls into the above the court must consider in particular:[18]

(a) the nature of alleged circumstances of the offence to which the proceedings relate;

(b) the age of the witness;

(c) such of the following which to the court appears to be relevant:
   (i) social and cultural background and ethnic origins of the witness;
   (ii) the domestic and employment circumstances of the witness; and
   (iii) any religious beliefs or political opinions of the witness;

(d) any behaviour towards the witness on the part of—
   (i) the accused;
   (ii) members of the family or associates of the accused; or
   (iii) any other person who is likely to be an accused or a witness in the proceedings.

Further the court must take into account any views expressed by the witness themselves.[19]

9.17 Given the requirement in the CDA 1998 to read the YJCEA 1999 with 'necessary modifications' it is submitted that references to 'offence' in (a) above must be read as referring to the alleged anti-social behaviour. The remaining criteria are relatively self-explanatory.

---

[10] This exclusion has been held to be neither unfair nor in contravention of the European Convention on Human Rights: *R (on the application of D) v Camberwell Youth Court; R (on the application of the DPP) v Camberwell Youth Court* [2005] 1 WLR 393 and *R v Waltham Forest Youth Court* [2004] EWHC 715 Admin; [2004] 2 Cr App R 21.

[11] YJCEA 1999, s 16(1).

[12] YJCEA 1999, s 16(2)(a)(i).

[13] YJCEA 1999, s 16(2)(a)(ii).

[14] YJCEA 1999, s 16(2)(b).

[15] YJCEA 1999, s 16(1)(b).

[16] YJCEA 1999, s 16(5).

[17] YJCEA 1999, s 17(1).

[18] YJCEA 1999, s 17(2)(a)–(d).

[19] YJCEA 1999, s 17(3).

PROCEDURE FOR APPLICATIONS

9.18 The rules for applications for special measures in the magistrates' court in criminal proceedings are governed by Part 29 of the Criminal Procedure Rules 2005 (CPR 2005).[20] There are no specific rules seemingly for ASBOs and therefore it is assumed that the same rules must apply to them by reason of the 'necessary modifications' permitted by the CDA 1998. Any application for special measures must therefore be made in writing on the prescribed practice direction form[21] and, depending on which direction is sought, information in the appropriate section must be completed.[22] Any application must be sent to the court officer and at the same time a copy must be sent by the applicant to every other party to the proceedings.[23] The time by which the application must be brought is unclear as the time-limits in the CPR 2005 apply to criminal proceedings time references, eg entering a plea of not guilty. It is submitted that the appropriate time period is at worst 28 days after the defendant at the first instance hearing states that the application is to be opposed.[24] The Rules do however allow an application to be made to extend the time-limit but must be made accompanied by a statement explaining the reason why the application was late and must be served on all parties.[25] The application is determined by a justice without a hearing unless they order otherwise.[26] Further there is a save-all provision that an application for special measures can be made orally at trial or even raised by the court itself. However, if an oral application is made reasons will have to be given why the application is late and the court has to be satisfied that the applicant was unable to make an application under CPR 2005, r 29.1.[27] The court does have to decide if the parties should be allowed oral representations and/or a hearing. It seems to us to be contrary to Art 6(2) of the ECHR not to allow the defendant to make representations especially as they would have been allowed a hearing if the application had been made earlier.[28] The statutory language of requiring the application to show that they were 'unable' to apply before does however mean that it will be in only rare cases of emerging intimidation, etc that an oral application would be appropriate.

OPPOSING AN APPLICATION

9.19 The procedure is governed by the CPR 2005 in the magistrates' court.[29] The defendant must make any objections to an application in writing and within 14 days of receipt of the application to both the court and the applicant.[30] The objections must set out whether (and the reasons why) the defendant:[31]

(i) disputes that the witness is eligible for assistance by virtue of s 16 or 17 of YJCEA 1999;

(ii) disputes that any of the special measures available would be likely to improve the quality of evidence given by the witness or that such measures (or a combination of them) would be likely to maximise the quality of that evidence; and

(iii) opposes the granting of a special measures direction.

---

[20] See Appendix 1(G).
[21] CPR 2005, r 29.1(1).
[22] CPR 2005, r 29.1(2).
[23] CPR 2005, r 29.1(3).
[24] Comparison CPR 2005, r 29.1(4)(b).
[25] CPR 2005, r 29.2.(3).
[26] CPR 2005, r 29.2(4).
[27] CPR 2005, r 29.3(2).
[28] CPR 2005, r 29.1(10).
[29] CPR 2005, r 29.1(5).
[30] CPR 2005, r 29.1(6).
[31] CPR 2005, r 29.1(8).

9.20 In addition where a video recording is served by an applicant to be played as the witnesses' evidence the defendant must within 14 days of its receipt, notify the applicant and the court officer, in writing whether:[32]

(a) he objects to the admission under s 27 of YJCEA 1999 of any part of the video recording or recordings disclosed, giving his reasons why it would not be in the interests of justice for the recording or any part of it to be admitted;

(b) he would agree to the admission of part of the video recording or recordings and, if so, which part or parts; and

(c) he wishes to be represented at any hearing of the application.

9.21 Where no objection is received within the time-limits to an application for special measures directions a single justice may grant the application without a hearing[33] or direct that there be a hearing.[34] Where the defendant files an application the court must direct that there is a hearing.[35]

SPECIAL MEASURES DIRECTIONS

9.22 Section 18 states that those measures in ss 23–30 will be available to those falling into s 16 above and those in ss 23–28 are available to those eligible by falling into s 17.

9.23 Special Measures are granted by the making of a direction by the court. The procedure for doing so is governed by s 19. The direction can be made either on the application of a party[36] or by the court's own motion in raising the issue of whether a direction should be made.[37]

9.24 Where the court determines that a witness is eligible for special measures under either s 16 or 17 it is obliged to determine:[38]

(a) whether any of the measures (or combination) would be likely to improve the quality of the evidence; and if so

(b) which would be likely to maximise so far as practicable, the quality of their evidence; and

(c) give a direction providing for those measures.

If, however, the witness is a child then the court must consider measures in s 21 before considering the above[39] and those in s 21 are to be considered as if they *are* measures which would be likely to maximise the quality of the child witnesses' evidence.[40]

9.25 In determining whether measures would be likely to improve the quality of a witness' evidence the court must consider all the circumstances of the case and in particular:

---

32 CPR 2005, r 29.7(7).
33 CPR 2005, r 29.1(9)(a).
34 CPR 2005, r 29.1(9)(b).
35 CPR 2005, r 29.1(10).
36 YJCEA 1999, s 19(1)(a).
37 YJCEA 1999, s 19(1)(b).
38 YJCEA 1999, s 19(2)(b).
39 YJCEA 1999, s 21(2)(a) and (b).
40 YJCEA 1999, s 21(2)(b).

(a)   any views expressed by the witness; and

(b)   whether the measure or measures might tend to inhibit such evidence being effectively tested by a party.

Any direction which is made must specify the particulars of the provision made by the direction in respect of each special measure which is to apply to the evidence.[41] Once made the direction lasts until determination by acquittal, conviction or abandoned. The court has the power to discharge or vary a special measure if it is in the interests of justice to do so.[42] Such power can be exercised of the court's own motion or on application by a party if there has been a material change of circumstances.[43] The court must state in open court its reasons for giving or varying, refusing or discharging a special measures application/provision.[44]

SPECIAL MEASURES FOR CHILD WITNESSES

9.26   If a witness is a child then the primary rule is that unless the court is satisfied that the special measures direction would not be likely to maximise the quality of the witness' evidence or is unavailable in that court,[45] the court *must* give a special measures direction for any video-recorded evidence in chief to be admitted[46] pursuant to s 27 *and* it must provide for any evidence which is not given by video recording to be by means of a live link in accordance with s 24.[47]

9.27   A direction made for a child witness ceases to have effect when they reach 17 years of age unless the direction relates to a relevant recording to be admitted and that recording was made when the child was under 17.

Available measures

Screens

9.28   A screen may be provided for a witness so that the defendant cannot see them.[48] The screens must, however, not prevent the judge, magistrates or legal representative from being able to see the witness.[49] If the defendant has more than one legal representative only one need be able to see the witness.[50] In pre-1999 cases the instances of use of screens was in more serious criminal cases but included one where a young witness had a fear of reprisals albeit in a murder trial.[51] It is suggested that the use of screens in ASBO cases will be more easily obtained especially where witnesses make statements and have stated that they are worried about reprisals or that they do not want the defendant staring at them as they give evidence as it scares them. In *R v X*[52] the Court of Appeal approved the erection of a screen in a courtroom to prevent young children seeing, or being seen by, the defendants. Social workers had been permitted to sit alongside the child witnesses when they gave evidence to comfort and console them when

---

[41]   YJCEA 1999, s 19(4).
[42]   YJCEA 1999, s 20(2).
[43]   YJCEA 1999, s 20(2)(a).
[44]   YJCEA 1999, s 20(5).
[45]   YJCEA 1999, s 21(4).
[46]   YJCEA 1999, s 20(3)(a).
[47]   YJCEA 1999, s 20(3)(b).
[48]   YJCEA 1999, s 23(1).
[49]   YJCEA 1999, s 23(2).
[50]   YJCEA 1999, s 23(3).
[51]   *R v HM Coroner for Newcastle upon Tyne ex parte P A* (1998) 162 JP 387.
[52]   (1990) 91 Cr App R 36.

necessary. The Court of Appeal said that plainly this was a course of conduct which had to be undertaken with considerable care and the court had to be astute to see that nothing improper passed and no undue encouragement was given to the witness to say anything other than the truth.

9.29 In *KL and LK v DPP*[53] Mr Justice Richards held that the fact that, on an application to a magistrates' court for permission for use of a screen, material adverse to the defendant was placed before the court did not necessarily preclude fair-minded consideration of the case. The magistrates were not debarred from continuing the hearing thereafter and where they had asked for the screen to be brought into court before the application the High Court would not go behind their statement that this was done as a precautionary measure and not a sign that they had pre-judged the issue. From this it can be seen that it would be advisable for a defendant to seek to have the application determined before the day of the final hearing to avoid any such potential disclosure to the magistrates trying the main application.

Live link

9.30 This is where the witness gives evidence by a live television link from a place not in the courtroom and can see and hear and can be heard and seen only by the judge, magistrates or legal representative.[54] The defendant is not mentioned, however, presumably the defendant can hear the evidence even if they cannot see or be seen by the witness. Once a direction has been given for evidence to be given in this way then the evidence from that witness can only be given in that way unless the court gives permission.[55] An application can be made due to a material change in the circumstances or of the court's own motion.[56] In *R v Richards*[57] the Court of Appeal held that any limitation on the principle of open justice caused by a special measures order was countered by the more fundamental rule that the principal object of the courts was to secure that justice was done. The court considered it was proper for the judge to order that the public gallery be cleared save for press when an important prosecution witness was likely to refuse to give evidence.

Evidence to be given in private

9.31 A direction can be given to exclude certain persons including the press (although if this made then one person nominated by the press must be allowed to be present unless no nomination is made)[58] during the evidence of a witness if the court considers that there are reasonable grounds for believing that any person other than the accused has sought or will seek to intimidate the witness in connection with testifying.[59] The defendant or his legal representative can not be excluded.[60]

Removal of wigs and gowns

9.32 A direction can be given that wigs and gowns can be dispensed with during the evidence from a witness.[61]

---

[53] (2002) 166 JP 369.
[54] YJCEA 1999, s 24(8).
[55] YJCEA 1999, s 24(2).
[56] YJCEA 1999, s 24(3).
[57] 163 JP 246, CA.
[58] YJCEA 1999, s 24(3).
[59] YJCEA 1999, s 24(5).
[60] YJCEA 1999, s 24(2).
[61] YJCEA 1999, s 26.

Video-recorded evidence-in-chief

9.33 The court may direct that unless the interests of justice dictate otherwise the whole or part of an interview of any witness may be admitted as the witness' evidence-in-chief.[62] If any part is not to be played then the court must consider whether the prejudice to the defendant in that part being admitted is outweighed by the desirability of showing the whole or substantially the whole.[63] Where a recording is admitted the witness must be called by the party tendering it unless a direction is given contrary to that effect and the witness cannot give further evidence-in-chief as to any matter which the court considers has been dealt with adequately in the recording.[64]

Video-recorded cross-examination or re-examination

9.34 Where the cross-examination is video recorded it is almost inevitable that the re-examination will have been as well. A direction can be given for such evidence to be given in the recorded form.[65] This provision is not yet in force at the time of this publication and no date is given for commencement.

Examination of a witness through an intermediary

9.35 This provision was brought into force on 23 February 2004. It would allow a direction to be made that examination of a witness would be put through an interpreter or other court approved person to communicate questions put to the witness and to explain questions which are put to the witness.[66]

Aids to communication

9.36 A direction may be given for the witness to be provided with any device which the court considers appropriate enabling questions or answers to be communicated to or by the witness despite any disability, disorder or other impairment suffered by the witness.[67] Presumably this relates to a deaf person having written questions or other means.

Status of evidence

9.37 Evidence which is given in accordance with a special measures direction is to be treated as if given by a witness in direct oral testimony in court.[68] Evidence given by recordings and not on oath are to be treated as if it was so given. The court in estimating the weight, if any, to be attached to evidence given pursuant to special measures directions should have regard to all the circumstances from which an inference could be reasonably drawn as to the accuracy of the statement or otherwise.[69]

---

[62] YJCEA 1999, s 27.
[63] YJCEA 1999, s 27(3).
[64] YJCEA 1999, s 27(5).
[65] YJCEA 1999, s 28.
[66] YJCEA 1999, s 29.
[67] YJCEA 1999, s 30.
[68] YJCEA 1999, s 31(2).
[69] YJCEA 1999, s 31(4).

Restrictions on reporting directions under Chapter I

9.38 Unless the court gives permission, any special measures directions given by the court under s 19 cannot be reported.[70] Any person, newspaper editor or corporate body doing so commits a criminal offence which can be punished on summary conviction to a fine not exceeding level 5 on the standard scale.[71]

COUNTY COURT

9.39 Neither CPR Part 65 nor the accompanying Practice Direction[72] provides any guidance on the procedure in the county court and, therefore, it must be assumed that the usual principles and procedures of a civil trial will apply. This means that the applicant will in almost every case make an opening speech (the court may dispense with the need for one but in almost every case will expect one) and the statements of the witnesses will stand as the evidence-in-chief. The defendant will make the first closing speech, with the applicant having the last speech. The defendant, however, has the right to the final speech if he or she calls no evidence of his or her own. Given that applications for ASBOs have to be made ancillary to other proceedings, the evidence in support of the ASBO will be heard before the submissions are made. The situation, however, could well arise where a defendant to an ASBO application is represented separately to the defendant to the main proceedings. The defendant to the ASBO proceedings will, of course, be permitted to cross-examine witnesses and make submissions after the defendant to the main application. The applicant should, however, generally make the final speech.

Vulnerable witnesses in the county court

9.40 The special measures provisions in the YJCEA 1999 do not apply to the county court nor are they made applicable by the CDA 1998. Therefore the only power to protect vulnerable witnesses when making an application for an order under s 1B will be those in place under the CPR or common law.

9.41 The county court has the power pursuant to CPR, r 32.3 to allow a witness to give evidence 'through a video link or by other means'. No further details are given; however, in *Rowland v Bock*[73] Mr Justice Newman held that the discretion in CPR, r 32.3 was unfettered and to be exercised in accordance with considerations of cost, time and convenience relevant to the overriding objective and the need to ensure, so far as practicable, that the parties are on an equal footing. The discretion was not limited to circumstances in which witnesses were not able to attend due to illness or pressing need. This presumably means that in appropriate cases, witnesses who are children or afraid of facing the defendant can be allowed to give their evidence in this way. What 'other means' refers to is not clear, however, there is no reason why this could not apply to a recorded examination in chief and also to the use of screens. Essentially this rule appears to give the court a very wide discretion.

9.42 The power of the county court to keep the identity of a witness anonymous comes from CPR, r 32.2(4) if it considers that non-disclosure was necessary in order to protect the interests of that party or witness.

---

[70] YJCEA 1999, s 47.
[71] YJCEA 1999, ss 49 and 51.
[72] See Appendix 1(F).
[73] [2002] EWHC 692 (QB).

9.43   There is no set procedure for applying for the use of the above powers and therefore it is suggested that the correct course is either to raise them at a case management conference hearing (with notice of intention to do so having been given some time before) or preferably in a Part 23 application supported by evidence which could be heard at the CMC or at a separate hearing.

ON CRIMINAL CONVICTION

9.44   The procedure is unspecified. The current Home Office Guidance simply states that an interested relevant applicant body may request the making of an order or that the court may make one of its own volition. It is submitted that, unless the facts are incontrovertible, a separate 'sentencing' hearing will probably have to be arranged for evidence to be produced for the sentencing court to decide if the criteria in s 1C(2) of CDA 1998 are satisfied. This is because there is unlikely to be sufficient time allowed for what is, in effect, a fully contested hearing, often including evidence. It is unclear what the procedure at that hearing will be. However, it seems likely that the format will be very similar to that of a normal application, although with limited evidence called. A failure to allow the defendant to challenge evidence relied on by the applicant, including allowing him or her to give evidence and call witnesses, is likely to be a breach of Art 6(1) and incompatible with the HRA 1998. For this reason, it is unlikely that a criminal court will be willing to make an order at the sentencing hearing, unless it can do so without having to hear substantial evidence. Following the amendments to the CDA 1998 introduced by the SOCPA 2005,[74] the criminal court has the power to adjourn any application for a post-conviction order even after sentencing the offender.[75] There does not appear to be any power to remand, however, the court does have the power to make an interim order pending such an adjourned hearing.[76] If the defendant does not attend the adjourned proceedings then the court may further adjourn the proceedings or may issue a warrant for his or her arrest[77] but only if it is satisfied that the defendant has had adequate notice of the time and place of the adjourned proceedings.[78] Applications for ASBOs on criminal conviction including the fair procedure to be adopted are discussed in greater detail in chapter 6.

PUBLICITY AND REPORTING RESTRICTIONS

9.45   Publicising the making of an ASBO and its terms serves two important functions. The first is to maximise the effectiveness of the order in that breaches are much more likely to be reported if the terms are known to the wider community and, secondly, it shows that effective action will be taken against those who commit anti-social behaviour. An order against an adult can be publicised without difficulty and should be disseminated to police stations and other relevant bodies.

9.46   ASBOs made against a juvenile pose considerations of balancing the interests of the child against the public interest. The prohibition against publicity in s 39 of the Children and Young Persons Act 1933 is a discretionary one. It is very important to note that there is no *automatic* restriction on reporting and, unless an order is made, every detail may be published. Whilst it is very hard to argue that a restriction should not be imposed until the main application is heard, if an order is granted, the converse is true. The current Home Office Guidance suggests that the court should have a good reason, aside from age alone, to impose the order. However, this is not quite in accordance with the case-law which has developed. The clearest authority is the

---

[74]   CDA 1998, s 1D(4A–4C), inserted by SOCPA 2005, s 139(1), 4(a), in force 1 July 2005, SI 2005/1521, art 3(1)(s).
[75]   CDA 1998, s 1D(4A).
[76]   CDA 1998, s 1D(1)(c) and (d).
[77]   CDA 1998, s 1D(4B).
[78]   CDA 1998, s 1D(4C).

judgment of Elias J, who gave a single judgment in respect of two cases,[79] which he heard separately, argued on similar points but with very different facts. The judge explored the various cases[80] which had previously dealt with the competing public and child's interests in relation to publicity after criminal conviction and applied them to the unique situation that arose in ASBOs. The main points in his decision were as follows:

- there is a conflict which must be balanced between the public interest in disclosure and the welfare of the young person who may require anonymity;

- the court should consider whether there are good reasons for naming the defendant;

- considerable weight should be given to the age of the offender and the potential damage of being identified as a criminal before adulthood;

- the court must have regard to the welfare of the child or young person;[81]

- the prospect of being named in court with accompanying disgrace is a powerful deterrent and the naming serves as a deterrent;

- the public has a particular interest in knowing who in their midst has been responsible for outrageous behaviour. This is not simply 'naming and shaming', which is, in any event, a relevant legitimate factor;

- disclosure of the identity of an individual may well make an order efficacious, as the community would be aware that an order has been made and report breaches;

- there is strong public interest in open justice;

- the fact that an appeal has been made may be a material consideration;

- whilst the court need not refer to every factor above, it should briefly summarise relevant factors and the competing interests before setting out its determination;

- there is no presumption against making an order but the strong public interest is a weighty factor against upholding any claim for anonymity; and

- in general, it is not appropriate or relevant to have regard to the effect on members of the defendant's family.

9.47 Of particular note is the concern that the judge had about the lack of a fully reasoned decision by the Crown Court in the *St Albans* case. On the facts of that case, he suggested that the extreme youth of the child (an 11-year-old) should have been expressly referred to and, further, the apparent improvement in the period after the order had been made required special consideration. For applicant authorities, this case makes it clear that it will be important to ensure that the court has a copy of the decision of Elias J and that the need for full reasons is explained. For defendant's representatives, it would seem that it is unlikely that an order can be obtained unless there are good reasons which outweigh the strong arguments of public interest and efficacy of enforcement. The latter may possibly be addressed by arguing for an order which allows the naming of the child but not disclosure of his or her address, or arguing that disclosure of the terms of the order to the wider community can be permitted but reporting in the

---

[79] *R (on the application of T) v St Albans Crown Court; Chief Constable of Surrey v JHG and DHG* [2002] EWHC Admin 1129, (unreported) 20 May 2002.

[80] In particular, *R v Winchester Crown Court, ex parte B* [1999] 1 WLR 788, [2000] 1 Cr App R 11.

[81] Children and Young Persons Act 1933, s 44.

newspapers should not. In practice, however, it is now unusual to be successful in obtaining an order if an ASBO is made. The one exception is if an appeal is to be lodged, in which case it is highly unlikely that the order will be refused. In this case, the applicant should ensure that the wording of the prohibition is such that the order will expire at the appeal hearing or if the appeal is withdrawn. This prevents the defendant from simply appealing and withdrawing the appeal to secure an order preventing publicity.

Stanley v London Borough of Brent

9.48   The issue of publicity using leaflets and its compliance with the European Convention has been considered by the court in *Stanley v London Borough of Brent*.[82] Brent council applied for ASBOs against a number of youths alleged to have conducted anti-social behaviour in their area. Interim orders were granted and before the main applications were heard the council prepared a draft leaflet which they wanted to distribute if the orders were granted. The leaflets contained images of the defendants taken on arrest, their names, ages and details of the orders issued against them. A district judge made orders and referred to convictions of three youths. The media publicised the orders and the local authority posted details on its community website. Leaflets were distributed by local authority and by police community safety officers. The local authority also published a report of the proceedings in its newsletter to its tenants. Three defendants sought judicial review of the decision to publicise. They sought a declaration that the publicity was unlawful and in breach of their right under Art 8 of the European Convention.

Defendants' case

9.49

(i)   Publicity interfered with their human rights under Art 8 (right to family life) and any interference should only be that necessary and proportionate to the legitimate aim being pursued.

(ii)   The council and police had failed to identify the legitimate ends which were sought to be achieved and therefore used unnecessary and disproportionate publicity.

(iii) It was not necessary to provide photographs or personal details of the individuals especially as they used photographs taken on arrest.

(iv)   The leaflets were distributed to an area wider than the individual exclusion order area.

(v)   A website was publicity to the world in general and not necessary.

(vi)   The newsletter did nothing to aid enforcement as whilst it included photographs, names and partial addresses, it did not spell out the terms of the orders.

(vii) The defendants also contended they should have had an opportunity to vet the material before it was publicised.

---

[82]   [2004] EWHC 2229 (Admin), (2005) EMLR 3, (2005) UKHRR 115, (2005) HLR 8, (2005) ACD 13, (2004) *The Times*, October 22.

Respondents' arguments

9.50

(i) Article 8 rights of the defendants were engaged but also those of the community and especially the victims of anti-social behaviour.

(ii) Further the community had rights under Art 10 (freedom to receive information), Art 11 (freedom of assembly – there was evidence that the public was afraid to go out in the area) and Art 17 (prohibition of the abuse of rights).

(iii) The state could be held to be under a positive obligation to protect the rights of the community so these had to be balanced against the defendants' rights.

(iv) The publicity was reasonable and proportionate and aided enforcement and legitimate aims including reassuring and informing the public.

Court of Appeal ruling

9.51

(i) The ASBOs were not limited to an exclusion zone but included general clauses without geographical constraint so publicity need not be limited to the exclusion area especially as most defendants lived outside the area.

(ii) The need for assistance in enforcement was an important consideration.

(iii) The use of arrest photographs was acceptable as the images were not secretly obtained or stored.

(iv) Publication by leaflet was neither unnecessary nor disproportionate as to be effective the orders needed to be better targeted than the media could provide.

(v) Use of photographs was necessary and proportionate for a specific public purpose. The identification of the defendants was critical both in relation to enforcement and as the impact of the orders on real people needed to demonstrated. Also the defendants could otherwise easily transfer their activities elsewhere where they were not known.

(vi) Cases may arise in which consultation as to publicity was a realistic possibility especially for those who are very young but not in this case.

(vii) A simple desire to name and shame would never be an appropriate justification for publicity, however, where the decision had been carefully taken some deference had to be accorded to those entrusted with that decision. The results of this process of consideration should, however, be carefully recorded.

(viii)If there had been significant criminal behaviour for years there was no reason why the publicity should not say so.

(ix) The council should have expressly considered whether the publicity was necessary and proportionate to the legitimate aims. Aims, however, did overlap and a resident who was informed about the orders to reassure may end up helping to enforce.

(x)   The website was informative and specifically invited assistance in enforcement. Only local residents would be likely to access the website.

(xi)   The newsletter was plainly intended to provide information and reassurance to all of the local authority's tenants. Many would not have seen the website or leaflet.

9.52   Every authority will therefore have to ensure that there is a designated officer in each case who takes the appropriate decision as to the type, form and extent of publicity. The decision-making process will have to be recorded. There is no reason why this process cannot be commenced from an early stage, however, it can only be concluded when the court has heard the evidence and made its findings of fact. The designated officer will have to record exactly why they have reached their decisions as to the publicity being given in that particular case. Caution should be taken so as to avoid any suggestion that the decisions are formulaic and any discretion is effectively fettered by policy. The Home Office has produced some guidance on the issue of publicity which is included at Appendix 6.

9.53   Lord Justice Kennedy also observed that it was perhaps now necessary to consider imposing time-limits on ASBO proceedings, and requiring that permission to bring an appeal to the Crown Court to prevent a different form of abuse by perpetrators of ASB. This is something which has been brought to the Home Office's attention previously, however, it has not led to any change despite several substantive amendments to the CDA 1998.

COSTS

Magistrates' court

9.54   Whether the proceedings have been in the magistrates' civil capacity or following a criminal conviction, there is power to award costs. Where the application is by way of complaint, the court may, in its discretion, make an order for costs to be paid by either party to the other, as it thinks just and reasonable.[83] The court may determine the quantum of the costs and in consideration of what is just and reasonable the court shall consider all relevant facts and circumstances of the case. It may be that costs follow the event, however, it may not be so.[84] Where, however, the defendant has successfully challenged an administrative decision made by police regulatory authority who were acting honestly, reasonably, properly and on grounds that appeared to be sound in the exercise of its public duty, the Court of Appeal has stated that the deciding court should consider particularly:

(a)   the financial prejudice to the particular complainant in the particular circumstances if an order for costs is not made in his or her favour; and

(b)   the need to encourage public authorities to make and stand by honest, reasonable and apparently sound administrative decisions made in the public interest without fear of exposure to undue financial prejudice if the decision is successfully challenged.[85]

It therefore follows that ASBO applications which are generally brought by local authorities or police will fall into the above. It seems likely that if the application was brought by a relevant authority based on ostensibly credible evidence without any indication of a lack of honesty or reasonableness then costs will not follow the event. Conversely if the defendant is able to show that the actions of the authority have been improper in bringing the proceedings or that they

---

[83]   MCA 1980, s 64(1).
[84]   *City of Bradford MDC v Booth* [2000] 164 JP 485, per Lord Justice Bingham at paras 24–25.
[85]   *City of Bradford MDC v Booth* [2000] 164 JP 485, per Lord Justice Bingham at para 26.

have in some way acted dishonestly then a costs order may be made against them. It is doubtful that this would be the case if the lay witnesses simply did not come up to proof or the court did not accept their evidence to the criminal standard of proof. In *Manchester City Council v Manchester Crown Court, Jerome Braithwaite, Zack Pinnock*[86] Mr Justice Burnton referred to the Bradford case where a local authority had properly brought proceedings but had withdrawn the final application due to the progress made by the defendants. The deputy district judge's order that the council pay the costs of the application was reversed as the decision to withdraw the applications were proper exercises of the local authority's discretion.

9.55 It should be noted that a legally aided defendant to a civil action in the magistrates' court is still liable to pay costs as the proceedings are deemed criminal proceedings for the purposes of such considerations.[87] If the court does make a costs order, it must specify the sum in the order.[88] The costs must be fixed by the court as part of the adjudication and may include fees for the attendance of witnesses and also legal costs but limited to those properly incurred. Any costs awarded in this way are enforceable as a civil debt.[89] Civil debts are enforced through the magistrates' court; however, a person may not be committed to prison in default unless it is proved to the satisfaction of the court that the defendant, having the means to pay the sums, has defaulted, refused or neglected to pay.[90]

9.56 On criminal conviction, the power to award costs is not clear. However, there is power for the criminal court to award prosecution costs. This does not, of course, include the costs of bringing the application for a post-conviction ASBO, which are not strictly those of the prosecution. The costs of providing the court with the additional information to pursue a post-conviction ASBO could be minimal, but could also be little different from the costs of a full application if the defendant contests the making of the order and requires evidence to be called on the issue of necessity or other alleged anti-social behaviour. The CPS is not a relevant authority for applications and, therefore, costs cannot be recovered as prosecution costs. This is another reason why it is most unlikely that the intention of Parliament was for post-conviction ASBO applications to be used in any but the most straightforward cases.

County court

9.57 In the county court, the power to award costs is governed by CPR Parts 43–48. The general principle is that the losing party should pay the costs of the winning party. However, similar difficulties in recovering any actual costs arise where the defendant is legally aided. If the main application has been allocated to the fast track, the costs will be assessed summarily at the end of the hearing. These applications are allocated to the multi-track and therefore the amount of costs will be assessed at a later date.

Crown Court

9.58 When hearing an appeal from the magistrates' court sitting in its civil capacity, the Crown Court has the power to make all orders which the magistrates' court could have made. This must, therefore, include costs orders. On criminal conviction in the Crown Court, the court has the same powers to award prosecution costs, as discussed above.

---

[86] [2009] EWHC 1866 (Admin).
[87] Criminal Defence Service (General) (No 2) Regulations 2001, SI 2001/1437, reg 3(2)(b).
[88] MCA 1980, s 64(2).
[89] MCA 1980, s 64(3).
[90] MCA 1980, s 96(1).

Enforcement of costs orders

9.59 In the county court, unpaid costs orders can be pursued by the court's enforcement provisions. These are contained in the CPR and include the following:

- *Warrant of execution (CPR Sch 2, CCR Ord 26)* – bailiffs seize and sell the goods of the defendant (known as 'the judgment debtor') to satisfy the costs order.[91]

- *Charging order (CPR Part 73)* – the costs order can be secured by registering a charge against any property or home of the judgment debtor. The cost order can be satisfied from the net sale proceeds when the house is sold.[92]

- *Third party debt orders (CPR Part 72)* – if the judgment debtor is owed money by a third party, the applicant (known as 'the judgment creditor') can obtain an order so that the third party pays their debt to the judgment debtor direct to the judgment creditor (or as much as is necessary to satisfy the order). It is most often used against a bank where the defendant has an account. The bank pays money from the defendant's bank account directly to the applicant body, to pay off the costs.[93]

- *Attachment of earnings order (CPR Sch 2, CCR Ord 27)* – if the judgment debtor is employed, the judgment creditor can obtain an order that the judgment debtor's employer should pay the judgment creditor directly from the judgment debtor's salary, until the costs order is satisfied.[94]

---

[91] Relevant forms: N42, N323 and N326.
[92] Relevant forms: N86, N87 and N379.
[93] Relevant forms: N85, N84 and N349.
[94] Relevant form: N337.

CHAPTER 10

TERMS AND DURATION OF AN ORDER

TERMS OF THE ORDER

10.1   If the conditions in s 1(1) of CDA 1998 are satisfied, the magistrates' court may make an order which prohibits the defendant from doing anything described in the order.[1] Whilst the applicant body will, as matter of good practice,[2] have filed with its application the prohibitions it seeks, the court may make some, all or entirely different prohibitions. In reality, however, it is very unusual for a court to make prohibitions which have not been applied for.

10.2   The terms of the order must be negative and prohibitory in nature. They may not be positive or mandatory.[3] This was re-stated in *Lonergan (Ashley) v (1) Lewes Crown Court (2) Brighton & Hove City Council & Secretary of State for the Home Department (Interested Party)*[4] where Lord Justice Maurice Kay stated that the statute required the order to be 'substantially and not just formally prohibitory'. However, the court found nothing objectionable in a term which stated that the defendant was forbidden from 'Being in any place other than … [three addresses] … or moving between those addresses, between the hours of 11.30 p.m. and 6.00 a.m.'. Lord Justice Maurice held that he was satisfied that a restraint upon leaving or travelling between specified premises between particular times met that test. As a matter of logical construction this is rather difficult to accept as essentially it requires a person to be in one of three places which would seem mandatory and, if not, certainly if only one place is specified that would seem so.

10.3   Clearly, the requirement for the term to be prohibitory should cover attempts by negative wording to impose a truly mandatory term (eg you must not fail to attend school). The terms which are sought should be carefully and properly drafted. The court has repeatedly made it clear that terms should be specifically drafted for each defendant and not applied formulaically to ASBOs.[5] There are far too many applications which include terms which are simply incapable of enforcement. For instance, one application contained the proposed prohibition that the defendant must not 'sing loudly' and another that he should not appear in public where more than two people were present. The former is imprecise and the latter would prevent the defendant catching a bus.

10.4   Another common problem is the use of inappropriate language in orders. The order is directed to the defendant, and the defendant's understanding and nature must be considered when drafting the order. In *R v P*,[6] the Court of Appeal was rightly critical of a term directed at the 16-year-old P, which read:

---

1   CDA 1998, s 1(4).
2   Mandatory for county court applications.
3   *R (on the application of M, a child) v Sheffield Magistrates' Court* [2004] EWHC 1830 (Admin), per Mr Justice Newman at [57]. The case is unreported at date of publication but available at: www.bailii.org/ew/cases/EWHC/Admin/2004/1830.html.
4   [2005] EWHC 457 (Admin), [2005] 2 All ER 362, [2005] 1 WLR 2570.
5   *R v Dean Boness & 10 ors* [2005] EWCA Crim 2395, 169 JP 621, (2005) *The Times*, October 24, [2005] All ER (D) 153 (Oct) para 29.
6   [2004] EWCA Crim 287, (2004) *The Times*, February 19.

'... either by himself or by instructing, encouraging or inciting any other person to engage in any conduct that tends to prevent the public from passing freely along the highway or enjoying free access to any place to which the public has access.'

10.5 Simple, plain language should be employed. Two terms rather than one overly complicated one are preferable. If necessary, professional help can be sought to formulate the terms of an order to ensure that the defendant can understand them. In a case brought by Bradford Metropolitan Borough Council, a psychologist specialising in Asperger's syndrome assisted in drafting the agreed terms of the order for a defendant with that condition and provided an additional pictorial representation to supplement the defendant's understanding of the court order. This was, however, an extreme example and, in the vast majority of cases, plain, simple, ordinary language will be sufficient. The current Home Office Guidance provides a very useful checklist of principles and practical points to be considered when drafting terms of an order. It states that the order should:[7]

- cover the range of anti-social acts committed by the defendant;

- be necessary to protect person(s) within a defined area from the anti-social acts of the defendant;

- be reasonable and proportionate;

- be realistic and practical;

- be clear, concise and easy to understand;

- be specific when referring to matters of time, if, for example, prohibiting the offender from being outside or in particular areas at certain times;

- be specific when referring to exclusion from an area, include street names and clear boundaries such as the side of the street included in the order (a map with identifiable street names should also be provided);

- be in terms which make it easy to determine and prosecute a breach;

- contain a prohibition on inciting/encouraging others to engage in anti-social behaviour; and

- protect all person who are in the area covered by the order from the behaviour (as well as specific individuals).

CRIMINAL OFFENCES AS TERMS

10.6 The above list reflects what, in practice, applicants have applied for and what the courts have granted in the years following the commencement of the CDA 1998. Of note in the current Home Office Guidance are the specific references and approval of terms which seek to prevent the defendant from doing something which is already a criminal offence. It was a common argument in the magistrates' court that any term preventing the defendant from committing an act which was already a criminal offence should not be made. It was thought that this point had been conclusively addressed by the Court of Appeal in *R v P*, however recent case-law has revived this issue and there is now an apparent inconsistency between various higher court

---

[7]   See current Home Office Guidance, reproduced in Appendix 3.

authorities. Whilst there is potentially some common ground which can be traced between the judgments, it remains the case that the law on whether criminal offences can be terms of an ASBO is in desperate need of clarification by means of either statutory amendment or by the House of Lords. Another conflicting Court of Appeal authority is not likely to assist unless it is made with the express intention of setting authoritative guidance. As there does not seem to be any pending judgment on the issue at the time of publication it is appropriate to set out the present conflicting case-law before offering views as to the possible correct approach.

10.7 The arguments against having criminal offences as terms of an order are based on two primary points. The first is that as each term has to be necessary and proportionate to prevent further anti-social behaviour by the defendant, how can it be necessary to impose a term the breach of which would already be punishable by criminal law? The second point is allied to the first and links with a hotly disputed assumption about breach and sentence (see chapter 13) and is: how can it be necessary to impose a term which when breached can only be punished by a sentence no more than that which would be imposed for the criminal offence?

10.8 The starting point for this review of the case-law is the Court of Appeal decision in *R v P*, where Mr Justice Henriques, giving the judgment of a court which included the Lord Chief Justice, Lord Woolf, said:

> 'Next, it is submitted that the prohibitions imposed by paragraphs 2 and 7 are redundant as they prohibit conduct which is already subject to a general prohibition by the Public Order Act 1986 and the Prevention of Crime Act 1953 respectively. In that regard we are by no means persuaded that the inclusion of such matters is to be actively discouraged. So far as more minor offences are concerned, we take the view that there is no harm in reminding offenders that certain matters do constitute criminal conduct, although we would only encourage the inclusion of comparatively minor criminal offences in the terms of such orders.' (at [30])

This was of course said in the context of a case where the defendant had committed offences of robbery from the person.

10.9 The next decision in time is that of *R v Hall*[8] which was decided in October 2004. The defendant was sentenced to 12 months for driving whilst disqualified and dangerous driving. The defendant had an appalling record of previous convictions for driving offences. The court also imposed an indefinite ASBO prohibiting the appellant from driving any mechanically propelled vehicle on a public road in the UK without being the holder of a valid driving licence and certificate of insurance. The defendant appealed against the making of the ASBO citing *R v P* and arguing that it was unnecessary to deal with the conduct which was the subject of the criminal offence. The defendant's representatives argued that the judge had only made the order so that in the event of him driving whilst disqualified he would be liable to 5 years instead of 6 months.

10.10 The court held that a principle emerging from *R v P* was that:

> 'There is nothing wrong in principle in making such an order when they are driving offences of such a regularity and type and in such an area that they do constitute anti social behaviour.'

And further that:

> 'In our view, as we say, it was not wrong in principle for the judge to make this order and the order followed the principles set out in P.'

---

8   [2004] EWCA Crim 2671, [2005] 1 Cr App Rep (S) 671, [2005] Crim LR 152, [2004] All ER (D) 377 (Nov).

They held that the judge was obliged to spell out to the defendant the consequences of breach. Presumably, therefore, they were of the view that the court had not made the order simply to increase the sentence, albeit that this was the practical effect. Finally, it should be noted that the court limited the duration of the order to 2 years.

10.11 The Court of Appeal in *R v Kirby*,[9] however, in January 2005 considered a defendant who had been sentenced to 20 months' imprisonment for dangerous driving and driving whilst disqualified and had an ASBO imposed on him for 10 years. This defendant also had numerous convictions for motoring offences. The court made an ASBO on the terms that he must not drive or allow himself to be carried in a motor vehicle which had been taken without consent of the owner or drive until the expiration of his period of disqualification. The judge in making the order specifically said when explaining the order that breach of the order actually increased the penalty to 5 years and counsel in the Court of Appeal made it clear that the judge did this with the purpose that if he committed those offences again the court would have a greater sentencing power.

10.12 The Court of Appeal (Maurice Kay LJ, David Clark J and Judge Saunders QC) said that in considering the making of a post-order conviction an ASBO should not be a normal part of the sentencing process, particularly in sentencing for offences which do not in themselves specifically involve intimidation, harassment or distress (given that in this case the defendant drove the wrong way around a roundabout and collided with an island in the centre of the road and then, driving on, crashed into railings it is hard to see how this would not cause distress!). It was an exceptional course to be taken in particular circumstances. The court held that there was nothing to justify the use of the power in this case which merely had the effect of increasing the potential penalty and in such a case was unwarranted in the absence of exceptional circumstances.

10.13 In the face of these seemingly conflicting decisions, the Court of Appeal in *R v Williams*[10] (Mance LJ, Elias J and Sir Charles Mantell) considered the appeal of a defendant who had a very long history of offending, including driving offences, but also mental health problems including diagnosis of a personality disorder. The defendant was sentenced to a community order for an offence of dangerous driving but did not attend and was sectioned under the Mental Health Act 1983. When those restrictions were lifted he caused criminal damage in the hospital and assaulted a member of staff. On sentencing for breach of the community order the judge sentenced him to a day already served and made an ASBO preventing him driving a motor vehicle in a public place until the date of the end of his driving disqualification. In so doing the judge made it clear that he was re-enforcing the driving ban and increasing the possible sentence.

10.14 The Court of Appeal noted that *Hall* had not been cited to the court in *Kirby* but followed the principle in the latter saying that there were not exceptional reasons to impose such an order increasing the sentence. No reasons were given for the preference but one can infer that the reasoning in *Hall* was doubted by this court.

10.15 *Williams* was decided on 28 June 2005 and the issue was again considered in *R v Morrison*[11] (Hughes J, Goldring J) which was decided on 26 July 2005. This was an appeal against sentence to the Court of Appeal and therefore there was only counsel for the appellant in attendance. The defendant had an appalling record of driving whilst disqualified (50 occasions) and other motoring matters. On the last occasion of this the magistrates' court disqualified him for 5 years and made an ASBO prohibiting him indefinitely from being in either of the front seats (either the passenger's or the driver's seat) of any motor vehicle anywhere in England and Wales. The

9   [2005] EWCA 1228, [2005] Crim LR 732.
10   [2005] EWCA Crim 1796, 169 JP 588, Crim LR 872, [2005] All ER (D) 03 (Oct).
11   [2005] EWCA Crim 2237.

defendant breached this term very soon after imposition when he drove whilst disqualified. On committal to the Crown Court for sentence the court imposed for the breach of the ASBO, 12 months' imprisonment. For all the summary offences, including driving while disqualified, no separate penalty was imposed. The defendant appealed arguing that since the breach of the ASBO in this case consisted of no more than driving while disqualified, it was wrong in principle to impose on the appellant the sentence of 12 months which is double the statutory maximum for driving while disqualified.

10.16 Before dealing with the above point Mr Justice Hughes considered the making of the ASBO itself and said:

> 'It seems to us, however, that an Anti-Social Behaviour Order to restrain driving while disqualified alone would (usually at least) be unlikely to be within the terms of the statute. Driving while disqualified is an offence, and rightly so, but it is not normally one which is likely to cause harassment, alarm or distress to persons not in the offender's household – at least unless some other offence was committed at the same time or perhaps there was an unusual public nuisance occasioned by the frequently repeated manner of the offender's driving.
>
> 12.   This Anti-Social Behaviour Order was, however, made against a man whose appalling driving record involved frequent offences of driving with excess alcohol. As to that, it seems to us that it could be that an Anti-Social Behaviour Order might be appropriate. This order was made on the occasion when the appellant had committed that offence as well as driving while disqualified. The terms of this order went beyond prohibiting driving while disqualified. Indeed, they went beyond prohibiting any criminal offence because the order prevented the appellant from travelling in the front passenger seat of any vehicle.'

10.17 With respect to the Court of Appeal it would seem to us that in fact there is more than a reasonable argument that if a member of the public knew that someone was driving whilst disqualified then this would or would be likely to cause harassment, alarm or distress given that this would mean that the person had been banned for some form of motoring offences in the past and was driving without insurance. The latter having the effect that full compensation (the Motor Insurers' Bureau (MIB) pays no property damage and maximum of £500,000 for personal injuries) may not be payable if he collided with their property or them.

10.18 In any event the Court of Appeal in *Morrison*, in considering the main issue of the appeal of what sentence should be imposed if an ASBO term which was also a criminal offence was breached, stated that in principle the sentence should not normally exceed the statutory maximum for the criminal offence but went on to consider the cases of *Williams*, *Hall* and *Kirby*. Mr Justice Hughes concluded:

> 'The maximum has been fixed by Parliament; it is fixed at six months. It is not open to this court to evade that maximum by imposing an Anti-Social Behaviour Order and then taking advantage of the maximum for breach of that order in the event that a further offence is committed. That, we are satisfied, follows from *R v Kirby* and *R v Williams*, and we are satisfied also that it follows from elementary principles.'

Mr Justice Hughes, however, continued to leave open an exceptional position saying:

> 'There may be exceptional cases in which it can properly be said that the vice of the breach of an ASBO, although it amounts to an offence, goes beyond that offence. We do not attempt to foresee circumstances in which that may occur but we have in mind, for example, repeated offences of criminal damage directed against a particular and perhaps vulnerable victim or group of victims.'

10.19 In neither *Morrison* nor *Williams* was an earlier case of *R v Curtis Braxton (aka Kamorudeen Owodunni)*[12] (Hooper LJ, Leveson J, Mettyear HHJ), which had been decided on 21 May 2005, cited (case of the same name in April 2003).[13] The omission is unfortunate but even more surprising when we later consider the case of *Boness* in which Lord Justice Hooper also sat. In *Braxton* the Court of Appeal had to consider the appeal from the breach of an ASBO the relevant term of which was not to use threatening, abusive, intimidating or insulting language. The defendant had been sentenced to 4 years' imprisonment concurrent on two breaches. The Court of Appeal (Tuckey LJ, Keith J, Sir Brian Smedley) held that a sentence close to the maximum should be reserved for persistent and prolonged breaches and reduced it to 2 years. The point of course is that the term was effectively a repetition of s 4 of the Public Order Act 1986 for which the maximum is 6 months. In the second appeal by *Braxton* in respect of further breaches, Mr Justice Leveson giving the judgment of the court (with which Lord Justice Hooper agreed) said as follows:

> '3. It is undeniable that this represents a serious infringement upon the liberty of the applicant, not only because it represents a restriction on his right of free movement, but also because breach constitutes a criminal offence punishable with a term of up to five years' imprisonment, which is greater than the maximum penalty which could be imposed for offences which might otherwise be reflected within the terms of the order. It is, however, a response by Parliament to the increasing concern about the impact on the public of antisocial behaviour in its many constituent forms. It follows that this concern must be reflected in the sentences which the court imposes for breach of the order.'

He then continued:

> '17. Unfortunately, the applicant still does not appear to understand the nature or effect of the order made against him. The anti-social behaviour order is specifically designed to protect the public from frequent and distressing repeated misbehaviour of the type which is the subject of this order, and the applicant was indeed committing a serious criminal offence, even entering the City of Birmingham within the confines set out within the map served upon him when the order was made. He acted in deliberate breach of that order not once but twice (which led to the four year term reduced to two years) and yet again twice more within weeks of his release from that prison sentence. He must understand that what he might consider as trivial in his case, because of the persistence of his conduct, is now treated seriously, specifically to protect the public. It is thus vital that he address this issue and his behaviour in public if he is to avoid further conflict with the law.'

10.20 Another case of the Court of Appeal which followed the reasoning in *Braxton* was *R v Tripp*[14] which was decided on 17 August 2005. The defendant was in breach of an ASBO which had prohibited him from 'using threatening, abusive or insulting words or behaviour or disorderly conduct within the hearing or sight of a person'. He had been drunk and verbally abusive to shelter project staff and was sentenced to 12 months' imprisonment. He appealed to the Court of Appeal. The single judge giving leave to appeal noted 'for being drunk and disorderly: a year's imprisonment ... Can this be right?'. The Court of Appeal gave this short shrift:

> '[7] The short answer to that question, as a matter of law is of course yes. Where an anti-social behaviour order has been made and is breached, the breach consisting of conduct which is itself a criminal offence, the potential sentence may be far longer than the maximum for that basic offence.

> [8] As Leveson J remarked when giving the judgment of *R v Braxton* [2004] EWCA Crim 1374, [2005] 1 Cr App Rep (S) 167, to which we have been helpfully referred, the anti-social behaviour order

---

[12]   [2004] EWCA Crim 1374.
[13]   [2003] EWCA Crim 1037.
[14]   [2005] EWCA Crim 2253.

provisions were a response by Parliament to increasing concerns about the impact on the public of anti-social behaviour in its many forms. That concern must therefore be reflected by the courts in the sentences which it imposes for breaches.'

BONESS

10.21 Very few cases seem to have created as many problems as they have solved, however *R v Boness and 10 others* is definitely one of them. Unfortunately, to some extent, it has become inaccurately summarised and relied on for incorrect submissions. A careful consideration is therefore essential for practitioners as the judgment does not say that terms which are criminal offences cannot be made only that they should be made when necessary.

10.22 There were ten defendants in the case and the behaviour was wide ranging, from football hooligans to burglars. In each of the cases there were ASBOs imposed post conviction and the court was provided with no wider allegations of anti-social behaviour or community impact statements. The Court of Appeal (Hooper LJ, Evans J, Pitchers J) in hearing the appeals firstly decided to quash the majority of the ASBOs in light of the sentences and also gave detailed judgment on many aspects of ASBOs including the terms. As the ASBOs were quashed it could be said that the aspects of the judgment on the terms of the order is only per curiam, however this would be to ignore the way in which subsequent appellate courts have considered the judgment.

10.23 On the issue above of whether a criminal offence can be included as a term of an ASBO, *Boness* has been generally taken to be authority that it cannot. On closer reading of the actual judgment this is not entirely correct. Lord Justice Hooper actually said as follows:

'31. It follows from the requirement that the order must be necessary to protect persons from further anti-social acts by him, that the court should not impose an order which prohibits an offender from committing a specified criminal offence if the sentence which could be passed following conviction for the offence should be a sufficient deterrent. If following conviction for the offence the offender would be liable to imprisonment then an ASBO would add nothing other than to increase the sentence if the sentence for the offence is less than 5 years' imprisonment. But if the offender is not going to be deterred from committing the offence by a sentence of imprisonment for that offence, the ASBO is not likely (it may be thought) further to deter and is therefore not necessary. In *P*, Henriques J said (paragraph 30):

"Next, it is submitted that [two of] the prohibitions ... are redundant as they prohibit conduct which is already subject to a general prohibition by the Public Order Act 1986 and the Prevention of Crime Act 1953 respectively. In that regard we are by no means persuaded that the inclusion of such matters is to be actively discouraged. So far as more minor offences are concerned, we take the view that there is no harm in reminding offenders that certain matters do constitute criminal conduct, although we would only encourage the inclusion of comparatively minor criminal offences in the terms of such orders."

32. We would only make one comment on this passage. The test for making an order is not whether the offender needs reminding that certain matters do constitute criminal conduct, but whether it is necessary.

33. It has been held, rightly in our view, that an ASBO should not be used merely to increase the sentence of imprisonment which an offender is liable to receive.'

10.24 In so saying the Court of Appeal has not said that criminal offences cannot be included as terms; only that it should be necessary to do so. As a bald statement this must be correct as it is the statutory wording. It must also be correct that if the only purpose of imposing the term was to make a person liable to greater sentence then this would not be necessary. However, this cannot then be equated with *Boness* being an authority that none should ever be made. If the sentence is less than would deter the defendant from committing the act but the court considered that the increased sentence on breach of an ASBO would and therefore would protect relevant persons, why should it not be made?

10.25 The judgment in *Boness* does not actually exclude ever making terms which are criminal offences and it is submitted that there are several reasons why this must be correct. First, the powerful judgment (the Lord Chief Justice being in agreement) in *R v P* which is cited with approval (but qualification) in *Boness*. Secondly, if no term which is a criminal offence could be made then the fact that the court in *Boness* approved a general anti-social behaviour term, which is of course an offence under s 5 of the Public Order Act 1986 (POA 1986) and carries only 6 months' imprisonment, would make no sense. Thirdly, to do so would be to ignore all the impact of anti-social behaviour and the intention of Parliament in making the legislation. There is also the point that in passing the CDA 1998 and all its amendments Parliament can be said to have shown its intention for the greater punishment of people who continue to cause harassment, alarm or distress to the community.

10.26 The defendant who commits such an act, which is also a criminal offence, is not in the same position as someone who has an order preventing it. If the court has before it a defendant who has repeatedly committed acts causing harassment, alarm or distress why should it not make a term of an ASBO breach of which makes it punishable by more than the sentence? Consider the position of a person who breaches an anti-social behaviour injunction or non-molestation order. The maximum sentence is 2 years' imprisonment which is almost always more than would be imposed for a criminal act which forms the breach, e g harassment pursuant to s 4 of the POA 1986. There is, however, abundant case-law giving such sentences for which part of the rationale is that the defendant has ignored the warning and order of the court not to repeat such conduct. It might be said that this is the same position as a defendant who has such a term imposed in an ASBO is in breach. The defendant appearing in breach of the ASBO does not appear in a vacuum. The breach may also be a criminal act but the breach is of an order of the court given to him personally with the gravest of warnings. The defendant knows the possible consequences and has been differentiated from other members of the public who may commit that act by reason of his past conduct. Therefore, provided the court makes terms which are also criminal acts only in those cases where the conduct is repeated, causes harassment, alarm or distress and is necessary to protect the community, why should the sentence for breach not exceed that for the actual offence? This point was made by the Court of Appeal in *R v Cyril Stevens*[15] where Mr Justice Burton held:

> ' . . . the anti-social behaviour order was made in order to stop persistent low level offending . . . The gravamen of this offence is not simply what the appellant did on this occasion, but his flagrant breaches of court orders which are always regarded as serious.' [paragraph 7]

R V LAMB

10.27 A more recent judgment of the Court of Appeal is that in *R v Lamb*[16] (Hallet LJ, Leveson J and Judge Patience QC) which was decided on 10 November 2005 when they considered the issue of whether a sentence of imprisonment for breach of an ASBO could exceed the maximum for the specific criminal offence. Lady Justice Hallet cited the above passage from *Braxton* (see **10.19**) and then held:

> '[11] … The justification for imposing punishment was and can only have been based on the appellant's persistent and deliberate failures to comply with the order of the court. That justification is perfectly sufficient …

---

[15] [2007] EWCA Crim 1128.
[16] [2005] EWCA Crim 2487, [2005] All ER (D) 132 (Nov), (2005) *The Times*, December 1.

[...]

[16]   We are conscious that in *Morrison* [2005] EWCA Crim 2237, this Court held that if the breach of an ASBO is no more than the commission of an offence for which the maximum penalty is prescribed by statute, it is normally wrong in principle to pass a sentence for a breach calculated by reference to the maximum for breach of an ASBO. With respect, that appears to ignore the impact of anti-social behaviour on the wider public which was the purpose of the legislation in the first place; it also means that anti-social behaviour short of a criminal offence could be more heavily punished than anti-social behaviour that coincidentally was also a criminal offence. We thus prefer the contrary approach of this Court in *Tripp* [2005] EWCA Crim 2253 which itself reflects *Braxton*.'

R V STEVENS[17]

10.28 The conflict between *Morrison* and *Lamb* has now effectively been resolved in the very recent case of *R v Stevens*[18] (Sir Igor Judge (President QB), Dobbs J, Sir Douglas Brown). The defendant had been made the subject of an ASBO which prohibited him from being drunk in a public place, and defecating or urinating in a public place other than a public toilet. He had many previous convictions for alcohol-related offences and theft before the making of the ASBO. The defendant breached that order admitting that he was drunk in the street and had urinated. The sentencing judge deferred sentence to allow him to rehabilitate but said that he would have otherwise imposed a 9-month sentence. Three days later the defendant stole a bottle of whisky and the judge imposed 9 months for the original breach and 3 months consecutive for theft. The defendant appealed, relying on *Morrison*, arguing that the criminal offence carried only a fine.

10.29 The Court of Appeal held that any sentence for breach of the ASBO should be commensurate to the breach. Therefore, if the conduct constituting the breach was also a distinct criminal offence, and the offence had carried a statutory maximum sentence, that was a feature to be borne in mind in the interests of proportionality. However, the court's power was not limited to the statutory maximum sentence that the offence that gave rise to the breach of the ASBO carried with it. Breach of an ASBO was an offence in its own right, created by Parliament, and which attracted a statutory maximum sentence of 5 years' imprisonment. It was said to be obvious that when the court was passing sentence for breach of an ASBO it was sentencing for the breach and not the basic offence which made up the factual basis. The other authorities on this issue had wholly undermined the decision in *Morrison*, which should not be followed. The Court of Appeal expressly approved the decisions in *Lamb* and *Braxton*. An ASBO should not, however, be imposed as a device to circumvent maximum penalties that may be considered to have been too modest. The Court of Appeal approved *Boness* insofar as the test to be applied when imposing any term was whether it was necessary.

10.30 In *Hills v Chief Constable of Essex* the defendant had brandished knives in a play area and threatened to stab a pupil whilst holding a penknife up to him. Amongst the terms made where that he was prohibited from carrying any knife or bladed article in public. The defendant argued that the term was already prohibited by the criminal law. Mr Justice Keith held that

'...there is no absolute bar on anti-social behaviour orders containing terms which prohibit specific acts which would have amounted to a criminal offence. It all depends on whether the particular prohibition is really necessary to protect members of the public from anti-social behaviour by the person who is the subject of the order.'

The judge went on to cite *R v Stevens* (above) as an example of this, noting that the court did not doubt that an anti-social behaviour could contain prohibitions of that kind. In this case whilst

---

[17]   [2006] All ER (D) 23 (Feb); decided on 2 February 2006, Lawtel Document No. AC9300667.
[18]   2 February 2006, Lawtel Document No. AC9300667.

the term included offences the criminal offence only applied to a penknife if the blade was more than 3 inches long. Here the defendant had been found to threaten with one and so the term was necessary. He did have the protection of the 'reasonable excuse' defence in any event.

DISCUSSION

10.31 Where possible, it is good practice to impose terms which are not criminal acts in themselves, however, in some cases the conduct is so often repeated that it is the only sensible term. It seems to the authors that if there is necessity to make a term which is also a criminal offence there is no absolute prohibition against doing so. *Boness* does not say that an order which includes such a term cannot be made, only that it should not be unless it is necessary to do so and not if the only purpose is merely to increase the sentence. The final point is of course covered by the fact that the term should not be made if it was not necessary. *Boness* did not cite or consider *Morrison*, *Tripp* or *Braxton* probably because that was not an issue which it was deciding. That was perhaps unfortunate and the shortcomings of the wider view of *Boness* are highlighted in *Lamb*, particularly in the passages above. It should be noted in the first appeal of *Braxton* that Hooper LJ delivered a concurring judgment. It seems to us that following the case of *Stevens* the decision in *Williams* has to be ignored. In addition, for the reasons given in *Lamb* and the additional matters which have been discussed above, it would seem to the authors that the rationale for not imposing sentences greater than the criminal statute was never a valid one. We would suggest that where conduct is repeated then the court can, as appropriate, make a term which is a criminal offence even if the punishment for breach would be greater than for the crime itself. Following the decisions in *Lamb*, and now *Stevens*, it would seem that on sentence the court can properly impose a sentence greater than that for the criminal offence itself. It should of course be noted the 'general prohibition' is a prohibition routinely imposed[19] and is a criminal offence in itself. The use of the term was approved in *Boness* and in fact the current Home Office Guidance makes it plain that there is no difficulty in making such a prohibition provided it is detailed and clear enough (see **10.51** below). We would, however, suggest that wherever possible the terms should not simply be criminal offences and attempts are made to formulate terms which prohibit the actions before the crime, for instance the carrying of spray cans or paint to prevent graffiti being written as advocated in *Boness*. Sometimes, however, this is not feasible and where the conduct is persistent, causes harassment, alarm or distress, and it is necessary to protect the community, the applicant should seek terms which are also minor criminal offences.

IMPROPER TERMS

10.32 In a number of cases appellate courts have considered terms which have imposed in the lower courts and provided some guidance as to what can be a term and what should not. In *R v McGrath*[20] the terms of the ASBO prohibited M from entering any car park in three specified counties; trespassing on any land belonging to any person whether legal or natural within those three counties; and having in his possession in any public place any tool or implement which could be used for the purpose of breaking into motor vehicles.

10.33 The court held that there was nothing to prevent a term being made which prohibited acts which were not anti-social in themselves (indeed this is what *Boness* suggests most terms should be). The terms should, however, be commensurate with the risk to be guarded against and hence

---

[19]   Although see contrary views in *R v Pedder* [2005] EWCA Crim 3163, 26 October 2005.
[20]   [2005] EWCA Crim 353, [2005] 2 Cr App Rep (S) 525, [2005] NLJ 826, [2005] All ER (D) 81 (May).

not disproportionate. What was proportionate must depend on the facts of each case, having regard both to the restrictions to be imposed on the offender and the risk against which the ASBO is seeking to protect the public.

10.34 The term of not entering car parks was too wide and unjustifiably draconian as it prevented the defendant being a passenger in a car in any supermarket car park (or presumably getting to the supermarket as you would have to cross the car park). The term relating to trespass was even worse as if he took a wrong turn he would be at risk of a 5-year prison term. The fact that the prosecutor had discretion to prosecute was not the correct approach. He should not be at the discretion of a prosecutor in those circumstances. Finally, the term about tools, etc was too wide as 'any tool or implement' was impossible to ascertain and where it stated 'for the purpose of breaking into motor vehicles' this was an overlap with the offence of going equipped.

10.35 Other terms which were considered to be improper in *Boness* included:

(i)   'doing anything which may cause damage' – too wide and includes scuffing his own shoes;

(ii)   'wearing, having with you anything which covers or could be used to cover the face or part of the face ...' – too wide as carrying a newspaper would put them in breach;

(iii)   'having any item with you in public which could be used in the commission of a burglary or theft of or from vehicle ...' – too wide and included items such as credit cards, gloves, etc;

(iv)   'having possession of any article in public ... that could be used as a weapon. This will include glass bottles, drinking bottles and tools' – too wide and prevents the person having a drink in a public bar.

10.36 Terms that were approved in principle in *Boness* included:

(i)   remaining on any shop, commercial or hospital premises if asked to leave by staff or entering any premises from which he had been barred from entry;

(ii)   touching or entering any unattended vehicle without the express permission of the owner;

(iii)   congregating in groups of people in a manner causing or likely to cause any person to fear for their safety.

In the context of inappropriate use of emergency services, one term which was upheld on case stated by the administrative court[21] prevented the defendant from:

> 'Calling NHS Direct or the Emergency services for medical advice or aid, or encouraging by her actions or reports anyone else to do so on her behalf, including staff at NHS Direct, save when there is a genuine need for those services and assistance.'

10.37 In *R v Harriman*[22] the defendant was convicted of offences of theft and battery against his ex-partner. He had numerous previous convictions by the age of conviction at 23 including burglary, criminal damage and disorderly behaviour. The sentencing order made an ASBO preventing him from entering an area within the ring road of Leicester city centre and that he should not co-habit with any woman without first disclosing to her the list of his previous convictions. Both terms were to last until further order.

---

[21]   *R (on the application of Delaney) v Calderdale Magistrates' Court*, (unreported) 25 August 2009, His Honour Judge Kay QC sitting as a High Court Judge of the administrative court at Leeds.

[22]   [2007] EWCA Crim 1185.

10.38 Mrs Justice Rafferty held that the terms were too wide. The former as to scope and the latter that he would be compelled to disclose his convictions to any woman he lived with regardless of whether he was in a relationship with her and that they would require disclosure of convictions wholly different from those which the court was concerned with at sentence. The court quashed the terms but imposed an exclusion zone of 200 yards about his ex-partner's home.

Specific terms and considerations

10.39 It is suggested that, when seeking to draft orders, the general prohibition from anti-social behaviour and the prohibition from approaching or harassing named lay witnesses who provided statements for the application are included as a matter of course. Thereafter, the prohibitions sought should reflect the incidents which have been alleged and proved. This could mean simple prohibitions against abusive or threatening language, but may also prevent the defendant from entering an area where the incidents have occurred. A common prohibition is to prevent a defendant from returning to an estate from which he has been evicted or a young person to a school from which he has been permanently excluded.

Exclusion zones

10.40 Exclusion zones are now popular and in regular use. Commonly, they exclude a defendant from a defined zone, giving relief to specific communities. They are easy to prosecute, as it is not necessary to prove that the defendant was acting in an anti-social manner. Such schemes were pioneered in Liverpool, where minors were banned from named streets. In Kirklees, a defendant had been banned from a named street despite the fact that family members resided there. The use of exclusion zones is often an important part of the process to curb anti-social behaviour. By denying the defendant access to the places where he or she has displayed anti-social behaviour in the past, the relevant persons in that area are being afforded a measure of direct protection. Exclusion zones will not always be appropriate but, where the acts are localised, then, even if the defendant lives in that area, the courts are willing to consider and make orders. In the multiple 'Little London' ASBOs, made in Leeds magistrates' court, an exclusion zone was made against all the defendants and often provided the defendants with a single route in and out of the area from their homes. The divisional court and the Court of Appeal did not comment adversely on these exclusions and the final orders that were made almost always included that exclusion zone.

10.41 If an exclusion zone is to be sought, then certain practical matters should be attended to by the applicant authority. First, the court should be provided with a clear, coloured map of the area from which the applicant seeks to exclude the defendant. If possible, the authority should indicate the size of the area and mark where the incidents of anti-social behaviour are alleged to have occurred. The map should also indicate the defendant's home (if within the area) and other key locations, eg witnesses' homes (assuming that the addresses were known to the defendant). The maps to be used with the order should, however, not be marked, save with the exclusion area being clearly marked by a coloured outline. The map should be marked with the defendant's name and its purpose, ie 'map to show exclusion area for "X"'. The term prohibiting entry to the exclusion zone should provide the defendant (where appropriate) with exceptions when attending pre-arranged medical appointments, schools, solicitors and when accompanied by probation or YOT workers.

Non-association

10.42 There is a difference between a term which requires a defendant not to associate generally in groups of x or more and a term which prevents him associating (generally in public places) with named individuals who also display anti-social behaviour when with the defendant. General terms of non-association with groups of set numbers are rather difficult to impose without raising issues of proportionality. A term which just prevents the defendant being in a group with more than a set number of people means that they cannot go to sporting events, queue up in a supermarket or go to church. It is unlikely that sufficient exceptions can be made that do not make the term unworkable, however there are some local authorities who have had success with them. In *Boness* a term preventing the defendant from 'congregating in groups of people in a manner causing or likely to cause any person to fear for their safety or congregating in groups of 6 or more in an outdoor public place' was said to be justified as regards the first part of the term but the second part of the term was not.

10.43 The use of terms preventing a defendant associating with specified individuals has rapidly increased in recent years and, indeed, where actions against youths are concerned, it is now commonplace to have such a term included in the application. The obvious purpose is to keep defendants away from others with whom they are liable to commit anti-social behaviour. The equally clear balance to be applied is that it prevents a person from having free choice over his or her associates or friends. One way to limit the restriction posed by this term is to limit the non-association requirement to public places, ie the defendant may associate with whom they like, provided it is not in public (or a place to which the public have access). This allows a measure of conformity with the ECHR in that there is no general right of freedom to associate with others protected by the Convention – only where the association is for political or demonstration ends – see *Anderson v UK*.[23] If a non-association clause is sought, then it is important to ensure that only those persons against whom there is evidence of anti-social behaviour when together with the defendant are included in the list of names. Often, this is not adhered to and there is little, if any, evidence to link the defendant to any of the persons named.

10.44 In *Hills v Chief Constable of Essex*[24] the court was asked to consider whether it was lawful to make a term preventing the defendant from associating with a person against whom there was no reciprocal order or term. The defendant had argued that the term went much further than that necessary to protect the public and could result in a breach through no fault of the defendant, eg if the other party came up to him in the street and insisted on walking with him. In this case the other party had been present when a number of the incidents had occurred and had been the subject of an interim order. Due to improvement in her behaviour no final order was argued for.

10.45 Mr Justice Keith noted that the report from the working group led by Thomas LJ had considered a non-association clause was a reasonable one. Further that in the situation put forward by the defendant he would have a reasonable excuse for being in her company.

10.46 In *N v DPP*[25] the Crown Court imposed a term which prevented the defendant from 'congregating in groups of 3 or more in a public place other than when with adults over 21 years'. The divisional court noted the guidance on this term in *Boness* above and that the term would put the defendant in breach when at a sporting event. They concluded that it was insufficient protection for the defendant to be able to assert 'reasonable excuse' and amended the term to effectively mirror that in *Boness*.

---

23   [1998] EHRLR 218.
24   [1998] EHRLR 218.
25   [2007] EWHC 833 (Admin).

Curfew

10.47 Curfews and prohibitions on drinking in public places can all be used as terms. The use of curfews was challenged in *Lonergan*[26] (see **10.2**). Having decided that the curfew term was prohibitory and not mandatory the court considered whether the term was a penalty and therefore improper. The court concluded that the proper consideration of whether a term was a penalty was to consider the purpose of its imposition. Whilst, when imposed as a sentence in criminal proceedings it was intended to punish as a prohibition in an ASBO its purpose was preventative and protective. Therefore the court concluded that there was nothing legally objectionable in the inclusion of a curfew provision if it was necessary for the protection of relevant persons. The court did go on to say, however:

> 'Having said that I do think that it behoves magistrates' courts to consider carefully the need for and duration of a curfew provision when making an ASBO. Just because the ASBO must run for a minimum of two years it does not follow that each and every prohibition within a particular order must endure for the life of the order. A curfew for two years in the life of a teenager is a very considerable restriction of freedom. It may be necessary but in many cases I consider it likely that either the period of curfew could properly be set at less than the full life of the order or that, in the light of behavioural progress, an application to vary the curfew under section 1(8) might well succeed.'

10.48 The above raises a point of interest, namely whether the court can make terms which last for less than the full term of the order. Clearly Lord Justice Kay envisaged that this could be done, however this was doubted by the Lord Chief Justice Thomas' working group which followed the decision and produced some Guidance on ASBOs to the courts. The reason for this is quite simply the wording of the CDA 1998 which provides that an order shall have effect for not less than 2 years. In *Boness*,[27] however, Lord Justice Hooper observed, albeit per curiam, that he considered *Lonergan* to be correctly decided on this point.

(Further examples of ASBO terms can be found on the Crime Reduction website, the details of which can be found in Appendix 5.)[28]

Clothing

10.49 In *R (on the application of B) v Greenwich Magistrates' Court v The Commissioner of Police of the Metropolis*[29] the district judge made an order that the defendant was prohibited from:

> '. . .wearing any article of clothing with an attached hood in any public place in the London Borough of Greenwich, whether the hood is up or down.'

The district judge in his reasons noted that the defendant was part of a gang which gathered together in the street, railway stations, bus stops and other locations where members intimidated members of the public through language and gestures and wore hooded tops to help conceal their identity. He concluded that he was 'satisfied that a prohibition would reduce the swagger, menace and fear of anti-social behaviour'. The defendant appealed by way of judicial review contending that the condition was unreasonable in that its purpose and effect was not to reduce anti-social behaviour but to prohibit or restrict a particular appearance or style of clothing the claimant would wish to wear. Further that the claimant's freedom of expression under article 10 was infringed.

---

[26]   [2005] EWHC 457 (Admin), [2005] 2 All ER 362, [2005] 1 WLR 2570.
[27]   [2005] EWCA Crim 2395, 169 JP 621, (2005) *The Times*, October 24, [2005] All ER (D) 153 (Oct).
[28]   See current Home Office Guidance, reproduced in Appendix 3.
[29]   [2008] EWHC 2882 (Admin).

10.50 Mr Justice Mitting with Lord Justice Latham held that the imposition was to reduce swagger, menace and fear and could do so by either prohibiting the wearing of what appeared to be part of a gang uniform and secondly by diminishing the confidence of those who wear the uniform that they may escape the identification by wearing and raising the hood. It was clear on the district judge's findings that the claimant wore the hooded tops deliberately for both of those purposes. The prohibition satisfied the tests of clarity, necessity and proportionality identified in *Boness*. Further that the judge had rightly considered that merely prohibiting the raising of the hood would be an ineffective prohibition.

GENERAL PROHIBITION AS TO ANTI-SOCIAL BEHAVIOUR

10.51 A consequence of the decision in *R v Boness* there has been an argument about whether a general term to prevent the defendant from engaging in anti-social behaviour offends a general principle that an order should not mirror a criminal offence unless 'necessary'. As discussed above it is not thought that the court in *Boness* could have intended such a conclusion given that it would contradict the direct wording of the statute and has been made and upheld in numerous cases which have followed *Boness*. There are however limits to the 'generality' of the term which can be imposed.

10.52 In *CPS v T*[30] the divisional court was asked, in a situation where on breach the court had held that the term was too vague to be enforced, to consider the validity of a term imposed by the district judge which held that the defendant must not:

'Act in an anti-social manner in the City of Manchester.'

10.53 Lord Justice Richards held that the above term would clearly have offended the principles in *R v Boness*. The term as made did not even include the explanatory words contained in the statutory definition, namely the words 'that is to say in a manner that caused or was likely to cause harassment, alarm or distress to one or more persons not of the same household as himself'. The term therefore lacked the essential element of clarity as to what the defendant was and was not permitted to do particularly as he was 13 years old. He would probably not even know the ambit of the City of Manchester. The court considered that such a wide provision as this without further definition or limitation should never be included in an ASBO. It should be noted that the court was not concerned that the term might be in breach of the restriction against criminal offences as terms, only as to its clarity.

10.54 In *CPS v T* the court noted with approval the Home Office Guidance on the proper forms of prohibitions. That Guidance has now been amended and on the issue of a general term states an order:

'may include a general condition prohibiting behaviour which is likely to cause harassment, alarm and distress, but where this is done there must be further clarification of what type of behaviour is prohibited.'

10.55 In *R (on the application of Rabess) v The Commissioner of Police for the Metropolis*[31] the defendant and his partner were the subject of an application for an ASBO based on their having been in a volatile and abusive relationship which gave rise to a large number of incidents of violence and abuse which required numerous attendances by the police and often spilt out into the public streets at night. The district judge imposed terms to prevent the defendant 'using abusive, offensive, threatening or intimidating language or behaviour; threatening violence

---

30 [2006] EWHC 728 (Admin).
31 [2007] EWHC 208 (Admin).

towards each other or other residents; unlawfully damaging property...'. The defendant argued that the first 2 of these mirrored public order offences under ss 4 and 5 of the Public Order Act 1986 and therefore the terms should not be imposed especially as the punishment for breach of an ASBO would be more severe than the statutory maximum for the criminal offence.

10.56 It was argued by the applicant authority that offences under ss 4 and 5 could not take place within a dwelling (which it is submitted is a good reason in many cases for imposing the term in an ASBO) but moreover that:

> '...this prohibits behaviour which falls short of an offence under section 4 because proof of intent is not necessary. The absence of this element is intended to protect third parties, irrespective of the effect on the other person [the partner]... The same principles apply to section 5 and indeed to any offence of assault. It means, effect, that in order to successfully prosecute, the police would need the co-operation of [the partner]...

> ...The effect of the prohibition is that a member of the public who is affected and is distress or alarmed would be able to urge the police to something about it – a vehicle enabling something to be done about the behaviour which falls short of a criminal offence thus is outwith the principle in *Boness*. Indeed, dealing in particular with the section 5 offence, that only carries a fine, and it is arguable that this is not a sufficient deterrent when one considers the necessary balancing act and the necessity for such a prohibition.'

10.57 Mrs Justice Dobbs held that:

> 'It was clear from the authorities that the mere fact that the terms may include behaviour which amounts to a criminal offence is no bar to the prohibition being made, although caution must be exercised. One has to look at the facts of each individual case to see what is appropriate.'

10.58 She also held that the whilst the terms here mirrored the criminal law to a certain extent, as argued by the applicant authority above, they did not fully mirror the law and had added value. The criminal law would not be an adequate substitute. However, in the as yet unreported case of *Heron v Plymouth City Council*[32] the Court of Appeal seems to have rejected a term in the form of the general prohibition on the grounds that it was '... too broad and of no real efficacy'. The judgment was however extempore and has not been fully reported as of publication. It may be that the term was insufficiently precise or focused on the actual anti-social behaviour.

Drunkenness

10.59 In *R v Blackwell*[33] the defendant pleaded guilty to an offence of harassment and was sentenced to a rehabilitation order and an ASBO which prevented him from 'abusing, threatening or acting in such a manner as to cause distress to any person; consuming, being under the influence of or in possession of any intoxicating liquor, drug or solvent in a public place and entering any premises [listed in the order]'.

10.60 The defendant had a long history of alcohol dependence and depressive mood disorder. It was argued on appeal that the terms of the order relating to alcohol were too wide, punishing conduct which need not lead to ASB, eg simple possession of alcohol in a public place and that 'under the influence of alcohol' was uncertain and difficult to enforce.

10.61 Mr Justice Penry-Davey considered that the terms could be said to be too wide but that in general a term was necessary and was amended to read 'Not to be in a state of drunkenness in any public place in England and Wales'.

---

[32] [2009] All ER (D) 149 (Nov).
[33] [2006] EWCA Crim 1671.

PRACTICAL CONSIDERATIONS FOR APPLICANTS

10.62 Deciding suitable terms of the order is a crucial element of court preparation for applicant authorities. It is good practice to consult with witnesses and victims about the proposed terms, as it is for their benefit that the order is being sought.

10.63 Applicants should give thought to the geographical terms of the order, particularly since it is now possible for an ASBO to cover all of England and Wales.[34] Clearly, the wider the geographical area sought in the application for an ASBO, the more compelling the evidence will need to be to secure the term. Where there is reason to believe that the defendant may move, or has already moved, a wider geographical area will be more easily justified. Evidence of an itinerant lifestyle, a possible move by the defendant, or evidence showing a wide geographical spread of anti-social behaviour can be used to support such an order. The Home Office Guidance states that an applicant does not have to prove that the conduct *will* occur elsewhere, only that it is likely to. It goes on to say that the more serious the behaviour, the more likely it will be that the court will grant a geographically wide order.[35] It is submitted that this must be correct as, having shown that an order is necessary to protect relevant persons from further anti-social behaviour, the likelihood of further acts has been established. It would seem a misguided argument to assert that a narrow geographical area should be imposed where an exclusion order is made, as, inevitably, there will be a displacement of the defendant into uncertain areas. The wider geographical area will be necessary to protect the relevant persons from any future anti-social behaviour. This argument is to be contrasted with that of the need for an exclusion zone which should be limited to the areas where the incidents have occurred *and* the immediate areas surrounding it, where ready displacement and continuation of the problems giving rise to the application may occur.

10.64 Specific terms, tailor-made for the situation in hand, are essential; whilst many terms are commonly used they are no substitute for individualisation. As highlighted in *Boness*, terms which are only criminal are to be avoided where possible, however, there are clearly many situations where such a term is necessary and should be made.

PRACTICAL CONSIDERATIONS FOR DEFENDANTS

Grounds for challenging the order

10.65 The defendant will wish to ensure that the least possible interference is caused by the terms of the ASBO. General terms not to cause harassment, alarm or distress are the least intrusive. A defendant can safeguard his or her interest by checking that the current Home Office Guidance has been adhered to, namely:

- Are the terms (sufficiently) specific?

- Are they discriminatory to the defendant in any way?

- Are they justifiable interferences with the defendant's human rights?

- Are the terms necessary, reasonable and/or proportionate in the light of the evidence against the defendant?

---

[34] CDA 1998, s 1B(6), as amended by the PRA 2002, with effect from 2 December 2002. See the current Home Office Guidance, reproduced in Appendix 3.

[35] See Appendix 3.

- If the term sought is a criminal one, is it necessary given the conduct alleged?

- Is the geographical area commensurate with the seriousness of the alleged anti-social behaviour and/or locations?

- Is the exclusion zone necessary? Does the defendant need access to the area for work or pass through it on a bus route?

- If an exclusion zone is necessary can the defendant reach essential services such as doctors or dentists; does he or she need to visit relatives in the area?

- Does the list of names in the non-association clause accord with the evidence of anti-social behaviour?

- Are the terms drafted in a clear and simple language that the defendant can understand?

Remember that any terms not couched as prohibitions are not permissible.

Negotiating and bargaining

10.66 The defendant may wish to negotiate with the applicant body about the terms sought. For example, the defendant can agree not to challenge part of the evidence, so long as the applicant body negotiates as to the terms sought at court. Similarly, the defendant may be willing to accept the making of an order provided certain incidents are removed and/or certain terms can be altered to make the order less restrictive.

Appeals

10.67 This issue is discussed in chapter 12.

Variation and discharge

10.68 This issue is discussed in chapter 11.

DURATION OF THE ORDER

10.69 An ASBO must be made for a minimum period of 2 years, but may be for any period of time, including an indefinite one. Ultimately, the length of the order is a matter for the court, but the Guidance suggests that the applicant body should propose a period as part of its application. We would not suggest that any proposal is made in writing prior to the hearing as this would make it difficult to reach any form of compromise with the defendant. It is often the case that if the defendant will agree to an order and prevent the witnesses (often lay) from having to give evidence, the authority can afford to be less demanding on the terms it would seek from the court and/or the duration of the order. This is both sensible and effective, and whilst the decision is for the court alone, it is usually guided by what the applicant body is willing to accept. The court will usually realise that the applicant will have a better knowledge of the strength of its evidence and witnesses' fears and not lightly interfere.

10.70 There is now authority for the court's ability to make a term of the order for a lesser period than 2 years albeit the conflict with the statutory wording, see **10.48** above. The Government has, however, taken some heed of the views of the court in *Lonergan* when proposing further planned amendments to ASBOs. Those amendments include introducing a mandatory review of ASBOs made against young people after one year to allow changes in their behaviour to be taken into account. At the time of writing, no further details were available.[36]

10.71 If the proceedings are to be contested, then it is appropriate for the applicant body to state in its opening remarks for what period of time it believes the order should be made. The assessment of the duration of the award will take into account all the circumstances of the case; however, the following are probably most relevant:[37]

- the severity of the anti-social behaviour proved;

- the history of the anti-social behaviour (ie for how long it has continued);

- the age of the defendant;

- the number of warnings and other remedies which have been attempted;

- whether there have been breaches of interim orders; and

- the effect of the behaviour on others in the community.

---

[36] Home Office press release dated 20 December 2005, quoting Home Office Minister Hazel Blears.
[37] See current Home Office Guidance, reproduced in Appendix 3.

CHAPTER 11

POST-ORDER PROCEDURE AND ANCILLARY ORDERS

SERVICE OF THE ORDER ON THE DEFENDANT

11.1 The 2-year duration period of an ASBO, during which no order can be discharged, except with the consent of both parties, runs from the date of service.[1] Ideally, the defendant should therefore wait in court until the order is signed by the chair of the justices or their clerk. The West Yorkshire court service level agreement advocates such an approach.[2] It is important that the magistrates are asked to sign both the order and any map which is attached. Further, when served, the court file should be endorsed to prevent future possible arguments about service in the event of a breach of the order. A number of courts have adopted the policy of requiring defendants to sign a note on the court file that they have been provided with a copy of the order. This would seem a very sensible procedure if it can be achieved. If the defendant does not wait inside court after the order has been made, the court should be asked to serve the order personally,[3] as soon as possible. This will remove any doubts as to whether service has been effected. A defendant who refuses to wait to be served with the order will, however, be most unlikely to be able to rely upon lack of service if he commits a breach. This mirrors the approach of the county court in relation to committal proceedings for breach of an injunction or undertaking. The importance of the court having read out the terms and explained the consequences of breach are of course all the more obvious if the defendant has not been served with the order. By virtue of s 10C, as introduced into the CDA 1998 by the SOCPA 2005, in any breach proceedings a copy of the original ASBO, certified by a proper officer of the court which made it, is admissible as evidence of its having been made and the contents as if oral evidence was given. It should be noted, however, that this does not defeat a defendant who says that he or she was not the person in court when the order was made and never had notice of the same. This is why it is important that personal service takes place and also the defendant is asked to sign the order retained by the court. This would of course provide another means to prove that the defendant was in court if his signature matches that on the order. If a defendant is persistent in avoiding personal service of an order, it may be sufficient if the order is brought to his or her attention by other means, eg personally delivering it to a known address.

11.2 It is important that the terms of the orders which are pronounced in open court, recorded in the court register and served on the defendant are the same. It is likely, however, that the order pronounced in court will be the one accepted as correct. In *Walking v Director of Public Prosecutions*,[4] Mr Justice Stanley Burnton held that, whilst s 1(9) referred to service of the order and that this might make it appear that a written document was involved, injunctions and undertakings were often referred to in similar terms, and injunctions made in open court were effective to bind the parties. The general rule was that the order of the court was as pronounced in open court, and this applied to ASBOs. It should also be noted that there is no power in the magistrates' court to correct an error on the court documents, as the county court slip rule does

---

[1]   CDA 1998, ss 1(9), 1B(6) and 1C(8), as amended. See current Home Office Guidance, reproduced in Appendix 3.
[2]   See Appendix 2(G).
[3]   See current Home Office Guidance, reproduced at Appendix 3.
[4]   [2003] All ER (D) 57 (Dec).

not apply[5] to the magistrates' court and its power to amend errors applies only to criminal matters.[6] Therefore, extra care must be taken to ensure that the wording is correct on the order (as read by the court), as any amendment, however obvious or simple, will require an application to vary the order.

11.3 In the interests of certainty, it is good practice for the defendant to be reminded of the terms of the ASBO in a letter from his or her own advisers or the applicant body. If the defendant is a minor, a copy of the ASBO should also be given to his or her parent, guardian or an appropriate adult. All parties should check carefully the ASBO at court to ensure that it accurately reflects the terms and duration of the order, as well as the proven incidents of harassment, alarm or distress recorded by the court. Maps should be attached securely to the order and edged or hatched, as described in the order. Interim orders made in the magistrates' court (other than without notice orders) can be served by post to the last known address[7] and, therefore, it cannot be invalid to serve a full ASBO by the same method. We would suggest that, whilst this can be done, every effort should be made to try to serve the order on the defendant personally, as well. It should be noted, however, that orders made in the county court, whether interim or final, *must* be served on the defendant personally.[8]

11.4 A certificate of service should be kept with the original order and all copies. A copy should be retained by the court which made the ASBO and a copy sent to the defendant's solicitor, if represented. An accompanying letter can highlight the terms of the order, and reinforce the fact that an ASBO will not be suspended pending an appeal.

11.5 Where the defendant is a minor, special considerations apply to ensure that he or she understands the terms of an order. See chapter 14, where this is dealt with more fully.

SERVICE OF AN ASBO ON THE POLICE AND WITNESSES

Applicants' considerations

11.6 Standard post-order procedure should involve serving a copy of the order on the police and relevant agencies and interested parties (eg schools or YOT). In *all* cases, *when*, and *only when*, the defendant has been served with the order (or it is clear that the terms are known to him or her) should the defendant be arrested for a breach of the order. Whilst postal service is effective for an order made in the magistrates' court (see **11.3**), we would strongly advise that the order is served on the defendant personally and a certificate of service prepared, and preferably that the defendant asked to sign a document to acknowledge receipt.

11.7 The lead agency, if not the police, should give a copy of the ASBO to the police immediately, as well as to the anti-social behaviour co-ordinator of the local CDRP[9] and any other partnership agency.[10] The police should then notify the appropriate police command area on the same working day.

11.8 Effective dissemination of ASBO information may differ according to local practice and the organisation of local police divisions. One proven method is to serve a copy on every main police division in the local authority district area by handing it in at the front desk, addressed to a named police officer who is responsible for dissemination throughout that police station or

---

[5]   See *R v Brighton Magistrates' Court* [1986] 1 FLR 426, [1986] Fam Law 134.
[6]   MCA 1980, s 142.
[7]   Magistrates' Courts (Anti-social Behaviour Order) Rules 2002, r 7(1).
[8]   CPR PD 65, para 13.1.
[9]   See current Home Office Guidance, reproduced in Appendix 3.
[10] See current Home Office Guidance, reproduced in Appendix 3.

area. A copy of the ASBO should also be given to the police community safety team and local community safety police officers, as the police's local eyes and ears on the ground.

11.9 The recording of ASBOs on the Police National Computer (PNC) will assist the police in enforcing orders, which is essential to the overall effectiveness of the ASBO regime. Arrangements for this are currently being made as a matter of priority.[11] West Yorkshire police have had this capacity since 1 December 2002. By agreement in West Yorkshire, councils will provide designated police departments with details of each ASBO for the PNC record. This record will have a unique reference number. In many cases, however, the full details cannot be recorded on the PNC and therefore contact details for a holder of the full terms will be given.

Defence considerations

11.10 The defence may have a more limited role in checking that information held by the police or local authority on computer is accurate. A personal data access request under the DPA 1998 may provide this information (subject to possible exemptions from disclosure on the grounds of prevention or detection of crime), or the defence may seek an assurance from the police or other agency that any ASBO details held are accurate.

EFFECTIVE MONITORING

Applicants' considerations

11.11 '[O]btaining … the order is not the end of the process. The order must be monitored and enforced.'[12] The challenge facing applicants is to promote public awareness of specific ASBOs and maintain awareness in the local population when the glare of publicity has faded. This is an essential element of breach monitoring as the local community plays a vital role in informally policing ASBOs. The Home Office recommends the promotion of awareness strategies, including an effective media strategy.[13]

11.12 Suggestions for achieving public awareness of ASBOs include leaflet drops of ASBOs obtained in the local community (used to great effect in Manchester), features on the partner agencies' websites and use of tenants' and residents' newsletters. It is also suggested that local housing officers, neighbourhood wardens and community constables are informed of all ASBOs in their area. However, any publicity will have to comply with the guidelines given in the case of *Stanley v London Borough of Brent* (see **9.48**) and the subsequent Home Office Guidance as to the same.[14]

11.13 For the local ASBO group, current orders should be a standing item for review. How this should be done is a matter for local agreement. An ASBO should last only as long as is necessary to protect the public. If the need for the order no longer exists, it should be discharged.

11.14 Effective awareness is also a necessary part of policing ASBOs by agencies' officers. Until the recording of ASBOs on the PNC is rolled out nationwide, other methods will have to be used. Some police forces use local intelligence systems, which a number have indicated they will retain in addition to the PNC system. For the first time, in 2002, tackling anti-social behaviour appeared as a key performance indicator in the National Policing Plan. This is likely to result in

---

[11]   See current Home Office Guidance, reproduced in Appendix 3.
[12]   See current Home Office Guidance, reproduced in Appendix 3.
[13]   See current Home Office Guidance, reproduced in Appendix 3.
[14]   See www.together.gov.uk.

an increased awareness and allocation of resources to deal with the problems. Other police initiatives include retaining copies of all ASBOs in the custody suite for routine checking by the custody sergeant on processing defendants, and identifying subjects of ASBOs as a routine item on all shift briefings.

11.15 Providing staff with comprehensive training is essential to the successful use of ASBOs. Defence solicitors should not underestimate the need for specialist training. The Social Landlords' Crime and Nuisance Group is available to give training and guidance in this field. The Home Office's new Anti Social Behaviour Unit may also be willing to assist with seminars or workshops on good practice. Details of the Home Office telephone advice line and website for further information about tackling anti-social behaviour and ASBOs generally are contained in Appendix 7.

Defendants' considerations

11.16 ASBO publicity can stigmatise a defendant, especially a minor. Defendants may wish to restrict the method of publicity and awareness by asking the court to impose reporting restrictions. This is now particularly relevant as a consideration (rather than a bar) following the case of *Stanley*. Publicity and reporting restrictions are dealt with at **9.45** et seq.

11.17 General concerns can be raised directly with applicants by defendants or other interested parties, such as human rights organisations. Applicant authorities, when acting as public bodies, must take reasonable account of objections, otherwise they could face human rights challenges or judicial review. ASBO protocols, together with media or publicity strategies, are usually public documents made available on request or on relevant websites. (See chapter 2 for more details of protocols and policies.)

11.18 Applicants and their partner agencies should check regularly whether the defendant is complying with the terms of the ASBO. This not only protects the public, but can be used to actively consider what help can be given to the defendant. This could include the provision of youth groups, drop-in centres, mentoring schemes, sporting activities and activities in the school holidays. This can also be coupled with specific work with the defendant.

11.19 For defendants with mental health issues, drug or alcohol addictions, specialist help should be considered to address their problem. Whilst it is not permissible to make an order requiring the defendant to attend for treatment, there may be an opportunity to see if the council can provide services or treatment which the defendant needs but which has been delayed or denied before. The role of the defence should be to enquire what help is available and check whether it is appropriate for their client or challenge non-provision of appropriate assistance.

MONITORING AND RECORDING INFORMATION RELATING TO ASBOS

11.20 Local procedures should be introduced to monitor all ASBO applications.[15] The current Home Office Guidance recommends a minimum level of information to be recorded by the anti-social behaviour working group, as follows:

- the original application for an ASBO (or prosecution details if a post-conviction ASBO), including the name, date of birth, address, gender and ethnicity of the defendant;

---

[15]　See current Home Office Guidance, reproduced in Appendix 3.

- the ASBO details and any exclusion maps;

- date and details of any variation or discharge of the ASBO; and

- any breach action.

11.21 Additional voluntary recording may include details of victims or complainants, contributory factors such as drugs or alcohol, aggravating factors such as racial issues, and whether the anti-social conduct has ceased.

VARIATION AND DISCHARGE OF ORDER

11.22 Parties may make an application to vary or discharge an order for a variety of reasons, eg the defendant may wish to vary the terms of an order because an exclusion clause precludes him or her from visiting family members or because of a non-association clause with friends. The applicant may wish to extend the terms of an exclusion clause or request new terms if the defendant displaces his or her anti-social behaviour to another area. Applications to discharge ASBOs prior to the relevant date should be considered when a defendant has complied with the terms of the ASBO for a significant period of time. An assessment can be made by the relevant bodies as to whether his or her behaviour has been controlled by the orders or has been permanently changed. It is good practice to review at reasonable intervals all orders made to see if discharge is appropriate or if a variation to tighten or relax the prohibitions is necessary. An example of the need for a variation may be where the defendant's behaviour has improved so that the exclusion area, or perhaps the restriction on attending particular shops or restaurants, is no longer needed.

Practice and case-law

11.23 In *Samuda v Birmingham Magistrates' Court*[16] the defendant applied to vary or discharge an ASBO which had been made against him in 2003. The terms had included a large exclusion zone and prohibition against begging in England and Wales and the order was unlimited in time. The defendant applied to discharge or vary the order. The CPS accepted that the terms were too vague and needed amendment. They also accepted that the order should be limited to 10 years. The defendant's argued that it was no longer necessary and its continued existence was disproportionate. If the order was to remain in existence, it should be varied so as to prohibit begging in one street only and be limited to a much shorter period than ten years. The district judge had evidence before him of convictions since 2003 for begging in 3 streets in Birmingham, 3 counts of theft together with a number of convictions for breach of ASBO. The defendant had received fines, community penalties (which he had failed to perform) and custodial sentences.

11.24 The defendant argued that there was no evidence that his begging had caused any alarm, harassment or distress. The CPS contended that it was unnecessary to adduce such evidence on an application for variation or discharge, and that the applicant's convictions since the order was made demonstrated the need for the order to continue. The district judge rejected the defendant's contentions. He appealed by way of case stated.

11.25 Mr Justice Sullivan giving the judgment of the Divisional Court held that if the original ASBO had not been successfully challenged, either on appeal or by way of judicial review, it must be treated as having been lawfully made unless and until it is quashed by a court of competent jurisdiction. The only very exceptional case would be where the behaviour described

---

[16] [2008] EWHC 205 (Admin).

on the face of the order could not possibly on any reasonable basis have caused or been likely to cause harassment, alarm or distress. In the absence of this the court's finding that the behaviour described in the order had caused or been likely to cause harassment, alarm or distress had to be the starting point for any application to vary or discharge the order.

11.26 In this case whilst begging did not necessarily cause or is not necessarily likely to cause harassment, alarm or distress, certain methods of begging may well do so. This was therefore not one of those exceptional cases. The convictions of the defendant post order, as where available to the district judge, were sufficient to justify his conclusion that the applicant had not made out a case for the discharge of the order. They held that there appeared to have been no material change in circumstances since the order was made in December 2003. The conduct then complained of, and which was considered to justify the order at that time, was simply being repeated by the applicant. The court considered that the order should not however have lasted for 10 years as proposed by the CPS and varied it so that it ended on the hearing date, ie about 5 years. The district judge's view that the burden of proof rested on the applicant was not dealt with by the Divisional Court however would seem to us to be a reasonable proposition even that the court did decide that it was not for the respondent to show that the defendant's behaviour at the date of the application was likely to cause harassment, alarm or distress.

VARIATION AND EXTENSION

11.27 The issue of whether an ASBO could be extended in length by application to vary the length of the order was considered by the court in the case of *Leeds City Council v RG*.[17] The magistrates' court had been asked to vary a 2 year ASBO but extending the end date for a further 3 years. The magistrates' court heard a preliminary issue and determined that it did not have any power in law to do so. The council appealed to the Divisional Court by way of case stated.

11.28 The council argued that as the power was given to the court to vary the order, this had to include the duration. They argued that there was a similar section in the Protection from Harassment Act 1997 which had been considered by the court[18] and a wide construction had been preferred. The defendant argued that this was effectively an application for a new ASBO and that the statute could not have been intended to be so especially given that the sub-sections dealing with interim orders[19] specifically included power to 'renew' and the material section did not.

11.29 Lord Justice Latham held that 'varied' in s 1(8) had to be given its ordinary meaning and not a restrictive one. The reference to 'renewed' in the interim ASBO legislation was explained by the fact that those orders were by their nature short duration ones. They accepted that the statute did not allow an appeal from an application to vary however the protection for the defendant was provided by the fact that an application to vary, it imposed more stringent terms or extended duration, could only succeed if the applicant could put before the court material which justified the extension as being 'necessary to achieve the statutory objective'. Further the usual burden and standard of proof would apply to the application, ie on the applicant to the criminal standard on allegations of further ASB.

11.30 The court went on to say that if the application was to vary the length of the ASBO they would have to persuade the magistrates' that it was appropriate to vary the length of the ASBO rather than make application for a new one. There would have to be a clear rationale for this, eg an extension for less than 2 years was being sought.

---

[17]   [2007] 1 WLR 3025, (2007) 4 All ER 652, (2007) *The Times*, 11 September.
[18]   *DPP v Hall* [2005] EWHC 2621 (Admin).
[19]   CDA 1998, s 1D(4).

11.31 The judgment of the court in *RG* confirms what has been the advice of the authors to relevant authorities seeking an extension of the duration of an ASBO, namely that unless the period of extension sought is short, say 1 year, a fresh free-standing application pursuant to s 1 should be made with further consultation, etc.

11.32 The issue of whether there is a right of appeal from an application to vary was argued in *RG* and was simply accepted by the court in its judgment. However, the absence of explanation prompted the court to consider the matter again and more fully in *R (on the application of Langley) v Preston Crown Court*.[20] There the defendant had been made subject to a 2 year order which was extended on application by the local authority for a further 2 years. The defendant sought to appeal to the Crown Court relying on s 4 of the Crime and Disorder Act 1998. The Crown Court held that it had no jurisdiction to hear that appeal and the defendant sought judicial review of that decision arguing about the proper construction of s 4 and the impact of a restrictive construction would have on the defendant's rights under Art 6 of the ECHR.

11.33 The defendant argued that the granting by the magistrates' court of a variation of an ASBO was a further order which was itself an ASBO. This would allow an appeal under s 4. Lord Justice Scott Baker concluded that there was no right appeal against a decision of the magistrates' court to vary an ASBO. The application to vary focused not on whether the past behaviour had warranted the making of an order but whether it continued to be necessary. The court noted that Lord Justice Latham had in *RG* (above) come to the same conclusion. Further that if the defendant was correct any minor variation such as adjusting an exclusion zone or curfew time would result in an order which had to continue for 2 further years unless the parties consented to discharge.

11.34 Further the fact that there was no right of appeal from orders made in the county court provided support for the fact that there need not be any right of appeal. In those cases permission was needed to appeal and any appeal would generally be by way of review rather than re-hearing. From the Crown Court there would have to be leave and then only granted if the decision was wrong in principle or in some way manifestly excessive.

11.35 The court concluded that as ASBOs were civil in nature there did not have to be any right of appeal and that Parliament would have intended no more right of appeal than for the county court or Crown Court. They considered that it was therefore logical that there should be an appeal on fact from an application to vary to the magistrates' court but there would be a right of review by case stated or judicial review. Further they would consider it to be an abuse of process, save in the most exceptional circumstances, to attempt to circumvent the above conclusion by seeking leave out of time to appeal against the original ASBO.

11.36 In relation to the issue of whether there was a breach of Article 6 if there was no right of appeal, Lord Justice Latham held that it was common ground that the right to a fair hearing did not require a right of appeal.[21] The defendant submitted that the unfairness in this case was that the application effectively imposed a new order without the rights which were available to the defendant when it was first made. In response it was submitted that it was unusual to have a right of appeal by re-hearing in civil proceedings and in this case there had been a full hearing before the magistrates' court which was Art 6 compliant. Lord Justice Latham dismissed that there was anything approaching a violation of Art 6 giving no reasons for this view.

---

[20]   [2008] All ER (D) 300 (Oct), [2008] EWHC 2623 (Admin).
[21]   *Delcourt v Belgium* (1970) 1 EHRR 355.

MAGISTRATES' COURTS IN THEIR CIVIL CAPACITY

11.37 An ASBO, whether interim or final, can be varied or discharged on application:

- either applicant or defendant can make the application;

- an application to vary or discharge the order must be made to the court that first made the ASBO;

- a post-conviction ASBO may be heard by any magistrates' court in the same petty sessions area;

- no ASBO can be discharged within 2 years of service of the order without both parties' consent;

- a post-conviction order cannot be discharged before 2 years;

- if the defendant brings the application, the applicant body must give the court a 'considered' response to the application;[22]

- for a contested application, reasons and appropriate evidence on the ASBO's effectiveness should be given.

11.38 The procedure for applying to vary or discharge an ASBO is set out at r 6 of the 2002 Rules, which came into force on 2 December 2002. The main principles are as follows:

- any application, with reasons, must be in writing to the magistrates' court which made the order (or any magistrates' court in the same petty sessions area for post-conviction ASBOs);

- if the court thinks there are *no* grounds to vary or discharge the ASBO, it can determine the case without hearing *anyone* in person (*except* when an interim ASBO was made without notice to the defendant – the court *must* give him or her the chance to be heard before deciding on the application);

- if there *are* grounds to hold a hearing, unless the application is withdrawn, a summons for a hearing will be issued giving at least 14 days' notice of the hearing. The clerk will send a copy of the application to vary or discharge with the summons.

11.39 Where a defendant has an ASBO in place but continues a course of anti-social behaviour, the appropriate procedure for extending or varying the terms of the original ASBO is unclear. Is the length of the order a term which can be varied? Or should the authority make a fresh application? It is suggested that, as the Act refers to applications to vary the order rather than its terms, extending the end date of the order is more properly a variation application rather than a fresh application. In practice, it is submitted that the best course is to file both a r 6 application and a completed Sch 1 application, setting out the previous order and then the subsequent breaches and anti-social behaviour alleged. The new proposed terms can then be included in the application so that the defendant has an opportunity to respond fully to the proposed variation and/or extension.

---

[22] See current Home Office Guidance, reproduced in Appendix 3.

POST-CONVICTION ORDERS

11.40 The applications to vary or discharge have to be made in accordance with CDA 1998, s 1CA. This is dealt with in more detail in chapter 6 (**6.36** et seq).

COUNTY COURT ORDERS

11.41 Either the defendant or the relevant authority may apply to the county court for the order to be varied or discharged[23] save that without the consent of the relevant authority the order cannot be discharged before 2 years have elapsed.[24] There is no specific rule as to how the application is to be made, however, it would seem that in accordance with the CPR, an application under Part 23 would be most appropriate.

ANCILLARY ORDERS

Intervention orders

11.42 These orders are introduced into the CDA 1998 by amendment from the Drugs Act 2005 (DA 2005). The DA 2005 inserts ss 1G and 1H into the CDA 1998, however, there is no commencement date given at the date of publication of this third edition. The Home Office has, however, indicated on the 'together' website that it intends for the orders to be available by April 2006.

11.43 An intervention order is an order which requires the defendant to comply with requirements in the order for no more than 6 months[25] and to comply with directions given by an authorised person with a view to implementing the requirements in the order.[26] The order can require the defendant to participate in activities specified at given times[27] and/or to present him or herself to a person at specified times.[28] The requirements must, so far as practicable, be such as to avoid any conflict with the defendant's religious beliefs and any interference with the times at which he or she normally works or attends an educational establishment.[29]

When?

11.44 The power to make an intervention order dovetails to a great extent with Individual Support Orders (ISOs) (see **11.60**) and can only be made if the defendant is aged 18 or over.[30] The application may be made by a relevant authority but only if:

- it has applied for an ASBO or order under s 1B (county court ASBO); *and*

- it has obtained a report from an appropriately qualified person relating to the effect on the person's behaviour of the misuse of controlled drugs or such other factors as the Secretary of State by order prescribes;[31] *and*

---

[23] CDA 1998, s 1B(5).
[24] CDA 1998, s 1B(6).
[25] CDA 1998, s 1G(5)(a).
[26] CDA 1998, s 1G(5)(b).
[27] CDA 1998, s 1G(6)(a).
[28] CDA 1998, s 1G(6)(b).
[29] CDA 1998, s 1G(7).
[30] CDA 1998, s 1G(1).
[31] CDA 1998, s 1G(1)(b).

- has engaged in consultation with such person as the Secretary of State by order prescribes to ascertain that if the report recommends that an order is made, appropriate activities will be available.[32]

11.45 There is no guidance as yet as to what format the report about the effect on the behaviour or the misuse of drugs is required to take. It would seem, however, that unless all that is required is a general report that misuse of a particular drug makes people potentially anti-social, the report will have to be personal to the defendant. This would include how it affects them including what drugs they use, how often, etc. This information, however, is only likely to be available if the defendant co-operates with the making of the report. It is unlikely that such admissions are going to be made if the defendant is contesting the report. If not, then why would they not have sought the assistance voluntarily rather than having the court potentially impose a further order on them for which they could be punished? Certainly any defendant's representative would advise them to do so before any hearing.

11.46 If the relevant authority makes an application and the court is satisfied that relevant conditions are met and the court makes an ASBO or order under s 1B it *may* make an intervention order as well.[33] It should be noted that unlike ISOs the court does not have to consider whether to make an order unless there is an application.

Relevant conditions

11.47 The relevant conditions are, first, that an intervention order is desirable in the interests of preventing a repetition of the behaviour which led to the ASBO being made.[34] This is called the 'trigger behaviour'. Second, that appropriate activities relating to the trigger behaviour or its cause are available for the defendant.[35] Third, that the defendant is not already subject to another intervention order or to any treatment relating to the trigger behaviour whether voluntary or compulsory[36] and, finally, that the court has been notified by the Secretary of State that arrangements for implementing an intervention order are available in the area in which the defendant resides or will reside.[37]

Procedure

11.48 Prior to making an intervention order the court must explain to the defendant in ordinary language the effect of the order and the requirements proposed to be included.[38] Further, the court must explain the consequences of a failure to comply and the power of the court to review the order on either the defendant's or relevant authority's application.[39]

Breach

11.49 If a defendant fails to comply with a requirement of the order or a direction given under the order the person responsible for the provision or supervision of the appropriate activity must inform the relevant authority of that fact.[40] If without reasonable excuse the defendant fails

---

[32]   CDA 1998, s 1G(1)(c).
[33]   CDA 1998, s 1G(3).
[34]   CDA 1998, s 1G(4)(a).
[35]   CDA 1998, s 1G(4)(b).
[36]   CDA 1998, s 1G(4)(c).
[37]   CDA 1998, s 1G(4)(d).
[38]   CDA 1998, s 1H(1).
[39]   CDA 1998, s 1H(1)(b) and (c).
[40]   CDA 1998, s 1G(8).

to comply with a requirement included in the order he or she is guilty of an offence and liable on summary conviction to a fine not exceeding level 4 on the standard scale.[41]

Variation and discharge

11.50 An intervention order will be discharged automatically if the ASBO or s 1B order is discharged.[42] Further if the ASBO order was varied then the court making the variation could vary or discharge the intervention order as well.[43] The intervention order can also be varied or discharged on application by the defendant or the relevant authority.[44] The application is made to the court which made the order and, in the magistrates' court, must be made by way of complaint.[45]

Parenting orders

11.51 A parenting order is an order which requires the parent to comply with requirements in an order for not more than 12 months and to attend for not more than 3 months such counselling or guidance programme as might be specified in directions given by the responsible officer under the order.[46] The court may order the parent to attend a residential course in respect of a counselling or guidance programme[47] but only if it is satisfied that this would be likely to be more effective than a non-residential course in preventing repetition of the behaviour or criminal offending[48] *and* that any interference with family life which would result from such attendance was proportionate in all the circumstances.[49]

11.52 Any requirements imposed in a parenting order must, as far as is practicable, be such as to avoid any conflict with the parent's religious beliefs and any interference with the defendant's work or educational attendance.[50]

11.53 A responsible officer in relation to parenting orders means a person specified in the order who is a probation officer, social worker in the social services department or member of a YOT or person nominated by a person appointed as a direction of children's services under s 18 of the Children Act 2004.[51]

When?

11.54 In any court proceedings where a child or young person is convicted of a criminal offence, a child safety order is made, parental compensation order or ASBO is made, the court may make a parenting order if it is satisfied that the relevant condition has been satisfied. The relevant condition is that the court considers that a parenting order would be desirable in the interests of preventing behaviour which led to the proceedings as a result of which the order was being considered, eg anti-social behaviour for ASBO proceedings. If the defendant is aged 15 or less

---

[41]   CDA 1998, s 1H(3).
[42]   CDA 1998, s 1H(4).
[43]   CDA 1998, s 1H(7).
[44]   CDA 1998, s 1H(5).
[45]   CDA 1998, s 1H(6).
[46]   CDA 1998, s 8(4).
[47]   CDA 1998, s 8(7A).
[48]   CDA 1988, s 8(7A)(a).
[49]   CDA 1998, s 8(7A)(b).
[50]   CDA 1998, s 9(4).
[51]   CDA 1998, s 8(8).

then the court must obtain and consider information about the defendant's family circumstances and the likely effect of the order on those circumstances before making a parenting order.[52]

11.55 If a defendant aged 15 or less is convicted of an offence for which a referral order is not made *or* an ASBO is made and the court is satisfied that the relevant condition is satisfied it must make a parenting order.[53] If it is not satisfied that the condition is satisfied then the court must state in open court why it is not.[54]

Variation or discharge

11.56 The court may, if it considers it is appropriate, vary or discharge a parenting order on application by the parent or the responsible officer.[55] This can include removing a provision or adding any requirement which the original court could lawfully have made.[56] If an application to discharge an order is dismissed by the court then no further application can be made by *any* person except with the consent of the court.[57] This is a very strange requirement for two reasons. First, the prohibition applies to both parent and responsible officer regardless of who applied. This seems nonsensical and could mean that if a parent made a hopeless application to discharge one week into an order but then did very well thereafter so that the responsible officer saw no reason for the order in, say, 3 months the court's permission would be needed for the officer's application to dismiss. There is no reason that we can see for such a hurdle. Further, the hurdle itself is unspecified and without indication as to the test; inevitably the application for permission will be the same hearing as the application to discharge. The evidence, if any, and submissions will be exactly the same. In reality this is a meaningless subsection.

Breach

11.57 Any parent who without reasonable excuse fails to comply with any requirement in the order or specified in directions given by the responsible officer shall be liable on summary conviction to a fine not exceeding level 3 on the standard scale.[58]

Appeals

11.58 If a parenting order is made following proceedings involving a child safety order then any appeal by a parent is to the High Court.[59] In respect of one imposed following an ASBO it is to the Crown Court.[60] There does not seem to be any right of appeal against one made consequential to a parental compensation order, however, judicial review proceedings would be available or a case stated. Appeals against parenting orders following criminal conviction or offences relating to school attendance are governed in the same way as appeals against the sentence for the criminal offences,[61] ie to the Crown Court as of right from the magistrates' court or Court of Appeal from the Crown Court with permission.

---

[52] CDA 1998, s 9(2).
[53] CDA 1998, s 9(1)(a) and 9(1B)(a) respectively.
[54] CDA 1998, s 9(a)(b) and 9(1B)(b) respectively.
[55] CDA 1998, s 9(5)(a).
[56] CDA 1998, s 9(5)(b).
[57] CDA 1998, s 9(6).
[58] CDA 1998, s 9(7).
[59] CDA 1998, s 10(1)(a).
[60] CDA 1998, s 10(1)(b).
[61] CDA 1998, s 10(4) and (5) respectively.

11.59 The Crown or High Court may make orders as if they were the original court or may direct that the application be re-heard by the magistrates' court in the case of an appeal to the High Court.

Individual support orders

11.60 On 1 May 2004 individual support orders (ISOs) were introduced.[62] They have been amended recently by s 124 of the Criminal Justice and Immigration Act 2008. Where the court makes an ASBO against a young person or child (ie a 10–17-year-old) it must consider whether the individual support conditions are fulfilled[63] and, if not, state this in open court, giving reasons.[64] It should be noted that ISOs whilst previously not available in respect of post-conviction ASBOs they are now so available to the court following the amendment of section 1AA.[65] Further where a young person is before the youth court charged with a criminal offence the YOT has a duty to recommend suitable penalties and interventions in the PSR. Where the YOT is aware of an application for a post-conviction order it should always consider the implications and possible conditions. ISOs are also available to the county court[66] if the necessary conditions are met where the court in its sentencing powers is expected to address those matters in any event. The conditions which need to be met in all cases for an ISO to be imposed are:[67]

(a)   that an ISO is desirable in the interests of preventing repetition of the behaviour which led to the orders being made; and

(b)   that there is not already such an order in place; and

(c)   that the court has been notified by the Secretary of State that arrangements for the implementation of such orders are in place for the area where the child lives.

11.61 ISOs have been available to the court to make in every local authority area since 2005, and following the above amendments can be made more than once provided the defendant is still a child at the time of the hearing of the application.

11.62 Before making an ISO, the court shall obtain from a social worker or YOT worker any information which the court considers necessary to decide if the conditions are fulfilled or what requirements should be imposed in the ISO.[68] This requirement is likely to involve consideration of the additional strain on the social services and YOT officers, and it remains to be seen whether the present structure could cope with the additional workload of assessment and supervision of requirements imposed under this legislation.

11.63 If the conditions are met, the court *must* make an order which requires the defendant to comply with requirements in the order for not more than 6 months and to comply with directions given by the responsible officer with a view to the implementation of the order's

---

[62]   Criminal Justice Act 2003, s 322, inserting s 1AA into the CDA 1998.
[63]   CDA 1998, s 1AA(1).
[64]   CDA 1998, s 1AA(4).
[65]   CDA 1998, s 1C(9AA).
[66]   CDA 1998, s 1B(8)–(9).
[67]   CDA 1998, s 1AA(3)(a)–(c).
[68]   CDA 1998, s 1AA(9).

requirements.[69] A responsible officer is defined as a social worker, personally nominated by a person appointed as chief education officer or member of a YOT.[70] An ISO may not extend beyond the length of the ASBO.[71]

11.64 The requirements contained in an ISO should be those which are desirable to prevent repetition of the conduct which gave rise to the ASBO and may require the defendant:[72]

- to participate in activities specified in the ISO or as directed by the responsible officer at times as specified; and/or

- to attend at specified places at specified times and/or meet with specified persons; and/or

- to comply with specified arrangements for education.

An ISO or directions given pursuant to it, however, cannot require a defendant to attend (the same place or others) on more than 2 days in any week (Sunday to Saturday).[73] Further, the requirements and directions given under them shall, as far as is practicable, avoid conflict with the defendant's religious beliefs or school attendance.[74] ISOs are civil orders and are intended to help young people address the causes of their anti-social behaviour. An ISO could, for example, require a young person to attend counselling for substance abuse or anger management sessions which are overseen by the responsible officer.

11.65 Before the court makes an ISO, it must explain to the defendant in ordinary language the effects and requirements of the ISO and the consequences which may follow in the event of breach and that the court has the power to review the ISO on the application of either the defendant or the responsible officer.[75] Whilst an ISO can be varied or discharged on the defendant's or responsible officer's application,[76] it can also occur if the court varies the ASBO following which the ISO was made.[77]

11.66 Following the amendments in the Criminal Justice and Immigration Act 2008 where an ASBO has previously been made in respect of a child or young person (and even if no ISO was made then) the relevant authority which applied for the ASBO can apply to the court by complaint for an ISO to be made. Where the ASBO was made pursuant to s 1C then the application can be made by the body responsible under s 1K(2)(a) or (b) for conducting the review.

Breach

11.67 Breach of the requirements of an ISO without a reasonable excuse is a criminal offence and can result in a fine of up to £250 for 10–13-year-olds and up to £1,000 for those aged 14 and over.[78] Any fine imposed on a person under 16 years of age must be paid by the parent or guardian.[79] For 16–17-year-olds, the court has a discretion as to whether to make the parent pay.

---

[69] CDA 1998, s 1AA(2)(a) and (b).
[70] CDA 1998, s 1AA(10).
[71] CDA 1998, s 1AB(5A).
[72] CDA 1998, s 1AA(6).
[73] CDA 1998, s 1AA(7).
[74] CDA 1998, s 1AA(8).
[75] CDA 1998, s 1AB(1), inserted by Criminal Justice Act 2003, s 322, in force from 1 May 2004: see SI 2004/829, art 3(1), (2)(b).
[76] CDA 1998, s 1AB(6).
[77] CDA 1998, s 1AB(7).
[78] CDA 1998, s 1AB(3).
[79] Powers of Criminal Courts (Sentencing) Act 2000, s 137(3).

A referral order is not available for breach of an ISO. This will, of course, mean that for children under 16 the emphasis will be placed on the parents to ensure the child's compliance with the terms of the ISO. Whilst a desire for parental control is laudable, it is difficult to see it being achieved by this means, although time will show whether it is successful or not. The Home Office has indicated, however, that it does not expect first breaches to be prosecuted.

11.68 The imposition of an ISO may well be a very significant part of the means to assist that young person to abide by the terms of the ASBO and end the anti-social behaviour.

CHAPTER 12

APPEALS AGAINST
ANTI-SOCIAL BEHAVIOUR ORDERS

APPEALS BY THE DEFENDANT

Magistrates' courts' decisions

12.1 Where the ASBO has been made by the magistrates' court, sitting either in its civil capacity or following a criminal conviction, appeal primarily lies to the Crown Court.[1] The same provisions which govern appeals from criminal matters are applied, namely rr 74 and 75 of the MCR 1981 regarding the documents to be sent to the Crown Court and rr 6–11 of the Crown Court Rules 1982 regarding the procedure and notices of appeal.

12.2 The appeal by a defendant to the Crown Court is as of right. In *R (on the application of T) v Manchester Crown Court*[2] the Divisional Court was asked to determine whether the fact that a defendant consented to the ASBO being made prevented him bringing an appeal. The 15-year-old defendant had been the subject of an application for an ASBO in the magistrates' court at which he was represented and accompanied by his mother. The defendant's mother was under pressure from work commitments and having spoken to counsel on the day decided that she would not oppose the making of the order. The district judge in the magistrates' court on hearing this considered the papers and made the order. Once the order had been made the defendant's mother changed her mind and wished to challenge the order. An appeal was therefore lodged on the basis that the order was not necessary.

12.3 At the appeal hearing counsel for the council took a preliminary point that as the order had been consented to there was a bar to any appeal. The Crown Court applied a test that unless there was mutual mistake of fact or undue pressure there would be no right to appeal from an order obtained by consent.

12.4 At the judicial review hearing no objections were raised to the application by either the council or the Home Office. Mr Justice Moses held that:

> '[16] In those circumstances it is clear to me that an order cannot be made merely on the basis of the consent of the Claimant. The court considering the making of an order must itself be satisfied to the required standard of proof as to the matters under s 1(1)(a) and, further, must exercise its own judgment pursuant to s 1(1)(b) as to the necessity of making such an order.
>
> [17] Of course, the cooperation and consent of the person who it is suggested should be made the subject of an order is welcome and relevant. If an applicant is prepared to consent, it would not only show a cooperative state of mind, but would afford considerable saving of time and money. In requiring the proof of those matters that the statute requires to be proved it is not intended in any

---

[1]   CDA 1998, s 4, as amended; for post-conviction orders, the order is ancillary to the sentence on the criminal conviction and the right of appeal lies to the Crown Court in the same way.

[2]   [2005] EHWC 1396 (Admin), [2005] All ER (D) 03 (Jun).

way to discourage such cooperation or consent. But consent is only a factor, both in relation to the matters that are required to be proved, and as to the value judgment that the court must exercise in deciding whether an order is necessary.

…

[20] Further, and more generally, as I have said, the order is made in the interests of the public at large whose interests must be considered by the court. In those circumstances, whilst, as I have said, the attitude either of the Claimant or the parent is relevant, it cannot be dispositive of the issue.'

He continued that as the hearing before the Crown Court was a complete re-hearing if the defendant appealed then the appeal must be heard, however:

'[22] If the Claimant did consent in the court below, that will be powerful evidence that there is absolutely nothing in the appeal. It will be evidence, even if there is something in the appeal, as to the merits of an ASBO as granted in the court below. In those circumstances it would, I hope, be rare indeed, that the time and effort of the Crown Court will be spent in considering an appeal where consent has been given to an ASBO before.'

Notice of appeal and time-limits

12.5 Notice of appeal is made in writing and should be made to the justices' chief executive for the relevant magistrates' court (specimen forms can be found in *Stone's Justices Manual* (LexisNexis)). A notice of appeal must be lodged no later than 21 days after the ASBO was made.[3] With the exception of post-conviction ASBOs these are appeals against the making of a civil order and, therefore, no actual grounds of appeal are needed save that the court erred in law or reached a decision that it should not have done on the weight of evidence. It would, however, seem sensible for limited grounds to be given by a defendant, if only to guide the Crown Court when it is considering the papers. Appeals against post-conviction orders are appeals against sentence and the notice of appeal should specify this along with the grounds of appeal. There is power to extend the time of filing a notice of appeal, both before and after the 21 days.[4] Any application to extend time is made to the Crown Court, to an appropriate officer, and should be made in writing, specifying the grounds of the application.[5] If the application is granted, then the Crown Court officer will give notice of this to the appellant and the magistrates' court. It is the appellant's responsibility to give notice of the extension to the other party.[6]

Format of Crown Court appeal hearing

12.6 The hearing at the Crown Court is an entirely fresh one and, by s 79(3) of the Supreme Court Act 1981, is a full re-hearing of the evidence and law. Section 79(3) is an unusual section, which states that the customary practice and procedure with respect to appeals to the Crown Court, particularly as to the extent to which an appeal was a re-hearing of the case, should continue to be observed. It is regrettable that the Government ignored the feedback and complaints made by a number of applicant bodies and did not make ASBOs an exception to this 'customary practice'. It is incompatible with the repeatedly expressed desire to protect vulnerable and unwilling witnesses, to provide the defendant with a right of a re-hearing. It is hard enough to persuade witnesses to attend court, without having to tell them, when asked, that this is not the end and the witness could undergo a second cross-examination in the Crown

---

[3]   Crown Court Rules 1982, r 7(3).
[4]   Crown Court Rules 1982, r 7(5).
[5]   Crown Court Rules 1982, r 7(6).
[6]   Crown Court Rules 1982, r 7(7).

Court. The poor drafting leading to the omission of special measures at appeal hearings compounds this problem. It would have been a simple step, and a considerable improvement, had there been a right of appeal which was limited to the usual appellate discretion where the decision was wrong in law or perverse. This is the usual appeal jurisdiction in the civil courts. There has been judicial comment from Lord Justice Kennedy[7] that the time has come for such right of appeal to be limited, however, seemingly there are no plans to consider the same.

12.7   At the re-hearing either party may submit further evidence in support of their case. As the hearing is a re-hearing, the applicant body may rely upon any evidence of recent alleged incidents. The Home Office Guidance suggests that, when determining an appeal, the Crown Court should have before it a copy of the original application for an order, the full order and the notice of appeal. The applicant body has responsibility for ensuring that copies are sent to the court. With the greatest respect to the authors of the current Home Office Guidance, this appears to be incomplete or incorrect. It cannot be right that the Crown Court does not have before it all the evidence that was before the magistrates' court. It would be strange in the extreme if the magistrates were entitled to consider the statements from the witnesses and to accept them as their evidence-in-chief, but judges in the Crown Court were not. The invariable practice that we have adopted is that the entire trial bundle is sent to the Crown Court, together with a copy of the notice of appeal and the perfected order. It should also be remembered that most Crown Court judges have had little or no exposure to ASBOs, and few have been given the appropriate training. The common situation is that the hearing is before a Crown Court judge and two lay magistrates, who would not normally read any statements before hearing an appeal. The difference for ASBO appeals should be carefully and politely pointed out in a letter. It is also advisable to give a sensible time estimate in this first letter as, unless the case can be dealt with in a short time, it will normally be listed along with another 10–12 cases in a rolling list, which will almost inevitably lead to an adjournment and disaffected witnesses and defendant. The letter can also be produced to the court and the Ministry of Justice if a case is unnecessarily adjourned due to 'impossible' listing.

12.8   The Crown Court may, on appeal, make any orders it wishes as are necessary to give effect to its findings. It may also make any incidental or consequential orders as are just. If the Crown Court makes an ASBO, then it is treated as if it was made by the magistrates' court for the purposes of applications to vary and/or discharge.

Case stated

12.9   The defendant has the right, pursuant to s 111 of MCA 1980, to ask for a case to be stated to the Divisional Court in respect of a decision of the magistrates' court (see **12.13** for procedure). However, if the defendant does so, he or she then loses the right to appeal as of right for a re-hearing before the Crown Court[8] and, therefore, it would not normally be in the defendant's interests to use this avenue of appeal first, as this option remains open even if the Crown Court subsequently rules against the defendant.

Appeal from the Crown Court

12.10 Appeal from the Crown Court is only by way of case stated, pursuant to s 28 of the Supreme Court Act 1981,[9] or judicial review, pursuant to s 29(3), both of which lie to the High Court. The grounds of appeal for case stated are that the Crown Court was 'wrong in law or is in

---

7   See *Stanley v London Borough of Brent* [2004] EWHC 2229 (Admin), (2005) EMLR 3, (2005) UKHRR 115, (2005) HLR 8, (2005) ACD 13, (2004) *The Times*, October 22.

8   MCA 1980, s 111(4).

9   Crown Court Rules 1982, r 26.

excess of jurisdiction'.[10] The principles of the remedies of the mandatory order, prohibiting order and quashing order, which an application for judicial review allows, are beyond the scope of this book. The practical difference is unlikely to be significant: to succeed in an application for judicial review, the court would have to be satisfied of an error of law or that the decision was '*Wednesbury*' unreasonable.[11] It should be noted that, as discussed in chapter 6, appeals from the Crown Court from post-conviction orders lie only to the Court of Appeal and then only if the sentence was wrong in principle or manifestly excessive.[12]

APPROPRIATE VENUE OF APPEAL

12.11 This section is concerned with the appropriate venue for an appeal from an ASBO imposed by a magistrates' court. Whilst there are three possible choices for appeal, discussed above, it has become common for any challenge to the making of the order to result in a judicial review application. Although there are undoubtedly cases where this is appropriate, it is by no means the correct route for the majority of cases. The court in *C (by his Mother and Litigation Friend, C) v Sunderland Youth Court, Northumbria Police, and Crown Prosecution Service*[13] made it clear that there was a right of appeal under s 108 of MCA 1980 and they would not wish to encourage applications for judicial review when there was an alternative remedy to appeal against sentence to the Crown Court.

12.12 This has been further explored by the administrative court in the case of *R (on the application of A) v Leeds Magistrates' Court and Leeds City Council*,[14] where the defendant applied for judicial review of two decisions made by a district judge, first, when making interim without notice orders and then when renewing the orders at a later on notice renewal hearing. The application was on the basis that whilst the defendant did not dispute that there was prima facie evidence before him to justify an interim order, the judge had failed on the without notice hearing to have any regard to A's best interests as a child (held to be a primary consideration by the administrative court in related proceedings, after the making of the without notice orders)[15] and, at the renewal notice hearing, to have both applied the wrong test and erred in law.

12.13 Mr Justice Stanley Burnton noted that a defendant who had had a without notice ASBO imposed could:

(a)   apply to the magistrates' court for the order to be discharged or varied;

(b)   appear and oppose the making of a further order, as the defendant had done here;

(c)   appeal to the Crown Court;

(d)   appeal to the High Court by way of case stated; or

(e)   apply to the High Court for judicial review. However, he considered (e) to be the least suitable option, stating:

> '30   Of these procedures, judicial review is the least suitable in a case such as the present, where it is not disputed that the evidence before the magistrates' court justified (although it did not necessarily

---

[10]   Supreme Court Act 1981, s 28(1).
[11]   *Associated Provincial Picture Houses v Wednesbury Corporation* [1948] 1 KB 223, [1947] 2 All ER 680, CA.
[12]   Criminal Appeal Act 1968, s 9(1).
[13]   [2003] EWHC 2385 (Admin), (2004) Crim LR 75.
[14]   [2004] EWHC 554 (Admin), (2004) *The Times*, March 31.
[15]   *R (on the application of Kenny) v Leeds Magistrates' Court; R (on the application of M) v Secretary of State for Constitutional Affairs and Lord Chancellor and another* [2003] EWHC 2963 (Admin), [2004] 1 All ER 1333.

require) the making of the order. In such a case, if the claimant establishes that the District Judge applied an incorrect test, the only relief this court can grant is to quash the ASBO. In judicial review proceedings, the High Court cannot consider the evidence before the District Judge (or any evidence subsequently available) and itself decide whether, applying the correct legal test, the order should be upheld, save in cases in which no District Judge properly applying the law could have come to any conclusion other than that the order should be made. Nor can the High Court vary the terms of the ASBO so as to accommodate the contentions successfully made by the claimant. The High Court cannot substitute its discretion for that of the magistrates' court.

…

32   … Judicial review proceedings have a further disadvantage. There is often no reliable record of the reasons given by the magistrates' court for its decision. The decision of 11 December 2003 is a case in point: I shall have to refer to the evidence below. Where however a case is stated, the District Judge has the opportunity to set out the facts on which he based his decision and his reasons for making the order.

33   Parliament has specifically provided in the 1998 Act for applications to the magistrates' court to discharge or to vary interim orders and for appeals to the Crown Court. In my judgment, it follows that these are the primary routes for challenging an interim order. Appeal by way of case stated is appropriate where a legal issue arises which is suitable for determination by the High Court …'

12.14 The judge concluded that judicial review was appropriate only where there was procedural unfairness or bias (to which we would add where an urgent remedy is needed). Here the alleged failure by the district judge to apply the correct legal test to the facts before him would not, in general, be an appropriate subject for judicial review. He dismissed the argument that judicial review was the preferable remedy for the defendant, as this would, if granted, have led to a quashing of the order, thereby sparing him the breach proceedings. The judge stated that an ASBO was an order of the court and must be complied with unless and until discharged or set aside. Indeed, he considered that breach of an ASBO by a defendant who has not applied for its variation or discharge may well be good reason for the court to refuse judicial review. The judge dismissed the application for judicial review on the grounds of delay, alternative remedy and on the merits – the latter is discussed in chapters 13 and 14.

12.15 *A* was a case involving interim orders; however, the principles set out must, as a matter of logic, apply to the making of full orders as well. What is clear is that the courts, whilst willing to exercise supervisory administrative control of the magistrates' courts in appropriate cases, consider that challenges to orders, whether interim or full orders, should be brought using the mechanism of appeal to the Crown Court for arguments on the facts or application of discretion or by way of case stated for points of law.

APPEALS BY THE APPLICANT BODY

12.16 The applicant body has only one avenue of appeal against a refusal by a magistrates' court to grant an ASBO: to apply by way of case stated to the Divisional Court for review of the decision on the grounds that the decision is wrong in law or in excess of jurisdiction.[16] The application must be made within 21 days of the decision of the magistrates.[17] The application is made with the proposed terms of the case stated for the magistrates to consider. The magistrates may refuse to state a case but only if they consider the application to be frivolous. If so, they must provide a certificate of refusal, and the applicant body may apply to the High Court for an order of mandamus to require the magistrates to state the case.[18]

---

[16]   MCA 1980, s 111.
[17]   MCA 1980, s 111(2).
[18]   MCA 1980, s 111(6).

Appeals from the county court

12.17 Any appeal from the decision of the county court in 'bolt-on' proceedings will have to be made by reference to CPR, Part 52. Here the appeals are generally to the next 'tier' of judge, namely to a circuit judge from a district judge, and from a circuit judge to a High Court judge. If, however, the case is allocated to the multi-track, then the appeal is with permission to the Court of Appeal.[19] This will not apply to the majority of county court orders, as the rule is not applicable to appeals in Part 55 possession proceedings,[20] where the appeal will actually lie to the High Court. It remains to be seen whether any alteration to Part 52 will occur but, at present, there is no right of appeal from an ASBO hearing; the appellant needs permission to appeal.[21] This permission can be granted by the court which hears the ASBO application or by the appeal court[22] but should be made initially to the court making the order.[23] The application for permission in the appeal court is generally dealt with on paper, and the appellant must show a real prospect of success or some other compelling reason why the appeal should be heard. The application must be made within 14 days of the decision of the lower court.[24]

12.18 The hearing before the higher court will be limited to a review of the decision of the lower court[25] (ie an appellate jurisdiction) as to whether the trial judge erred in law or fact, or there was a serious procedural or other irregularity, unless the court considers that, in the circumstances of an individual appeal, it would be in the interests of justice to hold a re-hearing. Unless it orders otherwise, the court will not hear any oral evidence or accept any evidence which the lower court did not hear. It may be possible to argue that, as an application in the magistrates' court would have allowed an appeal which would have resulted in a fresh hearing, the appellate court in an appeal from the county court application should also hear the matter afresh. It is unlikely, however, that the court will deviate readily from the usual appeal procedure in the county court.

Appeal from post-conviction orders

12.19 If the order imposed by the magistrates' court, then the appeal is one to the Crown Court, by virtue of the same statutory powers as for ASBOs made in free-standing applications.[26] However, if the order is imposed by the Crown Court, then, although not part of the criminal sentence, the correct venue for the appeal is the Court of Criminal Appeal. This has been confirmed in the case of *R v P*,[27] where Mr Justice Henriques, giving the decision of a Court of Appeal, including the Lord Chief Justice, stated:

> '36   Finally, it should be noted that whilst the making of such an order is strictly not part of the sentencing process, the appropriate venue for an appeal against the making of such an order when made in the Crown Court is plainly to the Court of Appeal Criminal Division. So much is plain from a reading of section 9(1) of the Criminal Appeal Act 1968 together with section 50(1) of the same Act.'

---

[19]   CPR PD 52, para 2A.2.
[20]   Although Part 65 has been added to the CPR 1998, it does not seem to affect the appeal route.
[21]   CPR, r 52.3(1).
[22]   CPR, r 52.3(2).
[23]   CPR PD 52, para 4.6.
[24]   CPR, r 52.4.
[25]   CPR, r 52.11.
[26]   MCA 1980, s 108, even though the order is not a conviction or sentence.
[27]   [2004] EWCA Crim 287, (2004) *The Times*, February 19.

APPEALS FROM VARIATION OF ORDERS

12.20 As discussed at para **11.32** there is no automatic appeal from the variation of an ASBO. Any order made by the magistrates' court either on conviction or on application can only be appealed by case stated or judicial review. Any appeal from the Crown Court or county court would have to be made with permission to the Court of Appeal and High Court respectively. Any appeal hearing would be by way of review not re-hearing unless the court exceptionally ordered otherwise in the later case.

RECTIFICATION OF MISTAKES

12.21 In the situation where there has been an error by the court in completing the order as made or failing to do something which was agreed the issue arises as to how this can be dealt with. In the county court the slip rule applies and there is no difficultly. Similarly in the Crown Court. The magistrates' court however being a creature of statute only has the power to amend by virtue of s 142 of the Magistrates' Court Act 1980. In *Samuda v Birmingham Magistrates' Court*[28] the court considered this section and re-iterated that it can only be used within the magistrates' criminal jurisdiction and not their civil jurisdiction.[29] The rationale being that the intention of Parliament appears to have been to deprive the magistrates' court of a general power to re-open civil proceedings.

12.22 The Home Office Guidance at page 47 seems to agree with the above save that it states that the power would be available to orders made on conviction as they are dealing with an offender in criminal proceedings. This would seem to be wrongly stated. There is no doubt from the case-law[30] that even in post-conviction applications the court, when making or considering the application for an order, is doing so in its civil and not criminal jurisdiction. Therefore, there can be no scope for using section 142 to rectify an error.

12.23 The only way to amend an error would be to make an application to vary the original order following the appropriate procedure. The court can of course be asked to use its powers under the Criminal Procedure Rules 2005[31] to shorten a time limit and allow a notice or application to be presented orally. Unfortunately there does not appear to be such a power within the Magistrates' Courts (Anti-social Behaviour) Order Rules 2002 although if all parties agree this would not be an impediment.

---

[28] [2008] EWHC 205 (Admin).
[29] [2008] EWHC 205 (Admin) at para 10 affirming *R (Perisamy Mathialagan v London Borough of Southwark)* [2004] EWCA Civ 1689.
[30] *R (on the application of W) v Acton Youth Court* [2005] All ER (D) 284.
[31] CPR 2005, r 50.3.

CHAPTER 13

BREACH OF AN ANTI-SOCIAL BEHAVIOUR ORDER

GENERAL PRINCIPLES

13.1 Breach of the terms of an ASBO without reasonable excuse is a criminal offence and renders the offender liable to be arrested and prosecuted. If proved, the breach is a recordable offence. Breach of an interim order is a criminal offence in the same way without distinction as to procedure or penalties.

13.2 As the breach is a criminal offence, the CPS will ordinarily prosecute all alleged breaches. Usually, the defendant will have been arrested and charged by a police officer and, therefore, the police will liaise directly with the CPS. Prosecutions for breach of ASBO terms will have to be proved to the criminal standard and will also have to pass the public interest test which the CPS applies to all prosecutions. In practice, this has sometimes led to problems owing to the lack of training and/or familiarity with ASBOs and their prosecution. On a number of occasions, the situation has arisen where evidence of a breach has been compiled and the defendant charged, only for the defendant to be bound over or the charge dropped by representatives of the CPS (sometimes as leverage to obtain a guilty plea on other offences), as they considered that the conduct was not significant and not likely to result in tangible punishment. This misconception seems to come from the view that a breach should not be proceeded with unless the defendant has caused harassment, alarm or distress on that occasion. This is not the correct approach, as any breach of an ASBO should be considered to be a serious matter and the courts are encouraged to take that view (indeed, a number of custodial sentences have been imposed for first instances of breach even though the conduct was 'merely' entering an exclusion area, with nothing more).[1] At any breach hearing, the court's attention should be drawn to the fact that the order has been made after the defendant has embarked on a course of behaviour which has made an order necessary. Whilst a defendant who simply enters an area from which he or she is forbidden by the order does not necessarily cause any harassment, alarm or distress, it is contrary to the principles behind the imposition of the order for there not to be a prosecution of that breach. This would make the order irrelevant and ignores the reason for prohibiting him or her from the area in the first place. A first breach of this nature may not result in a custodial sentence but must be prosecuted. Otherwise, that term of the order may as well not have been made. The effect of the public perception of the effectiveness of ASBO proceedings should not be underestimated if much publicised terms are breached and no action is taken.

13.3 In practice, complaints about breaches in the community are often made to the local authority or RSL officers. It is important that the officers who receive the complaints obtain as much information as possible about witnesses, as the nature of the proceedings is now criminal and, therefore, hearsay evidence will normally be excluded, save for limited exceptions. The investigation of a breach of an ASBO is an investigation of a criminal offence, and care must be taken, as an investigation will be subject to the provisions of the Criminal Procedure and Investigations Act 1996 and the Police and Criminal Evidence Act 1984. Ideally, the investigation of whether a breach has occurred and the taking of statements should be left to the police.

---

[1]   But see *R v Lamb* at **13.23** below.

13.4   Care must be taken by the prosecuting authority that prosecutions are brought together if allegations of both a breach of an ASBO and a criminal offence are to be founded on the same or similar facts. To do otherwise may well be an abuse of process or lead to an instance of *autrefois convict*. Defence representatives should seek at an early stage to try to put the prosecution to an election as to charges and to challenge attempts made to bring duplicitous charges.

CHALLENGING THE ORDER IN BREACH PROCEEDINGS

13.5   In *W v DPP*[2] the administrative court considered a case where an ASBO had been made including a term that he must not 'commit any criminal offence'. The defendant did not appeal against that order and then stole sweets and a bottle of Lucozade from a shop. The district judge considered the prohibition in the ASBO to have been far too wide and unnecessary, however felt himself compelled by its unambiguous wording and sentenced him to an absolute discharge.

13.6   Lord Justice Brooke giving the decision of the court considered that the clause was plainly too wide and that, although it might not have been inappropriate to include a term restraining him from stealing, a general prohibition was too widely drawn. He held that in accordance with *Boddington v British Transport Police*,[3] if the ASBO was 'plainly invalid' the magistrates could properly consider submissions that the ASBO or term was invalid and not convict. He was however at pains to limit the width of such arguments in saying:

> 'I would stress that anything I say in this case must be understood as referring only to an order as plainly invalid as one which contains a restraint preventing a defendant from committing any criminal offence. There is great force, in my judgment, in the submission that we have received from Mr Gelbart to the effect that there will be a danger of opening floodgates if challenges to anti-social behaviour orders could be made in breach proceedings, but in all these cases there are exceptions which are as plain as the exception in this case.'

13.7   The position was re-considered by the Divisional Court in *CPS v T*[4] when a district judge in hearing breach proceedings considered that an ASBO term prohibiting the defendant from acting in an anti-social manner was too vague and lacking in clarity so that he held it was invalid and therefore unenforceable relying by analogy on *W v DPP* above.

13.8   At the case stated hearing in *CPS v T* the CPS sought to argue that the concession in *DPP v W* was improperly made and that the ASBO made by a competent court was valid on its face and any challenge should have been by appeal or variation from the original order. Mr Justice Richards held that the normal rule is that an order is valid unless and until it is set aside and that even if the order should not have been made in the first place a person may be liable for any breach before it is set aside. Any person who has an ASBO imposed against them has rights of appeal and variation. There was no good reason why the magistrates' court should be held to have jurisdiction to rule on the validity of the original order. Although the court may have made an order which was unduly wide and uncertain it did not take the order beyond its jurisdiction to have made one.

13.9   Mr Justice Richards concluded as a result of consideration of case-law which was not cited to the court in *W v DPP*, the concession in it was wrong and that it was *not* open to the district judge, a matter of jurisdiction, to rule that the original order was invalid. However the district judge could have considered whether the term lacked sufficient clarity to warrant a finding that the defendant's conduct amounted to a breach of the order or whether the lack of clarity

---

[2]   [2005] EWCA Civ 1333.
[3]   [1999] 2 AC 143.
[4]   [2006] EWHC 728 (Admin).

provided a reasonable excuse for non-compliance. Finally he could have considered whether it was appropriate to have imposed any penalty for the breach.

PROVING THE ORDER

13.10 Some difficulties have been encountered by the CPS and local authorities when attempting to prosecute breaches of ASBOs where the defendant has denied that an order was made or alleged that the terms in the purported order were not those made. As the magistrates' court is not a court of record and no tape recording is made, proof has been at the whim of the clerks' notes of hearing and indeed has often required witness statements from representatives (and even clerks) as to the order which was made. As a result of the amendments to the CDA 1998 by the Serious Organised Crime and Police Act 2005 to prove that an ASBO was made, all that is required is the court register[5] (see **13.13** below).

13.11 In *R v English*[6] the Court of Appeal had to consider the position in relation to proof before those amendments to the CDA 1998 in the Serious Organised Crime and Police Act 2005 (SOCPA 2005). The appellant had been convicted of two counts of breach of an ASBO and appealed on the grounds that the prosecution had failed to establish that a valid ASBO was in force at the relevant time of breach. The ASBO was in fact a post-conviction order imposed by the magistrates' court. The court completed a document in which the fact of the conviction was set out but the details of behaviour found by the court were left blank in the standard form. The terms of the order were then properly set out. The appellant's submission was that as the details of the anti-social behaviour said to have been found by the court were blank the order was invalidly made. The appellant cited both *R v P* and *C v Sunderland Youth Court, Northumbria Police and Crown Prosecution Service* in respect of the principles of fairness (see, further, chapter 6).

13.12 Lord Justice Latham, in giving the decision of the Court of Appeal, agreed that the principles of fairness in the above cases were of importance, however, pointed out that the order which was the basis for any subsequent breach proceedings must be the order which was made in court.[7] He found that the form signed by the magistrates was admissible evidence of the order which was made and that, in the absence of any evidence that it was not the order made, the order was validly made as were the breach proceedings. He affirmed that it could only be in exceptional cases where the order was 'plainly invalid' that the court hearing a breach be entitled to look at the validity of the underlying order as in *W v DPP*.[8] He concluded:

> '12.   The presumption that any document such as the one in question here is recording a valid order is one which, in our judgment, should prevail in all other cases and that the only other way to challenge an order which is apparently valid on its face can be by way of an appeal under section 108 of the Magistrates' Courts Act or (if the underlying facts justify it) an application for judicial review on the basis of some failure or defect in procedure.'

13.13 The court in *English* was considering breach proceedings heard in February 2005. As of 1 July 2005, however, there has been a material amendment to the CDA 1998 by SOCPA 2005. Section 1(10C) has been inserted into the CDA 1998 and provides that in breach proceedings a copy of the original ASBO, certified as such by the proper officer of the court which made it, is admissible as evidence of its having been made and of its contents to the same extent that oral evidence of those facts would be admissible. This must presumably include any maps and terms which were attached to the order.

5   CDA 1998, s 1(10C).
6   [2005] EWCA Crim 2690, [2005] All ER (D) 115 (Oct).
7   [2005] EWCA Crim 2690, [2005] All ER (D) 115 (Oct), para 9.
8   [2005] EWCA Civ 1333.

13.14 Proof of an ASBO at breach proceedings was further considered more recently in *W v DPP*.[9] The defendant had been subject to ASBO in February but in March had tried to enter a shop from which he was barred, then loitered with others outside and threw a stone which broke the shop window. At the criminal trial the prosecution asserted that the defendant was subject to the ASBO but called no evidence to prove the making of the ASBO, nor that the defendant was the person against whom it was made. They also did not seek an admission of those facts from the defence. The defendant made a submission of no case to answer which was refused. He appealed to the Divisional Court.

13.15 Mr Justice Openshaw held that the CPS could have easily adduced the court register in evidence which showing a person with the same full name as the defendant, same date of birth and address would have allowed the court to conclude as a matter of fact that an ASBO had been made against him. They also noted that it may also have been possibly appropriate for the CPS to apply to re-open their case but this had not been done. They approved *Kingsnorth & Kenny v DPP*.[10] He held that the prosecuting authority *must* prove formally that an ASBO had been made *and* that the person named in the order was the person before the court.

DEFENCE OF REASONABLE EXCUSE

13.16 In the recent case of *R v Chuck Charles*[11] the Court of Appeal was asked to rule on the novel point in ASBO breach proceedings as to who bore the legal burden of proving whether a defendant had acted without reasonable excuse. The defendant had assaulted a police officer and had imposed on him a post conviction ASBO including the 'general prohibition' against ASB. Subsequently during the duration of the ASBO the defendant had gone to property which he rented out and waking a tenant had demanded rent and told him to move outside or be locked inside when the locks were changed. The tenant's back was scratched with a screwdriver during the incident and the defendant was charged with s 47 assault and breach of his ASBO.

13.17 The defendant's case was that he had gone to the house to clear up after some work had been done to the bathroom of the house, to deal with a complaint about noise and ask the tenant to pay overdue rent. He claimed he had been changing the lock so that the room could not be locked to persuade the complainant to pay his rent. The jury could not decide as to whether he had assaulted the tenant but convicted him of breach of the ASBO.

13.18 The Court of Appeal held that the legal burden of proving that the defendant acted without reasonable excuse must in the absence of clear statutory provisions to the contrary, lie on the prosecution. It could not in their view have been intended by Parliament to place any burden of proof on the defendant under s 1(10) which criminalised conduct which Parliament itself had not criminalised (the term here not being a criminal offence). The Act did however impose an evidential burden on the defendant to raise the defence.

BREACH OF INTERIM ORDERS

13.19 Breach of an interim order carries the same sentence as breach of a full order. Further, as made clear in *Parker v DPP*,[12] the breach of a term in an interim order which is subsequently not made as a condition in the final order is still a criminal offence and no less serious for not being

---

9   [2006] EWHC 1211 (Admin).
10 [2003] EWHC 786 (Admin).
11 [2009] EWCA Crim 1570.
12 [2005] EWHC 1485 (Admin).

continued. In *Parker* the term in the interim order was one against association with another youth. Lord Justice Rose (Vice President of the Court of Appeal, Criminal Division) held:

> 'In my judgment, however, it by no means follows that the absence from the final ASBO of a condition inserted at the interim stage itself affects the gravity or otherwise of the breach of that condition. The gravity of the breach of the interim condition depends on all the circumstances of the case by reference, for example without purporting to be exhaustive, to the nature of the conduct giving rise to the breach and the flagrancy of the breach having regard, for example, to the relevant time scale – that is to say, a breach which occurs very soon after an order has been made may very well be a good deal more serious than a breach occurring some time later. Equally, the repetition of the same breach may well result in the sentencing court taking a graver view of the quality of the breach for which sentence is to be passed.
>
> 11 … For my part, in spite of Mr Lofthouse's elegant submissions, I am wholly unpersuaded that omission of a condition from the final order of itself is a matter to which the court should properly have regard when sentencing for the breach of a condition in an interim order …'

Breaches by young people

13.20 As proceedings for breach of an ASBO by young people are heard in the youth court, where the reporting restrictions are generally automatic[13] and are far less likely to be lifted than on the making of an ASBO, a further amendment was made to the CDA 1998 by SOCPA 2005. Section 10D is inserted[14] and provides that in relation to breach proceedings against a child or young person automatic reporting restrictions will not apply, however, the court will have the power under s 45 of the Youth Justice and Criminal Evidence Act 1999 to make an order preventing reporting. Strangely, that section is not yet in force at the time of publication with no commencement date available. Save that the court must have regard to the welfare of the defendant[15] in considering whether to make an order under s 45 no test is given within the subsection. It seems likely, however, that there will have to be good reason to impose restrictions given that Parliament's intentions as to reporting have seemingly been signalled by removing the automatic restriction. If the court does impose reporting restrictions under s 45 then it must give its reasons for doing so.[16] If reporting restrictions were imposed in making the ASBO then it would seem proper, however, that prima facie there should be no reporting of the criminal proceedings. This may change if the conduct of the defendant is contrary to the reasons why the s 39 order was made, e g if made on the basis of a submission that the defendant was doing well and would be more likely to offend if publicity was given to the order. At the time of publication s 45 is *not* in force and the Home Office has not been able to give any date when it is likely to come into force. Until it does, therefore, reporting restrictions will not apply.

13.21 The proceedings before the youth court follow the same course as any criminal prosecution before that court and require the attendance of the defendant's parent or legal guardian if they are aged 15 or under. The maximum sentence of detention for a breach of an ASBO term for a young person is a 2-year detention and training order (only 12 months of this can be served in custody). A young person may only be sentenced to a detention and training order if he or she is aged 15 or over, or is a persistent offender and aged 12–14 years of age. A minor aged 10–11 who is in breach of an ASBO may not, at present, be sentenced to a term of detention but may be made subject to a community penalty. CDA 1998, s 1(11) applies to young people as well, preventing the making of a conditional discharge. In sentencing a person under the age of 16, the youth court must now consider whether a parenting order (see **11.51** et seq)

---

[13] Children and Young Persons Act 1933, s 49.
[14] Inserted by s 141 of SOCPA 2005.
[15] Youth Justice and Criminal Evidence Act 1999, s 45(6).
[16] CDA 1998, s 1(10E).

should be made and, if not, it should state the reasons why. In relevant circumstances it must also consider whether to make an individual support order (see **11.60**).

Who can prosecute?

13.22 If the defendant has been arrested by the police, then the CPS, through its director, has the statutory responsibility for the conduct of all criminal proceedings instituted on behalf of a police force.[17] This will mean, therefore, that any person who is charged by the police will be prosecuted by the CPS. This is what Parliament originally intended and is confirmed in the current Home Office Guidance. With the above problems arising from prosecution of breaches of ASBOs by the CPS, the CDA 1998 has been further amended by the ASB Act 2003,[18] with additional subsections being inserted into s 1 to permit a council which is a relevant authority and a council for the local government area in which the defendant resides or appears to reside to prosecute for an offence under s 1(10), namely breach of an order. This amendment came into force on 31 March 2004. Further, from 20 January 2004, where breach proceedings are brought against a young person, s 47 of the Children and Young Persons Act 1933 is to be read by virtue of the ASB Act 2003 to allow a single person, authorised by the relevant authority, to be present. This deals with the anomalous situation whereby the relevant authority could not be present in the youth court in any criminal proceedings. This amendment, therefore, allows representation from the relevant authority to prosecute a breach.

13.23 The CDA 1998 has been further amended[19] to allow the council for the local government area in which the defendant resides or appears to reside to bring proceedings under s 1(10) for breach of a post-conviction order. At first blush, this seems strange, as it would appear that by applying s 1(10) for the purposes of making and effecting post-conviction orders (see s 1C(9)), this would already allow a council or local government area council to bring a prosecution by virtue of s 1(10A). A possible reason could have been the reference to 'an anti-social behaviour order' in s 1(10). However, this cannot be valid, due to the 'applying' of s 1C(9) and, if correct, then breaches of county court ASBOs cannot be prosecuted by the council as, whilst there is a similar 'applying' subsection at s 1B(7), there is no similar amendment to allow prosecution of breaches. The reason therefore would seem to be that, as s 1C(9) brings in only s 1(10), this does not include s 1(10A). It is submitted that s 1C(9A) is clumsily drafted and is unnecessary. All that was needed was to add s 1(10A) to the list of sections in s 1C(9A). This is another example of the poor drafting which affects the CDA 1998 (as amended).

13.24 There is, however, an alternate way in which a body other than the CPS can bring or conduct proceedings. Section 6(1) of the Prosecution of Offences Act 1985 expressly preserves the right of any person to institute or conduct any criminal proceedings, although the Director of the CPS may take over their conduct at any time, whether or not he has a duty to do so.[20] Local authorities also have a specific reserved power to initiate proceedings under s 222 of the Local Government Act 1972, which provides:

> 'Where a local authority considers it expedient for the promotion or protection of the interests of the inhabitants of their area –
>
> (a) they may prosecute or defend or appear in any legal proceeding ....'

13.25 From a practical standpoint, however, if the police have charged a person with the breach of an ASBO term and the local authority wish to conduct the proceedings, they must seek to

---

17 Prosecution of Offences Act 1985, s 3(2).
18 ASB Act 2003, s 85(1) and (4), amending CDA 1998, s 10, and inserting ss 10A and 10B.
19 Section 1D(9A)–(9C), inserted by ASB Act 2003, s 86(3).
20 Prosecution of Offences Act 1985, s 6(2).

have the charge withdrawn and prosecution proceedings begun by the council. Caution must be taken to ensure that a not guilty verdict is not entered on the withdrawal of the police charge, otherwise the principles of *autrefois convict* will apply and no further charge can be brought. The alternative is to request that the CPS appoint someone in the local authority legal department to take over the conduct of the criminal proceedings pursuant to s 5(1) of the 1985 Act. The person must, however, be someone who holds a general legal qualification, that is to say, a person who has a right of audience in any part of the Supreme Court or all county or magistrates' courts.[21] Alternatively, some local authorities are considering investigating, and prosecuting, breaches of ASBOs themselves. We would suggest it is preferable wherever possible to allow the police and CPS to perform this task as they have greater experience in this field and it is also generally more cost-effective. Building good relationships with the police and CPS is therefore vital, and use should be made of the specialist anti-social behaviour Crown Prosecutors. It should, however, be noted that these prosecutors are not specialists in ASBOs and therefore, where appropriate, it may be sensible to arrange for either the CPS to instruct specialist counsel or for the local authority to take over the prosecution at that stage. If the relationship between local authority and the police/CPS is not fruitful the option does of course remain for the local authority itself to bring the prosecution.

SENTENCING

13.26 On summary conviction, an adult defendant (see **13.35** for young people) can be sentenced to a maximum of 6 months and a fine not exceeding the present statutory maximum of £5,000 and, on indictment, up to 5 years' imprisonment and/or a fine.[22] It should be noted that, whilst the court has the power to impose community penalties as well as fines or prison terms, it does not have the power to impose a conditional discharge,[23] although, presumably, an absolute discharge remains available. The penalty for breach is the same, whether the breach is of a final or an interim order. The Sentencing Guidelines Council has now produced 'Definitive' sentencing Guidelines for breach of ASBOs[24] after 5 January 2009 which every court is statutorily obliged to have regard to it when passing sentence.[25] The Guidelines states that whilst it applies to adults and youths the sentencing framework that applies to offenders aged under 18 is significantly different from that for older offenders and therefore the guidance for young offenders is in the form of principles particularly regarding the circumstances in which a custodial sentence might be justified. Sentencing Guidelines for youth sentences is expected in due course.

13.27 The Guidance gives the courts the following general statement:

'The main aim of sentencing for breach of a court order is to achieve the purpose of the order; in the case of an ASBO that is to protect the public from behaviour that is likely to cause harassment, alarm or distress. Any perception that the courts do not treat seriously a failure to comply with a court order can undermine public confidence and is therefore an important additional consideration.'

It continues:

'The main aim of sentencing for breach of a court order is to achieve the purpose of the order. Therefore, the sentence for breach of an ASBO should primarily reflect the harassment, alarm or distress involved; the fact that it constituted breach of a court order is a secondary consideration.'

---

21 Courts and Legal Services Act 1990, s 71.
22 CDA 1998, s 1(10).
23 CDA 1998, s 1(11).
24 See Appendix 5.
25 CJA 2003, s 172.

13.28 In determining how serious a breach is the Guideline states:

> 'The sentence for breach of an ASBO must be commensurate with the seriousness of the offence; that is determined by assessing the culpability of the offender and any harm which the offence caused, was intended to cause or might foreseeably have caused.'

13.29 The Guidelines note that the breach may itself cause harassment, alarm or distress, which can reduce the quality of life in a community. Further that breach of an ASBO contravenes an order of the court, and this can undermine public confidence in the effective administration of justice. The assessment of the seriousness of an individual offence must take into account not only the harm actually caused by an offence but also any harm that was intended or might foreseeably have been caused. If the defendant was unaware of the breach due to a misunderstanding of the terms this could be a mitigating feature.

13.30 At Annex B the Guidelines set out the factors indicating a more serious breach as being as follows:

- Offence committed whilst on bail for other offences.

- Failure to respond to previous sentences.

- Offence was racially or religiously aggravated.

- Offence motivated by, or demonstrating, hostility to the victim based on his or her sexual orientation (or presumed sexual orientation).

- Offence motivated by, or demonstrating, hostility based on the victim's disability (or presumed disability).

- Previous conviction(s), particularly where a pattern of repeat offending is disclosed.

- Planning of an offence.

- An intention to commit more serious harm than actually resulted from the offence.

- Offenders operating in groups or gangs.

- 'Professional' offending.

- Commission of the offence for financial gain (where this is not inherent in the offence itself).

- High level of profit from the offence.

- An attempt to conceal or dispose of evidence.

- Failure to respond to warnings or concerns expressed by others about the offender's behaviour.

- Offence committed whilst on licence.

- Offence motivated by hostility towards a minority group, or a member or members of it.

- Deliberate targeting of vulnerable victim(s).

- Commission of an offence while under the influence of alcohol or drugs.

- Use of a weapon to frighten or injure victim.

- Deliberate and gratuitous violence or damage to property, over and above what is needed to carry out the offence.

13.31 An even higher degree of seriousness would be indicated by any of the following:

- Multiple victims.

- An especially serious physical or psychological effect on the victim, even if unintended.

- A sustained assault or repeated assaults on the same victim.

- Victim is particularly vulnerable.

- Location of the offence (for example, in an isolated place).

- Offence is committed against those working in the public sector or providing a service to the public.

- Presence of others eg relatives, especially children or partner of the victim.

- Additional degradation of the victim (eg taking photographs of a victim as part of a sexual offence).

- In property offences, high value (including sentimental value) of property to the victim, or substantial consequential loss (eg where the theft of equipment causes serious disruption to a victim's life or business).

13.32 As to factors indicating a less serious breach the Guidelines indicate the following:

- A greater degree of provocation than normally expected.

- Mental illness or disability.

- Youth or age, where it affects the responsibility of the individual defendant.

- The fact that the offender played only a minor role in the offence.

13.33 Further in terms of personal mitigation the Guidelines indentify the following as non-exhaustive relevant matters:

- the offender has a lower level of understanding due to mental health issues or learning difficulties;

- the offender was acting under the influence of an older or more experienced offender; or

- there has been compliance with an Individual Support Order or Intervention Order imposed when the ASBO was made.

Sentencing starting points

13.34 The Guidelines set out in tabular form[26] the starting points for a first time offender after a trial. It should be noted that a first time offender is within the context of a breach of an ASBO not someone without previous convictions but someone who has not breached an ASBO before. The court is required to assess the nature of the failure and harm intended and caused by the defendant before considering the starting point for sentence within 3 brackets. The Guidelines make it plain that if there are repeated breaches or where there are several aggravating features a sentence beyond the range given would be justified. The court should then consider the defendant's credit for guilty plea, if any, and personal mitigation before determining sentence. There is a duty on the court to state why it passes any sentence which is of a different kind or outside the range in the Guidelines.[27]

Youths

13.35 The Guidelines states that whilst the above criteria and mechanism of determining seriousness apply to youths, in most cases of breach by a young offender convicted after a trial, the appropriate sentence will be a community sentence. The Guidelines also state that the particular stage of intellectual or emotional maturity of the defendant (which may not correspond with actual age) will also influence sentence. A young offender is likely to perceive a particular time period as being longer in comparison with an adult, and this may be of relevance dependent on how much time has elapsed between imposition and breach of the order.

13.36 The Guidelines state that where a 'first time offender' (normal meaning) pleads guilty it must make a referral order[28] unless it makes a custodial sentence, absolute discharge or hospital order. In some less serious cases, such as where the breach has not involved any harassment, alarm or distress, a fine may be appropriate if it will be paid by the offender, or otherwise a reparation order should be made. The custody threshold should be set at a significantly higher level than the threshold applicable to adult offenders and usually will not be crossed unless the breach involved serious harassment, alarm or distress through either the use of violence, threats or intimidation or the targeting of individuals/groups in a manner that led to a fear of violence. In exceptional cases the custody threshold may also be crossed where a youth is being sentenced for more than one offence of breach (committed on separate occasions within a short period) involving a lesser but substantial degree of harassment, alarm or distress. The Guidelines even go on to say that where the custody threshold is crossed, the court should normally impose a community sentence in preference to a DTO, as custody should be used only as a measure of last resort.

13.37 If the court is to impose a custodial sentence on a youth the Guidelines state the starting point for sentencing should be 4 months detention, with a range of up to 12 months. Where a youth is being sentenced for more than one breach involving serious harassment, alarm or distress, the sentence may go beyond that range. Where a custodial sentence is imposed in the youth court, it must be a detention and training order (DTO), which can only be for 4, 6, 8, 10, 12, 18 or 24 months. Where the offender is aged 10 or 11, no custodial sentence is available in the youth court. Where the offender is aged between 12 and 14, a custodial sentence may be imposed only if the child is a 'persistent offender'.[29]

---

[26]   See Appendix 5.
[27]   CJA 2003, s 174(2)(a).
[28]   Referral is to a youth offender panel, and the court may (or 'shall' in the case of a child aged under 16) require at least one parent or guardian to attend the panel meetings unless this would be unreasonable.
[29]   Powers of Criminal Courts (Sentencing) Act 2000, s 100.

13.38 The court may request reports prior to sentencing in the usual way. However, it may also take them from a relevant applicant body. In this way, the court is told of the reasons why the ASBO was made originally, which will have an effect on the impact of the breach that has been proved. It is important for any applicant body to have close links with the CPS with regard to prosecutions of breaches (if not prosecuting itself), as the overall conduct of the defendant is only likely to be known to the applicant and not to the CPS representatives. One means of providing more information which has been instituted by some local authorities in the provision of a case summary to the CPS for each ASBO made, including both details of the proved schedule and those incidents outside the 6 months used to show necessity. This ensures that the sentencing court is appraised on the full background before reaching a decision. Further, if the breach has highlighted the need for an extension or variation of the original terms, it is worthwhile ensuring that the application for the same is made prior to any sentence hearing, so that both matters can be heard by the same tribunal. It will, in those circumstances, generally be appropriate for the CPS to allow the sentence hearing to be conducted by the solicitor or barrister whom the applicant body has instructed to deal with the variation or extension application.

SENTENCING CASE-LAW

13.39 The issue of whether the court can impose a greater sentence of imprisonment on breach of a term of an ASBO which prohibits actions which constitute a criminal offence than for the crime alone has been considered in detail in chapter 10 (**10.6–10.31**).

13.40 In terms of actual sentences imposed for breaches of ASBOs the Court of Appeal has on a number of occasions upheld significant sentences of imprisonment, however, it has made it clear that the starting point must be to consider why the ASBO was made and its effect. Whilst every breach is potentially serious the greater sentences of imprisonment have to be reserved for breaches which cause harassment, alarm or distress. In *R v Curtis Braxton*[30] the Court of Appeal in considering the purpose and effect of an ASBO held that:

> 'It is undeniable that [an ASBO] represents a serious infringement upon the liberty of the applicant, not only because it represents a restriction on his right of free movement, but also because breach constitutes a criminal offence punishable with a term of up to five years' imprisonment, which is greater than the maximum penalty which could be imposed for offences which might otherwise be reflected within the terms of the order. It is, however, a response by Parliament to the increasing concern about the impact on the public of antisocial behaviour in its many constituent forms. It follows that this concern must be reflected in the sentences which the court imposes for breach of the order.'

13.41 In *Braxton* the Court of Appeal was considering a defendant who engaged in repeated, aggressive begging addressed at pedestrians in Birmingham city centre which clearly caused both real concern and distress. The appellant was a man with nine convictions for public order offences and nine convictions for minor violence who had served 2 years' imprisonment for breach of the ASBO imposed on him. He was refused leave to appeal a sentence of 3½ years' imprisonment for two identical breaches of the ASBO with 3 months' imprisonment consecutive for common assault (also on a pedestrian who would not engage with him) all committed soon after his release from prison. The court went on to say:

> '[17] ... Unfortunately, the applicant still does not appear to understand the nature or effect of the order made against him. The anti-social behaviour order is specifically designed to protect the public from frequent and distressing repeated misbehaviour of the type which is the subject of this order, and the applicant was indeed committing a serious criminal offence, even entering the City of

---

30   [2004] EWCA Crim 1374, [2005] 1 Cr App R (S) 36.

Birmingham within the confines set out within the map served upon him when the order was made. He acted in deliberate breach of that order not once but twice (which led to the four year term reduced to two years) and yet again twice more within weeks of his release from that prison sentence. He must understand that what he might consider as trivial in his case, because of the persistence of his conduct, is now treated seriously, specifically to protect the public. It is thus vital that he address this issue and his behaviour in public if he is to avoid further conflict with the law.'

13.42 The above passages were expressly approved by the Court of Appeal in *R v Lamb*[31] where the defendant was 18 years of age but had a substantial criminal record. He had been made the subject of an ASBO that prevented him entering a town centre and from using the metro system and from consuming alcohol in a public place. Six days after it was made he was found on the metro and sentenced to 6 months' custody. This was successfully appealed one month later and reduced to a conditional discharge. That evening, however, he was again seen at the metro station. He was then sentenced to 12 months' custody for this second breach which was reduced on appeal to 6 months. Shortly after release he was again found inside the exclusion area and sentenced to 3 months and on release from this sentence was found to be drunk in public on the same day within the prohibited area. For these he received a sentence of 2 years' imprisonment. When released from this sentence he was immediately seen in the metro on three occasions. None of the breaches involved any actual anti-social behaviour but the Crown Court imposed a 22-month sentence.

13.43 The Court of Appeal recognised that this was a defendant who was neither committing a crime nor actually causing harassment or distress but was repeatedly breaching his order which was a serious matter. They held that *Braxton* was illustrative as the court was prepared there to uphold long sentences for breach. However, they held that the vital distinction between *Lamb* and *Braxton* was that the social impact of this appellant's offending was very much less and, indeed, did not impact on the public in any way. The ever-longer sentences had been driven only by the determination of the court to ensure that its orders limiting the appellant's movements are not flouted. In this regard, however, they did say:

> '19. We recognize that this is an important objective in itself. An order of the court must be obeyed. We do not accept, however, that being found in a place within the proscribed area without any evidence of associated antisocial behaviour deserves to be visited with a sentence as long as 22 months imprisonment. Where breaches do not involve harassment, alarm or distress, community penalties should be considered in order to help the offender learn to live within the terms of the ASBO to which he or she is subject. In those cases when there is no available community penalty (into which category we include this case given the appellant's refusal to engage with agencies prepared to help him and the frequency of his breaches), custodial sentences which are necessary to maintain the authority of the court can be kept as short as possible. This approach is consistent with that adopted by the court in the albeit unrelated area of shoplifting: see *Page and others* [2004] EWCA Crim 3358 in which the Vice President spoke of the need for proportionality between the sentence and the particular offence.'

13.44 The Court of Appeal therefore reduced the sentence to 8 months (2 months on each breach) to commence after his period of licence to be served on recall. They concluded, however:

> '20. ... We underline, however, that such short sentences are not appropriate if the breach of the ASBO itself involves harassment, alarm or distress to the public of the type that the legislation was designed to prevent of which Braxton is a good example.'

13.45 In *R v Ward*[32] the Court of Appeal upheld a sentence of 6 months' consecutive imprisonment (to 3 years for theft) for breach of a term prohibiting the defendant from carrying articles in connection with the removal of motor car alloy wheels saying that the breach was

---

[31] [2005] EWCA Crim 2487; [2005] All ER (D) 132 (Nov).
[32] [2005] EWCA Crim 2713.

flagrant. In *R v Kearns*[33] the defendant had been made the subject of an order which prevented him from entering certain shops. In breach, he entered a shop and was told to leave and did. He had eight previous breaches of the order for which sentences ranging from a fine for the first to 4 months' imprisonment had been passed. The judge in the Crown Court sentenced him to 15 months for this latest breach. The defendant appealed on the ground that the sentence was manifestly excessive when regard was taken to the behaviour which occasioned the actual breach. The Court of Appeal held that whilst the breach was minor in itself it was a breach of an order made in very clear terms but reduced the sentence to 9 months.

13.46 In *R v Anthony*[34] the defendant was in breach of an order which prohibited her from abusing any member of staff working in a GP's office or hospital and/or being drunk or consuming alcohol in a public place. The breach occurred the day after the order was made when the defendant shouted racial abuse at a nurse in hospital, pushed a security officer and spat in his face. She was arrested but found to be unfit to be detained and was taken back to the hospital for examination where she struck a doctor in the face, spat at a police officer and kicked a female security officer three times. The defendant pleaded guilty to breach of the ASBO and four common assaults denying the racial abuse. The Court of Appeal imposed a sentence of 3 years and 3 months for the breach and 6 months concurrently on the other charges. This case shows that the courts are prepared in the right cases to take very severe action as this sentence could not have been imposed for any of the possible criminal charges.

13.47 In *R v Stevens*[35] (see further **10.28**) the Court of Appeal has confirmed that the approach in *Lamb* and *Braxton* was correct and *Morrison* had been wholly undermined and should not be followed. The Court of Appeal upheld a sentence of 9 months for a breach of ASBO in circumstances where the defendant had been in breach of an ASBO to prevent him being drunk or urinating in public.

13.48 In *R v Swain*[36] the defendant was convicted of breach of an ASBO when he was abusive to police officers, struggled when arrested, attempted to head-butt them and threatening to bite the face of an arresting officer. He was given an 18 month sentence consecutive to 4 months for other matters. The defendant had been in breach of ASBOs on 3 occasions before and had been sentenced to custody each time, reaching 8 months on a previous occasion.

13.49 On appeal before the Court of Appeal it was held that the actions of the defendant constituted bad behaviour but of itself would not had led to a sentence of anywhere near 18 months. He had not deliberately or recklessly disregarded the order. He had however continuously breached the order and therefore 12 months was substituted.

13.50 In *R v Cyril Stevens*[37] the Court of Appeal was once again faced with Mr Stevens having breached his ASBO, this time 2 days after a new ASBO had been imposed. He was drunk and abusive in a place which he was excluded from by the order. The judge imposed a sentence of 8 months imprisonment. He appealed to the Court of Appeal arguing that the length of sentence was disproportionate to the nature of the offence and the level of harm which was caused and/or that this was cruel and inhuman treatment in breach of the European Convention on Human Rights because he was an alcoholic and was being sentenced without sufficient regard to his disease.

13.51 The Court of Appeal held that the flaw in the defendant's argument was that:

---

[33]   [2005] EWCA Crim 2038.
[34]   [2005] EWCA Crim 2055.
[35]   [2006] All ER (D) 23 (Feb); decided on 2 February 2006, Lawtel Document No. AC9300667.
[36]   [2006] EWCA Crim 1621.
[37]   [2007] EWCA Crim 1128.

' . . .by its very nature a breach of an Anti-social Behaviour Order may well be a matter which in itself is relatively trivial. But the ASBO was made in order to stop persistent, relatively low-level offending. [Defendant's counsel] undervalues the damage done to the community by this sort of persistent anti-social behaviour. It is by no means trivial. It is a considerable interference with the liberty of other members of the public when this sort of behaviour is allowed to go on unchecked. The gravamen of this offence is not simply what the appellant did on this occasion, but his flagrant breaches of court orders, which are always regarded as serious . . .

. . . Parliament has decided that, even where the offences are relatively minor, courts should take action to prevent the public having to suffer continually the nuisance of someone like this appellant being drunk in public places, causing a disturbance, and causing problems for the authorities when they seek to prevent that happening . . . .'

13.52 In *R v Harris*[38] the defendant had been made subject to an ASBO due to inappropriate behaviour towards young females. He had approached three 12 year old girls asking for oral sex. The order included a term that he was not to associate when a female under 16. He went on to commit two offences of sexual activity in the presence of a child (masturbating) and a breach of the ASBO. He received 18 months for the sexual offences and 4 years concurrent for the breach of the ASBO. He appealed against the sentence arguing that he had pleaded guilty and the maximum was only 5 years and this breach was over a year into the order's duration.

13.53 The defendant had a large number of previous offences of this nature and he was assessed as having a high risk of re-offending. The Court of Appeal adopted the approach in *R v H Stevens and Lovegrove*[39] that it could not be right that the court was limited to the maximum imprisonment for the criminal offence. However the appropriate level of credit had not been given and a sentence of 3 years and 4 months was substituted.

Consecutive or concurrent

13.54 In *R v Craig Lawson*[40] the defendant had been made subject to an ASBO which had a general prohibition against anti-social behaviour which he breached by committing an offence of common assault. This offence had involved the defendant being with a group of people who assaulted 2 members of the public in the street. When a police officer came to arrest him he resisted arrest and tried to lunge at them. The court imposed a sentence of 6 months for the assault and 10 months consecutive for the breach of ASBO. The judge held that the defendant was drunk and out to make trouble. He had pleaded guilty at the last minute. The defendant appealed on the grounds that where the breach of an ASBO was a criminal offence the sentencing court should bear in mind the maximum sentence in the interests of proportionality. Also that 16 months overall was manifestly excessive.

13.55 Mr Justice Simon and Lord Justice Hooper following the case of *Braxton* held that there was nothing inherently wrong in passing a consecutive sentence for breach of an ASBO. Where consecutive sentences were to be passed there would usually be identifiable and discrete breaches other than those which comprised the index offence or an egregious breach of the ASBO. The 10 month sentence for the breach of ASBO was fully deserved but as the breach and the offences derived from the same course of conduct the sentences should have been concurrent, ie overall 10 months.

---

[38] [2006] EWCA Crim 1864.
[39] [2006] EWCA Crim 255, 2 Cr App R (S) 68, (2006) *The Times*, February 24.
[40] [2006] EWCA Crim 2674.

CHAPTER 14

ANTI-SOCIAL BEHAVIOUR ORDERS
AND YOUNG PEOPLE

14.1   The introduction of ASBOs has provided an effective civil tool to deal with minors who act in an anti-social manner. ASBOs may be made against defendants as young as 10 years of age. There are, however, special considerations in respect of applications against young persons which will be explored further in this chapter.

ASSESSMENT OF YOUNG PEOPLE'S NEEDS AND CIRCUMSTANCES

14.2   The Home Office Guidance calls for an assessment of a young person's needs and circumstances when applying for an ASBO.[1] An assessment is not strictly required by the Act, but is desirable and complies with other duties, eg under s 17 of the Children Act 1989. A young person is defined as a person between the ages of 10 and 17. The Guidance contains the following useful general remarks about assessments.

- The aim is twofold – to get information for the court *and* to ensure that the young person is provided with appropriate services.

- Assessments should not delay an application. Close liaison is therefore needed with the YOT or social services from the outset.

- Social services have a duty *in any event* to safeguard and promote the welfare of children in their area who may be 'in need'.[2]

- The assessment should be carried out in accordance with the guidance contained in the *Framework for the Assessment of Children in Need and their Families 2000*.[3]

- An initial assessment should be carried out within 7 working days. The Guidance does not specify when the 7 days commence, but, presumably, this is from the date of the initial referral.

- If the initial assessment identifies that a child is in need, a core assessment should be carried out within 35 working days.

- An assessment should deal with the child's needs and circumstances, the capacities of his or her parents and wider family, and any environmental factors.

- The assessment should run in parallel with the ASBO process.

---

[1]   See Home Office Guidance, reproduced in Appendix 3.
[2]   Children Act 1989, s 17.
[3]   Published by Department for Education and Employment.

14.3 The Guidance makes it clear that agencies have responsibilities to young people, irrespective of the ASBO process (eg social services, the local education authority or the health authority).

14.4 There is often a conflict of ideology between local authority agencies when ASBOs against young people are considered. Previous Home Office Guidance stated that the court hearing the application should satisfy itself that social services have been consulted and that the child's needs have been assessed before deciding whether an ASBO is appropriate. This was interpreted by some as giving social services or the YOT a veto on the decision whether or not to proceed with an ASBO. The current Guidance makes it clear that no one agency has a veto over an applicant's decision to apply for an ASBO (see chapter 3, dealing with consultation). It should be remembered that the guidance remains only that, and there is no requirement in the Act to conduct an assessment.

14.5 The defence may raise the lack of an assessment as proof that the underlying ASBO process has not been carried out properly. The point can be made that the court will not be able to make a judgment as to the necessity of an ASBO if the applicant has not carried out an assessment to see whether there are alternatives to an order (eg intensive social work input). Whilst the Home Office Guidance does not have the force of law, applicants are advised to be in a position to provide a good reason for not carrying out an assessment. There may not have been time to prepare a report or, perhaps, the child has recently been seen by the YOT or another agency, which has rendered a further assessment otiose. A matter sometimes raised by social workers is that the young person concerned is little different from many of the other children whom they see and that the imposition of an ASBO will stigmatise rather than reform. This is more often a personal perception of ASBOs, which also fails to consider the wider picture of the harm that the young person's behaviour causes to others, not least the other young persons in the area. However, the Home Office Guidance is clear:[4]

> '... there should be no confusion as to the purpose of the order, which is to protect the community. The welfare of a child is ... to be considered but ... is not the principal purpose of the order hearing.'

14.6 The issue of what weight the court should place on the welfare of the child has been raised in two cases. First, in *R (on the application of Kenny) v Leeds Magistrates' Court; R (on the application of M) v Secretary of State for Constitutional Affairs and another*,[5] as Kenny was aged 17 years and 360 days at the imposition of the without notice interim order, the defendant argued that, in considering whether it was just to impose an interim ASBO, the court must consider the interests of the child as a primary consideration. Mr Justice Owen, in agreeing, cited, with approval, the decision of Mr Justice Mumby,[6] where it was said that the youth court had to strike a fair balance between the competing interests of the particular child and the community but always having regard to the principle that the best interests of the child were a primary consideration. In relation to Kenny, the order was discharged for unrelated reasons but the judge failed to deal with the issue in relation to M (and most of the other defendants). It was not raised on appeal by M, but was raised as a test point by another defendant, A (aged 16), in *R (on the application of A) v Leeds Magistrates' Court and Leeds City Council*.[7] Whilst A's application for judicial review was refused on other grounds (see **12.12–12.15**), the judge, Mr Justice Stanley Burnton, expressly went on to consider the merits of the application. He concluded that, whilst the interests of the child were a primary consideration, they were not the primary consideration, and, further, that the interests of the public were themselves a primary consideration.[8] This is an important

---

4   See current Home Office Guidance, reproduced in Appendix 3.
5   [2004] 1 All ER 1333.
6   *R (on the application of the Howard League for Penal Reform v Secretary of State for the Home Dept* [2002] EWHC 2497 (Admin), [2002] All ER (D) 465 (Nov), at [67].
7   [2004] EWHC 554 (Admin), (2004) *The Times*, March 31.
8   [2004] EWHC 554 (Admin), (2004) *The Times*, March 31, at [49].

clarification of the bare principle which Mr Justice Owen stated. The judge, however, continued further to give more important guidance, saying:

> 'Secondly, it is by no means obvious that any of the prohibitions contained in the first order or the second order were contrary to the best interests of the claimant. This applies in particular to prohibitions 3, 5 to 7 and 9 and 10. At the hearing on 11 December 2003, Mr Message, not being able to call the claimant, and not having a witness statement from him, could only make a submission in the most general terms that (as summarised in his note) "it was not just to make an order which restricted his liberty, freedom of movement and associations." There was thus nothing before the District Judge to show that any prejudice, except of the most general kind, was caused by the imposition of any of the prohibitions, including prohibitions 4 and 8.

> If it is contended that the special interests of a child require either that there be no order, or an order in terms different from those proposed by the local authority, it is incumbent on a defendant to provide an explanation of his case and some relevant evidence. There will be cases where it is inappropriate to make any ASBO in respect of a child by reason of his age. That is not the present case: as I have stated, it is not contended that the evidence before the District Judge did not justify the making of an order against the Claimant, who was aged 16 and was allegedly participating in seriously anti-social behaviour. The phrase "the best interests of the child as a prime consideration" is not a magic talisman which, if not pronounced in a case concerning a child, will necessarily invalidate the order made.'[9]

14.7   The prohibitions referred to related to several forms of behaviour which were already criminal offences, save for one which prevented the defendant's being present when controlled drugs were traded, sold or supplied, and another which prevented him from possessing or distributing drug supplier (dealer) cards. There was also an exclusion zone and a general term mirroring the terms of s 1(1).

14.8   The point which emerges from the above cases is that the balance of the interests of the community and the child in ASBO applications is an equal one and not weighted either way. In practical terms, however, as most interim terms should be confined to only those terms which are necessary pending a full hearing, the interests of the community should be higher, unless the restrictions sought of the defendant are so draconian that they fundamentally interfere with his or her life. Even if those restrictions are present, it will be the defendant's responsibility to show more than just general objection and restriction. It is submitted that the defendant will have to show that his or her welfare (as a child) would be detrimentally affected by the term. This could be shown, perhaps, if it prevented attendance at school, a job programme or other important place in his or her development. Other than for exclusion zones, it is hard to see how, in the light of the above judgment, interim orders preventing criminal offences could be contrary to a child's welfare more than the obvious prejudice in the imposition of the interim order. Finally, whilst this reported case concerned interim orders, it is submitted that the basic principle must apply to the making of final orders as well.

14.9   The importance of a proper assessment, in appropriate circumstances, of a child's needs at a final hearing was underlined in the case of *R (on the application of AB and SB) v Nottingham City Council*.[10] This was an application for judicial review for alleged ongoing failure by the council to assess and provide for the applicants' needs. One of the applicants in this case was also the subject of an application for an ASBO, which had been adjourned pending the judicial review hearing. Part of the defence to the ASBO application was that an order should not be made because the local authority had failed to assess the child's needs or to consider other ways of dealing with the anti-social behaviour. Richards J underlined the importance of undertaking a systematic assessment of the child's needs, which he described as a three-stage process, including 'identification of needs, production of a care plan, and provision of identified

---

[9]   [2004] EWHC 554 (Admin), (2004) *The Times*, March 31, at [50]–[51].
[10]   [2001] EWCA Admin 235, [2001] 3 FCR 350.

services'. On the facts, it was held that there had been a failure properly to assess the child's needs. Richards J issued a warning to all applicant bodies:

> '... on the general issue of assessment of need, I have to say that I am left with the impression that the defendant [Nottingham City Council] has concentrated unduly on the anti-social behaviour order proceedings and insufficiently on the discharge of its duty, in particular under s 17 of the Children Act, to assess SB's needs and to make provision for them. No doubt the focus has been the result of SB's very serious behavioural problems, but those problems cannot excuse a failure to comply with the s 17 duty.'

14.10 This case pre-dates *Kenny* and *A* but is still valid and highlights the importance of an open-minded approach to cases of anti-social behaviour. It is unlikely, however, that failure to perform a s 17 assessment is sufficient to defeat an ASBO application. The Guidance has always stated that the court should be given all the relevant information about a child, and not that there has to be an assessment. Further, it is now clear that there is no claim which arises from a failure to make a s 17 assessment, as it is a 'target' duty and not an absolute one.[11] Finally, it would seem to us that if a court did not feel that it had sufficient information about a child to make an order which it otherwise would have considered (ie other elements of the test being proved), it is open to it to adjourn the proceedings in order for further information to be provided to it.

14.11 CDA 1998, s 37 states that the principal aim of the YOT is to prevent youth offending. If diversionary or other methods do not change a young person's behaviour, there may be little option left but to consider supporting an ASBO to fulfil this statutory function.

What form should the assessment take?

14.12 In Kirklees, the YOT carries out 'asset' assessments to fulfil the requirements of the Guidance. It is doubted if the core assessment, referred to in the Guidance, should be openly disclosed in ASBO application hearings, as they are open proceedings, which do not enjoy the same protection from publicity as other proceedings involving children (eg care proceedings). Core assessments are directed to the welfare of the child and are likely to contain sensitive information whose publication may harm the child and his or her immediate family (reporting restrictions could not be made to prevent details relating to the family being published). A better option may be to use a report based on the YOT's asset assessment, which can be written in a manner which more effectively provides the type of information that the court requires and can direct the appropriate authority to offer services which should be made available to the young person. For post-conviction ASBOs, if no asset assessment has been undertaken, the YOT representative in court can obtain information about the young person.

14.13 Many local authorities are finding it difficult to resource all the assessments that ASBO applications now demand. Initial statistics relating to ASBOs showed the national proportion of orders made against young people to be 78%, although the Home Office's most recent information is that the figure has dropped to 43%. Nonetheless, it is likely that additional resources may be needed for busy social services departments and YOTs to meet the challenges and expectations laid down by the current Home Office Guidance. In particular, the timescales envisaged would be beyond many departments. Agreements between divisional heads as to the appropriate protocols for referrals and allocation of resources will become more important as the number of applications against young persons increases.

---

[11]   See *R (on the application of G) v Barnet London Borough Council* [2003] 3 WLR 1194.

APPLICATIONS AGAINST CHILDREN IN THE CARE OF THE LOCAL AUTHORITY

14.14 Where a local authority has parental responsibility for a defendant who is either in its care or placed at home under the protection of a care order, there is an obvious conflict between the potential need to apply for an ASBO and the local authority's duty to the child in its care. The procedure which a local authority should follow in such circumstances is not addressed in the Act nor in the Home Office Guidance, despite the issues raised by such applications. It has, however, recently been considered by the courts in *R (on the application of M (a child)) v Sheffield Magistrates' Court v Sheffield City Council*.[12] The defendant was made the subject of a care order at the age of 6 and placed in various care homes until he came to be living without statutory authority with his grandmother. The defendant had been convicted of numerous criminal offences and was alleged to be responsible for many other acts of anti-social behaviour in his community. The defendant's social worker recorded that the placement was not meeting the child's needs. Shortly after this was noted, the council's anti-social behaviour panel met and were told by the social worker that she believed he may have Attention Deficit Hyperactivity Disorder (ADHD) and his grandmother was to take him for assessment. The local anti-social behaviour panel decided that the first limb of the test was satisfied (ie that he had acted in an anti-social manner), but adjourned the final decision to await a report from social services as to whether an order was necessary.

14.15 The panel sent the social worker a proforma report form which was duly completed. The social worker having answered the prescribed questions on the form added that she did not feel that an ASBO was likely to solve the child's problems and that he was making some progress. The panel subsequently met without the social worker present and decided that an order was necessary so as to protect other persons from the child's behaviour and that the application would be led by the housing department. There was no further contact with the social services, other than to serve proceedings on the social worker. This was despite the fact that the application was not made for a further 5 months and further ISSP conditions were imposed.

14.16 When the application came to be heard, the defendant's solicitor properly requested disclosure of the social services files. The solicitor attempted to contact the YOT team but was informed that he could not contact them as they were employed by the council, the applicant. The social worker (who had now changed) made it clear that he would only appear as a witness for his employer, the applicant, and at the interview with the defendant's solicitor was attended by the local authority solicitor who was prosecuting the ASBO.

14.17 The magistrates' court was asked to rule on a preliminary point as to whether the proceedings could continue given the conflict of interests and/or abuse of process. The district judge ruled that the local authority could continue with the application. As there was now insufficient time to hear the main application this was adjourned for 6 weeks. The applicant then for the first time applied for an interim order which the district judge duly granted. The defendant applied for judicial review of both decisions.

14.18 Mr Justice Newman held that the statutory purpose of the ASBO legislation was to protect the community and whilst making an order could be of benefit to a defendant this did not prevent a conflict of interest arising in these circumstances. He held that where a local authority discharged its duties in relation to a child in care it had to act so as to promote the welfare of the child in question and must consult with the child and give due consideration to the wishes and

---

[12] *R (on the application of M, a child) v Sheffield Magistrates' Court* [2004] EWHC 1830 (Admin), 27 July 2004, per Mr Justice Newman at [57]. The case is available at www.bailii.org/ew/cases/EWHC/Admin/2004/1830.html, and is reported in *The Times Law Reports*, August/September 2004.

feelings of those consulted.[13] The effect of an ASBO was to render the defendant at risk of penal sanction and any parent, whether natural or statutory, would hesitate to place their child at risk of detention in custody. This therefore gave rise to a conflict of interests, which had caused prejudice to the defendant in this case. However, the judge considered that the existence of a conflict did not preclude an application for an ASBO by a council against a child in its care.

14.19 The court stopped short of prescribing detailed measures and procedures to ensure that such conflict can be avoided. It did, however, attempt to identify the problem areas and define the relevant legal principles.

(a) *Consultation:* Mr Justice Newman held that the decision to apply for an ASBO was one within the meaning of s 22(4) of the Children Act 1989 and therefore the 'wishes and feelings' of the child and the person with parental responsibility or other relevant person should have been sought. In this case that had not been done. The person who conducted such 'consultation' should be the social worker, who should provide a full report to the panel. The report should not be dictated by the panel but should be a report for the authority on behalf of the child. The information before this panel was deficient given the detailed information and assessments which social services had and were expected to be conducting (in relation to ADHD assessment).

(b) *Social services report:* the decision of the panel as to whether to continue with the application should have been made with the benefit of the report from social services but without their participation in that discussion. If the social worker participated then there was a risk to actual and perceived independence (from the child's view). If an application was to be made, then this should be communicated to all. Where there were exceptional circumstances a further report could be prepared.

(c) *Role of the solicitor:* the solicitor bringing the application should not attend meetings between the defendant's solicitor and the social worker. Further it should be rare for the social worker to need a solicitor in attendance. Once it has been decided to make an application there should be no contact on the issue between the ASBO team and the social services section unless the defendant's solicitor consents.

(d) *Role of the social worker:* the social worker should be available to assist the child at court and to be a witness if requested. Orders should not be made (save in exceptional circumstances) against children in care without the presence of someone from social services.

The judge further stated that if, after detailed consideration with the child and relevant persons, social services wished to support an ASBO application, different considerations may apply; however, the court was not in a position to deal with that possibility.

14.20 The judgment of Mr Justice Newman in this case provides welcome guidance as to the procedures to be adopted by local authorities in making applications against children in their care. The need to comply with s 22(4) is one which needs careful consideration and may not be possible if there is an urgent situation which requires a without notice interim order application or even where there is a group application where notice of a potential application is likely to lead to significant problems for residents. The requirement applies only so far as is reasonably practicable and is not an absolute duty. It is suggested, however, that if such situations arise in which it is not reasonably practicable it is important that very careful notes are taken by the social worker and the ASBO solicitors as to the steps taken and the reasons why the requirement was not complied with.

---

[13]   Children Act 1989, s 22, particularly s 22(4).

14.21 Where the social services support the making of an order it is important that their reasoning is properly recorded and the reasons explained to the child. Whilst left open by the court, it is submitted that it would still be preferable for the social services and the ASBO legal department not to contact each other after the decision has been made, save for making requests for updates, etc. which should be sent to the defendant's solicitor as well. For those authorities which have a separate police team applying for ASBOs, the best course will always be for the application to be made by the police. This would allow the social services department to maintain actual and perceived independence.

SERVICE OF COURT FORMS

14.22 A copy of the summons should be served on any person with parental responsibility for the defendant. This is defined as a parent, which can include a social worker in the case of a 'looked after' child. A 'parent' has the same meaning as in s 3 of the Family Law Reform Act 1987. 'Guardian' is as defined in s 107 of the Children and Young Persons Act 1933. Both of these definitions are set out in full in the Guidance.[14]

COURT PROCEDURE

14.23 The current Home Office Guidance makes the age of the defendant a specific factor for the court to consider in determining the duration of an ASBO. Further, it provides the following advice:

- Evidence is given on oath, save for those aged under 14, who should give unsworn testimony (s 98 of MCA 1980 and s 55(2) of the YJCEA 1999).

- If the young person is aged under 16, the parent or legal guardian *must* attend. It is not considered that the warrant and arrest powers of the court to compel attendance (ss 54–57 of MCA 1980) are available; therefore, the applicant must use best endeavours to secure the attendance of a natural parent or guardian if the defendant is not a 'looked after' child.

- The court will need a home circumstances report (the reason why is not given in the Guidance). The asset assessment referred to above should satisfy this.

- There are no automatic reporting restrictions, as ASBO applications are heard in the magistrates' court, and not in the youth court. Exceptions to the normal rules of the youth court have also been made since the Guidance was published. Publicity issues are dealt with in more detail in chapter 9.

- There is no longer an automatic reporting restriction imposed on breach proceedings in the youth court and defendant's representatives will have to be alive to the commencement date for the discretionary provisions in s 45 of the YJCEA 1999 (see further chapter 13 at **13.19**).

14.24 If an ASBO is made, it is advisable to serve a copy of the order on the child's parent or guardian. Additionally, the YOT should receive a copy of the order on the day on which it is made. They should arrange for the appropriate agency to ensure that the young person understands the seriousness of the ASBO, as well as considering appropriate support programmes and diversionary schemes to help prevent breaches of the order.

---

[14] See current Home Office Guidance, reproduced in Appendix 3.

WHICH COURT?

14.25 The following courts have the power to impose ASBOs against young people:

- the magistrates' court, sitting in its civil capacity, hearing stand-alone applications;

- the youth court, making an order post-conviction;

- the county court. It is rare that a young person will be a party in his or her own right (eg a juvenile tenant in a possession proceedings case or an injunction sought against a minor to curb criminal activity). With the amendments brought by ASB Act 2003 (see **6.3–6.4**), it is likely that many more applications will be made in the county court against juveniles when possession proceedings are brought against their parents.

14.26 Steps can and should be taken to make the procedure less arduous for young persons. The Guidance states that 'the officer in charge of the application should contact the justices' clerk in advance of the hearing, to ensure that it will be conducted in a way that is suitable for the child or young person'.[15] Methods of achieving this include:

- the use of the youth court setting;

- the use of magistrates with youth court experience;

- regular breaks;

- the avoidance of jargon; and

- more informal court procedures (eg no robes on appeal, seated advocates).

REVIEW OF ASBOS IMPOSED AGAINST YOUNG PERSONS

14.27 The Home Office Guidance in August 2006 stated that where an ASBO was made against a minor then it should be reviewed every year. This was to take account of the fact that the defendant would have greater changing circumstances than an adult. In addition the review is to ensure that the defendant receives the support that they need to prevent a breach of the ASBO. The form of the review is not a judicial hearing but an administrative function and should be considered by the same team that made the application for an ASBO. The Guidance suggests that if possible YOT should conduct a further assessment of the defendant for the consideration of the group. The intention is to move to variation or discharge of the order if appropriate. The overriding considerations were to remain the safety and needs of the community, and the review would have to incorporate the community's views on the order's effectiveness.

14.28 Since the publication of the Guidance, the Crime and Disorder Act 1998 was yet again amended[16] adding sections 1J and 1K. The provisions came into force on 1 February 2009. In essence they provide that if an order (whether on application to the magistrates' court, county court or on conviction[17]) is made against a defendant who was aged 16 years or less at the date

---

[15]   See current Home Office Guidance, reproduced in Appendix 3.
[16]   Section 123 of the Criminal Justice and Immigration Act 2008.
[17]   CDA 1998 1J(1).

of making[18] and is not yet 18 years of age[19] at the end of various 'review periods' and the order runs to the end of that period, or beyond, then a review of the operation of the order must be carried out.[20]

14.29 The requirement to review will apply to any ASBO whose first review period (12 months) falls after 1 February 2009. However this only applies to an ASBO which was less than 9 months old when the provisions came into force or was varied in that time. The reason for this is not immediately apparent on the face of s 123 of the 2008 Act but is due to the transitional and commencement provisions within the Act.[21]

Review periods

14.30 Review periods are defined as being:

(i)   12 months from the date of the making of the order;[22] or

(ii) if there was a supplemental order (or more than one), the date of the supplemental order (or the last of them);[23] and

(iii) a 12 month period commencing the day after the previous review period;[24] or

(iv) if there was a supplemental order (or more than one), the date of the supplemental order (or the last of them).[25]

14.31 A supplemental order is defined as being any further order varying the order or any individual support order made on application under section 1AA(1A).[26]

14.32 The above definitions lead to potentially unfortunate outcomes which Parliament is unlikely to have intended but poor drafting seems to create. In essence the primary review period is 12 months from trial. However if there is any variation (for any reason) then the 12 months begins again from that time. This has the potential to adversely affect defendants in that say an order has to be varied because a defendant moves home or obtains employment the right he had to a 12 month review is lost. If this occurred at say 9 months post order it would be approaching 2 years before any review was required in law. Similarly if the order has to be varied due to administrative error in drafting then the period will re-commence. Whilst a defendant could apply to discharge an order themselves no application could succeed within 2 years unless the applicant authority agreed. This was the situation which one would have thought the new section was intended to deal with but now in certain circumstances cannot. The Home Office Guidance issued in January 2009[27] states that it was open for the agencies to reconsider the ASBO at any time at the young person's request however that is of course voluntary and unenforceable. The Guidance seems to suggest that the first review would be the date of any supplemental order made within 12 months of the making of the order however this is plainly at odds with the wording of the statute.

---

[18]   CDA 1998 1J (1).
[19]   CDA 1998 1J(2)(a).
[20]   CDA 1998 1J(2)(b).
[21]   Schedule 27, Part 8, Paragraph 33(1) & (2) of the Criminal Justice and Immigration Act 2008.
[22]   CDA 1998 1J(3)(i).
[23]   CDA 1998 1J(3)(a)(ii).
[24]   CDA 1998 1J(3)(b)(i).
[25]   CDA 1998 1J(3)(b)(ii).
[26]   CDA 1998 1J(4).
[27]   http://www.respect.gov.uk/uploadedFiles/Members_site/Documents_and_images/
       Enforcement_tools_and_powers/ASBO_ISOReviewGuideJan09_0157.pdf.

Nature of the review

14.33 Any review conducted under section 1J must include consideration of the extent to which the defendant has complied with the order, the adequacy of the support available to the defendant to comply with the order and any other matters relevant to whether the order should be varied or discharged. Further the person(s) conducting the review must have regard to the Guidance which the Secretary of State issues about how the review should be done, what should be addressed in the review and what action should be taken as a consequence.

14.34 The Guidance does however confirm that the review is to be administrative and not judicial and that whilst there is no appeal mechanism the applicant is subject to judicial review. The Guidance also makes it clear that a 'specified individual' within the lead agency takes responsibility for the ownership and management of the case. It is therefore suggested that where an ASBO is made against a minor one person should immediately be charged with the review process so that all information and evidence pertinent to that process will be properly directed. The appointed person should be charged with co-ordinating other appropriate agencies such as social services, probation, YOT, the Childrens' Fund, Surestart, etc. It goes on to state that as local authorities have a duty under s 17 of the Children Act 1989 to safeguard and promote the welfare of children who may be in need an assessment in accordance with the guidelines at 14.2 should be done to assess whether the child is in need and what services may be necessary to address those needs.

Who does the review?

14.35 Any order obtained on conviction shall be reviewed by the chief officer of police[28] where the defendant resides even if the order was on the initiative of the court unless the reviewing authority is specified by the court under section 1C(9ZA).[29] Any order imposed by the county court is reviewed by the applicant authority.[30]

14.36 The local authority has a duty to co-operate with the chief officer of police, and vice versa, in the conducting of a review.[31] If the relevant authority conducting the review is not the local authority or the chief officer of police then they have a duty to act in co-operate with both of them.[32] Any relevant authority or chief officer of police may invite a person or body to participate in the review.[33]

SENTENCING

14.37 Sentencing for breach is dealt with in chapter 13. In summary, in the case of a young person, the maximum sentence for breach is:

- a 24-month detention and training order (with 12 months served in the community and 12 months in custody) for defendants between 12 and 17 years of age (note that if a detention and training order is to be imposed for 12–14-year-olds, they must also be persistent criminal offenders); and

---

[28]   CDA 1998 1K(2)(a).
[29]   CDA 1998 1K(2(b) inserted by s 123 of the Criminal Justice and Immigration Act 2008 and provides that where an order on conviction is made or varied the court can specify a relevant authority other than the chief officer of police to be responsible for carrying out the review process pursuant to section 1J.
[30]   CDA 1998 1K(1).
[31]   CDA 1998 1K(3) and (4).
[32]   CDA 1998 1K(5).
[33]   CDA 1998 1J(6).

- a community order for those aged 10 or 11 years.

14.38 Sentencing should be proportionate and reflect the impact of the anti-social conduct. Proportionality may lead to the consideration of a lighter sentence for the young defendant and makes age *per se* a mitigating factor.

OTHER AVAILABLE ORDERS

14.39 Other orders are available in the CDA 1998 and elsewhere for tackling anti-social behaviour by youths. The following is a non-exhaustive list of other court options, more details of which can be found in chapter 1:

- care orders;[34]

- supervision orders;[35]

- local child curfew schemes;[36]

- child safety orders;[37]

- parenting orders (see further chapter 11 (**11.51** et seq);[38]

- intensive surveillance and supervision programmes (ISSPs);

- criminal sentencing, including supervision orders, community penalties and reparation orders;

- individual support orders (see **11.60** et seq).

14.40 Interventionist work also remains available, which can work instead of, or alongside, the more formal court remedies (see further chapter 11).

CONCLUSION

14.41 The majority of ASBO applications are made against young people. Whilst it is clear that some young people's anti-social behaviour causes real misery for their community, some have questioned whether ASBOs are being correctly brought against this age group and why the number of applications against them is so high. What is clear is that, in appropriate cases, ASBOs against young persons have proved highly effective in deterring further anti-social behaviour. Provided that proper assessment of the young person's needs is made and the appropriateness of an application verified, ASBOs can and should be pursued against young person.

---

[34] Children Act 1989, s 33.
[35] Children and Young Persons Act 1969, s 12.
[36] CDA 1998, s 14.
[37] CDA 1998, s 11.
[38] CDA 1998, s 8.

CHAPTER 15

DRINKING BANNING ORDERS

15.1 Drinking Banning Orders (DBOs) were introduced by the Violent Crime Reduction Act 2006 (VCRA 2006). They however only came into force on 31 August 2009.[1] Their use therefore remains untested at the time of publication.

WHAT ARE THEY?

15.2 DBOs are orders which have obvious parallels with ASBOs. They are prohibitory orders which can be made by magistrates, county or criminal courts in certain prescribed circumstances, breach of which will be a criminal offence. The Home Office Guidance states that a DBO is not an ASBO but that they would be similar to an ASBO in terms of the procedure.

WHEN CAN THEY BE MADE?

15.3 A DBO can only be made against a person who is aged 16 years or over. Where the defendant is 16 or 17 years of age the Home Office Guidance makes it plain that YOT should be involved at a very early stage and that their views as to the appropriateness or otherwise of an application should be considered prior to application.

15.4 They can only be made where it is necessary for the purpose for protecting other persons from criminal or disorderly conduct by the subject of the order while he is under the influence of alcohol.[2] Anti-social behaviour which is not alcohol related is not suitable for a DBO. The Home Office Guidance suggests that they may appropriate in cases of alcohol misuse including binge drinking where this is associated with crime or disorder conduct. Typically an application for a DBO may be made against a person who is drunk and disorderly on a regular basis and where other intervention has not worked. Another example given in the Home Office Guidance is where the person commits criminal damage whilst under the influence of alcohol. A DBO would not be appropriate where an order of more than 2 years is appropriate (an ASBO would be then sought), where the behaviour is linked to football match attendance (seek a Football Banning Order) or where the person is subject to proceedings relating to domestic violence proceedings.

VULNERABLE INDIVIDUALS

15.5 The Home Office Guidance states that where a person is considered vulnerable particularly due to alcohol or drug dependency, or when they have mental health problems then it would generally be unlikely to be appropriate to seek a DBO. Dependency is said to be difficult to define but includes those who had a chronic psychological need or dependence for alcohol. Where a person is vulnerable or alcohol dependent then the relevant authority is expected to identify them at the statutory consultation stage and before making an application

---

[1]   Violent Crime Reduction Act 2006 (Commencement) (No. 7) Order 2009.
[2]   VCRA 2006, s 1(2).

should provide support through social services or other support agencies. The Guidance reminds readers of the duty of local authorities under s 47 of the National Health Service and Community Care Act 1990 to assess though who may be in need of community care services. Finally the Guidance states that rough sleepers should be dealt with through existing arrangements between local authorities and by a DBO.

15.6 The statutory conditions for the making of an order are:

(a)   that the defendant has since the commencement of the section engaged in criminal or disorderly conduct whilst under the influence of alcohol;[3] and

(b)   an order is necessary to protect other persons from further conduct of that kind whilst he is under the influence of alcohol.[4]

15.7 The conduct relied on must therefore have occurred after 31 August 2009 however as in ASBO applications it is likely that pre-commencement date conduct can be taken into account in assessing whether an order is necessary. It should be noted that the definition of 'relevant' conduct is somewhat different to that required for an ASBO. There is no requirement for a person to be caused or be likely to be caused harassment, alarm or distress by the behaviour complained of. There is no definition of 'disorderly' conduct however it seems likely that it will have the same meaning as in criminal law. The necessity of an order that is required in the test for an ASBO is retained however the conduct has to be of the same kind. There is no need for the conduct to relate specifically to simply drunk and disorderly behaviour but could include where a person is involved in any offence or disorder if alcohol was involved.

15.8 There is nothing within the statute as to whether the orders are civil in nature, however it seems improbable that they will not be deemed so by the court. Indeed the Home Office Guidance does state that they are civil orders and that the standard of proof to be applied by the courts in considering the above tests would be appropriate for the court to apply the same tests as in an ASBO. This seems only logical given that the consequences for breach are the same. This means that the first part of the test would require proof to the criminal standard by the applicant but the second part would have no standard or burden of proof and be a matter for the exercise of the court's judgment and evaluation.

WHO CAN APPLY?

15.9 The application for a DBO can only be made by a relevant authority. The definition of a relevant authority is defined in s 14(1) as:

(a)   the chief officer of police of a police force for a police area;

(b)   the chief constable of the British Transport Police Force;

(c)   a local authority.

WHAT CAN BE ORDERED?

15.10 The prohibitions which can be imposed by the DBO can be any order necessary for the purpose of protecting other persons from criminal or disorderly conduct by the subject of the

---

3   VCRA 2006, s 3(2)(a).
4   VCRA 2006, s 3(2)(b).

order while he is under the influence of alcohol.[5] The statute however goes on to prescribe at least one term of the order. However, the section is badly drafted and so its meaning is unclear. At this time there is no Home Office Guidance nor was the point raised in Parliament and therefore it remains unqualified and unexplained.

15.11 The section states that the

> 'prohibitions imposed by such an order must include such prohibition as the court making it considers necessary, for that purpose, on the subject entering:
>
> (a) premises in respect of which there is a premises licence authorising the use of the premises for the sale of alcohol by retail; and
> b)   premises in respect of which there is a club premises certificate authorising the use of the premises for the supply of alcohol to members or guests.'

15.12 One reading of the above section would be that the court must make an order banning the defendant from entering any of the above types of premises. An alternative view is that it must make orders which will take effect on a person when they enter such premises. The latter would seem to be difficult to formulate other than a simple requirement not to cause disorder whilst in those premises. The plain reading of the section would seem to require a court to make orders as are necessary to prevent the defendant from having access to those types of premises. This could therefore be by way of an order which simply prevented access to all premises of that type or perhaps all those in a particular area. It could presumably also simply be an exclusion zone for a problem area. The Home Office Guidance does not deal with the above point at all. It only goes on to consider other orders that may be made for instance preventing a person entering particular streets or areas. It does however note that a person could be prohibited from entering a particular area for a shorter period than the period for which they are prohibited from entering a specified set of licensed premises. This might be said to be support for the first of the 2 interpretations above.

15.13 A DBO may not however impose a prohibition which prevents a defendant from having access to a place where he lives;[6] from attending any place where he is required to attend for work;[7] from attending any place where he is expected to attend during the order's duration for education or training or for the purpose of receiving medical treatment;[8] from attending any place which he is required to attend by court or tribunal.[9] The Home Office Guidance notes that prohibitions banning a person from all licensed premises within a specific area would result in the person being banned from all premises holding a premises licence including supermarkets, cinemas etc. They suggest naming the premises or specifying the streets. It also notes that where displacement of the problem may be an issue consideration should be given to a larger geographical area.

DURATION

15.14 A DBO has effect for a specified period which must be not less than 2 months and not more than 2 years.[10] There are therefore orders which fall below ASBOs in terms of 'severity' given the 2 year minimum duration for an ASBO. The Act now specifically states that different

---

5   VCRA 2006, s 1(2).
6   VCRA 2006, s 1(4)(a).
7   VCRA 2006, s 1(4)(b).
8   VCRA 2006, s 1(4)(c).
9   VCRA 2006, s 1(4)(d).
10 VCRA 2006, s 2(1).

terms of an order can have different terms of duration[11] however no term can be stated to last for less than 2 months or more than 2 years. If the person completes an approved course successfully the duration of the DBO can be reduced by up to half. The court must specify in its order what the reduction on successful completion will be.

15.15 The court can specify that either the whole order or any particular provision will come to an end earlier than the specified period if the defendant satisfactorily completes an approved course.[12] The limitation on this is that the order or term must be specified to last at least half of the specified period even if the course is completed satisfactorily. Conversely if the defendant does not complete the course by the time half of the order has expired, the order or term will continue until the course has been completed or the full specified period elapses.[13]

15.16 Before the above can be included in an order the court has to be satisfied that there is a place on one of the approved courses available for the defendant and that he has agreed to it being made.[14] Before the provision can be made the defendant has to inform the defendant in ordinary language (in writing or otherwise) about the effect of the provision, in general terms what the course will entail, any fees that he will be required to pay and when he will have to pay such fees.[15]

15.17 This seems to be a very strange requirement in that there is nothing within the remainder of the Act nor any of the guidance information to say when a defendant might be required to pay, ie is it means tested. The Secretary of State has now set down charge limits in that a course provider may not require a person to pay more than £250 or less than £120 for a course.[16] It seems unlikely that a defendant will agree to any such provision if the cost is more than minimal given that his or her permission is needed to make such a provision.

15.18 If the court makes a DBO but does not make a provision for a course and reduced order term that it must gives its reason for not including such provision in open court.[17] The most likely reason will be the refusal of the defendant to comply. It will be very important for the defendant's solicitors to ensure that the court makes its determination as to the appropriate length of the DBO without knowing of the defendant's refusal to agree to such a provision. Logically it should not interfere with the order of the decision making however it is likely that the court will attempt to ascertain the defendant's wishes before setting duration.

APPROVED COURSES AND COMPLETION CERTIFICATES

15.19 Approved courses are established by the 2006 Act and the recent statutory instrument[18]. It would seem from the statutory provisions that independent companies will be asked to provide approved courses. They will have to apply to the Secretary of State to approve or reject their course as being approved.[19] The approval can last no more than 7 years[20] and can be withdrawn by him at any time.[21] Some courses have already seemingly been approved[22] but more will be needed if DBOs prove popular with the courts. The Secretary of State may also issue guidance

---

[11]   VCRA 2006, s 2(2).
[12]   VCRA 2006, s 2(3).
[13]   VCRA 2006, s 2(4) and (5).
[14]   VCRA 2006, s 2(6).
[15]   VCRA 2006, s 2(7).
[16]   Violent Crime Reduction Act 2006 (Drinking Banning Orders) (Approved Courses) Regulations 2009 No. 1839, r 4.
[17]   VCRA 2006, s 2(8).
[18]   Violent Crime Reduction Act 2006 (Drinking Banning Orders) (Approved Courses) Regulations 2009, SI 2009/1839.
[19]   VCRA 2006, s 12(1).
[20]   VCRA 2006, s 12(4)(a).
[21]   VCRA 2006, s 12(4)(b).
[22]   www.crimereduction.homeoffice.gov.uk/dbo001.htm.

about the conduct of approved courses and a court must have regard to that guidance in determining what constitutes reasonable instructions or reasonable requirements by a person providing an approved course. The Home Office Guidance contains details of the content of approved courses to form the essential minimum national model requirements however it can only be a generic guidance as each course will presumably differ as the provider's approach varies. What it does state is that the Home Office requires there to be at least one, 1-1 session at the beginning of each course including an assessment. The Guidance goes on to state that a full review of approved courses would be held in 2 years time and was likely to result in changes to the national model and will take account of the effectiveness of the courses on recipients.

15.20 A person can only be regarded as having completed a course satisfactorily of the person providing the course has provided a certificate.[23] The certificate has to be in such form and contain such particulars as are specified in regulations made by the Secretary of State.[24] The defendant is entitled to a certificate as a matter of right unless he has failed to pay the fees; failed to attend the course in accordance with the reasonable instructions of the person providing the course or has failed to comply with any other reasonable requirement of that person.[25]

15.21 The course is however only deemed complete in time when the certificate has been received by the justices' clerk or clerk of the court in other courts.[26] This a potential problem for defendants as they may believe having completed the last of the courses and/or been handed a certificate that they are free to enter a premises or otherwise act in breach of the order.

APPLICATIONS TO THE MAGISTRATES' COURT

15.22 Applications are made to the court by complaint only.[27] Complaints must be lodged within 6 months of the alleged conduct otherwise they will be out of time in accordance with s 127 of the Magistrates' Court Act 1980.[28] The Home Office Guidance states that whilst a court could deal with the applicant in the absence of the defendant this would be in exceptional cases and the court would usually consider an adjournment and use its powers to issue warrants to secure court attendance.[29] The Home Office Guidance states that there will be further Magistrates' Court Rules regarding procedure but at publication they had not been published although it is likely that they will simply follow the same rules as exist for ASBOs in the magistrates' court and are detailed earlier in this book.

15.23 Prior to an application being made the applicant must consult[30] the 'appropriate persons'. These are defined as any of the following who are not party to the proceedings:

(a)   the chief officer of police of the area where the conduct occurred;

(b)   the chief officer of police of the area in which the defendant normally resides;

(c)   local authority where the defendant normally resides;

(d)   the chief constable of the British Transport Police.[31]

---

23   VCRA 2006, s 13(1)(a).
24   VCRA 2006, s 13(2).
25   VCRA 2006, s 13(3).
26   VCRA 2006, s 13(1)(b).
27   VCRA 2006, s 3(3).
28   VCRA 2006, s 3(6).
29   MCA 1980, ss 54–57.
30   VCRA 2006, s 3(4).
31   VCRA 2006, s 14(1).

15.24 No detailed guidance is given on the manner or extent of consultation which must be undertaken however it is submitted that it would be appropriate to follow the guidance and case law which has emerged in relation to ASBOs, see **2.3–2.20**. The Home Office Guidance does state that as in ASBOs there is no requirement for the agencies to agree but consultation should ensure at a very minimum that actions taken by the agency did not conflict. It is also to be used to consider whether the proposed defendant is a vulnerable person.

COUNTY COURT

15.25 There are two main situations in which an application could be made to the county court for a DBO. First, where proceedings have been brought in a county court and a relevant party is already a party to proceedings (effectively limiting it to local authorities) and it considers that another party in the proceedings is someone who it would be reasonable to make an application for a DBO it can apply in the extant proceedings.[32] If a relevant authority is not a party to the proceedings but considers that it would be reasonable to make an application for a DBO it can apply to become a party and if joined can make the application.[33]

15.26 Second, if the relevant authority is a party to proceedings and the intended defendant is not but has committed conduct which is criminal or disorderly which is material to those proceedings under the influence of alcohol,[34] the relevant authority may apply for the person to be joined and apply for an order.[35]

15.27 Prior to making any of the above applications to join or for an order the relevant authority must consult with the appropriate persons at **15.23** above.

15.28 The test to be applied by the county court is that in s 3(2) at paragraph **15.5** above and further that the conduct was material in those proceedings.[36]

PROCEDURE

15.29 The procedure to be followed in application to the county court for a DBO is governed by the CPR in the new provisions at ss 65.31–65.36. All applications for DBOs must be accompanied by written evidence which must include evidence that the consultation requirements have been complied with.[37] The Rules do however seem to impose a rather strict procedural bar to applications in the county court in that if a relevant authority wishes to apply for an order and knows of the circumstances which lead it to apply for an order then it *must* do so in the claim form[38] if the claimant or by application notice filed with the defence, if the defendant.[39] Only if the circumstances are not known can an application be brought later and then it must be made by application notice as soon as possible thereafter.[40] This means that no application to amend a particulars of claim or later application will succeed if the information was 'known' to the relevant authority at the time of filing of the statement of case. It is likely that this will result in

---

[32] VCRA 2006, s 4(2).
[33] VCRA 2006, s 4(3).
[34] VCRA 2006, s 4(4).
[35] VCRA 2006, s 4(5).
[36] VCRA 2006, s 4(7).
[37] CPR 1998, r 65.35.
[38] CPR 1998, r 65.32(1)(a).
[39] CPR 1998, r 65.32(1)(b).
[40] CPR 1998, r 65.32(2).

arguments about what knowledge is needed, who needs to have it and when was it received as for the respondent it would defeat the application against them completely without recourse to the merits.

15.30 The CPR does not specifically comment on whether a DBO can be made without notice however it does say that where the application is made by application notice it should be made on notice to the respondent.[41] The inference being that it can in appropriate circumstances be made without notice.

15.31 If the relevant authority is not a party to the original proceedings then it must apply to become joined to the proceedings[42] pursuant to CPR 19[43] and make its application for a DBO in the same application notice.[44] The applications must be made as soon as possible after the relevant authority becomes aware of the relevant principal proceedings and normally be on notice to the respondent.[45] Where the relevant authority wishes to join a person to the principal proceedings to seek a DBO against them, similar requirements apply in that the application must be made in accordance with CPR 19, be made as soon as possible after the authority considers that the criteria have been met and with the applications to join and for a DBO in the same notice.[46] The relevant authority must also state in the notice both the reasons for claiming that the alleged conduct is material in relation to the existing principal proceedings and details of the conduct which is to be alleged.[47]

APPLICATIONS ON CRIMINAL CONVICTION

15.32 When a person over 16 is convicted of an offence which he committed whilst under the influence of alcohol[48] the court is required to consider whether the test for the imposition of a DBO (see **15.3–15.4** above) is satisfied.[49] If it is then it may make an order. If it decides that the criteria are fulfilled but does not make an order it must state its reasons for not doing so in open court.[50] Even if it decides that the conditions are not satisfied it must state that fact in open court and give reasons.[51]

15.33 The above section would seem to be likely to result in a significantly increased work load for the magistrates' court as a large number of offences before it are committed whilst in drink. The need for reasons to be given even when it does not believe that the conditions are not satisfied is unexpected but is largely likely to be ignored. The likelihood is that the court in most cases will not consider an order save where it is clearly appropriate in any event. It should be noted that both the magistrates' court and the Crown Court on committal has the power to make a DBO.[52]

15.34 In deciding whether or not to make a DBO the criminal court may consider evidence from the prosecution and the defendant and it is immaterial if the evidence was inadmissible in the relevant criminal conviction proceedings.

---

41   CPR 1998, r 65.32(3).
42   CPR 1998, r 65.33(1)(a).
43   In practice specifically CPR 1998, r 19.4.
44   CPR 1998, r 65.33(1)(b).
45   CPR 1998, r 65.33(2).
46   CPR 1998, r 65.34(1).
47   CPR 1998, r 65.34(2).
48   VCRA 2006, s 6(1).
49   VCRA 2006, s 6(2).
50   VCRA 2006, s 6(4).
51   VCRA 2006, s 6(5).
52   VCRA 2006, s 7(11).

15.35 A DBO cannot be made if the defendant is discharged unconditionally or is bound over to keep the peace.[53] The court has the power to adjourn the hearing of the DBO application after sentence for the offence[54] and if the defendant does not appear at the adjourned proceedings it can further adjourn or if satisfied that the defendant had adequate notice of the time and place of the adjourned proceedings it can issue a warrant for his arrest.[55]

15.36 A DBO made post conviction in criminal proceedings will take effect on the day it is made unless the defendant is sentenced to a term of custody in which case it commences on the day of his release.[56]

PUBLICITY

15.37 Given that DBOs are said to be similar to ASBOs it is not surprising that the Home Office Guidance contains a section on publicity and the need for the same. In fact it describes publicity as 'essential'. The Guidance provides in brief the same considerations for a relevant authority to consider before publicising that should apply after an ASBO is made.

If the defendant is under 18 then s 49 of the Children and Young Persons Act 1933 does not apply but s 39 of the same Act does. This therefore mirrors the situation with ASBOs on publicity so that the court has the power to order a restriction on identification of the defendant but it is not an automatic process. The likelihood is that given that the defendant should not be drinking anyway the court will allow full publicity to follow.

VARIATION OR DISCHARGE OF DBOS

15.38 Different rules apply to variation and discharge of DBOs made on application magistrates' and county court and those made on conviction by the criminal courts.

15.39 Where the DBO is made on application to the magistrates or county court then the defendant or the relevant authority can apply to vary or discharge the DBO. The application to the magistrates' court is by compliant and no application can be made to extend the period beyond 2 years.[57] This therefore removes any doubt as to whether an order can be extended by variation.

15.40 An application to discharge a DBO cannot succeed unless half the specified period has elapsed or the relevant authority consents.[58] There is no guidance as to the test to be applied by the court in considering an application for variation or discharge however it would seem probable that a court would not discharge an order unless it could be shown that there was no longer a need for the order.

15.41 Where the DBO was made following criminal conviction the defendant or relevant authority can apply to vary or discharge the order or terms however so may the Director of Public Prosecutions (DPP). If a defendant (not a relevant authority) makes an application to vary

---

[53] VCRA 2006, s 7(3).
[54] VCRA 2006, s 7(4).
[55] VCRA 2006, s 7(5) and (6).
[56] VCRA 2006, s 7(7).
[57] VCRA 2006, s 5(5).
[58] VCRA 2006, s 5(6).

or discharge he is required to send a copy of his application to the DPP.[59] Any application by the DPP or a relevant authority need only be served on the defendant.[60]

15.42 As in the case of applications to vary orders made on application to the magistrates' and county courts, an order can be extended but not beyond 2 years.[61] A DBO made on conviction cannot be discharged until half the specified period has elapsed or the DPP consents.[62]

INTERIM ORDERS

15.43 The court may make an interim DBO either before hearing the full application in the magistrates' or county court or before considering whether the conditions are satisfied following a relevant criminal conviction, if it considers it just to do so.[63] There is a form which forms Annex C to the Home Office Guidance which it seems likely will be the prescribed form and therefore practitioners would be advised to use the same. An application for an interim order in the county court must be made in accordance with CPR 25[64] and should normally be made in the claim form and on notice.[65]

15.44 The above situation obviously mirrors the provisions for the making of interim ASBOs and with further parallels, an interim DBO can be made without notice being given to the defendant and be heard in his absence.[66]

15.45 As for without notice applications for ASBOs in the magistrates' court, before an application can be heard the justices' clerk must give permission for it to be heard without notice to the defendant and then only if he or she is satisfied that it is necessary for the application to be made without notice to the defendant and that it is not necessary for the defendant to be present.[67] This is a rather strange piece of drafting given that if it is necessary for it to be heard without the defendant being present then by inevitable conclusion it is not necessary for the defendant to be present. It could perhaps be surmised that the drafter was intending to reinforce that it is a balance for the justices' clerk to consider.

15.46 In applications to the county court the same test as to whether a without notice application can be heard applies however permission is sought from the court.[68] Presumably the same court could hear the permission hearing followed by the main hearing.

15.47 An interim DBO may contain any term which might be contained in a full DBO[69] however it must be made for no more than 4 weeks in the first instance[70] but can be renewed once or more times for a maximum of a further 4 weeks on each occasion.[71] The Home Office Guidance in fact specifically states that whilst this can be done technically it was 'not the best use of courts' time' and should be avoided. This would seem to be a pointless comment which has no bearing on reality as interim orders are only made if necessary and just.

---

[59] VCRA 2006, s 8(2).
[60] VCRA 2006, s 8(3).
[61] VCRA 2006, s 8(5).
[62] VCRA 2006, s 8(6).
[63] VCRA 2006, s 9(1) and (2).
[64] CPR 1998, r 65.36(1).
[65] CPR 1998, r 65.36(2).
[66] VCRA 2006, s 9(3).
[67] VCRA 2006, s 9(4)(b) and (5).
[68] CPR 1998, r 65.36(3).
[69] VCRA 2006, s 9(6)(a).
[70] VCRA 2006, s 9(6)(b).
[71] VCRA 2006, s 9(7).

15.48 An interim DBO will cease to have effect on the earliest of either on the expiry of the above set periods or on determination of the main application or consideration by the court of whether the conditions are satisfied following conviction.[72]

15.49 The provisions with regard to variation and discharge of full orders apply equally to interim DBOs save that half the set period does not have to have expired before an application to discharge can be made.[73]

APPEAL

15.50 An appeal lies as of right to the Crown Court against the making of a DBO by the magistrates' court.[74] Note that there is no right of appeal given to the relevant authority as in ASBO applications. On hearing an appeal the Crown Court may make any order which the lower court could have done.[75] Any application to vary or discharge an order varied by Crown Court on appeal is made to the magistrates' court and not the Crown Court.[76]

BREACH

15.51 Any defendant acting in breach of the terms of a full or interim DBO without reasonable excuse is guilty of an offence for which they are liable on conviction to a fine not exceeding level 4 on the standard scale.[77] The court may not make a conditional discharge on conviction[78] but could presumably order an absolute discharge. It would seem to us that the possible strength and use of DBOs is effectively removed by limiting the punishment to a financial penalty. It is hardly likely to have the effect sought with the defendant having another long period of having to pay £10 per fortnight as the only sanction. The only possible argument may be that on conviction an ASBO could be applied for on the basis that it is necessary because the defendant has failed to comply with the DBO. This would seem however to defeat the object of the orders.

15.52 Proceedings can be brought by a local authority or if the Secretary of State were to use his powers to make an order other described persons could do so.

15.53 In breach proceedings a copy of the original order which has been certified as accurate by the justices' clerk or clerk of the county court as appropriate is admissible in evidence of it having made and its contents as if the person had given oral evidence.[79]

15.54 In breach proceedings against youths, s 47(2) of the Children and Young Persons Act 1933 has effect so that one person from the relevant authority may be present. Automatic restrictions on reporting pursuant to s 49 of the 1933 Act are not in force but the court has power under s 45 of the Youth Justice and Criminal Evidence Act 1999[80] to order such a restriction however if it does so then it must give reasons for doing so.

---

[72]   VCRA 2006, s 9(7).
[73]   VCRA 2006, s 9(8) and (9).
[74]   VCRA 2006, s 10(1).
[75]   VCRA 2006, s 10(2).
[76]   VCRA 2006, s 10(3).
[77]   VCRA 2006, s 11(2).
[78]   VCRA 2006, s 11(3).
[79]   VCRA 2006, s 11(6).
[80]   Note that if not in force the power is contained in s 39 of the 1933 Act and applies in the alternative.

CHAPTER 16

DESIGNATED PUBLIC PLACE ORDERS

WHAT ARE THEY?

16.1 Designated Public Place Orders ('DPPOs') were introduced by the Criminal Justice and Police Act 2001 (CJPA 2001)[1] and amended by the Violent Crime Reduction Act 2006 (VCRA 2006)[2] which removed a conflict between open air alcohol licences and DPPOs.

16.2 The orders permit a local authority to designate a public place where restrictions on public drinking may apply. The power is granted with an intention to address nuisance associated with consumption of alcohol. DPPOs 'replace' drinking byelaws which were often used by local authorities to attempt to control public drinking problems. All drinking byelaws are deemed repealed as of 31 August 2006.[3]

WHO CAN MAKE ONE?

16.3 Only a local authority may make a DPPO and then only in certain circumstances and after following certain procedures laid down in the Local Authorities (Alcohol Consumption in Designated Public Places) Regulations 2007.[4]

DESIGNATING A DPPO

16.4 A local authority can designate by order a public place as a DPPO if they are satisfied that nuisance or annoyance to the public (or a section of it) has been associated with drinking of alcohol in that area.[5] It can also be made if it is satisfied that alcohol-related disorder is associated with the area.[6]

16.5 A public place is defined as any place to which the public or any section of it has access, on payment, as of right or by express or implied permission.[7] This is a very wide definition and is seemingly open to contradiction in that by including those places after payment is given it could be said to include those places which the layperson would consider private property.

---

[1] CJPA 2001, s 13.
[2] VCRA 2006, s 26, which amended CJPA 2001, s 14.
[3] CJPA 2001, s 15(2) and (3) (commencement 31 August 2001).
[4] SI 2007/806.
[5] CJPA 2001, s 13(2)(a).
[6] CJPA 2001, s 13(2)(b).
[7] CJPA 2001, s 16(1).

CONSULTATION

16.6 A local authority has a legal obligation[8] to consult with the following:[9]

(a) chief office of police for the police area;

(b) the parish or community council if any for the area;

(c) the chief office of police, local authority and/or parish or community council of an area close to the area if it may be affected by the order;

(d) premises licence holder, club certificate holder, premises user of every premises for which appropriate licences or certificates pursuant to the 2003 Act have been granted and which it is considered might be affected by the order.

16.7 Further before an order is made a local authority must take reasonable steps to consult with the owners or occupiers of any land proposed to be identified.[10] Where a residential area is to be included in a DPPO consultation should be attempted perhaps by means of a residents' meeting or leaflet drop.

16.8 When consulting the local authority should describe in writing the effect that the order is intended to have at particular times in relation to each various categories of premises designated in CJPA 2001, s 14(1)(a)–(e),[11] namely as set out in those provisions:

- Premises in respect of which a premises licence has effect which authorises the premises to be used for the sale or supply of alcohol[12] (but where CJPA 2001, s 14(1)(b) does not apply). This provision covers licensed premises at all times of the day.

- Premises in respect of which a premises licence has effect which authorises the premises to be used for the sale or supply of alcohol but only at times when it is being used for the sale or supply of alcohol or at times falling within 30 minutes after the end of a period during which it has been so used. This provision covers licensed premises during the times of operation of the licence and 30 minutes thereafter – so for example they are not covered at times that they are not licensed to sell or supply alcohol.

- Premises in respect of which a club premises certificate has effect which certifies that the premises may be used by the club for the sale or supply of alcohol.[13] This provision covers clubs that have club premises certificates.

- A place within the boundary of licensed premises or club premises.[14] This provision covers any place within the enclosed area of licensed premises or club premises.

- Premises which by virtue of Part 5 of the Licensing Act 2005 may for the time being be used for the supply of alcohol or which, by virtue of that Part, could have been so used within

---

[8] Bizarrely the Home Office Guidance of December 2008 states that a local authority 'should' (not 'shall') consult. This is plainly wrong and should be ignored.

[9] Local Authorities (Alcohol Consumption in Designated Public Places) Regulations 2007, reg 3(1)(a)–(d).

[10] Local Authorities (Alcohol Consumption in Designated Public Places) Regulations 2007.

[11] Local Authorities (Alcohol Consumption in Designated Public Places) Regulations 2007, reg 3(3)(a).

[12] CJPA 2001, s 14(1)(a).

[13] CJPA 2001, s 14(1)(aa).

[14] CJPA 2001, s 14(1)(b).

the last 30 minutes.[15] This includes premises for which there is a valid temporary event notice in force and for 30 minutes after the period ends. This was something that was a lacuna in the 2001 statutory instrument.

- A place where facilities or activities relating to the sale or consumption of alcohol which has been allowed by the local authority under its power in s 115E of the Highways Act 1980.[16]

16.9 Further, it shall identify in writing by postal address (or by ordinance survey map reference or description) any premises within the public place to which the exception to being a DPPO is allowed pursuant to CJPA 2001, s 14(1B) when those premises are being used for the sale or supply of alcohol or 30 minutes after so used.[17]

PUBLICITY

16.10 Twenty-eighty days[18] prior to the making of an order the local authority is required to publish a notice in a newspaper circulating in its area.[19] The notice must:

(a) identify the proposed area;

(b) set out the effect of an order being made in relation to that place, including the effect that order will have at particular times in relation to each category as above;

(c) identify any premises within that place to which an exception under CJPA 2001, s 14(1B) applies; and

(d) invite representations as to whether or not an order should be made.

16.11 The Home Office Guidance indicates that it is good practice to include publication of a notice in the council's own publication however this would not comply with the legal requirement to publish in a local newspaper and therefore must additionally be done. The Guidance also suggests that whilst the minimum period is 28 days, best practice would allow 4–6 weeks for representations to be made concerning the making of the order. There is no statutory procedure for dealing with representations however it is a matter of common legal practice for there to be a written record of all representations and the response of the council to each one. Where appropriate further enquiries including speaking directly to the person(s) concerned may be required and if necessary further evidence in support of the order may be needed. The Home Office Guidance suggests that it would be good practice to send a letter to each person who makes representations setting out the council's response to their objection/comment.

16.12 If an order is made then a notice shall be published in the same way as above including details of the effects to premises in (a) to (d) as above. It would make sense for the notice to include the whole of the order which has been made.

---

15 CJPA 2001, s 14(1)(c).
16 CJPA 2001, s 14(1)(e).
17 Local Authorities (Alcohol Consumption in Designated Public Places) Regulations 2007, reg 3(3)(c).
18 Local Authorities (Alcohol Consumption in Designated Public Places) Regulations 2007, reg 6.
19 Local Authorities (Alcohol Consumption in Designated Public Places) Regulations 2007, reg 5.

SIGNS

16.13 It is a legal requirement that prior to any order taking effect that a local authority shall erect signs as it considers sufficient to bring the effect of the order to the public's attention.[20] It is however a requirement that every sign shall set out the effect the order will have at particular times in relation to each premises in (a) to (d) above.[21]

16.14 It would seem that if there are several types of premises falling into (a) to (d) then the sign would either have to be very large indeed or have very small print. The Guidance suggests consideration be given to local requirements such as other languages but accepts that there may be budgetary constraints although size may be more of an issue if more than one language is to be used on a sign.

NOTIFICATION TO THE GOVERNMENT

16.15 Any order must be sent to the Secretary of State as soon as practicable after it has been made.[22] However, the Home Office Guidance specifies the name and address[23] to which the order should be sent. The Guidance states that the Home Office would ordinarily send an acknowledgment of receipt within 2 weeks. Whilst this should be done for best practice purposes, the Act clearly states that it should be sent to the Secretary of State and not to a nominated person. The order should in our view be sent to the Secretary of State as per statute.

EXTENSION AND REVOCATION OF A DPPO

16.16 It is not possible to simply extend a DPPO to cover new areas. Each area would need a further consultation and publicity as well as individual proof as to the need. The Home Office Guidance also properly cautions against any consideration of deeming a whole Borough as a DPPO. There must be evidence to support the statutory test for all parts. It should be noted that whilst the Home Office Guidance states that there is no power to extend the area and this has to be considered as assistance in interpretation. The statute specifically gives the power to amend a DPPO to the local authority.[24] There is nothing within the statute or the 2007 Regulations which indicates any need to consult or publicise an amendment but it must be necessary as a matter of common sense for that to be done. To allow otherwise would be to drive a coach and horses through the protection. It is however another poor piece of drafting amongst many others.

16.17 A DPPO can be revoked by a local authority[25] however the Home Office Guidance states that it is a requirement for the authority to perform the same process of consultation and publicity before revoking an order. The Guidance states that if an order is revoked notice must be sent to the Secretary of State. There is no support for this requirement within either statute or statutory instrument however it would seem sensible to do so.

---

[20] Local Authorities (Alcohol Consumption in Designated Public Places) Regulations 2007, reg 8(1).
[21] Local Authorities (Alcohol Consumption in Designated Public Places) Regulations 2007, reg 8(2).
[22] Local Authorities (Alcohol Consumption in Designated Public Places) Regulations 2007, reg 9.
[23] Joanne French, Home Office, Alcohol Strategy Unit, 4th Floor, Peel Building, 2 Marsham Street, London, SW1P 4DF.
[24] CJPA 2001, s 13(3).
[25] CJPA 2001, s 13(3).

ENFORCEMENT

16.18 Consuming alcohol within a DPPO is *not* an offence. Care should be taken to ensure that no such impression is given within consultation, notice, order or signage. If however a police officer (or community support officer in certain circumstances) reasonably believes that a person is, has been or intends to consume alcohol in a DPPO[26] then they may require them not to consume anything which is, or the constable believes is, alcohol and to surrender it or any container for alcohol.[27] The officer may dispose of the alcohol or container in any manner they think appropriate.[28] Failure to comply with any requirement is a criminal offence liable on summary conviction to a fine not exceeding level 2.[29] The officer must however on giving the person an order to comply inform them of the fact that failure to do so is an offence.[30]

---

[26] CJPA 2001, s 12(1).

[27] CJPA 2001, s 12(2).

[28] CJPA 2001, s 12(3).

[29] CJPA 2001, s 12(4). On 4 March 2008 the Culture Secretary announced that the maximum fine would be increased to £2,500 however this has not been implanted as of writing.

[30] CJPA 2001, s 12(5).

APPENDIX 1

STATUTORY MATERIAL

A1.1

Crime and Disorder Act 1998

(1998 C 37)

PART I
PREVENTION OF CRIME AND DISORDER

Chapter I

England And Wales

Crime and disorder: general

1 Anti-social behaviour orders

(1) An application for an order under this section may be made by a relevant authority if it appears to the authority that the following conditions are fulfilled with respect to any person aged 10 or over, namely –

 (a) that the person has acted, since the commencement date, in an anti-social manner, that is to say, in a manner that caused or was likely to cause harassment, alarm or distress to one or more persons not of the same household as himself; and
 (b) that such an order is necessary to protect relevant persons from further anti-social acts by him.

(1A) In this section and sections 1AA, 1B, 1C, 1CA, 1E. 1F and 1K'relevant authority' means –

 (a) the council for a local government area;
 (aa) in relation to England, a county council;
 (b) the chief officer of police of any police force maintained for a police area;
 (c) the chief constable of the British Transport Police Force,
 (d) any person registered under section 1 of the Housing Act 1996 (c 52) as a social landlord who provides or manages any houses or hostel in a local government area; or
 (e) a housing action trust established by order in pursuance of section 62 of the Housing Act 1988.

(1B) In this section 'relevant persons' means –

 (a) in relation to a relevant authority falling within paragraph (a) of subsection (1A), persons within the local government area of that council;
 (aa) in relation to a relevant authority falling within paragraph (aa) of subsection (1A), persons within the county of the county council;
 (b) in relation to a relevant authority falling within paragraph (b) of that subsection, persons within the police area;
 (c) in relation to a relevant authority falling within paragraph (c) of that subsection –

  (i) persons who are within or likely to be within a place specified in section 31(1)(a) to (f) of the Railways and Transport Safety Act 2003 in a local government area; or

(ii)   persons who are within or likely to be within such a place;

(d)   in relation to a relevant authority falling within paragraph (d) or (e) of that subsection –

(i)   persons who are residing in or who are otherwise on or likely to be on premises provided or managed by that authority; or

(ii)   persons who are in the vicinity of or likely to be in the vicinity of such premises.

(2) ...

(3) Such an application shall be made by complaint to a magistrates' court.

(4) If, on such an application, it is proved that the conditions mentioned in subsection (1) above are fulfilled, the magistrates' court may make an order under this section (an 'anti-social behaviour order') which prohibits the defendant from doing anything described in the order.

(5) For the purpose of determining whether the condition mentioned in subsection (1)(a) above is fulfilled, the court shall disregard any act of the defendant which he shows was reasonable in the circumstances.

(5A) Nothing in this section affects the operation of section 127 of the Magistrates' Courts Act 1980 (limitation of time in respect of informations laid or complaints made in magistrates' court).

(6) The prohibitions that may be imposed by an anti-social behaviour order are those necessary for the purpose of protecting persons (whether relevant persons or persons elsewhere in England and Wales) from further anti-social acts by the defendant.

(7) An anti-social behaviour order shall have effect for a period (not less than two years) specified in the order or until further order.

(8) Subject to subsection (9) below, the applicant or the defendant may apply by complaint to the court which made an anti-social behaviour order for it to be varied or discharged by a further order.

(9) Except with the consent of both parties, no anti-social behaviour order shall be discharged before the end of the period of two years beginning with the date of service of the order.

(10) If without reasonable excuse a person does anything which he is prohibited from doing by an anti-social behaviour order, he is guilty of an offence and liable –

(a)   on summary conviction, to imprisonment for a term not exceeding six months or to a fine not exceeding the statutory maximum, or to both; or

(b)   on conviction on indictment, to imprisonment for a term not exceeding five years or to a fine, or to both.

(10A) The following may bring proceedings for an offence under subsection (10) –

(a)   a council which is a relevant authority;

(b)   the council for the local government area in which a person in respect of whom an anti-social behaviour order has been made resides or appears to reside.

(c)   Transport for London, where the anti-social behaviour order was made on an application by Transport for London.

(10B) If proceedings for an offence under subsection (10) are brought in a youth court section 47(2) of the Children and Young Persons Act 1933 (c 12) has effect as if the persons entitled to be present at a sitting for the purposes of those proceedings include one person authorised to be present by a relevant authority.

(10C) In proceedings for an offence under subsection (10), a copy of the original anti-social behaviour order, certified as such by the proper officer of the court which made it, is admissible as evidence of its having been made and of its contents to the same extent that oral evidence of those things is admissible in those proceedings.

(10D) In relation to proceedings brought against a child or a young person for an offence under subsection (10) –

    (a)   section 49 of the Children and Young Persons Act 1933 (restrictions on reports of proceedings in which children and young persons are concerned) does not apply in respect of the child or young person against whom the proceedings are brought;

    (b)   section 45 of the Youth Justice and Criminal Evidence Act 1999 (power to restrict reporting of criminal proceedings involving persons under 18) does so apply.

(10E) If, in relation to any such proceedings, the court does exercise its power to give a direction under section 45 of the Youth Justice and Criminal Evidence Act 1999, it shall give its reasons for doing so.

(11) Where a person is convicted of an offence under subsection (10) above, it shall not be open to the court by or before which he is so convicted to make an order under subsection (1)(b) (conditional discharge) of section 12 of the Powers of Criminal Courts (Sentencing) Act 2000 in respect of the offence.

(12) In this section –

'British Transport Police Force' means the force of constables appointed under section 53 of the British Transport Commission Act 1949 (c xxix);
'child' and 'young person' shall have the same meaning as in the Children and Young Persons Act 1933;
'the commencement date' means the date of the commencement of this section;
'local government area' means –

    (a)   in relation to England, a district or London borough, the City of London, the Isle of Wight and the Isles of Scilly;

    (b)   in relation to Wales, a county or county borough,

Amendments—Powers of Criminal Courts (Sentencing) Act 2000, s 165(1), Sch 9, para 192; Police Reform Act 2002, ss 61(1), (3), 107(2), Sch 8; Anti-social Behaviour Act 2003, s 85(1), (2)(a); Criminal Justice and Immigration Act 2008, s 124(4).

1A Power of Secretary of State to add to relevant authorities

(1) The Secretary of State may by order provide that the chief officer of a body of constables maintained otherwise than by a police authority is, in such cases and circumstances as may be prescribed by the order, to be a relevant authority for the purposes of section 1 above.

(2) The Secretary of State may by order –

    (a)   provide that a person or body of any other description specified in the order is, in such cases and circumstances as may be prescribed by the order, to be a relevant authority for the purposes of such of sections 1 above and 1B, 1CA and 1E below as are specified in the order; and

    (b)   prescribe the description of persons who are to be 'relevant persons' in relation to that person or body.

Amendments—Police Reform Act 2002, s 62(1); Serious Organised Crime and Police Act 2005, s 139(1), (3).

1AA Individual support orders

(1) This section applies where a court makes an anti-social behaviour order in respect of a defendant who is a child or young person when that order is made.

(1A) This section also applies where –

    (a)   an anti-social behaviour order has previously been made in respect of such a defendant;

    (b)   an application is made by complaint to the court which made that order, by the relevant authority which applied for it, for an order under this section; and

    (c)   at the time of the hearing of the application –

        (i)   the defendant is still a child or young person, and

        (ii)   the anti-social behaviour order is still in force.

(1B) The court must consider whether the individual support conditions are fulfilled and, if satisfied that they are, must make an individual support order.

(2)   An individual support order is an order which –

    (a)   requires the defendant to comply, for a period not exceeding six months, with such requirements as are specified in the order; and

    (b)   requires the defendant to comply with any directions given by the responsible officer with a view to the implementation of the requirements under paragraph (a) above.

(3)   The individual support conditions are –

    (a)   that an individual support order would be desirable in the interests of preventing any repetition of the kind of behaviour which led to the making of

        (i)   the anti-social behaviour order, or

        (ii)   an order varying that order (in a case where the variation is made as a result of further anti-social behaviour by the defendant);

    (b)   that the defendant is not already subject to an individual support order; and

    (c)   that the court has been notified by the Secretary of State that arrangements for implementing individual support orders are available in the area in which it appears to it that the defendant resides or will reside and the notice has not been withdrawn.

(4)   If the court is not satisfied that the individual support conditions are fulfilled, it shall state in open court that it is not so satisfied and why it is not.

(5)   The requirements that may be specified under subsection (2)(a) above are those that the court considers desirable in the interests of preventing any repetition of the kind of behavioue mentioned in subsection (3) (a) above.

(6)   Requirements included in an individual support order, or directions given under such an order by a responsible officer, may require the defendant to do all or any of the following things –

    (a)   to participate in activities specified in the requirements or directions at a time or times so specified;

    (b)   to present himself to a person or persons so specified at a place or places and at a time or times so specified;

    (c)   to comply with any arrangements for his education so specified.

(7)   But requirements included in, or directions given under, such an order may not require the defendant to attend (whether at the same place or at different places) on more than two days in any week; and 'week' here means a period of seven days beginning with a Sunday.

(8)   Requirements included in, and directions given under, an individual support order shall, as far as practicable, be such as to avoid –

    (a)   any conflict with the defendant's religious beliefs; and

    (b)   any interference with the times, if any, at which he normally works or attends school or any other educational establishment.

(9)   Before making an individual support order, the court shall obtain from a social worker of a local authority or a member of a youth offending team any information which it considers necessary in order –

    (a)   to determine whether the individual support conditions are fulfilled, or

    (b)   to determine what requirements should be imposed by an individual support order if made,

and shall consider that information.

(10)   In this section and section 1AB below 'responsible officer', in relation to an individual support order, means one of the following who is specified in the order, namely –

    (a)   a social worker of a local authority;

(b)   a person nominated by a person appointed as chief education officer under section 532 of the Education Act 1996 (c 56);

(c)   a member of a youth offending team.

Amendments—Inserted by the Criminal Justice Act 2003, s 322, Children Act 2004, s 64, Sch 5, Pt 4; Criminal Justice and Immigration Act 2008, s 124(1), s 148(2), Sch 27, Pt 8, para 34.

1AB Individual support orders: explanation, breach, amendment etc

(1) Before making an individual support order, the court shall explain to the defendant in ordinary language –

(a)   the effect of the order and of the requirements proposed to be included in it;

(b)   the consequences which may follow (under subsection (3) below) if he fails to comply with any of those requirements; and

(c)   that the court has power (under subsection (6) below) to review the order on the application either of the defendant or of the responsible officer.

(2) The power of the Secretary of State under section 174(4) of the Criminal Justice Act 2003 includes power by order to –

(a)   prescribe cases in which subsection (1) above does not apply; and

(b)   prescribe cases in which the explanation referred to in that subsection may be made in the absence of the defendant, or may be provided in written form.

(3) If the person in respect of whom an individual support order is made fails without reasonable excuse to comply with any requirement included in the order, he is guilty of an offence and liable on summary conviction to a fine not exceeding –

(a)   if he is aged 14 or over at the date of his conviction, £1,000;

(b)   if he is aged under 14 then, £250.

(4) No referral order under section 16(2) or (3) of the Powers of Criminal Courts (Sentencing) Act 2000 (referral of young offenders to youth offender panels) may be made in respect of an offence under subsection (3) above.

(5) If the anti-social behaviour order as a result of which an individual support order was made ceases to have effect, the individual support order (if it has not previously ceased to have effect) ceases to have effect when the anti-social behaviour order does.

(5A) The period specified as the term of an individual support order made on an application under section 1AA(1A) above must not be longer than the remaining part of the term of the anti-social behaviour order as a result of which it is made.

(6) On an application made by complaint by –

(a)   the person subject to an individual support order, or

(b)   the responsible officer,

the court which made the individual support order may vary or discharge it by a further order.

(7) If the anti-social behaviour order as a result of which an individual support order was made is varied, the court varying the anti-social behaviour order may by a further order vary or discharge the individual support order.

Amendments—Criminal Justice Act 2003, s 322; Criminal Justice and Immigration Act 2008, s 124(5).

1B Orders in county court proceedings

(1) This section applies to any proceedings in a county court ('the principal proceedings').

(2) If a relevant authority –

    (a)   is a party to the principal proceedings, and

    (b)   considers that a party to those proceedings is a person in relation to whom it would be reasonable for it to make an application under section 1,

it may make an application in those proceedings for an order under subsection (4).

(3) If a relevant authority –

    (a)   is not a party to the principal proceedings, and

    (b)   considers that a party to those proceedings is a person in relation to whom it would be reasonable for it to make an application under section 1,

it may make an application to be joined to those proceedings to enable it to apply for an order under subsection (4) and, if it is so joined, may apply for such an order.

(3A) Subsection (3B) applies if a relevant authority is a party to the principal proceedings and considers –

    (a)   that a person who is not a party to the proceedings has acted in an anti-social manner, and

    (b)   that the person's anti-social acts are material in relation to the principal proceedings.

(3B) The relevant authority may –

    (a)   make an application for the person mentioned in subsection (3A)(a) to be joined to the principal proceedings to enable an order under subsection (4) to be made in relation to that person;

    (b)   if that person is so joined, apply for an order under subsection (4).

(3C) But a person must not be joined to proceedings in pursuance of subsection (3B) unless his anti-social acts are material in relation to the principal proceedings.

(4) If, on an application for an order under this subsection, it is proved that the conditions mentioned in section 1(1) are fulfilled as respects that other party, the court may make an order which prohibits him from doing anything described in the order.

(5) Subject to subsection (6), the person against whom an order under this section has been made and the relevant authority on whose application that order was made may apply to the county court which made an order under this section for it to be varied or discharged by a further order.

(6) Except with the consent of the relevant authority and the person subject to the order, no order under this section shall be discharged before the end of the period of two years beginning with the date of service of the order.

(7) Subsections (5) to (7) and (10) to (12) of section 1 apply for the purposes of the making and effect of orders made under this section as they apply for the purposes of the making and effect of anti-social behaviour orders.

(8) Sections 1AA and 1AB apply in relation to orders under this section, with any necessary modifications, as they apply in relation to anti-social behaviour orders.

(9) In their application by virtue of subsection (8), sections 1AA(1A)(b) and 1AB(6) have effect as if the words 'by complaint' were omitted.

Amendments—Police Reform Act 2002, s 63; Anti-social Behaviour Act 2003, s 85(1), (5); Criminal Justice and Immigration Act 2008, s 124(6).

1C Orders on conviction in criminal proceedings

(1) This section applies where a person (the 'offender') is convicted of a relevant offence.

(2) If the court considers –

(a)   that the offender has acted, at any time since the commencement date, in an anti-social manner, that is to say in a manner that caused or was likely to cause harassment, alarm or distress to one or more persons not of the same household as himself, and

(b)   that an order under this section is necessary to protect persons in any place in England and Wales from further anti-social acts by him,

it may make an order which prohibits the offender from doing anything described in the order.

(3) The court may make an order under this section –

(a)   if the prosecutor asks it to do so, or

(b)   if the court thinks it is appropriate to do so.

(3A) For the purpose of deciding whether to make an order under this section the court may consider evidence led by the prosecution and the defence.

(3B) It is immaterial whether evidence led in pursuance of subsection (3A) would have been admissible in the proceedings in which the offender was convicted.

(4) An order under this section shall not be made except –

(a)   in addition to a sentence imposed in respect of the relevant offence; or

(b)   in addition to an order discharging him conditionally.

(4A) The court may adjourn any proceedings in relation to an order under this section even after sentencing the offender.

(4B) If the offender does not appear for any adjourned proceedings, the court may further adjourn the proceedings or may issue a warrant for his arrest.

(4C) But the court may not issue a warrant for the offender's arrest unless it is satisfied that he has had adequate notice of the time and place of the adjourned proceedings.

(5) An order under this section takes effect on the day on which it is made, but the court may provide in any such order that such requirements of the order as it may specify shall, during any period when the offender is detained in legal custody, be suspended until his release from that custody.

(6) ...

(7) ...

(8) ...

(9) Subsections (7), (10), (10C), (10D), (10E) and (11) of section 1 apply for the purposes of the making and effect of orders made by virtue of this section as they apply for the purposes of the making and effect of anti-social behaviour orders.

(9ZA) An order under this section made in respect of a person under the age of 17, or an order varying such an order, may specify a relevant authority (other than the chief officer of police mentioned in section 1K(2)(a)) as being responsible for carrying out a review under section 1J of the operation of the order.

(9A) The council for the local government area in which a person in respect of whom an anti-social behaviour order has been made resides or appears to reside may bring proceedings under section 1(10) (as applied by subsection (9) above) for breach of an order under subsection (2) above.

(9AA) Sections 1AA and 1AB apply in relation to orders under this section, with any necessary modifications, as they apply in relation to anti-social behaviour orders.

(9AB) In their application by virtue of subsection (9AA), sections 1AA(1A)(b) and 1AB(6) have effect as if the words "by complaint" were omitted.

(9AC) In its application by virtue of subsection (9AA), section 1AA(1A)(b) has effect as if the reference to the relevant authority which applied for the anti-social behaviour order were a reference to the chief officer of police, or other relevant authority, responsible under section 1K(2)(a) or (b) for carrying out a review of the order under this section.

(9B) Subsection (9C) applies in relation to proceedings in which an order under subsection (2) is made against a child or young person who is convicted of an offence.

(9C) In so far as the proceedings relate to the making of the order –

  (a)   section 49 of the Children and Young Persons Act 1933 (c 12) (restrictions on reports of proceedings in which children and young persons are concerned) does not apply in respect of the child or young person against whom the order is made;
  (b)   section 39 of that Act (power to prohibit publication of certain matter) does so apply.

(10) In this section –

  'child' and "young person" have the same meaning as in the Children and Young Persons Act 1933 (c 12);
  'the commencement date' has the same meaning as in section 1 above;
  'the court' in relation to an offender means –

      (a)   the court by or before which he is convicted of the relevant offence; or
      (b)   if he is committed to the Crown Court to be dealt with for that offence, the Crown Court; and

  'relevant offence' means an offence committed after the coming into force of section 64 of the Police Reform Act 2002 (c 30).

Amendments—Anti-social Behaviour Act 2003, s 86(4); Serious Organised Crime and Police Act 2005, s 139(1), (4)(a); Criminal Justice and Immigration Act 2008, s 124(7).

1CA Variation and discharge of orders under section 1C

(1) An offender subject to an order under section 1C may apply to the court which made it for it to be varied or discharged.

(2) If he does so, he must also send written notice of his application to the Director of Public Prosecutions.

(3) The Director of Public Prosecutions may apply to the court which made an order under section 1C for it to be varied or discharged.

(4) A relevant authority may also apply to the court which made an order under section 1C for it to be varied or discharged if it appears to it that –

  (a)   in the case of variation, the protection of relevant persons from anti-social acts by the person subject to the order would be more appropriately effected by a variation of the order;
  (b)   in the case of discharge, that it is no longer necessary to protect relevant persons from anti-social acts by him by means of such an order.

(5) If the Director of Public Prosecutions or a relevant authority applies for the variation or discharge of an order under section 1C, he or it must also send written notice of the application to the person subject to the order.

(6) In the case of an order under section 1C made by a magistrates' court, the references in subsections (1), (3) and (4) to the court by which the order was made include a reference to any magistrates' court acting in the same local justice area as that court.

(7) No order under section 1C shall be discharged on an application under this section before the end of the period of two years beginning with the day on which the order takes effect, unless –

(a)   in the case of an application under subsection (1), the Director of Public Prosecutions consents, or
(b)   in the case of an application under subsection (3) or (4), the offender consents.

Amendments—Inserted by the Serious Organised Crime and Police Act 2005, s 140(1), (4).

1D Interim orders

(1) This section applies where –

(a)   an application is made for an anti-social behaviour order;
(b)   an application is made for an order under section 1B;
(c)   a request is made by the prosecution for an order under section 1C; or
(d)   the court is minded to make an order under section 1C of its own motion.

(2) If, before determining the application or request, or before deciding whether to make an order under section 1C of its own motion, the court considers that it is just to make an order under this section pending the determination of that application or request or before making that decision, it may make such an order.

(3) An order under this section is an order which prohibits the defendant from doing anything described in the order.

(4) An order under this section –

(a)   shall be for a fixed period;
(b)   may be varied, renewed or discharged;
(c)   shall, if it has not previously ceased to have effect, cease to have effect on the determination of the application or request mentioned in subsection (1), or on the court's making a decision as to whether or not to make an order under section 1C of its own motion.

(5) In relation to cases to which this section applies by virtue of paragraph (a) or (b) of subsection (1), subsections (6), (8) and (10) to (12) of section 1 apply for the purposes of the making and effect of orders under this section as they apply for the purposes of the making and effect of anti-social behaviour orders.

(6) In relation to cases to which this section applies by virtue of paragraph (c) or (d) of subsection (1) –

(a)   subsections (6) and (10) to (12) of section 1 apply for the purposes of the making and effect of orders under this section as they apply for the purposes of the making and effect of anti-social behaviour orders; and
(b)   section 1CA applies for the purposes of the variation or discharge of an order under this section as it applies for the purposes of the variation or discharge of an order under section 1C.

Amendments—Police Reform Act 2002, s 65(1); Serious Organised Crime and Police Act 2005, s 139(1), (5), (9).

1E Consultation requirements

(1) This section applies to –

(a)   applications for an anti-social behaviour order; and
(b)   applications for an order under section 1B.

(2) Before making an application to which this section applies, the council for a local government area shall consult the chief officer of police of the police force maintained for the police area within which that local government area lies.

(3) Before making an application to which this section applies, a chief officer of police shall consult the council for the local government area in which the person in relation to whom the application is to be made resides or appears to reside.

(4) Before making an application to which this section applies, a relevant authority other than a council for a local government area or a chief officer of police shall consult –

(a) the council for the local government area in which the person in relation to whom the application is to be made resides or appears to reside; and
(b) the chief officer of police of the police force maintained for the police area within which that local government area lies.

(5) Subsection (4)(a) does not apply if the relevant authority is a county council for a county in which there are no districts.

Amendments—Police Reform Act 2002, s 66; Anti-social Behaviour Act 2003, s 85(1), (7).

1F   Contracting out of local authority functions

(1)   The Secretary of State may by order provide that a relevant authority which is a local authority may make arrangements with a person specified (or of a description specified) in the order for the exercise of any function it has under sections 1 to 1E above –

(a) by such a person, or
(b) by an employee of his.

(2)   The order may provide –

(a) that the power of the relevant authority to make the arrangements is subject to such conditions as are specified in the order;
(b) that the arrangements must be subject to such conditions as are so specified;
(c) that the arrangements may be made subject to such other conditions as the relevant authority thinks appropriate.

(3)   The order may provide that the arrangements may authorise the exercise of the function –

(a) either wholly or to such extent as may be specified in the order or arrangements;
(b) either generally or in such cases or areas as may be so specified.

(4)   An order may provide that the person with whom arrangements are made in pursuance of the order is to be treated as if he were a public body for the purposes of section 1 of the Local Authorities (Goods and Services) Act 1970.

(5)   The Secretary of State must not make an order under this section unless he first consults –

(a) the National Assembly for Wales, if the order relates to a relevant authority in Wales;
(b) such representatives of local government as he thinks appropriate;
(c) such other persons as he thinks appropriate.

(6)   Any arrangements made by a relevant authority in pursuance of an order under this section do not prevent the relevant authority from exercising the function to which the arrangements relate.

(7)   The following provisions of the Deregulation and Contracting Out Act 1994 apply for the purposes of arrangements made in pursuance of an order under this section as they apply for the purposes of an authorisation to exercise functions by virtue of an order under section 70(2) of that Act –

(a) section 72 (effect of contracting out);
(b) section 73 (termination of contracting out);

(c)   section 75 and Schedule 15 (provision relating to disclosure of information);

(d)   paragraph 3 of Schedule 16 (authorised persons to be treated as officers of local authority).

(8)   For the purposes of subsection (7), any reference in the provisions specified in paragraphs (a) to (d) to a person authorised to exercise a function must be construed as a reference to a person with whom an arrangement is made for the exercise of the function in pursuance of an order under this section.

(9)   Relevant authorities and any person with whom arrangements are made in pursuance of an order under this section must have regard to any guidance issued by the Secretary of State for the purposes of this section.

(10)   An order under this section may make different provision for different purposes.

(11)   An order under this section may contain –

(a)   such consequential, supplemental or incidental provisions (including provision modifying any enactment), or

(b)   such transitional provisions or savings,

as the person making the order thinks appropriate.

(12)   Each of the following is a local authority –

(a)   a local authority within the meaning of section 270 of the Local Government Act 1972;

(b)   the Common Council of the City of London;

(c)   the Council of the Isles of Scilly.

Amendments—Inserted by Serious Organised Crime and Police Act 2005, s 142(1).

1G   Intervention orders

(1)   This section applies if, in relation to a person who has attained the age of 18, a relevant authority –

(a)   makes an application for an anti-social behaviour order or an order under section 1B above (the behaviour order),

(b)   has obtained from an appropriately qualified person a report relating to the effect on the person's behaviour of the misuse of controlled drugs or of such other factors as the Secretary of State by order prescribes, and

(c)   has engaged in consultation with such persons as the Secretary of State by order prescribes for the purpose of ascertaining that, if the report recommends that an order under this section is made, appropriate activities will be available.

(2)   The relevant authority may make an application to the court which is considering the application for the behaviour order for an order under this section (an intervention order).

(3)   If the court –

(a)   makes the behaviour order, and

(b)   is satisfied that the relevant conditions are met,

it may also make an intervention order.

(4)   The relevant conditions are –

(a)   that an intervention order is desirable in the interests of preventing a repetition of the behaviour which led to the behaviour order being made (trigger behaviour);

(b)   that appropriate activities relating to the trigger behaviour or its cause are available for the defendant;

(c)   that the defendant is not (at the time the intervention order is made) subject to another intervention order or to any other treatment relating to the trigger behaviour or its cause (whether on a voluntary basis or by virtue of a requirement imposed in pursuance of any enactment);

(d)   that the court has been notified by the Secretary of State that arrangements for implementing intervention orders are available in the area in which it appears that the defendant resides or will reside and the notice has not been withdrawn.

(5)   An intervention order is an order which –

(a)   requires the defendant to comply, for a period not exceeding six months, with such requirements as are specified in the order, and

(b)   requires the defendant to comply with any directions given by a person authorised to do so under the order with a view to the implementation of the requirements under paragraph (a) above.

(6)   An intervention order or directions given under the order may require the defendant –

(a)   to participate in the activities specified in the requirement or directions at a time or times so specified;

(b)   to present himself to a person or persons so specified at a time or times so specified.

(7)   Requirements included in, or directions given under, an intervention order must, as far as practicable, be such as to avoid –

(a)   any conflict with the defendant's religious beliefs, and

(b)   any interference with the times (if any) at which he normally works or attends an educational establishment.

(8)   If the defendant fails to comply with a requirement included in or a direction given under an intervention order, the person responsible for the provision or supervision of appropriate activities under the order must inform the relevant authority of that fact.

(9)   The person responsible for the provision or supervision of appropriate activities is a person of such description as is prescribed by order made by the Secretary of State.

(10)   In this section –

'appropriate activities' means such activities, or activities of such a description, as are prescribed by order made by the Secretary of State for the purposes of this section;

'appropriately qualified person' means a person who has such qualifications or experience as the Secretary of State by order prescribes;

'controlled drug' has the same meaning as in the Misuse of Drugs Act 1971;

'relevant authority' means a relevant authority for the purposes of section 1 above.

(11)   An order under this section made by the Secretary of State may make different provision for different purposes.

(12)   This section and section 1H below apply to a person in respect of whom a behaviour order has been made subject to the following modifications–

(a)   in subsection (1) above paragraph (a) must be ignored;

(b)   in subsection (2) above, for 'is considering the application for' substitute 'made';

(c)   in subsection (3) above paragraph (a), the word 'and' following it and the word 'also' must be ignored.

Amendments—Inserted by Drugs Act 2005, s 20(1).

1H   Intervention orders: explanation, breach, amendment etc

(1)   Before making an intervention order the court must explain to the defendant in ordinary language –

(a)   the effect of the order and of the requirements proposed to be included in it,

(b)   the consequences which may follow (under subsection (3) below) if he fails to comply with any of those requirements, and

(c)   that the court has power (under subsection (5) below) to review the order on the application either of the defendant or of the relevant authority.

(2)   The power of the Secretary of State under section 174(4) of the Criminal Justice Act 2003 includes power by order to –

(a)   prescribe cases in which subsection (1) does not apply, and

(b)   prescribe cases in which the explanation referred to in that subsection may be made in the absence of the defendant, or may be provided in written form.

(3)   If a person in respect of whom an intervention order is made fails without reasonable excuse to comply with any requirement included in the order he is guilty of an offence and liable on summary conviction to a fine not exceeding level 4 on the standard scale.

(4)   If the behaviour order as a result of which an intervention order is made ceases to have effect, the intervention order (if it has not previously ceased to have effect) ceases to have effect when the behaviour order does.

(5)   On an application made by –

(a)   a person subject to an intervention order, or

(b)   the relevant authority,

the court which made the intervention order may vary or discharge it by a further order.

(6)   An application under subsection (5) made to a magistrates' court must be made by complaint.

(7)   If the behaviour order as a result of which an intervention order was made is varied, the court varying the behaviour order may by a further order vary or discharge the intervention order.

(8)   Expressions used in this section and in section 1G have the same meaning in this section as in that section.

Amendments—Inserted by Drugs Act 2005, s 20(1).

1I   Special measures for witnesses

(1)   This section applies to the following proceedings –

(a)   any proceedings in a magistrates' court on an application for an anti-social behaviour order,

(b)   any proceedings in a magistrates' court or the Crown Court so far as relating to the issue whether to make an order under section 1C, and

(c)   any proceedings in a magistrates' court so far as relating to the issue whether to make an order under section 1D.

(2)   Chapter 1 of Part 2 of the Youth Justice and Criminal Evidence Act 1999 (special measures directions in the case of vulnerable and intimidated witnesses) shall apply in relation to any such proceedings as it applies in relation to criminal proceedings, but with –

(a)   the omission of the provisions of that Act mentioned in subsection (3) (which make provision appropriate only in the context of criminal proceedings), and

(b)   any other necessary modifications.

(3)   The provisions are –

(a)   section 17(4),

(b)   section 21(1)(b) and (5) to (7),

(c)   section 22(1)(b) and (2)(b) and (c),

(d)   section 27(10), and

(e)   section 32.

(4)   Any rules of court made under or for the purposes of Chapter 1 of Part 2 of that Act shall apply in relation to proceedings to which this section applies –

(a)   to such extent as may be provided by rules of court, and

(b)   subject to such modifications as may be so provided.

(5)   Section 47 of that Act (restrictions on reporting special measures directions etc) applies, with any necessary modifications, in relation to –

(a)   a direction under section 19 of the Act as applied by this section, or
(b)   a direction discharging or varying such a direction,

and sections 49 and 51 of that Act (offences) apply accordingly.

Amendments—Inserted by Serious Organised Crime and Police Act 2005, s 143.

1J Review of orders under sections 1, 1B and 1C

(1) This section applies where –

(a)   an anti-social behaviour order,
(b)   an order under section 1B, or
(c)   an order under section 1C,

has been made in respect of a person under the age of 17.

(2) If –

(a)   the person subject to the order will be under the age of 18 at the end of a period specified in subsection (3) (a "review period"), and
(b)   the term of the order runs until the end of that period or beyond,

then before the end of that period a review of the operation of the order shall be carried out.

(3) The review periods are –

(a)   the period of 12 months beginning with –

(i)   the day on which the order was made, or
(ii)   if during that period there is a supplemental order (or more than one), the date of the supplemental order (or the last of them);

(b)   a period of 12 months beginning with –

(i)   the day after the end of the previous review period, or
(ii)   if during that period there is a supplemental order (or more than one), the date of the supplemental order (or the last of them).

(4) In subsection (3) 'supplemental order' means –

(a)   a further order varying the order in question;
(b)   an individual support order made in relation to the order in question on an application under section 1AA(1A).

(5) Subsection (2) does not apply in relation to any review period if the order is discharged before the end of that period.

(6) A review under this section shall include consideration of –

(a)   the extent to which the person subject to the order has complied with it;
(b)   the adequacy of any support available to the person to help him comply with it;
(c)   any matters relevant to the question whether an application should be made for the order to be varied or discharged.

(7) Those carrying out or participating in a review under this section shall have regard to any guidance issued by the Secretary of State when considering –

(a)   how the review should be carried out;

(b)   what particular matters should be dealt with by the review;

(c)   what action (if any) it would be appropriate to take in consequence of the findings of the review.

Amendments—Inserted by the Criminal Justice and Immigration Act 2008, s 123(1).

1K Responsibility for, and participation in, reviews under section 1J

(1) A review under section 1J of an anti-social behaviour order or an order under section 1B shall be carried out by the relevant authority that applied for the order.

(2) A review under section 1J of an order under section 1C shall be carried out –

(a)   (except where paragraph (b) applies) by the appropriate chief officer of police;

(b)   where a relevant authority is specified under section 1C(9ZA), by that authority.

(3) A local authority, in carrying out a review under section 1J, shall act in co-operation with the appropriate chief officer of police; and it shall be the duty of that chief officer to co-operate in the carrying out of the review.

(4) The chief officer of police of a police force, in carrying out a review under section 1J, shall act in co-operation with the appropriate local authority; and it shall be the duty of that local authority to co-operate in the carrying out of the review.

(5) A relevant authority other than a local authority or chief officer of police, in carrying out a review under section 1J, shall act in co-operation with –

(a)   the appropriate local authority, and

(b)   the appropriate chief officer of police;

and it shall be the duty of that local authority and that chief officer to co-operate in the carrying out of the review.

(6) A chief officer of police or other relevant authority carrying out a review under section 1J may invite the participation in the review of a person or body not required by subsection (3), (4) or (5) to co-operate in the carrying out of the review.

(7) In this section –

'the appropriate chief officer of police' means the chief officer of police of the police force maintained for the police area in which the person subject to the order resides or appears to reside;

'the appropriate local authority' means the council for the local government area (within the meaning given in section 1(12)) in which the person subject to the order resides or appears to reside.

Amendments—Criminal Justice and Immigration Act 2008, s 123(1).

2 ...

Amendments—Repealed by the Sexual Offences Act 2003, ss 139, 140, Sch 6, para 38(1), (2), Sch 7.

2A ...

Amendments—Repealed by the Sexual Offences Act 2003, ss 139, 140, Sch 6, para 38(1), (2), Sch 7.

2B ...

Amendments—Repealed by the Sexual Offences Act 2003, ss 139, 140, Sch 6, para 38(1), (2), Sch 7.

3 ...

Amendments—Repealed by the Sexual Offences Act 2003, ss 139, 140, Sch 6, para 38(1), (2), Sch 7.

4 Appeals against orders

(1) An appeal shall lie to the Crown Court against the making by a magistrates' court of an anti-social behaviour order, an individual support order, an order under section 1D above,

(2) On such an appeal the Crown Court –

(a) may make such orders as may be necessary to give effect to its determination of the appeal; and

(b) may also make such incidental or consequential orders as appear to it to be just.

(3) Any order of the Crown Court made on an appeal under this section (other than one directing that an application be re-heard by a magistrates' court) shall, for the purposes of section 1(8), 1AB(6), be treated as if it were an order of the magistrates' court from which the appeal was brought and not an order of the Crown Court.

Amendments—Criminal Justice Act 2003, s 323(1), (2)(a); Police Reform Act 2002, s 65(2); Sexual Offences Act 2003, ss 139, 140, Sch 6, para 38(1), (3)(a), Sch 7.

Crime and disorder strategies

5 Authorities responsible for strategies

(1) Subject to the provisions of this section, the functions conferred by or under section 6 below shall be exercisable in relation to each local government area by the responsible authorities, that is to say –

(a) the council for the area and, where the area is a district and the council is not a unitary authority, the council for the county which includes the district;

(b) every chief officer of police any part of whose police area lies within the area;

(c) every police authority any part of whose police area so lies;

(d) every fire and rescue authority any part of whose area so lies;

(e) if the local government area is in England, every Primary Care Trust the whole or any part of whose area so lies; and

(f) if the local government area is in Wales, every Local Health Board the whole or any part of whose area so lies.

(1A) The Secretary of State may by order provide in relation to any two or more local government areas in England –

(a) that the functions conferred by or under section 6 or by section 7 below are to be carried out in relation to those areas taken together as if they constituted only one area; and

(b) that the persons who for the purposes of this Chapter are to be taken to be responsible authorities in relation to the combined area are the persons who comprise every person who (apart from the order) would be a responsible authority in relation to any one or more of the areas included in the combined area.

(1B) The Secretary of State shall not make an order under subsection (1A) above unless –

(a) an application for the order has been made jointly by all the persons who would be the responsible authorities in relation to the combined area or the Secretary of State has first consulted those persons; and

(b) he considers it would be in the interests of reducing crime and disorder, or of combatting the misuse of drugs, alcohol and other substances, to make the order.

(1C) An order under subsection (1A) above –

(a) may require the councils for the local government areas in question to appoint a joint committee of those councils (the "joint crime and disorder committee") and to arrange for crime and disorder scrutiny functions in relation to any (or all) of those councils to be exercisable by that committee;

(b) may make provision applying any of the relevant provisions, with or without modifications, in relation to a joint crime and disorder committee.

(1D) In subsection (1C) –

'crime and disorder scrutiny functions', in relation to a council, means functions that are, or, but for an order under subsection (1A) above, would be, exercisable by the crime and disorder committee of the council under section 19 of the Police and Justice Act 2006 (local authority scrutiny of crime and disorder matters);

'the relevant provisions' means –

(a)   section 19 of the Police and Justice Act 2006;
(b)   section 20 of that Act and any regulations made under that section;
(c)   Schedule 8 to that Act;
(d)   section 21 of the Local Government Act 2000.

(2) In exercising those functions, the responsible authorities shall act in co-operation with the following persons and bodies, namely –

(b)   every local probation board any part of whose area lies within the area;
(ba) every provider of probation services operating within the area in pursuance of arrangements under section 3 of the Offender Management Act 2007 which provide for it to co-operate under this subsection with the responsible authorities;
(c)   every person or body of a description which is for the time being prescribed by order of the Secretary of State under this subsection; and
(d)   where they are acting in relation to an area in Wales, every person or body which is of a description which is for the time being prescribed by an order under this subsection of the National Assembly for Wales;

and it shall be the duty of those persons and bodies to co-operate in the exercise by the responsible authorities of those functions.

(3) The responsible authorities shall also invite the participation in their exercise of those functions of at least one person or body of each description which is for the time being prescribed by order of the Secretary of State under this subsection and, in the case of the responsible authorities for an area in Wales, of any person or body of a description for the time being prescribed by an order under this subsection of the National Assembly for Wales.

(4) In this section and sections 6 and 7 below 'local government area' means –

(a)   in relation to England, each district or London borough, the City of London, the Isle of Wight and the Isles of Scilly;
(b)   in relation to Wales, each county or county borough.

(5) In this section –

'fire and rescue authority' means –

(a)   a fire and rescue authority constituted by a scheme under section 2 of the Fire and Rescue Services Act 2004 or a scheme to which section 4 of that Act applies;
(b)   a metropolitan county fire and rescue authority; or
(c)   the London Fire and Emergency Planning Authority; and

'police authority' means –

(a)   any police authority established under section 3 of the Police Act 1996 (c 16); or
(b)   the Metropolitan Police Authority.

(6) The appropriate national authority may by order amend this section by –

(a)   adding an entry for any person or body to the list of authorities in subsection (1),
(b)   altering or repealing an entry for the time being included in the list, or
(c)   adding, altering or repealing provisions for the interpretation of entries in the list.

(7) In this section the 'appropriate national authority', in relation to a person or body, means –

(a) the National Assembly for Wales, if all the functions of the person or body are devolved Welsh functions;

(b) the Secretary of State and the Assembly acting jointly, if the functions of the person or body include devolved Welsh functions and other functions; and

(c) the Secretary of State, if none of the functions of the person or body are devolved Welsh functions.

(8) In subsection (7), 'devolved Welsh functions' means functions which are dischargeable only in relation to Wales and relate to matters in relation to which the Assembly has functions.

Amendments—Police Reform Act 2002, s 107(2), Sch 8; Civil Contingencies Act 2004, s 32(1), Sch 2, Pt 1, para 10(1), (2); Police and Justice Act 2006, s 22, Sch 9, paras 1, 2(1), (2); SI 2008/912, art 3, Sch 1, Pt 1, para 13(1), (2).

6 Formulation and implementation of strategies

(1) The responsible authorities for a local government area shall, in accordance with section 5 and with regulations made under subsection (2), formulate and implement –

(a) a strategy for the reduction of crime and disorder in the area (including anti-social and other behaviour adversely affecting the local environment); and

(b) a strategy for combatting the misuse of drugs, alcohol and other substances in the area.

(2) The appropriate national authority may by regulations make further provision as to the formulation and implementation of a strategy under this section.

(3) Regulations under subsection (2) may in particular make provision for or in connection with –

(a) the time by which a strategy must be prepared and the period to which it is to relate;

(b) the procedure to be followed by the responsible authorities in preparing and implementing a strategy (including requirements as to the holding of public meetings and other consultation);

(c) the conferring of functions on any one or more of the responsible authorities in relation to the formulation and implementation of a strategy;

(d) matters to which regard must be had in formulating and implementing a strategy;

(e) objectives to be addressed in a strategy and performance targets in respect of those objectives;

(f) the sharing of information between responsible authorities;

(g) the publication and dissemination of a strategy;

(h) the preparation of reports on the implementation of a strategy.

(4) The provision which may be made under subsection (2) includes provision for or in connection with the conferring of functions on a committee of, or a particular member or officer of, any of the responsible authorities.

(5) The matters referred to in subsection (3)(d) may in particular include guidance given by the appropriate national authority in connection with the formulation or implementation of a strategy.

(6) Provision under subsection (3)(e) may require a strategy to be formulated so as to address (in particular) –

(a) the reduction of crime or disorder of a particular description; or

(b) the combatting of a particular description of misuse of drugs, alcohol or other substances.

(7) Regulations under this section may make –

(a) different provision for different local government areas;

(b) supplementary or incidental provision.

(8) For the purposes of this section any reference to the implementation of a strategy includes –

(a) keeping it under review for the purposes of monitoring its effectiveness; and

(b) making any changes to it that appear necessary or expedient.

(9) In this section the 'appropriate national authority' is –

- (a) the Secretary of State, in relation to strategies for areas in England;
- (b) the National Assembly for Wales, in relation to strategies for combatting the misuse of drugs, alcohol or other substances in areas in Wales;
- (c) the Secretary of State and the Assembly acting jointly, in relation to strategies for combatting crime and disorder in areas in Wales.

Amendments—Police and Justice Act 2006, s 22, Sch 9, paras 1, 3.

6A...

Amendments—Police Reform Act 2002, s 98.

7 Supplemental

(1) The responsible authorities for a local government area shall, whenever so required by the Secretary of State, submit to the Secretary of State a report on such matters connected with the exercise of their functions under section 6 above as may be specified in the requirement.

(2) A requirement under subsection (1) above may specify the form in which a report is to be given.

(3) The Secretary of State may arrange, or require the responsible authorities to arrange, for a report under subsection (1) above to be published in such manner as appears to him to be appropriate.

Youth crime and disorder

8 Parenting orders

(1) This section applies where, in any court proceedings –

- (a) a child safety order is made in respect of a child or the court determines on an application under section 12(6) below that a child has failed to comply with any requirement included in such an order;
- (aa) a parental compensation order is made in relation to a child's behaviour;
- (b) an anti-social behaviour order or sexual offences prevention order is made in respect of a child or young person;
- (c) a child or young person is convicted of an offence; or
- (d) a person is convicted of an offence under section 443 (failure to comply with school attendance order) or section 444 (failure to secure regular attendance at school of registered pupil) of the Education Act 1996.

(2) Subject to subsection (3) and section 9(1) below, if in the proceedings the court is satisfied that the relevant condition is fulfilled, it may make a parenting order in respect of a person who is a parent or guardian of the child or young person or, as the case may be, the person convicted of the offence under section 443 or 444 ('the parent').

(3) A court shall not make a parenting order unless it has been notified by the Secretary of State that arrangements for implementing such orders are available in the area in which it appears to the court that the parent resides or will reside and the notice has not been withdrawn.

(4) A parenting order is an order which requires the parent –

- (a) to comply, for a period not exceeding twelve months, with such requirements as are specified in the order, and
- (b) subject to subsection (5) below, to attend, for a concurrent period not exceeding three months, such counselling or guidance programme as may be specified in directions given by the responsible officer.

(5) A parenting order may, but need not, include such a requirement as is mentioned in subsection (4)(b) above in any case where a parenting order under this section or any other enactment has been made in respect of the parent on a previous occasion.

(6) The relevant condition is that the parenting order would be desirable in the interests of preventing –

    (a)   in a case falling within paragraph (a), (aa) or (b) of subsection (1) above, any repetition of the kind of behaviour which led to the child safety order, parental compensation order, anti-social behaviour order or sexual offences prevention order being made;

    (b)   in a case falling within paragraph (c) of that subsection, the commission of any further offence by the child or young person;

    (c)   in a case falling within paragraph (d) of that subsection, the commission of any further offence under section 443 or 444 of the Education Act 1996.

(7) The requirements that may be specified under subsection (4)(a) above are those which the court considers desirable in the interests of preventing any such repetition or, as the case may be, the commission of any such further offence.

(7A) A counselling or guidance programme which a parent is required to attend by virtue of subsection (4)(b) above may be or include a residential course but only if the court is satisfied –

    (a)   that the attendance of the parent at a residential course is likely to be more effective than his attendance at a non-residential course in preventing any such repetition or, as the case may be, the commission of any such further offence, and

    (b)   that any interference with family life which is likely to result from the attendance of the parent at a residential course is proportionate in all the circumstances.

(8) In this section and section 9 below 'responsible officer', in relation to a parenting order, means one of the following who is specified in the order, namely –

    (a)   an officer of a local probation board or an officer of a provider of probation services;

    (b)   a social worker of a local authority; and

    (bb)   a person nominated by a person appointed as director of children's services under section 18 of the Children Act 2004 or by a person appointed as chief education officer under section 532 of the Education Act 1996;

    (c)   a member of a youth offending team.

(9) In this section 'sexual offences prevention order' means an order under section 104 of the Sexual Offences Act 2003 (sexual offences prevention orders.

Amendments—Criminal Justice and Court Services Act 2000, s 74, Sch 7, Pt I, para 4(1)(a), (2); Children Act 2004, s 60(1), (2); Serious Organised Crime and Police Act 2005, s 144, Sch 10, Pt 1, paras 1, 3(1), (2); Violent Crime Reduction Act 2006, s 60(1), (2)(a); Powers of Criminal Courts (Sentencing) Act 2000, s 165(1), Sch 9, para 194; Criminal Justice Act 2003, ss 324, 332, Sch 34, para 1, Sch 37, Pt 12; Anti-social Behaviour Act 2003, s 18(1), (2).

9 Parenting orders: supplemental

(1) Where a person under the age of 16 is convicted of an offence, the court by or before which he is so convicted –

    (a)   if it is satisfied that the relevant condition is fulfilled, shall make a parenting order; and

    (b)   if it is not so satisfied, shall state in open court that it is not and why it is not.

(1A) The requirements of subsection (1) do not apply where the court makes a referral order in respect of the offence.

(1B) If an anti-social behaviour order is made in respect of a person under the age of 16 the court which makes the order –

    (a)   must make a parenting order if it is satisfied that the relevant condition is fulfilled;

    (b)   if it is not so satisfied, must state in open court that it is not and why it is not.

(2) Before making a parenting order –

(a)   in a case falling within paragraph (a) of subsection (1) of section 8 above;

(b)   in a case falling within paragraph (b) or (c) of that subsection, where the person concerned is under the age of 16; or

(c)   in a case falling within paragraph (d) of that subsection, where the person to whom the offence related is under that age,

a court shall obtain and consider information about the person's family circumstances and the likely effect of the order on those circumstances.

(2A) In a case where a court proposes to make both a referral order in respect of a child or young person convicted of an offence and a parenting order, before making the parenting order the court shall obtain and consider a report by an appropriate officer –

(a)   indicating the requirements proposed by that officer to be included in the parenting order;

(b)   indicating the reasons why he considers those requirements would be desirable in the interests of preventing the commission of any further offence by the child or young person; and

(c)   if the child or young person is aged under 16, containing the information required by subsection (2) above.

(2B) In subsection (2A) above 'an appropriate officer' means –

(a)   an officer of a local probation board or an officer of a provider of probation services;

(b)   a social worker of a local authority; or

(c)   a member of a youth offending team.

(3) Before making a parenting order, a court shall explain to the parent in ordinary language –

(a)   the effect of the order and of the requirements proposed to be included in it;

(b)   the consequences which may follow (under subsection (7) below) if he fails to comply with any of those requirements; and

(c)   that the court has power (under subsection (5) below) to review the order on the application either of the parent or of the responsible officer.

(4) Requirements specified in, and directions given under, a parenting order shall, as far as practicable, be such as to avoid –

(a)   any conflict with the parent's religious beliefs; and

(b)   any interference with the times, if any, at which he normally works or attends an educational establishment.

(5) If while a parenting order is in force it appears to the court which made it, on the application of the responsible officer or the parent, that it is appropriate to make an order under this subsection, the court may make an order discharging the parenting order or varying it –

(a)   by cancelling any provision included in it; or

(b)   by inserting in it (either in addition to or in substitution for any of its provisions) any provision that could have been included in the order if the court had then had power to make it and were exercising the power.

(6) Where an application under subsection (5) above for the discharge of a parenting order is dismissed, no further application for its discharge shall be made under that subsection by any person except with the consent of the court which made the order.

(7) If while a parenting order is in force the parent without reasonable excuse fails to comply with any requirement included in the order, or specified in directions given by the responsible officer, he shall be liable on summary conviction to a fine not exceeding level 3 on the standard scale.

(7A) In this section 'referral order' means an order under section 16(2) or (3) of the Powers of Criminal Courts (Sentencing) Act 2000 (referral of offender to youth offender panel).

Amendments—Youth Justice and Criminal Evidence Act 1999, s 67(1), Sch 4, paras 25, 27; Criminal Justice Act 2003, s 324, Sch 34, para 2(1), (2); Children Act 2004, s 64, Sch 5, Pt 4.

10 Appeals against parenting orders

(1) An appeal shall lie –

    (a)   to the High Court against the making of a parenting order by virtue of paragraph (a) of subsection (1) of section 8 above; and

    (b)   to the Crown Court against the making of a parenting order by virtue of paragraph (b) of that subsection.

(2) On an appeal under subsection (1) above the High Court or the Crown Court –

    (a)   may make such orders as may be necessary to give effect to its determination of the appeal; and

    (b)   may also make such incidental or consequential orders as appear to it to be just.

(3) Any order of the High Court or the Crown Court made on an appeal under subsection (1) above (other than one directing that an application be re-heard by a magistrates' court) shall, for the purposes of subsections (5) to (7) of section 9 above, be treated as if it were an order of the court from which the appeal was brought and not an order of the High Court or the Crown Court.

(4) A person in respect of whom a parenting order is made by virtue of section 8(1)(c) above shall have the same right of appeal against the making of the order as if –

    (a)   the offence that led to the making of the order were an offence committed by him; and

    (b)   the order were a sentence passed on him for the offence.

(5) A person in respect of whom a parenting order is made by virtue of section 8(1)(d) above shall have the same right of appeal against the making of the order as if the order were a sentence passed on him for the offence that led to the making of the order.

(6) The Lord Chancellor may, with the concurrence of the Lord Chief Justice, by order make provision as to the circumstances in which appeals under subsection (1)(a) above may be made against decisions taken by courts on questions arising in connection with the transfer, or proposed transfer, of proceedings by virtue of any order under paragraph 2 of Schedule 11 (jurisdiction) to the Children Act 1989 ('the 1989 Act').

(7) Except to the extent provided for in any order made under subsection (6) above, no appeal may be made against any decision of a kind mentioned in that subsection.

(8) The Lord Chief Justice may nominate a judicial office holder (as defined in section 109(4) of the Constitutional Reform Act 2005) to exercise his functions under this section.

Amendments—Constitutional Reform Act 2005, s 15(1), Sch 4, Pt 1, paras 276, 277(1), (3).

11 Child safety orders

(1) Subject to subsection (2) below, if a magistrates' court, on the application of a local authority, is satisfied that one or more of the conditions specified in subsection (3) below are fulfilled with respect to a child under the age of 10, it may make an order (a 'child safety order') which –

    (a)   places the child, for a period (not exceeding the permitted maximum) specified in the order, under the supervision of the responsible officer; and

    (b)   requires the child to comply with such requirements as are so specified.

(2) A court shall not make a child safety order unless it has been notified by the Secretary of State that arrangements for implementing such orders are available in the area in which it appears that the child resides or will reside and the notice has not been withdrawn.

(3) The conditions are –

(a) that the child has committed an act which, if he had been aged 10 or over, would have constituted an offence;

(b) that a child safety order is necessary for the purpose of preventing the commission by the child of such an act as is mentioned in paragraph (a) above;

(c) that the child has contravened a ban imposed by a curfew notice; and

(d) that the child has acted in a manner that caused or was likely to cause harassment, alarm or distress to one or more persons not of the same household as himself.

(4) The maximum period permitted for the purposes of subsection (1)(a) above is twelve months.

(5) The requirements that may be specified under subsection (1)(b) above are those which the court considers desirable in the interests of –

(a) securing that the child receives appropriate care, protection and support and is subject to proper control; or

(b) preventing any repetition of the kind of behaviour which led to the child safety order being made.

(6) Proceedings under this section or section 12 below shall be family proceedings for the purposes of the 1989 Act or section 65 of the Magistrates' Courts Act 1980 ('the 1980 Act'); and the standard of proof applicable to such proceedings shall be that applicable to civil proceedings.

(7) In this section 'local authority' has the same meaning as in the 1989 Act.

(8) In this section and section 12 below, 'responsible officer', in relation to a child safety order, means one of the following who is specified in the order, namely –

(a) a social worker of a local authority; and

(b) a member of a youth offending team.

Amendments—Children Act 2004, s 60(1), (3).

12 Child safety orders: supplemental

(1) Before making a child safety order, a magistrates' court shall obtain and consider information about the child's family circumstances and the likely effect of the order on those circumstances.

(2) Before making a child safety order, a magistrates' court shall explain to the parent or guardian of the child in ordinary language –

(a) the effect of the order and of the requirements proposed to be included in it;

(b) the consequences which may follow (under subsection (6) below) if the child fails to comply with any of those requirements; and

(c) that the court has power (under subsection (4) below) to review the order on the application either of the parent or guardian or of the responsible officer.

(3) Requirements included in a child safety order shall, as far as practicable, be such as to avoid –

(a) any conflict with the parent's religious beliefs; and

(b) any interference with the times, if any, at which the child normally attends school.

(4) If while a child safety order is in force in respect of a child it appears to the court which made it, on the application of the responsible officer or a parent or guardian of the child, that it is appropriate to make an order under this subsection, the court may make an order discharging the child safety order or varying it –

(a) by cancelling any provision included in it; or

(b) by inserting in it (either in addition to or in substitution for any of its provisions) any provision that could have been included in the order if the court had then had power to make it and were exercising the power.

(5) Where an application under subsection (4) above for the discharge of a child safety order is dismissed, no further application for its discharge shall be made under that subsection by any person except with the consent of the court which made the order.

(6) Where a child safety order is in force and it is proved to the satisfaction of the court which made it or another magistrates' court acting in the same local justice area, acting for the same petty sessions area, on the application of the responsible officer, that the child has failed to comply with any requirement included in the order, the court –

    (a)   ...
    (b)   may make an order varying the order –

          (i)   by cancelling any provision included in it; or
          (ii)   by inserting in it (either in addition to or in substitution for any of its provisions) any provision that could have been included in the order if the court had then had power to make it and were exercising the power.

(7) ...

Amendments—Courts Act 2003 (Consequential Provisions) Order 2005, SI 2005/886; Children Act 2004, ss 60(1), (4), 64, Sch 5, Pt 6.

13 Appeals against child safety orders

(1) An appeal shall lie to the High Court against the making by a magistrates' court of a child safety order; and on such an appeal the High Court –

    (a)   may make such orders as may be necessary to give effect to its determination of the appeal; and
    (b)   may also make such incidental or consequential orders as appear to it to be just.

(2) Any order of the High Court made on an appeal under this section (other than one directing that an application be re-heard by a magistrates' court) shall, for the purposes of subsections (4) to (6) of section 12 above, be treated as if it were an order of the magistrates' court from which the appeal was brought and not an order of the High Court.

(3) Subsections (6) and (7) of section 10 above shall apply for the purposes of subsection (1) above as they apply for the purposes of subsection (1)(a) of that section.

13A Parental compensation orders

(1) A magistrates' court may make an order under this section (a 'parental compensation order') if on the application of a local authority it is satisfied, on the civil standard of proof –

    (a)   that the condition mentioned in subsection (2) below is fulfilled with respect to a child under the age of 10; and
    (b)   that it would be desirable to make the order in the interests of preventing a repetition of the behaviour in question.

(2) The condition is that the child has taken, or caused loss of or damage to, property in the course of –

    (a)   committing an act which, if he had been aged 10 or over, would have constituted an offence; or
    (b)   acting in a manner that caused or was likely to cause harassment, alarm or distress to one or more persons not of the same household as himself.

(3) A parental compensation order is an order which requires any person specified in the order who is a parent or guardian of the child (other than a local authority) to pay compensation of an amount specified in the order to any person or persons specified in the order who is, or are, affected by the taking of the property or its loss or damage.

(4) The amount of compensation specified may not exceed £5,000 in all.

(5) The Secretary of State may by order amend subsection (4) above so as to substitute a different amount.

(6) For the purposes of collection and enforcement, a parental compensation order is to be treated as if it were a sum adjudged to be paid on the conviction by the magistrates' court which made the order of the person or persons specified in the order as liable to pay the compensation.

(7) In this section and sections 13B and 13C below, 'local authority', has the same meaning as in the 1989 Act.

Amendments—Inserted by the Serious Organised Crime and Police Act 2005, s 144, Sch 10, Pt 1, paras 1, 2. Date in force (in relation to certain specified areas): 20 July 2006 (except in relation to any conduct which occurred before that date); see SI 2006/1871, art 2. Date in force (for remaining purposes); to be appointed, see the Serious Organised Crime and Police Act 2005, s 178(8).

13B Parental compensation orders: the compensation

(1) When specifying the amount of compensation for the purposes of section 13A(3) above, the magistrates' court shall take into account –

   (a)   the value of the property taken or damaged, or whose loss was caused, by the child;
   (b)   any further loss which flowed from the taking of or damage to the property, or from its loss;
   (c)   whether the child, or any parent or guardian of his, has already paid any compensation for the property (and if so, how much);
   (d)   whether the child, or any parent or guardian of his, has already made any reparation (and if so, what it consisted of);
   (e)   the means of those to be specified in the order as liable to pay the compensation, so far as the court can ascertain them;
   (f)   whether there was any lack of care on the part of the person affected by the taking of the property or its loss or damage which made it easier for the child to take or damage the property or to cause its loss.

(2) If property taken is recovered before compensation is ordered to be paid in respect of it –

   (a)   the court shall not order any such compensation to be payable in respect of it if it is not damaged;
   (b)   if it is damaged, the damage shall be treated for the purposes of making a parental compensation order as having been caused by the child, regardless of how it was caused and who caused it.

(3) The court shall specify in the order how and by when the compensation is to be paid (for example, it may specify that the compensation is to be paid by instalments, and specify the date by which each instalment must be paid).

(4) For the purpose of ascertaining the means of the parent or guardian, the court may, before specifying the amount of compensation, order him to provide the court, within such period as it may specify in the order, such a statement of his financial circumstances as the court may require.

(5) A person who without reasonable excuse fails to comply with an order under subsection (4) above is guilty of an offence and is liable on summary conviction to a fine not exceeding level 3 on the standard scale.

(6) If, in providing a statement of his financial circumstances pursuant to an order under subsection (4) above, a person –

   (a)   makes a statement which he knows to be false in a material particular;
   (b)   recklessly provides a statement which is false in a material particular; or
   (c)   knowingly fails to disclose any material fact,

he is liable on summary conviction to a fine not exceeding level 4 on the standard scale.

(7) Proceedings in respect of an offence under subsection (6) above may, despite anything in section 127(1) of the 1980 Act (limitation of time), be commenced at any time within two years from the date of the commission of the offence or within six months of its first discovery by the local authority, whichever period expires earlier.

Amendments—Inserted by the Serious Organised Crime and Police Act 2005, s 144, Sch 10, Pt 1, paras 1, 2. Date in force (in relation to certain specified areas): 20 July 2006 (except in relation to any conduct which occurred before that date); see SI 2006/1871, art 2. Date in force (for remaining purposes); to be appointed, see the Serious Organised Crime and Police Act 2005, s 178(8).

13C Parental compensation orders: supplemental

(1) Before deciding whether or not to make a parental compensation order in favour of any person, the magistrates' court shall take into account the views of that person about whether a parental compensation order should be made in his favour.

(2) Before making a parental compensation order, the magistrates' court shall obtain and consider information about the child's family circumstances and the likely effect of the order on those circumstances.

(3) Before making a parental compensation order, a magistrates' court shall explain to the parent or guardian of the child in ordinary language –

    (a)   the effect of the order and of the requirements proposed to be included in it;

    (b)   the consequences which may follow (under subsection (4)(b) below) as a result of failure to comply with any of those requirements;

    (c)   that the court has power (under subsection (4)(a) below) to review the order on the application either of the parent or guardian or of the local authority.

(4) A magistrates' court which has made a parental compensation order may make an order under subsection (5) below if while the order is in force –

    (a)   it appears to the court, on the application of the local authority, or the parent or guardian subject to the order, that it is appropriate to make an order under subsection (5); or

    (b)   it is proved to the satisfaction of the court, on the application of the local authority, that the parent or guardian subject to it has failed to comply with any requirement included in the order.

(5) An order under this subsection is an order discharging the parental compensation order or varying it –

    (a)   by cancelling any provision included in it; or

    (b)   by inserting in it (either in addition to or in substitution for any of its provisions) any provision that could have been included in the order if the court had then had power to make it and were exercising the power.

(6) Where an application under subsection (4) above for the discharge of a parental compensation order is dismissed, no further application for its discharge shall be made under that subsection by any person except with the consent of the court which made the order.

(7) References in this section to the magistrates' court which made a parental compensation order include any magistrates' court acting in the same local justice area as that court.

Amendments—Inserted by the Serious Organised Crime and Police Act 2005, s 144, Sch 10, Pt 1, paras 1, 2. Date in force (in relation to certain specified areas): 20 July 2006 (except in relation to any conduct which occurred before that date); see SI 2006/1871, art 2. Date in force (for remaining purposes); to be appointed, see the Serious Organised Crime and Police Act 2005, s 178(8).

13D Parental compensation orders: appeal

(1) If a magistrates' court makes a parental compensation order, the parent or guardian may appeal against the making of the order, or against the amount of compensation specified in the order.

(2) The appeal lies to the Crown Court.

(3) On the appeal the Crown Court –

    (a)   may make such orders as may be necessary to give effect to its determination of the appeal;

    (b)   may also make such incidental or consequential orders as appear to it to be just.

(4) Any order of the Crown Court made on an appeal under this section (other than one directing that an application be re-heard by a magistrates' court) shall, for the purposes of section 13C above, be treated as if it were an order of the magistrates' court from which the appeal was brought and not an order of the Crown Court.

(5) A person in whose favour a parental compensation order is made shall not be entitled to receive any compensation under it until (disregarding any power of a court to grant leave to appeal out of time) there is no further possibility of an appeal on which the order could be varied or set aside.

Amendments—Inserted by the Serious Organised Crime and Police Act 2005, s 144, Sch 10, Pt 1, paras 1, 2. Date in force (in relation to certain specified areas): 20 July 2006 (except in relation to any conduct which occurred before that date); see SI 2006/1871, art 2. Date in force (for remaining purposes); to be appointed, see the Serious Organised Crime and Police Act 2005, s 178(8).

13E Effect of parental compensation order on subsequent award of damages in civil proceedings

(1) This section has effect where –

  (a) a parental compensation order has been made in favour of any person in respect of any taking or loss of property or damage to it; and
  (b) a claim by him in civil proceedings for damages in respect of the taking, loss or damage is then to be determined.

(2) The damages in the civil proceedings shall be assessed without regard to the parental compensation order, but the claimant may recover only an amount equal to the aggregate of the following –

  (a) any amount by which they exceed the compensation; and
  (b) a sum equal to any portion of the compensation which he fails to recover.

(3) The claimant may not enforce the judgment, so far as it relates to such a sum as is mentioned in subsection (2)(b) above, without the permission of the court.

Amendments—Inserted by the Serious Organised Crime and Police Act 2005, s 144, Sch 10, Pt 1, paras 1, 2. Date in force (in relation to certain specified areas): 20 July 2006 (except in relation to any conduct which occurred before that date); see SI 2006/1871, art 2. Date in force (for remaining purposes); to be appointed, see the Serious Organised Crime and Police Act 2005, s 178(8).

14 Local child curfew schemes

(1) A local authority or a chief officer of police may make a scheme (a 'local child curfew scheme') for enabling the authority or (as the case may be) the officer –

  (a) subject to and in accordance with the provisions of the scheme; and
  (b) if, after such consultation as is required by the scheme, the authority or (as the case may be) the officer considers it necessary to do so for the purpose of maintaining order,

to give a notice imposing, for a specified period (not exceeding 90 days), a ban to which subsection (2) below applies.

(2) This subsection applies to a ban on children of specified ages (under 16) being in a public place within a specified area –

  (a) during specified hours (between 9 pm and 6 am); and
  (b) otherwise than under the effective control of a parent or a responsible person aged 18 or over.

(3) Before making a local child curfew scheme, a local authority shall consult –

  (a) every chief officer of police any part of whose police area lies within its area; and
  (b) such other persons or bodies as it considers appropriate.

(3A) Before making a local child curfew scheme, a chief officer of police shall consult –

  (a) every local authority any part of whose area lies within the area to be specified; and
  (b) such other persons or bodies as he considers appropriate.

(4) A local child curfew scheme shall, if made by a local authority, be made under the common seal of the authority.

(4A) A local child curfew scheme shall not have effect until it is confirmed by the Secretary of State.

(5) The Secretary of State –

(a)　may confirm, or refuse to confirm, a local child curfew scheme submitted under this section for confirmation; and

(b)　may fix the date on which such a scheme is to come into operation;

and if no date is so fixed, the scheme shall come into operation at the end of the period of one month beginning with the date of its confirmation.

(6) A notice given under a local child curfew scheme (a 'curfew notice') may specify different hours in relation to children of different ages.

(7) A curfew notice shall be given –

(a)　by posting the notice in some conspicuous place or places within the specified area; and

(b)　in such other manner, if any, as appears to the local authority or (as the case may be) the chief officer of police[1] to be desirable for giving publicity to the notice.

(8) In this section –

'local authority' means –

(a)　in relation to England, the council of a district or London borough, the Common Council of the City of London, the Council of the Isle of Wight and the Council of the Isles of Scilly;

(b)　in relation to Wales, the council of a county or county borough;

'public place' has the same meaning as in Part II of the Public Order Act 1986.

Amendments—Criminal Justice and Police Act 2001, ss 48, 49(1)–(5).

15 Contravention of curfew notices

(1) Subsections (2) and (3) below apply where a constable has reasonable cause to believe that a child is in contravention of a ban imposed by a curfew notice.

(2) The constable shall, as soon as practicable, inform the local authority for the area that the child has contravened the ban.

(3) The constable may remove the child to the child's place of residence unless he has reasonable cause to believe that the child would, if removed to that place, be likely to suffer significant harm.

(4) In subsection (1) of section 47 of the 1989 Act (local authority's duty to investigate) –

(a)　in paragraph (a), after sub-paragraph (ii) there shall be inserted the following sub-paragraph –

'(iii)　as contravened a ban imposed by a curfew notice within the meaning of Chapter I of Part I of the Crime and Disorder Act 1998; or'; and

(b)　at the end there shall be inserted the following paragraph –

'In the case of a child falling within paragraph (a)(iii) above, the enquiries shall be commenced as soon as practicable and, in any event, within 48 hours of the authority receiving the information'.

16 Removal of truants and excluded pupils to designated premises etc

(1) This section applies where a local authority –

(a) designates premises in a police area ('designated premises') as premises to which children and young persons of compulsory school age may be removed under this section; and

(b) notifies the chief officer of police for that area of the designation.

(2) A police officer of or above the rank of superintendent may direct that the powers conferred on a constable by subsections (3) and (3ZA) below –

(a) shall be exercisable as respects any area falling within the police area and specified in the direction; and

(b) shall be so exercisable during a period so specified;

and references in each of those subsections to a specified area and a specified period shall be construed accordingly.

(3) If a constable has reasonable cause to believe that a child or young person found by him in a public place in a specified area during a specified period –

(a) is of compulsory school age; and

(b) is absent from a school without lawful authority,

the constable may remove the child or young person to designated premises, or to the school from which he is so absent.

(3ZA) If a constable has reasonable cause to believe that a child or young person found by him in a public place in a specified area during a specified period and during school hours –

(a) is of compulsory school age,

(b) has been excluded on disciplinary grounds from a relevant school for a fixed period or permanently,

(c) remains excluded from that school,

(d) has not subsequently been admitted as a pupil to any other school, and

(e) has no reasonable justification for being in the public place,

the constable may remove the child or young person to designated premises.

(3A) Subsection (2) shall have effect in relation to The British Transport Police Force; and for that purpose the reference to any area falling within the police area shall be treated as a reference to any area in a place specified in section 31(1)(a) to (f) of the Railways and Transport Safety Act 2003.

(3B) In subsection (3ZA), 'school hours' means any time during a school session of the school referred to in paragraph (b) of that subsection or during a break between sessions of that school on the same day.

(4) A child's or young person's absence from a school shall be taken to be without lawful authority unless the child or young person is prevented from attending by sickness or other unavoidable cause or the absence falls within subsection (3) (leave or day set apart for religious observance) of section 444 of the Education Act 1996.

(5) In this section –

'British Transport Police' means the force of constables appointed under section 53 of the British Transport Commission Act 1949 (c xxix);
'local authority' means –

(a) in relation to England, a county council, a district council whose district does not form part of an area that has a county council, a London borough council or the Common Council of the City of London;

(b) in relation to Wales, a county council or a county borough council;

'public place' has the same meaning as in section 14 above;
'relevant school' has the meaning given by section 111 of the Education and Inspections Act 2006;[1]
'school' has the same meaning as in the Education Act 1996.

Amendments—Police Reform Act 2002, s 75(1), (2)(a) and (b); SI 2004/1573, art 12(5); Education and Inspections Act 2006, s 109(10), (11); s 108(1)–(6).

Miscellaneous and supplemental

17 Duty to consider crime and disorder implications

(1) Without prejudice to any other obligation imposed on it, it shall be the duty of each authority to which this section applies to exercise its various functions with due regard to the likely effect of the exercise of those functions on, and the need to do all that it reasonably can to prevent,

   (a)　crime and disorder in its area (including anti-social and other behaviour adversely affecting the local environment); and
   (b)　the misuse of drugs, alcohol and other substances in its area.

(2) This section applies to each of the following –

   a local authority;
   a joint authority;
   the London Fire and Emergency Planning Authority;
   a fire and rescue authority constituted by a scheme under section 2 of the Fire and Rescue Services Act 2004 or a scheme to which section 4 of that Act applies;
   a metropolitan county fire authority;
   a police authority;
   a National Park authority;
   the Broads Authority;
   the Greater London Authority;
   the London Development Agency;
   Transport for London.

(3) In this section –

   'local authority' means a local authority within the meaning given by section 270(1) of the Local Government Act 1972 or the Common Council of the City of London;
   'joint authority' has the same meaning as in the Local Government Act 1985;
   'National Park authority' means an authority established under section 63 of the Environment Act 1995.

(4) The appropriate national authority may by order amend this section by –

   (a)　adding an entry for any person or body to the list of authorities in subsection (2),
   (b)　altering or repealing any entry for the time being included in the list, or
   (c)　adding, altering or repealing provisions for the interpretation of entries in the list.

(5) In subsection (4) 'the appropriate national authority' has the same meaning as in section 5.

Amendments—Police and Justice Act 2006, s 22, Sch 9, paras 1, 4(1), (4); SI 2008/78, art 2.

17A Sharing of information

(1) A relevant authority is under a duty to disclose to all other relevant authorities any information held by the authority which is of a prescribed description, at such intervals and in such form as may be prescribed.

(2) In subsection (1) 'prescribed' means prescribed in regulations made by the Secretary of State.

(3) The Secretary of State may only prescribe descriptions of information which appears to him to be of potential relevance in relation to the reduction of crime and disorder in any area of England and Wales (including anti-social or other behaviour adversely affecting the local environment in that area).

(4) Nothing in this section requires a relevant authority to disclose any personal data (within the meaning of the Data Protection Act 1998).

(5) In this section 'relevant authority' means an authority in England and Wales which is for the time being a relevant authority for the purposes of section 115.

Amendments—Inserted by the Police and Justice Act 2006, s 22, Sch 9, paras 1, 5.

****

Supplemental

114 Orders and regulations

(1) Any power of a Minister of the Crown or of the National Assembly for Wales to make an order or regulations under this Act –

(a) is exercisable by statutory instrument; and
(b) includes power to make such transitional provision as appears to him necessary or expedient in connection with any provision made by the order or regulations.

(2) A statutory instrument containing an order under section 1A, 1G, 5(1A), (2) or (3), 10(6), 66C(1) or 66H(e)(vi) above (other than one made by the National Assembly for Wales), or containing regulations under section 6 or 17A or paragraph 1 of Schedule 3 to this Act, shall be subject to annulment in pursuance of a resolution of either House of Parliament.

(2A) Subsection (2) also applies to a statutory instrument containing

(a) an order under section 66C(4) unless the order makes provision of the kind mentioned in subsection (3A)(a) below, or
(b) an order under section 66G(5) other than the first such order.

(3) No order under section 1F, 5(6), 135A(5), 17(4), 38(5), 41(6), 66A(6) or 115(3) above shall be made unless a draft of the order has been laid before and approved by a resolution of each House of Parliament.

(3A) Subsection (3) also applies to –

(a) an order under section 66C(4) which makes provision increasing the figure in section 66C(3) by more than is necessary to reflect changes in the value of money, and
(b) the first order under section 66G(5).

(4) The Secretary of State must consult the National Assembly for Wales before making an order under section 5(6), 17(4) or 115(3) that relates to a person or body any of whose functions are dischargeable in relation to Wales (not being functions of the kind referred to in section 5(8)).

Amendments—Police Reform Act 2002, s 62(2); Drugs Act 2005, s 20(2); Police and Justice Act 2006, s 22, Sch 9, paras 1, 6(1), (4); Criminal Justice and Immigration Act 2008, s 148(2), Sch 27, Pt 4, para 18.

115 Disclosure of information

(1) Any person who, apart from this subsection, would not have power to disclose information

(a) to a relevant authority; or
(b) to a person acting on behalf of such an authority,

shall have power to do so in any case where the disclosure is necessary or expedient for the purposes of any provision of this Act.

(2) In this section 'relevant authority' means –

(a) the chief officer of police for a police area in England and Wales;
(b) the chief constable of a police force maintained under the Police (Scotland) Act 1967;
(c) a police authority within the meaning given by section 101(1) of the Police Act 1996;
(d) a local authority, that is to say –

(i) in relation to England, a county council, a district council, a London borough council, a parish council or the Common Council of the City of London;

(ii) in relation to Wales, a county council , a county borough council or a community council;

(iii) in relation to Scotland, a council constituted under section 2 of the Local Government etc (Scotland) Act 1994;

(da) a person registered under section 1 of the Housing Act 1996 as a social landlord;

(e) a local probation board in England and Wales;

(ea) a Strategic Health Authority;

(eb) probation trust;

(ec) a provider of probation services (other than a probation trust or the Secretary of State), in carrying out its statutory functions or activities of a public nature in pursuance of arrangements made under section 3(2) of the Offender Management Act 2007;

(f) a Local Health Board;

(g) a Primary Care Trust;

(h) the London Fire and Emergency Planning Authority;

(i) a fire and rescue authority constituted by a scheme under section 2 of the Fire and Rescue Services Act 2004 or a scheme to which section 4 of that Act applies;

(j) a metropolitan county fire and rescue authority;

(k) Transport for London.

(3) The appropriate national authority may by order amend this section so far as it extends to England and Wales by –

(a) adding an entry for any person or body to the list of authorities in subsection (2),

(b) altering or repealing any entry for the time being included in the list, or

(c) adding, altering or repealing provisions for the interpretation of entries in the list.

(4) In subsection (3) 'the appropriate national authority' has the same meaning as in section

Amendments—SI 2000/90, arts 2(1), 3(1), Sch 1, para 35(1), (7); Police and Justice Act 2006, s 22, Sch 9, paras 1, 7(1), (2); Police Reform Act 2002, s 97(1), (14)(b); Housing Act 2004, s 270(3)(a); Criminal Justice and Court Services Act 2000, s 74, Sch 7, Pt II, paras 150, 151; SI 2002/2469, reg 4, Sch 1, Pt 1, para 25(1), (6); SI 2007/961, art 3, Schedule, para 29(1), (2)(f); SI 2008/912, art 3, Sch 1, Pt 1, para 13(1), (7).

A1.2

Civil Evidence Act 1995

Admissibility of hearsay evidence

1 Admissibility of hearsay evidence

(1) In civil proceedings evidence shall not be excluded on the ground that it is hearsay.

(2) In this Act –

(a) 'hearsay' means a statement made otherwise than by a person while giving oral evidence in the proceedings which is tendered as evidence of the matters stated; and

(b) references to hearsay include hearsay of whatever degree.

(3) Nothing in this Act affects the Admissibility of evidence admissible apart from this section.

(4) The provisions of sections 2 to 6 (safeguards and supplementary provisions relating to hearsay evidence) do not apply in relation to hearsay evidence admissible apart from this section, notwithstanding that it may also be admissible by virtue of this section.

Safeguards in relation to hearsay evidence

2 Notice of proposal to adduce hearsay evidence

(1) A party proposing to adduce hearsay evidence in civil proceedings shall, subject to the following provisions of this section, give to the other party or parties to the proceedings –

  (a)   such notice (if any) of that fact, and
  (b)   on request, such particulars of or relating to the evidence,

as is reasonable and practicable in the circumstances for the purpose of enabling him or them to deal with any matters arising from its being hearsay.

(2) Provision may be made by rules of court –

  (a)   specifying classes pf proceedings or evidence in relation to which subsection (1) does not apply, and
  (b)   as to the manner in which (including the time within which) the duties imposed by that subsection are to be complied with in the cases where it does apply.

(3) Subsection (1) may also be excluded by agreement of the parties; and compliance with the duty to give notice may in any case be waived by the person to whom notice is required to be given.

(4) A failure to comply with subsection (1), or with rules under subsection (2)(b), does not affect the Admissibility of the evidence but may be taken into account by the court –

  (a)   in considering the exercise of its powers with respect to the course of proceedings and costs, and
  (b)   as a matter adversely affecting the weight to be given to the evidence in accordance with section 4.

3 Power to call witness for cross-examination on hearsay statement

Rules of court may provide that where a party to civil proceedings adduces hearsay evidence of a statement made by a person and does not call that person as a witness, any other party to the proceedings may, with the leave of the court, call that person as a witness and cross-examine him on the statement as if he had been called by the first-mentioned party and as if the hearsay statement were his evidence in chief.

4 Considerations relevant to weighing of hearsay evidence

(1) In estimating the weight (if any) to be given to hearsay evidence in civil proceedings the court shall have regard to any circumstances from which any inference can reasonably be drawn as to the reliability or otherwise of the evidence.

(2) Regard may be had, in particular, to the following –

  (a)   whether it would have been reasonable and practicable for the party by whom the evidence was adduced to have produced the maker of the original statement as a witness;
  (b)   whether the original statement was made contemporaneously with the occurrence or existence of the matters stated;
  (c)   whether the evidence involves multiple hearsay;
  (d)   whether any person involved had any motive to conceal or misrepresent matters;
  (e)   whether the original statement was an edited account, or was made in collaboration with another or for a particular purpose;
  (f)   whether the circumstances in whch the evidence is adduced as hearsay are such as to suggest an attempt to prevent proper evaluation of its weight.

Supplementary provisions as to hearsay evidence

5 Competence and credibility

(1) Hearsay evidence shall not be admitted in civil proceedings if or to the extent that it is shown to consist of, or to be proved by means of, a statement made by a person who at the time he made the statement was not competent as a witness.

For this purpose 'not competent as a witness' means suffering from such mental or physical infirmity, or lack of understanding, as would render a person incompetent as a witness in civil proceedings; but a child shall be treated as competent as a witness if he satisfies the requirements of section 96(2)(a) and (b) of the Children Act 1989 (conditions for reception of unsworn evidence of child).

(2) Where in civil proceedings hearsay evidence is adduced and the maker of the original statement, or of any statement relied upon to prove another statement, is not called as a witness –

    (a)   evidence which if he had been so called would be admissible for the purpose of attacking or supporting his credibility as a witness is admissible for that purpose in the proceedings; and

    (b)   evidence tending to prove that, whether before or after he made the statement, he made any other statement inconsistent with it is admissible for the purpose of showing that he had contradicted himself.

Provided that evidence may not be given of any matter of which, if he had been called as a witness and had denied that matter in cross-examination, evidence could not have been adduced by the cross-examining party.

6 Previous statements of witnesses

(1) Subject as follows, the provisions of this Act as to hearsay evidence in civil proceedings apply equally (but with any necessary modifications) in relation to a previous statement made by a person called as a witness in the proceedings.

(2) A party who has called or intends to call a person as a witness in civil proceedings may not in those proceedings adduce evidence of a previous statement made by that person, except –

    (a)   with the leave of the court, or

    (b)   for the purpose of rebutting a suggestion that his evidence has been fabricated.

This shall not be construed as preventing a witness statement (that is, a written statement of oral evidence which a party to the proceedings intends to lead) from being adopted by a witness in giving evidence or treated as his evidence.

(3) Where in the case of civil proceedings section 3, 4 or 5 of the Criminal Procedure Act 1865 applies, which make provision as to –

    (a)   how far a witness may be discredited by the party producing him,

    (b)   the proof of contradictory statements made by a witness, and

    (c)   cross-examination as to previous statements in writing,

this Act does not authorise the adducing of evidence of a previous inconsistent or contradictory statement otherwise than in accordance with those sections.

This is without prejudice to any provision made by rules of court under section 3 above (power to call witness for cross-examination on hearsay statement).

(4) Nothing in this Act affects any of the rules of law as to the circumstances in which, where a person called as a witness in civil proceedings is cross-examined on a document used by him to refresh his memory, that document may be made evidence in the proceedings.

(5) Nothing in this section shall be construed as preventing a statement of any description referred to above from being admissible by virtue of section 1 as evidence of the matters stated.

7 Evidence formerly admissible at common law

(1) The common law rule effectively preserved by section 9(1) and (2)(a) of the Civil Evidence Act 1968 (Admissibility of admissions adverse to a party) is superseded by the provisions of this Act.

(2) The common law rules effectively preserved by section 9(1) and (2)(b) to (d) of the Civil Evidence Act 1968, that is, any rule of law whereby in civil proceedings –

    (a)   published works dealing with matters of a public nature (for example, histories, scientific works, dictionaries and maps) are admissible as evidence of facts of a public nature stated in them,

    (b)   public documents (for example, public registers, and returns made under public authority with respect to matters of public interest) are admissible as evidence of facts stated in them, or

    (c)   records (for example, the records of certain courts, treaties, Crown grants, pardons and commissions) are admissible as evidence of facts stated in them,

shall continue to have effect.

(3) The common law rules effectively preserved by section 9(3) and (4) of the Civil Evidence Act 1968, that is, any rule of law whereby in civil proceedings –

    (a)   evidence of a person's reputation is admissible for the purpose of proving his good or bad character, or

    (b)   evidence of reputation or family tradition is admissible –

        (i)   for the purpose of proving or disproving pedigree or the existence of a marriage, or

        (ii)   for the purpose of proving or disproving the existence of any public or general right or of identifying any person or thing,

shall continue to have effect in so far as they authorise the court to treat such evidence as proving or disproving that matter.

Where any such rule applies, reputation or family tradition shall be treated for the purposes of this Act as a fact and not as a statement or multiplicity of statements about the matter in question.

(4) The words in which a rule of law mentioned in this section is described are intended only to identify the rule and shall not be construed as altering it in any way.

Other matters

8 Proof of statements contained in documents

(1) Where a statement contained in a document is admissible as evidence in civil proceedings, it may be proved –

    (a)   by the production of that document, or

    (b)   whether or not that document is still in existence, by the production of a copy of that document or of the material part of it,

authenticated in such manner as the court may approve.

(2) It is immaterial for this purpose how many removes there are between a copy and the original.

9 Proof of records of business or public authority

(1) A document which is shown to form part of the records of a business or public authority may be received in evidence in civil proceedings without further proof.

(2) A document shall be taken to form part of the records of a business or public authority if there is produced to the court a certificate to that effect signed by an officer of the business or authority to which the records belong.

For this purpose –

(a)   a document purporting to be a certificate signed by an officer of a business or public authority shall be deemed to have been duly given by such an officer and signed by him; and

(b)   a certificate shall be treated as signed by a person if it purports to bear a facsimile of his signature.

(3) The absence of an entry in the records of a business or public authority may be proved in civil proceedings by affidavit of an officer of the business or authority to which the records belong.

(4) In this section –

'records' means records in whatever form;

'business' includes any activity regularly carried on over a period of time, whether for profit or not, by any body (whether corporate or not) or by an individual;

'officer' includes any person occupying a responsible position in relation to the relevant activities of the business or public authority or in relation to its records; and

'public authority' includes any public or statutory undertaking, any government department and any person holding office under Her Majesty.

(5) The court may, having regard to the circumstances of the case, direct that all or any of the above provisions of this section do not apply in relation to a particular document or record, or description of documents or records.

10 Admissibility of proof of Ogden Tables

(1) The actuarial tables (together with explanatory notes) for use in personal injury and fatal accident cases issued from time to time by the Government Actuary's Department are admissible in evidence for the purpose of assessing, in an action for personal injury, the sum to be awarded as general damages for future pecuniary loss.

(2) They may be proved by the production of a copy published by Her Majesty's Stationery Office.

(3) For the purposes of this section –

(a)   'personal injury' includes any disease and any impairment of a person's physical or mental condition; and

(b)   'action for personal injury' includes an action brought by virtue of the Law Reform (Miscellaneous Provisions) Act 1934 or the Fatal Accidents Act 1976.

General

11 Meaning of 'civil proceedings'

In this Act 'civil proceedings' means civil proceedings, before any tribunal, in relation to which the strict rules of evidence apply, whether as a matter of law or by agreement of the parties.

References to 'the court' and 'rules of court' shall be construed accordingly.

12 Provisions as to rules of court

(1) Any power to make rules of court regulating the practice or procedure of the court in relation to civil proceedings includes power to make such provision as may be necessary or expedient for carrying into effect the provisions of this Act.

(2) Any rules of court made for the purposes of this Act as it applies in relation to proceedings in the High Court apply, except in so far as their operation is excluded by agreement, to arbitration proceedings to which this Act applies, subject to such modifications as may be appropriate.

Any question arising as to what modifications are appropriate shall be determined, in default of agreement, by the arbitrator or umpire, as the case may be.

13 Interpretation

In this Act –

'civil proceedings' has the meaning given by section 11 and 'court' and 'rules of court' shall be construed in accordance with that section;
'document' means anything in which information of any description is recorded, and 'copy', in relation to a document, means anything onto which information recorded in the document has been copied, by whatever means and whether directly or indirectly;
'hearsay' shall be construed in accordance with section 1(2);
'oral evidence' includes evidence which, by reason of a defect of speech or hearing, a person called as a witness gives in writing or by signs;
'the original statement', in relation to hearsay evidence, means the underlying statement (if any) by –

(a) in the case of evidence of fact, a person having personal knowledge of that fact, or
(b) in the case of evidence of opinion, the person whose opinion it is; and

'statement' means any representation of fact or opinion, however made.

14 Savings

(1) Nothing in this Act affects the exclusion of evidence on grounds other than that it is hearsay.

This applies whether the evidence falls to be excluded in pursuance of any enactment or rule of law, for failure to comply with rules of court or an order of the court, or otherwise.

(2) Nothing in this Act affects the proof of documents by means other than those specified in section 8 or 9.

(3) Nothing in this Act affects the operation of the following enactments –

(a) section 2 of the Documentary Evidence Act 1868 (mode of proving certain official documents);
(b) section 2 of the Documentary Evidence Act 1882 (documents printed under the superintendence of Stationery Office);
(c) section 1 of the Evidence (Colonial Statutes) Act 1907 (proof of statutes of certain legislatures);
(d) section 1 of the Evidence (Foreign, Dominion and Colonial Documents) Act 1933 (proof and effect of registers and official certificates of certain countries);
(e) section 5 of the Oaths and Evidence (Overseas Authorities and Countries) Act 1963 (provision in respect of public registers of other countries).

15 Consequential amendments and repeals

(1) The enactments specified in Schedule 1 are amended in accordance with that Schedule, the amendments being consequential on the provisions of this Act.

(2) The enactments specified in Schedule 2 are repealed to the extent specified.

16 Short title, commencement and extent

(1) This Act may be cited as the Civil Evidence Act 1995.

(2) The provisions of this Act come into force on such day as the Lord Chancellor may appoint by order made by statutory instrument, and different days may be appointed for different provisions and for different purposes.

(3) Subject to subsection (3A), the provisions of this Act shall not apply in relation to proceedings begun before commencement.

(3A) Transitional provisions for the application of the provisions of this Act to proceedings begun before commencement may be made by rules of court or practice directions.

(4) This Act extends to England and Wales.

(5) Section 10 (admissibility and proof of Ogden Tables) also extends to Northern Ireland.

As it extends to Northern Ireland, the following shall be substituted for subsection (3)(b)—

> "(b) "action for personal injury" includes an action brought by virtue of the Law Reform (Miscellaneous Provisions) (Northern Ireland) Act 1937 or the Fatal Accidents (Northern Ireland) Order 1977."

(6) The provisions of Schedules 1 and 2 (consequential amendments and repeals) have the same extent as the enactments respectively amended or repealed.

Amendments—SI 1999/1217.

A1.3

Youth Justice and Criminal Evidence Act 1999

CHAPTER 23

PART II

GIVING OF EVIDENCE OR INFORMATION FOR PURPOSES OF CRIMINAL PROCEEDINGS

Chapter I

Special Measures Directions in Case of Vulnerable and Intimidated Witnesses

Preliminary

16 Witnesses eligible for assistance on grounds of age or incapacity

(1) For the purposes of this Chapter a witness in criminal proceedings (other than the accused) is eligible for assistance by virtue of this section –

(a)   if under the age of 17 at the time of the hearing; or
(b)   if the court considers that the quality of evidence given by the witness is likely to be diminished by reason of any circumstances falling within subsection (2).

(2) The circumstances falling within this subsection are –

(a)   that the witness –

      (i)   suffers from mental disorder within the meaning of the Mental Health Act 1983, or

      (ii)   otherwise has a significant impairment of intelligence and social functioning;

  (b)   that the witness has a physical disability or is suffering from a physical disorder.

(3) In subsection (1)(a) 'the time of the hearing', in relation to a witness, means the time when it falls to the court to make a determination for the purposes of section 19(2) in relation to the witness.

(4) In determining whether a witness falls within subsection (1)(b) the court must consider any views expressed by the witness.

(5) In this Chapter references to the quality of a witness's evidence are to its quality in terms of completeness, coherence and accuracy; and for this purpose 'coherence' refers to a witness's ability in giving evidence to give answers which address the questions put to the witness and can be understood both individually and collectively.

17 Witnesses eligible for assistance on grounds of fear or distress about testifying

(1) For the purposes of this Chapter a witness in criminal proceedings (other than the accused) is eligible for assistance by virtue of this subsection if the court is satisfied that the quality of evidence given by the witness is likely to be diminished by reason of fear or distress on the part of the witness in connection with testifying in the proceedings.

(2) In determining whether a witness falls within subsection (1) the court must take into account, in particular –

  (a)   the nature and alleged circumstances of the offence to which the proceedings relate;

  (b)   the age of the witness;

  (c)   such of the following matters as appear to the court to be relevant, namely –

      (i)   the social and cultural background and ethnic origins of the witness,

      (ii)   the domestic and employment circumstances of the witness, and

      (iii)   any religious beliefs or political opinions of the witness;

  (d)   any behaviour towards the witness on the part of –

      (i)   the accused,

      (ii)   members of the family or associates of the accused, or

      (iii)   any other person who is likely to be an accused or a witness in the proceedings.

(3) In determining that question the court must in addition consider any views expressed by the witness.

(4) Where the complainant in respect of a sexual offence is a witness in proceedings relating to that offence (or to that offence and any other offences), the witness is eligible for assistance in relation to those proceedings by virtue of this subsection unless the witness has informed the court of the witness' wish not to be so eligible by virtue of this subsection.

18 Special measures available to eligible witnesses

(1) For the purposes of this Chapter –

  (a)   the provision which may be made by a special measures direction by virtue of each of sections 23 to 30 is a special measure available in relation to a witness eligible for assistance by virtue of section 16; and

  (b)   the provision which may be made by such a direction by virtue of each of sections 23 to 28 is a special measure available in relation to a witness eligible for assistance by virtue of section 17;

but this subsection has effect subject to subsection (2).

(2) Where (apart from this subsection) a special measure would, in accordance with subsection (1)(a) or (b), be available in relation to a witness in any proceedings, it shall not be taken by a court to be available in relation to the witness unless –

(a)   the court has been notified by the Secretary of State that relevant arrangements may be made available in the area in which it appears to the court that the proceedings will take place, and
(b)   the notice has not been withdrawn.

(3) In subsection (2) 'relevant arrangements' means arrangements for implementing the measure in question which cover the witness and the proceedings in question.

(4) The withdrawal of a notice under that subsection relating to a special measure shall not affect the availability of that measure in relation to a witness if a special measures direction providing for that measure to apply to the witness's evidence has been made by the court before the notice is withdrawn.

(5) The Secretary of State may by order make such amendments of this Chapter as he considers appropriate for altering the special measures which, in accordance with subsection (1)(a) or (b), are available in relation to a witness eligible for assistance by virtue of section 16 or (as the case may be) section 17, whether –

(a)   by modifying the provisions relating to any measure for the time being available in relation to such a witness,
(b)   by the addition –

(i)   (with or without modifications) of any measure which is for the time being available in relation to a witness eligible for assistance by virtue of the other of those sections, or
(ii)   of any new measure, or

(c)   by the removal of any measure.

Special measures directions

19 Special measures direction relating to eligible witness

(1) This section applies where in any criminal proceedings –

(a)   a party to the proceedings makes an application for the court to give a direction under this section in relation to a witness in the proceedings other than the accused, or
(b)   the court of its own motion raises the issue whether such a direction should be given.

(2) Where the court determines that the witness is eligible for assistance by virtue of section 16 or 17, the court must then –

(a)   determine whether any of the special measures available in relation to the witness (or any combination of them) would, in its opinion, be likely to improve the quality of evidence given by the witness; and
(b)   if so –

(i)   determine which of those measures (or combination of them) would, in its opinion, be likely to maximise so far as practicable the quality of such evidence; and
(ii)   give a direction under this section providing for the measure or measures so determined to apply to evidence given by the witness.

(3) In determining for the purposes of this Chapter whether any special measure or measures would or would not be likely to improve, or to maximise so far as practicable, the quality of evidence given by the witness, the court must consider all the circumstances of the case, including in particular –

(a)   any views expressed by the witness; and
(b)   whether the measure or measures might tend to inhibit such evidence being effectively tested by a party to the proceedings.

(4) A special measures direction must specify particulars of the provision made by the direction in respect of each special measure which is to apply to the witness's evidence.

(5) In this Chapter 'special measures direction' means a direction under this section.

(6) Nothing in this Chapter is to be regarded as affecting any power of a court to make an order or give leave of any description (in the exercise of its inherent jurisdiction or otherwise) –

    (a)   in relation to a witness who is not an eligible witness, or

    (b)   in relation to an eligible witness where (as, for example, in a case where a foreign language interpreter is to be provided) the order is made or the leave is given otherwise than by reason of the fact that the witness is an eligible witness.

20 Further provisions about directions: general

(1) Subject to subsection (2) and section 21(8), a special measures direction has binding effect from the time it is made until the proceedings for the purposes of which it is made are either –

    (a)   determined (by acquittal, conviction or otherwise), or

    (b)   abandoned,

in relation to the accused or (if there is more than one) in relation to each of the accused.

(2) The court may discharge or vary (or further vary) a special measures direction if it appears to the court to be in the interests of justice to do so, and may do so either –

    (a)   on an application made by a party to the proceedings, if there has been a material change of circumstances since the relevant time, or

    (b)   of its own motion.

(3) In subsection (2) 'the relevant time' means –

    (a)   the time when the direction was given, or

    (b)   if a previous application has been made under that subsection, the time when the application (or last application) was made.

(4) Nothing in section 24(2) and (3), 27(4) to (7) or 28(4) to (6) is to be regarded as affecting the power of the court to vary or discharge a special measures direction under subsection (2).

(5) The court must state in open court its reasons for –

    (a)   giving or varying,

    (b)   refusing an application for, or for the variation or discharge of, or

    (c)   discharging,

a special measures direction and, if it is a magistrates' court, must cause them to be entered in the register of its proceedings.

(6) Criminal Procedure Rules may make provision –

    (a)   for uncontested applications to be determined by the court without a hearing;

    (b)   for preventing the renewal of an unsuccessful application for a special measures direction except where there has been a material change of circumstances;

    (c)   for expert evidence to be given in connection with an application for, or for varying or discharging, such a direction;

    (d)   for the manner in which confidential or sensitive information is to be treated in connection with such an application and in particular as to its being disclosed to, or withheld from, a party to the proceedings.

Amendments—Words substituted: Courts Act 2003, s 109(1), Sch 8, para 384(a), with effect from 1 September 2004, (except in relation to the operation of this section in relation to rules of court other than Criminal Procedure Rules during the period between that date and the coming into force of the first Criminal Procedure Rules made under the Courts Act 2003, s 69) (see Courts Act 2003 (Commencement No 6 and Savings) Order 2004, SI 2004/2066, arts 2(c)(xix), 3.

21 Special provisions relating to child witnesses

(1) For the purposes of this section –

    (a)   a witness in criminal proceedings is a 'child witness' if he is an eligible witness by reason of section 16(1)(a) (whether or not he is an eligible witness by reason of any other provision of section 16 or 17);

    (b)   a child witness is 'in need of special protection' if the offence (or any of the offences) to which the proceedings relate is –

        (i)   an offence falling within section 35(3)(a) (sexual offences etc.), or

        (ii)   an offence falling within section 35(3)(b), (c) or (d) (kidnapping, assaults etc.); and

    (c)   a 'relevant recording', in relation to a child witness, is a video recording of an interview of the witness made with a view to its admission as evidence in chief of the witness.

(2) Where the court, in making a determination for the purposes of section 19(2), determines that a witness in criminal proceedings is a child witness, the court must –

    (a)   first have regard to subsections (3) to (7) below; and

    (b)   then have regard to section 19(2);

and for the purposes of section 19(2), as it then applies to the witness, any special measures required to be applied in relation to him by virtue of this section shall be treated as if they were measures determined by the court, pursuant to section 19(2)(a) and (b)(i), to be ones that (whether on their own or with any other special measures) would be likely to maximise, so far as practicable, the quality of his evidence.

(3) The primary rule in the case of a child witness is that the court must give a special measures direction in relation to the witness which complies with the following requirements –

    (a)   it must provide for any relevant recording to be admitted under section 27 (video recorded evidence in chief); and

    (b)   it must provide for any evidence given by the witness in the proceedings which is not given by means of a video recording (whether in chief or otherwise) to be given by means of a live link in accordance with section 24.

(4) The primary rule is subject to the following limitations –

    (a)   the requirement contained in subsection (3)(a) or (b) has effect subject to the availability (within the meaning of section 18(2)) of the special measure in question in relation to the witness;

    (b)   the requirement contained in subsection (3)(a) also has effect subject to section 27(2); and

    (c)   the rule does not apply to the extent that the court is satisfied that compliance with it would not be likely to maximise the quality of the witness's evidence so far as practicable (whether because the application to that evidence of one or more other special measures available in relation to the witness would have that result or for any other reason).

(5) However, subsection (4)(c) does not apply in relation to a child witness in need of special protection.

(6) Where a child witness is in need of special protection by virtue of subsection (1)(b)(i), any special measures direction given by the court which complies with the requirement contained in subsection (3)(a) must in addition provide for the special measure available under section 28 (video recorded cross-examination or re-examination) to apply in relation to –

    (a)   any cross-examination of the witness otherwise than by the accused in person, and

    (b)   any subsequent re-examination.

(7) The requirement contained in subsection (6) has effect subject to the following limitations –

(a)   it has effect subject to the availability (within the meaning of section 18(2)) of that special measure in relation to the witness; and

(b)   it does not apply if the witness has informed the court that he does not want that special measure to apply in relation to him.

(8) Where a special measures direction is given in relation to a child witness who is an eligible witness by reason only of section 16(1)(a), then –

(a)   subject to subsection (9) below, and

(b)   except where the witness has already begun to give evidence in the proceedings,

the direction shall cease to have effect at the time when the witness attains the age of 17.

(9) Where a special measures direction is given in relation to a child witness who is an eligible witness by reason only of section 16(1)(a) and –

(a)   the direction provides –

    (i)   for any relevant recording to be admitted under section 27 as evidence in chief of the witness, or

    (ii)   for the special measure available under section 28 to apply in relation to the witness, and

(b)   if it provides for that special measure to so apply, the witness is still under the age of 17 when the video recording is made for the purposes of section 28,

then, so far as it provides as mentioned in paragraph (a)(i) or (ii) above, the direction shall continue to have effect in accordance with section 20(1) even though the witness subsequently attains that age.

22 Extension of provisions of section 21 to certain witnesses over 17

(1) For the purposes of this section –

(a)   a witness in criminal proceedings (other than the accused) is a 'qualifying witness' if he –

    (i)   is not an eligible witness at the time of the hearing (as defined by section 16(3)), but

    (ii)   was under the age of 17 when a relevant recording was made;

(b)   a qualifying witness is 'in need of special protection' if the offence (or any of the offences) to which the proceedings relate is –

    (i)   an offence falling within section 35(3)(a) (sexual offences etc.), or

    (ii)   an offence falling within section 35(3)(b), (c) or (d) (kidnapping, assaults etc.); and

(c)   a 'relevant recording', in relation to a witness, is a video recording of an interview of the witness made with a view to its admission as evidence in chief of the witness.

(2) Subsections (2) to (7) of section 21 shall apply as follows in relation to a qualifying witness –

(a)   subsections (2) to (4), so far as relating to the giving of a direction complying with the requirement contained in subsection (3)(a), shall apply to a qualifying witness in respect of the relevant recording as they apply to a child witness (within the meaning of that section);

(b)   subsection (5), so far as relating to the giving of such a direction, shall apply to a qualifying witness in need of special protection as it applies to a child witness in need of special protection (within the meaning of that section); and

(c)   subsections (6) and (7) shall apply to a qualifying witness in need of special protection by virtue of subsection (1)(b)(i) above as they apply to such a child witness as is mentioned in subsection (6).

Special measures

23 Screening witness from accused

(1) A special measures direction may provide for the witness, while giving testimony or being sworn in court, to be prevented by means of a screen or other arrangement from seeing the accused.

(2) But the screen or other arrangement must not prevent the witness from being able to see, and to be seen by –

    (a)   the judge or justices (or both) and the jury (if there is one);
    (b)   legal representatives acting in the proceedings; and
    (c)   any interpreter or other person appointed (in pursuance of the direction or otherwise) to assist the witness.

(3) Where two or more legal representatives are acting for a party to the proceedings, subsection (2)(b) is to be regarded as satisfied in relation to those representatives if the witness is able at all material times to see and be seen by at least one of them.

24 Evidence by live link

(1) A special measures direction may provide for the witness to give evidence by means of a live link.

(2) Where a direction provides for the witness to give evidence by means of a live link, the witness may not give evidence in any other way without the permission of the court.

(3) The court may give permission for the purposes of subsection (2) if it appears to the court to be in the interests of justice to do so, and may do so either –

    (a)   on an application by a party to the proceedings, if there has been a material change of circumstances since the relevant time, or
    (b)   of its own motion.

(4) In subsection (3) 'the relevant time' means –

    (a)   the time when the direction was given, or
    (b)   if a previous application has been made under that subsection, the time when the application (or last application) was made.

(5) ...

(6) ...

(7) ...

(8) In this Chapter 'live link' means a live television link or other arrangement whereby a witness, while absent from the courtroom or other place where the proceedings are being held, is able to see and hear a person there and to be seen and heard by the persons specified in section 23(2)(a) to (c).

Amendments—Courts Act 2003, s 109(1), (3), Sch 8, para 385, Sch 10.

25 Evidence given in private

(1) A special measures direction may provide for the exclusion from the court, during the giving of the witness's evidence, of persons of any description specified in the direction.

(2) The persons who may be so excluded do not include –

    (a)   the accused,

(b) legal representatives acting in the proceedings, or

(c) any interpreter or other person appointed (in pursuance of the direction or otherwise) to assist the witness.

(3) A special measures direction providing for representatives of news gathering or reporting organisations to be so excluded shall be expressed not to apply to one named person who –

(a) is a representative of such an organisation, and

(b) has been nominated for the purpose by one or more such organisations,

unless it appears to the court that no such nomination has been made.

(4) A special measures direction may only provide for the exclusion of persons under this section where –

(a) the proceedings relate to a sexual offence; or

(b) it appears to the court that there are reasonable grounds for believing that any person other than the accused has sought, or will seek, to intimidate the witness in connection with testifying in the proceedings.

(5) Any proceedings from which persons are excluded under this section (whether or not those persons include representatives of news gathering or reporting organisations) shall nevertheless be taken to be held in public for the purposes of any privilege or exemption from liability available in respect of fair, accurate and contemporaneous reports of legal proceedings held in public.

26 Removal of wigs and gowns

A special measures direction may provide for the wearing of wigs or gowns to be dispensed with during the giving of the witness's evidence.

27 Video recorded evidence in chief

(1) A special measures direction may provide for a video recording of an interview of the witness to be admitted as evidence in chief of the witness.

(2) A special measures direction may, however, not provide for a video recording, or a part of such a recording, to be admitted under this section if the court is of the opinion, having regard to all the circumstances of the case, that in the interests of justice the recording, or that part of it, should not be so admitted.

(3) In considering for the purposes of subsection (2) whether any part of a recording should not be admitted under this section, the court must consider whether any prejudice to the accused which might result from that part being so admitted is outweighed by the desirability of showing the whole, or substantially the whole, of the recorded interview.

(4) Where a special measures direction provides for a recording to be admitted under this section, the court may nevertheless subsequently direct that it is not to be so admitted if –

(a) it appears to the court that –

(i) the witness will not be available for cross-examination (whether conducted in the ordinary way or in accordance with any such direction), and

(ii) the parties to the proceedings have not agreed that there is no need for the witness to be so available; or

(b) any Criminal Procedure Rules requiring disclosure of the circumstances in which the recording was made have not been complied with to the satisfaction of the court.

(5) Where a recording is admitted under this section –

(a) the witness must be called by the party tendering it in evidence, unless –

(i)   a special measures direction provides for the witness's evidence on cross-examination to be given otherwise than by testimony in court, or

(ii)   the parties to the proceedings have agreed as mentioned in subsection (4)(a)(ii); and

(b)   the witness may not give evidence in chief otherwise than by means of the recording –

(i)   as to any matter which, in the opinion of the court, has been dealt with adequately in the witness's recorded testimony, or

(ii)   without the permission of the court, as to any other matter which, in the opinion of the court, is dealt with in that testimony.

(6) Where in accordance with subsection (2) a special measures direction provides for part only of a recording to be admitted under this section, references in subsections (4) and (5) to the recording or to the witness's recorded testimony are references to the part of the recording or testimony which is to be so admitted.

(7) The court may give permission for the purposes of subsection (5)(b)(ii) if it appears to the court to be in the interests of justice to do so, and may do so either –

(a)   on an application by a party to the proceedings, if there has been a material change of circumstances since the relevant time, or

(b)   of its own motion.

(8) In subsection (7) 'the relevant time' means –

(a)   the time when the direction was given, or

(b)   if a previous application has been made under that subsection, the time when the application (or last application) was made.

(9) The court may, in giving permission for the purposes of subsection (5)(b)(ii), direct that the evidence in question is to be given by the witness by means of a live link; and, if the court so directs, subsections (5) to (7) of section 24 shall apply in relation to that evidence as they apply in relation to evidence which is to be given in accordance with a special measures direction.

(10) *A magistrates' court inquiring into an offence as examining justices under section 6 of the Magistrates' Courts Act 1980 may consider any video recording in relation to which it is proposed to apply for a special measures direction providing for it to be admitted at the trial in accordance with this section.*

(11) Nothing in this section affects the admissibility of any video recording which would be admissible apart from this section.

Amendments—Courts Act 2003, s 69.

Prospective amendments—Criminal Justice Act 2003, ss 41, 332, Sch 3, Pt 2, para 73(1), (2), Sch 37, Pt 4.

28 Video recorded cross-examination or re-examination

(1) Where a special measures direction provides for a video recording to be admitted under section 27 as evidence in chief of the witness, the direction may also provide –

(a)   for any cross-examination of the witness, and any re-examination, to be recorded by means of a video recording; and

(b)   for such a recording to be admitted, so far as it relates to any such cross-examination or re-examination, as evidence of the witness under cross-examination or on re-examination, as the case may be.

(2) Such a recording must be made in the presence of such persons as Criminal Procedure Rules or the direction may provide and in the absence of the accused, but in circumstances in which –

(a)   the judge or justices (or both) and legal representatives acting in the proceedings are able to see and hear the examination of the witness and to communicate with the persons in whose presence the recording is being made, and

(b)   the accused is able to see and hear any such examination and to communicate with any legal representative acting for him.

(3) Where two or more legal representatives are acting for a party to the proceedings, subsection (2)(a) and (b) are to be regarded as satisfied in relation to those representatives if at all material times they are satisfied in relation to at least one of them.

(4) Where a special measures direction provides for a recording to be admitted under this section, the court may nevertheless subsequently direct that it is not to be so admitted if any requirement of subsection (2) or Criminal Procedure Rules or the direction has not been complied with to the satisfaction of the court.

(5) Where in pursuance of subsection (1) a recording has been made of any examination of the witness, the witness may not be subsequently cross-examined or re-examined in respect of any evidence given by the witness in the proceedings (whether in any recording admissible under section 27 or this section or otherwise than in such a recording) unless the court gives a further special measures direction making such provision as is mentioned in subsection (1)(a) and (b) in relation to any subsequent cross-examination, and re-examination, of the witness.

(6) The court may only give such a further direction if it appears to the court –

(a)   that the proposed cross-examination is sought by a party to the proceedings as a result of that party having become aware, since the time when the original recording was made in pursuance of subsection (1), of a matter which that party could not with reasonable diligence have ascertained by then, or
(b)   that for any other reason it is in the interests of justice to give the further direction.

(7) Nothing in this section shall be read as applying in relation to any cross-examination of the witness by the accused in person (in a case where the accused is to be able to conduct any such cross-examination).

Amendments—Courts Act 2003, s 109(1), Sch 8, para 384(c).

29 Examination of witness through intermediary

(1) A special measures direction may provide for any examination of the witness (however and wherever conducted) to be conducted through an interpreter or other person approved by the court for the purposes of this section ('an intermediary').

(2) The function of an intermediary is to communicate –

(a)   to the witness, questions put to the witness, and
(b)   to any person asking such questions, the answers given by the witness in reply to them,

and to explain such questions or answers so far as necessary to enable them to be understood by the witness or person in question.

(3) Any examination of the witness in pursuance of subsection (1) must take place in the presence of such persons as Criminal Procedure Rules or the direction may provide, but in circumstances in which –

(a)   the judge or justices (or both) and legal representatives acting in the proceedings are able to see and hear the examination of the witness and to communicate with the intermediary, and
(b)   (except in the case of a video recorded examination) the jury (if there is one) are able to see and hear the examination of the witness.

(4) Where two or more legal representatives are acting for a party to the proceedings, subsection (3)(a) is to be regarded as satisfied in relation to those representatives if at all material times it is satisfied in relation to at least one of them.

(5) A person may not act as an intermediary in a particular case except after making a declaration, in such form as may be prescribed by Criminal Procedure Rules, that he will faithfully perform his function as intermediary.

(6) Subsection (1) does not apply to an interview of the witness which is recorded by means of a video recording with a view to its admission as evidence in chief of the witness; but a special measures direction may provide for such a recording to be admitted under section 27 if the interview was conducted through an intermediary and –

(a)   that person complied with subsection (5) before the interview began, and
(b)   the court's approval for the purposes of this section is given before the direction is given.

(7) Section 1 of the Perjury Act 1911 (perjury) shall apply in relation to a person acting as an intermediary as it applies in relation to a person lawfully sworn as an interpreter in a judicial proceeding; and for this purpose, where a person acts as an intermediary in any proceeding which is not a judicial proceeding for the purposes of that section, that proceeding shall be taken to be part of the judicial proceeding in which the witness's evidence is given.

Amendments—Courts Act 2003, s 109(1), Sch 8, para 384(d).

30 Aids to communication

A special measures direction may provide for the witness, while giving evidence (whether by testimony in court or otherwise), to be provided with such device as the court considers appropriate with a view to enabling questions or answers to be communicated to or by the witness despite any disability or disorder or other impairment which the witness has or suffers from.

Supplementary

31 Status of evidence given under Chapter I

(1) Subsections (2) to (4) apply to a statement made by a witness in criminal proceedings which, in accordance with a special measures direction, is not made by the witness in direct oral testimony in court but forms part of the witness's evidence in those proceedings.

(2) The statement shall be treated as if made by the witness in direct oral testimony in court; and accordingly –

(a)   it is admissible evidence of any fact of which such testimony from the witness would be admissible;
(b)   it is not capable of corroborating any other evidence given by the witness.

(3) Subsection (2) applies to a statement admitted under section 27 or 28 which is not made by the witness on oath even though it would have been required to be made on oath if made by the witness in direct oral testimony in court.

(4) In estimating the weight (if any) to be attached to the statement, the court must have regard to all the circumstances from which an inference can reasonably be drawn (as to the accuracy of the statement or otherwise).

(5) Nothing in this Chapter (apart from subsection (3)) affects the operation of any rule of law relating to evidence in criminal proceedings.

(6) Where any statement made by a person on oath in any proceeding which is not a judicial proceeding for the purposes of section 1 of the Perjury Act 1911 (perjury) is received in evidence in pursuance of a special measures direction, that proceeding shall be taken for the purposes of that section to be part of the judicial proceeding in which the statement is so received in evidence.

(7) Where in any proceeding which is not a judicial proceeding for the purposes of that Act –

(a)   a person wilfully makes a false statement otherwise than on oath which is subsequently received in evidence in pursuance of a special measures direction, and

(b)   the statement is made in such circumstances that had it been given on oath in any such judicial proceeding that person would have been guilty of perjury,

he shall be guilty of an offence and liable to any punishment which might be imposed on conviction of an offence under section 57(2) (giving of false unsworn evidence in criminal proceedings).

(8) In this section 'statement' includes any representation of fact, whether made in words or otherwise.

****

Chapter IV

Reporting Restrictions

Reports relating to persons under 18

44 Restrictions on reporting alleged offences involving persons under 18

(1) This section applies (subject to subsection (3)) where a criminal investigation has begun in respect of –

(a)   an alleged offence against the law of –

(i)   England and Wales, or
(ii)   Northern Ireland; or

(b)   an alleged civil offence (other than an offence falling within paragraph (a)) committed (whether or not in the United Kingdom) by a person subject to service law.

(2) No matter relating to any person involved in the offence shall while he is under the age of 18 be included in any publication if it is likely to lead members of the public to identify him as a person involved in the offence.

(3) The restrictions imposed by subsection (2) cease to apply once there are proceedings in a court (whether a court in England and Wales, a service court or a court in Northern Ireland) in respect of the offence.

(4) For the purposes of subsection (2) any reference to a person involved in the offence is to –

(a)   a person by whom the offence is alleged to have been committed; or
(b)   if this paragraph applies to the publication in question by virtue of subsection (5) –

(i)   a person against or in respect of whom the offence is alleged to have been committed, or
(ii)   a person who is alleged to have been a witness to the commission of the offence;

except that paragraph (b)(i) does not include a person in relation to whom section 1 of the Sexual Offences (Amendment) Act 1992 (anonymity of victims of certain sexual offences) applies in connection with the offence.

(5) Subsection (4)(b) applies to a publication if –

(a)   where it is a relevant programme, it is transmitted, or
(b)   in the case of any other publication, it is published,

on or after such date as may be specified in an order made by the Secretary of State.

(6) The matters relating to a person in relation to which the restrictions imposed by subsection (2) apply (if their inclusion in any publication is likely to have the result mentioned in that subsection) include in particular –

(a)   his name,
(b)   his address,
(c)   the identity of any school or other educational establishment attended by him,

(d)   the identity of any place of work, and
(e)   any still or moving picture of him.

(7) Any appropriate criminal court may by order dispense, to any extent specified in the order, with the restrictions imposed by subsection (2) in relation to a person if it is satisfied that it is necessary in the interests of justice to do so.

(8) However, when deciding whether to make such an order dispensing (to any extent) with the restrictions imposed by subsection (2) in relation to a person, the court shall have regard to the welfare of that person.

(9) In subsection (7) 'appropriate criminal court' means –

(a)   in a case where this section applies by virtue of subsection (1)(a)(i) or (ii), any court in England and Wales or (as the case may be) in Northern Ireland which has any jurisdiction in, or in relation to, any criminal proceedings (but not a service court unless the offence is alleged to have been committed by a person subject to service law);
(b)   in a case where this section applies by virtue of subsection (1)(b), any court falling within paragraph (a) or a service court.

(10) The power under subsection (7) of a magistrates' court in England and Wales may be exercised by a single justice.

(11) In the case of a decision of a magistrates' court in England and Wales, or a court of summary jurisdiction in Northern Ireland, to make or refuse to make an order under subsection (7), the following persons, namely –

(a)   any person who was a party to the proceedings on the application for the order, and
(b)   with the leave of the Crown Court, or in Northern Ireland a county court, any other person,

may, in accordance with Criminal Procedure Rules in England and Wales, or rules of court in Northern Ireland, appeal to the Crown Court, or in Northern Ireland a county court against that decision or appear or be represented at the hearing of such an appeal.

(12) On such an appeal the Crown Court or in Northern Ireland a county court –

(a)   may make such order as is necessary to give effect to its determination of the appeal; and
(b)   may also make such incidental or consequential orders as appear to it to be just.

(13) In this section –

(a)   'civil offence' means an act or omission which, if committed in England and Wales, would be an offence against the law of England and Wales;
(b)   any reference to a criminal investigation, in relation to an alleged offence, is to an investigation conducted by police officers, or other persons charged with the duty of investigating offences, with a view to it being ascertained whether a person should be charged with the offence;
(c)   any reference to a person subject to service law is to –

    (i)   *a person subject to military law, air-force law or the Naval Discipline Act 1957, or*
    (ii)   *any other person to whom provisions of Part II of the Army Act 1955, Part II of the Air Force Act 1955 or Parts I and II of the Naval Discipline Act 1957 apply (whether with or without any modifications).*
    [(i)   a person subject to service law within the meaning of the Armed Forces Act 2006; or
    (ii)   a civilian subject to service discipline within the meaning of that Act].

Amendments—SI 2003/1247, art 36(1), Sch 1, para 23(a); Courts Act 2003, s 109(1), Sch 8, para 386.

Prospective Amendments—Sub-s (13): para (c)(i), (ii) substituted by the Armed Forces Act 2006, s 378(1), Sch 16, para 158. Date in force: to be appointed: see the Armed Forces Act 2006, s 383(2).

45 Power to restrict reporting of criminal proceedings involving persons under 18

(1) This section applies (subject to subsection (2)) in relation to –

(a)   any criminal proceedings in any court (other than a service court) in England and Wales or Northern Ireland; and

(b)   any proceedings (whether in the United Kingdom or elsewhere) in any service court.

(2) This section does not apply in relation to any proceedings to which section 49 of the Children and Young Persons Act 1933 applies.

(3) The court may direct that no matter relating to any person concerned in the proceedings shall while he is under the age of 18 be included in any publication if it is likely to lead members of the public to identify him as a person concerned in the proceedings.

(4) The court or an appellate court may by direction ('an excepting direction') dispense, to any extent specified in the excepting direction, with the restrictions imposed by a direction under subsection (3) if it is satisfied that it is necessary in the interests of justice to do so.

(5) The court or an appellate court may also by direction ('an excepting direction') dispense, to any extent specified in the excepting direction, with the restrictions imposed by a direction under subsection (3) if it is satisfied –

(a)   that their effect is to impose a substantial and unreasonable restriction on the reporting of the proceedings, and

(b)   that it is in the public interest to remove or relax that restriction;

but no excepting direction shall be given under this subsection by reason only of the fact that the proceedings have been determined in any way or have been abandoned.

(6) When deciding whether to make –

(a)   a direction under subsection (3) in relation to a person, or

(b)   an excepting direction under subsection (4) or (5) by virtue of which the restrictions imposed by a direction under subsection (3) would be dispensed with (to any extent) in relation to a person,

the court or (as the case may be) the appellate court shall have regard to the welfare of that person.

(7) For the purposes of subsection (3) any reference to a person concerned in the proceedings is to a person –

(a)   against or in respect of whom the proceedings are taken, or

(b)   who is a witness in the proceedings.

(8) The matters relating to a person in relation to which the restrictions imposed by a direction under subsection (3) apply (if their inclusion in any publication is likely to have the result mentioned in that subsection) include in particular –

(a)   his name,

(b)   his address,

(c)   the identity of any school or other educational establishment attended by him,

(d)   the identity of any place of work, and

(e)   any still or moving picture of him.

(9) A direction under subsection (3) may be revoked by the court or an appellate court.

(10) An excepting direction –

(a)   may be given at the time the direction under subsection (3) is given or subsequently; and

(b)   may be varied or revoked by the court or an appellate court.

(11) In this section 'appellate court', in relation to any proceedings in a court, means a court dealing with an appeal (including an appeal by way of case stated) arising out of the proceedings or with any further appeal.

Reports relating to adult witnesses

46 Power to restrict reports about certain adult witnesses in criminal proceedings

(1) This section applies where –

    (a)   in any criminal proceedings in any court (other than a service court) in England and Wales or Northern Ireland, or

    (b)   in any proceedings (whether in the United Kingdom or elsewhere) in any service court,

a party to the proceedings makes an application for the court to give a reporting direction in relation to a witness in the proceedings (other than the accused) who has attained the age of 18.

In this section 'reporting direction' has the meaning given by subsection (6).

(2) If the court determines –

    (a)   that the witness is eligible for protection, and

    (b)   that giving a reporting direction in relation to the witness is likely to improve –

        (i)   the quality of evidence given by the witness, or

        (ii)   the level of co-operation given by the witness to any party to the proceedings in connection with that party's preparation of its case,

the court may give a reporting direction in relation to the witness.

(3) For the purposes of this section a witness is eligible for protection if the court is satisfied –

    (a)   that the quality of evidence given by the witness, or

    (b)   the level of co-operation given by the witness to any party to the proceedings in connection with that party's preparation of its case,

is likely to be diminished by reason of fear or distress on the part of the witness in connection with being identified by members of the public as a witness in the proceedings.

(4) In determining whether a witness is eligible for protection the court must take into account, in particular –

    (a)   the nature and alleged circumstances of the offence to which the proceedings relate;

    (b)   the age of the witness;

    (c)   such of the following matters as appear to the court to be relevant, namely –

        (i)   the social and cultural background and ethnic origins of the witness,

        (ii)   the domestic and employment circumstances of the witness, and

        (iii)   any religious beliefs or political opinions of the witness;

    (d)   any behaviour towards the witness on the part of –

        (i)   the accused,

        (ii)   members of the family or associates of the accused, or

        (iii)   any other person who is likely to be an accused or a witness in the proceedings.

(5) In determining that question the court must in addition consider any views expressed by the witness.

(6) For the purposes of this section a reporting direction in relation to a witness is a direction that no matter relating to the witness shall during the witness's lifetime be included in any publication if it is likely to lead members of the public to identify him as being a witness in the proceedings.

(7) The matters relating to a witness in relation to which the restrictions imposed by a reporting direction apply (if their inclusion in any publication is likely to have the result mentioned in subsection (6)) include in particular –

(a) the witness's name,
(b) the witness's address,
(c) the identity of any educational establishment attended by the witness,
(d) the identity of any place of work, and
(e) any still or moving picture of the witness.

(8) In determining whether to give a reporting direction the court shall consider—

(a) whether it would be in the interests of justice to do so, and
(b) the public interest in avoiding the imposition of a substantial and unreasonable restriction on the reporting of the proceedings.

(9) The court or an appellate court may by direction ('an excepting direction') dispense, to any extent specified in the excepting direction, with the restrictions imposed by a reporting direction if –

(a) it is satisfied that it is necessary in the interests of justice to do so, or
(b) it is satisfied –

   (i) that the effect of those restrictions is to impose a substantial and unreasonable restriction on the reporting of the proceedings, and
   (ii) that it is in the public interest to remove or relax that restriction;

but no excepting direction shall be given under paragraph (b) by reason only of the fact that the proceedings have been determined in any way or have been abandoned.

(10) A reporting direction may be revoked by the court or an appellate court.

(11) An excepting direction –

(a) may be given at the time the reporting direction is given or subsequently; and
(b) may be varied or revoked by the court or an appellate court.

(12) In this section –

(a) 'appellate court', in relation to any proceedings in a court, means a court dealing with an appeal (including an appeal by way of case stated) arising out of the proceedings or with any further appeal;
(b) references to the quality of a witness's evidence are to its quality in terms of completeness, coherence and accuracy (and for this purpose 'coherence' refers to a witness's ability in giving evidence to give answers which address the questions put to the witness and can be understood both individually and collectively);
(c) references to the preparation of the case of a party to any proceedings include, where the party is the prosecution, the carrying out of investigations into any offence at any time charged in the proceedings.

Chapter 1, 1A or 2

47 Restrictions on reporting directions under Chapter 1, 1A or 2

(1) Except as provided by this section, no publication shall include a report of a matter falling within subsection (2).

(2) The matters falling within this subsection are –

(a) a direction under section 19, 33A or 36 or an order discharging, or (in the case of a direction under section 19) varying, such a direction;
(b) proceedings –

    (i)   on an application for such a direction or order, or

    (ii)   where the court acts of its own motion to determine whether to give or make any such direction or order.

(3) The court dealing with a matter falling within subsection (2) may order that subsection (1) is not to apply, or is not to apply to a specified extent, to a report of that matter.

(4) Where –

    (a)   there is only one accused in the relevant proceedings, and

    (b)   he objects to the making of an order under subsection (3),

the court shall make the order if (and only if) satisfied after hearing the representations of the accused that it is in the interests of justice to do so; and if the order is made it shall not apply to the extent that a report deals with any such objections or representations.

(5) Where –

    (a)   there are two or more accused in the relevant proceedings, and

    (b)   one or more of them object to the making of an order under subsection (3),

the court shall make the order if (and only if) satisfied after hearing the representations of each of the accused that it is in the interests of justice to do so; and if the order is made it shall not apply to the extent that a report deals with any such objections or representations.

(6) Subsection (1) does not apply to the inclusion in a publication of a report of matters after the relevant proceedings are either –

    (a)   determined (by acquittal, conviction or otherwise), or

    (b)   abandoned,

in relation to the accused or (if there is more than one) in relation to each of the accused.

(7) In this section 'the relevant proceedings' means the proceedings to which any such direction as is mentioned in subsection (2) relates or would relate.

(8) Nothing in this section affects any prohibition or restriction by virtue of any other enactment on the inclusion of matter in a publication.

Amendments—Police and Justice Act 2006, s 52, Sch 14, para 37(1), (2); Criminal Evidence (Northern Ireland) Order 1999, SI 1999/2789, art 40(1), Sch 1, para 6.

****

A1.4

Magistrates' Courts (Hearsay Evidence in Civil Proceedings) Rules 1999

SI 1999/681

1 Citation and commencement

These Rules may be cited as the Magistrates' Courts (Hearsay Evidence in Civil Proceedings) Rules 1999 and shall come into force on 1st April 1999.

2 Application and interpretation

(1) In these Rules, the "1995 Act" means the Civil Evidence Act 1995.

(2) In these Rules –

"hearsay evidence" means evidence consisting of hearsay within the meaning of section 1(2) of the 1995 Act;

"hearsay notice" means a notice under section 2 of the 1995 Act.

(3) These Rules shall apply to hearsay evidence in civil proceedings in magistrates' courts.

3 Hearsay notices

(1) Subject to paragraphs (2) and (3), a party who desires to give hearsay evidence at the hearing must, not less than 21 days before the date fixed for the hearing, serve a hearsay notice on every other party and file a copy in the court by serving it on the designated officer for the court.

(2) Subject to paragraph (3), the court or the justices' clerk may make a direction substituting a different period of time for the service of the hearsay notice under paragraph (1) on the application of a party to the proceedings.

(3) The court may make a direction under paragraph (2) of its own motion.

(4) A hearsay notice must –

(a) state that it is a hearsay notice;
(b) identify the proceedings in which the hearsay evidence is to be given;
(c) state that the party proposes to adduce hearsay evidence;
(d) identify the hearsay evidence;
(e) identify the person who made the statement which is to be given in evidence; and
(f) state why that person will not be called to give oral evidence.

(5) A single hearsay notice may deal with the hearsay evidence of more than one witness.

Amendments—SI 2005/617.

4 Power to call witness for cross-examination on hearsay evidence

(1) Where a party tenders as hearsay evidence a statement made by a person but does not propose to call the person who made the statement to give evidence, the court may, on application, allow another party to call and cross-examine the person who made the statement on its contents.

(2) An application under paragraph (1) must –

(a) be served on the designated officer for the court with sufficient copies for all other parties;
(b) unless the court otherwise directs, be made not later than 7 days after service of the hearsay notice; and
(c) give reasons why the person who made the statement should be cross-examined on its contents.

(3) On receipt of an application under paragraph (1) –

(a) the justices' clerk must –

(i) unless the court otherwise directs, allow sufficient time for the applicant to comply with paragraph (4); and
(ii) fix the date, time and place of the hearing; and

(b) the designated officer for the court must –

(i) endorse the date, time and place of the hearing on the copies of the application filed by the applicant; and

(ii) return the copies to the applicant forthwith.

(4) Subject to paragraphs (5) and (6), on receipt of the copies from the designated officer for the court under paragraph (3)(c), the applicant must serve a copy on every other party giving not less than 3 days' notice of the hearing of the application.

(5) The court or the justices' clerk may give directions as to the manner in which service under paragraph (4) is to be effected and may, subject to the designated officer's giving notice to the applicant, alter or dispense with the notice requirement under paragraph (4) if the court or the justices' clerk, as the case may be, considers it is in the interests of justice to do so.

(6) The court may hear an application under paragraph (1) ex parte if it considers it is in the interests of justice to do so.

(7) Subject to paragraphs (5) and (6), where an application under paragraph (1) is made, the applicant must file with the court a statement at or before the hearing of the application that service of a copy of the application has been effected on all other parties and the statement must indicate the manner, date, time and address at which the document was served.

(8) The court must notify all parties of its decision on an application under paragraph (1).

Amendments—SI 2001/615; SI 2005/617.

5 Credibility and previous inconsistent statements

(1) If –

(a) a party tenders as hearsay evidence a statement made by a person but does not call the person who made the statement to give oral evidence, and

(b) another party wishes to attack the credibility of the person who made the statement or allege that the person who made the statement made any other statement inconsistent with it,

that other party must notify the party tendering the hearsay evidence of his intention.

(2) Unless the court or the justices' clerk otherwise directs, a notice under paragraph (1) must be given not later than 7 days after service of the hearsay notice and, in addition to the requirements in paragraph (1), must be served on every other party and a copy filed in the court.

(3) If, on receipt of a notice under paragraph (1), the party referred to in paragraph (1)(a) calls the person who made the statement to be tendered as hearsay evidence to give oral evidence, he must, unless the court otherwise directs, notify the court and all other parties of his intention.

(4) Unless the court or the justices' clerk otherwise directs, a notice under paragraph (3) must be given not later than 7 days after the service of the notice under paragraph (1).

6 Service

(1) Where service of a document is required by these Rules it may be effected, unless the contrary is indicated –

(a) if the person to be served is not known by the person serving to be acting by solicitor –

(i) by delivering it to him personally, or

(ii) by delivering at, or by sending it by first-class post to, his residence or his last known residence, or

(b) if the person to be served is known by the person serving to be acting by solicitor –

(i) by delivering the document at, or sending it by first-class post to, the solicitor's address for service,

(ii) where the solicitor's address for service includes a numbered box at a document exchange, by leaving the document at that document exchange or at a document exchange which transmits documents on every business day to that document exchange, or

(iii) by sending a legible copy of the document by facsimile transmission to the solicitor's office.

(2) In this rule, "first-class post" means first-class post which has been pre-paid or in respect of which pre-payment is not required.

(3) A document shall, unless the contrary is proved, be deemed to have been served –

(a) in the case of service by first-class post, on the second business day after posting,

(b) in the case of service in accordance with paragraph (1)(b)(ii), on the second business day after the day on which it is left at the document exchange, and

(c) in the case of service in accordance with paragraph (1)(b)(iii), where it is transmitted on a business day before 4 pm, on that day and in any other case, on the next business day.

(4) In this rule, "business day" means any day other than –

(a) a Saturday, Sunday, Christmas Day or Good Friday; or

(b) a bank holiday under the Banking and Financial Dealings Act 1971, in England and Wales.

7 Amendment to the Justices' Clerks Rules 1970

The Justices' Clerks Rules 1970 shall be amended by the insertion, after paragraph 18 of the Schedule, of the following paragraph –

> "**19** The giving, variation or revocation of directions in accordance with rules 3(2), 4(5), 5(2) and (4) of the Magistrates' Courts (Hearsay Evidence in Civil Proceedings) Rules 1999.".

A1.5

Magistrates' Courts (Anti-social Behaviour Orders) Rules 2002

SI 2002/2784

2[1] Citation, interpretation and commencement

(1) These Rules may be cited as the Magistrates' Courts (Anti-social Behaviour Orders) Rules 2002 and shall come into force on 2nd December 2002.

(2) In these Rules any reference to a numbered section is a reference to the section so numbered in the Crime and Disorder Act 1998, any reference to a 'form' includes a form to like effect, and, unless otherwise stated, reference to a 'Schedule' is a reference to a Schedule hereto.

3 Transitional provisions

After these Rules come into force, rules 6 and 7 of, and Schedules 5 and 6 to the Magistrates' Courts (Sex Offender and Anti-Social Behaviour Orders) Rules 1998 shall (notwithstanding their revocation) continue to apply to proceedings commenced prior to the commencement of these Rules.

---

[1] The numbering of these Rules is as per the Queen's Printers copy. It is thought that this is a drafting error.

4 Forms

(1)   An application for an anti-social behaviour order may be in the form set out in Schedule 1.

(2)   ...

(3)   ...

(4)   ...

(5)   An application for an interim anti-social behaviour order made under section 1D [may] be in the form set out in Schedule 5.

(6)   ...

Amendments—SI 2003/1236, rr 88, 89(1).

5   Interim orders

(1)   An application for an interim order under section 1D, may, with leave of the justices' clerk, be made without notice being given to the defendant.

(2)   The justices' clerk shall only grant leave under paragraph (1) of this rule if he is satisfied that it is necessary for the application to be made without notice being given to the defendant.

(3)   If an application made under paragraph (2) is granted, then the interim order and the application for an anti-social behaviour order under section 1 (together with a summons giving a date for the defendant to attend court) shall be served on the defendant in person as soon as practicable after the making of the interim order.

(4)   An interim order which is made at the hearing of an application without notice shall not take effect until it has been served on the defendant.

(5)   If such an interim order made without notice is not served on the defendant within seven days of being made, then it shall cease to have effect.

(6)   An interim order shall cease to have effect if the application for an anti-social behaviour order is withdrawn.

(7)   Where the court refuses to make an interim order without notice being given to the defendant it may direct that the application be made on notice.

(8)   If an interim order is made without notice being given to the defendant, and the defendant subsequently applies to the court for the order to be discharged or varied, his application shall not be dismissed without the opportunity for him to make oral representations to the court.

6   Application for variation or discharge

(1)   This rule applies to the making of an application for the variation or discharge of an order made under section 1, 1C or, subject to rule 5(8) above, 1D.

(2)   An application to which this rule applies shall be made in writing to the magistrates' court which made the order, or in the case of an application under section 1C to any magistrates' court in the same local justice area, and shall specify the reason why the applicant for variation or discharge believes the court should vary or discharge the order, as the case may be.

(3) Subject to rule 5(8) above, where the court considers that there are no grounds upon which it might conclude that the order should be varied or discharged, as the case may be, it may determine the application without hearing representations from the applicant for variation or discharge or from any other person.

(4) Where the court considers that there are grounds upon which it might conclude that the order should be varied or discharged, as the case may be, the designated officer for the court shall, unless the application is withdrawn, issue a summons giving not less than 14 days' notice in writing of the date, time and place appointed for the hearing.

(5) The designated officer shall send with the summons under paragraph 4 above a copy of the application for variation or discharge of the anti-social behaviour order.

Amendments—SI 2005/617, art 1.

7 Service

(1) Subject to rule 5(3), any summons, or copy of an order or application required to be sent under these Rules to the defendant shall be either given to him in person or sent by post to the last known address, and, if so given or sent, shall be deemed to have been received by him unless he proves otherwise.

(2) Any summons, copy of an order or application required to be sent to the defendant under these Rules shall also be sent by the designated officer for the court to the applicant authority, and to any relevant authority whom the applicant is required by section 1E to have consulted before making the application and, where appropriate, shall invite them to make observations and advise them of their right to be heard at the hearing.

Amendments—SI 2005/617, art 2, Schedule, para 202.

8 Delegation by justices' clerk

(1) In this rule, 'employed as a clerk of the court' has the same meaning as in rule 2(1) of the Justices' Clerks (Qualifications of Assistants) Rules 1979.

(2) Anything authorised to be done by, to or before a justices' clerk under these Rules, may be done instead by, to or before a person employed as a clerk of the court where that person is appointed by the Lord Chancellor to assist him and where that person has been specifically authorised by the justices' clerk for that purpose.

(3) Any authorisation by the justices' clerk under paragraph (2) shall be recorded in writing at the time the authority is given or as soon as practicable thereafter.

Amendments—SI 2005/617, art 2, Schedule, para 203.

Schedule 1

Form

Rule 4(1)

Application for Anti-Social Behaviour Order (Crime and Disorder Act 1998, s 1(1))

Magistrates' Court

(Code)

Date:

Defendant:

Address:

Applicant Authority:

Relevant authorities consulted:

And it is alleged

(a) that the defendant has acted on

[dates(s)] at [place(s)] in an anti-social manner, that is to say, in a manner that caused or was likely to cause harassment, alarm or distress to one or more persons not of the same household as himself; and

(b) that an anti-social behaviour order is necessary to protect relevant persons from further anti-social acts by him, and accordingly application is made for an anti-social behaviour order containing the following prohibition(s):—

Short description of acts:

The complaint of:

Name of Applicant Authority:

Address of Applicant Authority:

who [upon oath] states that the defendant was responsible for the acts of which particulars are given above, in respect of which this complaint is made.

Taken [and sworn] before me

Justice of the Peace

[By order of the clerk of the court]

Schedule 2

****

Schedule 3

****

Schedule 4

****

Schedule 5

Form

Rule 4(5)

Application for an Interim Order

(Crime and Disorder Act 1998, s 1D)

Magistrates' Court

(Code)

Date:

Defendant:

Address:

Applicant Authority:

Relevant Authorities Consulted:

Reasons for applying for an interim order:

Do you wish this application to be heard: without notice being given to the defendant

with notice being given to the defendant

If you wish the application to be heard without notice state reasons:

The complaint of:

Address of Applicant Authority:

Who [upon oath] states that the information given above is correct.

Taken [and sworn] before me.

Justice of the Peace

[By order of the clerk of the court]

NOTE: This application must be accompanied by an application for an anti-social behaviour order (Crime and Disorder Act 1998, s 1).

Schedule 6

****

A1.6

Civil Procedure Rules 1998

SI 1998/3132

****

PART 19

PARTIES AND GROUP LITIGATION

19.1 Parties – general

Any number of claimants or defendants may be joined as parties to a claim.

Amendments—Inserted by SI 2000/221.

I Addition and Substitution of Parties

19.2 Change of parties – general

(1) This rule applies where a party is to be added or substituted except where the case falls within rule 19.5 (special provisions about changing parties after the end of a relevant limitation period$^{(GL)}$).

(2) The court may order a person to be added as a new party if –

    (a)   it is desirable to add the new party so that the court can resolve all the matters in dispute in the proceedings; or

    (b)   there is an issue involving the new party and an existing party which is connected to the matters in dispute in the proceedings, and it is desirable to add the new party so that the court can resolve that issue.

(3) The court may order any person to cease to be a party if it is not desirable for that person to be a party to the proceedings.

(4) The court may order a new party to be substituted for an existing one if –

    (a)   the existing party's interest or liability has passed to the new party; and

    (b)   it is desirable to substitute the new party so that the court can resolve the matters in dispute in the proceedings.

Amendments—Inserted by SI 2000/221.

****

19.4 Procedure for adding and substituting parties

(1) The court's permission is required to remove, add or substitute a party, unless the claim form has not been served.

(2) An application for permission under paragraph (1) may be made by –

    (a)   an existing party; or

    (b)   a person who wishes to become a party.

(3) An application for an order under rule 19.2(4) (substitution of a new party where existing party's interest or liability has passed) –

(a)   may be made without notice; and
(b)   must be supported by evidence.

(4) Nobody may be added or substituted as a claimant unless –

(a)   he has given his consent in writing; and
(b)   that consent has been filed with the court.

(4A) The Commissioners for HM Revenue and Customs may be added as a party to proceedings only if they consent in writing.

(5) An order for the removal, addition or substitution of a party must be served on –

(a)   all parties to the proceedings; and
(b)   any other person affected by the order.

(6) When the court makes an order for the removal, addition or substitution of a party, it may give consequential directions about –

(a)   filing and serving the claim form on any new defendant;
(b)   serving relevant documents on the new party; and
(c)   the management of the proceedings.

Amendments—Inserted by SI 2000/221; SI 2005/2292.

****

PRACTICE DIRECTION –
PD19: ADDITION AND SUBSTITUTION OF PARTIES

This Practice Direction supplements CPR Part 19 (PD19)

A party applying for an amendment will usually be responsible for the costs of and arising from the amendment.

CHANGES OF PARTIES

General

1.1 Parties may be removed, added or substituted in existing proceedings either on the court's own initiative or on the application of either an existing party or a person who wishes to become a party.

1.2 The application may be dealt with without a hearing where all the existing parties and the proposed new party are in agreement.

1.3 The application to add or substitute a new party should be supported by evidence setting out the proposed new party's interest in or connection with the claim.

1.4 The application notice should be filed in accordance with rule 23.3 and, unless the application is made under rule 19.2(4) [1], be served in accordance with rule 23.4.

1.5 An order giving permission to amend will, unless the court orders otherwise, be drawn up. It will be served by the court unless the parties wish to serve it or the court orders them to do so.

Addition or Substitution of Claimant

2.1 Where an application is made to the court to add or to substitute a new party to the proceedings as claimant, the party applying must file:

(1)   the application notice,
(2)   the proposed amended claim form and particulars of claim, and
(3)   the signed, written consent of the new claimant to be so added or substituted.

2.2 Where the court makes an order adding or substituting a party as claimant but the signed, written consent of the new claimant has not been filed:

(1)   the order, and
(2)   the addition or substitution of the new party as claimant,

will not take effect until the signed, written consent of the new claimant is filed.

2.3 Where the court has made an order adding or substituting a new claimant, the court may direct:

(1)   a copy of the order to be served on every party to the proceedings and any other person affected by the order,
(2)   copies of the statements of case and of documents referred to in any statement of case to be served on the new party,
(3)   the party who made the application to file within 14 days an amended claim form and particulars of claim.

Addition or Substitution of Defendant

3.1 The Civil Procedure Rules apply to a new defendant who has been added or substituted as they apply to any other defendant (see in particular the provisions of Parts 9, 10, 11 and 15).

3.2 Where the court has made an order adding or substituting a defendant whether on its own initiative or on an application, the court may direct:

(1)   the claimant to file with the court within 14 days (or as ordered) an amended claim form and particulars of claim for the court file,
(2)   a copy of the order to be served on all parties to the proceedings and any other person affected by it,
(3)   the amended claim form and particulars of claim, forms for admitting, defending and acknowledging the claim and copies of the statements of case and any other documents referred to in any statement of case to be served on the new defendant,
(4)   unless the court orders otherwise, the amended claim form and particulars of claim to be served on any other defendants.

3.3 A new defendant does not become a party to the proceedings until the amended claim form has been served on him.

****

PART 25

INTERIM REMEDIES AND SECURITY FOR COSTS

I Interim remedies

25.1 Orders for interim remedies

(1) The court may grant the following interim remedies –

(a)   an interim injunction[GL];

(b)   an interim declaration;

(c)   an order –

 (i)   for the detention, custody or preservation of relevant property;

 (ii)   for the inspection of relevant property;

 (iii) for the taking of a sample of relevant property;

 (iv) for the carrying out of an experiment on or with relevant property;

 (v)   for the sale of relevant property which is of a perishable nature or which for any other good reason it is desirable to sell quickly; and

 (vi) for the payment of income from relevant property until a claim is decided;

(d)   an order authorising a person to enter any land or building in the possession of a party to the proceedings for the purposes of carrying out an order under sub-paragraph (c);

(e)   an order under section 4 of the Torts (Interference with Goods) Act 1977 to deliver up goods;

(f)   an order (referred to as a 'freezing injunction[GL]') –

 (i)   restraining a party from removing from the jurisdiction assets located there; or

 (ii)   restraining a party from dealing with any assets whether located within the jurisdiction or not;

(g)   an order directing a party to provide information about the location of relevant property or assets or to provide information about relevant property or assets which are or may be the subject of an application for a freezing injunction[GL];

(h)   an order (referred to as a 'search order') under section 7 of the Civil Procedure Act 1997 (order requiring a party to admit another party to premises for the purpose of preserving evidence etc);

(i)   an order under section 33 of the Supreme Court Act 1981 or section 52 of the County Courts Act 1984 (order for disclosure of documents or inspection of property before a claim has been made);

(j)   an order under section 34 of the Supreme Court Act 1981 or section 53 of the County Courts Act 1984 (order in certain proceedings for disclosure of documents or inspection of property against a non-party);

(k)   an order (referred to as an order for interim payment) under rule 25.6 for payment by a defendant on account of any damages, debt or other sum (except costs) which the court may hold the defendant liable to pay;

(l)   an order for a specified fund to be paid into court or otherwise secured, where there is a dispute over a party's right to the fund;

(m) an order permitting a party seeking to recover personal property to pay money into court pending the outcome of the proceedings and directing that, if he does so, the property shall be given up to him;

(n)   an order directing a party to prepare and file accounts relating to the dispute;

(o)   an order directing any account to be taken or inquiry to be made by the court; and

(p)   an order under Article 9 of Council Directive (EC) 2004/48 on the enforcement of intellectual property rights (order in intellectual property proceedings making the continuation of an alleged infringement subject to the lodging of guarantees).

(Rule 34.2 provides for the court to issue a witness summons requiring a witness to produce documents to the court at the hearing or on such date as the court may direct)

(2) In paragraph (1)(c) and (g), 'relevant property' means property (including land) which is the subject of a claim or as to which any question may arise on a claim.

(3) The fact that a particular kind of interim remedy is not listed in paragraph (1) does not affect any power that the court may have to grant that remedy.

(4) The court may grant an interim remedy whether or not there has been a claim for a final remedy of that kind.

Amendments—SI 2002/2058; SI 2005/3515.

25.2 Time when an order for an interim remedy may be made

(1) An order for an interim remedy may be made at any time, including –

    (a)   before proceedings are started; and
    (b)   after judgment has been given.

(Rule 7.2 provides that proceedings are started when the court issues a claim form)

(2) However –

    (a)   paragraph (1) is subject to any rule, practice direction or other enactment which provides otherwise;
    (b)   the court may grant an interim remedy before a claim has been made only if –

        (i)   the matter is urgent; or
        (ii)   it is otherwise desirable to do so in the interests of justice; and

    (c)   unless the court otherwise orders, a defendant may not apply for any of the orders listed in rule 25.1(1) before he has filed either an acknowledgment of service or a defence.

(Part 10 provides for filing an acknowledgment of service and Part 15 for filing a defence)

(3) Where it grants an interim remedy before a claim has been commenced, the court should give directions requiring a claim to be commenced.

(4) In particular, the court need not direct that a claim be commenced where the application is made under section 33 of the Supreme Court Act 1981 or section 52 of the County Courts Act 1984 (order for disclosure, inspection etc before commencement of a claim).

Amendments—SI 2005/3515.

25.3 How to apply for an interim remedy

(1) The court may grant an interim remedy on an application made without notice if it appears to the court that there are good reasons for not giving notice.

(2) An application for an interim remedy must be supported by evidence, unless the court orders otherwise.

(3) If the applicant makes an application without giving notice, the evidence in support of the application must state the reasons why notice has not been given.

(Part 3 lists general powers of the court)

(Part 23 contains general rules about making an application)

****

PRACTICE DIRECTION –
PD25: INTERIM INJUNCTIONS

This Practice Direction supplements CPR Part 25 (PD25)

JURISDICTION

1.1 High Court judges and any other judge duly authorised may grant 'search orders'[1] and 'freezing injunctions'[2].

1.2 In a case in the High Court, masters and district judges have the power to grant injunctions:

(1)   by consent,
(2)   in connection with charging orders and appointments of receivers,
(3)   in aid of execution of judgments.

1.3 In any other case any judge who has jurisdiction to conduct the trial of the action has the power to grant an injunction in that action.

1.4 A master or district judge has the power to vary or discharge an injunction granted by any judge with the consent of all the parties.

MAKING AN APPLICATION

2.1 The application notice must state:

(1)   the order sought, and
(2)   the date, time and place of the hearing.

2.2 The application notice and evidence in support must be served as soon as practicable after issue and in any event not less than 3 days before the court is due to hear the application[1].

2.3 Where the court is to serve, sufficient copies of the application notice and evidence in support for the court and for each respondent should be filed for issue and service.

2.4 Whenever possible a draft of the order sought should be filed with the application notice and a disk containing the draft should also be available to the court in a format compatible with the word processing software used by the court This will enable the court officer to arrange for any amendments to be incorporated and for the speedy preparation and sealing of the order.

EVIDENCE

3.1 Applications for search orders and freezing injunctions must be supported by affidavit evidence.

3.2 Applications for other interim injunctions must be supported by evidence set out in either:

(1)   a witness statement, or
(2)   a statement of case provided that it is verified by a statement of truth[1], or
(3)   the application provided that it is verified by a statement of truth,

unless the court, an Act, a rule or a practice direction requires evidence by affidavit.

3.3 The evidence must set out the facts on which the applicant relies for the claim being made against the respondent, including all material facts of which the court should be made aware.

3.4 Where an application is made without notice to the respondent, the evidence must also set out why notice was not given.

URGENT APPLICATIONS AND APPLICATIONS WITHOUT NOTICE

4.1 These fall into two categories:

(1)   applications where a claim form has already been issued, and
(2)   applications where a claim form has not yet been issued,

and, in both cases, where notice of the application has not been given to the respondent.

4.2 These applications are normally dealt with at a court hearing but cases of extreme urgency may be dealt with by telephone.

4.3 Applications dealt with at a court hearing after issue of a claim form:

(1)   the application notice, evidence in support and a draft order (as in 2.4 above) should be filed with the court two hours before the hearing wherever possible,

(2)   if an application is made before the application notice has been issued, a draft order (as in 2.4 above) should be provided at the hearing, and the application notice and evidence in support must be filed with the court on the same or next working day or as ordered by the court, and

(3)   except in cases where secrecy is essential, the applicant should take steps to notify the respondent informally of the application.

4.4 Applications made before the issue of a claim form:

(1)   in addition to the provisions set out at 4.3 above, unless the court orders otherwise, either the applicant must undertake to the court to issue a claim form immediately or the court will give directions for the commencement of the claim[1],

(2)   where possible the claim form should be served with the order for the injunction,

(3)   an order made before the issue of a claim form should state in the title after the names of the applicant and respondent 'the Claimant and Defendant in an Intended Action'.

4.5 Applications made by telephone:

(1)   where it is not possible to arrange a hearing, application can be made between 10.00 am and 5.00 pm weekdays by telephoning the Royal Courts of Justice on 020 7947 6000 and asking to be put in contact with a High Court judge of the appropriate Division available to deal with an emergency application in a High Court matter. The appropriate district registry may also be contacted by telephone. In county court proceedings, the appropriate county court should be contacted,

(2)   where an application is made outside those hours the applicant should either –

(a)   telephone the Royal Courts of Justice on 020 7947 6000 where he will be put in contact with the clerk to the appropriate Duty Judge in the High Court (or the appropriate area circuit judge where known), or

(b)   the Urgent Court Business Officer of the appropriate circuit who will contact the local Duty Judge,

(3)   where the facility is available it is likely that the judge will require a draft order to be faxed to him,

(4)   the application notice and evidence in support must be filed with the court on the same or next working day or as ordered, together with two copies of the order for sealing,

(5)   injunctions will be heard by telephone only where the applicant is acting by counsel or solicitors.

****

PART 65

PROCEEDINGS RELATING TO ANTI-SOCIAL BEHAVIOUR AND HARRASSMENT

65.1 Scope of this Part

This Part contains rules –

(a)   in Section I, about injunctions under the Housing Act 1996;

(b)   in Section II, about applications by local authorities under section 91(3) of the Anti-social Behaviour Act 2003 for a power of arrest to be attached to an injunction;

(c)   in Section III, about claims for demotion orders under the Housing Act 1985 and Housing Act 1988 and proceedings relating to demoted tenancies;

(d)   in Section IV, about anti-social behaviour orders under the Crime and Disorder Act 1998;

(e)   in Section V, about claims under section 3 of the Protection from Harassment Act 1997;and

...

(g)   in Section VII, about parenting orders under sections 26A and 26B of the Anti-social Behaviour Act 2003.

Amendments—Inserted by SI 2004/1306; amended by SI 2007/2204; SI 2008/2178.

****

II Applications by Local Authorities for Power of Arrest to be Attached to Injunction

65.8 Scope of this Section and interpretation

(1) This Section applies to applications by local authorities under section 91(3) of the Anti-social Behaviour Act 2003 or under section 27(3) of the Police and Justice 2006 Act for a power of arrest to be attached to an injunction.

> (Section 91 of the 2003 Act and section 27 of the 2006 Act apply to proceedings in which a local authority is a party by virtue of section 222 of the Local Government Act 1972 (power of local authority to bring, defend or appear in proceedings for the promotion or protection of the interests of inhabitants in their area)

(2) In this Section 'the 2003 Act' means the Anti-social Behaviour Act 2003.

(3) In this Section 'the 2006 Act' means the Police and Justice Act 2006.

Amendments—Inserted by SI 2004/1306; SI 2007/2204.

65.9 Applications under section 91(3) of the 2003 Act or section 27(3) of the 2006 Act for a power of arrest to be attached to any provision of an injunction

(1) An application under section 91(3) of the 2003 Act or section 27(3) of the 2006 Act for a power of arrest to be attached to any provision of an injunction must be made in the proceedings seeking the injunction by –

    (a)   the claim form;
    (b)   the acknowledgment of service;
    (c)   the defence or counterclaim in a Part 7 claim; or
    (d)   application under Part 23.

(2) Every application must be supported by written evidence.

(3) Every application made on notice must be served personally, together with a copy of the written evidence, by the local authority on the person against whom the injunction is sought not less than 2 days before the hearing.

(Attention is drawn to rule 25.3(3) – applications without notice)

Amendments—Inserted by SI 2004/1306.

65.10 Injunction containing provisions to which a power of arrest is attached

(1) Where a power of arrest is attached to a provision of an injunction on the application of a local authority under section 91(3) of the 2003 Act, the following rules in Section I of this Part shall apply –

    (a)   rule 65.4; and
    (b)   paragraphs (1), (2), (4) and (5) of rule 65.6.

(1A) Where a power of arrest is attached to a provision of an injunction on the application of a local authority under section 27(3) of the 2006 Act, the following rules in Section I of this Part apply –

    (a)   rule 65.4;
    (b)   paragraphs (1), (2), (4) and (5) of rule 65.6;

(c)   paragraph (1) of rule 65.7, as if the reference to paragraph 2(2)(b) of Schedule 15 to the Housing Act 1996 was a reference to paragraph 2(2)(b) of Schedule 10 to the 2006 Act; and

(d)   paragraph (2) of rule 65.7.

(2) CCR Order 29, rule 1 shall apply where an application is made in a county court to commit a person for breach of an injunction.

Amendments—Inserted by SI 2004/1306; SI 2007/2204.

****

IV *Anti-Social Behaviour Orders under the Crime and Disorder Act 1998*

65.21 Scope of this Section and interpretation

(1) This Section applies to applications in proceedings in a county court under sub-sections (2), (3) or (3B) of section 1B of the Crime and Disorder Act 1998 by a relevant authority, and to applications for interim orders under section 1D of that Act.

(2) In this Section –

(a)   'the 1998 Act' means the Crime and Disorder Act 1998;

(b)   'relevant authority' has the same meaning as in section 1(1A) of the 1998 Act; and

(c)   'the principal proceedings' means any proceedings in a county court.

Amendments—Inserted by SI 2004/1306.

65.22 Application where the relevant authority is a party in principal proceedings

(1) Subject to paragraph (2) –

(a)   where the relevant authority is the claimant in the principal proceedings, an application under section 1B(2) of the 1998 Act for an order under section 1B(4) of the 1998 Act must be made in the claim form; and

(b)   where the relevant authority is a defendant in the principal proceedings, an application for an order must be made by application notice which must be filed with the defence.

(2) Where the relevant authority becomes aware of the circumstances that lead it to apply for an order after its claim is issued or its defence filed, the application must be made by application notice as soon as possible thereafter.

(3) Where the application is made by application notice, it should normally be made on notice to the person against whom the order is sought.

Amendments—Inserted by SI 2004/1306.

65.23 Application by a relevant authority to join a person to the principal proceedings

(1) An application under section 1B(3B) of the 1998 Act by a relevant authority which is a party to the principal proceedings to join a person to the principal proceedings must be made –

(a)   in accordance with Section I of Part 19;

(b)   in the same application notice as the application for an order under section 1B(4) of the 1998 Act against the person; and

(c)   as soon as possible after the relevant authority considers that the criteria in section 1B(3A) of the 1998 Act are met.

(2) The application notice must contain –

   (a)   the relevant authority's reasons for claiming that the person's anti-social acts are material in relation to the principal proceedings; and

   (b)   details of the anti-social acts alleged.

(3) The application should normally be made on notice to the person against whom the order is sought.

Amendments—Inserted by SI 2004/1306.

65.24 Application where the relevant authority is not party in principal proceedings

(1) Where the relevant authority is not a party to the principal proceedings –

   (a)   an application under section 1B(3) of the 1998 Act to be made a party must be made in accordance with Section I of Part 19; and

   (b)   the application to be made a party and the application for an order under section 1B(4) of the 1998 Act must be made in the same application notice.

(2) The applications –

   (a)   must be made as soon as possible after the authority becomes aware of the principal proceedings; and

   (b)   should normally be made on notice to the person against whom the order is sought.

Amendments—Inserted by SI 2004/1306.

65.25 Evidence

An application for an order under section 1B(4) of the 1998 Act must be accompanied by written evidence, which must include evidence that section 1E of the 1998 Act has been complied with.

Amendments—Inserted by SI 2004/1306.

65.26 Application for an interim order

(1) An application for an interim order under section 1D of the 1998 Act must be made in accordance with Part 25.

(2) The application should normally be made –

   (a)   in the claim form or application notice seeking the order; and

   (b)   on notice to the person against whom the order is sought.

Amendments—Inserted by SI 2004/1306.

****

VI Drinking Banning Orders Under the Violent Crime Reduction Act 2006

Amendments—Inserted by SI 2009/2092.

65.31 Scope of this Section and interpretation

(1) This Section applies to applications in proceedings in a county court under sub-sections (2), (3) or (5) of section 4 of the Violent Crime Reduction Act 2006 by a relevant authority, and to applications for interim orders under section 9 of that Act.

(2) In this Section –

   (a)   'the 2006 Act' means the Violent Crime Reduction Act 2006;

   (b)   'relevant authority' has the same meaning as in section 14(1) of the 2006 Act; and

   (c)   'the principal proceedings' means any proceedings in a county court.

Amendments—Inserted by SI 2009/2092.

65.32 Application where the relevant authority is a party in principal proceedings

(1) Subject to paragraph (2) –

  (a) where the relevant authority is the claimant in the principal proceedings, an application under section 4(2) of the 2006 Act for an order under section 4(7) of the 2006 Act must be made in the claim form; and

  (b) where the relevant authority is a defendant in the principal proceedings, an application for an order must be made by application notice which must be filed with the defence.

(2) Where the relevant authority becomes aware of the circumstances that lead it to apply for an order after its claim is issued or its defence filed, the application must be made by application notice as soon as possible thereafter.

(3) Where the application is made by application notice, it should normally be made on notice to the person against whom the order is sought.

Amendments—Inserted by SI 2009/2092.

65.33 Application where the relevant authority is not a party in principal proceedings

(1) Where the relevant authority is not a party to the principal proceedings –

  (a) an application under section 4(3) of the 2006 Act to be made a party must be made in accordance with Section I of Part 19; and

  (b) the application to be made a party and the application for an order under section 4(7) of the 2006 Act must be made in the same application notice.

(2) The applications –

  (a) must be made as soon as possible after the relevant authority becomes aware of the principal proceedings; and

  (b) should normally be made on notice to the person against whom the order is sought.

Amendments—Inserted by SI 2009/2092.

65.34 Application by a relevant authority to join a person to the principal proceedings

(1) An application under section 4(5) of the 2006 Act by a relevant authority which is a party to the principal proceedings to join a person to the principal proceedings must be made –

  (a) in accordance with Section I of Part 19;

  (b) in the same application notice as the application for an order under section 4(7) of the 2006 Act against the person; and

  (c) as soon as possible after the relevant authority considers that the criteria in section 4(4) of the 2006 Act are met.

(2) The application notice must contain –

  (a) the relevant authority's reasons for claiming that the person's conduct is material in relation to the principal proceedings; and

  (b) details of the conduct alleged.

(3) The application should normally be made on notice to the person against whom the order is sought.

Amendments—Inserted by SI 2009/2092.

65.35 Evidence

An application for an order under section 4(7) of the 2006 Act must be accompanied by written evidence, which must include evidence that section 4(6) of the 2006 Act has been complied with.

Amendments—Inserted by SI 2009/2092.

65.36 Application for an interim order

(1) An application for an interim order under section 9 of the 2006 Act must be made in accordance with Part 25.

(2) The application should normally be made –

    (a)   in the claim form or application notice seeking the order; and

    (b)   on notice to the person against whom the order is sought.

(3) An application for an interim order may be –

    (a)   made without a copy of the application notice being served on the person against whom the order is sought;

    (b)   heard in the absence of the person against whom the order is sought,

with the permission of the court.

Amendments—Inserted by SI 2009/2092.

SECTION IV

ANTI-SOCIAL BEHAVIOUR ORDERS UNDER THE CRIME AND DISORDER ACT 1998

Service of an order under sections 1B(4) or 1D of the 1998 Act

13.1 An order under section 1B(4) or an interim order under section 1D of the 1998 Act must be served personally on the defendant.

****

A1.7

Criminal Procedure Rules 2005

SI 2005/384

PART 29

SPECIAL MEASURES DIRECTIONS

Contents of this Part

Application for special measures directions	rule 29.1
Application for an extension of time	rule 29.2
Late applications	rule 29.3
Discharge or variation of a special measures direction	rule 29.4
Renewal application following change of circumstances	rule 29.5
Vulnerable witness to give evidence by live television link	rule 29.6

Video recording of testimony from witnesses   rule 29.7

Expert evidence   rule 29.8

Intermediaries   rule 29.9

29.1 Application for special measures directions

(1) An application by a party in criminal proceedings for a magistrates' court or the Crown Court to give a special measures direction under section 19 of the Youth Justice and Criminal Evidence Act 1999 must be made in writing in the form set out in the Practice Direction.

(2) If the application is for a special measures direction –

- (a)   enabling a witness to give evidence by means of a live link, the information sought in Part B of that form must be provided;
- (b)   providing for any examination of a witness to be conducted through an intermediary, the information sought in Part C of that form must be provided; or
- (c)   enabling a video recording of an interview of a witness to be admitted as evidence in chief of the witness, the information sought in Part D of that form must be provided.

(3) The application under paragraph (1) above must be sent to the court officer and at the same time a copy thereof must be sent by the applicant to every other party to the proceedings.

(4) The court officer must receive the application –

- (a)   in the case of an application to a youth court, within 28 days of the date on which the defendant first appears or is brought before the court in connection with the offence;
- (b)   in the case of an application to a magistrates' court, within 14 days of the defendant indicating his intention to plead not guilty to any charge brought against him and in relation to which a special measures direction may be sought; and
- (c)   in the case of an application to the Crown Court, within 28 days of

  - (i)   the committal of the defendant, or
  - (ii)   the consent to the preferment of a bill of indictment in relation to the case, or
  - (iii) the service of a notice of transfer under section 53 of the Criminal Justice Act 1991, or
  - (iv) where a person is sent for trial under section 51 of the Crime and Disorder Act 1998, the service of copies of the documents containing the evidence on which the charge or charges are based under paragraph 1 of Schedule 3 to that Act, or
  - (v)   the service of a Notice of Appeal from a decision of a youth court or a magistrates' court.

(5) A party to whom an application is sent in accordance with paragraph (3) may oppose the application for a special measures direction in respect of any, or any particular, measure available in relation to the witness, whether or not the question whether the witness is eligible for assistance by virtue of section 16 or 17 of the 1999 Act is in issue.

(6) A party who wishes to oppose the application must, within 14 days of the date the application was served on him, notify the applicant and the court officer, as the case may be, in writing of his opposition and give reasons for it.

(7) Paragraphs (5) and (6) do not apply in respect of an application for a special measures direction enabling a child witness in need of special protection to give evidence by means of a live link if the opposition is that the special measures direction is not likely to maximise the quality of the witness's evidence.

(8) In order to comply with paragraph (6) –

- (a)   a party must in the written notification state whether he –

  - (i)   disputes that the witness is eligible for assistance by virtue of section 16 or 17 of the 1999 Act,

(ii) disputes that any of the special measures available would be likely to improve the quality of evidence given by the witness or that such measures (or a combination of them) would be likely to maximise the quality of that evidence, and

(iii) opposes the granting of a special measures direction; and

(b) where the application relates to the admission of a video recording, a party who receives a recording must provide the information required by rule 29.7(7) below.

(9) Except where notice is received in accordance with paragraph (6), the court (including, in the case of an application to a magistrates' court, a single justice of the peace) may –

(a) determine the application in favour of the applicant without a hearing; or

(b) direct a hearing.

(10) Where a party to the proceedings notifies the court in accordance with paragraph (6) of his opposition to the application, the justices' clerk or the Crown Court must direct a hearing of the application.

(11) Where a hearing of the application is to take place in accordance with paragraph (9) or (10) above, the court officer shall notify each party to the proceedings of the time and place of the hearing.

(12) A party notified in accordance with paragraph (11) may be present at the hearing and be heard.

(13) The court officer must, within 3 days of the decision of the court in relation to an application under paragraph (1) being made, notify all the parties of the decision, and if the application was made for a direction enabling a video recording of an interview of a witness to be admitted as evidence in chief of that witness, the notification must state whether the whole or specified parts only of the video recording or recordings disclosed are to be admitted in evidence.

(14) In this Part:

'an intermediary' has the same meaning as in section 29 of the 1999 Act; and
'child witness in need of protection' shall be construed in accordance with section 21(1) of the 1999 Act.

29.2 Application for an extension of time

(1) An application may be made in writing for the period of 14 days or, as the case may be, 28 days specified in rule 29.1(4) to be extended.

(2) The application may be made either before or after that period has expired.

(3) The application must be accompanied by a statement setting out the reasons why the applicant is or was unable to make the application within that period and a copy of the application and the statement must be sent to every other party to the proceedings.

(4) An application for an extension of time under this rule shall be determined by a single justice of the peace or a judge of the Crown Court without a hearing unless the justice or the judge otherwise directs.

(5) The court officer shall notify all the parties of the court's decision.

29.3 Late applications

(1) Notwithstanding the requirements of rule 29.1 –

(a) an application may be made for a special measures direction orally at the trial; or

(b) a magistrates' court or the Crown Court may of its own motion raise the issue whether a special measures direction should be given.

(2) Where an application is made in accordance with paragraph (1)(a) –

(a) the applicant must state the reasons for the late application; and

    (b)   the court must be satisfied that the applicant was unable to make the application in accordance with rule 29.1.

(3) The court shall determine before making a special measures direction –

    (a)   whether to allow other parties to the proceedings to make representations on the question;
    (b)   the time allowed for making such representations (if any); and
    (c)   whether the question should be determined following a hearing at which the parties to the proceedings may be heard.

(4) Paragraphs (2) and (3) do not apply in respect of an application made orally at the trial for a special measures direction –

    (a)   enabling a child witness in need of special protection to give evidence by means of a live link; or
    (b)   enabling a video recording of such a child to be admitted as evidence in chief of the witness,

if the opposition is that the special measures direction will not maximise the quality of the witness's evidence.

Amendments—SI 2006/2636.

29.4 Discharge or variation of a special measures direction

(1) An application to a magistrates' court or the Crown Court to discharge or vary a special measures direction under section 20(2) of the Youth Justice and Criminal Evidence Act 1999 must be in writing and each material change of circumstances which the applicant alleges has occurred since the direction was made must be set out.

(2) An application under paragraph (1) must be sent to the court officer as soon as reasonably practicable after the change of circumstances occurs.

(3) The applicant must also send copies of the application to each party to the proceedings at the same time as the application is sent to the court officer.

(4) A party to whom an application is sent in accordance with paragraph (3) may oppose the application on the ground that it discloses no material change of circumstances.

(5) Rule 29.1(6) to (13) shall apply to an application to discharge or vary a special measures direction as it applies to an application for a direction.

29.5 Renewal application following a material change of circumstances

(1) Where an application for a special measures direction has been refused by a magistrates' court or the Crown Court, the application may only be renewed ('renewal application') where there has been a material change of circumstances since the court refused the application.

(2) The applicant must –

    (a)   identify in the renewal application each material change of circumstances which is alleged to have occurred; and
    (b)   send the renewal application to the court officer as soon as reasonably practicable after the change occurs.

(3) The applicant must also send copies of the renewal application to each of the parties to the proceedings at the same time as the application is sent to the court officer.

(4) A party to whom the renewal application is sent in accordance with paragraph (3) above may oppose the application on the ground that it discloses no material change of circumstances.

(5) Rules 29.1(6) to (13), 29.6 and 29.7 apply to a renewal application as they apply to the application which was refused.

29.6 Application for special measures direction for witness to give evidence by means of a live television link

(1) Where the application for a special measures direction is made, in accordance with rule 29.1(2)(a), for a witness to give evidence by means of a live link, the following provisions of this rule shall also apply.

(2) A party who seeks to oppose an application for a child witness to give evidence by means of a live link must, in order to comply with rule 29.1(5), state why in his view the giving of a special measures direction would not be likely to maximise the quality of the witness's evidence.

(3) However, paragraph (2) does not apply in relation to a child witness in need of special protection.

(4) Where a special measures direction is made enabling a witness to give evidence by means of a live link, the witness shall be accompanied at the live link only by persons acceptable to the court.

(5) If the special measures directions combine provisions for a witness to give evidence by means of a live link with provision for the examination of the witness to be conducted through an intermediary, the witness shall be accompanied at the live link only by –

(a)   the intermediary; and
(b)   such other persons as may be acceptable to the court.

29.7 Video recording of testimony from witnesses

(1) Where an application is made to a magistrates' court or the Crown Court for a special measures direction enabling a video recording of an interview of a witness to be admitted as evidence in chief of the witness, the following provisions of this rule shall also apply.

(2) The application made in accordance with rule 29.1(1) must be accompanied by the video recording which it is proposed to tender in evidence and must include –

(a)   the name of the defendant and the offence to be charged;
(b)   the name and date of birth of the witness in respect of whom the application is made;
(c)   the date on which the video recording was made;
(d)   a statement as to whether, and if so at what point in the video recording, an oath was administered to, or a solemn declaration made by, the witness;
(e)   a statement that, in the opinion of the applicant, either –

        (i)   the witness is available for cross-examination, or
        (ii)   the witness is not available for cross-examination and the parties have agreed that there is no need for the witness to be so available;

(f)   a statement of the circumstances in which the video recording was made which complies with paragraph (4) of this rule; and
(g)   the date on which the video recording was disclosed to the other party or parties.

(3) Where it is proposed to tender part only of a video recording of an interview with the witness, the application must specify that part and be accompanied by a video recording of the entire interview, including those parts which it is not proposed to tender in evidence, and by a statement of the circumstances in which the video recording of the entire interview was made which complies with paragraph (4) of this rule.

(4) The statement of the circumstances in which the video recording was made referred to in paragraphs (2)(f) and (3) of this rule shall include the following information, except in so far as it is contained in the recording itself –

(a)   the times at which the recording commenced and finished, including details of interruptions;

(b)   the location at which the recording was made and the usual function of the premises;

(c)   in relation to each person present at any point during, or immediately before, the recording –

    (i)   their name, age and occupation,

    (ii)   the time for which each person was present, and

    (iii)   the relationship, if any, of each person to the witness and to the defendant;

(d)   in relation to the equipment used for the recording –

    (i)   a description of the equipment,

    (ii)   the number of cameras used,

    (iii)   whether the cameras were fixed or mobile,

    (iv)   the number and location of the microphones,

    (v)   the video format used; and

    (vi)   whether it offered single or multiple recording facilities and, if so, which were used; and

(e)   the location of the mastertape if the video recording is a copy and details of when and by whom the copy was made.

(5) If the special measures directions enabling a video recording of an interview of a witness to be admitted as evidence in chief of the witness with provision for the examination of the witness to be conducted through an intermediary, the information to be provided under paragraph (4)(c) shall be the same as that for other persons present at the recording but with the addition of details of the declaration made by the intermediary under rule 29.9.

(6) If the special measures directions enabling a video recording of an interview of a witness to be admitted as evidence in chief of the witness with provision for the witness, in accordance with section 30 of the Youth Justice and Criminal Evidence Act 1999, to be provided with a device as an aid to communication during the video recording of the interview the information to be included under paragraph (4)(d) shall include also details of any such device used for the purposes of recording.

(7) A party who receives a recording under paragraph (2) must within 14 days of its receipt, notify the applicant and the court officer, in writing –

(a)   whether he objects to the admission under section 27 of the 1999 Act of any part of the video recording or recordings disclosed, giving his reasons why it would not be in the interests of justice for the recording or any part of it to be admitted;

(b)   whether he would agree to the admission of part of the video recording or recordings and, if so, which part or parts; and

(c)   whether he wishes to be represented at any hearing of the application.

(8) A party who seeks to oppose an application for a special measures direction enabling a video recording of an interview of a child witness to be admitted as evidence in chief of the witness must, in order to comply with rule 29.1(6), state why in his view the giving of a special measures direction would not be likely to maximise the quality of the witness's evidence.

(9) However, paragraph (8) does not apply if the witness is a child witness in need of special protection.

(10) Notwithstanding the provisions of rule 29.1 and this rule, any video recording which the defendant proposes to tender in evidence need not be sent to the prosecution until the close of the prosecution case at the trial.

(11) The court may determine an application by the defendant to tender in evidence a video recording even though the recording has not, in accordance with paragraph (10), been served upon the prosecution.

(12) Where a video recording which is the subject of a special measures direction is sent to the prosecution after the direction has been made, the prosecutor may apply to the court for the direction to be varied or discharged.

(13) An application under paragraph (12) may be made orally to the court.

(14) A prosecutor who makes an application under paragraph (12) must state –

    (a)   why he objects to the admission under section 27 of the 1999 Act of any part of the video recording or recordings disclosed, giving his reasons why it would not be in the interests of justice for the recording or any part of it to be admitted; and

    (b)   whether he would agree to the admission of part of the video recording or recordings and, if so, which part or parts.

(15) The court must, before determining the application –

    (a)   direct a hearing of the application; and

    (b)   allow all the parties to the proceedings to be present and be heard on the application.

(16) The court officer must notify all parties to the proceedings of the decision of the court as soon as may be reasonable after the decision is given.

(17) Any decision varying a special measures direction must state whether the whole or specified parts of the video recording or recordings subject to the application are to be admitted in evidence.

29.8 Expert evidence in connection with special measures directions

Any party to proceedings in a magistrates' court or the Crown Court who proposes to adduce expert evidence (whether of fact or opinion) in connection with an application or renewal application for, or for varying or discharging, a special measures direction must, not less than 14 days before the date set for the trial to begin –

    (a)   furnish the other party or parties and the court with a statement in writing of any finding or opinion which he proposes to adduce by way of such evidence and notify the expert of this disclosure; and

    (b)   where a request is made to him in that behalf by any other party to those proceedings, provide that party also with a copy of (or if it appears to the party proposing to adduce the evidence to be more practicable, a reasonable opportunity to examine) the record of any observation, test, calculation or other procedure on which such finding or opinion is based and any document or other thing or substance in respect of which any such procedure has been carried out.

Amendments—SI 2006/2636.

29.9 Intermediaries

The declaration required to be made by an intermediary in accordance with section 29(5) of the Youth Justice and Criminal Evidence Act 1999 shall be in the following form:

> 'I solemnly, sincerely and truly declare that I will well and faithfully communicate questions and answers and make true explanation of all matters and things as shall be required of me according to the best of my skill and understanding.'

Form of application for a special measures direction under s.19 Youth Justice and Criminal Evidence Act 1999
(Criminal Procedure Rules, r 29.1(1), (2))

This form must be used when applying for a special measures direction in a magistrates' court or in the Crown Court.

An application in a **magistrates' court** must be made –

  (a)   where the application is made to a youth court, within 28 days of the date on which the defendant first appeared or was brought before a court in connection with an offence; or

  (b)   on any other application, within 14 days of the date the defendant first indicated his intention to plead not guilty to any offence.

An application in the **Crown Court** must be made within 28 days of –

  (a) the committal of the defendant;

  (b) the consent to the preferment of the bill of indictment;

  (c) a notice of transfer;

  (d) the service of copies of the documents containing the evidence on which the charge or charges are based under the Crime and Disorder Act 1998; or

  (e) the notice of appeal.

This form may also be used where an extension of time has been granted for the making of this application.

A copy of this form must be given at the same time to the other party or parties to the case.

PART A

To be completed by all applicants

Details required	*Notes*
Details of witness:	
Name of witness Date of birth of witness:	An application by the defence for evidence to be given through a live television link or by means of a video recording need not disclose who that witness is, except where the witness is to give evidence in support of an alibi.
If a previous application has been made to tender in evidence a video recording of testimony from the witness, give the date and (if known) result of that application.	If the applicant is the prosecutor, give the name of the witness (otherwise leave blank).

Case details:	
Name of Crown Prosecution Service office:	
Crown Prosecution Service number:	
Defendant(s): surname: Forenames:	
Case reference numbers: (a) unique reference number assigned by police: (b) trial number:	
Court area:	The area in which the court hearing the case is situated.
Charges:	Give brief details of those charges to which this application applies.
Details of application:	
Specify the special measures being sought:	
State the grounds on which the witness relies in support of the application for a special measures direction:	The statement should make clear whether the applicant seeks automatic eligibility (see Reasons for application section below) or whether the applicant alleges that the quality of the evidence will be reduced unless a direction is given. In the latter case, the grounds on which the applicant alleges that the quality of the witness's evidence is likely to be diminished in terms of completeness, coherence and accuracy should be clearly stated.
	Give a description of evidence submitted in support of this application:
	This requirement is optional. Examples of evidence might be: birth certificate; medical report; expert evidence; police report.
Arrangements which may be made available Give a brief description of the arrangements relevant to the measures applied for which may be made available in the area in which it is likely the hearing will take place:	
Reasons for application	
A Is the application for special measures for any of the following? (i) video recorded evidence in chief only; (ii) live link only; (iii) both these measures? Yes/No	
B Is the witness a child witness in need of special protection at the time that any relevant recording was made? Yes/No	A child in need of special protection is defined by section 21 of the Youth Justice and Criminal Evidence Act 1999

C Is the witness a child under 17 but not a child in need of special protection? Yes/No	
If the answer to both A and B is "Yes", information concerning the grounds of application and any views of the witness need not be provided.	Section 21 of the Youth Justice and Criminal Evidence Act 1999
If the answer to C is "Yes" and there is no application for either video recorded evidence in chief or live link, (or both) state the reasons why it is said that the special measures of video evidence in chief, live link, (or both) would NOT maximise the quality of the child's evidence.	Section 21 of the Youth Justice and Criminal Evidence Act 1999 sets out a primary rule in favour of providing child witnesses with video recorded evidence in chief and live link unless, for witnesses who are not child witnesses in need of special protection, this would not be likely to maximise the quality of the witness's evidence.
For all witnesses over 17 years and for applications for witnesses under 17 years for measures other than video recorded evidence in chief or live link:	
Give the grounds for believing the special measures being sought in this application will improve the quality of the witness's evidence:	
Give the views of the witness as to why the measures sought in this application are required:	
Material change of circumstances	
Give a description of any material change of circumstances relied upon to support this application:	This requirement applies only where (a) a special measures direction is already in force and application is being made to discharge or vary the direction, or (b) a previous application for a special measures direction was refused and this application seeks to reverse that decision.

PART B

To be completed if the application is for evidence to be given through a live television link

Details required	*Notes*
Details of application	
Give – (a) the address of any venue from which the witness will give evidence if the court's own live television link is not used:	
(b) the name of the person who it is proposed will accompany the witness:	An application by the defence need not disclose the name of the person proposed to accompany the witness if disclosure could lead to the identification of the witness.
(c) the occupation of this person; (d) the relationship (if any) of this person to the witness:	
Grounds State why it is believed that this person should accompany the witness:	

PART C

To be completed if the application is to tender in evidence a video recording under section 27 of the Youth Justice and Criminal Evidence Act 1999

Details required	*Notes*
Video recording(s)	
Statement as to circumstances in which video recording made:	These details need to be completed only to the extent that the information is not contained in the video recording itself. °
Date(s) of video recording(s):	
Time(s) of video recording(s):	Give the times at which recording began and finished, including details of any interruptions.
Location and normal function of premises where video recording made:	Give address of premises where recording made and state the usual function of those premises.
Details of those present while recording made	
Give details of each person present at any point during the recording.	Include name, age and occupation of anyone present; time for which present; relationship (if any) to witness and to the defendant.

- page 4 -

Use of an intermediary	
1 Was any person used as an intermediary in the making of the video recording?	
If so, has the court's approval for the purposes of section 29 of the Youth Justice and Criminal Evidence Act 1999 been given?	The court's approval for the purposes of section 29 of the Youth Justice and Criminal Evidence Act 1999 must be given before the Special Measures Direction is given. The court's approval may be sought at the hearing of the application for the Special Measures Direction.
If it has, give details.	If the court's approval has not been obtained the information required in Part C of this Form must be given
2 Did the intermediary make the appropriate declaration before the interview began?	
Is the declaration recorded on the video recording?	The declaration is – "I solemnly, sincerely and truly declare that I will well and faithfully communicate questions and answers and make true explanation of all matters and things as shall be required of me according to the best of my skill and understanding."
Equipment used	
Give a description of	The description must include the following information –
(a) the equipment used for the recording:	number and type of cameras used (fixed or mobile); the number and location of microphones; the video format used;
(b) any devices used as an aid to communication:	and whether it offered single or multiple recording facilities and if it did which were used. In the case of communication aids, describe how the device was operated. State also whether the equipment was provided for or owned by the witness or the intermediary and whether any additional needs arose for the witness or the intermediary as a result of using the devices (Refer to the examples given in Part C, paragraph 9(b)).
Recordings of part only of an interview	
State whether the video recording contains part only of the interview with the witness:	A copy of any video recordings of other parts of the interview with the witness which it is not proposed to tender in evidence must also be provided to the court and the other parties. The details of each such recording must be given as above. Use separate sheets where necessary.
Details of copy	
State in respect of each video recording whether it is a copy, and give the following details in respect of each copy –	
Name and address of person who has the master tape:	
When, and by whom, the copy was made:	

Attendance and supply of copies	
In the opinion of the applicant – (a) is the witness available for cross-examination? (b) if the witness is not available for cross-examination, have the parties agreed that the witness need not be available?	
Has the agreement of the other parties to the video recording(s) being tendered as evidence been sought?	
Have copies of the video recording(s) to which this application relates been disclosed to the other parties?	
Has a copy of this notice and the video recording(s) to which it relates been served on each party to the proceedings? °	Where the application is by the defendant, the video recording(s) do not have to be served on the prosecution until the close of the prosecution case at the trial.
Signature of applicant or applicant's Solicitor:	Date:

PART D	
To be completed if the application is for the examination of the witness to be conducted through an intermediary or if the court's approval is being sought retrospectively to the use of an intermediary in a video recording	
Details required	*Notes*
Details of application	
1 Give a description of the communication needs of the witness:	Where an assessment has been undertaken by a relevant professional, give details of where and by whom the assessment was carried out.
2 State why you consider that the quality of the evidence given by the witness would be improved by use of an intermediary:	
3 Give the name of the person through whom it is proposed the examination of the witness be conducted:	
4 What is the occupation of this person and what is the person's area of specialism:	
5 Is this person related to the witness? If not related to the witness, does the intermediary know the witness and, if so, how and to what extent?	
6 Is this person registered with the Intermediary Registration Board?	If the person is not registered with the IRB, give the reason why this person is preferred to an IRB registered person.
7 Why do you consider this person has the necessary skills to meet the particular communication needs of the witness:	
8 Has this person been used in the pre-trial investigation?	If so, give reasons why it is proposed to use the same person throughout the proceedings.
- page 7 -	

9 Communication aids	
(a) give details of any devise used or which it is intended to use as a communication aid:	Give details of any devices that may be used and how they are operated.
(b) are there any issues which arise as a result of this device being used?	Examples might be: (a) whether breaks might be needed for the witness and/or the intermediary: (b) the facilities that may be needed for the use of the devices, for example power sources.
- page 8 —	

[Note: Formerly in the Schedule to the Magistrates' Courts (Special Measures Directions) Rules 2002 (SI 2002/1687, as amended), relating to rule 2 of those Rules and in the Schedule to the Crown Court (Special Measures Directions and Directions Prohibiting Cross-examination) (Amendments) Rules 2004 (SI 2004/185), relating to rule 2 of the Crown Court (Special Measures Directions and Directions Prohibiting Cross-examination) Rules 2002]

PART 50

CIVIL BEHAVIOUR ORDERS AFTER VERDICT OR FINDING

Contents of this Part

When this Part applies   rule 50.1
Behaviour orders: general rules   rule 50.2
Application for behaviour order: special rules   rule 50.3
Evidence to assist the court: special rules   rule 50.4
Application to vary or revoke behaviour order   rule 50.5
Notice of hearsay evidence   rule 50.6
Cross-examination of maker of hearsay statement   rule 50.7
Credibility and consistency of maker of hearsay statement   rule 50.8
Court's power to vary requirements under this Part   rule 50.9
Amendments—SI 2007/3662.

50.1 When this Part applies

(1) This Part applies in magistrates' courts and in the Crown Court where the court could decide to make, vary or revoke a civil order –

    (a)   under a power that the court can exercise after reaching a verdict or making a finding, and
    (b)   that requires someone to do, or not do, something.

(2) A reference to a 'behaviour order' in this Part is a reference to any such order.

(3) A reference to 'hearsay evidence' in this Part is a reference to evidence consisting of hearsay within the meaning of section 1(2) of the Civil Evidence Act 1995.

Amendments—SI 2007/3662.

50.2 Behaviour orders: general rules

(1) The court must not make a behaviour order unless the person to whom it is directed has had an opportunity –

    (a)   to consider what order is proposed and why; and
    (b)   to make representations at a hearing (whether or not that person in fact attends).

(2) That restriction does not apply to making an interim behaviour order.

(3) But an interim behaviour order has no effect unless the person to whom it is directed –

    (a)   is present when it is made; or
    (b)   is handed a document recording the order not more than 7 days after it is made.

Amendments—SI 2007/3662.

50.3 Application for behaviour order: special rules

(1) This rule applies where a prosecutor wants the court to make –

    (a)   an anti-social behaviour order; or
    (b)   a serious crime prevention order,

if the defendant is convicted.

(2) The prosecutor must serve a notice of intention to apply for such an order on –

(a) the court officer;

(b) the defendant against whom the prosecutor wants the court to make the order; and

(c) any person on whom the order would be likely to have a significant adverse effect,

as soon as practicable (without waiting for the verdict).

(3) The notice must be in the form set out in the Practice Direction and must –

(a) summarise the relevant facts;

(b) identify the evidence on which the prosecutor relies in support;

(c) attach any written statement that the prosecutor has not already served; and

(d) specify the order that the prosecutor wants the court to make.

(4) The defendant must then –

(a) serve written notice of any evidence on which the defendant relies on –

(i) the court officer, and

(ii) the prosecutor,

as soon as practicable (without waiting for the verdict); and

(b) in the notice, identify that evidence and attach any written statement that has not already been served.

(5) This rule does not apply to an application for an interim anti-social behaviour order.

Amendments—SI 2007/3662.

50.4 Evidence to assist the court: special rules

(1) This rule applies where the court indicates that it may make on its own initiative –

(a) a football banning order;

(b) a restraining order;

(c) an anti-social behaviour order; or

(d) a drinking banning order.

(2) A party who wants the court to take account of any particular evidence before making that decision must –

(a) serve notice in writing on –

(i) the court officer, and

(ii) every other party,

as soon as practicable (without waiting for the verdict); and

(b) in that notice identify that evidence and attach any written statement that has not already been served.

Amendments—SI 2007/3662.

50.5 Application to vary or revoke behaviour order

(1) The court may vary or revoke a behaviour order if –

(a) the legislation under which it is made allows the court to do so; and

(b) one of the following applies –

(i) the prosecutor,

(ii) the person to whom the order is directed,

(iii) any other person mentioned in the order,

(iv) the relevant authority or responsible officer,

(v) the relevant Chief Officer of Police, or

(vi) the Director of Public Prosecutions.

(2) A person applying under this rule must –

(a) apply in writing as soon as practicable after becoming aware of the grounds for doing so, explaining why the order should be varied or revoked; and

(b) serve the application, and any notice under paragraph (3), on the court officer and, as appropriate, anyone listed in paragraph (1)(b).

(3) A party who wants the court to take account of any particular evidence before making its decision must, as soon as practicable –

(a) serve notice in writing on –

(i) the court officer, and
(ii) as appropriate, anyone listed in paragraph (1)(b); and

(b) in that notice identify the evidence and attach any written statement that has not already been served.

(4) The court may decide an application under this rule with or without a hearing.

(5) But the court must not –

(a) dismiss an application under this rule unless the applicant has had an opportunity to make representations at a hearing (whether or not the applicant in fact attends); or

(b) allow an application under this rule unless everyone served with the application has had at least 14 days in which to make representations, including representations about whether there should be a hearing.

(6) Where a person applies under this rule to a magistrates' court –

(a) the application must be by complaint; and
(b) the court officer must give notice by summons of any hearing.

Amendments—SI 2007/3662.

50.6 Notice of hearsay evidence

(1) A party who wants to introduce hearsay evidence must –

(a) serve notice in writing on –

(i) the court officer, and
(ii) every other party directly affected; and

(b) in that notice –

(i) explain that it is a notice of hearsay evidence,
(ii) identify that evidence,
(iii) identify the person who made the statement which is hearsay, or explain why if that person is not identified, and
(iv) explain why that person will not be called to give oral evidence.

(2) A party may serve one notice under this rule in respect of more than one statement and more than one witness.

Amendments—SI 2007/3662.

50.7 Cross-examination of maker of hearsay statement

(1) This rule applies where a party wants the court's permission to cross-examine a person who made a statement which another party wants to introduce as hearsay.

(2) The party who wants to cross-examine that person must –

(a) apply in writing, with reasons, not more than 7 days after service of the notice of hearsay evidence; and
(b) serve the application on –

    (i) the court officer,
    (ii) the party who served the hearsay evidence notice, and
    (iii) every party on whom the hearsay evidence notice was served.

(3) The court may decide an application under this rule with or without a hearing.

(4) But the court must not –

(a) dismiss an application under this rule unless the applicant has had an opportunity to make representations at a hearing (whether or not the applicant in fact attends); or
(b) allow an application under this rule unless everyone served with the application has had at least 7 days in which to make representations, including representations about whether there should be a hearing.

Amendments—SI 2007/3662.

50.8 Credibility and consistency of maker of hearsay statement

(1) This rule applies where a party wants to challenge the credibility or consistency of a person who made a statement which another party wants to introduce as hearsay.

(2) The party who wants to challenge the credibility or consistency of that person must –

(a) serve a written notice of intention to do so on –

    (i) the court officer, and
    (ii) the party who served the notice of hearsay evidence
    not more than 7 days after service of that hearsay evidence notice; and

(b) in the notice, identify any statement or other material on which that party relies.

(3) The party who served the hearsay notice –

(a) may call that person to give oral evidence instead; and
(b) if so, must serve a notice of intention to do so on –

    (i) the court officer, and
    (ii) every party on whom he served the hearsay notice

    not more than 7 days after service of the notice under paragraph (2).

Amendments—SI 2007/3662.

50.9 Court's power to vary requirements under this Part

The court may –

(a) shorten a time limit or extend it (even after it has expired);
(b) allow a notice or application to be given in a different form, or presented orally.

Amendments—SI 2007/3662.

PRACTICE DIRECTION

8 JULY 2002

Consolidated Criminal Practice

As amended and reissued 18 May 2004.

****

III.29 Support for witnesses giving evidence by live television link

(III.29.1) This section of the Practice Direction is made pursuant to Rule 7 of the Crown Court (Special Measures Directions and Directions Prohibiting Cross-examination) Rules 2002 and Rule 7 of the Magistrates' Courts (Special Measures Directions) Rules 2002 and supersedes previous guidance given by the Senior Presiding Judges, Lord Justice Tasker Watkins in 1991 and Lord Justice Auld in 1998.

(III.29.2) An increased degree of flexibility is now appropriate as to who can act as supporter of a witness giving evidence by live television link. Where a special measures direction is made enabling a vulnerable, intimidated or child witness to give evidence by means of a live television link, the trial judge will make a direction as to the identity of the witness supporter. Where practical, the direction will be made before the trial commences. In giving the direction, the trial judge will balance all relevant interests – see paragraph 1.11 of the guidance 'Achieving Best Evidence'. The witness supporter should be completely independent of the witness and his or her family and have no previous knowledge of or personal involvement in the case. The supporter should also be suitably trained so as to understand the obligations of, and comply with, the National Standards relating to witness supporters. Providing these criteria are met, the witness supporter need not be an usher or court official. Thus, for example, the functions of the witness supporter may be performed by a representative of the Witness Service.

(III.29.3) Where the witness supporter is someone other than the court usher, the usher should continue to be available both to assist the witness and the witness supporter, and to ensure that the judge's requirements are properly complied with in the CCTV room.

****

IV.40 Video recorded evidence in chief

(IV.40.1) The procedure for making application for leave to adduce a video recording of testimony from a witness under section 27 of the Youth Justice and Criminal Evidence Act 1999 is laid down in rule 8 of the Crown Court (Special Measures Directions and Directions Prohibiting Cross-Examination) Rules 2002 (S.I. 2002 No. 1688).

(IV.40.2) Where a court, on application by a party to the proceedings or of its own motion, grants leave to admit a video recording in evidence under section 27(1) of the 1999 Act it may direct that any part of the recording be excluded (section 27(2) and (3)). When such direction is given, the party who made application to admit the video recording must edit the recording in accordance with the judge's directions and send a copy of the edited recording to the appropriate officer of the Crown Court and to every other party to the proceedings.

(IV.40.3) Where a video recording is to be adduced during proceedings before the Crown Court, it should be produced and proved by the interviewer, or any other person who was present at the interview with the witness at which the recording was made. The applicant should ensure that such a person will be available for this purpose, unless the parties have agreed to accept a written statement in lieu of attendance by that person.

****

APPENDIX 2

PRECEDENTS

A2.1

DRAFT ASBO APPLICATION

SCHEDULE 1
FORM
Application for Anti-Social Behaviour Order
Crime and Disorder Act 1998, Section 1(1)

In the ………………… Magistrates' Court

[*address of the court*] [*court code*]

Date ……………………………………………

Defendant: **Fred Anti-Social** DOB 7 June 1994
[*Defendant's address*]

Local government area in respect ………………… council
of which application is made:

Relevant authorities consulted: ………………… police
………………… council etc.

And it is alleged:

(a)   That the defendant has acted on the dates and at the places listed in the schedule below in an anti-social manner, that is to say, in a manner that has caused or is likely to cause harassment, alarm or distress to one or more persons not of the same household as himself; and

(b)   That an anti-social behaviour order is necessary to protect relevant persons from further anti-social acts by him,

The applicant applies for an order that:

Fred Anti-social must not

1   Engage in conduct which causes or is likely to cause alarm, distress or harassment to others or inciting or encouraging others to do so within the ………………… council area;

2   Buy, attempt to buy or to possess fireworks;

3   Have any contact with, and/or attempt to communicate with Mr and Mrs White;

4   Enter or attempt to enter the Careful Secondary School or its grounds without the express written permission of the headmaster or deputy headmaster at the time;

5   Enter or attempt or enter and/or remain in any place within the area bordered in green as marked on the attached map.

Schedule/Short Description of Acts

Date	Details
21 May 2008	Was verbally abusive to Mrs Black calling her a 'bitch'.

5 June 2008	Threatened Mr White and said 'I'll punch you and your son's going to get a punch'.
6 July 2008	Shouted abuse repeatedly at Mrs Pink.
10 Aug 2008	Left the classroom without permission, disrupted other lessons by banging on windows and doors and being verbally abusive. Climbed onto the roof and caused damage to the roof and then absconded.
13 Aug 2008	Re-entered the Careful Secondary School having been excluded from the same. Whilst there, was abusive to staff and threatened them.
19 Aug 2008	Re-entered the Careful Secondary School and was verbally abusive banging on objects to disrupt other classes and threw apples at staff.
1 Sept 2008	Punched another child in the face without provocation at school.
2 Sept 2008	Assaulted a pupil and repeated this although removed by staff. Was abusive to staff and damaged 2 cars when leaving.
12 Sept 2008	Verbally abused and/or was part of a group that verbally abused Mr Black and fired fireworks at his house and later told Mr Black that he was going to chin him.
13 Sept 2008	Made an obscene gesture and shouted 'Oi Wanker' at Mr Green.
13 Sept 2008	Made an obscene finger gesture to Mrs White.
31 Oct 2008	Assaulted a fellow pupil at the Careful Secondary School. When challenged was extremely violent threatening people and threw bricks at the school and staff.
30 Nov 2008	Shouted abuse and threw an egg at Mr and Mrs White's home.

The applicant will also rely on the defendant's criminal convictions and incidents of anti-social behaviour prior to the above incidents in support of the application. The details of the same are contained in the attached schedule.

The complaint of:　　　　　　　　　　　　...

Applying body
[*Address of applying body*]

Who [upon oath] states that the defendant was responsible for the acts of which the particulars are given above, in respect of which this complaint is made.

Taken before me,　　　　　　　　　...

Justice of the Peace/Justices' Clerk

A2.2

DRAFT ASBO

**Anti-social Behaviour Order
Crime and Disorder Act 1998, Section 1(1)**

In the .... Magistrates' Court
[*Court address*] [*court code*]

Date ....

Defendant: **Fred Anti-Social** DOB 7 June 1994
[Defendant's address]

Local government area in respect
of which application is made: .... council

Relevant authorities consulted: .... police

.... council etc.

The .... Magistrates' Court having found:

(a) that Fred Anti-Social has acted on the dates and at the places listed in the schedule below/attached in an anti-social manner, that is to say, in a manner that has caused or is likely to cause harassment, alarm or distress to one or more persons not of the same household as himself; and

(b) that an anti-social behaviour order is necessary to protect relevant persons from further anti-social acts by him.

Fred Anti-Social is prohibited from [*delete as appropriate from sample terms below*]:

1 Acting in a manner which causes or is likely to cause nuisance, harassment, alarm or distress to any person in the .... council area as shown on the attached map bordered in red.

2 Entering or attempting to enter the area marked and outlined in red on the attached map save:

(a) to and from his place of residence and then only by means of the route marked blue on the attached map;

(b) for the purposes attending pre-arranged doctors or dentists appointments within the area and then by and returning by the most direct route [or marked route if appropriate];

(c) when in the company of or under the direction of the probation service or youth offending team workers.

3 Painting, drawing, spraying, writing, or otherwise putting graffiti on any surface not belonging to you, except with the express permission of the owner of the surface.

4 Possessing a can of spray paint, marker pen in a public place.

5 Having contact with, in public, whether by being in a group with, talking to or otherwise associating with [*insert names*].

6 Touching or attempting to enter any unoccupied vehicle without the express permission of the owner.

7 Being in possession of alcohol in open bottles, cans, cups or containers in a public place.

8 Being in possession of any solvent, for example glue, thinner, petrol, butane gas, etc, in a public place.

9 Begging in the areas edged in red on the attached map.

10 Not to possess, light or throw fireworks or attempt to do so.

11 Wearing clothing within the ...... area, whether a balaclava, hood, mask, scarf or other item of clothing so as to hide your facial features or identity.

12   Possessing or using a '2-way' radio, walkie-talkie, open band radio, police radio or radio scanner.

13   Encouraging or inciting others to carry out any of the prohibited acts on your behalf.

14   Not to be part of a group of 4 or more people in [*insert street name*].

15   Not to be abusive to any member of staff in any GP's office or hospital.

16   Contacting, whether directly or indirectly [*insert names of witnesses*].

17   Being away from [*insert address*] between the hours of 22:00 and 8:00 the next morning unless accompanied by one or both parents, social worker, youth team worker or person authorised as a carer by social services.

18   Not to drink alcohol in a public place save on licensed premises.

19   Not to be in possession of opened cans or bottles of alcohol in a public place.

THIS ORDER SHALL REMAIN IN FORCE
UNTIL . . . .

IF WITHOUT REASONABLE EXCUSE, YOU DO ANYTHING WHICH YOU MUST NOT DO BY REASON OF THIS ORDER YOU WILL BE LIABLE ON CONVICTION TO IMPRISONMENT FOR A TERM NOT EXCEEDING 5 YEARS (2 years if a minor) OR TO A FINE OR BOTH

. . . .
Justice of the Peace/District Judge (Magistrates' Courts)

A2.3

APPLICATION FOR INTERIM ANTI-SOCIAL BEHAVIOUR ORDER

SCHEDULE 5 FORM
Application for interim order
Crime and Disorder Act 1988, s 10

In the .... Magistrates' Court
[*Court address*] [*Court code*]

Date ....

Defendant: **Fred Anti-Social** DOB: 7 June 1994

Defendant's address: ....

Local government area in respect .... council
of which application is made:

Relevant authorities consulted: .... police

.... council etc.

Reasons for applying for an interim order:

The defendant has been responsible for anti-social behaviour in the area which has been of a serious nature. Many witnesses are too intimidated by fear of reprisals if they give evidence. His conduct has caused severe distress to several of the witnesses, one of whom is seriously ill and it is feared that if the application is delayed for any reason, e g pending criminal charges, then the witnesses will be at severe risk of intimidation. Further the defendant has conducted such a large number of acts of anti-social behaviour despite being served with an intention to seek an order that it is feared that the behaviour will not cease unless an interim order is granted. The defendant's response to being challenged is to be aggressive and to commit further acts. There is an urgent need for an interim order to prevent further acts pending the hearing of the full application.

Do you wish this application to be heard: [ ] without notice being given to the defendant

[ ] with notice being given to the defendant

If you wish the application to be heard without notice state reasons:

The order has been made without notice because the defendant's acts of anti-social behaviour are serious and escalating and there is a significant risk that he will further intimidate witnesses if he is given notice of the intention to apply for an interim order. There is therefore an urgent need to obtain protection for the community and witnesses.

Reasons for applying without notice

Sample reasons:

This interim order is required to be made initially without notice as the defendant has committed and continues to commit acts against the main witnesses which include physical threats and verbal abusive and intimidation. If the defendant is given notice of this hearing there is a real likelihood that he will commit acts of anti-social behaviour particularly against the witnesses before any hearing of the application for an interim order could take place. Therefore, there is an urgent need for an interim order without notice.

The complaint of: ....

[name and address of applying body]

Who [upon oath] states that the defendant was responsible for the acts of which the particulars are given above, in respect of which this complaint is made.

Taken [and sworn] before me, ...

Justice of the Peace/Justices' Clerk/District Judge
(Magistrates' Court)

A2.4

INTERIM ANTI-SOCIAL BEHAVIOUR ORDER

[   ] **Magistrates' Courts Service**
Interim Order
(Crime and Disorder Act 1998, s 1D)

In the .... Magistrates' Court
[*Court address*] [*Court code*]

Date:

Defendant: **Fred Anti-social** DOB 2 October 1983

Address:

On the complaint of:

Applicant authority:

Address of the applicant:

Authority:

The court makes an Interim Anti-Social Behaviour Order against the defendant.

Reasons for making this order are:

The defendant is alleged to have conducted a number of acts of anti-social behaviour and it is feared that this behaviour will not cease prior to the full hearing of this matter unless an interim order is granted.

And the court found that it is just to make this order pending the determination of the application for an anti-social behaviour order, which application is attached to this order.

This order has been made with notice.

The court orders that **Fred Anti-social** is prohibited from:

1   Acting in a manner which causes or is likely to cause nuisance, harassment, alarm or distress to any person in the area of ....;

2   Leaving [*insert address*] between the hours of 21:00 and 07:00 the next morning;

3   Not to enter the area marked in green on the attached map as the exclusion zone;

4   Encouraging or inciting others to carry out any of the prohibited acts on your behalf.

Address of the applicant authority:

This order will end on

The court also orders all parties to attend at .... Magistrates' Court, ...
On [*insert date if pre-trial review date or further consideration of interim order*]
Or [*use if main application date is fixed*]
A hearing will take place in respect of the main application on .... Magistrates' Court on
.... at .... am/pm

....
District Judge (Magistrates' Courts)/Justice of the Peace

Note—If, without reasonable excuse, the defendant does anything which she is prohibited from doing by this order, he shall be liable on conviction to a term of imprisonment not exceeding five years (two if a minor) or to a fine or to both.

About this Order

This is an interim anti-social behaviour order. The court has made this order because it considers it just to do so pending the determination of an application for an anti-social behaviour order against you. The court believes that you have acted in an anti-social manner, and that this order is necessary to protect people from further anti-social acts by you. Anti-social behaviour is behaviour which caused or was likely to cause harassment, alarm or distress to people outside of your household.

If, without reasonable excuse, you do anything which is prohibited by this order you will be guilty of an offence, for which you could be punished by a term of imprisonment or by a fine or by both.

The order will end on the date specified unless a further order is made.

You may apply to the court to end or to vary this order. You should consult a solicitor or the court office to find out how to do this.

You must attend court for the next hearing date, which is specified in the summons accompanying this order.

A2.5

ORDERS ON CONVICTION

(a) Crown Court Post-conviction Order

Order on Conviction
(Crime and Disorder Act 1998, s 1C)

.... Crown Court

[*Court code*]

1   On the .... [*date*] Crown Court sitting at .... convicted:

Name: .... [*the defendant*] of

Address: ....
                 ....

Date of   .... of
birth:

Offences: .... [*relevant offence(s)*]

and imposed the following sentence/conditional discharge ....

2   The court found that:

    (i)   the defendant had acted in an anti-social manner which caused or was likely to cause harassment, alarm or distress to one or more persons not of the same household as himself

....
....
....

[*details of behaviour*]

and that:

    (ii)   an order was necessary to protect persons in England and Wales from further anti-social acts by him.

3   It is ordered that the defendant .... [*name*] is prohibited from:

....
....
....

[Where appropriate, the court must specify whether any of the requirements of the order are suspended until the defendant's release from custody]

....
....
....

Until [ ] [further order]

The Judge

Note—If without reasonable excuse the defendant does anything which he is prohibited from doing by this order, he shall be liable on conviction to a term of imprisonment not exceeding five years or to a fine or to both.

(b) Suggested Precedent for Post-convicton Order in the Magistrates' court

Order on Conviction
(Crime and Disorder Act 1998, s 1C)

.... Magistrates' Court/Youth Court

[*Court code*]

1   On the: .... [date] the Magistrates' Court/Youth Court
     sitting at .... convicted

Name: .... [*the defendant*] of

Address: ....

               ....

Date of   .... of
birth:

Offences: .... [*relevant offence(s)*]

and imposed the following sentence/conditional discharge ....

2   The court found that:

     (i)   the defendant had acted in the following anti-social manner, which caused or was likely to
            cause harassment, alarm or distress to one or more persons not of the same household as
            himself,

....

....

[*details of behaviour*] (see attached schedule)

and that

     (ii)   an order was necessary to protect persons in England and Wales from further anti-social
            acts by him.

3   It is ordered that the defendant

....

[*name*] is prohibited from:

....

[Where appropriate, the court must specify whether any of the requirements of the order are suspended
until the defendant's release from custody]

Until [   ]/[further order]

Justice of the Peace/District Judge (Magistrates' Courts)

Note—If without reasonable excuse the defendant does anything which he is prohibited from doing by this order, he shall be liable on
conviction to a term of imprisonment not exceeding five years (two years if a minor) or to a fine or to both.

A2.6

COUNTY COURT ANTI-SOCIAL BEHAVIOUR ORDER (FORM N113)

Anti-social behaviour
(Order under section 1B(4) of
the Crime and Disorder Act 1998)

In the	
	County Court
Claim No.	
Claimant	
Applicant	
Defendant	

SEAL

On   20   , District Judge
sitting at

considered the application of the [claimant] [applicant] [defendant] and found that
the [claimant] [defendant] has acted in an anti-social manner that caused or was likely to cause
harassment, alarm or distress to one or more persons not of the same household as [himself] [herself]; **and**
that this order is necessary to protect persons from further anti-social acts by the [claimant] [defendant]
and the court ordered that the [claimant] [defendant] is forbidden from:-

until [   ] [further order]

[The [claimant] [applicant] [or] [defendant] may apply to the court for this order to be varied or discharged.
Unless both parties consent, this order may not be discharged within two years of the order being served.]

To

You **must** obey this order. If, without reasonable excuse, you do anything which you are forbidden from doing
by this order, you will be liable on conviction to a term of imprisonment not exceeding five years or to a
fine or to both.

[Notice of further hearing [(see also note overleaf)]
The court will re-consider the application and whether the order should continue at a further hearing
at

on   the   day of   20 at   o'clock

If you do not attend at the time shown the court may make an order in your absence.]

N113 Anti-social behaviour (Order under s1B(4) of the Crime and Disorder Act 1998) (04.03)

Anti social behaviour order - Record of hearing   Claim No.

On   the   day of   20

Before District Judge

The court was sitting at

The   [claimant]   [applicant]

was   ☐ represented by counsel
         ☐ represented by a solicitor
         ☐ in person

The   [claimant]   [defendant]

was   ☐ represented by counsel
         ☐ represented by a solicitor
         ☐ in person
         ☐ not given notice of this hearing

or

         ☐ did not appear having been given notice of this hearing

The court read the statements of
         ☐ the claimant
         ☐ the applicant
         ☐ the defendant

[And of]

[The court heard spoken evidence on oath from]

Signed_____ Dated_____

[**Note:** This order was made without notice being given to you. You may apply for it to be set aside, varied or stayed. If you wish to apply, do not delay. You must make your application to the court within 7 days of the date you received it. You may make your application by writing to the court or asking the court for a Form N244 Application Notice. You will have to pay a fee to make your application unless you qualify for fee exemption or remission]

A2.7

HEARSAY NOTICE

IN AN APPLICATION FOR AN ANTI-SOCIAL BEHAVOUR ORDER
PURSUANT TO
Crime and Disorder Act 1998, s 1(1) and the Magistrates' Courts (Hearsay Evidence in Civil Proceedings) Rules 1999

BETWEEN

[applicant authority]	Applicant
and	
V. ANTI-SOCIAL	Defendant

**NOTICE OF INTENTION TO
RELY ON
HEARSAY EVIDENCE**

1   The complainant intends to rely on hearsay evidence at trial and that evidence is contained in the witness statement of Mr Blue dated 3 January 2009 which has already been served but is also attached to this notice for reference.

2   Mr Blue is a Tenancy Enforcement Officer who has been provided with information that has been relayed to him by other housing officers who can no longer be traced or by witnesses to incidents who are have either moved away and cannot be contacted or are too frightened due to fear of reprisals by the defendant. Those witnesses who names are known and were content for their identity to be disclosed are given in the statement. The remaining witnesses names are either not known to the applicant or the witnesses were too afraid to have their names disclosed. The statement indicates in each case the source of the evidence and whether as above the identity of the giver is known and/or can be disclosed.

3   The applicant seeks rely on the above evidence in its application for an anti-social behaviour order against the defendant.

Signed   Dated
....

NOTICE OF INTENTION TO APPLY FOR AN ANTI-SOCIAL BEHAVIOUR ORDER IF THE DEFENDANT IS CONVICTED

AND

PROPOSED APPLICATION

Criminal Procedure Rules 2005, r 50.3

R v FRED BLOGGS

Case reference number: ……………………………..

In the Crown Court

at………………………………………………(*or*)

In the ALL RISE Magistrates' Court/Youth Court

1 **THIS NOTICE is to tell you** [*name and address of the defendant against whom the prosecutor intends to apply to the court for an anti-social behaviour order*]

FRED BLOGGS OF 2 THE VALES, NOWHERE

that if you are convicted of one or more offences with which you have been charged, the prosecutor intends to apply to the court for an anti-social behaviour order to be made against you.[1]

2 **THE TERMS OF THE ORDER** the prosecutor wants the court to make are:

The defendant must not: [*prosecutor to specify here the prohibitions required*]

………………………………………………………………………………………………

………………………………………………………………………………………………

3 **NOTICE TO THE DEFENDANT SERVED** with this document:

If you are convicted, you will have an opportunity to explain to the court why you think the proposed order should not be made. (Written notice of any evidence you rely on needs to be served on the court officer and the prosecutor.)[2]

1Acting in a manner which causes or is likely to cause nuisance, harassment, alarm or distress to any person in the area of Nowhere as bordered in the attached map

2Leaving [*insert address*] between the hours of 21:00 and 07:00 the next morning;

4 **Name and address of prosecutor:**

Name: [Mr Prosecutor]

Address: [Prosecution Street]

Prosecuting authority (*if applicable*):

………………………………………………………………………………………………

5 **Offence(s) with which the defendant is charged/has been convicted:**

(a)   Assault occasioning actual bodily harm

(b)   Burglary of a dwelling house

6 **Attachments in support of the proposed application:**

(i)   **Description of behaviour** [*a list, with dates, of the specific acts of anti-social behaviour upon which the prosecutor will rely in making this application*]

21 May 2008	Was verbally abusive to Mrs Black calling her a 'bitch'
5 June 2008	Threatened Mr White and said 'I'll punch you and your son's going to get a punch'
13 Aug 2008	Was abusive to Careful Secondary school staff, Mrs Black and Pink and threatened them.
1 Sept 2008	Punched another child in the face without provocation at school
2 Sept 2008	Assaulted a pupil. Was abusive to staff and damaged 2 cars when leaving
12 Sept 2008	Verbally abused Mr Black and fired fireworks at his house
13 Sept 2008	Made an obscene gesture and shouted 'Oi Wanker' at Mr Green
13 Sept 2008	Made an obscene finger gesture to Mrs White

(ii)   **Evidence to be relied on** (eg witness statements, any previous convictions):

    (a)   a list of such evidence that has already been served;

Witness statements of:

Mrs Smith dated 1.11.08

Mr Black dated 2.11.08

Mr Green dated 3.11.08

    (b)   a list of such evidence that has not yet been served and is attached to and served with this notice.

Witness statement from Mr Blue dated 1.3.09

Mrs Pink dated 1.3.09

School log

Police log

Photographs of injuries

(iii)   Notice of any hearsay evidence to be relied on.

See attached notice

(iv)   Other documents served with this notice [*The prosecutor is required to list and attach all other documents now served, such as a map of the proposed exclusion area*].

Signed

....

Prosecutor

Date: ....

This notice and proposed application must be served, with the listed attachments upon which the application will be based, as soon as possible

APPENDIX 3

A GUIDE TO ANTI-SOCIAL BEHAVIOUR ORDERS

CONTENTS

Ministerial foreword

Introduction

1. **Anti-social behaviour orders: the basics**

   What are anti-social behaviour orders?

   What sort of behaviour can be tackled by ASBOs?

   Legal definition of anti-social behaviour for the purpose of obtaining an order

   Standard of proof

   Against whom can an order be made?

   Who can apply for an order?

   Which courts can make ASBOs?

   Length of orders

   Anti-social behaviour response courts

   Orders made in county court proceedings (section 1B of the Crime and Disorder Act 1998)

2. **Taking a strategic approach**

   Orders made on conviction in criminal proceedings

   Where is an ASBO valid?

   Can interim orders be made?

   Interim orders made in the county courts

   Orders against children and young people

   Breach of an order

   Expert prosecutors

   Standard ASBO form

   Disposals

3. **Managing the application process**

   Partnership working

   Taking ownership

   Other considerations

   Collection of evidence

   Together campaign fact sheet

4. **Time limits**

   Magistrates' courts (acting in their civil capacity)

5. **Use of hearsay and professional witness evidence**

   Hearsay evidence

   Professional witnesses

   Vulnerable and intimidated witnesses

   Witness development and support

   Improving protection of witnesses in court

6. **Information sharing**

   Information sharing and registered social landlords

   Information sharing protocols

7. **The terms of the order (the prohibitions)**

The role of the agencies

The courts

Effective prohibitions

Length of prohibitions

Targeting specific behaviour

Duration of an order

8. **Applying to the courts**

Summons procedure

Disclosure

Court procedures

Orders made on conviction in criminal proceedings

Interim orders on conviction

Step-by-step guide 37 Public funding for defendants

9. **Children and young people**

Who can apply for an order?

Individual support orders

10. **Immediate post-order procedure (adults and young people)**

Good practice – managing procedures and timescales

Enforcing the order

One year review of juveniles' ASBOs

Police National Computer (PNC)

11. **Appeals**

Magistrates' court (acting in its civil capacity) and orders on conviction in criminal proceedings

County court

Appeals to the High Court by case stated

Appeals before the Crown Court

Rectification of mistakes

Application for judicial review

12. **Breaches**

Breaches by adults

Breaches by children and young people

13. **Variation and discharge of an order**

14. **Monitoring and recording**

15. **Promoting awareness of orders**

Suggested aims of the strategy

Publicity

Principles

Benefits of publicity

The decision to publish

The decision-making process

What publicity should look like: are the contents proportionate?

Type of information to include in publicity

Age consideration

Photographs

Distribution of publicity

Consideration of human rights

Consideration of data protection

Type of publicity

Working with the media

Appendices
Appendix A Early intervention and tackling offending behaviour by under-10s
Appendix B County court Practice Direction according to the Civil Procedure Rules
Appendix C Order form
Appendix D Summons form
Appendix E Step-by-step process for anti-social behaviour orders and orders on conviction
Appendix F Public funding for defendants
Further reading

Ministerial foreword

It is now seven years since anti-social behaviour orders (ASBOs) were introduced following the Crime and Disorder Act 1998. Since then over 7,300 ASBOs have been issued. We often hear from residents up and down the country about how useful they are in bringing respite to communities suffering anti-social behaviour. The drive to tackle anti-social behaviour has been pioneered by anti-social behaviour practitioners and other interested parties all over England and Wales.

During this time much has happened:

- For our part we have adjusted policy and response to changing demands prompted by practitioners to ensure that the tool continues to be effective.

- The Together ActionLine, website and Academy events have provided an excellent source of advice and ensured spread of good practice.

- Practitioners have developed protocols and helpful leaflets to improve communication between themselves.

- A number of organisations have also organised seminars and conferences to bring practitioners together, debate problem areas and resolve issues between them.

- The courts have responded and played their part and we particularly welcome Lord Justice Thomas's guidance, which has been referred to substantially for the revision of this guidance, and which provides the latest case law for practitioners in a very clear and methodical manner.

The fundamental ethos of ASBOs remains that they combine the twin-track approach of enforcement and support.

However, there have also been some developments and policy adjustments as the courts have interpreted ASBO legislation as more and more cases come before them.

After ASBOs were first introduced, orders on conviction were introduced to improve access and timing; and interim orders for extreme cases where communities needed protecting urgently. Since May 2004 courts have been able to issue individual support orders to juveniles issued with ASBOs on application. This is a positive measure, attaching positive conditions to ensure that young people get all the support they need to change their behaviour. I urge agencies to make the greatest possible use of them.

We are also extending the power to apply for orders to the Environment Agency and Transport for London.

We continue to listen to the views of practitioners and stakeholders and to adjust policy and legislation accordingly. One illustration of this has been the development of the one-year review of ASBOs issued to young people, which is explained in this guidance. Although it is not yet enshrined in legislation, we feel that this formalises existing good practice to ensure that young people are provided with the right support throughout the duration of their ASBO. We also hope to introduce later this year measures to empower the courts to apply rigorous case management in ASBO proceedings.

This guidance is also issued in the context of the Respect programme which builds on the Government's anti-social behaviour strategy. Under the Respect drive, we will maintain and build on the strong enforcement action that has helped us make so much progress, but extend this further through a comprehensive strategy to deliver:

- a new approach to tackling problem families;

- a wide-ranging programme to address poor parenting;

- measures to improve behaviour and attendance in schools;

- initiatives to provide constructive activities for young people; and

- a drive to strengthen communities through more responsive public services.

I am delighted to introduce this new guidance which I am sure everyone working in the field of anti-social behaviour will find to be a source of reference that is both useful and informative.

TONY McNULTY
August 2006

Introduction

This guidance on ASBOs draws on the experience of the police service, local authorities, youth offending teams, the courts and other organisations. It is intended for use by practitioners – people with a professional responsibility for tackling anti-social behaviour, whether they represent local authorities, the police, youth offending teams, registered social landlords, prosecutors, the courts, or any other agency which seeks to tackle the problem of anti-social behaviour.

The crime and disorder reduction partnership lies at the heart of the Government's approach to the reduction of both crime and anti-social behaviour (much of which is of course criminal in nature).All crime and disorder reduction partnerships have an anti-social behaviour co-ordinator and access to them is published on the Together website (www.together.gov.uk).All partnerships, too, are required to draw up strategies for the reduction of anti-social behaviour in their areas, and the anti-social behaviour co-ordinators are in the best position to ensure that those strategies genuinely reflect the needs of the community served by the partnerships.

Anti-social behaviour is given a wide meaning by the legislation – to paraphrase the Crime and Disorder Act 1998, it is behaviour that causes or is likely to cause harassment, alarm or distress to one or more people who are not in the same household as the perpetrator. Among the forms it can take are:

- graffiti – which can on its own make even the tidiest urban spaces look squalid, and can act as a magnet for further anti-social behaviour and crime;

- abusive and intimidating language, too often directed at minority groups;

- excessive noise, particularly late at night;

- fouling the street with litter;

- drunken behaviour in the streets, and the mess it can result in; and

- dealing drugs, with all the problems to which it gives rise.

There has been considerable criticism of the current wording being too wide. However, the House of Commons Select Committee looked at this in its report on anti-social behaviour and concluded[1] that it would be a mistake to make it more specific because:

- the definitions work well from an enforcement point of view and no significant practical problems appear to have been encountered;

- exhaustive lists of the kind of behaviour considered anti-social by central government would be unworkable and anomalous; and

- anti-social behaviour is inherently a local problem and may be of a different nature in different localities.

This flexibility is therefore a major strength of the current statutory description of anti-social behaviour.

Anti-social behaviour is an issue that concerns everyone in the community. Incidents that cause harassment, alarm and distress cannot be written off as generational issues – they impact on the quality of life of young and old alike. And they require a response that puts partnership into action.

Just as the problems of anti-social behaviour are wide-ranging, the solutions too must operate equally effectively on many levels. While an energetic and constructive police response is essential, it must be supplemented by engagement from a wide variety of partners. To take only the most obvious, schools need to have effective policies in place against truancy and bullying, and the police need to work closely with licensing authorities in order to tackle alcohol-related problems. Local authorities and registered social landlords need to take responsibility for acting against anti-social behaviour by their tenants and against their tenants. Social services need to ensure that they are taking the welfare of the whole community fully into account when making decisions, as well as taking care of the perpetrators. And, just as important, all of these bodies need to be sharing information with each other to the fullest possible extent in order to act fairly and decisively against the problems of anti-social behaviour.

1. Anti-social behaviour orders: the basics

What are anti-social behaviour orders?

Anti-social behaviour orders (ASBOs) were introduced by section 1 of the Crime and Disorder Act 1998 in England and Wales and have been available since April 1999.The powers to deal with anti-social behaviour were strengthened and extended by the Police Reform Act 2002, which introduced the power to make similar orders on conviction in criminal proceedings, and in county court proceedings, and the power to make interim orders. Orders can now also extend across any defined part of England and Wales. The provisions relating to orders on conviction under section1C and interim orders under section1D in the magistrates' courts were inserted in the 1998 Act by the Police Reform Act 2002 and came into force on 2 December 2002.

The provisions relating to orders in county court proceedings (section 1B) were also inserted in the 1998 Act by the Police Reform Act 2002 and came into force on 1 April 2003.

ASBOs are civil orders to protect the public from behaviour that causes or is likely to cause harassment, alarm or distress. An order contains conditions prohibiting the offender from carrying out specific anti-social acts or from entering defined areas and is effective for a minimum of two years. The orders are not criminal sanctions and are not intended to punish the offender.

Applications for ASBOs are made to the magistrates' court by 'relevant authorities' which include local authorities, chief officers of police, registered social landlords, housing action trusts or any other person or body specified by the order of the Secretary of State (as previously mentioned, it is intended that the Environment Agency and Transport for London be specified for this purpose). A similar order can be

---

[1] House of Commons Select Committee, *Anti-Social Behaviour: 5th Report of Session 2004–05*, recommendation 7.

applied for during related proceedings in the county court, and can be requested on conviction of certain offences in the criminal courts. It remains a civil order irrespective of the issuing court.

ASBOs are community-based orders that involve local people not only in the collection of evidence to support an application but also for the purpose of helping to enforce breaches. By their nature they encourage local communities to become actively involved in reporting crime and disorder and to contribute actively to building and protecting the community. The civil status of ASBOs has implications for the nature of the proceedings at which applications are heard. For example, hearsay and professional witness evidence can be heard. This is an extremely important feature of ASBOs that can help protect victims and witnesses of anti-social behaviour.

What sort of behaviour can be tackled by ASBOs?

Anti-social behaviour that can be tackled by ASBOs includes:

- harassment of residents or passers-by;

- verbal abuse;

- criminal damage;

- vandalism;

- noise nuisance;

- writing graffiti;

- engaging in threatening behaviour in large groups;

- racial abuse;

- smoking or drinking alcohol while under age;

- substance misuse;

- joyriding;

- begging;

- prostitution;

- kerb-crawling;

- throwing missiles;

- assault; and

- vehicle vandalism.

The terms of each order should be tailored to the circumstances of the individual case.

Tackling prostitution and drug-related anti-social behaviour at Kings Cross

Issue

Kings Cross was one of the most infamous drug and vice hotspots in the country. For years the authorities had struggled to improve the area.   ➡

Approach

The anti-social behaviour partners meet to discuss individual cases and offer appropriate help, including housing and rehabilitation services. If the perpetrators of the anti-social behaviour fail either to engage or to change their behaviour, acceptable behaviour agreements (ABAs) are often used to bring to the offenders' attention the impact of their behaviour on the community.

Outcomes

This worked very well with only 4 out of 32 ABAs progressing to ASBO applications. But where the ASBO was deemed necessary by the partners, Camden police officers put together bundles of evidence, with Camden Council's legal team making the ASBO application. Impact statements were taken from local community activists and councillors to prove the need for the orders. Since then, having issued 45 ASBOs with prohibitions within the area, Kings Cross is completely unrecognisable from its previous image. The partners have also been successful in working with perpetrators to facilitate a significant sustainable change in behaviour. One crack cocaine addict recently wrote to the local paper apologising to the people of Kings Cross for his behaviour. Another went on to be a drugs worker in Brixton while a third is now working in the Home Counties and has had her ASBO discharged with the consent of the authorities.

Contact

Ian Walker
Email: ian.walker@camden.gov.uk

Legal definition of anti-social behaviour for the purpose of obtaining an order

Under section 1 of the Crime and Disorder Act 1998, the agency applying for an ASBO must show that:

- the defendant behaved in an anti-social manner; and

- an order is necessary for the protection of people from further anti-social behaviour by the defendant.

This is sometimes referred to as the 'two-stage test'.

Section 1(1) of the Act describes acting in an 'anti-social manner' as acting in 'a manner which causes or is likely to cause harassment, alarm or distress to one or more persons not of the same household' as the perpetrator. The wording is intentionally wide-ranging to allow for the orders to be used in a variety of circumstances.

The expression 'likely to cause' has the effect that someone other than a victim of the anti-social behaviour can give evidence of the likelihood of its occurring. This is intended specifically to enable the use of professionals as witnesses where those targeted by the behaviour feel unable to come forward, for example for fear of reprisals or intimidation.

Standard of proof

In the case of *McCann (R v Crown Court at Manchester ex parte McCann (FC) and Others (FC))*, the House of Lords, while confirming that ASBOs were civil orders, set out the law on the standard of proof as follows:

> 'they [magistrates] must in all cases under section 1 apply the criminal standard . . . it will be sufficient for the magistrates, when applying section 1(1)(a) to be sure that the defendant has acted in an anti-social manner, that is to say in a manner which caused or was likely to cause harassment, alarm, or distress to one or more persons not of the same household as himself.' (Lord Steyn, paragraph 37)

This means that the criminal standard of proof applies to acts of anti-social behaviour alleged against the defendant.

However, Lord Steyn went on to explain:

> 'The inquiry under section 1(1)(b), namely that such an order is necessary to protect persons from further anti-social acts by him, does not involve a standard of proof: it is an exercise of judgement or evaluation.'

It should be noted that it is the effect or likely effect of the behaviour on other people that determines whether the behaviour is anti-social. The agency applying for the order does not have to prove an intention on the part of the defendant to cause harassment, alarm or distress. Under section 1(5) of the 1998 Act, the Court will, however, disregard any behaviour shown to be reasonable in the circumstances.

The most common behaviour tackled by ASBOs is general loutish and unruly conduct such as verbal abuse, harassment, assault, graffiti and excessive noise. ASBOs have also been used to combat racial harassment, drunk and disorderly behaviour, throwing fireworks, vehicle vandalism and prostitution. Many other problems, for instance the misuse of air guns, could also lend themselves to this approach.

The wide range of anti-social behaviour that can be tackled by ASBOs and the ability to tailor the terms of the order to each specific case illustrates their flexibility. There have been cases where the chief executive of a company has been issued with an ASBO for anti-social behaviour committed by the company. This is because ASBOs must be issued against individuals and not against organisations. ASBOs may also be used, for example in the misuse of mini motos, where warnings and other measures have failed.

Against whom can an order be made?

An order can be made against anyone aged 10 years or over who has acted in an anti-social manner, or is likely so to act, and where an order is needed to protect people and the wider community from further anti-social acts. A list of interventions available for children under 10 is at Appendix A.

The orders are tenure-neutral and can be used against perpetrators living in any type of housing (not just social housing). Because the order is specific to the person, if someone moves house, it still remains in force. ASBOs can be used to combat anti-social behaviour in a wide range of situations and settings. They are highly relevant to misconduct in public spaces such as parks, shopping centres and transport hubs, but they are by no means confined to such areas.

Where groups of people are engaged in anti-social behaviour, a case needs to be made against each individual against whom an order is sought. However, the cases can be heard together by the court. Agencies have found that targeting ringleaders with orders is an effective deterrent to other members of the group.

When investigating complaints about anti-social behaviour, it is vital that agencies satisfy themselves that complaints are well founded. In particular, they should consider the possibility that complaints may have been motivated by discrimination, perhaps on racist grounds, or to further a pre-existing grudge. However, failing to act against instances of anti-social behaviour can lead to an escalation of the problem by increasing fear of crime or leading those subjected to the anti-social behaviour to retaliate. Nipping unacceptable behaviour in the bud is therefore the best option.

Who can apply for an order?

Agencies able to apply for orders are referred to as 'relevant authorities' in the legislation (section 1(1A) of the Crime and Disorder Act 1998). These are:

- local authorities – by virtue of sections 1(A) and 1(12) of the 1998 Act, a local authority is, in England, the council of a county, district or London Borough, the Isle of Wight or the Isles of Scilly, or, in Wales, the council of a county or county borough;

- police forces, including the British Transport Police (BTP);

- registered social landlords (RSLs), that is a body registered as a social landlord under section 1 of the Housing Act 1996; and

- Housing Action Trusts (HATs).

The Environment Agency and Transport for London are to be designated as relevant authorities in due course.

Local authorities and the police may apply for an order where they consider it necessary to protect persons in their area ('relevant persons') from further anti-social behaviour irrespective of where the original anti-social behaviour took place. An order can be sought which provides protection not just to the relevant persons but also, where necessary, to any persons in England and Wales.

The BTP, RSLs and HATs are empowered to apply for orders by virtue of changes introduced under the Police Reform Act 2002, which enable these agencies to deal with their particular problems of anti-social behaviour in a more effective and timely manner. RSLs and HATs may apply for orders against non-residents as well as residents and should consider doing so where the anti-social behaviour of non-residents is affecting the quality of life for residents.

Applications from the BTP, RSLs or HATs must concern anti-social behaviour related to the premises for which they are responsible by persons who are on or in the vicinity of such premises or likely to be either on or in the vicinity of such premises.

The BTP, RSLs and HATs are required to consult both the local authority and local police force when applying for an order. The agencies are not compelled to use the power. The police or local authority may still apply for ASBOs on their behalf.

Under section 17 of the 1998 Act, the police and local authorities have a joint responsibility to develop and implement strategies for tackling anti-social behaviour and disorder in the local area. This responsibility is not changed in any way by allowing the BTP, RSLs and HATs to apply for orders.

Which courts can make ASBOs?

ASBOs can be made by:

- magistrates' courts (acting in their civil capacity);

- county courts (where the relevant authority or the person against whom the order is sought is a party to the proceedings and the non-party is joined to these proceedings);

- magistrates' courts (on conviction in criminal proceedings);

- the Crown Court (on conviction in criminal proceedings);

- youth courts (on conviction in criminal proceedings); and

- at the time this guidance was being revised, 11 county courts, which were trialling hearings for ASBO cases for children and young people. These are as follows:
  Bristol
  Central London
  Clerkenwell
  Dewsbury
  Huddersfield
  Leicester
  Manchester
  Oxford
  Tameside

Wigan
Wrexham

The pilot will be evaluated in autumn 2006.

The table overleaf sets out what each type of court can do.

Length of orders

Orders are issued for a minimum of two years and can be issued for an indefinite period pending a further order. They can also be varied or discharged on application by either party, although they cannot be discharged in the first two years without the consent of both parties. In the case of young people, ASBOs should be reviewed each year as explained on page 45.

Anti-social behaviour response courts

Within Her Majesty's Courts Service there is now a network of specialist anti-social behaviour response courts across the country – existing courts that are better able to respond to the issue of anti-social behaviour. They ensure that magistrates and court staff are specially trained and follow a framework – including specialist sessions, witness care, local community engagement and appropriate media strategies. This ensures courts are able to respond properly to anti-social behaviour cases in a visible and consistent way.

	Magistrates' court – acting in their . . .		County court	Youth court
	. . . Civil capacity	**. . . Criminal capacity**		
Which ASBO?	No restrictions	Only on conviction in criminal proceedings	Pilots taking place for children and young people until September 2006	Only on conviction in criminal proceedings as it has no civil jurisdiction
Disposals available if ASBO breached – under-18s	n/a	n/a	n/a	Sections 90 and 91 cases – Powers of Criminal Courts (Sentencing) Act 2000, detention and training order, action plan order, referral order, attendance centre order, supervision order, reparation order, parenting order, fine, community punishment and rehabilitation order (16–17 year olds), absolute discharge. All sentences to the community are open to the following orders: curfew order, parenting order, drug testing and treatment order

	Magistrates' court – acting in their . . .		County court	Youth court
	---	---	---	---
	. . . Civil capacity	. . . Criminal capacity		
Disposals available if ASBO breached – adult	Maximum five years' imprisonment; community order, absolute discharge, fine, compensation order, deferred sentence	Maximum five years' imprisonment; community order, absolute discharge, fine, compensation order, deferred sentence	Maximum five years' imprisonment; community order, absolute discharge, fine, compensation order, deferred sentence	n/a

Untouchable gang's reign of terror on a Merseyside street ends in the anti-social behaviour response courts

Issue

A gang of 10 youths who believed they were beyond the reach of the law were regularly terrorising vulnerable residents on a street in Thornton, Merseyside. The youths had been smashing windows, breaking into and throwing missiles at vehicles, and verbally abusing people. Victims included the young, elderly and vulnerable and the gang's behaviour created such fear locally that residents would not go out after dark or leave their properties unattended. Many of them installed CCTV. Only the most serious incidents were reported at the time they occurred but victims would not press charges for fear of being singled out and targeted by the gang.

Approach

The neighbourhood police officer carried out a detailed investigation of the problem to bring a case for arresting the perpetrators and bringing them before the courts. Previous police logs and reports were scrutinised and impact statements taken from the majority of witnesses in anonymity to use as hearsay evidence. One family, which had been singled out by the perpetrators, was given support by the police with daily contact and visits. The victims installed CCTV and kept a diary of all the incidents which was exhibited as evidence.

The police and Crown Prosecution Service (CPS) worked closely together to prepare the case and the police gathered strong evidence. Interviews with perpetrators were carefully planned so that when faced with the evidence against them all 10 to perpetrators admitted their responsibility.

In advance of the case, the CPS specialist prosecutor for the area worked to set up a special anti-social behaviour response court. Advance disclosure of evidence to the judge and other parties prior to the court hearing meant that the case was dealt with quickly once in court.

At the hearing, nine perpetrators were charged on criminal offences ranging from disorderly behaviour to attempted arson. Three of the gang were given ASBOs and six of the gang signed acceptable behaviour agreements.

Conditions attached to the ASBOs were designed to protect the community from any recurrence of the behaviour. The perpetrators were restricted to sleeping at their nominated address and were not allowed out between 6.00pm and 6.00am unless accompanied by a parent or appropriate adult. They were clearly instructed not to approach or interfere with any prosecution witnesses. They were also prohibited from being verbally abusive and from throwing missiles at any residential property or from carrying anything which they could use launch a missile.

The CPS advised the local media of the anti- social behaviour response court and the press reported this operation on the front pages of the local papers. This is part of a strategy to publicise successful➡

action of the police, CPS and judiciary working in partnership to tackle anti-social behaviour. Its aim is to encourage the community to report anti-social behaviour, knowing that it will be dealt with effectively.

Outcome

The operation provided much needed relief for the residents in the area. A parent of one of the gang members has since become proactive in a local community action group which is working to increase diversionary activities for young people in the area.

For the professionals involved in the case, the operation has underlined the importance of taking impact statements as a matter of course when victims fail to press charges due to fear of reprisals. The multi-agency partnership approach works best if one officer who is aware of all the facts of the case co-ordinates the case.

Orders made in county court proceedings (section 1B of the Crime and Disorder Act 1998)

For an application to be made in the county court, both the applicant and the person against whom the application is made must be parties to the 'principal proceedings' (such as an eviction).Where the relevant authority is not a party to the principal proceedings, an application to be made a party and the application for an order should be made as soon as possible after the authority becomes aware of the principal proceedings. Where the person alleged to have committed the anti-social behaviour is not a party but the relevant authority thinks that his anti-social acts are material to the principal proceedings, the authority can apply to have him joined in the proceedings and apply for an order. The county court will be able to grant orders where the principal proceedings involve evidence of anti-social behaviour.

Enabling the county courts to make orders may remove the need for a separate legal process in the magistrates' court and make it possible for the public to be protected from anti-social behaviour more quickly and more efficiently.

An order made in county court proceedings might, for example, be useful to prevent an individual, evicted from his accommodation for harassing his neighbours and/or others in the area, from returning to the same area to continue the abusive behaviour.

2. Taking a strategic approach

Orders can only work properly when they are based on partnership in action. They are powerful instruments, and they will be at their most effective when all the agencies confronted by an individual's anti-social behaviour collaborate to make the best possible use of them.

Orders made on conviction in criminal proceedings

Criminal courts – the magistrates' court, the Crown Court and the youth court – can make orders against an individual who has been convicted of a criminal offence, and this is known as an 'order on conviction' (sometimes also called a 'CRASBO'). Some county courts are currently trialling stand-alone ASBO cases for children and young people until the end of September 2006. These are not proceedings on conviction.

The order on conviction is considered at a civil hearing after the verdict. It is not part of the sentence the offender receives for the criminal offence.

The order will be granted on the basis of the evidence presented to the court during the criminal proceedings and any additional evidence provided to the court after the verdict, although it is possible for the order to be granted on the basis of the criminal proceedings alone. There is a statutory requirement for a conviction to be for an offence committed after the date on which the insertion of the relevant provisions by the Police Reform Act took effect.

The court may make an order on conviction either on its own initiative or following an application by the prosecutor (see section1C(3) of the Crime and Disorder Act 1998).Alternatively, the order can be requested by the police or local authority, who may make representations to the court in support of the request. Orders on conviction cannot be made if there is a deferred sentence for the relevant offence.

The court may adjourn the proceedings following conviction to allow an application for an order on conviction to be made. By virtue of section 1D(1)(b) of the 1998 Act (inserted by the Serious Organised Crime and Police Act 2005), the court may also make an interim order.

The order on conviction is a civil order and has the same effect as an ASBO made on application – it contains prohibitions rather than penalties and is made in civil proceedings. It is similar to the football banning order on conviction in that it is a civil order made following a criminal procedure.[2]

If the offender is detained in custody, the court may make provision for requirements of the order on conviction to become effective on their release. For this period the order takes effect immediately but its terms are suspended until release.

Where is an ASBO valid?

Before the changes introduced by the Police Reform Act 2002, the conditions an order could impose extended only to the applicant's area and adjoining areas. An order can now extend across any defined area within England and Wales.[3]

The power to make an order over a wide area is for use where there is reason to believe that the person concerned may move or has already moved. It goes some way to addressing the problem of offenders moving to other areas and continuing the behaviour.

An order covering a wider area could address problems such as ticket touting at different train stations or anti-social behaviour on trains, and could help deal with the minority of the travelling community who persistently engage in anti-social behaviour around the country. Careful thought needs to be given to the consequences of extending the exclusion area so that it does not simply result in displacing the behaviour into a neighbouring area.

Any evidence of the itinerant nature of the defendant's lifestyle, of the likelihood of the individual moving to another area, or of wide geographical spread of offending behaviour should be submitted with the application file. The applicant does not have to prove that anti-social behaviour will occur elsewhere, just show that it is likely to.

The more serious the behaviour, the greater the likelihood that the court will grant a geographically wide order. Orders that seek to operate in the whole of England and Wales will not be granted without evidence that that is the actual or potential geographical extent of the problem. Further detail about effective prohibitions is given in Chapter 7.

Can interim orders be made?

Interim orders are available under section 1D of the Crime and Disorder Act 1998 (as amended by section 65 of the Police Reform Act 2002 and the Serious Organised Crime and Police Act (SOCPA) 2005) in both the magistrates' court and the county court. This is an order made at an initial court hearing held in advance of the full hearing. This temporary order can impose the same prohibitions and has the same penalties for breach as a full order.

---

[2] Section 1C(2) of the Crime and Disorder Act 1998 states that the court may make an order which prohibits the offender from doing anything described in the order. Section 14A of the Football Spectators Act 1989 places a duty on the court to impose a football banning order if a person is convicted of a relevant offence or to state in open court why such an order has not been made.

[3] The geographical area which an order may cover is indicated by section 1(6) for ASBOs and orders made in county court proceedings; and by section 1C(2)(b) for orders made on conviction in criminal proceedings.

The interim order can, with leave of the justices' clerk, be made without notice of proceedings being given to the defendant. A without notice interim order has no effect until it has been served on the defendant. If it is not served within seven days, it will cease and will not have effect. The benefit of the interim order is that it enables the courts to order an immediate stop to anti-social behaviour and thereby to protect the public more quickly. It reduces the scope for witness intimidation by making it unlawful for the offender to continue the behaviour while the ASBO application is being processed. It also removes any delay in the proceedings.

Section 139 of SOCPA 2005 gives the court the power to grant an interim order pending an adjourned hearing for an order on conviction.

The interim order will send a clear message to the community that swift action against anti-social behaviour is possible.

The order can be made at the outset of proceedings for an ASBO application if the court considers that it is just to make such an order. The applicant authority should, if possible, request an interim order at the same time as submitting an application for a full order.

When considering whether to make an interim order, the court will be aware that it may not be possible at the time of the interim order application to compile all the evidence which would prove that a full ASBO is necessary. Rather the court will determine the application for the interim order on the question of whether the application for the full order has been properly made and where there is sufficient evidence of an urgent need to protect the community.

Applications for interim orders will be appropriate, for example, in cases where the applicant feels that persons need to be protected from the threat of further anti-social acts which might occur before the main application can be determined. Where an interim order is granted without notice of proceedings to the defendant, it is expected that the court will usually arrange an early return date.

An individual who is subject to an interim order will have the opportunity to respond to the case at the hearing for the full order. The defendant is also able to apply to the court for the interim order to be varied or discharged. In this instance the matter will be dealt with at a hearing dealing specifically with the interim order.

The interim order:

- will be for a fixed period;

- can be varied or discharged on application by the defendant;

- will cease to have effect if the application for the ASBO or county court order is withdrawn or refused;

- may extend over any defined area of England and Wales; and

- has the same breach penalties as for a full order.

The court procedures and forms to be used when applying for or making an interim order are set out in the Magistrates' Courts (Anti-Social Behaviour Orders) Rules 2002 (available at www.opsi.gov.uk/si/si2002/20022784.htm).

Interim orders made in the county courts

A relevant authority may apply for an interim order in the county court once it is party to the 'principal proceedings'. The application for an interim order should be made early in the proceedings.

The procedure for making applications for orders in the county court is set out in the Practice Direction of the updated Civil Procedure Rules 65. 24 to 26 (Appendix B).

Orders against children and young people

Under the Crime and Disorder Act 1998, applications for ASBOs against young people aged 10 to 17, and in certain circumstances 18-year-olds, can be heard in the magistrates' court. As a result of the recent practice direction (the Magistrates' Courts (Anti-Social Behaviour Orders) Composition of Benches practice direction, February 2006), the justices constituting the court should normally be qualified to sit in the youth court unless to do so would result in a delayed hearing. Applications for orders are not heard in the youth court as a matter of course because of the civil status of the orders, although youth courts may make orders where appropriate on conviction.

Practitioners familiar with dealing with young people's cases will be aware of the restrictions on reporting that apply under the Children and Young Persons Act 1933. However, automatic reporting restrictions do not apply to stand-alone ASBOs as they are civil orders. In orders on conviction cases, the court does have discretion under section 39 of the Children and Young Persons Act 1933 to impose reporting restrictions. Reporting restrictions will always apply to the criminal proceedings on which the order on conviction is based but in all other cases, the presumption is that publicity will be allowed. See page 52 for detailed guidance on promoting awareness of orders.

A court making an ASBO does have the power to impose restrictions to protect the identity of a person under 18. But the imposition of reporting restrictions may restrict the effectiveness of the order if the effectiveness of the ASBO will largely depend on the wider community knowing the details. Please see the separate sections on publicity and on children and young people.

Breach of an order

Breach of an order is a criminal offence; criminal procedures and penalties apply. The standard of proof required is the criminal standard. Guilt must be established beyond reasonable doubt. Breach proceedings are heard in the magistrates' court and may be committed to the Crown Court. Such proceedings are the same irrespective of whether the order is a full or interim order made on application to the magistrates' court or the county court, or an order on conviction in criminal proceedings.

Expert prosecutors

A team of 14 anti-social behaviour expert prosecutors has been set up with funding from the Together campaign to support all Crown Prosecution Service (CPS) prosecutors dealing with anti-social behaviour-related cases. The team drives improvements in performance across the country.

The team:

- promotes better partnership working between local prosecutors, the police, local authorities, registered social landlords and others involved in taking action against anti-social behaviour;

- delivers training to prosecutors on the new powers to obtain orders on conviction;

- provides advice to prosecutors on the full range of enforcement measures and key issues such as prosecution of ASBO breach; and

- works with court clerks and magistrates in improving their response to anti-social behaviour.

In addition to the 14 specialist prosecutors, anti-social behaviour co-ordinators have now been appointed CPS-wide to ensure that there is a focus on anti-social behaviour issues in every CPS area. Their role is to drive this work forward. Further information can be obtained from Sarah Johnston at sarah.johnston@cps.gsi.gov.uk.

Standard ASBO form

A copy of the order form used by the magistrates' courts can be found at Appendix C.

Disposals

The maximum penalty for breach of an order is five years' imprisonment for an adult offender. A conditional discharge is not available for breach of an ASBO.

The full range of disposals of the youth court is available, and custody should only be considered as a last resort in cases of serious and persistent breach (if appropriate, breach may be dealt with by way of a final warning). Where custody is deemed by the court to be necessary, the maximum sentence for breach by children and young people is a detention and training order (DTO), which has a maximum term of 24 months – 12 months of which is custodial and 12 months is in the community. The DTO is available for 12 to 17-year-olds (although 12 to 14-year-olds must be persistent (criminal) offenders to be given a DTO).A 10 to 11-year-old can be given a community order for breach of an ASBO. The sentence given should be proportionate and reflect the impact of the anti-social behaviour. It must relate to all the relevant circumstances, such as the number of breaches and how the breach relates to the finding of anti-social behaviour. Proceedings should be swift and not fractured by unnecessary adjournments either during the proceedings or before sentencing. Information on how to handle breaches of ASBOs by young people is contained in page 26 of the anti-social behaviour guidance issued by the Youth Justice Board, Home Office and Association of Chief Police Officers.[4]

The leading precedent for the approach on sentencing on this point is *R v Lamb* [2005] EWCA Crim 2487. In this judgment the court drew the distinction between a breach that represents further anti-social behaviour and those that are merely breaches of the terms of an order, for instance, as in that case, not to enter a particular metro system. Differing from earlier decisions – in particular from the case of *R v Morrison* [2005] EWCA Crim 2237 – the court held that the orders are properly designed to protect the public from frequent and distressing repeated misbehaviour.

In the case of *Morrison*, it was determined that if the breach amounted to a specific criminal offence that carried a particular penalty, the sentence for breach of the ASBO could not be greater than that.

As the court in *Lamb* pointed out, this would merely encourage people to commit criminal offences rather than breach their ASBOs in other ways. The court has therefore laid down a series of steps for consideration prior to the imposition of a sentence.

Where a breach does not involve harassment, alarm or distress, a community order may be considered to assist the defendant to learn to live with the terms of the ASBO. This is entirely consistent with the guideline on breach proceedings issued by the Sentencing Guidelines Council, where it is pointed out that custody should be used as a last resort, and the primary purpose of breach proceedings should be to ensure that the order itself is observed.

However, *Lamb* confirmed that where there is a persistent breach without harassment, alarm or distress, it may become necessary to impose custody to preserve the authority of the court. In those circumstances, the sentence should be as short as possible, and in *Lamb* the individual sentences were reduced to two months in custody. However, where the new breach amounts to further harassment, alarm or distress, then the court thought orders of eight months, on a guilty plea, were appropriate, applying *R v Braxton* [2005] 1 CR APP R (S) 36, *R v Tripp* [2005] EWCA Crim 2253 and *R v Dickinson* [2005] 2 CR APP R (S) 488.

When the offender has been found guilty of breaching an order, and before sentencing, the court may take reports from the local authority or police and any applicant agency. The court should also consider the original reasons for the making of the order.

---

[4]   Youth Justice Board, Home Office and Association of Chief Police Officers (2006) *Anti-social Behaviour: A guide to the role of Youth Offending Teams in dealing with anti-social behaviour.* This can be downloaded at www.youth-justice-board.gov.uk/Publications/Scripts/prodView.asp?idproduct=212&ep=

A copy of the court order (ASBO) as granted (including any maps and details of any prohibitions) can be put before the court during breach proceedings as evidence that an order has been made without the need for a statement formally proving that an order was made. This provision was introduced by SOCPA 2005 on 1 July 2005.

3. Managing the application process

This section focuses on the main issues involved in applying for an order. For an ASBO to be effective, the process of evidence gathering and applying to the courts should be as swift as possible.

Groups of organisations and partnerships such as crime and disorder reduction partnerships (CDRPs) may wish to consider buying specialist legal advice in blocks or pooling expertise and experience. This is likely to be more cost effective than buying in legal advice on a case-by-case basis.

Partnership working

A fully co-ordinated approach is essential if anti-social behaviour is to be tackled. Effective defence of communities depends on all agencies – including housing organisations, social services, education authorities and youth services – accepting that the promotion of safe and orderly neighbourhoods is a priority, and working together to agree a response to unacceptable behaviour. The consultation arrangements are important but should be organised so that they do not cause delays in dealing with cases.

Agencies and communities join to tackle anti-social behaviour in Slade Green

Issue

Slade Green in Bexley was once described as 'a cluster of low-rise estates centred on a precinct of shops and Slade Green railway station, where vandalism, burglary and drugs blight the lives of residents'. Slade Green has experienced high levels of crime and social deprivation and features among the top 16% of the most deprived wards in England. Bexley Police identified Slade Green as a hot spot for residential and non-residential burglary, auto crime, disorder, domestic violence and race crime. Residents, local housing providers and the leader of the Slade Green Community Safety Forum were alarmed at the escalation of anti-social behaviour in the area. Residents regularly experienced threats and actual violence, making them afraid of giving evidence to the police.

Approach

A meeting between residents and the local partnership team produced an outline action plan. Community meetings, local press coverage and 'Have A Say' days led to key witnesses being willing to give evidence.

The partnership team applied for ASBOs against the six men identified as the most prolific perpetrators. In total, 30 witnesses gave evidence, most in the form of hearsay, with nine giving evidence in person at the court hearing. The policing team involved in the case supported witnesses by being at court to provide additional reassurance. Victim Support's witness support service also helped. Strong witness evidence and a compelling case prepared by the police and the council legal department convinced the court to agree to all six applications.

Outcome

The impact of these ASBOs on crime and fear of crime in the area was significant. For the period 2003/04, robbery incidents fell by 53%, burglary by 21% and auto crime by 40%. Of the original six to receive an ASBO, one person has been prosecuted for breach of the ASBO condition relating to criminal damage to a car, for which he received a custodial sentence. ➡

A community safety action zone (CSAZ) was established in Slade Green with the aim of reducing crime and disorder in the area. A multi-agency operations group was formed to find the grass roots issues leading to these problems. The addition of environmental and security improvements have enhanced the appearance of the area and have made it a safer and more secure place to live. These improvements have included improved street lighting, removal of graffiti, removal of fly-tipping, removal of abandoned and unlicensed cars and improvements to play areas.

A survey was carried out before the start of the CSAZ which found that 22% of residents in Slade Green who responded felt safe at night in their area. After the CSAZ had been set up, 93% of residents surveyed in Slade Green felt safe at night in their area.

Contact

Charlotte Shrimpton
Telephone: 020 8284 5505

Taking ownership

It is vital that a specified individual within the lead agency takes on a lead role with responsibility for the ownership, direction and management of the case. This will help ensure that there is no confusion about who is expected to make sure that the necessary actions are taken on the right timescale.

The lead individual should manage and co-ordinate the involvement of other agencies so that they add value by contributing their own specialist knowledge and expertise.

A multi-agency approach should be adopted so that all agencies that could hold information on the individual in question are involved in the process at an early stage.

Such agencies include the Probation Service, social services, health services, the youth offending team (YOT) and voluntary organisations, all of which may have come into contact with the individual or members of their family.

CDRPs should consider adopting the anti-social behaviour action group (ASBAG) approach developed by Watford Borough Council.

Watford's partnership approach involves all relevant statutory and voluntary agencies and engages the local community in taking a stand against the perpetrators of anti-social behaviour.

They have developed a problem-solving approach to issues and apply the SARA model:

- Scan for all available intelligence in relation to the anti-social behaviour issue.

- Analyse the intelligence, looking for the root cause of the problem.

- Respond with a clear action plan designed to address the behaviour.

- Assess the progress/success of the action plan on a monthly basis.

Delivery is through the monthly multi-agency ASBAG, which includes cross-boundary working as required.

Watford's anti-social behaviour strategy allows for a range of diversionary activities and intervention as alternatives to enforcement, if the ASBAG agrees they are appropriate to effectively tackle an individual and their anti-social behaviour, such as:

- verbal warnings;

- written warnings;

- acceptable behaviour contracts (ABCs);

- mentoring programmes;

- intervention programmes;

- educational programmes;

- supporting youths and their parents; and

- restorative justice (when and where appropriate for victims and localities).

Information is exchanged between stakeholders and members of the CDRP at each monthly ASBAG meeting.

This strategy works in parallel with the prolific and priority offender strategy and a representative from the prolific offender unit is represented on the ASBAG to avoid duplication of work.

If the level of anti-social behaviour is such that the risk of further behaviour or escalation of behaviour is imminent, the Watford anti-social behaviour co-ordinator may convene an immediate action plan meeting with the police anti-social behaviour officer and a legal representative from Watford Borough Council acting on the ASBAG's behalf in the interests of managing the risk to public safety without delay.

Watford CDRP works to the principles of the National Intelligence Model for tasking and co-ordination.

Each action plan is performance-managed by the ASBAG and is subject to monitoring and scrutiny by quarterly feedback to the Watford responsible authority group by the Watford Borough Council anti-social behaviour co-ordinator. The ASBAG performs a full self-evaluation and review every 12 months.

Contact

Matt Leng
Anti-social Behaviour Coordinator
Watford Borough Council
Matt.Leng@watford.gov.uk

Other considerations

Local authorities have a duty under the NHS and Community Care Act 1990 to assess any person who may be in need of community care services. If there is any evidence to suggest that the person against whom the order is being sought may be suffering from drug, alcohol or mental health problems or an autistic spectrum disorder, the necessary support should be provided by social services or other support agencies. Such support should run parallel with the collection of evidence and application for an order, where an application for an order is deemed necessary. This ensures that the court can balance the needs of the community with the needs of any alleged perpetrator.

From December 2006, provisions in the Disability Discrimination Act 2005 will come into force which make unlawful discrimination by a public authority in the exercise of public functions. There are some exemptions for listed persons and certain acts including (in broad terms) legislation, prosecution and judicial acts. However, the new prohibition of discrimination covers functions carried out, for example, by local authorities and the police. The definition of discrimination includes, in some circumstances, not making a reasonable adjustment to the way a function is carried out. Chapter 11 of the guidance, which the Disability Rights Commission will issue shortly (entitled *Code of Practice – Rights of Access: services to the public, public authority functions, private clubs and premises*) includes advice on how the Act now impacts on those carrying out public authority functions. It will be available on the Commission's website (www.drc.org.uk).

Statutory consultation requirements

Section 1E of the Crime and Disorder Act 1998 (as amended by section 66 of the Police Reform Act 2002) sets out the consultation requirements for agencies applying for orders. These are that:

- the police and local authorities must consult each other; and

- the British Transport Police (BTP), registered social landlords, housing action trusts and any other person or body designated by the Secretary of State as a relevant authority must consult both the local authority and the police force for the area.

Consultation takes place with the authority or force whose area includes the address where the subject of the order resides or appears to reside. Each district or borough council and police division/basic command unit should have a nominated contact. Care should be taken (where the local authority is the applicant) that if the subject is under local authority care there is no conflict of interest. They must ensure that the social worker involved in the case is consulted. Where a young person is the alleged perpetrator, the YOT should be consulted.

Consultation is required to inform the appropriate agency or agencies of the intended application for the order and to check whether they have any relevant information. The agencies must take into consideration at the earliest possible opportunity the relevant information necessary to apply for an individual support order or a parenting order. Information on these is contained in a separate section on children and young people.

Where the partnership working arrangements recommended in earlier paragraphs are in force, they will normally satisfy (and exceed) the statutory requirement for consultation.

The statutory requirement for consultation does not mean that the agencies must agree to an application being made but rather that they should be told of the intended application and given the opportunity to comment. This should ensure at the very minimum that actions taken by each agency regarding the same individual do not conflict.

While no agency has a veto over another agency's application for an order, the expectation is that any reservations or alternative proposals should be discussed carefully against the background of the overriding need to bring the anti-social behaviour to a speedy end. Again, the case conference procedure is designed to ensure that this happens.

A signed document of consultation is all that is required by the court. This should **not** indicate whether the party consulted was or was not in agreement. This is not required by the legislation. Supporting statements or reports from partner agencies should be provided separately.

The changes introduced by the Police Reform Act 2002 reduce bureaucracy by removing the need for applying agencies to consult with every local authority and police service whose areas are included in the order.

In addition to the consultation requirements set out above, it may be helpful for police forces to contact the BTP, which may hold information on the anti-social behaviour of the subject. The availability of this information may assist the evidence-gathering process for an order. The BTP holds a national database of offenders committing summary offences (these include railway-specific summary offences as well as those included in Home Office counting rules).

Police forces can request a search on a particular offender, in writing, from the Force Crime Registrar, British Transport Police, Force Headquarters, 15 Tavistock Place, London WC1H 9SJ.

Collection of evidence

When applying for an order, the lead agency will be required to gather evidence to prove its case beyond reasonable doubt. This evidence can include hearsay evidence. Further advice on hearsay evidence is provided later in the guidance.

The evidence in support of an application for an order should prove:

- that the defendant acted in a specific way on specific dates and at specific places;

- that these acts caused or were likely to cause harassment, alarm or distress to one or more persons not in the same household as the defendant.

The court then needs to evaluate whether an order is necessary to protect persons from further anti-social acts by the defendant. This is not a test to which a standard of proof will be applied. Instead, it is an assessment of future risk. The applicant can present evidence or argument to assist the court in making this evaluation. Witness evidence need not prove that they were alarmed or distressed themselves, but only that the behaviour they witnessed was likely to produce such an effect on others. As hearsay evidence is allowed, it may be given by 'professional witnesses' – officers of public agencies whose job it is to prevent anti-social behaviour. Since civil rules apply to these orders, it is unnecessary to disclose the names of the witnesses.

Experience has shown that elaborate court files are not normally required or advantageous. Where the anti-social behaviour has been persistent, agencies should focus on a few well-documented cases. A large volume of evidence and/or a large number of witnesses creates its own problems. There is more material for the defence to contest and timetabling issues may increase delays in the process.

Agencies applying for orders should strike a balance and focus on what is most relevant and necessary to provide sufficient evidence for the court to arrive at a clear understanding of the matter.

Evidence may include:

- breach of an ABC;

- witness statements of officers who attended incidents;

- witness statements of people affected by the behaviour;

- evidence of complaints recorded by the police, housing providers or other agencies;

- statements from professional witnesses, for example council officials, health visitors or truancy officers;

- video or CCTV evidence (effective where resolution is high and high-quality still images can be used);

- supporting statements or reports from other agencies, for example probation reports;

- previous successful civil proceedings that are relevant, such as an eviction order for similar behaviour;

- previous relevant convictions;

- copies of custody records of previous arrests relevant to the application; and

- information from witness diaries.

Together campaign fact sheet

The Together campaign has produced a fact sheet giving step-by-step guidance on evidence collection which is available on the website www.together.gov.uk

---

Southampton shopping area blighted by anti-social behaviour

Issue

Lordshill centre was suffering from a large amount of anti-social behaviour, especially around the local supermarket. There was a substantial amount of shoplifting, criminal damage and harassment of visitors and shoppers. At the other end of the centre was a large bingo hall frequented by older patrons who were becoming increasingly afraid to go after 6pm. The supermarket was also shutting earlier in response to these incidents.

Approach

The local anti-social behaviour team's senior investigator met with the manager of the supermarket, together with the local police, and discussed possible ways of working more closely to deal with the issues. They were provided with a log book to record all incidents and this was checked weekly by the anti-social behaviour investigator and the police. This information was then put into a schedule to identify times and dates of the issues and also the perpetrators. Log books were provided to the local library and the bingo hall, as well as the supermarket, in an attempt to collate a large amount of evidence. 'It's Your Call' posters were put up in all shops in the area and premises were visited regularly by a member of the multiagency team.

Outcome

Because of the joint working and shared support, the stores felt able to tackle those causing the problem. As a result of information provided by the shops, an ASBO was obtained against the main perpetrator, with an exclusion from the whole shopping area.

There was also a Crime Reduction and Environment Week in the area, and a youth project has been funded by the supermarket, which has also provided paint to repaint the subway. This has prevented graffiti reappearing. There is also a dispersal order in place now to complement the ASBO and the perpetrator has not returned to the area. Residents and visitors can now shop in peace and the supermarket is looking to invest more money in the area.

Contact

Jane Mielnicezek
Anti-social Behaviour Manager
Telephone: 023 8083 3988

---

4.   Time limits

Magistrates' courts (acting in their civil capacity)

Under section 127 of the Magistrates' Court Act 1980, a complaint must be made within six months of the time when the matter of the complaint (the behaviour) arose. One incidence of serious anti-social behaviour may be sufficient for an order to be made. Earlier incidents may be used as background information to support a case and show a pattern of behaviour. As long as the complaint is made within the six-month timeframe, a summons may be served outside this time period, although delay is not encouraged.

5.   Use of hearsay and professional witness evidence

Hearsay and professional witness evidence allow for the identities of those too fearful to give evidence to be protected. This is especially vital as cases often involve anti-social behaviour in residential areas by local people and those targeted by the behaviour feel unable to come forward for fear of reprisals. Hearsay evidence cannot be excluded (at the request of defence lawyers) simply on the grounds that it is hearsay.

Hearsay evidence

Evidence of anti-social behaviour which occurs at any time after the commencement of section 1[5] may be taken into account when the court considers whether or not to grant an order on conviction under section 1C.

The House of Lords judgment in the McCann case confirmed that hearsay evidence is admissible. Lord Steyn stated that:[6]

> 'Having concluded that the proceedings in question are civil under domestic law and article 6, it follows that the machinery of the Civil Evidence Act 1995 and the Magistrates' Courts (Hearsay Evidence in Civil Proceedings) Rules 1999 allow the introduction of such evidence under the first part of section 1.

> ' . . . use of the Civil Evidence Act 1995 and the Rules in cases under the first part of section 1 are not in any way incompatible with the Human Rights Act 1998.

> ' . . . hearsay evidence will often be of crucial importance. For my part, hearsay evidence depending on its logical probativeness is quite capable of satisfying the requirements of section 1(1).'

It is a matter for the judge or magistrate to decide what weight they attach to hearsay evidence.

Hearsay allows a police officer to provide a statement on behalf of a witness or witnesses who remain anonymous. Hearsay evidence must be relevant to the matters to be proved. It could include details such as dates, places, times, specific descriptions of actions, who was present and who said what.

Hearsay can include evidence from the person taking the statement. The person giving the hearsay evidence may attest to the observable conditions of the witness, for example that the witness appeared upset, and may give evidence based on their own judgement of the situation.

Where an applicant intends to rely on hearsay evidence in the county court, they must act in accordance with part 33 of the Civil Procedure Rules. Written notice must be given at least 21 days before the hearing to the other party and to the court.

Professional witnesses

Professional witnesses can be called to give their opinions as to matters within their expertise and can give evidence about their assessments of the respondent or his/her behaviour. Examples of witnesses who may be called as professional witnesses include council officials, health visitors, railway staff, teachers, doctors and police officers.

Care should be taken to ensure that a professional witness does not inadvertently enable vulnerable or intimidated witnesses to be identified, for example from their home address.

---

[5]   Section 1 of the Crime and Disorder Act 1998 came into force on 1 April 1999.
[6]   Taken from paragraphs 35, 36 and 37 of *Clingham (formerly C (a minor)) v Royal Borough of Kensington and Chelsea (on Appeal from a Divisional Court of the Queen's Bench Division); R v Crown Court at Manchester ex parte McCann (FC) and Others (FC).*

Vulnerable and intimidated witnesses

Witnesses who are willing to testify in court provide the best form of evidence and, where possible, should be encouraged to come forward. The new provisions introduced in the Serious Organised Crime and Police Act 2005 make it easier for victims of anti-social behaviour to attend court and give evidence in person. The Act permits the 'special measures' that were formerly reserved for criminal hearings to be used in anti-social behaviour cases. This will enable witnesses who wish to give direct evidence to do so in private, from behind a screen or by video link.

Vulnerable witnesses are all witnesses aged under 17 years or whose quality of evidence is likely to be diminished because they have a mental disorder or learning disability or have a physical disability or physical disorder.

Intimidated witnesses are witnesses whose quality of evidence is likely to be diminished because they are in fear or distress about testifying. It is for the court to decide whether the quality of a witness's evidence is likely to be diminished.

Witness development and support

The principal purpose of an order is to protect those who directly experience anti-social behaviour. The protection provided should include, where necessary, those who are personally targeted by perpetrators, other witnesses who see this happen and the wider local community. It follows that engaging, developing and supporting these individuals and groups of people must be a primary concern for any agency managing a case and seeking to use these orders. Without the initial complaint of the witness, the agency will have no detailed knowledge of the problem. Without their continuing engagement, there will be no evidence on which to build a case.

Local strategies to promote the use of orders should have the interests of the witnesses and the community at their centre. The welfare and safety of residents whose complaints form the basis of any action must at every stage of the process be the first consideration. The use of hearsay evidence and professional witnesses is one way of achieving this (see section on hearsay evidence above).

While professional witnesses may have a duty to engage, lay witnesses can only be expected to do so if they can see a point in doing it; if the agency is credible and authoritative; if the case work is visibly focused on the interests of the witnesses; if the order protects them and stops the anti-social behaviour quickly and effectively; and if the case manager offers them well-informed, practical personal support throughout the period of evidence collection, court proceedings and afterwards, as necessary.

The experience of witnesses must be given value and significance by case managers. The status and importance of witnesses in case development must be made clear. They should be provided, as appropriate, with:

- a simple method of capturing information – diaries, video/audio recording facilities and translation services;

- information on services and procedures – about the way witness support services work, service access points, telephone numbers and the name of the case manager working on the case;

- an active and respected role in developing the case – the case strategy should reflect their needs, particularly for reassurance about their safety, and they should have control over any information they provide, including agreeing the form in which it will be provided to the defence;

- protection for themselves and their family – security for door and window access, emergency contact equipment, panic alarms and mobile phones may all be appropriate in particularly serious cases;

- regular contact from the case manager, including telephone contact as agreed with the witness (daily, weekly, etc);

- support for any court appearance – a briefing on court procedures and what they should expect, the presence with them in court of the case manager, transport to and from court (if necessary) and a secure space separate from perpetrators in which they can wait to be called; and

- support after a court appearance – speedy delivery of information, copies of any orders which have been made and an explanation of the implications of the court decision.

Each key witness should also be engaged in a face-to-face meeting with the agencies, including those who do not wish to give a statement or attend court.

Agencies should publicise positive results – one way this can be done is through leaflet drops (these can be cost effective when targeted appropriately).

Witness support is an area where the benefits of partnership working can be clearly seen: local authorities and the police have different skills and resources and can combine them to give well-rounded support.

Methods of supporting witnesses currently being used by agencies also include:

- enclosing a letter with the summons advising the respondent to stay away from witnesses;

- a higher police presence in the vicinity;

- giving witnesses the personal mobile telephone number of a named police officer who can be called if they are threatened;

- visits from neighbourhood wardens at pre-arranged times (sometimes daily); and

- phone calls from the local authority at pre-arranged times.

The interim order enables witnesses to be protected from the outset of the court process. Sections 48 and 49 of the Criminal Justice and Police Act 2001 make it an offence to intimidate witnesses in civil proceedings such as those for ASBOs.

Improving protection of witnesses in court

Manchester City Council protects witnesses

Issue

Witnesses felt anxious about giving evidence. Their concerns included the prospect of appearing in court, coming face to face with defendants and being threatened by defendants at the court building, as well as uncertainties about waiting room and refreshment facilities.

Approach

Manchester City Council negotiated the following arrangements with local courts for anti-social behaviour cases:

- access to a quiet room for witnesses;

- a video link for perpetrators in prison where it would be expensive to bring them back for an ASBO or injunction hearing (this also has the benefit of being less stressful for the witnesses);

- a video link for children and young people; and

- police presence, where appropriate.

➡

In addition, the council provides practical information and support to witnesses. They are made aware of what to expect, including the court layout, where they and the defendant(s) will be sitting and how people will be dressed. Practical support also includes transport to and from the court, being met by a council officer on arrival and information about refreshment and bathroom facilities.

Outcome

The result has been reassurance and physical security for witnesses. This has led to a reduction in the anxiety about the prospect of appearing in court or accidentally meeting a defendant. Witnesses are better able to focus on the case. The case manager is also able to keep witnesses informed of progress and to manage the case more effectively.

Contact

Nuisance Strategy Group Telephone: 0161 234 4611

6. Information sharing

Section 115 of the Crime and Disorder Act 1998 empowers any person to disclose information, where necessary or expedient for the purposes of the Act, to a 'relevant authority', namely a chief officer of police, police force, local authority, probation service or health authority, or to a person acting on their behalf. Where the agency requesting the information clearly needs it for the purposes of reducing anti-social behaviour, the presumption should normally be that it will be supplied.

As a result of the findings of the Crime and Disorder Act review, the Police and Justice Bill before Parliament seeks to strengthen section 115 of the Crime and Disorder Act further. For example, the power to disclose personal information has not changed but it places a duty on relevant authorities to share depersonalised data which is relevant for community safety purposes and already held in a depersonalised format.

Information sharing and registered social landlords

A 'relevant authority' (as defined by section 115 of the Crime and Disorder Act 1998) may disclose information to a registered social landlord where the landlord is acting on behalf of the relevant authority for the purposes of the provisions of the Act.

In order to be 'acting on behalf of' the relevant authority, the person or body so acting must have authority and must have consented to do so. Such authority may be given in writing or orally. Authority may also be implied from the conduct of the parties or from the nature of employment. Authority may be confined to a particular act or be general in its character. If authority is general, then it will that be confined to acts that the relevant authority itself has power to do.

Information sharing protocols

It may be useful for partners to negotiate information sharing protocols, examples of which can be obtained from the Home Office Information Sharing Team at informationsharing@homeoffice.gsi.gov.uk www.crimereduction.gov.uk/informationsharing

If possible, the protocol should be published, so that the public can see that information is being shared in an appropriate way.

The model protocol can be accessed at www.crimereduction.gov.uk/infosharing21.htm

Information sharing issues can also be discussed with the Information Commissioner's Office, whose website (www.ico.gov.uk) gives further details.

7. The terms of the order (the prohibitions)

The role of the agencies

Although it is for the court to decide what prohibitions are to be imposed by the order, the applicant agency should propose conditions (including duration) to the court. A full order should be drawn up using the form in the court rules. The courts find it helpful if applicants can ensure that they are equipped to amend and print off the final version of the order at the end of the hearing. This improves efficiency and helps ensure that the defendant leaves the court with a clear understanding of the prohibitions.

In the county court, the proposed order should accompany the application. The process for the county court is set out in the Practice Direction at Appendix B.

Where the order is made on conviction in criminal proceedings, an agency concerned in the case, such as the police, may propose prohibitions or the court may draw them up of its own volition. It should be noted that the order may not impose positive requirements, only prohibitions.

Careful thought needs to be given to the formulation of the conditions so they cannot be easily circumvented, and can be easily understood by the perpetrator.

The prohibitions

The prohibitions:

- should cover the range of anti-social acts committed by the defendant;

- should be necessary for protecting person(s) within a defined area from the anti-social acts of the defendant (but, as a result of the recent changes, that defined area may be as wide as necessary and could in appropriate cases include the whole of England and Wales);

- should be reasonable and proportionate;

- should be realistic and practical;

- should be clear, concise and easy to understand;

- should be specific when referring to matters of time if, for example, prohibiting the offender from being outside or in particular areas at certain times;

- should be specific when referring to exclusion from an area, including street names and clear boundaries such as the side of the street included in the order (a map with identifiable street names should also be provided);

- should be in terms that make it easy to determine and prosecute a breach;

- should contain a prohibition against inciting/encouraging others to engage in anti-social behaviour;

- should protect all people who are in the area covered by the order from the behaviour (as well as protecting specific individuals);

- may cover acts that are anti-social in themselves and those that are precursors to a criminal act, for example a prohibition on entering a shopping centre rather than on shoplifting;

- may include a general condition prohibiting behaviour which is likely to cause harassment, alarm and distress, but where this is done there must be further clarification of what type of behaviour is prohibited; and

- may include a prohibition from approaching or harassing any witnesses named in the court proceedings.

Examples of ASBO prohibitions can be found on the Crime Reduction website at www.crimereduction.gov.uk

The courts

The absence of a precise definition of anti-social behaviour within the legislation means that orders can be used to tackle a wide range of behaviour. In recent years, courts have imposed orders to prevent behaviour such as joyriding, verbal abuse, vandalism, begging, drinking under age and assault. While the proceedings and the making of the order itself can curb behaviour, the extent to which the order succeeds also depends on the prohibitions imposed, which in turn require effective wording.

It is good practice for the applicant to provide a draft of the prohibitions sought, but the final wording of the order will be a matter for the court. Problems have arisen when prohibitions have been drafted too widely or in such ways that enforcement is made difficult, if not impossible. Guidance and general principles on drafting prohibitions have come from legislation, case law and shared best practice. The following section draws together these principles and provides suggestions and comments for consideration.

There is now a requirement for the court to set out its findings of fact in relation to anti-social behaviour on the face of the order, following the cases of Wadmore and Foreman.

Effective prohibitions

If the conditions for making an order are met, the court may make an order which prohibits the defendant from doing anything described in the order (section 1(4) Crime and Disorder Act 1998 (CDA)).The facts leading to the order should be recorded and the court should provide its reasons for making the order (*C v Sunderland Youth Court* [2003] EWHC 2385).

The effect of the order should be explained to the defendant and the exact terms pronounced in open court. Most courts now have a practice of serving the defendant with a copy of the court order before he or she leaves court and may also require his or her acknowledgement. The order should set out in full the anti-social behaviour in relation to which the order was made (*R v Shane Tony P* [2004] EWCA Crim 287).

Once the court has decided that the order is necessary to protect persons from further anti-social acts by the defendant, the court must then consider what prohibitions are appropriate to include. Each order and therefore prohibition will need to be targeted to the individual and the type of anti-social behaviour it is to prevent.

The prohibitions that may be imposed are those necessary to protect persons from further anti-social behaviour by the defendant (section 1(6) CDA) and must not impose positive obligations. Therefore each prohibition must be:

- negative in nature;

- precise and target the specific behaviour that has been committed by the defendant;

- proportionate to the legitimate aim pursued and commensurate with the risk to be guarded against, which is particularly important where an order may interfere with an ECHR right (*R v Boness* [2005] EWCA 2395); and

- expressed in simple terms and easily understood.

Identification of some of the best practice used within the courts suggests that the following issues should be borne in mind when formulating prohibitions:

- A court should ask itself before making an order: 'Are the terms of this order clear so that the offender will know precisely what it is he or she is prohibited from doing?' (*R v Boness* [2005] EWCA 2395).

- Less common phrases such as 'curtilage', 'paraphernalia' or 'environs' should be avoided as they may cause confusion.

- Can it be enforced? Those who will enforce the order must be able to identify and prove a breach.

- Are any excluded areas clearly delineated? Most courts require a map to be included and it may be necessary to delineate which side of the road forms the boundary. If a line is drawn down the middle of a road, there may be arguments as to which side of the road the defendant was standing.

- Does the prohibition clearly identify those whom the defendant must not contact or associate with?

- Where the defendant is a foreign national, some courts consider it good practice for the order to be translated into the native tongue.

- Testing the prohibition by considering ways in which it could be breached may highlight its limitations (*R v McGrath* [2005] EWCA Crim 353).

- There is no requirement that the acts prohibited by an order should by themselves give rise to harassment, alarm or distress (*R v McGrath* [2005] EWCA Crim 353).

- Curfews are substantially prohibitive and, while also a sentence of the court, there is nothing legally objectionable to a curfew as a prohibition if the necessary protection of the public justifies its inclusion (*R (Lonerghan) v Lewes Crown Court* [2005] EWHC 457 (Admin)).

A prohibition can prohibit behaviour that is in any event unlawful, although previously the courts have encouraged inclusion of comparatively minor offences only (*R v Shane Tony P* [2004] EWCA Crim 287). However, recently the Court of Appeal has indicated that prohibiting behaviour that is in any event a crime does not necessarily address the aim of an order, which is to prevent anti-social behaviour. Prohibitions should enable agencies to take action before the anti-social behaviour takes place rather than waiting for a crime to be committed (*R v Boness* [2005] EWCA 2395).Therefore, bail conditions provide a useful analogy when considering what prohibitions to impose.

The Court of Appeal provided some hypothetical examples by way of guidance. If faced with a defendant who causes criminal damage by spraying graffiti, then the order should be aimed at facilitating action to be taken to prevent graffiti spraying by him before it takes place. For example, the prohibition could prevent the offender from being in possession of a can of spray paint in a public place, giving an opportunity to take action in advance of the actual spraying. This makes it clear to the defendant that he has lost the right to carry such a can for the duration of the order.

If a court wished to make an order prohibiting a group of youngsters from racing cars or motor bikes on an estate or driving at excessive speed (anti-social behaviour for those living on the estate), then the order should not (normally) prohibit driving while disqualified. It should prohibit, for example, the offender while on the estate from taking part in, or encouraging, racing or driving at excessive speed. It might also prevent the group from congregating with named others in a particular area of the estate. Such an order gives those responsible for enforcing the order on the estate the opportunity to take action to prevent the anti-social conduct before it takes place. Neighbours can alert the police, who will not have to wait for the commission of a particular criminal offence.

The order will be breached not just by the offender driving but by his giving encouragement by being a passenger or a spectator.

The court also seemed to leave open the door for the continued use of a prohibition to prevent conduct that also amounts to an existing offence which carries only a monetary penalty, for example loitering for the purpose of prostitution. The court should not impose such a prohibition merely to increase the sentence for the offence, but must go through all the steps to make sure that an order is necessary.

Further details can be found on the Together website at www.together.gov.uk

Length of prohibitions

In *R (Lonerghan) v Lewes Crown Court* [2005] EWHC 457 (Admin), Maurice Kay LJ referred to the duration of prohibitions, saying:

> 'A curfew for two years in the life of a teenager is a very considerable restriction of freedom. It may be necessary, but in many cases I consider it likely that either the period of curfew could properly be set at less than the full life of the order or that, in the light of behavioural progress, an application to vary the curfew under section 1(8) might well succeed.'

Consequently, just because an order must run for a minimum of two years, it does not follow that each and every prohibition within the order must endure for the life of the order. This approach was endorsed by the Court of Appeal in *R v Boness* [2005] EWCA 2395 which considered that it might be necessary to amend or remove a prohibition after a period of time, for example if the defendant started work.

ASBOs on juveniles should be reviewed yearly, and further details are given on page 45.

Targeting specific behaviour

As noted above, prohibitions must target the defendant's specific anti-social behaviour. But assuming the prohibitions are negative, specific and enforceable, the appropriateness of the prohibitions imposed can be judged only on the facts of each case. Therefore, a number of common scenarios are included below for consideration. These are based on orders made by the courts, although facts and prohibitions have been altered to highlight specific issues. While these types of behaviour have been made the subject of orders, this should not imply that such behaviour will automatically be held to be subject to orders in the future.

Further examples of prohibitions can be found on the Crime Reduction website at www.crimereduction-.gov.uk

The following are examples of prohibitions that were drawn up but were found to be too wide or poorly drafted:

- Not to be a passenger in or on any vehicle, while any other person is [sic] committing a criminal offence in England or Wales. (A breach could be occasioned by travelling in a bus, the driver of which, unknown to the subject of the order, was driving without a licence (*R (W) v Acton Magistrates' Court* [2005] EWHC 954 (Admin)).

- Not to associate with any person or persons while such a person or persons is engaged in attempting or conspiring to commit any criminal offence in England or Wales. (A similar result to the above, in that he could be associating with someone who, unknown to him, was conspiring to commit an offence.)

- Entering any other car park, whether on payment or otherwise, within the counties of [. . .]. (This was considered to be too draconian as it would prevent the defendant from entering, even as a passenger, any car park in a supermarket (*R v McGrath* [2005] EWCA Crim 353).)

- Trespassing on any land belonging to any person, whether legal or natural, within those counties. (As above, in that any wrong turn onto someone else's property would risk custody.)

- Having in his possession in any public place any window hammer, screwdriver, torch or any tool or implement that could be used for the purpose of breaking into motor vehicles. (Unacceptably wide, as the meaning of 'any tool or implement' is impossible to ascertain.)

- Entering any land or building on the land that forms a part of educational premises, except as an enrolled pupil with the agreement of the head of the establishment or in the course of lawful employment. (It was held that the term 'educational premises' lacked clarity, for example it could have included teaching hospitals or premises where night classes were held. Also, there was a danger that the defendant might unwittingly breach the order if he played on playing fields associated with educational premises (*R v Boness* [2005] EWCA 2395).)

- In any public place, wearing, or having with you, anything that covers, or could be used to cover, the face or part of the face. This will include hooded clothing, balaclavas, masks or anything else that could be used to hide identity. (This was found to be too wide and a breach could occur by wearing a scarf or carrying a newspaper.)

- Doing anything that may cause damage. (Far too wide, as it may include the defendant scuffing his shoes.)

- Committing any criminal offence. (Taken with other prohibitions, the divisional court commented that this was very plainly too wide (*R (on application of W) v DPP* [2005] EWHC 1333 (Admin).)

Further examples and consideration of prohibitions made for football-related violence may be found in the case of (*R v Boness* [2005] EWCA 2395).

Duration of an order

The minimum duration of an order is two years, which was set in order to give respite to communities from anti-social behaviour. There is no maximum period and an order may be made for an indefinite period. It is for the court to decide the duration of an order, but the applicant agency should propose a time period as part of its application.

The duration applied for should take into account the age of the recipient, any special conditions that might affect their behaviour, the severity of his or her anti-social behaviour, the length of time it has gone on for and the recipient's response to any previous measures to deal with the behaviour. A longer order will generally be appropriate in the case of more serious or persistent anti-social behaviour. Orders issued to children and young people should be reviewed annually and careful consideration must be given to the case for applying for such orders to last beyond two years.

8.   Applying to the courts

Summons procedure

Magistrates' court (acting in its civil capacity)

The lead individual in charge of the case should arrange for an application form and three copies of the summons form to be completed and served upon the court. Once these proceedings have been issued, the applicant should serve the defendant with the following:

- the summons;

- a copy of the completed application form;

- documentary evidence of statutory consultation;

- guidance on how the defendant can obtain legal advice and representation;

- notice of any hearsay evidence;

- details of evidence in support of the application as agreed with the applicant agency's solicitor; and

- a warning to the defendant that it is an offence to pervert the course of justice, and that witness intimidation is liable to lead to prosecution.

Wherever possible, the lead officer in charge will ensure that service of the summons is made on the defendant in person. If personal service is not possible, the summons should be served by post as soon as possible to the last known address.

Where a child or a young person is concerned, a person with parental responsibility must also receive a copy of the summons. This could be a local authority social worker in the case of a looked-after child as well as, or instead of, the parent. ('Parent' has the same meaning as under section 1 of the Family Law Reform Act 1987, and 'guardian' is defined in section 107 of the Children and Young Persons Act 1933.)

The summons forms are set out within the Magistrates' Courts (Anti-Social Behaviour Orders) Rules 2002. See Appendix D.

County court

The process for the county court is set out in the Practice Direction of the updated Civil Procedure Rules at 65.21–65.26.

Disclosure

Before evidence is disclosed, the applicant should consult the police and other agencies to ensure that all reasonable steps have been taken to support witnesses and minimise any potential for witness intimidation. Evidence should not be disclosed without the express permission of the witness. However, evidence that is not disclosed cannot be relied on.

The applicant should seek to maintain witness anonymity and ensure that it does not identify them by default (for example through details of location, race, personal characteristics or age).

Court procedures

It is important that those hearing the case are fully briefed on the purpose of an order. There should be no confusion as to the purpose of the order, which is to protect the community. Where the case concerns a child, the welfare of the child is, of course, to be considered, and indeed the making of the order should contribute to this by setting standards of expected behaviour. But the welfare of the child is not the principal purpose of the order hearing.

Whether or not the subject of the application is present, the court should be asked to make the order. Adjournments should be avoided unless absolutely necessary.

Magistrates' court (acting in its civil capacity)

An application for an order in the magistrates' court is made by complaint. This means that the court will act in its civil capacity. The provisions governing civil applications for orders in magistrates' courts are set out in the Magistrates' Courts Act 1980.

The application, under section 1(3) of the Crime and Disorder Act 1998, should be made to the magistrates' court whose area includes the local government area or police area where people need to be protected from the anti-social behaviour.

The lead officer in charge of the case should ensure that all the evidence and witnesses are available at the hearing, including evidence in support of any need for the court to make an immediate order.

Under section 98 of the Magistrates' Courts Act 1980, evidence will be given on oath. Any magistrate or judge may hear the case.

Where a defendant fails to attend a hearing, the applicant may, after substantiating the complaint on oath, apply to the court to issue a warrant for the defendant's arrest. Various provisions for adjournment, non-attendance at court and the issue of a warrant for arrest are contained in sections 54 to 57 of the Magistrates' Courts Act 1980.

County court

An application for an order in the county court must be made in accordance with the procedure set out in the Practice Direction at Appendix B.

Where the applicant is the claimant in the principal proceedings, the application for the order should be included in the claim form. Where the applicant is the defendant in the principal proceedings, the application should be made by way of an application notice,

---

How to prepare a court file for an application

A file to support the application for an order should be prepared by the lead agency or the solicitor acting on their behalf. A minimum of eight identical court bundles will be required as follows:

- three for the magistrates;

- one for the legal adviser;

- one for the applicant's solicitor;

- one for the defence solicitor;

- one for the defendant; and

- one for the witness box.

The files are in loose-leaf format (in an A4 and ring binder) and should be indexed and paginated.

The index and contents should include, as appropriate:

- the summons for the order, together with the summons proof of service;

- the application for the order (in the format provided by the Magistrates' Court (Anti-Social Behaviour Orders) Rules 2002);

- the defendant's details;

- the defendant's previous convictions;

- the defendant's acceptable behaviour contract (ABC) agreements;

- a summary of the incidents being relied upon by the applicant;

- a map and description of the exclusion area;

- an association chart (showing relationships and connections where the alleged anti-social behaviour is by a group of people);

- documentation of statutory consultations; ➡

- supporting statements from any multi-agency consultation;

- a statement from the officer in the case;

- any other statements obtained;

- hearsay notices;

- a draft order for approval by the court;

- a home circumstances report where the subject of the order is a child or young person (if necessary and completed).

The bundle should be prepared and served on the solicitor for the defendant as soon as the summons is served. The applicant's solicitor should attempt to have the contents of the bundle agreed prior to any pre-trial review. Disclosure should be transparent and complete.

Contact

Niamh Noone, Lancashire Constabulary
Email: niamh.noone@lancashire.police.uk
Telephone: 01772 412919

which should accompany the defence. If the applicant is not a party to the principal proceedings, an application to be made a party and for the order must be made to the court in the same application notice.

Orders made on conviction in criminal proceedings

After a defendant has been convicted of an offence, the prosecutor may make an application for an order. Alternatively, the court may make an order of its own volition.

Orders on conviction can be made by the magistrates' court, the youth court or the Crown court. The form of these orders is set out in the Magistrates' Court Rules and the Crown Court Rules. An order may be made only if the court sentences or conditionally discharges the offender for a relevant offence.

The Crown Prosecution Service usually requests the court to make an order on conviction, as there is no formal application process for this order. The court has to consider that:

- the offender has acted in an anti-social manner, that is in a manner that caused or was likely to cause harassment, alarm or distress to one or more persons not of the same household as the offender; and

- an order is necessary to protect any persons in any place in England and Wales from further anti-social acts by him.

Evidence

Evidence should explain to the court the context of the anti-social behaviour and its effect on other people. It can include:

- direct witness statements;

The head of a noisy household gets an ASBO for ignoring repeated official warnings and threatening complaining neighbours and council officers

Issue

In March 2004, neighbours of a house in Lowestoft were subjected to frequent and persistent loud music, resulting in 17 complaints over the course of a month. The perpetrator, who was a housing association tenant, had intimidated, threatened and verbally abused her neighbours, council officers and visitors.

Approach

A noise abatement notice was served on the perpetrator by environmental health officers under section 80 of the Environmental Protection Act 1990. Audio equipment was confiscated following breach of the noise abatement notice. During the confiscation, the perpetrator verbally abused the council officers.

After seven warning letters, two abatement notices and the confiscation of more than£1,000 of musical equipment, the council was still receiving complaints.

Failure to comply with an abatement notice without reasonable excuse is an offence, and the noisy neighbour was taken to court. The council consulted Suffolk Police and the housing association and proposed terms for an order on conviction that achieved much more than the original abatement notice was capable of.

The magistrates granted the council's application for an order on conviction with the following prohibitions:

- not to play loud music that could be heard outside her dwelling; and

- not to verbally (or otherwise) abuse: employees or agents of the council; neighbours; or visitors to the neighbourhood.

Outcome

The order on conviction had several advantages over the noise abatement notice as an enforcement tool. It was easier to enforce as the evidence of experts such as environmental health officers to prove statutory noise nuisance would not be required. The order on conviction reduced the test of compliance to a simple (non-expert) factual observation of 'audibility' beyond the confines of the defendant's dwelling – a simple matter of observable fact that, say, a police officer could witness.

The second prohibition to deal with the tenant's threatening and abusive behaviour was beyond the scope of the original abatement notice. It was granted as the council was able to produce evidence of the tenant's behaviour to justify the restriction gained from early consultations with Suffolk Police and the housing association, which proved it was a reasonable restriction to impose on the defendant.

The resulting order on conviction did not cost any more than the noise prosecution would have cost on its own. Obtaining these restrictions in this way avoided the need for a stand-alone ASBO application in respect of the other aspects of the defendant's behaviour, saving money, avoiding several weeks' delay, and achieving faster and more readily enforceable relief for the wider community.

Valuable lessons were learnt by environmental health and other enforcement authorities in this action. In particular, early consultation with relevant agencies in the process of investigation and enforcement are important to an ASBO's success. And if the applicant for an order offers the other➡

relevant agencies the opportunity to assist in drafting appropriate prohibitions, a successful outcome, which offers relief for the community 'on all fronts', is more likely.

Contact

Andrew Reynolds, Principal Environmental Health Officer, Waveney District Council
Telephone: 01502 562111

- professional witness statements;

- hearsay evidence;

- CCTV footage;

- letters of complaint (including anonymous complaints) to the police, the council or a landlord;

- articles in the local press;

- the number and nature of the charges against the defendant;

- the defendant's character and conduct as revealed by the evidence;

- the content of the victim's personal statement;

- other offences that have been taken into consideration (TICs);

- details of final warnings or previous convictions;

- the risk assessment in any pre-sentence report;

- records of any non-compliance with other interventions, e g ABCs or warnings; and

- the community impact statement (CIS).

A CIS can be written by a caseworker (such as a housing officer or community safety officer) and/or by the local police. The purpose of a CIS is to outline the effect the anti-social behaviour is having on the wider community in a way that is clear and concise for the judge's consideration. In certain circumstances, some elements of evidence, such as hearsay, CCTV footage and letters of complaint, can be put in a CIS.

Adjournments

Section 10(3) of the Magistrates' Courts Act 1980 permits adjournments to be made after conviction and before sentence to enable enquiries to be made or, in this context, to determine the most suitable way of dealing with an application for an order under section 1C of the Crime and Disorder Act 1998.Where the court adjourns and delays sentencing to consider the order, it can impose bail conditions in the normal manner.

Section 139 of the Serious Organised Crime and Police Act 2005 has amended section 1C of the Crime and Disorder Act 1998 to allow for adjournments after sentencing the offender for the purpose of considering an order. Powers are also available to compel a defendant to return to court after sentencing to attend the adjourned hearing.

Interim orders on conviction

An interim order on conviction can be sought to protect vulnerable witnesses and communities from threats of violence, intimidation and further anti-social behaviour by the defendant pending the hearing of an application for a full order. This change to the Crime and Disorder Act 1998 was also introduced by section 139 of the Serious Organised Crime and Police Act 2005. For more information on interim orders, see the article 'What are interim anti-social behaviour orders?' on the Together website at www.together.gov.uk

Step-by-step guide

A step-by-step guide to the process can be found at Appendix E.

Public funding for defendants

A guide to public funding for defendants can be found at Appendix F.

9. Children and young people

The Home Office, Youth Justice Board and Association of Chief Police Officers have issued separate guidance on the role of the youth offending team (YOT) in dealing with anti-social behaviour.[7] There is also separate guidance on the interventions available for children under 10 at Appendix B.

This section sets out the procedures for applying for ASBOs and similar orders in respect of children and young people, and the procedures for managing the case afterwards.

Who can apply for an order?

Agencies able to apply for orders are the same as those for adults, and the consultation requirements are the same.

The role of the YOT needs to be clearly set out in terms of what it can offer in the prevention of anti-social behaviour, and in the ASBO process. All other agencies should involve the YOT in any consideration of an order at an early stage as it is likely to have much information to share about that young person. The YOT has a responsibility to prevent crime and anti-social behaviour by young people, and should help partners to obtain an order to stop the behaviour continuing where it is deemed appropriate. If there are any doubts about the option of obtaining an order, these should be explored at an early stage with the YOT and other partners, rather than in court. The YOT can also have a role in explaining the conditions of an order to the young person and their parents, explaining the impact of that person's behaviour on the community and making it clear that the order is the consequence of that behaviour. In addition, the YOT and other partners should offer support in order to aid compliance.

In cases of a breach of an order, the pre-sentence report (PSR) provided to the court by the YOT should outline the impact the behaviour has had on the community.

The YOT can also use the PSR in criminal proceedings to recommend an order on conviction where that course of action has been agreed and deemed appropriate.

The PSR should also address the issue of parenting and further support to the young person. Courts can make a parenting order with an ASBO or similar order, if a voluntary approach has failed and it will help improve behaviour, together with an individual support order (ISO).The YOT has a key role in both of these interventions. Details on these are set out below.

---

[7]   Youth Justice Board, Home Office and Association of Chief Police Officers (2006). *Anti-social Behaviour: A guide to the role of Youth Offending Teams in dealing with anti-social behaviour.* This can be downloaded at www.youth-justice-board.gov.uk/Publications/ Scripts/prodView.asp?idproduct=212&ep=

Applications to the magistrates' court acting in its civil capacity

Since the youth court has no civil jurisdiction, applications for orders against under-18s will be heard by the magistrates' court (except where the youth court is asked to impose an order on conviction). A pilot to allow children and young people to be joined to proceedings in the county court, for the purpose of obtaining an ASBO where the anti-social behaviour is material to the principal proceedings, is currently under way in 11 county courts and is due to run until September 2006.

The officer in charge of the application should contact the justices' clerk in advance of the hearing to ensure that it will be conducted in a way that is suitable for the child or young person.

- Where there is an application to a magistrates' court for an ASBO under section 1 of the Crime and Disorder Act 1998, or an application to a magistrates' court for an ASBO to be varied or discharged under section 1(8) of the Act, and the person against whom the order is sought is under 18, the justices constituting the court should normally be qualified to sit in the youth court.

- Unlike a youth court, which is closed to the general public, the magistrates' court is open to the general public and has no automatic restrictions to prevent public and press access or to prevent reporting of the proceedings or to protect the identity of a child or young person (or adult) who is the subject of an application.

- The court should have a good reason, aside from age alone, to impose a discretionary order under section 39 of the Children and Young Persons Act 1933 to prevent the identification of a child or young person concerned in the proceedings.

- The applicant may resist a call from the defendant's representatives for such restrictions if the effectiveness of the ASBO will largely depend on the wider community knowing the details.

The applicant should note the following.

- Under section 98 of the Magistrates' Courts Act 1980, evidence will be given on oath, except the evidence of a child under 14 years of age, which is given unsworn.

- Section 34A of the Children and Young Persons Act 1933 requires the attendance of a parent or legal guardian at court for any person under 16 years of age. Every effort should be made before a hearing to ensure that this takes place to avoid unnecessary adjournments.

- The court will require information about the child's or young person's background, home surroundings and family circumstances. Such information should be available to avoid the need for an adjournment.

Dealing effectively with persistent young perpetrators in Norfolk

Issue

Improved partnership working between the police and the YOT was key to effectively tackling anti-social behaviour by young people.

Approach

Regular liaison meetings of YOT and youth inclusion and support panel (YISP) staff were held at the Safer Communities Unit. Community reparation projects were planned which impacted on sensitive communities or resonated with vulnerable members of the community. Police officers forged contact with youth groups and educational centres. Part of the action plan required YISP workers to attend a police tasking and co-ordination meeting.   ➡

Outcomes

The YOT discussed, and was helpful to and supportive of, community reparation projects that added to increased public reassurance. Work commissioned included graffiti clearance in priority areas, and the cleaning of 'Home Watch' street signs that were covered in algae, and where householders were elderly and not able to carry out that work. Two respected local officers maintained their links with a local community youth project through a weekly radio broadcast, 'On the Beat', on the first community radio station in Norfolk. The Safer Communities inspector became a member of the steering group of that project. Community team officers enjoyed good relations with the Excellence Centre, a unit for excluded or disengaged children of school age, as evidenced by the support of the centre manager for the Constabulary's recent 'Chartermark' award.

Contact

Inspector Peter Walsh
Email: walshp@norfolk.pnn.police.uk

Assessment of needs

When applying for an order against a young person aged between 10 and 17, the YOT should make an assessment of their circumstances and needs. This will enable the local authority to ensure that the appropriate services are provided for the young person concerned and for the court to have the necessary information about them.

It is vital that any assessment does not delay the application for an order. The lead agency should therefore liaise closely with the local social services department or YOT from the start of the process so that, where a new assessment is required, it can be begun quickly. In some cases an up-to-date assessment may already be available.

Councils with social services responsibilities have a duty, arising from section 17 of the Children Act 1989, to safeguard and promote the welfare of children within their areas who may be in need. The assessment of the needs of such children is expected to be carried out in accordance with the *Framework for the assessment of children in need and their families*.[8] The guidance sets out the content and timescales of the initial assessment (seven working days) and the core assessment (35 working days). A core assessment is required when an initial assessment has determined that the child is in need. The assessment will cover the child's needs, the capacities of their parents and wider family, and environmental factors. This enables councils to determine whether the child is a 'child in need' and what services may be necessary in order to address the assessed needs.

The assessment of the child's needs should run in parallel with evidence gathering and the application process. Statutory agencies, such as social services, the local education authority or the health authority, have a statutory obligation to provide services to under-18s. They should do so irrespective of whether an ASBO application is to be made and the timing of that application. The ASBO application does not prevent such support and can proceed in parallel, or indeed prior to, that support.

Parenting orders

This section should be read in conjunction with Government guidance on parenting contracts and parenting orders.[9] There is also information on the Together website (www.together.gov.uk). The applicant for parenting orders is the YOT. (Provisions in the Police and Justice Bill currently before Parliament aim to extend to registered social landlords and local authorities the power to apply for parenting orders.)

---

[8] Department of Health (2000) *Framework for the assessment of children in need and their families*.
[9] Home Office, Youth Justice Board, Department for Constitutional Affairs. *Parenting Contracts and Orders Guidance*, February 2004.

Parenting orders are available alongside other court action where:

- an ASBO or a sex offender order has been made in respect of a child or young person; or

- a child or young person has been convicted of a criminal offence.

Parenting orders can be made for children aged between 10 and 17 provided that the conditions in section 8 of the Crime and Disorder Act 1998 are met. This section stipulates that a parenting order is desirable only if it is made 'in the interest of preventing repetition of the behaviour which led to the order being made.'

The court can decide to make the order; it is not necessary to obtain the consent of the parent or guardian.

It is essential that parents and guardians take responsibility for the behaviour of their children. If an ASBO or an order on conviction is made against a child or young person, the court must also consider making a parenting order in respect of the parents or guardians of the child or young person.[10] Where the parent or child has a disability, a practitioner with specialist knowledge should be involved in the assessment process to help establish whether the behaviour is a result of disability and whether it could or should be addressed.

Parenting orders are civil orders that help to engage parents[11] to address their child's offending or anti-social behaviour, and to establish discipline and build a relationship with their child. This may help the conditions of the ASBO to be met and thereby reduce the chances of the young person breaching the order.

The parenting order requires the parent or guardian to comply, for a period of not more than 12 months, with such requirements as are specified in the order, being those which the court considers desirable in the interests of preventing any repetition of the anti-social behaviour (for example ensuring that the child attends school regularly, avoids certain places, or is home by a certain time at night).

The parent or guardian is required to attend a counselling or guidance programme for up to three months. This element is compulsory and must be imposed in all cases when an order is made (except where the parent or guardian has previously received a parenting order – section 8(5)). Programmes can cover setting and enforcing consistent standards of behaviour and responding more effectively to unreasonable adolescent demands.

The court needs to consider an oral or written report before making a parenting order, unless the child or young person has reached the age of 16.To avoid unnecessary adjournments, such a report should be available early in the court process.

A 'responsible officer', who will generally be from the local YOT, social services, probation service or local education authority, supervises delivery of the parenting order. The officer will have responsibility for, among other things, arranging the provision of counselling or guidance sessions and ensuring that the parent complies with any other requirements which the court may impose.

If the parent does not comply with the order, the responsible officer can refer the matter to the police for investigation. Such action is generally expected only where non-compliance is sufficiently serious to warrant possible prosecution – the responsible officer is expected to work with the parent to improve compliance. But if prosecuted and convicted for non-compliance, the parent can be fined up to £1,000 (level 3 on the standard scale).

---

[10]   Provision for parenting orders is set out in sections 8, 9 and 10 of the Crime and Disorder Act 1998.The orders can be made in proceedings where a child safety order, an ASBO or sex offender order has been made; a child or young person is convicted of an offence; or a person is convicted of an offence under sections 443 or 444 of the Education Act 1996.

[11]   For the purposes of the 1998 Act, the term 'parent' has the same meaning as that contained within section 1 of the Family Law Reform Act 1987, that is either of the child's or young person's natural parents whether or not married to each other at the time of their birth. 'Guardian' is defined in section 117 of the 1998 Act with reference to section 107 of the Children and Young Persons Act 1933, and includes any person who, in the opinion of the court, has for the time being the care of the child or young person. This may include people who may not have parental responsibility for the child or young person as defined in the Children Act 1989, such as step parents.

Individual support orders

Section 1AA of the Crime and Disorder Act 1998, which was inserted by section 322 of the Criminal Justice Act 2003, provides for the making of ISOs, which have been available since May 2004.They are civil orders and can be attached to ASBOs made against young people aged between 10 and 17 years old. They impose positive requirements on the young person and are designed to tackle the underlying causes of their anti-social behaviour.

ISOs are available for stand-alone ASBOs made in the magistrates' courts only. Where a magistrates' court makes an ASBO against a young person, it must also make an ISO if it considers that an ISO would help to prevent further anti-social behaviour. ISOs are not available for orders on conviction, where it is expected that sentencing will address the underlying causes of the offence.

ISOs can last up to six months and require a young person to comply with such requirements as may be specified in the order and any directions given by the responsible officer to that end. Such requirements must be those which the court considers desirable in the interests of preventing repetition of the anti-social behaviour and may include requirements to participate in certain activities, to report to a specified person at specified times or to comply with educational arrangements, but in no case should they require attendance on more than two days a week. An example would be support sessions tailored to the individual's needs and designed to address the causes of the behaviour that led to the ASBO being made, such as counselling for substance misuse or an anger management programme. The ISO may name specific activities the individual must participate in and can also specify dates and places where attendance is required.

ISO application process

There is no need for a specific application for an ISO, although it might be helpful to raise the issue with the court. Where a magistrates' court is making an ASBO (stand-alone only) against a person under 18 years old, it is obliged to make an ISO at the same time if the following conditions are met:

- the ISO would be desirable in the interests of preventing any repetition of the anti-social behaviour which led to the ASBO being made;

- the young person is not already subject to an ISO; and

- the Secretary of State has notified the court that arrangements for implementing the ISO are available (this was done in April 2004 in Home Office Circular 025/2004).

The court should ensure the requirements of the ISO and the consequences of breach are explained to the defendant. If an ISO is not made, then the court must state why it considers that the conditions for making the order are not met. ISOs are not available for orders on conviction.

Role of the youth offending team

The YOT advises the magistrates' court on whether an ISO is necessary and the conditions an ISO should contain. This information is based on a needs assessment of the young person.

The YOT is responsible for co-ordinating delivery of the ISO and also has a role in ensuring that the terms and conditions of both the ASBO and ISO are understood by the defendant. The conditions within the ISO are overseen by a responsible officer who is usually a member of the YOT, social services or local education authority.

Variation and discharge

An application to vary or discharge the ISO may be made by either the young person subject to the ISO or the responsible officer. The need to vary an ISO may arise where support proves to be inappropriate or the individual moves out of the area. Equally, if the ASBO linked to the ISO is varied by a court, the court may also vary or discharge the ISO at the same time.

If the ASBO comes to an end or is discharged, the ISO also ceases to have effect.

Breach

Breach of an ISO is an offence and criminal penalties apply. For ISOs to be credible, breaches must be dealt with.

The responsible officer is responsible for ensuring compliance with an ISO. It will usually be appropriate for the responsible officer to encourage compliance using warning letters before instigating proceedings for a criminal prosecution.

The breach is taken forward by the Crown Prosecution Service and breach proceedings are heard in the youth court. If a court finds that the subject of the order has failed to comply with any requirement of the order, they are guilty of an offence. Breach is a summary offence and the court can impose a fine of up to:

- £1,000, if defendant aged 14 or over; or

- £250, if defendant aged under 14.

Where the defendant is under 16, the parent will usually be responsible for payment of the fine. The court also has the discretion to order the parent to pay if the defendant is aged between 16 and 18 (as set out in section 137 of the Powers of Criminal Court (Sentencing) Act 2000.

A referral order is not available for breach of an ISO.

Balcony games for the boys creates corridor of hell for neighbours: ASBOs, ISOs and a house move bring relief for all

Issue

Sons of two neighbouring families were responsible for persistent noise nuisance which caused neighbours great distress for over a year. The children of families X and Y, aged between 10 and 15, lived in first-floor council flats where they played rowdy games outside their flats. Family X had a secure tenancy while family Y had a short-term tenancy. Residents frequently complained to the housing office or to the local police community support officers (PCSOs).

Approach

Police and the housing office worked closely together on the case and discovered a pattern of nuisance. PCSOs and the estate manager mediated between families X and Y and their neighbours. When mediation failed, joint visits were made to warn the families of the consequences of their continued anti-social behaviour. Formal warnings followed, outlining the consequences of the boys' actions in terms of potential ASBOs and possible loss of their parents' tenancy. When all warnings had failed, a multi-agency team obtained an interim ASBO on the five boys to put an immediate stop to the nuisance.

Evidence provided by PCSOs and the estate manager was used at the hearing, and interim orders were granted.   ➡

Minor breaches over the Christmas period were reported to the police by witnesses between the interim and full hearing, and these strengthened the case for the ASBOs at the full hearing.

Witnesses who were previously fearful of giving evidence were willing to do so at the full hearing where the ASBOs were granted, and an ISO was attached to each ASBO to tackle some of the underlying causes of the behaviour.

The conditions of the ASBOs on the five boys ordered them:

- not to cause nuisance within the vicinity of their dwellings;

- to stop knocking on doors and windows; and

- not to play games on the balcony.

Outcome

The main benefit of the ASBOs was the relief that they brought to the neighbours, who felt they had been supported through the process by police and the housing office.

The ISO, devised and facilitated by Norfolk Youth Offending Team, consisted of four hour-long sessions aimed at helping the boys develop an understanding of how their anti-social behaviour, their constant shouting and banging, impacted on themselves as a group, on their immediate family, and on their neighbours.

The first session defined the ground rules for the group, including showing respect, listening with only one person talking at a time, no shouting, and with each member being allowed to voice an opinion. The second session got the boys listening to what people were saying around them. The third session introduced elements from a social skills game that focused on the boys' finding different ways of asking each other something without resorting to shouting. In the fourth session, a worker from Positive Futures helped the boys think about what leisure activities were available as alternatives to playing on the balcony. The youth worker kept the boys' parents up to date on what was happening in the sessions.

Family X, who were relocated away from family Y, kept their tenancy and no further problems were reported. Similarly, family Y succeeded in stopping their anti-social behaviour.

The ISO gave the boys an opportunity to understand the effect of their rowdy behaviour on themselves and others. As a result of the order and the interventions of the youth worker, the boys took up recreational activities and found constructive ways of spending their time.

Overall, the intervention package was a great success for the community, and for the families themselves.

Contact

Karl Hodgins
Youth Worker, Norfolk YOT
Karl.Hodgins@yot.norfolk.gov.uk

In a debate in the House of Commons on 28 June, Vernon Coaker MP, a Home Office Minister, said:

"ISOs are playing their part in the wider battle to combat anti-social behaviour and promote positive behaviour. They have proven potential to help young people to turn around their lives and move away from anti-social behaviour and offending. I share the enthusiasm for ISOs of my hon. Friend ➡

> the Member for Stockport, and I hope that she and the other hon. Members will encourage local agencies to make more use of such a highly effective intervention tool."

10. Immediate post-order procedure (adults and young people)

Where an ASBO or similar order is granted, it is preferable for a copy of the order to be served on the defendant in person prior to his or her departure from court. It is essential to ascertain that the defendant understands the nature of the prohibitions and the order.

Good practice – managing procedures and timescales

Practitioners handling such orders have taken a range of measures to minimise paperwork and delays, including:[12]

- breaking down the process into clear, manageable stages that are easy to follow for those unfamiliar with the process;

- setting timeframes for each stage of the application to keep the process focused, including a commitment to arrange problem-solving meetings at short notice;

- releasing key staff so that they can concentrate on the application process – this should result in evidence gathering being conducted quickly and efficiently;

- using other agencies, such as neighbourhood wardens and station staff, to collect additional evidence where required (evidence gathering and attending incidents are tasks that local authorities, registered social landlords (RSLs) and the police are already involved in and therefore involve no additional cost);

- adopting strategies to overcome challenges to witness evidence such as ensuring that witness statements corroborate;

- minimising court delays by forewarning the courts of application and using pre–trial reviews;

- sharing costs between partner agencies and utilising the expertise from each agency; and

- not engaging in non-essential problem-solving meetings in more serious cases in order to get to court more quickly.

Where an individual has not been personally served with the order at the court, the court should be asked to arrange for personal service as soon as possible thereafter.

In without notice proceedings, proof of service of an ASBO is important, since any criminal proceedings for breach may fail if service is challenged by the defence and cannot be proved by the prosecution. While all other orders do not need proof of service in order to prove breach of an order, lack of knowledge of existence of an order will contribute to a reasonable excuse for the defence. In the case of a child or young person, the order should also be served on the parent, guardian or an appropriate adult, and such service should be recorded.

An order comes into effect on the day it is made. But the two-year period during which no order shall be discharged except with the consent of both parties starts from the date of service.[13]

The lead agency, if not the police, should ensure that a copy of the order is forwarded immediately to the police. The agency should also give copies of the order to the anti-social behaviour co-ordinator of the local

---

12   Campbell, S. (2002) *Implementing Anti-social Behaviour Orders: messages for practitioners*. Home Office Findings 160.
13   Sections 1(9), 1B(6) and 1C of the Crime and Disorder Act 1998, as amended.

crime and disorder reduction partnership, the other partner agencies and the main targets and witnesses of the anti-social behaviour, so that breaches can be reported and acted upon. The Justices' Clerks' Society guidance states that it is the responsibility of the court to inform the police of the making of an order.[14]

The police should notify the appropriate police area command on the same working day so that details of the defendant and the conditions of the order can be recorded.

A copy of the order should be provided to the lead agency's legal representative on the same day as the court hearing, and in the case of a child or young person, the court will provide a further copy for the youth offending team (YOT).The YOT should arrange for action to be taken by an appropriate agency (for example social services) to ensure that the young person understands the seriousness of the order. It should also consider the provision of appropriate support programmes to help avoid a breach of the order by diverting the offender from the behaviour that led to it, although such programmes cannot, as the law currently stands, be a condition of the order.

Enforcing the order

The obtaining of the order is not the end of the process. The order must be monitored and enforced properly.

Partnership working after the order is made should include information exchange to ensure early warning of problems and clarification of who should do what to safeguard witnesses, as well as what other action should be taken to challenge the perpetrator in such cases.

It is essential that breaches of an order, appeals against the sentence and any other actions relating to the management of the case are reported to the agency responsible for the management of the case.

One year review of juveniles' ASBOs

Orders issued to young people should be reviewed each year, given young people's continually changing circumstances, to help ensure that they are receiving the support they need in order to prevent breach. The review should be administrative rather than judicial, and should be undertaken by the team that decided upon the initial application. Where practicable, the YOT should provide the group with an assessment of the young person. Depending upon progress towards improved behaviour, possible outcomes will include an application to discharge the order or a strengthening of the prohibitions. Applications to vary or discharge the order will have to be made to the court in the usual way. The overriding considerations remain the safety and needs of the community, and the review would have to incorporate the community's views on the order's effectiveness.

Agencies need to be alert to the prospect that this should become a statutory requirement in the near future. Adopting this as best practice now will enable them to achieve compliance more readily.

Police National Computer (PNC)

Recording of orders on the PNC will enable police forces to enforce breaches effectively. Local arrangements should be made for orders to be placed on the PNC so that police officers are in a position to access usable data to identify those who are subject to an order. Conditions of the order should be appended clearly along with the identity of the case officer so that the necessary action can be taken in case of a breach (which is an arrestable offence).

---

[14] Justices' Clerks' Society. *Good practice guide – Anti-Social Behaviour Orders. A Guide to Law and Procedure in the Magistrates' Court*, 4.5(V).

11. Appeals

Magistrates' court (acting in its civil capacity) and orders on conviction in criminal proceedings

Section 4 of the Crime and Disorder Act 1998 provides the offender with the right of appeal against the making of a stand-alone ASBO. Section 108 of the Magistrates' Courts Act 1980 provides a right of appeal against an on-conviction order. An appeal in both cases is to the Crown Court. Rules 74 and 75 of the Magistrates' Courts Rules 1981 and 6 to 11 of the Crown Court Rules 1982 apply to appeals against orders. Both parties may provide additional evidence. By virtue of section 79(3) of the Supreme Court Act 1981, an appeal is by way of a re-hearing of the case. In determining an appeal, the Crown Court should have before it a copy of the original application for an order (if applicable), the full order and the notice of appeal. The lead agency should ensure that copies are sent to the court.

Notice of appeal must be given in writing to the designated officer of the court and the applicant body within 21 days of the order (Crown Court Rules 1982, rule 7). But the Crown Court has the discretion to give leave to appeal out of time (rule 7(5)). The agency that brought the initial application should take charge of defending any appeal against the order. It should also lead in action to guard against witness intimidation.

The Crown Court may vary the order or make a new order. Any order made by the Crown Court on appeal shall be treated for the purpose of any later application for variation or discharge as if it were the original magistrates' court order, unless it is an order directing that the application be re-heard by the magistrates' court.

Although on hearing an appeal it is open to the Crown Court to make any incidental order, for example to suspend the operation of a prohibition pending the outcome of the appeal where this appears to the Crown Court to be just, there is no provision for automatic stay of an order pending appeal. The order remains in force pending the outcome of the appeal, and breach is a criminal offence even if the appeal subsequently succeeds.

An appeal against the ruling of the Crown Court is to the High Court by way of case stated under section 28 of the Supreme Court Act 1981, or by application for judicial review by virtue of section 29(3) of that Act. It is also open to the applying authority to seek to challenge a magistrates' decision to refuse to grant an order by way of case stated (judicial review of the decision to the divisional court) by virtue of section 111 of the Magistrates' Courts Act 1980.

County court

Any appeal against an order made in the county court must be made in accordance with part 52 of the Civil Procedure Rules. Appeals against orders made by district judges will be to a circuit judge and against orders made by circuit judges to the High Court.

Appeals to the High Court by case stated

Any person who was party to any proceedings or is aggrieved by the conviction, order, determination or other proceedings of the court may question the proceedings on the grounds that it is wrong in law or in excess of jurisdiction.

The court can then be asked to state a case for the opinion of the High Court.

The case stated is heard by at least two High Court judges, and more often three judges sit, including the Lord Chief Justice. No evidence is considered, so the hearing consists entirely of legal argument by counsel.

Having heard and determined the question(s) of law, the High Court may reverse, affirm or amend the original determination in respect of which the case has been stated, or remit the matter to the justices with the opinion of the court, or make such an order in relation to the matter as the court may see fit.

Appeals before the Crown Court

The hearing at the Crown Court is an entirely fresh one and, by virtue of section 79(3) of the Supreme Court Act 1981, is a full re-hearing of the case. The judgment in the case of *R v Lamb* [2005] EWCA Crim 2487 recommended that circuit judges and above should be dealing with these cases.

Rectification of mistakes

Section 142 of the Magistrates' Courts Act 1980 gives the court power to vary or rescind a sentence or other order imposed or made by it when dealing with an offender, if it appears to the court to be in the interests of justice to do so. However, this section is intended to rectify mistakes and applies only to orders made when dealing with an offender in criminal proceedings. Therefore, this power would only be applicable to orders made on conviction, rather than on a stand-alone application.

Application for judicial review

Judicial review looks at the lawfulness of actions and decisions. An application can be made for the High Court to consider whether the magistrates' court has failed to exercise its jurisdiction properly or whether it has made an error of law, which appears on the face of the record.

The High Court has the power to quash the order or make a mandatory prohibiting order.

An application must be made promptly, and in any event within three months of the date on which the grounds for the application arose.

12. Breaches

Breaches by adults

Breach of an order is a criminal offence, which is arrestable and recordable. Prosecutions for breaches of orders can be brought by the Crown Prosecution Service (CPS), although a local authority may also do so by virtue of section 1(10A) of the Crime and Disorder Act 1998 (as inserted by section 85(4) of the Anti-social Behaviour Act 2003), which states that prosecutions can also be brought by:

(a)   a council which is a relevant authority;

(b)   the council for the local government area in which a person in respect of whom an order has been made resides or appears to reside.

The lead officer managing the case should keep the other partner agencies informed of the progress and outcome of any breach investigation. A particular consideration will be the need to protect witnesses. The standard of proof for prosecution of a breach of an order is the criminal standard – 'beyond reasonable doubt'. Provision is made in section 1(10) of the Crime and Disorder Act 1998 for a defence of reasonable excuse.

The maximum penalty on conviction in the magistrates' court is six months in prison or a fine not exceeding £5,000 or both; at the Crown Court the maximum penalty is five years in prison or a fine or both. Community penalties are available but a conditional discharge is not.

Agencies and courts should not treat the breach of an order as just another minor offence. (It should be remembered that the order itself would normally have been the culmination of a course of persistent anti-social behaviour.) An order will only be seen to be effective if breaches are taken seriously.

Information on breaches can be received from any source, including the local authority housing department and other local authority officers, neighbours and other members of the public. Any information received by a partner agency should be passed immediately to the police and lead officer, who should inform the other agencies involved. Breach penalties are the same for all orders, including the interim order. Court proceedings should be swift and not fractured by unnecessary adjournments either during the proceedings or before sentencing.

Where the offender is found guilty of the breach, the court may take reports from the local authority or police and any applicant agency before sentencing. The court should also consider the original reasons for making the order. A copy of the original order as granted (including any maps and details of any prohibitions) can be put before the court as evidence that an order has been made without the need for a statement formally proving that an order was made (section 139 of the Serious Organised Crime and Police Act 2005).

The sentence given should be proportionate and reflect the impact of the behaviour complained of.

Breaches by children and young people

Breach proceedings for children and young people will be dealt with in the youth court. Breach proceedings in the youth court are not subject to automatic reporting restrictions. The Serious Organised Crime and Police Act 2005 removed automatic reporting restrictions for children and young people convicted of a breach of an ASBO (section 141), and thus details about the perpetrator can be made public. The court may still impose reporting restrictions, particularly if they were put in place when the order was initially imposed in a civil court.

Under section 98 of the Magistrates' Courts Act 1980, evidence will be given on oath, except the evidence of a child under 14, which is given unsworn. Section 34 of the Children and Young Persons Act 1933 requires the attendance of a parent or legal guardian at court for any person under 16 years of age. The court will require information about the young person's background, home surroundings and family circumstances prior to sentence. This should be provided by the youth offending team or social services.

As with adults, community penalties are available but a conditional discharge is not. In addition, the youth court should consider whether to make a parenting order, or whether the individual support order should be amended.

13. Variation and discharge of an order

Variation or discharge of an order, including an interim order, may be made on application to the court that originally made it. An application to vary or discharge an order made on conviction in criminal proceedings may be made to any magistrates' court within the same petty sessions areas as the court that made the order. The application can be made either by the original applicant in the case or the defendant. An order cannot be discharged within two years of its service without the consent of both parties. An order made on conviction cannot be discharged before the end of two years. Prohibitions, however, can be varied, removed or added within that initial two year period.

The procedure for variation or discharge is set out in the Magistrates' Courts (Anti-Social Behaviour Orders) Rules 2002, the Crown Court (Amendment) Rules 2002 and the Civil Procedure Rules. These are published separately from this guidance and are available on the crime reduction website at www.crimereduction.gov.uk

If the individual who is subject to the order asks for its variation or discharge, the agency that obtained the order needs to ensure that a considered response is given to the court. If it is decided that the lead agency should contest the application for variation or discharge, it should give the court its reasons, supported as appropriate by evidence gathered in the course of monitoring the effectiveness of the order. The magistrates' legal adviser will send details of the variation or discharge of any order to the local police force and local authority. The police should record any discharge or variation of the order on their computer system and arrange for any changes to be reflected in the Police National Computer record.

14. Monitoring and recording

Local agencies should agree common procedures for recording and monitoring both their successful and unsuccessful applications. Details of orders granted should be sent to the local crime and disorder reduction partnership (CDRP) anti-social behaviour co-ordinator and the local authority or police as appropriate, as well as to other agencies involved with the offender (including the local youth offending team if the offender is under 18 years old).

As a minimum there should be a record of:

- the original application (or details of the prosecution and hearing of any request for the order in the case of an order on conviction), including the name, address, date of birth, gender and ethnicity of the defendant;

- the order itself, including, where applicable, the map showing any exclusion area;

- the date and details of any variation or discharge of the order; and

- the action taken for any breach.

The following information could also be recorded:

- name, address, age, gender and ethnicity of any victim – or a statement that the case involved no identified victim;

- details of any person or persons who complained of the behaviour;

- details of any contributory issues, for example drugs, alcohol and substance misuse and/or mental health problems;

- details of any aggravating factors, for example racial motivation; and

- assessment of outcome in terms of whether or not the anti-social behaviour ceased.

Consistency of information will help to assess the effectiveness of orders and inform future local audits and crime reduction strategies.

Local authorities and other agencies, including the police, have a duty under the Race Relations (Amendment) Act 2000 to satisfy themselves and the public that their anti-social behaviour policies do not discriminate. The Act also imposes a duty to promote race equality. As part of this duty, local authorities and the police should therefore ensure that they monitor the impact of their anti-social behaviour policy on the promotion of race equality. Systems to monitor the ethnicity of both defendants and victims will therefore need to be in place. This information should, where possible, be collected on the basis of self-definition by the defendant.

From December 2006, the new general duty under the Disability Discrimination Act requires a public authority to pay due regard when carrying out its functions to: the need to eliminate unlawful discrimination against disabled people; the need to eliminate disability-related harassment of disabled people; the need to promote equality of opportunity for disabled people; and the need to take account of disabled persons' disabilities even where that involves more favourable treatment. Advice on the general duty can also be obtained from the leaflet issued by the Office for Disability Issues (ODI) entitled *Disability equality: a priority for all*. The Disability Rights Commission website at www.drc.org.uk contains information under the section on publications entitled 'Do the Duty'.

15. Promoting awareness of orders

The purpose of the orders is to protect local communities from the harassment, alarm or distress that can be caused by anti-social behaviour. An effective media strategy by the CDRP is therefore essential if local residents and businesses are to be aware of orders and their implications. Using the local press to ensure the community knows the subject and conditions of the order is often a cost-effective strategy. At the same time, the staff of the partner agencies need to understand how and when orders can be used, and how they relate to the other tools to combat anti-social behaviour available to the partnership.

Local agencies and CDRPs should, within the context of their overall strategies for combating anti-social behaviour, devise a strategy for promoting awareness of orders. A designated officer should have responsibility for its delivery. This might most naturally be the CDRP anti-social behaviour co-ordinator. Disclosure of information should be necessary and proportionate to the objective it seeks to achieve.

Suggested aims of the strategy

The aims of an effective local publicity strategy are to:

- increase community confidence in reporting anti-social behaviour and expectations that it can be reduced;

- deter potential offenders from anti-social behaviour;

- ensure that the local population is aware of orders; the powers of the local authority, registered social landlords, Housing Action Trusts, the Environment Agency and the police (including the British Transport Police) to apply for them; and whom to approach if they believe that an order may be appropriate;

- ensure that agency staff have confidence in using orders where they are deemed appropriate; and

- ensure that potential witnesses are aware of the support available to them.

Publicity

This part of the guidance reflects the judgment of Lord Justice Kennedy, presiding judge in the case of *R (on application of Stanley, Marshall and Kelly) v Commissioner of Police for the Metropolis and Chief Executive of London Borough of Brent* [2004] EWHC 2229 (Admin), commonly referred to as Stanley v Brent.

Principles

- There is no 'naming and shaming' – ASBOs are not intended to punish or embarrass individuals but to protect communities.

- Publicity is essential if local communities are to support agencies in tackling anti-social behaviour. There is an implied power in the Crime and Disorder Act 1998 and the Local Government Act 2000 to publicise an order so that it can be effectively enforced.

- Orders protect local communities.

- Obtaining the order is only part of the process; its effectiveness will normally depend on people knowing about the order.

- Information about orders obtained should be publicised to let the community know that action has been taken in their area.

- A case-by-case approach should be adopted, and each individual case should be judged on its merits as to whether or not to publicise the details of an individual who is subject to an order. Publicity should be expected in most cases.

- It is necessary to balance the human rights of individuals who are subject to orders against those of the community as a whole when considering publicising orders.

- Publicity should be the norm, not the exception. An individual who is subject to an order should understand that the community is likely to learn about it.

Benefits of publicity

The benefits of publicity include the following:

- *Enforcement* – Local people have the information they need to identify and report breaches.

- *Public reassurance about safety* – Victims and witnesses know that action has been taken to protect them and their human rights in relation to safety and/or quiet enjoyment of their property. Making local people aware of an order that is made for their own protection can make a real difference to the way in which they live their lives, especially when they have suffered from anti-social behaviour themselves or lived in fear of it.

- *Public confidence in local services* – Local people are reassured that if they report anti-social behaviour, action will be taken by local authorities, the police or other agencies.

- *Deterrent to the subject of the order* – The perpetrator is aware that breaches are more likely to be reported because details of the order are in the public domain.

- *Deterrent to other perpetrators* – Publicity spreads the message that orders are being used and is a warning to others who are causing a nuisance in the community.

The decision to publish

Each individual case should be judged on its merits as to whether or not to publicise the details of an individual who is subject to an order. There should be a correlation between the purpose of publicity and the necessity test: that is, what is the least possible interference with privacy in order to promote the purpose identified.

Decision-makers should ensure that the decisions to publicise orders are recorded. However, this should not be seen as an onerous, lengthy task, but merely a way of recording the process they go through to arrive at publication. To ensure it is achieved, it is good practice to identify an individual, such as the anti-social behaviour co-ordinator, to be in charge of the process.

The decision-making process should aim to consider and record several key factors:

- the need for publicity;

- a consideration of the human rights of the public;

- a consideration of the human rights of those against whom orders are made; and

- what the publicity should look like and whether it is proportionate to the aims of the publicity.

The decision-making process should be carried out early on so as to avoid any delay in publicity following the granting of the order.

The decision-making process

Publicity must be necessary to achieve an identified aim – this will involve a necessity test. The identified aim for publicising could be (1) to notify the public that an order has been obtained, to reassure the public that action has been taken; (2) to notify the public of a specific order so that they can help in its enforcement; or (3) to act as a deterrent to others involved in anti-social behaviour. In some cases two or even all three aims will be relevant.

Disclosure of information should always be necessary and proportionate to achieving the desired aim(s). When identifying the aim(s), decision-makers should acknowledge, in those cases where it is relevant, the 'social pressing need' for effective enforcement of an order that prohibits anti-social behaviour to protect the community. In effect, this is a consideration of the human rights of the wider community, including past and potential victims. The decision-maker should recognise and acknowledge that for publicity to achieve its aim, it might engage the human rights of the individual who is subject to the order and potentially those of his or her family. Publicity should be proportionate to ensure that any interference is kept to a minimum. For example, if the legitimate aim is enforcement of the order then personal information, such as the terms of the order, the identity of the individual (including a photograph) and how to report any breach of the terms should normally be included. Usually the consideration of the effect of publicity on family members should not deter decision-makers from the stated aim of publicising the order. However, consideration of the impact of publicity on vulnerable family members should be made and recorded. The defendant and his or her family should be warned of the intention to publish details.

What publicity should look like: are the contents proportionate?

The contents of the publicity should also be considered and decisions about them recorded. Disclosure of information should always be proportionate to achieving the desired aim. The contents of publicity should include factual and accurate material.

The content and tone of the publicity should be considered carefully. Information must be based on facts, and appropriate language used: for example, the order itself does not mean that an individual has been found guilty of a criminal offence. Words such as 'criminal' and 'crime' to describe the individual and their behaviour must be used with care and only when appropriate. If the anti-social behaviour was, as a matter of fact, also criminal, then it is permissible to describe it as criminal. Breach of an order is an offence and should be described as such. Publicity should be consistent with the character of the order itself: that is, a civil prohibition (rather than a criminal order) restricting anti-social behaviour (which may be criminal, but need not be).

It would be prudent to rehearse the facts of the case and agree on appropriate language to use. Some consideration should be given to the personal circumstances of individuals named on the order when deciding whether to include them in any publicity leaflet, particularly if they are under 18. However, any arguments for not including their names must be balanced with the need to enable those who receive the leaflet to be able to identify a breach.

Details of conditions of non-association named on the order, particularly where those named are also subject to orders or have a recent history of anti-social behaviour, can be included in publicity. Even in cases where the named individuals with whom association is prohibited are not subject to an ASBO it will usually be appropriate to name them once some consideration has been given to their personal circumstances.

Type of information to include in publicity

The type of personal information that might be included in any publicity would be:

- the name of the individual; and/or

- a description; and/or

- the age; and/or

- a photograph; and/or

- his/her address;

- a summary of the individual's anti-social behaviour; and/or

- a summary of, or extracts from, the findings of the judge when making the ASBO; and/or

- a summary of, or extracts from, the terms of the ASBO;

- the identification of any relevant exclusion zone (as illustrated on a map);

- details of conditions of non-associations named on the order, particularly where those named are also subject to ASBOs or have a recent history of anti-social behaviour;

- the expiry date of the order;

- the manner in which the public can report breaches (for example names, telephone numbers, addresses, possibility of anonymous reporting, etc); and/or

- the names of local agencies responsible for obtaining the ASBO;

- local contact numbers, such as those for Victim Support, local police and housing services, with reassurance that reports will be treated in confidence;

- date of publication;

- the identity of the group to be targeted by the publicity (for example businesses or residents in the vicinity); and/or

- those who are suspected to have been subject to anti-social behaviour by the individual; and/or

- those individuals or businesses within and immediately adjacent to an area identified in the ASBO; and

- details of the publication area, for example within the area of any exclusion zone and the area immediately adjacent to the exclusion zone, within the borough.

Age consideration

The age of the person against whom the order was obtained should be a consideration when deciding whether or how to inform people about the order. Factual information should be obtained about whether an individual is particularly vulnerable. This should be done as early as possible, to avoid delays in informing the public once an order has been obtained. The fact that someone is under the age of 18 does not mean that their anti-social behaviour is any less distressing or frightening than that of an adult.

An order made against a child or young person under 18 is usually made in open court and is not usually subject to reporting restrictions. The information is in the public domain and newspapers are entitled to publish details. But if reporting restrictions have been imposed, they must be scrupulously adhered to. In applications involving children and young people where evidence has consisted of details of their past convictions, and reporting restrictions were not lifted for the proceedings leading to those convictions, the publicity should not make reference to those convictions. Similarly, where an order on conviction has been imposed on a child or young person in the youth court, unless reporting restrictions are lifted, details of the offences or behaviour alluded to in that hearing cannot be reported. However, details of the behaviour outlined in the order on conviction hearing can be used, unless the court orders otherwise. Where the court making the order does impose reporting restrictions under section 39 of the Children and Young Persons Act 1933, the press must scrupulously observe these.

A court must have a good reason to make a section 39 order. Age alone is insufficient to justify reporting restrictions being imposed. Section 141 of the Serious Organised Crime and Police Act 2005 reverses the presumption in relation to reporting restrictions in the youth court in cases for breach of ASBOs. Automatic reporting restrictions will not apply but the court retains the discretion to impose them. The prosecutor can make an application to the court for this. While it is the case that from 1 July 2005 no automatic reporting restrictions have applied in cases for breach of ASBOs relating to children and young people, when dealing with the case the court will consider whether reporting restrictions were imposed when the original order was granted. As ASBOs are civil orders, reporting restrictions will not have applied (unless imposed by the court).

If reporting restrictions were imposed at the original ASBO hearing, then unless there has been a significant change in the intervening period, it is likely that the court will impose reporting restrictions at the hearing for the breach. If no reporting restrictions were imposed at the original ASBO hearing, it is still open to the court to impose reporting restrictions at the hearing of the breach case. If reporting restrictions are not imposed, publicity can be considered, taking into account all the matters that are relevant when considering publicising the ASBO itself.

Photographs

A photograph of the subject of the ASBO will usually be required so that they can be identified. This is particularly necessary for older people or housebound witnesses who may not know the names of those causing a nuisance in the area. The photograph should be as recent as possible.

Distribution of publicity

This should be primarily within the area(s) that suffered from the anti-social behaviour and that are covered by the terms of the order, including exclusion zones. People who have suffered from anti-social behaviour, for example residents, local businesses, shop staff, staff of local public services, particular groups or households should be the intended audience.

All orders should be recorded on the Police National Computer to assist enforcement. This is particularly relevant where the order extends across England and Wales. It may be appropriate to extend publicity beyond the area where the anti-social behaviour was focused if there is a general term prohibiting harassment, alarm or distress in a wider area. It may also be appropriate if there is a danger of displacement of the anti-social behaviour to distribute it just beyond the area covered by the order.

The timescale over which publicity is anticipated to occur should also be given due consideration and decisions recorded. It is important that publicity does not become out of date or irrelevant. Special attention needs to be paid to posters that are distributed to other organisations, as posters should not be left up when the need for them has expired. It will usually be appropriate to issue publicity when a full order is made, rather than an interim order. However, exceptions can be made, for example where the anti-social behaviour is severe, where there has been extreme intimidation or where there is a delay between the making of the interim order and the outcome of the final hearing. In the case of *Keating v Knowsley Metropolitan Borough Council* [2004] EWHC 1933 (Admin), the judge held that publicity could be used for interim orders. In these circumstances it should be stated in the publicity that the order is temporary and that a hearing for a 'full' order will follow, and distribution should be extremely localised.

Consideration of human rights

Consideration of the human rights of the individual who is subject to the order and of the human rights of the public, including the victim(s) and potential victims, should be carried out. Appropriate and proportionate publicity is compliant with the human rights of the individual who is subject to the order. The *Stanley v Brent* case accepted that publicity was needed for effective enforcement of the order. Individuals do not welcome publicity and may view the effect of publicity as a punishment. However, a subjective assessment by the individual of the effect of publicity is irrelevant in determining the purpose of the publicity. Consideration of the human rights implications of publicity should be recorded.

Consideration of data protection

Publicity is not contrary to the Data Protection Act 1998 as long as authorities are operating in accordance with the Act. There is an exemption in section 29 of the Act to the processing of personal data for the purposes of prevention or detection of crime. This means that personal data can be processed with a view to compliance with a statutory function, where the data has been obtained from a person who possessed it for the purposes of the prevention or detection of crime. This will be the case when considering publicising an ASBO.

Type of publicity

No one directly involved in the case (witnesses and victims) should wait unnecessarily for information about an order. They should be informed immediately when an order is made. This is in addition to keeping them informed of progress throughout the court process and can be done by visits, letters and community meetings or by phone. Victims and witnesses may also be given a copy of the order. It is recommended that publicity be distributed to targeted households immediately after the order has been granted and by at least a week after the court date. Local people should be informed when variation or discharge of an order relevant to them is made.

The method of publicity can include the following:

- local print and television media;

- local leaflet drop; and

- local newsletter.

Practitioners need to apply the proportionality test when deciding which method is appropriate.

Leaflets and other printed materials, such as posters or residents' newsletters, allow local agencies to target particular neighbourhoods, streets or households with information.

The public can be informed about an ASBO at any time – publicity can be issued and re-issued according to the circumstances. However, publicity needs to be timely to ensure that people are able to enforce the order as soon as it has been granted and to reassure the public that something is being done.

Working with the media

It is usual for local statutory agencies to have working relationships with local and regional media, including press, television and radio. This is particularly relevant to issues such as anti-social behaviour and where the media are keen to report how local agencies are tackling these issues through the deployment of dispersal orders, ASBOs, 'crack house' closures, etc.

It is important to work with local media and to make them understand that it is not the purpose of any publicity to punish the individual. Media coverage has the potential to go to a wider audience than leaflets or posters. It is good practice to identify newspapers that report on city, borough and neighbourhood issues, free local press and local radio and television and to develop working relationships with them. This could include being aware of their publication deadlines, giving them exclusives and making sure that the complainant's (victim's) point of view is put across. However, it is important to keep close control of the material. Witnesses should not be put at risk by disclosing dates of hearings, and your relationships with the courts should not be jeopardised. Those subject to an ASBO who are considered vulnerable should also not be put at risk.

Issuing a press release is a way of retaining control of the material. There should be an agreed process for authorisation of the press releases. The press release should contain information that meets the identified aim of the publicity. For example, if the aim is to help enforce the order, the information in the press release will be more detailed than the information needed for publicity whose aim is to reassure the community that something is being done. It is good practice to identify a spokesperson to liaise with the press.

Appendix A

Early intervention and tackling offending behaviour by under-10s

Interventions available

Acceptable behaviour contract (ABC)

An ABC (also known as an acceptable behaviour agreement) is an intervention designed to engage an individual in acknowledging his or her anti-social behaviour and its effect on others, with the aim of stopping that behaviour. An ABC is a written agreement made between a person who has been involved in anti-social behaviour and their local authority, youth inclusion support panel (YISP), landlord or the police. ABCs are not set out in law, which is why they are sometimes called agreements. Any agency is able to use and adapt the model. An ABC or acceptable behaviour agreement is completely flexible and can be adapted for the particular local need. It can include conditions that the parties agree to keep. It may also contain the agreed consequences of a breach of the agreement.

Parenting contracts (section 25 of the Anti-Social Behaviour Act 2003)

Parenting contracts are voluntary written agreements between youth offending teams (YOTs) and the parent/guardian of a child/young person involved, or likely to be involved, in anti-social behaviour or criminal conduct. They are a two-sided arrangement where both the parents and the agency will play a part in improving the young person's behaviour. The contract contains a statement by the parent(s) agreeing to comply with the requirements for the period specified and a statement by the YOT agreeing to provide support to the parent(s) for the purpose of complying with those requirements. It is important that there is a clear agreement about the consequences if the terms of the parenting contract are not adhered to. If the contract is broken, the YOT may apply to the court for a parenting order (see below), which would include compulsory requirements.

Child safety order (sections 11–13 of the Crime and Disorder Act 1998 as amended by section 60 of the Children Act 2004)

A child safety order (CSO) allows compulsory intervention with a child under 10 years of age who has committed an act which, had they been aged 10 or over, would have constituted an offence. It is designed to prevent anti-social behaviour when it is not possible to engage on a voluntary basis with a child under 10. A CSO is made in family proceedings in the magistrates' court on application by a local authority. The order places the child under the supervision of a responsible officer, who may be a local authority social worker or a member of a youth offending team and can include requirements designed to improve the child's behaviour and address underlying problems. If the order is not complied with, the parent can be made the subject of a parenting order if that would be in the interests of preventing repetition of the behaviour that led to the CSO being made.

Parenting order

A parenting order can be made in respect of a parent of a child under 10 years of age. It can require parents to attend a parenting programme (lasting up to three months) and specify requirements for the parent regarding supervision of the child (lasting up to 12 months). Failure to comply with a parenting order is a criminal offence punishable by a fine of up to £1,000 and/or a community sentence.

Under section 8 of the Crime and Disorder Act 1998 as amended by the Children Act 2004, a parenting order can be imposed on a parent of a child who is subject to a CSO or when a CSO has been breached.

Section 26 of the Anti-social Behaviour Act 2003 enables YOTs to apply to the magistrates' court for a 'free-standing' parenting order. The court must be satisfied that the child or young person has engaged in anti-social behaviour or criminal conduct and that the order would be desirable in preventing further occurrences of such behaviour.

There is provision in the current Police and Justice Bill to extend the power to apply for parenting orders to local authorities and registered social landlords.

For further information on parenting orders, refer to the guidance on parenting contracts and orders at www.homeoffice.gov.uk/documents/ parenting-orders-guidance

Local child curfew schemes (section 14 of the Crime and Disorder Act 1998 as amended by Criminal Justice and Police Act 2001)

These are designed for children and young people 15 years old and below, to help local authorities to deal with the problem of unsupervised children or young people involved in late-night, anti-social behaviour on the streets. Under a local child curfew scheme, a local authority or local police force can ban children under 16 from being in a public place during specified hours (between 9pm and 6am), unless they are under the control of a responsible adult. With children under 10, contravening a ban imposed by a curfew notice (for instance being found outside their homes after the curfew) is one of the conditions under which a family court could make the child subject to a CSO. A local child curfew can last for up to 90 days.

Junior youth inclusion projects

Junior youth inclusion projects are based on high-crime, high-deprivation neighbourhoods across England and Wales and work with the 8–13 age range. Projects aim to prevent youth crime in those neighbourhoods by targeting the 50 most at-risk children and young people in the area, assessing their needs and providing meaningful interventions aimed at addressing those risk factors. Young people typically are either on the cusp of offending or are already involved in low-level offending. In order to engage with the 50 most at-risk young people, projects work with around another 100 peers and siblings of core group members.

Youth inclusion support panels

Youth inclusion support panels (YISPs) are multi-agency planning groups that serve to identify those young people in the 8–13 age range who are most at risk of offending and engaging in anti-social behaviour. They offer an early intervention based on assessed risk and need. Parenting support in the form of contracts and programmes is offered as part of a range of tailored interventions.

The suggested criteria for a young person referred to the YISP is as follows:

- The child is aged between 8 and 13 years inclusive (up to 17 in some areas).

- The behaviour of the child is of concern to two or more of the partner agencies and/or their parents/carers, and they consider that it requires a multi-agency response.

- The parent/carer and child are willing to take part, give consent to the referral and the child is willing to co-operate with an integrated support plan.

- The child is exposed to four or more risk factors.

- There is known offending behaviour up to and including a police reprimand or ASBO, or there is concern over potential involvement in criminal or anti-social behaviour.

The panel is made up of representatives from a variety of agencies which can include YOTs; police; social services; housing, probation and education services; Connexions; voluntary sector organisations; anti-social behaviour units; and the fire service. (This list is not exhaustive and can be tailored to local circumstances.) The panel will meet on a regular basis and consider referrals made to it in order to devise an integrated support plan. The YISP must ensure that a mechanism is in place for the sharing of information. The method, criteria and considerations for this can be found by referring to the Association of Chief Police Officers/Youth Justice Board guidance.[15]

Appendix B

County court Practice Direction according to the Civil Procedure Rules

IV. Anti-social behaviour orders under the Crime and Disorder Act 1998

Scope of this Section and interpretation

65.21   (1)   This Section applies to applications in proceedings in a county court under sub-sections (2), (3) or (3B) of section 1B of the Crime and Disorder Act 1998 by a relevant authority, and to applications for interim orders under section 1D of that Act.

      (2)   In this Section –

          (a)   'the 1998 Act' means the Crime and Disorder Act 1998;

          (b)   'relevant authority' has the same meaning as in section 1(1A) of the 1998 Act; and

          (c)   'the principal proceedings' means any proceedings in a county court.

Application where the relevant authority is a party in principal proceedings

65.22   (1)   Subject to paragraph (2) –

          (a)   where the relevant authority is the claimant in the principal proceedings, an application under section 1B(2) of the 1998 Act for an order under section 1B(4) of the 1998 Act must be made in the claim form; and

          (b)   where the relevant authority is a defendant in the principal proceedings, an application for an order must be made by application notice which must be filed with the defence.

      (2)   Where the relevant authority becomes aware of the circumstances that lead it to apply for an order after its claim is issued or its defence filed, the application must be made by application notice as soon as possible thereafter.

      (3)   Where the application is made by application notice, it should normally be made on notice to the person against whom the order is sought.

Application by a relevant authority to join a person to the principal proceedings

65.23   (1)   An application under section 1B(3B) of the 1998 Act by a relevant authority which is a party to the principal proceedings to join a person to the principal proceedings must be made –

          (a)   in accordance with Section I of Part 19;

          (b)   in the same application notice as the application for an order under section 1B(4) of the 1998 Act against the person; and

          (c)   as soon as possible after the relevant authority considers that the criteria in section 1B(3A) of the 1998 Act are met.

      (2)   The application notice must contain –

          (a)   the relevant authority's reasons for claiming that the person's anti-social acts are material in relation to the principal proceedings; and

          (b)   details of the anti-social acts alleged.

      (3)   The application should normally be made on notice to the person against whom the order is sought.

Application where the relevant authority is not party in principal proceedings

65.24   (1)   Where the relevant authority is not a party to the principal proceedings –

          (a)   an application under section 1B(3) of the 1998 Act to be made a party must be made in accordance with Section I of Part 19; and

          (b)   the application to be made a party and the application for an order under section 1B(4) of the 1998 Act must be made in the same application notice.

---

15   Association of Chief Police Officers/Youth Justice Board (2005) *Sharing Personal and Sensitive Information in Respect of Children and Young People at Risk of Offending.* London: Youth Justice Board, p.11.

(2) The applications –

    (a)   must be made as soon as possible after the authority becomes aware of the principal proceedings; and

    (b)   should normally be made on notice to the person against whom the order is sought.

Evidence

65.25   An application for an order under section 1B(4) of the 1998 Act must be accompanied by written evidence, which must include evidence that section 1E of the 1998 Act has been complied with.

Application for an interim

65.26   (1)   An application for an interim order under section 1D of the 1998 Act must be made in accordance with Part 25.

    (2)   The application should normally be made –

        (a)   in the claim form or application notice seeking the order; and

        (b)   on notice to the person against whom the order is sought.

Appendix C

Order form

FORM

Anti-social behaviour order (Crime and Disorder Act 1998, s1)

Magistrates' Court
(Code)

Date:

Defendant:

Address:

On the complaint of
Complainant:

Applicant Authority:

Address of Applicant Authority:

_____

_____

The court found that:

(i) the defendant acted in the following anti-social manner, which caused or was likely to cause harassment, alarm or distress to one or more persons not of the same household as himself:

_____

_____

And (ii) this order is necessary to protect persons

_____

from further anti-social acts by him.
And it is ordered that the defendant

_____

[NAME]
is prohibited from

_____

_____

_____

Until [   ]

_____

[further order]

Justice of the Peace

[By order of the clerk of the court]

NOTE: If, without reasonable excuse, the defendant does anything which he is prohibited from doing by this order, he shall be liable on conviction to a term of imprisonment not exceeding five years or to a fine or to both.

Appendix D

Summons form

SCHEDULE 2

Rule 4(2)

FORM

Summons on application for anti-social behaviour order (Crime and Disorder Act 1998, s1)

Magistrates' Court
(Code)

Date:

To the defendant:

[name]

Address:

You are hereby summoned to appear on
[date] at

before the magistrates' court at

to answer an application for an anti-social behaviour order, which application is attached to this summons.

Justice of the Peace
[By order of the clerk of the court]

NOTE: Where the court is satisfied that this summons was served on you within what appears to the court to be a reasonable time before the hearing or adjourned hearing, it may issue a warrant for your arrest or proceed in your absence.

If an anti-social behaviour order is made against you and if, without reasonable excuse, you do anything you are prohibited from doing by such an order, you shall be liable on conviction to imprisonment for a term not exceeding five years or to a fine, or to both.

Appendix E

Step-by-step process for anti-social behaviour orders and orders on conviction

Process for anti-social behaviour orders

Collect evidence

Agencies applying for orders should strike a balance and focus on what is most relevant and necessary to provide sufficient evidence for the court to arrive at a clear understanding of the matter.

Undertake statutory consultation

Documentary evidence of consultation, not agreement, is required although it is not a statutory requirement for orders on conviction (see below).

The stages for orders in county court proceedings will be available on publication of the practice direction in the updated Civil Procedure Rules.

Partnership working

Lead agencies should liaise with other agencies which can add value to the application. Involve the youth offending team and social services at the start of the process if the subject of the application is a child or young person, in order to ensure that any assessment required is carried out in parallel with the application process. If the perpetrator is aged 10 to 17, the court is obliged to consider making an individual support order (ISO). Consideration needs to be given at an early stage to the positive interventions which could be included in such an order to address the individual's anti-social behaviour.

Identification of the need to protect the community

An order is necessary to protect person(s) from further anti-social acts by the perpetrator.

Identification of anti-social behaviour

There is behaviour that is causing, or likely to cause, harassment, alarm or distress to one or more person(s) not of the same household as the perpetrator.

The hearing

The lead officer in charge of the case should ensure that all the evidence and witnesses are available at the hearing, including any evidence in support of the need for the court to make an immediate order. The defendant(s) should attend but an order can be made in their absence.

Applying for an interim order

Where there is an urgent need to protect the community, an application for an interim order may be made with the application for the main order. The appropriate form in the Magistrates' Courts (Anti-Social Behaviour Orders) Rules 2002 should be used. An application for an order without notice to the defendant may be made subject to agreement of the justices' clerk or other court clerk with delegated authority. The clerk shall grant leave for an application for an interim order to be made where they are satisfied that it is necessary.

The hearing for a without notice interim order will take place without the presence of the defendant. Where the hearing is made on notice, the defendant should be summoned to attend the hearing.

If an interim order is granted, the application for the main order (together with a summons giving a date for the defendant to attend court) should be served on the defendant in person as soon as practicable after the making of the interim order. The interim order will not take effect until it has been served on the defendant. If the interim order is not served on the defendant within seven days of being made, then it shall be set aside. The interim order shall cease to have effect if the application for an anti-social behaviour order is withdrawn or refused.

Make an application to the magistrates' court

An application for an ASBO is by complaint to the magistrates' court using the appropriate form in the Magistrates' Courts (Anti-Social Behaviour Orders) Rules 2002. The complaint must be made within six months from the time when the matter of the complaint (the behaviour) arose. A complaint may be made on the basis of one incident if sufficiently serious. Earlier incidents may be used as background information to support the case and show a pattern of behaviour. The application may be made to any magistrates' court. A summons together with the application, as set out in the Rules, should be either given to the defendant in person or sent by post to the last known address.

Draw up prohibitions

The order should be drafted in full, including its duration, and a court file prepared.

Process for an order made on conviction in criminal proceedings (in the magistrates' court or the Crown Court)

Since the case of *R v Wadmore and Foreman* [2006] EWCA Crim 686 Court of Appeal Criminal Division, the court should record on the face of the order its findings of fact in relation to the alleged anti-social behaviour.

Verdict

If found guilty of breaching the order, the offender is convicted or given a conditional discharge.

Criminal hearing

This is to establish guilt of criminal charge only.

Signal intention to seek an order

Prior to, or at the start of, the criminal stage or hearing, the police, Crown Prosecution Service or local authority involved in the case may advise the subject and court that an order will be sought on conviction. This is not a requirement; the issue can be raised for the first time post-conviction.

Draw up prohibitions

The police or other agency involved in the case may draw up the prohibitions necessary to protect the community from the subject's anti-social behaviour for consideration by the court post-conviction. This is not a requirement.

Collect evidence

Evidence may be collected for presentation to the court post-conviction. This is not a requirement as the court may make an order on conviction on its own initiative.

Other matters

Application for variation or discharge by either the applicant or the defendant is to the same magistrates' court that made the order. Appeal is to the Crown Court. Breach of the order will go to the magistrates' court, which may refer it to the Crown Court in the more serious cases. Mode of trial decision determines whether breach of ASBO is dealt with in the magistrates' court or the Crown Court.

Immediate post-order procedure

Where an ASBO is granted, it is preferable for a copy of the order to be served on the defendant in person prior to their departure from court. If this is not possible, personal service should be arranged as soon as possible thereafter. In the case of a child or young person, the order should also be served on the parent, guardian or an appropriate adult. In all cases, service should be recorded.

The lead agency, if not the police, should ensure that a copy of the order is forwarded immediately to the police. Copies should also be given to the anti-social behaviour co-ordinator of the local crime and disorder reduction partnership, the other partner agencies, and to the main targets and witnesses of the anti-social behaviour.

An order comes into effect on the day it is made. But the two-year period during which no order shall be discharged starts from the date of service.

Other matters

Where the order is made on conviction in the magistrates' court, application for variation or discharge by either the applicant or the defendant may be made to any magistrates' court within the same local justice area as the court that made the order. Appeal is to the Crown Court. Breach of the order will go to the magistrates' court, which may refer it to the Crown Court in the more serious cases.

Where the order is made on conviction in the Crown Court, application for variation or discharge by either the applicant or the defendant is made to the same Crown Court which made the order. Appeal is to the Court of Appeal. Breach of the order will go to the magistrates' court, which may refer it to the Crown Court in the more serious cases.

Immediate post-order procedure

If the offender is given a custodial sentence, the court may make provision for the requirements of the order to come into effect when the offender is released from custody. See above for details for immediate post-order procedure for ASBOs.

Post verdict – hearing for order on conviction

The hearing for the order post-conviction is civil.

The issue of an order may be raised by the magistrates or judge without any request from the prosecution or the police or local authority; the Crown Prosecution Service may make an application for an order on conviction. Additional evidence relating to the request for the order and the need for the prohibitions may be produced.

Appendix F

Public funding for defendants

Criminal public funding is available for any proceedings under sections 1 and 4 of the Crime and Disorder Act (CDA) 1998 relating to ASBOs, including interim orders, where they are made in the magistrates' court or where an appeal is made in the Crown Court.

Advocacy assistance is available for an ASBO, an interim order under section 1D of the CDA, variation or discharge of an ASBO, or an appeal against the making of an ASBO under section 4 of the CDA, in accordance with the Criminal Defence Service General Criminal Contract. Solicitors can self-grant advocacy assistance for these matters. There are no financial criteria for the grant of advocacy assistance. Advocacy assistance may not be provided where it appears unreasonable that approval should be granted in the particular circumstances of the case, or where the interests of justice test, set out in Schedule 3 of the Access to Justice Act 1999, is not met. In applying this test, there is an additional factor of whether there is a real risk of imprisonment if an ASBO is made and subsequently breached.

A representation order may be sought on application to the Legal Services Commission in respect of these proceedings. Provision for representation is made under Regulation 3(2)(criminal proceedings for the purposes of section 12(2)(g) of the Access to Justice Act 1999) of the Criminal Defence Service (General)(No.2) Regulations 2001, and Regulation 6(3) of the same regulations.

An application to the Commission must be made on form CDS3. An application will be determined in accordance with the interests of justice criteria. The availability of advocacy assistance will be a relevant factor which the Legal Services Commission will take into account when considering the grant of representation.

Where an application for a representation order is refused, the Legal Services Commission shall provide written reasons for the refusal and details of the appeal process. The applicant may make a renewed application in writing to the Funding Review Committee, which may grant or refuse the application.

Advocacy assistance is available for proceedings in the Crown Court, where an appeal is made under section 4 of the CDA. The merits test is slightly different from that on application for an interim or a full ASBO. It is based only on the general reasonableness test. Advocacy assistance may not be granted if it appears unreasonable that approval should be granted in the particular circumstances of the case. The prospects and merits of an appeal should be taken into account as well as whether the individual has reasonable grounds for taking the proceedings. Representation is also available for an appeal against an order under section 4 of the CDA. An application should be made to the Legal Services Commission which will consider grant against the availability of advocacy assistance.

Any challenge against the ruling of the Crown Court to the High Court by way of case stated or by application for judicial review falls outside the scope of criminal funding. Legal representation would have to be applied for in accordance with the Funding Code procedures to the Legal Services Commission. This work is funded through the Community Legal Service although it falls within the scope of the General Criminal Contract.

Advocacy assistance is available for a breach of an interim order or full ASBO. Representation is also available for breach proceedings on application to the Commission as above.

Further reading

Anti-social Behaviour: A guide to the role of Youth Offending Teams in dealing with anti-social behaviour published by the Youth Justice Board, the Home Office and the Association of Chief Police Officers, which can be downloaded at www.youth-justice-board.gov.uk/ Publications/Scripts/prodView.asp?idproduct= 212&eP=

The Guidance for the Courts by Lord Justice Thomas can be found at:

www.youth-justice-board.gov.uk/NR/   rdonlyres/398987C5-E79A-491E-B912-DF3D4D   762293/0/
ASBOGuidanceforjudiciaryHMCS june05_2_.pdf

Websites

www.together.gov.uk

www.respect.gov.uk

www.crimereduction.gov.uk

www.youth-justice-board.gov.uk

APPENDIX 4

A GUIDE TO REVIEWING ANTI-SOCIAL BEHAVIOUR ORDERS GIVEN TO YOUNG PEOPLE AND INDIVIDUAL SUPPORT ORDERS

CONTENTS

Introduction
Definition of terms
Part 1: One-year review of Anti-social Behaviour Orders
    Case management
    Responsibility for, and participating in, reviews
    Conducting a review
    Review periods
    Discharging/varying an ASBO
Part 2: Individual Support Orders (ISOs)
    Applying for an ISO
    Conditions for making an ISO
    Requirements included in an ISO
    Courts
    Duration of an ISO
    Variation and discharge of an ISO
    Breach of an ISO
    Penalty for breach
    The role of the YOT
    Annex A: Criminal Justice and Immigration Act 2008 (c. 4)
    Annex B: Diversionary activities for young people
    Annex C: Other interventions available for parents and families
    Annex D: Perpetrators with health needs

Introduction

Anti-Social Behaviour Orders (ASBOs) were introduced by the Crime and Disorder Act 1998 in England and Wales and have been available since April 1999. The Orders last a minimum of two years and can be made against anyone aged 10 or over who has acted in an anti-social manner (i.e. behaving in a way that caused, or is likely to cause, harassment, alarm or distress to others not of the same household), and where an Order is needed to protect person(s) from further anti-social acts.

This guidance brings together two measures in the Criminal Justice and Immigration Act 2008 which are to be implemented on 1 February 2009. The one-year review for young people on ASBOs has been long-standing good practice by practitioners and is now being put on a legal footing. The extension of the Individual Support Order (ISO) legislation is in response to practitioners' requests to make ISOs more widely available.

Section 123 of the Criminal Justice and Immigration Act 2008 inserts two new sections, 1J and 1K, into Part 1 of the Crime and Disorder Act 1998 requiring agencies to carry out a one-year review of ASBOs issued to persons under 17 years of age and sets out how the review should be carried out. Section 1K sets out which agencies are responsible for carrying out and participating in the review.

Legislation sets out that, where a magistrates' court makes an ASBO against a young person under 18 years of age, it must also make an ISO if it considers that an ISO would help to prevent further anti-social behaviour.

Section 124 of the 2008 Act inserts new subsections into section 1AA of the Crime and Disorder Act 1998, which deals with ISOs. The new subsections allow ISOs to be made more than once within the lifetime of an ASBO, and to be made subsequent to the making of the original ASBO.

ISOs require the perpetrator to comply with positive conditions that tackle the root cause of their anti-social behaviour. For example, the perpetrator may be ordered to attend an anger management course.

The amendments made by section 124 do not apply in relation to an ASBO made more than nine months before 1 February 2009, but would apply if the ASBO has been varied by a further Order made no more than nine months before 1 February 2009.

This guidance is statutory. Practitioners carrying out or participating in a review shall have regard to the principles set out in this guidance.

This guidance relates to the provisions contained in Part 1 of the Crime and Disorder Act 1998 (as amended by Part 8, sections 123 and 124 of the Criminal Justice and Immigration Act 2008).

The 2008 Act received Royal Assent on 8 May 2008 and can be accessed at: www.opsi.gov.uk/acts/acts2008/ ukpga_20080004_en_1. See Annex A for sections 123 and 124 of the Criminal Justice and Immigration Act 2008.

This guidance is designed principally for:

- the courts;

- the police;

- local authorities; and

- Youth Offending Teams (YOTs).

This guidance is issued by the Home Office to assist with the use of ASBOs and has been written by the Anti-Social Behaviour and Crime Prevention Unit in collaboration with the Youth Justice Board for England and Wales (YJB) and Ministry of Justice. We are also grateful for the contribution to the guidance from colleagues across the Home Office, other government departments, police forces and the numerous practitioners who have provided advice and allowed us to use examples of their work.

For further information or advice on certain aspects of the powers, please contact:

Norah Kugblenu
Anti-Social Behaviour and Crime Prevention Unit
Crime and Drug Strategy Directorate
Home Office
Peel Building
2 Marsham Street
London SW1P 4DF

Definition of terms

Supplemental Order

Supplemental Order means:

- a further Order varying the Order in question; or

- an ISO made in relation to the Order in question.

The appropriate chief officer of police

The appropriate chief officer of police means the chief officer of police of the police force maintained for the police area in which the person subject to the Order resides or appears to reside.

The appropriate local authority

The appropriate local authority means the council for the local government area in which the person subject to the Order resides or appears to reside.

Local government area

Local government area means:

- in relation to England, a district or London borough, the City of London, the Isle of Wight and the Isles of Scilly; or

- in relation to Wales, a county or county borough.

Relevant authority

Relevant authority means:

- the council for the local government area, or, in relation to England, a county council;

- the chief officer of police of any police force maintained for a police area;

- the chief constable of the British Transport Police;

- any registered social landlord;

- a housing action trust; and/or

- the Environment Agency.

Anti-social Behaviour Orders (ASBOs)

ASBOs are civil Orders made by a court which prohibit the perpetrator from specific anti-social acts and from entering defined areas on a map, usually referred to as exclusion zones. An Order can be made against anyone aged 10 years or over who has acted in an anti-social manner (i.e. behaving in a way that caused, or is likely to cause, harassment, alarm or distress to others not of the same household), and where an Order is needed to protect persons from further anti-social acts. ASBOs should be used in conjunction with other measures of intervention and support as part of a tiered approach to tackling anti-social behaviour. The approach to ASBOs made against a young person is generally the same as for adults.

When used as part of a tiered approach with other measures, ASBOs are an effective measure, when other attempts to modify disruptive behaviour have failed. They are flexible tools which can be used in a variety of circumstances and to tackle a range of anti-social acts.

ASBOs are issued for a minimum period of two years to reflect the need for them to bring respite to communities and for behaviour to be changed. However, a year is a long time in the life of a young person and their needs and behaviour are more prone to change than those of adults. While ASBOs must be issued for a minimum of two years, prohibitions may last for less than this – see, for example, R (Lonerghan) v Lewes Crown Court [2005] England and Wales High Court 457.

ASBOs issued to young people must be reviewed each year to check progress with compliance with the terms of the Order. This review is an important safeguard to ensure that young people are receiving the support they need to prevent them breaching their ASBO and causing further harm to the community. The victims are often also young people and they, and the wider community, have a right to be protected. The one-year review may lead to an application to the court to modify or strengthen the ASBO by adding or removing prohibitions.

Comprehensive guidance on how to use ASBOs is available on the crime reduction website, which also has a separate section on children and young people (www.crimereduction.gov.uk/antisocialbehaviour/ antisocialbehaviour55.htm).

The YJB has also produced guidance which focuses on the role that YOTs can play in preventing and reducing anti-social behaviour. This guidance is available on the YJB website (www.yjb.gov.uk/ Publications/Scripts/ prodView.asp?idproduct=212&eP=YJB).

Individual Support Orders (ISOs)

ISOs were introduced in the Criminal Justice Act 2003 (sections 322 and 323) to be made in conjunction with an ASBO on a young person. They may last for up to six months and impose positive obligations on a young person with the aim of tackling the underlying causes that led to the ASBO being made. Breach of an ISO is a criminal offence punishable by a financial penalty.

It is essential that all young people who are given ASBOs receive as much support as possible. There will be occasions when an ASBO is sought on a young person who is already subject to a court Order, which enables the delivery of support to the young person by the YOT. In this case, a decision must be made whether an ISO is needed to complement the support that is already being delivered to the young person. An ISO can provide a statutory Order through which additional support is provided on top of what is already delivered through an existing YOT Order. YOTs are well placed to supervise such Orders because they offer a wealth of skill, experience and success in improving outcomes for both young people and the communities in which they live.

The engagement of the parents of perpetrators in tackling anti-social behaviour is crucial to encouraging young people's compliance with ASBOs and ISOs. Annex C of this guidance sets out a range of interventions available to help parents and families in addressing a young person's anti-social behaviour.

Part 1: One-year review of Anti-social Behaviour Orders

The applicant authority that made the ASBO against a young person is required to carry out a review one year into its operation. The purpose of this review is to assess the young person's progress in abiding by the prohibitions, to review the adequacy of the support provided, and to decide whether the Order should be varied. The one-year review also reflects the fact that young people's lives and circumstances can change rapidly as they develop. Applicant authorities should also look at what additional support might need to be offered to the young person or their family.

Section 1J(1) of the Criminal Justice and Immigration Act 2008 requires ASBOs issued to young people to be reviewed regardless of how they were obtained (on complaint, or on conviction), provided that:

- the perpetrator was aged under 17 on the day that the Order was made; and

- they will be under the age of 18 at the end of the review period.

The review should be administrative rather than judicial, and should be undertaken by the team that decided upon the initial application. Where practicable, the YOT should provide the group with an assessment of the young person.

The obligation to carry out this review applies to any ASBO whose first anniversary falls after the commencement of the new requirement (i.e. 1 February 2009). It will not apply to ASBOs whose first anniversary falls before 1 February 2009. To qualify for a review, an ASBO must be less than nine months old when these provisions come into force, or have been varied nine months (or less) before the requirement comes into force.

There is no appeal mechanism built into the review process. Applicant authorities are subject to the normal review mechanisms for their decisions.

Case management

ASBOs on young people require active case management through a multi-agency case conference. It is vital that a specified individual within the lead agency takes on responsibility for the ownership and management of the case. This will help ensure that there is no confusion about who is expected to ensure that the necessary actions are taken and within the right timescale.

The Crime and Disorder Act 1998 (as amended by the Police and Justice Act 2006) enshrined in statute the concept of partnership working to prevent and reduce crime, disorder and anti-social behaviour. The lead individual should manage and co-ordinate the involvement of other agencies so that they add value by contributing their own specialist knowledge and expertise. A multi-agency approach should be adopted so that all agencies that could hold information on the young person in question are involved in the process at an early stage. Such agencies include the probation service, social services, police, health services, the YOT and voluntary organisations. There are also a number of other partnerships that have a role to play in tackling anti-social behaviour. Some of these are focused on young people, such as the Children's Fund, Sure Start and Connexions, Targeted Youth Support, Youth Inclusion and Support Panels (YISPs) and Youth Inclusion Programme (YIP). This co-ordinated approach allows for ASBO prohibitions to be discussed and varied in some cases (see Annex B).

Dealing with anti-social behaviour in a structured and coherent way will provide long-term gains for the community and for young people. It can prevent young people entering the criminal justice system, and benefit all agencies and the communities they work for.

Where an ASBO is breached, the YOT has a responsibility to contribute to the pre-sentence report to ensure that the sentence handed down is proportionate and reflects the seriousness of the breach.

This should ensure that, at every stage, local services are working together to assess young people's needs and to offer appropriate support to young people involved in or at risk of anti-social behaviour to help them change their behaviour.

In England, local authorities with social services responsibilities have a duty, arising from section 17 of the Children Act 1989, to safeguard and promote the welfare of children within their areas who may be in need. The assessment of needs of such children is expected to be carried out in accordance with the *Framework for the Assessment of Children in Need and their Families*.[1] Parallel guidance exists in Wales[2] in pursuit of the Children First programme aims. Both sets of guidance, for England and Wales, set out the content and timescales of the initial assessment and the core assessment. The assessment will cover the child's needs,

---

[1]   Department of Health (2000) *Framework for the Assessment of Children in Need and their Families*. London: The Stationery Office.
[2]   National Assembly for Wales (2001) *Framework for the Assessment of Children in Need and their Families*. London: The Stationery Office.

the capacities of their parents/carer and wider family, and environmental factors. This enables the local authorities to determine whether the child is a child in need and what services may be necessary to address the assessed needs.

Section 44 of the Children and Young Persons Act 1933 requires the courts to have regard to the welfare of a young person.

Responsibility for, and participating in, reviews

A review of a stand-alone ASBO or an Order made by a county court should be carried out by the relevant authority that applied for the order.

Where the ASBO was obtained on conviction (where the applicant may be the Crown Prosecution Service (CPS), or the Order was made by the court itself), the review should be carried out by the appropriate chief officer of police, unless a relevant authority is specified by the court as being responsible for carrying out the review. This also applies to the task of making any further applications to the court (e.g. for an ISO, or to vary the Order).

A local authority is required to co-operate with the appropriate chief police officer for the area, when carrying out a review of an ASBO; and the chief officer has a duty to co-operate with the local authority. Likewise, the chief officer of a police force, in carrying out a review, is required to co-operate with the appropriate local authority for the area; and the local authority has a duty to co-operate with the chief police officer.

A relevant authority other than a local authority or chief police officer is obliged to co-operate with the appropriate local authority and the appropriate police chief officer when carrying out a review of an ASBO, and similarly both the police and the local authority are duty bound to co-operate with the relevant authority, for example a registered social landlord.

A chief officer of police or other relevant authority carrying out a review may invite a person or body other than a local authority or relevant authority to participate or co-operate in the review.

Conducting a review

When conducting a review, the case review team must consider:

- the extent to which the person subject to an ASBO has complied with the Order;

- the adequacy of any support available to the person to help them comply with the Order; and

- any matters relevant to the question of whether an application should be made for the Order to be varied or discharged.

Review periods

For persons under the age of 18, an ASBO should be reviewed before the end of each 'review period'. The review periods are as follows:

- The period of 12 months beginning with:
  - the day on which the Order was made; or
  - if during that period there is a supplemental Order (or more than one), the date of the supplemental Order (or the last of them).

- A period of 12 months beginning with:
  - the day after the end of the previous review period; or
  - if during that period there is a supplemental Order (or more than one), the date of the supplemental Order (or the last of them).

The first review is to be carried out for the period covering the first year of the ASBO. However, if during that period there is a further Order varying the ASBO, or an ISO is made in relation to the ASBO in question, the review period would be the date of the supplemental Order.

The second and subsequent reviews are to be carried out on a one-yearly cycle starting from the day after the first review period ended. However, again, the clock can be re-set if a supplemental Order is made within that second (or subsequent) review period. This will avoid a review having to be carried out when a similar process has already achieved the same end.

Twelve months represents the period within which a formal review must take place. However, it is open to the agencies to reconsider the ASBO at any time at the young person's request.

Discharging/varying an ASBO

Depending on the progress towards improved behaviour, possible outcomes will include an application to discharge the Order or a strengthening of the prohibitions.

Applications to vary or discharge the Order will have to be made to the court in the usual way. The procedures set out in Part 50 of the Criminal Procedure Rules 1995 must be followed in respect of section 1C orders. The overriding considerations remain the safety and needs of the community and the review would have to incorporate the community's views on the Order's effectiveness. It is also important to take into account how much progress the young person may have made in addressing their behaviour and how any support they and their parents/ carers may have received has helped in this respect.

Part 2: Individual Support Orders (ISOs)

Section 1AA of the Crime and Disorder Act 1998 (as amended by the Criminal Justice and Immigration Act 2008) provides for the making of ISOs. The Orders have been available since May 2004. They are civil Orders and can be attached to ASBOs made against young people aged between 10 and 17 years. ISOs impose positive conditions on the young person and are designed to tackle the underlying causes of their anti-social behaviour.

The above legislation sets out that, where a magistrates' court makes an ASBO against a young person aged under 18, it must also make an ISO if it considers that it would help to prevent further anti-social behaviour. ISOs are designed to underpin an ASBO with a package of support to help the young person adhere to the terms of the Order while at the same time providing positive requirements to improve the outcomes for both the young person and the community in which they live.

Section 124 of the Criminal Justice and Immigration Act 2008 inserts new subsections into section 1AA of the Crime and Disorder Act 1998. This enables ISOs to be made more than once, and to be made subsequent to the hearing at which the original ASBO was made.

Under section 1AA, subsection 1A of the Crime and Disorder Act 1998 as amended by the Criminal Justice and Immigration Act 2008, a relevant authority can make an application on complaint to the court for an ISO provided that:

- an ASBO has previously been made in respect of such defendant;

- it is on application from the original applicant agency (or, in respect of section 1C orders, the chief officer of police or other relevant authority, responsible under section 1K(2)(a) or (b) for carrying out a review of the Order);

- at the time of the hearing of the application the defendant is still a child or young person; and

- the ASBO is still in force.

The court must consider whether these conditions are fulfilled and, if satisfied that they are, must make an ISO.

ISOs last up to six months and require a young person to attend a maximum of two support sessions per week. These support sessions are tailored to the individual's needs and are designed to address the causes of the behaviour that led to the ASBO being made. For example, the Order can require an individual to attend counselling for substance misuse or attend an anger management programme. The ISO may name specific activities the individual must participate in and can also specify dates and places where attendance is required.

Applying for an ISO

Where a court makes an ASBO in respect of a child or a young person, it must also make an ISO if it considers that an ISO would help to prevent further anti-social behaviour.

In cases where an ASBO has previously been made in respect of a child or young person, the relevant authority which applied for the ASBO can apply to the court which made the ASBO for an ISO to be made.

Conditions for making an ISO

The conditions for making an ISO are that:

- it would be desirable in the interests of preventing any repetition of the kind of behaviour which led to the ASBO; or an Order varying the ASBO (in a case where the variation is made as a result of further anti-social behaviour by the defendant);

- the defendant is not already subject to an ISO; and

- the court has been notified by the Home Secretary that arrangements for implementing ISOs are available in the area in which it appears to the court that the defendant resides or will reside and the notice has not been withdrawn.

Requirements included in an ISO

The requirements that may be specified in the ISO are those that the court considers desirable in the interests of preventing any repetition of the kind of behaviour which led to the ASBO or an Order varying that ASBO (where the variation is made as a result of further anti-social behaviour).

The Order may require that the young person:

- participate in specified activities at specified times;

- present himself/herself to a specified person or persons at a specified place and time; and

- comply with specified arrangements for his/her education.

The support must be individually tailored to the causes of the person's anti-social behaviour in order to prevent its repetition.

The requirements of the Order and the consequences of failing to comply with it should be explained to the defendant by the court. If an ISO is not made, the court must state why it considers that the conditions for making the Order are not met.

Courts

Magistrates' court

Since May 2004, a magistrates' court making an ASBO on a young person aged between 10 and 17 years has been obliged to make an ISO, if it is satisfied that an ISO would be desirable in the interests of preventing any repetition of the kind of behaviour which led to the making of the ASBO; that the defendant is not already subject to an ISO; and that the court has been notified by the Home Secretary that arrangements for implementing ISOs are available in the area in which it appears to the court that the defendant resides or will reside (and the notice has not been withdrawn).

County court

The Criminal Justice and Immigration Act 2008 inserts new subsection 8 under section 1B of the Crime and Disorder Act 1998 to allow ISOs to be made and varied in the county court, where an ASBO is made as a result of proceedings there, either at the time or subsequently.

Youth court

When a young person is before the youth court charged with a criminal offence, the YOT has a duty to recommend suitable penalties and interventions in their pre-sentence report (PSR). Where the YOT is aware of an application for an Order on conviction, it should always consider the implications and possible conditions to be included when compiling a PSR. This will help the young person set clear boundaries to their behaviour, and will provide the necessary protection to the community.

The court may make an Order on conviction at the request of the prosecutor or of its own volition. There is no formal application process for such an Order. The CPS will usually request that the court makes the Order and leads the evidence in support of the request. Alternatively, the Order can be requested by the police or local authority which may make representations to the court in support of the request. The procedure set out in Part 50 of the Criminal Procedure Rules 2005 must be followed when an application is made.

Section 124, subsection 7 of the Criminal Justice and Immigration Act 2008 allows ISOs to be made for ASBOs obtained on conviction, provided that the criteria for doing so are met. The Act also allows whoever is carrying out the annual review of an ASBO to make an application for an ISO.

Duration of an ISO

ISOs last for up to six months and impose positive conditions designed to tackle the underlying causes of a young person's anti-social behaviour. However, an ISO cannot be made to last beyond the lifetime of the corresponding ASBO. The period specified as the term of an ISO made on application must not be longer than the remaining part of the term of the ASBO.

Section 1AA, subsection 5A of the Crime and Disorder Act 1998 (as amended by the Criminal Justice and Immigration Act 2008) sets a time limit on any ISO subsequent to the original hearing.

Variation and discharge of an ISO

An ISO can be varied or discharged on application by the young person or the responsible officer. Variation or discharge of the ISO may also occur if the ASBO to which it relates is varied.

An application to vary or discharge the ISO may be made by either the young person subject to the ISO or the responsible officer. The need to vary an ISO may arise where support proves to be inappropriate or the individual moves out of the area. Equally, if the ASBO linked to the ISO is varied by a court, the court may also vary the ISO at the same time. An Order can also be made if it is desirable in the interests of preventing repetition of the anti-social behaviour which led to a variation.

An ISO ceases to have effect if the corresponding ASBO comes to an end or is discharged.

Breach of an ISO

Breach of an ISO is a criminal offence and criminal penalties apply. The responsible officer is responsible for ensuring compliance with the ISO. It will usually be appropriate for the responsible officer to encourage compliance using warning letters before instigating proceedings for a criminal prosecution.

The breach is taken forward by the CPS and breach proceedings are heard in the youth court. If a court finds that the subject of the Order has failed to comply with any requirement of the Order then the defendant is guilty of a criminal offence. The breach hearing will be heard in the youth court.

Penalty for breach

The penalty on summary conviction for breach of an ISO is a fine of a maximum of £1,000 for a young person aged 14 years or over and a maximum of £250 for a young person aged between 10 and 13 years. If the young person is aged under 16 years, the court has a duty to order the parent or guardian to pay the fine imposed unless it is unreasonable to do so. If the young person is aged 16 or 17, the court can exercise its discretion as to whether to order the parent/guardian to pay the fine.

A Referral Order is not available for breach of an ISO.

The role of the YOT

YOTs play a central role in preventing and reducing anti-social behaviour by children and young people.

There is a YOT in every local authority area in England and Wales. They are made up of representatives from the police, probation service, social services, health, education, drugs and alcohol misuse and housing officers. Each YOT is managed by a YOT manager who is responsible for co-ordinating the work of the youth justice services in their area.

Because the YOT incorporates representatives from a wide range of services, it can respond to the needs of young offenders in a comprehensive way.

The YOT advises the magistrates' court on whether an ISO is necessary and the conditions an ISO should contain. This information is based on a needs assessment of the young person.

The YOT is responsible for co-ordinating delivery of the ISO and also has a role in ensuring that the terms and conditions of both the ASBO and ISO are understood by the defendant. The conditions within the ISO are overseen by a responsible officer who is usually a member of the YOT, social services or the local education authority.

ISOs form an integral part of the work of YOTs in providing support to young people subject to ASBOs. This is done by working with the young person to provide tailored interventions to prevent recurrence of the behaviour that led to the ASBO.

YOTs have the expertise to advise on the individual needs and circumstances of young people; and they have close links with other agencies such as the young person's school, social services, Connexions (in England), the youth service or other children's services, including those under the auspices of the Welsh Assembly Government. They will often have information on past interventions with individual young people, and knowledge about the young person's family, the behaviour of siblings, and the engagement of parents/carers in addressing their child's behaviour. Research has shown that children and young people who offend have multiple needs that must be identified and addressed to reduce their risk of offending or re-offending. YOTs use a range of assessments to identify the needs of young people, the risk they present to themselves and others, and the likelihood of them offending or re-offending.

YJB guidance *Anti-social Behaviour: A guide to the role of Youth Offending Teams in dealing with anti-social behaviour* is available on the YJB website at: www.yjb.gov.uk/Publications/Scripts/prodView.asp?idproduct=212&eP=YJB.

Further YJB guidance *Providing consistent advice to courts in Anti-Social Behaviour Order proceedings (Guidance for youth offending teams)* is available on the YJB website at: www.yjb.gov.uk/Publications/Scripts/prodView.asp?idproduct=378&eP=YJB.

Manchester YOT has also produced very clear and helpful guidance for magistrates, judges, court staff and other practitioners on ISOs and Parenting Orders and how they manage the application process. Importantly, it emphasises the positive requirements of ISOs, dispelling the myth that they are a punishment. The leaflet entitled *Parenting Orders and Individual Support Orders* is a helpful model for other areas producing similar guidance and is available at: www.respect.gov.uk/uploadedFiles/Members_site/Documents_and_images/Supportive_interventions/Parenting_ISOs_orders_ ManchesterYOT0003.pdf.

Annex A: Criminal Justice and Immigration Act 2008 (c. 4)

Anti-social Behaviour Orders etc. in respect of children and young persons

[omitted]

Annex B: Diversionary activities for young people

Diversionary activities/schemes

Making sure that young people have activities they can easily access, and which are appropriate for their age and particular needs, can help to prevent and reduce anti-social behaviour.

Activities can be in the form of generic provision, which helps ensure that young people make constructive use of their leisure time rather than becoming involved in anti-social behaviour.

Provision includes local authority detached youth work and drop-in clubs, voluntary activities run by parents and local community groups. These activities can play a valuable role in helping to set local standards of acceptable behaviour.

The following programmes aim to deal with risk factors, engage young people's interests and increase their knowledge:

- Youth Inclusion Programmes;

- Youth Inclusion and Support Panels;

- parenting interventions;

- Safer School Partnerships;

- Splash Cymru; and

- mentoring.

Youth Inclusion Programmes

Youth Inclusion Programmes (YIPs), established in 2000, are tailor-made programmes for 8- to 17-year-olds who are identified as being at high risk of involvement in offending or anti-social behaviour.

YIPs are also open to other young people in the local area. The programmes operate in 120 of the most deprived/high-crime estates in England and Wales. YIPs aim to reduce youth crime and anti-social behaviour in the neighbourhoods where they work. Young people on the YIP are identified through a number of different agencies including YOTs, police, social services, local education authorities or schools, and other local agencies.

The programmes give young people somewhere safe to go where they can learn new skills, take part in activities with others and get help with their education and careers guidance. Positive role models – the workers and volunteer mentors – help to change young people's attitudes to education and crime.

Youth Inclusion and Support Panels

Youth Inclusion and Support Panels (YISPs) aim to prevent anti-social behaviour and offending by 8 to 17-year-olds who are considered to be at high risk of offending.

YIPs and YISPs have been designed to help local areas reduce the number of first-time entrants to the youth justice system.

Panels are made up of a number of representatives of different agencies (e.g. police, schools, health and social services). The main emphasis of a panel's work is to ensure that children and their families, at the earliest possible opportunity, can access mainstream public services.

Safer School Partnerships

The Safer School Partnerships (SSP) programme enables local agencies to address significant behavioural and crime-related issues in and around a school. A result of the YJB's proposal to develop a new policing model for schools, the SSP programme was launched as a pilot in September 2002, and brought into mainstream policy in March 2006. All schools involved in the SSP initiative have a police officer based in their school.

The school-based officer works with school staff and other local agencies to:

- reduce victimisation, criminality and anti-social behaviour within the school and its community;

- work with schools on whole-school approaches to behaviour and discipline;

- identify and work with children and young people at risk of becoming victims or offenders;

- ensure the full-time education of young offenders (a proven preventative factor in keeping young people away from crime);

- support vulnerable children and young people through periods of transition, such as the move from primary to secondary school; and

- create a safer environment for children to learn in.

Close working between police and schools is crucial to keeping children in education, off the streets and away from a life of crime.

Mentoring

Mentoring pairs a volunteer with a young person at risk of offending. The volunteer's role is to motivate and support the young person on the scheme through a sustained relationship, over an extended period of time. The relationship is built upon trust and a commitment to confidentiality and equality between the mentor and the young person.

The relationship must be structured and have clearly identified objectives. These objectives should be to help the young person identify and achieve educational, vocational or social goals which address the factors in the young person's life that put them at risk of offending.

Splash Cymru

Splash Cymru is a programme of positive and constructive activities for 13- to 17-year-olds which runs in the school holidays in Wales. It was launched in 2002 (originally for ages 9 to 17), following the success of the Splash and Splash Extra programmes in England.

Funded and managed by the YJB, the programme consists of locally run schemes based in areas experiencing high levels of crime and deprivation.

Young people at high risk in Splash neighbourhoods are engaged in a range of appropriate activities and interventions aimed at preventing their involvement in anti-social behaviour and offending.

Positive Activities for Young People

Positive Activities for Young People (PAYP) is targeted specifically at young people not fully engaged in education, those with a low level of school achievement, and those at risk of becoming involved in crime and anti-social behaviour. Referral agencies include YOTs, Connexions and behaviour improvement programmes in schools. Key workers support young people with the greatest needs, encouraging them to participate.

PAYP is a targeted programme supported by the YJB which has provided diversionary activities since April 2003. Young people across the country aged 8 to 19 who are at risk of social exclusion and becoming involved in community crime are able to participate in positive activities during the school holidays and access out-of-school activities throughout the year. Those young people who are most at risk are encouraged to engage in learning and/or employment with key worker support.

The programme aims to give young people opportunities for personal development including the development of self-discipline, self-respect and self-confidence, enabling them to communicate more effectively with a range of people and work effectively in a team. The programme will be targeted to reach those young people most at risk. YOTs, Connexions partnerships, behaviour improvement programmes in schools and other agencies working with at-risk young people will be responsible for identifying the target group of young people in the referral process.

A child or young person who is identified as being at risk of anti-social behaviour, particularly after school and during the holidays, may benefit from referral to the PAYP scheme. This should be via the local YOT or Connexions.

Positive Futures

Positive Futures is a national social inclusion programme supported by the YJB using sport and leisure activities to engage with disadvantaged and socially marginalised young adults.

Sure Start

Sure Start offers targeted services for 0- to 4-year-olds and their families living in areas of high deprivation to ensure that they have the best start in life. Sure Start programmes may provide a useful support mechanism for families that are struggling and behaving anti-socially – especially when there are young children in the household. Intervening early and providing support helps prevent young children from behaving anti-socially in the future, and support their parents. To find out more about the Sure Start initiative, see the website at: www.surestart.gov.uk.

Education initiatives

For example behaviour improvement programmes, aimed at improving poor behaviour and attendance and supporting children most at risk of exclusion, truancy, criminality and anti-social behaviour.

It is essential that supportive work with young people helps them to learn about the boundaries of behaviour that are expected by society, and the impact that their anti-social behaviour can have on others.

Engaging youth services in outreach work early in the problem-solving stage can lead to effective solutions such as improved diversion activities and facilities for young people.

Targeted Youth Support

Targeted Youth Support is an initiative aimed at vulnerable young people and involves ensuring that agencies work together to meet young people's needs. The initiative's rationale is that a collaborative, joined-up approach is needed because young people may have complex and multiple needs which cannot be met by mainstream or specialist services in isolation. It is rooted in the principles expressed in *Youth Matters*, which was published in July 2005 as part of the Government's wider Every Child Matters agenda. The central thrust within *Youth Matters* is the reform of targeted support to children and young people.

Annex C: Other interventions available for parents and families

Parenting interventions

Preventing anti-social behaviour from a young age starts in the home. Parenting interventions are designed to help parents improve their parenting skills, including skills needed to deal with problems early on and to address the behaviour that puts their child at risk of offending. The intervention may involve a series of tailored sessions with a trained practitioner or a group-based programme.

Parenting programmes

Parenting programmes provide parents with an opportunity to improve their skills in dealing with the behaviour that puts their child at risk of offending. They provide parents/carers with one-to-one advice as well as practical support in handling the behaviour of their child, setting appropriate boundaries and improving communication. A parenting programme could be offered at the first sign of problems – perhaps when a warning about a child's behaviour is first given. Most parents will take up help voluntarily, but where they do not want help, a Parenting Order should be used to secure their engagement. By improving the parenting skills of parents/carers, these programmes are addressing one of the major risk factors associated with young people at risk of offending. Parenting programmes have proved successful in turning children and young people away from crime and anti-social behaviour.

Parenting programmes may also be important for young offenders who are parents. Young parents who are constructively engaged in parenting may be less likely to re-offend. When this outlook is combined with new parenting skills they have acquired, these young parents are likely to exercise a positive impact on their children which may prevent them from becoming offenders or engaging in anti-social behaviour.

Family intervention projects

Family intervention projects work with persistently anti-social families to change their behaviour. They take a whole-family approach which considers the needs of the whole household and assesses the underlying problems driving the family's behaviour, in order to identify which services need to be involved. Projects use a twin-track approach which includes help for families to address the causes of their behaviour, alongside supervision and enforcement tools to provide them with the incentives to change.

Agencies should think about referring when there are numerous complaints about the behaviour of a family and the impact they are having on their local community. Referrals might be made by statutory agencies, housing associations, voluntary sector organisations or even by families themselves. Referrals must be accepted into the projects from anti-social behaviour teams or their equivalent.

Further information on family intervention projects can be viewed at: www.respect.gov.uk/members/article.aspx?id=8678.

Parenting Contracts

Sections 19 and 25 of the Anti-Social Behaviour Act 2003 give certain agencies the power to enter into Parenting Contracts, offering a structured and balanced way for these agencies to work with parents on a voluntary basis. They are a two-sided arrangement where both the parents and the agency will play a part in improving the young person's behaviour.

The Act set out Parenting Contracts in legislation to make it clear that:

- schools and local education authorities can enter into Parenting Contracts with the parent(s) of a child who has truanted or been excluded from school; and

- YOTs can enter into Parenting Contracts with the parent(s) of a child who has engaged in or is likely to engage in criminal conduct or anti-social behaviour.

The Contract contains a statement by the parent(s) agreeing to comply with the requirements for the period specified and a statement by the YOT or the local education authority agreeing to provide the necessary support to the parent(s) to comply with the requirements. As with acceptable behaviour agreements/contracts, it is important that there is a clear agreement about the consequences if the Parenting Contract is not adhered to.

If the Contract is broken, then the agency may apply to the court for a Parenting Order which makes the requirements compulsory.

There is comprehensive information on the issue of parenting on the YJB website at: www.yjb.gov.uk.

Section 23 of the Police and Justice Act 2006, amending section 25 of the Anti-Social Behaviour Act 2003, inserts two new sections (25A, 25B) into Part 3 of the 2003 Act which allow local authorities and registered social landlords to enter into Parenting Contracts with a parent of a child to prevent that child engaging in anti-social behaviour.

A local authority can apply for a Parenting Order if it has reason to believe that:

- the child is engaged in anti-social behaviour; and

- the child resides in its area.

A registered social landlord can apply for a Parenting Order where that child's behaviour affects housing management functions of the housing association

Parenting Orders

Section 24 of the Police and Justice Act 2006, amending section 26 of the Anti-Social Behaviour Act 2003, inserts new sections 26A, 26B and 26C into Part 3 of the 2003 Act which allows local authorities and registered social landlords to apply for Parenting Orders where anti-social behaviour is the trigger. Local authorities can apply to the court for a Parenting Order on the same grounds as they can enter into a Parenting Contract.

Generally, a Parenting Contract should be agreed before resorting to court for an Order. Any failure to adhere to the terms of the Contract may be used in support of an application for a Parenting Order.

A registered social landlord can apply for Parenting Orders in similar situations but must first consult with the local authority in the area (to ensure that one isn't already in place or that other action is not planned). Section 26C covers procedures for applications in county court proceedings under 26A and 26B.

Annex D: Perpetrators with health needs

Some perpetrators of anti-social behaviour have been found to have an undiagnosed and treatable mental health problem. It is essential for anti-social behaviour practitioners to refer people for assistance in such circumstances, which may then resolve the problem for all concerned.

It is important that when health needs have been identified, partnership working commences to ensure that adequate support is provided. At a local level, general practitioners, community psychiatric nurses, drug and alcohol workers and health visitors all have a role to play. It is essential that at a strategic level the health authority and primary care trust are committed to tackling anti-social behaviour through partnership working and will ensure the sharing of information via information exchange protocols.

Local authorities have a duty under the NHS and Community Care Act 1990 to assess any person who may be in need of community care services. If there is any evidence to suggest that the person against whom the Order is being sought may be suffering from drug, alcohol or mental health problems, the necessary support should be provided by social services or other support agencies. Such support should run parallel with the collection of evidence and application for an Order, where an application for an Order is deemed necessary.

When applying for an Order against a young person aged between 10 and 17 years, an assessment should be made of their circumstances and needs. This will enable the local authority to ensure that the appropriate services are provided for the young person concerned and for the courts to have necessary information about him or her. The assessment of the child's needs should run in parallel with evidence gathering and the application process.

For more information, see the article 'Is a needs assessment required for an ASBO application under the Childrens Act 1989?' on the Respect website at: www.respect.gov.uk/members/article.aspx?id=7866.

From December 2006, the new general duty under the Disability Discrimination Act 1995 requires a public authority to pay due regard when carrying out its functions to the need to:

- eliminate unlawful discrimination against disabled people;

- eliminate disability-related harassment of disabled people;

- promote equality of opportunity for disabled people; and

- take account of disabled people's disabilities even where that involves more favourable treatment.

All programmes around anti-social behaviour will need to be designed to address specific needs. A child's disability, special educational needs or mental health problems will also have a bearing on any requirements set out in any Order.

The measures taken to prevent and tackle anti-social behaviour should ensure that young people with disabilities, mental health problems or special educational needs are not excluded or discriminated against, and are able to access the same quality and level of support as others.

Advice on the general duty can be obtained from a leaflet issued by the Office for Disability Issues entitled *Disability equality: a priority for all* at: www.officefordisability.gov.uk/ docs/disability-equality.pdf. The Equality and Human Rights Commission website at www.equalityhumanrights. com contains information under the publications section entitled 'The Disability Equality Duty and Involvement'.

It is also worth noting the case of Cooke v Department for Public Prosecuctions (21 October 2008) which concluded that it would be wrong to make an ASBO against a person who by reason of mental ill health would not have the capacity to understand or comply with the Order. For example, the fact that a person would be likely to breach an Order because he or she suffers from mental health problems is not, of itself, a good reason for not making the Order.

APPENDIX 5

BREACH OF AN ANTI-SOCIAL BEHAVIOUR ORDER

Foreword

In accordance with section 170(9) of the Criminal Justice Act (CJA) 2003, the Sentencing Guidelines Council issues this guideline as a definitive guideline. By virtue of section 172 of the CJA 2003, every court must have regard to a relevant guideline. This guideline applies to the sentencing of offenders convicted of breaching an anti-social behaviour order (ASBO) who are sentenced on or after **5 January 2009**.

The Council has previously set out the approach to dealing with breaches of orders in its guidelines on *New Sentences: Criminal Justice Act 2003*[1] and *Breach of Protective Orders*.[2] The main aim of sentencing for breach of a court order is to achieve the purpose of the order; in the case of an ASBO that is to protect the public from behaviour that is likely to cause harassment, alarm or distress.

Any perception that the courts do not treat seriously a failure to comply with a court order can undermine public confidence and is therefore an important additional consideration.

Since the ability of a court to deal appropriately with an order that has been breached depends on how it was made, Annex A to the guideline summarises the key principles and considerations applicable to the making of an ASBO.

This guideline applies to the sentencing of adult <u>and</u> young offenders. It is recognised that a large proportion of orders are imposed on persons under 18 years of age. Although the sentencing framework for youths is very different from that for adults, and a guideline for sentencing young offenders will follow in due course, the Council considered that sentencers would find it helpful to have guiding principles for sentencing young offenders for breach of an ASBO.

The Council has appreciated the work of the Sentencing Advisory Panel in preparing the advice on which this guideline is based and is grateful to those who responded to the consultation of both the Panel and Council. The advice and this guideline are available on www.sentencing-guidelines.gov.uk or can be obtained from the Sentencing Guidelines Secretariat at 4th Floor, 8–10 Great George Street, London SW1P 3AE. A summary of the responses to the Council's consultation also appears on the website.

Chairman of the Council
December 2008

---

[1]   *New Sentences: Criminal Justice Act 2003*, published 16 December 2004, www.sentencing-guidelines.gov.uk.
[2]   *Breach of a Protective Order*, published 7 December 2006, www.sentencing-guidelines.gov.uk.

CONTENTS

Foreword

A. Statutory provision

B. Introduction

C. Assessing seriousness

   (i)   Culpability and harm

   (ii)   Relevance of the originating conduct

   (iii)   Breach of an interim order

   (iv)   A breach that also constitutes another criminal offence

   (v)   Aggravating factors and mitigating factors

   (vi)Personal mitigation

D. Sentencing guideline – adult offenders

   Sentencing ranges and starting points

   The decision making process

   Factors to take into consideration and guideline

E. Sentencing principles – young offenders

Annex A   Summary of principles for making an anti-social behaviour order

Annex B   General aggravating and mitigating factors

Annex C   Summary of sentencing framework and principles relating to young offenders

A.   Statutory provision

1.   Section 1 of the Crime and Disorder Act 1998 provides:

> *"(10) If without reasonable excuse a person does anything which he is prohibited from doing by an anti-social behaviour order, he shall be liable-*
>
> *(a)   on summary conviction, to imprisonment for a term not exceeding six months or to a fine not exceeding the statutory maximum or to both; or*
> *(b)   on conviction on indictment, to imprisonment for a term not exceeding five years or to a fine, or to both."*

2.   Where a person is convicted of an offence of breach of an anti-social behaviour order (ASBO), it is not open to the court to make an order discharging the offender conditionally.[3]

B.   Introduction

3.   An ASBO is a preventative order that can be made in either civil or criminal proceedings; its aim is to protect the public from behaviour that causes, or is likely to cause, harassment, alarm or distress. An order may be made on application to a magistrates' court, on conviction, or in conjunction with other proceedings in the County Court.

4.   Since the ability of a court to deal appropriately with an order that has been breached depends on how it was made, <u>Annex A</u> summarises the key principles and considerations applicable to the making of an ASBO.

5.   This guideline relates to the sentencing of both adult and young offenders. As the sentencing framework that applies to offenders aged under 18 is significantly different from that for older offenders, the guidance for young offenders is in the form of principles particularly regarding the circumstances in which a custodial sentence might be justified. The maximum penalty in the case of a young offender is detention for 24 months.

---

3   Crime and Disorder Act 1998, s 1(11).

6. Breach of this type of order is different from breach of a community order or failure to surrender to custody because it has the potential to affect a community or the public at large in a way that causes direct harm.

    The main aim of sentencing for breach of a court order is to achieve the purpose of the order. Therefore, the sentence for breach of an ASBO should primarily reflect the harassment, alarm or distress involved; the fact that it constituted breach of a court order is a secondary consideration.

C. Assessing seriousness

7. The sentence for breach of an ASBO must be commensurate with the seriousness of the offence; that is determined by assessing the culpability of the offender and any harm which the offence caused, was intended to cause or might foreseeably have caused.[4]

8. A community sentence can be imposed only if a court considers that the offence is serious enough to justify it,[5] and a custodial sentence can be imposed only if a court considers that a community sentence or a fine alone cannot be justified in view of the seriousness of the offence.[6] The Council has published a definitive guideline on seriousness that guides sentencers through the process of determining whether the respective sentencing thresholds have been crossed.[7]

9. A wide range of prohibitions can be attached to an order; consequently the degree of harm resulting from a breach will vary greatly and may be experienced by the wider community as well as by individuals.

10. In order properly to assess the seriousness of a breach of an ASBO, a court needs to be aware of the purpose of the order and the context in which it was made. A breach may be of one or more prohibitions in an order; the approach to sentencing is based on an assessment of the seriousness of the harm arising from the breach (or intended by the offender) rather than the number of prohibitions not complied with.

(i) Culpability and harm

11. When a court is considering the seriousness of breach of an order such as an ASBO, it will need to consider two aspects of culpability:

    (a) The degree to which the offender intended to breach the order.

    Culpability is variable and an offender may have:
    *   intended the breach
    *   been reckless as to whether the order was breached
    *   been aware of the risk of breach; or
    *   been unaware of this risk due to an incomplete understanding of the terms of the order.

    (b) he degree to which the offender intended to cause the harm that resulted (or could have resulted).

    Culpability will be higher where the offender foresaw the harm likely to be caused by the breach and will be at its highest where such harm was intended.

12. There are also two dimensions to the harm involved in breach of an ASBO:

    (a) the breach may itself cause harassment, alarm or distress, which can reduce the quality of life in a community.

    (b) breach of an ASBO contravenes an order of the court, and this can undermine public confidence in the effective administration of justice.

13. The assessment of the seriousness of an individual offence must take into account not only the harm actually caused by an offence but also any harm that was intended or might foreseeably have been caused.[8]

---

4   Criminal Justice Act 2003, s 143(1).
5   Criminal Justice Act 2003, s 148(1).
6   Criminal Justice Act 2003, s 152(2).
7   *Overarching Principles: Seriousness*, published 16 December 2004, www.sentencing-guidelines.gov.uk.
8   Criminal Justice Act 2003, s 143(1).

14. The test of foreseeability is objective[9] but as the prohibitions imposed must have been considered by a court to be necessary to prevent anti-social behaviour, some degree of harm must always be foreseeable whenever an order is breached. Where a breach causes harm that was not readily foreseeable, the level of culpability should carry more weight than harm when assessing offence seriousness.[10]

(ii)   Relevance of the originating conduct

15. The **original conduct** that led to the making of an order is a relevant consideration in so far as it indicates the level of harm caused and whether this was intended.[11]

16. High culpability and/or harm may be indicated if the breach continues a pattern of behaviour against an identifiable victim. Conversely, where there is little connection between the breach and the behaviour that the order was aimed at, this may indicate a less serious offence.

17. The court should examine the prohibitions of the order itself (particularly those in older orders which may have been made without the benefit of the guidance summarised in <u>Annex A</u>), their necessity and reasonableness in all the circumstances.[12]

(iii) Breach of an interim order

18. Breach of an interim order or a final order is equally serious and the same approach to sentencing should be taken.

19. Sentence for a breach of an interim order should be imposed as soon as possible. If the hearing regarding the final order can be brought forward, this should be done so that the two issues can be considered together. However, sentencing for the breach of the interim order should not be delayed for this purpose.

20. Where an interim order is breached the court should consider the extent to which an urgent need for specific interim prohibitions was demonstrated, or if the interim order was sought principally to obtain additional time to prepare a case for the full hearing.[13]

21. Where an interim order has been made without notice to the subject, the order does not take effect until it has been served. If doubts arise about the extent to which the subject has understood the prohibitions but the defence of reasonable excuse is not made out, a lack of understanding of the terms of the order may still mitigate the seriousness of the offence through reducing culpability.

(iv) A breach that also constitutes another criminal offence

22. Whether one offence or two has been charged, the sentence should reflect all relevant aspects of the offence so that, provided the facts are not in issue, the result should be the same.[14]
     (a) if the substantive offence only has been charged, the fact that it constitutes breach of an ASBO should be treated as an aggravating factor;
     (b) if breach of the order only has been charged, the sentence should reflect the full circumstances of the breach, which will include the conduct that could have been charged as a substantive offence.

---

9   Harm must have been foreseeable by 'a reasonable person'.
10   *Overarching Principles: Seriousness*, published 16 December 2004, www.sentencing-guidelines.gov.uk.
11   *Breach of a Protective Order*, published 7 December 2006, www.sentencing-guidelines.gov.uk.
12   Where appropriate, an application may be made separately for the order to be varied: Crime and Disorder Act 1998, ss 1(8) or 1CA. See also the Magistrates' Courts (Anti-Social Behaviour Orders) Rules 2002. Where the subject/offender is aged under 18, Practice Direction (Magistrates' Courts: Anti-Social Behaviour Orders: Composition of Benches) [2006] 1 AER 886 provides for the constitution of the court.
13   A report commissioned by the YJB concluded that there may be grounds for interim ASBOs only where there is an urgent need for specific prohibitions: Aikta-Reena Solanki, Tim Bateman, Gwyneth Boswell and Emily Hill, Anti-social Behaviour Orders, YJB (2006).
14   *Breach of a Protective Order*, published 7 December 2006, www.sentencing-guidelines.gov.uk.

23. Where breach of an ASBO also constitutes another offence with a lower maximum penalty than that for breach of the order, this penalty is an element to be considered in the interests of proportionality, although the court is not limited by it when sentencing an adult or youth for breach.

(v) Aggravating and mitigating factors

24. The Council guideline *Overarching Principles: Seriousness* identifies a number of factors that might increase or mitigate the seriousness of an offence. For ease of reference, the factors are set out in Annex B.

(vi) Personal mitigation

25. Offender mitigation is particularly relevant to breach of an ASBO as compliance with the order depends on the ability to understand its terms and make rational decisions in relation to these. Sentence may be mitigated where:
    - the offender has a lower level of understanding due to mental health issues or learning difficulties
    - the offender was acting under the influence of an older or more experienced offender; or
    - there has been compliance with an Individual Support Order or Intervention Order imposed when the ASBO was made.

D. Sentencing guideline – adult offenders

Sentencing ranges and starting points

1. This guideline applies to a *"first time offender"* who has been **convicted after a trial**. In common with other proceedings based on breach of a court order,[15] it is likely that an offender in breach of an ASBO will have previous convictions. That has been taken into account in determining the starting points and ranges. Therefore, within this guideline, a "first time offender" is a person who does not have a conviction for breach of an ASBO rather than the usual approach which is based on the existence of any conviction which, by virtue of section 143(2) of the Criminal Justice Act 2003, must be treated as an aggravating factor.

2. As an aid to consistency of approach, the guideline describes a number of types of activity which would fall within the broad definition of the offence. These are set out in a column headed 'Nature of failure & harm'.

3. The expected approach is for a court to identify the description that most nearly matches the particular facts of the offence for which sentence is being imposed. This will identify a **starting point** from which the sentencer can depart to reflect aggravating or mitigating factors affecting the seriousness of the offence (beyond those contained within the column describing the nature of the failure or of the harm) to reach a **provisional sentence**.

4. The **sentencing range** is the bracket into which the provisional sentence will normally fall after having regard to factors which aggravate or mitigate the seriousness of the offence. The particular circumstances may, however, make it appropriate that the provisional sentence falls outside the range.

5. Where the offender has previous convictions which aggravate the seriousness of the current offence, that may take the provisional sentence beyond the range given particularly where there are significant other aggravating factors present.

6. Once the provisional sentence has been identified by reference to those factors affecting the seriousness of the offence, the court will take into account any relevant factors of personal mitigation, which may take the sentence beyond the range given.

---

[15] For example, failing to surrender to bail.

7. Where there has been a guilty plea, any reduction attributable to that plea will be applied to the sentence at this stage. Again, this reduction may take the sentence below the range provided.

8. A court must give its reasons for imposing a sentence of a different kind or outside the range provided in the guidelines.[16]

The decision making process

The process set out below is intended to show that the sentencing approach for the offence of breach of an anti-social behaviour order is fluid and requires the structured exercise of discretion.

1. Identify the appropriate starting point

Identify the description that most nearly matches the particular facts of the offence for which sentence is being imposed.

2. Consider relevant aggravating factors, both general and those specific to the type of offence

This may result in a sentence level being identified that is <u>higher</u> than the suggested starting point, sometimes substantially so.

3. Consider mitigating factors and personal mitigation

There may be offence or offender mitigation which could result in a sentence that is <u>lower</u> than the suggested starting point (possibly substantially so), or a sentence of a different type.

4. Reduction for guilty plea

The court will then apply any reduction for a guilty plea following the approach set out in the Council Guideline *Reduction in Sentence for a Guilty Plea* (revised July 2007).

5. Consider ancillary orders

The court should consider whether ancillary orders are appropriate or necessary.

6. The totality principle

The court should review the total sentence to ensure that it is proportionate to the offending behaviour and properly balanced.

7. Reasons

When a court imposes a sentence of a different type or outside the range provided, it should explain its reasons for doing so.

---

[16] Criminal Justice Act 2003, s 174(2)(a).

Factors to take into consideration

1. The starting points and sentencing ranges are for a *"first time offender"* who pleaded not guilty. In this guideline, a *"first time offender"* is one who does not have a previous conviction for breach of an ASBO.

2. Where a court determines that there are other convictions which it is reasonable to treat as a factor aggravating the seriousness of the breach,[17] that factor will be taken into account at stage 2 of the sentencing process set out on page 7.

3. An ASBO may be breached in a wide range of circumstances and may involve one or more prohibitions not being complied with. The examples given below are intended to illustrate how the scale of the conduct that led to the breach, taken as a whole, might come within the three levels of seriousness:
    *   **Serious harm caused or intended** – breach at this level of seriousness will involve the use of violence, significant threats or intimidation or the targeting of individuals or groups of people in a manner that leads to a fear of violence.
    *   **Lesser degree of harm intended or likely** – examples may include lesser degrees of threats or intimidation, the use of seriously abusive language, or causing more than minor damage to property.
    *   **No harm caused or intended** – in the absence of intimidation or the causing of fear of violence, breaches involving being drunk or begging may be at this level, as may prohibited use of public transport or entry into a prohibited area, where there is no evidence that harassment, alarm or distress was caused or intended.

4. The suggested starting points are based on the assumption that the offender had the highest level of culpability.

5. Aggravating and mitigating factors specifically relevant to sentencing for breach of an ASBO are included in the guideline. Care needs to be taken to ensure that there is no double counting where an element of the breach determines the level of seriousness where it might in other circumstances be an aggravating factor. When assessing the seriousness of an offence, the court must always refer to the full list of aggravating and mitigating factors in the Council guideline on Seriousness (see Annex B).[18]

6. In the most serious cases, involving repeat offending and a breach causing serious harassment together with the presence of several aggravating factors, such as the use of violence, a sentence beyond the highest range will be justified.

7. Once the provisional sentence has been identified by reference to factors affecting the seriousness of the offence, the court will take into account any relevant factors of personal mitigation (see paragraph 25 above), and, in accordance with the Council guideline[19] consider reducing the sentence where a guilty plea was entered.

8. When imposing a community order, the court must ensure that the requirements imposed are proportionate to the seriousness of the breach, compatible with each other,[20] and also with the prohibitions of the ASBO if the latter is to remain in force. Even where the threshold for a custodial sentence is crossed, a custodial sentence is not inevitable.[21]

9. An offender may be sentenced for more than one offence of breach, which occurred on different days. While consecutive sentences may be imposed in such cases, the overall sentence should reflect the totality principle.

---

[17] In accordance with Criminal Justice Act 2003, s 143(2).

[18] *Overarching Principles: Seriousness*, published 16 December 2004, www.sentencing-guidelines.gov.uk.

[19] *Reduction in Sentence for a Guilty Plea*, published 20 July 2007, www.sentencing-guidelines.gov.uk.

[20] *New Sentences: Criminal Justice Act 2003*, published 16 December 2004, www.sentencing-guidelines.gov.uk.

[21] *New Sentences: Criminal Justice Act 2003*, published 16 December 2004, www.sentencing-guidelines.gov.uk.

Breach of an Anti-social Behaviour Order

Crime and Disorder Act 1998 (section 1(10))

Maximum Penalty: 5 years imprisonment

Note: A conditional discharge is not available as a sentence for this offence

Nature of failure & harm	Starting point	Sentencing range
Serious harassment, alarm or distress has been caused or where such harm was intended	26 weeks custody	Custody threshold – 2 years custody
Lesser degree of harassment, alarm or distress, where such harm was intended, or where it would have been likely if the offender had not been apprehended	6 weeks custody	Community Order (MEDIUM) – 26 weeks custody
No harassment, alarm or distress was actually caused by the breach and none was intended by the offender	Community Order (LOW)	Fine Band B – Community Order (MEDIUM)

Aggravating factors

1. Offender has a history of disobedience to court orders.

2. Breach was committed immediately or shortly after the order was made.

3. Breach was committed subsequent to earlier breach proceedings arising from the same order.

4. Targeting of a person the order was made to protect or a witness in the original proceedings.

Mitigating factors

1. Breach occurred after a long period of compliance.

2. The prohibition(s) breached was not fully understood, especially where an interim order was made without notice.

E. Sentencing principles: young offenders

1. The approach to assessing the seriousness of a breach outlined above at paragraphs 7 to 25 applies equally to youths. A court must impose a community or custodial sentence only if such a sentence is warranted by the seriousness of the offence and no lesser sentence can be justified.

2. When sentencing a young offender, the normal approach is for the penalty to reflect both the reduction in culpability (for example, due to a lesser ability to foresee the consequences of actions) and the more onerous effects of punishments on education and personal development in comparison with an adult offender.

3. The sentencing framework that applies to offenders aged under 18 is significantly different from that for adult offenders and key principles are set out in Annex C. The maximum penalty for this offence when committed by a young offender is a 24 month detention and training order (DTO). With the exception of a conditional discharge,[22] the full range of disposals of the youth court is available, and these are also outlined in Annex C.[23]

---

[22]   Crime and Disorder Act 1998, ss 1(11) and 1C(9).

[23]   If the young offender has also been charged with a grave crime under s 91 Powers of Criminal Courts (Sentencing) Act 2000, the case may be committed to the Crown Court. Similarly, where the young offender is committed to the Crown Court for sentence under the dangerous offender provisions.

4. In most cases of breach by a young offender convicted after a trial, the appropriate sentence will be a community sentence.[24] Within the sentence(s) available, a range of requirements can be attached; the court will consider the seriousness of the breach, which requirement(s) will best prevent further offending and the individual circumstances of the offender.

5. The court must ensure that the requirements imposed are compatible both with each other and with the prohibitions of the ASBO if the latter is to remain in force, and that the combination of both is not so onerous as to make further breaches likely.

6. The particular stage of intellectual or emotional maturity of the individual (which may not correspond with actual age) will also influence sentence. A young offender is likely to perceive a particular time period as being longer in comparison with an adult, and this may be of relevance when considering how much time has elapsed between imposition and breach of the order.

7. The principles to be followed when sentencing a youth for breach of an ASBO are as follows:

"First time offender"[25] pleading guilty: the court[26] must make a referral order unless it imposes an absolute discharge, a custodial sentence or a hospital order;

In all other cases:

(i)   in some less serious cases, such as where the breach has not involved any harassment, alarm or distress, a fine may be appropriate if it will be paid by the offender, or otherwise a reparation order;

(ii)   in most cases, the appropriate sentence will be a community sentence;

(iii)   the custody threshold should be set at a significantly higher level than the threshold applicable to adult offenders;

(iv)   the custody threshold usually will not be crossed unless the breach involved serious harassment, alarm or distress through either the use of violence, threats or intimidation or the targeting of individuals/groups in a manner that led to a fear of violence;

(v)   exceptionally, the custody threshold may also be crossed where a youth is being sentenced for more than one offence of breach (committed on separate occasions within a short period) involving a lesser but substantial degree of harassment, alarm or distress;

(vi)   even where the custody threshold is crossed, the court should normally impose a community sentence in preference to a DTO, as custody should be used only as a measure of last resort; and

(vii)   where the court considers a custodial sentence to be unavoidable, the starting point for sentencing should be 4 months detention, with a range of up to 12 months. Where a youth is being sentenced for more than one breach involving serious harassment, alarm or distress, sentence may go beyond that range.

Aggravating and mitigating factors

8. As with adult offenders, factors that are likely to <u>aggravate</u> an offence of breach of an anti-social behaviour order are:
    *   history of disobedience of court orders
    *   the breach was committed immediately or shortly after the order was made
    *   the breach was committed subsequent to earlier breach proceedings arising from the same order
    *   targeting of a person the order was made to protect or of a witness in the original proceedings.

9. Factors that are likely to <u>mitigate</u> the seriousness of the breach are:
    *   the breach occurred after a long period of compliance
    *   the prohibition(s) breached was not fully understood, especially where an interim order was made without notice.

---

[24] Though see paragraph 7 below.

[25] For the purpose of this requirement, a "first time offender" is an offender who has never been convicted by or before a court in the United Kingdom of any offence other than the offence and any connected offence, or been bound over in criminal proceedings; Powers of Criminal Court (Sentencing) Act 2000, s 17(1)(b) and (c).

[26] A referral order may be made by a youth court or other magistrates' court; Powers of Criminal Courts (Sentencing) Act 2000, s 16(1).

Personal mitigation

10.   Offender mitigation is particularly relevant to breach of an ASBO as compliance with the order depends on the ability to understand its terms and make rational decisions in relation to these. Sentence may be mitigated where:

- the offender has a lower level of understanding due to mental health issues or learning difficulties
- the offender was acting under the influence of an older or more experienced offender; or
- there has been compliance with an Individual Support Order or Intervention Order imposed when the ASBO was made.

11.   Other offender mitigating factors that may be particularly relevant to young offenders include peer pressure and a lack of parental support.

Annex A: Summary of principles and other considerations relevant to the making of an anti-social behaviour order

1.   Proceedings for the imposition of an ASBO are civil in nature, so that hearsay evidence is admissible, but a court must be satisfied to a criminal standard that the individual has acted in the anti-social manner alleged.

2.   The test of 'necessity' requires the exercise of judgement or evaluation; it does not require proof beyond reasonable doubt that the order is "necessary".

3.   It is particularly important that the findings of fact giving rise to the making of the order are recorded by the court.

4.   As the ASBO is a preventative order it is unlawful to use it as a punishment; so, when sentencing an offender, a court must not allow itself to be diverted into making an ASBO as an alternative or additional sanction.

5.   The police have powers to arrest an individual for any criminal offence, and the court should not impose an order which prohibits the subject from committing an offence if it will not add significantly to the existing powers of the police to protect others from anti-social behaviour by the subject. An order must not prohibit a criminal offence merely to increase the sentence range available for that offence.

6.   The terms of the order made must be precise and capable of being understood by the subject.[27] Where the subject is aged under 18, it is important for both the subject and the parent or guardian to confirm their understanding of the order and its terms. The prohibitions must be enforceable in the sense that they should allow a breach to be readily identified and capable of being proved.

7.   An order should not impose a 'standard list' of prohibitions, but should identify and prohibit the particular type of anti-social behaviour that gives rise to the necessity of an ASBO. Each separate prohibition must be necessary to protect persons from anti-social behaviour by the subject, and each order must be specifically fashioned to deal with the individual concerned.

8.   The order must be proportionate to the legitimate aim pursued and commensurate with the risk guarded against. The court should avoid making compliance very difficult through the imposition of numerous prohibitions, and those that will cause great disruption to the subject should be considered with particular care. It is advisable to make an order for a specific period; when considering the duration of an order imposed on a youth, the potential for the subject to mature may be a relevant factor.

---

[27]   'A Guide for the Judiciary' produced by the JSB (third edition published January 2007, supplement published January 2008) provides a list of examples of prohibitions that the higher courts have found to be too wide or poorly drafted; www.jsboard.co.uk.

9. Not all prohibitions set out in an ASBO have to run for the full term of the ASBO itself. The test must always be what is necessary to deal with the particular anti-social behaviour of the offender and what is proportionate in the circumstances. At least one of the prohibitions must last for the duration of the order but not all are required to last for the 2 years that is the minimum length of an order. The court can vary the terms of an order at any time upon application by the subject (or the applicant in the case of an order made upon application).

10. When making an order upon conviction, the court has the power to suspend its terms until the offender has been released from a custodial sentence. However, where a custodial sentence of 12 months or more is imposed and the offender is liable to be released on licence and thus subject to recall, an order will not generally be necessary. There might be cases where geographical restraints could supplement licence conditions.

11. Other considerations:
    (i)   Where an ASBO is imposed on a subject aged 10-17, the court must consider whether a **parenting order** would be desirable in the interests of preventing repetition of the anti-social behaviour.[28] Such an order <u>must</u> be made where the offender is aged under 16 and the condition is met, but is discretionary where the offender is aged 16 or 17.
    (ii) Where a magistrates' court imposes a stand-alone ASBO, it must also consider whether an **individual support order** (ISO) would be desirable to tackle the underlying causes of the behaviour.[29]
    (iii) In the case of an adult, the court may make an **intervention order** if the underlying causes of the anti-social behaviour are drug-related and appropriate treatment is available.[30]
    12.   Interim orders:
    Where a decision to impose an order (either upon application or conviction) is pending, the court may make an interim order if it considers it just to do so.[31] The court must balance the seriousness of the behaviour and the urgency with which it is necessary to take steps to control it, with the likely impact of an interim order upon the potential subject.[32]

Annex B: Aggravating and mitigating factors identified in the council guideline overarching principles: seriousness

The factors below apply to a wide range of offences. Not all will be relevant to the offence of breach of an anti-social behaviour order

Factors indicating higher culpability:
- Offence committed whilst on bail for other offences
- Failure to respond to previous sentences
- Offence was racially or religiously aggravated
- Offence motivated by, or demonstrating, hostility to the victim based on his or her sexual orientation (or presumed sexual orientation)
- Offence motivated by, or demonstrating, hostility based on the victim's disability (or presumed disability)
- Previous conviction(s), particularly where a pattern of repeat offending is disclosed
- Planning of an offence
- An intention to commit more serious harm than actually resulted from the offence
- Offenders operating in groups or gangs
- 'Professional' offending
- Commission of the offence for financial gain (where this is not inherent in the offence itself)
- High level of profit from the offence
- An attempt to conceal or dispose of evidence

---

[28] Crime and Disorder Act 1998, s 8. The Anti-social Behaviour Act 2003 now provides for a court to impose stand-alone Parenting Orders, if it is satisfied that the child has engaged in criminal or anti-social behaviour. The ASBA also provides for certain agencies to enter into Parenting Contracts which, as an alternative to legal action, have much in common with the non-statutory Acceptable Behaviour Contracts.

[29] Crime and Disorder Act 1998, s 1AA.

[30] Crime and Disorder Act 1998, s 1G.

[31] Crime and Disorder Act 1998, s 1D.

[32] Leeds Magistrates' Court, ex parte Kenny; Secretary of State for Constitutional Affairs and another, ex parte M [2004] EWCA Civ 312.

- Failure to respond to warnings or concerns expressed by others about the offender's behaviour
- Offence committed whilst on licence
- Offence motivated by hostility towards a minority group, or a member or members of it
- Deliberate targeting of vulnerable victim(s)
- Commission of an offence while under the influence of alcohol or drugs
- Use of a weapon to frighten or injure victim
- Deliberate and gratuitous violence or damage to property, over and above what is needed to carry out the offence
- Abuse of power
- Abuse of a position of trust

Factors indicating a more than usually serious degree of harm:
- Multiple victims
- An especially serious physical or psychological effect on the victim, even if unintended
- A sustained assault or repeated assaults on the same victim
- Victim is particularly vulnerable
- Location of the offence (for example, in an isolated place)
- Offence is committed against those working in the public sector or providing a service to the public
- Presence of others e.g. relatives, especially children or partner of the victim
- Additional degradation of the victim (e.g. taking photographs of a victim as part of a sexual offence)
- In property offences, high value (including sentimental value) of property to the victim, or substantial consequential loss (e.g. where the theft of equipment causes serious disruption to a victim's life or business)

Factors indicating significantly lower culpability:
- A greater degree of provocation than normally expected
- Mental illness or disability
- Youth or age, where it affects the responsibility of the individual defendant
- The fact that the offender played only a minor role in the offence

Annex C: Summary of sentencing framework and principles relating to young offenders

1. The principal aim of the youth justice system is to prevent offending by children and young persons.[33]

2. Under domestic law, the court must have regard to the welfare of the child or young person when imposing sentence.[34] In accordance with obligations under international conventions and treaties, the best interests of the child must be a primary consideration.[35] A sentence designed to prevent re-offending also helps to promote the welfare of the young offender.

3. Restorative justice is an important underlying principle in all youth justice disposals, from referral and reparation orders to action plan and supervision orders;[36] as well as reducing the harm done, it can also help prevent re-offending.

---

[33] Crime and Disorder Act 1998, s 37.

[34] Children and Young Persons Act 1933, s 44. In *R (A) v Leeds Magistrates' Court* [2004] EWHC Admin 554 the High Court held that where the person against whom the order is sought is a child, the child's best interests are a primary consideration but so are the interests of the public.

[35] United Nations Standard Minimum Rules for the Administration of Juvenile Justice ('The Beijing Rules'), adopted by General Assembly resolution 40/33 of 29/11/1985; www.ohchr.org. See also United Nations Convention on the Rights of the Child, Article 3; www2.ohchr.org/english/law/crc.htm.

[36] YJB, *A guide to the role of youth offending teams in dealing with anti-social behaviour* (2006); www.yjb.gov.uk.

4. Where a young offender pleads guilty and is being sentenced for the first time, the court must impose a **referral order** unless either it considers the offence to be of such a nature that an absolute discharge or hospital order is appropriate or it considers the offence to be so serious that only a custodial sentence is appropriate.[37]

   - Such an order refers the offender to a youth offender panel, and the court may (or 'shall' in the case of a child aged under 16) require at least one parent or guardian to attend the panel meetings unless this would be unreasonable.[38]
   - Panel meetings are intended to result in a youth offender contract, which is aimed at repairing the harm caused by the offence and addressing the causes of the offending behaviour (including requirements such as unpaid work in the community).
   - The terms of the 'contract' are determined by the panel, but the court must specify the period for which it is to have effect (between 3 and 12 months), which will depend on the seriousness of the breach.
   - If the offender does not agree to the contract, fails to abide by its terms, or re-offends while it is in force, the case is returned to the youth court to be re-sentenced.

5. If the offender has previous convictions or has been found guilty after a trial the court has the following options:
   - absolute discharge
   - reparation order
   - fine
   - community sentence
   - detention and training order

6. A **reparation order** requires a young offender to make reparation to the victim(s) of the offence, and before making such an order the court will obtain the views of anyone so affected.[39] In the case of breach of an ASBO, there will often be no identifiable victim, but the legislation provides for reparation to be made to the community at large. This work must last no longer than 24 hours and be completed within 3 months.

7. The court may impose a **fine** of up to £250 for offenders aged between 10 and 14, and up to £1,000 for those aged 15-17. Where the offender is under 16, the court must order that the fine is paid by the offender's parent unless that would be unreasonable; in the case of an offender aged 16 or 17, the court has discretion to do so.

8. Where a community sentence is imposed, it may consist of one or more of five **youth community orders** set out in section 147(2) of the Criminal Justice Act 2003.[40] These are:
   - a **curfew order** – order to remain at a specified place for a designated period for a maximum of 6 months, or 3 months for those under 16
   - an **exclusion order** – available for offenders aged under 16, prohibits the offender from entering a specified place for a maximum of 3 months
   - an **attendance centre order** – attendance at a designated place for a total of 12-36 hours (maximum 24 hours for offenders under 16)
   - an **action plan order** – a short (3 months) but intensive period of supervision, intended to be individually tailored by means of a series of requirements
   - a **supervision order** – can impose a wide range of requirements and last for up to 3 years. A supervision order may also involve participation in the Intensive Supervision and Surveillance Programme (ISSP). Introduced in 2001, ISSP is the most rigorous non-custodial intervention available for young offenders, and offers the court an alternative to a short DTO.

9. Additionally, where the offender is 16 or 17, the court may impose a **community rehabilitation order** (which may require participation in the ISSP), a **community punishment order**, or a **community**

---

[37] Powers of Criminal Courts (Sentencing) Act 2000, s 16. When in force, the Criminal Justice and Immigration Act 2008 will widen the circumstances in which a referral order can be made, to include where the offender has been bound over previously, or where the offender has one conviction in respect of which a referral order was not imposed.

[38] Powers of Criminal Courts (Sentencing) Act 2000, s 20.

[39] Powers of Criminal Courts (Sentencing) Act 2000, s 73.

[40] When in force, the Criminal Justice and Immigration Act 2008 will replace these with the Youth Rehabilitation Order, a generic community order for youths.

rehabilitation and punishment order (combining both).[41] A community rehabilitation order lasts between six months and three years, and may involve reparation and/or programmes to address the offending behaviour. A community punishment order involves unpaid community work for a total of 40-240 hours.

10.   Where a custodial sentence is imposed in the youth court, it must be a **detention and training order (DTO)**, which can only be for 4, 6, 8, 10, 12, 18 or 24 months. Where the offender is aged 10 or 11, no custodial sentence is available in the youth court. Where the offender is aged between 12 and 14, a custodial sentence may be imposed only if the child is a "persistent offender".[42]

---

[41]   Powers of Criminal Courts (Sentencing) Act 2000, ss 41, 46 and 51 respectively. These orders will be replaced by a generic community order, the Youth Rehabilitation Order, when the relevant provisions in the Criminal Justice and Immigration Act 2008 are in force.

[42]   Powers of Criminal Courts (Sentencing) Act 2000, s 100.

APPENDIX 6

WORKING TOGETHER GUIDANCE ON PUBLICISING ANTI-SOCIAL BEHAVIOUR ORDERS

Aims of guidance

- To inform those individuals making a decision whether or not to publicise the personal information of those who are the subject of an ASBO, how to do it, what medium to consider and what should be taken into account.
  The decision to publish should not be onerous, or bureaucratic; but moreover easy, timely whilst considering the necessary safeguards.
  It is necessary to balance the human rights of those individuals subject to an ASBO against those of the community as a whole when considering publicising ASBOs.

- To inform individuals, who might find themselves subject to an ASBO, what they can expect in the way of publicity.

Anti-social Behaviour Orders – use of publicity

1. Statement of principles

- Publicity is essential if local communities are to support agencies tackling anti-social behaviour. There is an implied power in the Crime and Disorder Act 1998 and the Local Government Act 2000 to publicise an order so that the order can be effectively enforced.

- ASBOs protect local communities. Obtaining the order is only part of the process; its effectiveness will normally depend on people knowing about the order.

- Information about ASBOs obtained should be publicised to let the community know that action has been taken in their area.

- A case by case approach should be adopted and each individual case should be judged on its merits as to whether or not to publicise the details of an individual subject to an ASBO – **publicity should be expected in most cases.**

- It is necessary to balance the human rights of individuals subject to an ASBO against those of the community as a whole when considering publicising ASBOs.

- Publicising should be the norm not the exception. An individual who is subject to an ASBO should understand that the community is likely to learn about it.

2. Main objectives and benefits of publicity

Publicity is not intended to punish the individual. An ASBO is a civil order, which restrains future anti-social behaviour: it is not a punishment.

The benefits of publicity include:

- **Enforcement** – local people have the information they need to identify and report breaches.

- **Public reassurance about safety** – victims and witnesses know that action has been taken to protect them, and to protect their human rights in relation to safety and/or quiet enjoyment of their property. Making local people aware of an order that is made for their own protection can make a real difference to the way in which they live their lives, especially when they have suffered from anti-social behaviour themselves or lived in fear of it.

- **Public confidence in local services** – local people are reassured that if they report anti-social behaviour, action will be taken by local authorities, the police or other agencies.

- **Deterrent to the subject of the order** – the perpetrator is aware that breaches are more likely to be reported because details of the order are in the public domain.

- **Deterrent to other perpetrators** – publicity spreads the message that ASBOs are being used and is a warning to others who are causing a nuisance in the community.

3. The decision to publish

Each individual case should be judged on its merits as to whether or not to publicise the details of an individual subject to an ASBO.

There should be a correlation between the purpose of publicity and the necessity test: that is, what is the least interference with privacy that is possible in order to promote the purpose identified.

Decision-makers should ensure that the decisions to publicise ASBOs are recorded. However, decision-makers should not see this as an onerous, lengthy task but merely a way of recording the process they go through to arrive at a published document.

To ensure it is achieved, it is good practice to identify an individual, such as the Anti-social Behaviour Co-ordinator, to be in charge of the recording process.

The decision-making process should aim to consider and record several key factors:

- The need for publicity.

- A consideration of the human rights of the public.

- A consideration of the human rights of those against whom ASBOs are made.

- What the publicity should look like and whether it is proportionate to the aims of the publicity.

Carry out the decision making process early on so as to avoid any delay in publicity following the granting of the order.

4. The decision making process

Keep it simple

Publicity must be necessary to achieve the identified aim – this will involve a necessity test. The identified aim for publicising could be (1) to notify the public that ASBOs have been obtained in order to reassure the public that action has been taken; (2) to notify the public of specific ASBOs so that they can help in their enforcement; or (3) to act as a deterrent to others involved in anti-social behaviour. In some cases two or all three aims will be relevant.

Disclosure of information should always be necessary and proportionate to achieving the desired aim(s).

When identifying the aim(s) decision-makers should acknowledge, in those cases where it is relevant, the 'social pressing need' for effective enforcement of an injunction which prohibits anti-social behaviour in order to protect the community. In effect, this is a consideration of the human rights of the wider community, including past and potential victims.

The decision-maker should recognise and acknowledge that for publicity to achieve its aim it might interfere with the individual's human rights and potentially those of his or her family. Publicity should be proportionate to this interference.

For example, if the legitimate aim is enforcement of the ASBO then personal information, such as the terms of the ASBO, the identity of the individual (including a photograph) and how to report any breach of the terms should be included.

Normally the consideration of the effect of publicity on family members should not deter decision makers on the stated aim of publicising the ASBO. However consideration of the impact of publicity on vulnerable family members, should be made and recorded.

The defendant and his or her family should be warned of the intention to publish details.

5. *What publicity should look like and are the contents proportionate?*

The contents of the publicity should also be considered and decisions recorded.

Disclosure of information should always be proportionate to achieving the desired aim. The contents of publicity should include factual and accurate material.

Close regard should be had to the content and tone of the publicity. Information must be based on facts and appropriate language used: for example, the order itself does not mean that an individual has been found guilty of a criminal offence. Words such as 'criminal' and 'crime' to describe the individual and their behaviour must be used with care and only when appropriate. If the anti-social behaviour was, as a matter of fact, also criminal, then it is permissible to describe it as criminal. Breach of an order is a criminal offence and should be described as such.

Publicity should be consistent with the character of the ASBO itself: that is, a civil injunction (rather than a criminal order) restricting anti-social behaviour (which may be criminal but need not be criminal). It would be prudent to rehearse the facts of the case and agree on appropriate language to use.

Some consideration should be given to the personal circumstances of individuals named on the order when deciding whether to include them in the leaflet, particularly if they are under 18. However, any arguments for not including their names must be balanced with the need to enable those who receive the leaflet to be able to identify a breach.

Details of conditions of non-association named on the order, particularly where those named are also subject to ASBOs or have a recent history of anti-social behaviour can be included in publicity. Even in cases where the named individuals with whom association is prohibited are not subject to an ASBO it will usually be appropriate to name them once some consideration has been given to their personal circumstances.

Age consideration

The age of the person against whom the ASBO was obtained should be a consideration when deciding whether or how to inform people about the order.

Factual information should be obtained about whether an individual is particularly vulnerable. This should be done as early as possible so as to avoid delays in informing the public once an order has been obtained.

The fact that someone is under the age of 18 does not mean that their anti-social behaviour is any less distressing or frightening than that of an adult.

An ASBO made against a juvenile (a person under 18) is made in open court and is not usually subject to reporting restrictions. The information is in the public domain and newspapers are entitled to publish details. **But if reporting restrictions have been imposed they must be scrupulously adhered to.**

In applications involving juveniles where evidence has consisted of details of their past criminal convictions and reporting restrictions were not lifted for these convictions, the publicity should not make reference to those criminal convictions. Similarly where an order on conviction has been obtained in the Youth Court for a juvenile, unless reporting restrictions are lifted, details of the criminal offences or behaviour alluded to in the criminal hearing cannot be reported.

However, details of the behaviour outlined in the order on conviction hearing can be used.

Where the court making the order does impose **reporting restrictions** under section 39 of the Children and Young Persons Act 1933, the press must scrupulously observe these.

A court must have a good reason to make a section 39 order. Age alone is insufficient to justify reporting restrictions being imposed.

Section 141 of the Serious Organised Crime and Police Act 2005 reverses the presumption in relation to reporting restrictions in the Youth Court in cases for breach of ASBOs. Automatic reporting restrictions will not apply but the court retains the discretion to impose them.

Whilst it is the case that from 1 July 2005 no automatic reporting restrictions will apply in cases for breach of ASBOs relating to juveniles, the court when dealing with the case will consider whether reporting restrictions were imposed when the original order was granted. As ASBOs are civil orders, no reporting restrictions apply unless imposed by the court, so it is likely that reporting restrictions will not have been imposed.

If reporting restrictions were imposed at the original ASBO hearing then unless there has been a significant change in the intervening period, it is likely that the court will impose reporting restrictions at the hearing for the breach. If no reporting restrictions were imposed at the original ASBO hearing, it is still open to the court to impose reporting restrictions at the hearing of the breach case. If reporting restrictions are not imposed, publicity can be considered, taking into account all the matters which are relevant when considering publicising the ASBO itself.

Photographs

A photograph of the subject of the ASBO will usually be required so that they can be identified. This is particularly necessary for older people or housebound witnesses who may not know the names of those causing a nuisance in the area. The photograph should be as recent as possible.

Distribution of publicity

This should be primarily within the area(s), which suffered from the anti-social behaviour and which are covered by the terms of the order, including exclusion zones. People who have suffered from anti-social behaviour, for example residents, local businesses, shop staff, staff of local public services, particular groups or households should be the target of publicity.

All orders should be recorded on the Police National Computer to assist enforcement. This is particularly relevant where the order extends across England and Wales.

It may be appropriate to extend publicity beyond the area where the anti-social behaviour was focused if there is a general term prohibiting harassment, alarm or distress in a wider area. It may also be appropriate if there is a danger of displacement of the anti-social behaviour to distribute it just beyond the area covered by the order.

The **timescale** over which publicity is anticipated to occur should also be given due consideration and decisions recorded. It is important that publicity does not become out of date or irrelevant. Special attention needs to be paid to posters that are distributed to other organisations, as posters should not be left up when the need for them has expired.

It will usually be appropriate to issue publicity when a full order is made rather than an **interim order**. However, exceptions can be made, for example, where the anti-social behaviour is severe, where there has been extreme intimidation or where there is a delay between the making of the interim order and the outcome of the final hearing. In the case of Keating v Knowsley Metropolitan Borough Council (2004) the judge held that publicity could be used for interim orders.

In these circumstances it should be stated in the publicity that the order is temporary, that a hearing for a 'full' order will follow, and distribution should be extremely localised.

6. *Consideration of human rights*

Consideration of the human rights of the individual subject to the order and of the human rights of the public including the victim(s) and potential victims should be carried out.

Appropriate and proportionate publicity is compliant with the human rights of the individual subject to the order.

The Stanley v Brent case accepted that publicity was needed for effective enforcement of the order.

Individuals do not welcome publicity and may view the effect of publicity as a punishment. However, a subjective assessment by the individual of the effect of publicity is irrelevant in determining the purpose of the publicity.

Consideration of the human rights implications of publicity should be recorded.

7. *Consideration of data protection*

Publicity is not contrary to the Data Protection Act 1998, as long as authorities are operating in accordance with the Act. There is an exemption in section 29 of the Act to the processing of personal data for the purposes of prevention or detection of crime. This means that personal data can be processed with a view to compliance with a statutory function, where the data has been obtained from a person who possessed it for the purposes of the prevention or detection of crime. This will be the case when considering publicising an ASBO.

8. *Type of publicity*

No one directly involved in the case (witnesses and victims) should wait unnecessarily for information about an order. They should be informed immediately when an order is made. This is in addition to keeping them informed of progress throughout the court process, and can be done by visits, letters, and community meetings or by phone. Victims and witnesses may also be given a copy of the order.

It is recommended that publicity be distributed to targeted households immediately after the order has been granted and by at least a week after the court date. Local people should be informed when variation or discharge of an order relevant to them is made.

The method of publicity can include the following:

- local print and television media;

- local leaflet drop;

- local newsletter.

Practitioners need to apply the proportionality test when deciding which method is appropriate.

Leaflets and other printed materials such as posters or residents' newsletters allow local agencies to target particular neighbourhoods, streets or households with information.

The public can be informed about an ASBO at any time – publicity can be issued and re-issued according to the circumstances. However, publicity needs to be timely to ensure that people are able to enforce the order as soon as it has been granted and to reassure the public that something is being done.

9. Type of information to include in publicity

The type of personal information that might be included in any publicity would be:

- the name of the individual; and/or

- a description of the individual; and/or

- the age of the individual; and/or

- a photograph of the individual; and/or

- the address of the individual;

- a summary of the individual's anti-social behaviour; and/or

- a summary of, or extracts from, the findings of the judge when making the ASBO; and/or

- a summary of, or extracts from, the terms of the ASBO;

- the identification of any relevant exclusion zone (as illustrated on a map);

- details of conditions of non-associations named on the order, particularly where those named are also subject to ASBOs or have a recent history of anti-social behaviour;

- the expiry date of the order;

- the manner in which the public can report breaches (e.g. names, telephone numbers, addresses, possibility of anonymous reporting etc); and/or

- the names of local agencies responsible for obtaining the ASBO;

- local contact numbers such as those for victim support, local police and housing services, with reassurance that reports will be treated in confidence;

- date of publication;

- the identity of the group to be targeted by the publicity: for example, businesses or residents in the vicinity of; and/or

- those are suspected to have been subject to anti-social behaviour by the individual; and/or

- those individuals or businesses within and immediately adjacent to an area identified in the ASBO;

- the geography of where publication will occur: for example within the area of any exclusion zone and the area immediately adjacent to the exclusion zone, within the borough.

Decision-makers need to apply the proportionality test when deciding what information it is necessary to include in order to meet the aims of publicity.

Information must be based on facts and appropriate language used: for example, the order itself does not mean that an individual has been found guilty of a criminal offence. Words such as 'criminal' and 'crime' to describe the individual and their behaviour must be used with care and only when appropriate.

10. Working with the media

The media (including press, TV) are at liberty to report issues that affect the public.

However, their reporting of crimes committed by juveniles is regulated by legislation and there are automatic reporting restrictions in the Youth Court which the media must scrupulously observe. However, the court can remove these restrictions.

There are no automatic reporting restrictions on ASBOs made in any court and the media, especially the local press, have been keen to report ASBOs issued against local people. Significant benefits can arise from having a reputation as a firm but fair organisation, and such a reputation will be enhanced by media reporting of the way in which you use legal action to tackle anti-social behaviour.

An ASBO made against a juvenile (a person under 18) is made in open court and is not usually subject to reporting restrictions. The information is in the public domain and newspapers are entitled to publish details.

It is usual for local statutory agencies to have working relationships with local and regional media, including press, television and radio. This is particularly relevant to issues such as anti-social behaviour and where the media are keen to report how local agencies are tackling these issues through the deployment of dispersal orders, ASBOs, 'crack house' closures etc.

It is important to work with local media, and to make them understand the purpose of any publicity i.e. it is not to punish the individual.

Media coverage has the potential to go to a wider audience than leaflets or posters.

It is good practice to identify newspapers that report on city, borough and neighbourhood issues, free local press and local radio and television and to develop working relationships with them.

This could include being aware of their publication deadlines, giving them exclusives, making sure that the complainant's (victim's) point of view is put across.

However, it is important to keep close control of the material. Witnesses should not be put at risk by disclosing dates of hearings and your relationships with the courts should not be jeopardised. Those subject to an ASBO who are considered vulnerable should also not be put at risk.

Issuing a press release is a way of retaining control of the material.

There should be an agreed process for authorisation of the press releases.

The press release should contain information that meets the identified aim of the publicity. For example, if the aim is to help enforce the order the information in the press release will be more detailed than the information needed for publicity whose aim is to reassure the community that something is being done.

It is good practice to identify a spokesperson to liaise with the press.

APPENDIX 7

HOME OFFICE GUIDANCE ON DRINKING BANNING ORDERS ON APPLICATION FOR LOCAL AUTHORITIES, POLICE FORCES, MAGISTRATES AND COURSE PROVIDERS WITHIN ENGLAND AND WALES

Introduction

This guidance provides a single point of reference on Drinking Banning Orders (DBOs) for the police and local authorities, magistrates and approved course providers. This guidance document provides comprehensive information regarding the seeking, making and enforcement of a DBO, as well as covering matters relating to the recipient's attendance of an approved course.

DBO are to be used to address an individual's alcohol misuse behaviour and protect others and their property from such behaviour. Alcohol misuse, and particularly that associated with anti-social and disorderly behaviour, is a significant concern for many people in our communities. Such alcohol misuse behaviour is a strong contributory factor associated with a wide range of crimes or disorderly behaviour that can include:

- public order offences (often anti-social by nature, these offences can involve rowdy, threatening and abusive behaviour, disorderly groups of people, and urinating in public);

- criminal damage;

- minor and serious assaults;

- violent offences; and

- traffic offences.

DBOs are a new civil order that come into force on 31 August 2009 and are similar in their working to Anti-Social Behaviour Orders (ASBOs). These orders can be given for a duration of between two months and two years. They are available through the provisions of the Violent Crime Reduction Act 2006 (referred to in this guidance as the VCR Act 2006) that received Royal Assent on 8 November 2006. DBOs are intended to tackle alcohol-related criminal or disorderly behaviour. Individuals engaging in criminal or disorderly behaviour which is not alcohol related are not suitable for a DBO, and other sanctions such as ASBOs may be more appropriate.

DBOs can be applied for to the courts by either the police (including British Transport Police) or local authorities in England and Wales (referred to collectively in this guidance as 'relevant authorities') against individuals aged 16 and over who are responsible for alcohol-related crime or disorder.

The DBO is intended to deal with individuals who are involved in criminal and disorderly behaviour that is alcohol related, including alcohol-related anti-social behaviour and nuisance. In particular, they are intended for use in cases where other early intervention approaches have not worked. DBOs could also be relevant in cases of criminal damage to property, committed while under the influence of alcohol.

DBOs must include any prohibitions on entering licensed premises as are necessary for the purpose of protecting other persons from criminal or disorderly conduct that the individual may commit under the influence of alcohol. They may also include any other prohibitions that are necessary for that purpose.

Ultimately, DBOs are designed to protect the community from a specific range of behaviour that is associated with an individual's alcohol misuse.

From the 31 August 2009 the following courts can make a DBO on application:

- magistrates' courts (acting in their civil capacity); and

- county courts (where the principal proceedings involve alcohol misuse crime or disorderly behaviour by those who are party to the proceedings or could be made a party).

The VCR Act 2006 also has provision for the making of DBOs on conviction, where the courts can consider whether to make a DBO when a person is convicted of an offence that is committed while under the influence of alcohol. We are currently only commencing DBOs on application. This will enable the effectiveness of DBOs in tackling the problems of alcohol misuse behaviour to be proved before a wider roll-out for criminal cases on conviction. It will give the courts time to become more familiar with the legislation and for the government to monitor the effects of DBOs on application closely before a decision is made on the commencement of DBOs on conviction.

A separate application to the courts for a DBO will need to be made in all cases where a DBO is sought, even in cases where the individual has been convicted by the court of an offence that is alcohol related.

Approved courses

The VCR Act 2006 and the VCR Act 2006 (Drinking Banning Orders) (Approved Courses) Regulations 2009 make provision for the duration of a DBO to be reduced if an individual satisfactorily completes an approved course to address their alcohol misuse behaviour. This means that a court can propose to an individual that they attend a specified approved course to address their alcohol misuse. The court has to be satisfied that a place is available for the individual on a course, and the subject has voluntarily agreed to attend the course, and have it included in the DBO.

The Home Secretary has approved a number of course providers throughout England and Wales to follow a national model in the provision of approved courses. Details of the providers including the areas that they cover are available on the crime reduction website at www.crimereduction.homeoffice.gov.uk/dbo001.htm.

Other tools for tackling alcohol-related crime and disorder

There is now a wide range of tools and tactics that can be used to tackle the problems of alcohol-related crime and disorder, which enables authorities and courts to take action that targets the particular problem in question. Details of these tools and powers can be found at www.crimereduction.homeoffice.gov.uk/drugsalcohol/drugsalcohol104.htm.

It is important that where it is appropriate to do so these tools are used energetically and constructively to tackle those in our communities who are responsible for alcohol-related crime or disorder.

Updates to this guidance will be available from the crime reduction website as above.

Section 1: Drinking Banning Orders – the basics

What are DBOs, who can apply for them and who can they be made against?

DBOs are civil orders that can be sought by relevant authorities. These are the police (including British Transport Police) or local authorities in England and Wales. They are not criminal penalties and are not intended to punish the subject. DBOs can be made against an individual aged 16 years or over if:

- they have engaged in criminal or disorderly conduct while under the influence of alcohol; and

- the court considers that a DBO is necessary to protect persons and/or their property from further conduct by that person of that kind while under the influence of alcohol.

Local authorities will need to be clear as to who has delegated responsibility to act on behalf of the authority.

If a DBO is imposed, the court must include such prohibitions as it considers necessary for the purpose of protecting persons or their property from the subject's alcohol-related disorderly or criminal conduct, on the subject's entering licensed premises. The court may also impose any other prohibition that it believes is necessary for that purpose.

When a DBO might be appropriate

Alcohol misuse, particularly as a result of binge drinking, is associated with a wide range of crimes or disorderly behaviour. These can include:

- public order offences (often anti-social by nature);

- criminal damage;

- minor and serious assaults;

- violent offences; and

- traffic offences.

Typically, an application for a DBO may be made for drunk or disorderly behaviour, including persistent low-level, anti-social behaviour or nuisance that is alcohol related. In particular, an application may be made in cases where other early intervention approaches have not worked. DBOs could also be relevant (in addition to criminal sanctions) in cases of criminal damage to property committed while under the influence of alcohol, and some more serious alcohol-related crime and disorder or violence.

When a DBO would not be appropriate, including position on vulnerable individuals

DBOs are designed to protect individuals and their property from a specific type of behaviour that occurs as a result of alcohol misuse and is often associated with binge drinking. However, a DBO may not be appropriate if:

- A ban of longer than two years is needed. In such circumstances an ASBO may be considered more appropriate since DBOs can only be imposed for a maximum of two years (and a minimum of two months).

- The behaviour is alcohol related but clearly linked to attending a football match. It may be more appropriate to seek a Football Banning Order rather than a DBO, especially if an order is being sought on conviction.

- The individual is subject to proceedings relating to domestic violence or non-molestation proceedings.

Relevant authorities will need to take these factors into account when consulting each other on the appropriateness of seeking a DBO.

In addition, generally it is unlikely to be appropriate to seek a DBO for those individuals who are vulnerable, particularly if they are suffering from drug or alcohol dependency or mental health problems.[1] The VCR Act 2006 does not permit a DBO to be sought in respect of an individual who is only under the influence of drugs and not alcohol.

If an individual is vulnerable or suffering from alcohol dependency then such problems should be identified by the relevant authority at the statutory consultation stages of seeking a DBO (details are provided below) and during the collection of evidence stage prior to making an application for a DBO. Rather than seek a DBO, support should be provided for such individuals by social services or other support agencies. Local authorities also have a duty under section 47 of the National Health Service and Community Care Act 1990 to assess any person who may be in need of community care services. Rough sleepers should similarly be dealt with through existing arrangements between local authorities, homelessness agencies and the police for dealing with such individuals rather than through a DBO.

Prohibitions

A DBO prohibits the individual subject to the order from doing the things described in the order. The prohibitions must be necessary for protecting others from the individual's criminal or disorderly conduct (or their property from unlawful loss or damage by the defendant – see section 14(2) of the VCR Act 2006) while under the influence of alcohol. It will be for the court to decide what prohibitions are necessary.

The court making the DBO must (see section 1(3) of the VCR Act 2006) include such prohibitions as are necessary for that purpose on the person's entering:

(a)   premises in respect of which there is a premises licence authorising the use of the premises for the sale of alcohol by retail; and

(b)   premises in respect of which there is a club premises certificate authorising the use of the premises for the supply of alcohol to members or guests.

(Note: The expressions used in (a) and (b) referred to above in relation to premises have the same meaning as those in the Licensing Act 2003.)

The court may impose such other prohibitions (see section 1(2) of the VCR Act 2006) as it believes necessary for the purposes of protecting others or their property from the criminal or disorderly conduct of the subject when under the influence of alcohol. This could mean restrictions on individuals from entering particular streets or areas. Prohibitions may be limited to certain times only. For example, under the terms of the prohibitions an individual could be prohibited from entering licensed premises on certain days of the week or at certain times of the day/night. Different prohibitions within a DBO can take effect for different

---

[1]   Dependence is difficult to define, as it is not a single entity, but a constellation of behaviours and internal processes that combine to cause a chronic problem. The World Health Organization (WHO) defines dependence as: 'a cluster of physiological, behavioural, and cognitive phenomena in which the use of a substance or a class of substances takes on a much higher priority for a given individual than other behaviours that once had greater value. A central descriptive characteristic of the dependence syndrome is the desire (often strong, sometimes overpowering) to take psychoactive drugs (which may or may not have been medically prescribed), alcohol, or tobacco. There may be evidence that return to substance use after a period of abstinence leads to a more rapid reappearance of other features of the syndrome than occurs with nondependent individuals.' Alternatively, *Models of care for alcohol misusers* (MoCAM) (Department of Health/National Treatment Agency 2006) differentiates between moderate and severe dependence:
    • *Moderately dependent drinkers* have a level of psychological dependence 'with an increased drive to use alcohol and difficulty controlling its use, despite negative consequences'.
    • *Severely dependent drinkers* have a severe level of psychological dependence and often have physical withdrawal upon cessation. They may have formed the habit of drinking to stop withdrawal symptoms. Their drinking is likely to comprise 'habitual significant daily alcohol use or heavy use over long periods or bouts of drinking'.

periods within the overall period of the DBO. For example, a person can be prohibited from entering a particular area for a shorter period than the period for which they are prohibited from entering a specified set of licensed premises.

Proposing prohibitions

A relevant authority can propose the prohibitions it believes are necessary when making an application, or the court can do so of its own volition. Careful consideration should, however, be given to the formulation of the prohibitions so that they can be easily understood and enforced. The prohibitions should:

• cover the range of criminal or disorderly conduct committed by the defendant while under the influence of alcohol;

• be necessary for protecting other persons from the defendant's criminal or disorderly conduct (or property from unlawful loss or damage by the defendant) while they are under the influence of alcohol;

• be reasonable and proportionate;

• be realistic and practical;

• be clear, concise and easy to understand;

• be specific when referring to a named set of premises with a premises licence or club premises certificate in a given street (or streets) or within a defined geographic area;

• be specific when referring to matters of time if, for example, prohibiting the subject from being in a set of licensed premises at certain times;

• be specific when referring to exclusion from a geographic area, including street names and clear boundaries (a map with identifiable street names could be provided);

• be specific in the terms of the prohibitions in order for it to be easy to establish whether a breach had taken place; and

• seek to protect all people and property that need protection.

The prohibitions, however, must **not** (see section 1(4) of the VCR Act 2006) prevent the individual from:

• having access to their home;

• having access to their place of work;

• having access to a place where they need to attend to receive education, training or medical treatment; and

• having access to a place that they have been ordered to attend, by an enactment or by the order of a court or tribunal.

Prohibitions should be proportionate

Where appropriate, the relevant authorities should also ensure that prohibitions are not sought that could prevent an individual from being able to attend their normal place of worship, or for example taking wine as part of a religious service, or in rare cases prevent them from the need to fulfil any special dietary or medical requirements. Prohibitions should not be included that would prevent an individual from taking a child to a place where they may receive medical treatment or preventing a person from taking their child to school.

It should be noted that a prohibition on entering all licensed premises within a specific area would result in the individual being banned from entering all premises that hold a premises licence. This will include supermarkets, convenience stores, cinemas and other outlets that have a licence to sell alcohol. The relevant authority applying for the DBO may wish to consider instead banning the individual from named licensed premises, banning them from specific streets or, should the circumstances warrant it, banning them from purchasing alcohol within a specific area.

Prohibitions should not be sought to ban individuals completely from entering supermarkets that sell alcohol (or other food outlets that sell alcohol), or garages that have a licence to sell alcohol, unless this proves to be absolutely necessary given the circumstances of a particular case. Factors to take into account if proposing such a ban would be whether such premises would be the only convenient and easily accessible food or fuel outlets within a locality to which the individual would have access to buy food or fuel.

Prohibitions could include, where necessary and proportionate:

- exclusion from an individual set of licensed premises or a number of licensed premises;

- exclusion from consuming alcohol in public places. What 'public places' means will need to be carefully explained in the DBO. For example, it could be any place to which the public has access (whether as of right or by express or implied permission). It could also include places to which the person gains unlawful access;

- exclusion from all licensed premises in a geographically defined area such as a street or town centre, or for the whole of England and Wales; and

- exclusion from purchasing alcohol in a particular set of licensed premises or a number of licensed premises or any licensed premises in England and Wales.

When considering what prohibitions might be appropriate, relevant authorities will need to take into account the issue of possible displacement of alcohol-related problems from one area to another. If a small geographical area is considered as part of a DBO prohibition, the relevant authority will need to consider the possible effect on the surrounding areas. In some cases, it might be both necessary and proportionate to include a larger geographical area in order to take account of the risks of displacing the problem.

Where a DBO is valid

The prohibitions that a DBO could impose can apply to the subject within England and Wales if it is considered to be reasonable and proportionate. Clearly, the wider the area over which the prohibition extends, the greater the justification required. DBOs are not applicable to Scotland or Northern Ireland. However, where necessary the appropriate authorities each side of the border should work closely together to ensure that information is shared and that displacement is anticipated and dealt with as necessary.

A DBO is designed to protect any member of the public. Relevant authorities could therefore apply for a DBO if they are satisfied that a DBO is necessary to protect a person who is from a different geographical area. However, in the majority of cases it is expected that the persons who are to be protected by the DBO will reside in the same area as the subject of the order.

Duration of a DBO

The minimum period for which a DBO can apply is two months and the maximum is two years (see section 2(1) of the VCR Act 2006). The length of a DBO cannot be varied to extend it beyond its maximum two-year duration. The duration of the DBO should, however, take into account the severity of the individual's behaviour while under the influence of alcohol and the need to protect other people and their property from that behaviour, and the recipient's response to any previous measures to deal with the behaviour. A longer DBO will generally be appropriate in the case of more serious or persistent alcohol misuse behaviour. The length of a DBO will, however, ultimately be a matter for the courts.

As outlined above, different prohibitions within a DBO can take effect for different periods within the overall period of the DBO, subject to the requirement that each prohibition is no less than two months and no more than two years (see section 2(2) of the VCR Act 2006).

When deciding on the length of a DBO, consideration should be given as to whether an approved course would be beneficial to the recipient. Those who receive a short DBO are likely to be unable to attend an approved course because of the time it takes to register and attend sessions over a number of weeks.

Referral to an approved course

Approved courses are established under the provisions of sections 12 and 13 of the VCR Act 2006 and the VCR Act 2006 (Drinking Banning Orders) (Approved Courses) Regulations 2009.

Recipients of a DBO can be referred by the court to an approved course provider if the recipient consents (see section 2(6)(b) of the VCR Act 2006). Successful completion of an approved course can reduce the length of a DBO by up to half. Approved courses are undertaken on a voluntary basis as a means to address alcohol misuse behaviour. These courses focus on educating individuals about the serious social and health impacts of heavy alcohol consumption.

Information on course providers in a specific area will be supplied to the courts by the providers themselves; however, it is also available on the crime reduction website at www.crimereduction.homeoffice.gov.uk/dbo001.htm.

Relevant authorities that have applied for and been granted a DBO against an individual should seek to remind the court that they may refer the individual to an approved course. They should further remind the court of the requirement under section 2(8) of the VCR Act 2006 to give its reasons in open court for not referring an individual to an approved course.

A court making an order has to ensure that:

- it is appropriate for a recipient to attend an approved course, ie it may be not be appropriate if they have previously been allocated a place on a course and completed it/failed to attend, if it is perceived that they will not benefit from attendance on such a course;

- it has been explained to the recipient the effect of the order in ordinary language, what in general terms attendance on the course will involve, the fees for the course and that payment must be made in advance;

- a place is available on an approved course;

- if the recipient is under 18 years old, their age has been taken into consideration;

- consideration is given as to the proposed location of the course to be attended, ie how close to home, a place of work etc; and

- the recipient has agreed to the inclusion of the completion of the course in the order.

Courts are required to specify in the order the course to which a recipient has been referred. The exact period of reduction should the course be satisfactorily completed must also be specified in the order.

It is then the responsibility of the court to notify the provider that a recipient has been referred. Specific instructions on this process will be given on the HMCS intranet. However, before a DBO referral form is available on the LIBRA system, courts will have to send a copy of the order to the provider in their area. A list of providers can be found at www.crimereduction.homeoffice.gov.uk/dbo001.htm.

It is then for the provider to approach the recipient with an offer of a course – specifying the dates, times and location of attendance.

The details of those recipients referred to an approved course should be recorded in the court register. If a court decides not to refer a recipient to an approved course, the reasons for this decision must be given in court.

When notifying the relevant course provider of the referral of a recipient the courts should specify if the person concerned has any special needs, for example any accessibility problem or difficulty in understanding English.

The scheme is voluntary. There is no additional penalty if an offender does not agree to attend a course or consents to the inclusion of the course in the DBO but then fails to attend a course.

When DBOs take effect

A DBO on application to the magistrates' court would come into effect once the case had been heard in court and the court had approved the application, so that the individual is fully aware of its terms. A DBO granted in the county court must be served personally on the recipient of a DBO and would not come into effect until it is served and the individual is therefore fully aware of its terms. The relevant authority that has made the application for the DBO is responsible for ensuring that the DBO is served on the individual. In respect of interim DBOs, these will come into effect once the individual is made aware of its terms. (It is important therefore that applicants come to court able to print off an amended version of their draft order.) The Magistrates' Court Rules will provide further details on serving orders. We expect that these rules will come into force during Autumn 2009.

Variation and discharge

The VCR Act 2006 provides for the variation and discharge of DBOs made in the magistrates' court on complaint and in county court proceedings (see section 5 of the VCR Act 2006). An application to the court for variation or discharge can be made by the person subject to the DBO or the relevant authority on whose application the DBO was made.

Interim DBOs

The court can make an interim DBO (see section 9 of the VCR Act 2006) if they think it is just so to do, ie it is necessary to take immediate action to address the problem. Applications for interim DBOs will be appropriate where the relevant authorities believe that other persons or property are in need of urgent protection from further criminal or disorderly conduct by the subject while they are under the influence of alcohol before the main application for a full DBO can be determined.

Interim DBOs can be made at the outset of an application for a full DBO. The relevant authority should therefore request an interim DBO at the same time as making an application for a full DBO in the magistrates' court or the county court. An interim DBO can be made at an initial court hearing that is held in advance of the full hearing.

When considering whether to make an interim DBO the court will be aware that it may not be possible at the time of the interim DBO application to compile all the evidence that would prove that a full DBO is necessary. Rather, the court will determine the application for an interim DBO on the question of whether the application for the full DBO has been properly made and whether there is sufficient evidence of an urgent need to protect other persons or property from criminal or disorderly conduct by the subject while they are under the influence of alcohol.

An interim DBO can be applied for without notice of proceedings being given to the defendant (ex parte), and can be heard in the absence of the individual. Such an application can only be made with the permission of the court. In an application to the county court this means the court itself, and in the case of proceedings before a magistrates' court it means the permission of the proper officer (justices' clerk). Permission for an ex parte application for an interim DBO may only be given where the court or proper officer (justices' clerk) is satisfied that it is necessary – because of the urgent need for protection – for the application to be made without the individual concerned receiving notice, and without their presence.

Where an interim DBO is granted ex parte it is expected that that the court will usually arrange for an early return date for consideration of the interim DBO and full DBO. The recipient would have the opportunity to respond to the case at the hearing for the full DBO. The recipient is also able to apply to the court for the interim DBO to be varied or discharged. In this instance the matter will be dealt with at a hearing that deals specifically with the interim matter.

The interim DBO:

• will be for a specified time period not exceeding four weeks;

• may be renewed once or more but for a period not longer than four weeks from the time it would otherwise have expired. While it is technically possible for an interim DBO to continue to be renewed this is not the best use of the courts', or relevant authorities', time. This should therefore be avoided;

• will contain any prohibitions that could be in a full DBO;

• can be varied or discharged on application by the subject to the magistrates' court and in county court proceedings;

• will cease to have effect once the court has decided whether or not to make a full DBO; and

• will have the same breach penalties as for a full DBO.

If an interim DBO is made at a hearing of an application without notice, it will not take effect until it is served personally on the subject. The relevant authority that applied for the DBO will be responsible for serving the interim order on the recipient of the DBO.

Appeals

Appeals against a DBO being made on application (see section 10 of the VCR Act 2006) can be made through the following routes.

Appeal from an order made in the magistrates' court sitting in its civil capacity is to the Crown Court by virtue of section 10(1) of the VCR Act 2006. By virtue of section 79(3) of the Supreme Court Act 1981, appeal is by way of re-hearing.

The procedure for appeals against an order made in the county court must be made in accordance with Part 52 of the Civil Procedure Rules and the Supplementary Practice Direction. It therefore does not feature in the VCR Act 2006.

Breach of a DBO

Breach of a DBO (see section 11 of the VCR Act 2006) without reasonable excuse is an offence. A person found guilty of such an offence on summary conviction could be liable to a fine not exceeding level 4 on the standard scale. The Crown Prosecution Service (CPS) will be responsible for prosecuting any breach of a DBO. The police and local authorities will need to liaise with their local CPS contact to discuss what information the CPS will require for the prosecution file. As a minimum this should include:

• a copy of the DBO granted by the court;

• a summary of the evidence submitted to the court in the original DBO application;

• details/evidence of the alleged breach of the DBO eg witness statements, evidence from police officers, CCTV footage etc;

• the defendant's explanation (if any) for the alleged breach, whether this be in a formal interview, or in Q & A recorded in the officer's notebook contemporaneously and offered for signature; and

- details of any previous breaches.

Informing licensed premises

Relevant authorities should, where it is practical to do so, ensure that the licensed premises which an individual who is a recipient of a DBO is prohibited from entering or buying alcohol are made aware of those individuals and the specific nature and duration of the prohibitions that apply to their DBOs. Those licensed premises should, as soon as is practically possible, also be informed about when a DBO is due to end or when the terms of a DBO have been varied or the DBO discharged. This should help to enforce the prohibitions in DBOs. Licensed staff should be encouraged to inform the police if an individual is seen breaching a DBO, for example if they enter a premises that they were excluded from under the terms of their DBO.

Young people

DBOs apply to those aged 16 or over. When applying for a DBO against a young person aged 16 or 17 an assessment should be made of their circumstances and needs. This will enable the local authority to ensure that the appropriate services are provided for the young person concerned, and for the court to have the necessary information about them. It is vital, however, that any assessment made does not cause delay to the application for a DBO. The lead agency must therefore liaise closely with the local social services department and Youth Offending Team (YOT) from the start of the process, so that where a new assessment is required it can be done quickly.

Those under 16 years of age who have come to the attention of the relevant authorities for alcohol misuse may best be diverted to an intervention programme, for example run by a YOT.

Section 2: Drinking Banning Orders – seeking an order

Most effective route to seek a DBO

Relevant authorities need to consider and identify the most effective route that should be adopted to seek a DBO. If an individual has engaged in criminal or disorderly conduct while under the influence of alcohol and it is necessary to protect other persons (or property) from further acts by the perpetrator then a DBO could be sought. Relevant authorities should work in partnership and if necessary liaise with other agencies to add value to a DBO application. The main routes for seeking a DBO are on application to the magistrates' court (acting in its civil capacity), and in county court proceedings.

A DBO remains a civil order irrespective of the issuing court.

Applications to the magistrates' court (acting in its civil capacity)

An application for a DBO can be made (see section 3 of the VCR Act 2006) where an individual has engaged in some criminal or disorderly conduct while under the influence of alcohol within six months of the time when the matter of the complaint (the behaviour) arose. One incident may be sufficient for a DBO to be made. So, at least one incident of such behaviour must have occurred in the six months previous to the application to the court. If in addition there is relevant conduct outside the six-month period this can be relevant to support an application – to show, for example, that there is a pattern of behaviour that the DBO is intended to address. It will be for the court to then determine the weight to be given to that evidence in deciding whether the behaviour in question took place and whether it is necessary to make the DBO.

An application for a DBO can be made by a relevant authority to the magistrates' court acting in its civil capacity. An application for a DBO should, where it is practicable to do so, be made to the magistrates' court whose area includes the local authority area or police area where persons need to be protected from the individual's alcohol misuse behaviour. Under section 98 of the Magistrates' Courts Act 1980, evidence will be given on oath.

The lead police or local authority officer in charge of the case should ensure that all the evidence and witnesses are available at the hearing, including any evidence in support of the need for the court to make an immediate DBO. It is important to note that section 3(2)(a) of the VCR Act 2006 states that the criminal or disorderly conduct **must be committed after the commencement of section 3 of the Act**. Therefore DBOs will not be able to be applied for on the basis of criminal or disorderly conduct that took place before 31 August 2009.

Various provisions for adjournment, non-attendance at court and the issue of a warrant for arrest are contained in sections 54 to 57 of the Magistrates' Courts Act 1980.

The magistrates' court could, subject to some provisos about service, consider the complaint in the absence of the defendant (see section 55 of the Magistrates' Courts Act 1980) and make a full DBO in their absence. However, in practice this should only be done in exceptional cases. The court may consider an adjournment and use the powers to issue warrants to secure court attendance, but this will be a matter for the court to decide.

Where a number of individuals have engaged in alcohol misuse behaviour a case needs to be made against each individual on whom a DBO is sought, although cases can be heard together by the court.

The provisions governing applications for DBOs in the magistrates' court (in its civil capacity) will be set out in Magistrates' Court Rules. They have not yet been made, but we expect them to be available in Autumn 2009.

A diagram showing the passage of a DBO on application through the magistrates' court is shown in Annex A.

Consultation requirements

Before making an application to the magistrates' court (in its civil capacity) the relevant authority must (see section 3(4) of the VCR Act 2006) consult with the relevant 'appropriate persons' for their application. For this purpose 'appropriate persons' are such of the following who are not party to the proceedings:

(a)   the chief officer of police for the police area in which the conduct in question took place;

(b)   the chief officer of police for the police area in which the subject usually resides;

(c)   every local authority in whose area the subject usually resides; and

(d)   the Chief Constable of the British Transport Police.

A district or county council and police division/basic command unit may each wish to establish a nominated contact for these orders. Local authorities need to ensure that they are clear as to whom they have delegated responsibilities to act as an appropriate person and who will act on behalf of the relevant authority. This will avoid potential confusions when making and consulting on DBO applications.

Consultation is required to inform the appropriate agency or agencies of the intended application for the DBO and to check whether they have any relevant information. It may also assist in the evidence-gathering process. Any reservations about an application should be resolved quickly. There is no requirement for the agencies to agree to an application being made, but they must be told of the intended application and given the opportunity to comment. No agency has a veto over another agency's application. Consultation ensures at a very minimum that actions taken by each agency regarding the same individual do not unknowingly conflict. It also ensures that full consideration is given as to whether a DBO is appropriate in situations where the individual may be vulnerable, may be suffering from drug or alcohol dependency or mental health problems or is a rough sleeper. In these cases individuals might not be in a position to be able to understand or keep to the conditions that might be imposed under a DBO. Relevant authorities would therefore need to consider whether alternative community care services may be more appropriate in these circumstances.

As a matter of good practice a letter/document showing proof of consultation is all that is required by the court. This should not indicate whether the party consulted was or was not in agreement. This is not required by the legislation. Supporting statements or reports from partner agencies should be provided separately.

Pooling resources

Where a number of applications are being made for DBOs then relevant authorities may want to consider obtaining specialist legal advice in blocks or pooling expertise and experience. This is likely to be more cost-effective than paying for legal advice on a case-by-case basis. However, cases should not be stockpiled as this could lead to delays in seeking DBOs.

Collection of evidence

When applying for a DBO the lead agency will be required to gather evidence to prove its case. Evidence put forward by the applicant can include hearsay evidence. The evidence in support of a DBO application should prove:

(a)   that the individual has engaged in criminal or disorderly conduct while under the influence of alcohol; and

(b)   that a DBO is necessary to protect other persons (or property) from further conduct by the individual of that kind while they are under the influence of alcohol.

The court will need to be satisfied that (a) the behaviour complained of has occurred and will then determine (b) whether a DBO is necessary for protecting other persons (or property) from criminal or disorderly conduct by the subject while they are under the influence of alcohol. Limb (b) of the test is not one to which a standard of proof will be applied. Instead, it is an assessment of future risk. The applicant can present evidence or argument to assist the court in making this evaluation.

Elaborate court files are not normally required or advantageous. If the criminal or disorderly conduct while under the influence of alcohol has been persistent, relevant authorities should focus on a few well-documented incidents. A large volume of evidence and/or a large number of witnesses creates its own problems as there is more material for the defence to contest and timetabling issues may increase delays in the process. Relevant authorities applying for DBOs should therefore strike a balance and focus on what is most relevant and necessary to provide sufficient evidence for the court to arrive at a clear understanding of the matter.

Examples of evidence may include:

•   copies of custody records of previous arrests relevant to the application;

•   previous relevant convictions;

•   supporting statements or reports from other agencies;

•   witness statements of officers who attended incidents;

•   witness statements of people affected by the behaviour;

•   statements from professional witnesses, for example council officers, health workers in A&E departments;

•   video or CCTV evidence;

•   warning letters;

•   breach of acceptable behaviour contract or other non-statutory agreement;

- directions to leave (under section 27(1) of the VCR Act 2006); and

- Fixed Penalty Notices (FPNs)/Penalty Notices for Disorder (PNDs).

Interim DBOs made in the magistrates' court

An application for an ex parte interim DBO can only be made with the permission of the justices' clerk. If permission is given, a hearing may go ahead without notice being given to the individual. If the interim DBO is granted without notice to the individual, it should be served personally on the individual together with the application for the full DBO and a summons giving a date for the individual to attend court. Such an interim DBO will not have effect until it is served on the individual.

The forms to be used when applying for or making an interim DBO are provided at Annex C of this guidance.

Varying or discharging DBOs made on application

In certain circumstances an application can be made (see section 5 of the VCR Act 2006) to the court to vary or discharge a DBO which was made on application to the magistrates' court that made the order, or to any magistrates' court acting for the local justice area in which the subject normally resides. The application can be made by the person subject to the DBO or by the police or local authority on whose application the DBO was made. An application to vary or discharge the DBO has to be made by complaint. The DBO, however, may not be varied so as to extend the period for which it has effect to more than two years. An order also should not be discharged before the end of the period which is half the duration of its length, unless consent is given by the relevant authority on whose application the DBO was made. Therefore, for example, a two-month DBO could not normally be discharged until a month had elapsed.

Summons procedure

The lead police or local authority officer in charge of the case should arrange for a summons to be completed, with a copy retained on the application files, and for the defendant to be served with the following:

- the summons;

- a copy of the completed DBO application;

- documentary evidence of statutory consultation;

- guidance on how the defendant may obtain legal advice and representation;

- any notice of hearsay evidence;

- details of evidence in support of the application as agreed with the applicant agency's solicitor; and

- a warning to the defendant that it is an offence to pervert the course of justice, and that witness intimidation is liable to lead to prosecution.

Wherever possible the lead officer in charge will ensure that service of the summons is made on the defendant in person. If personal service is not possible, the summons should be served by post as soon as possible to the last known address.

Where a person under 18 is the subject of an application for a DBO, a person with parental responsibility must also be served with a copy of the summons. This could be a local authority social worker rather than the parent in the case of a young person who is cared for by that authority. ('Parent' has the same meaning as under section 1 of the Family Law Reform Act 1987 and 'guardian' is defined in section 107 of the Children and Young Persons Act 1933.)

The process for county court is set out in the Practice Direction of the Civil Procedure Rules published on www.opsi.gov.uk.

DBOs in county court proceedings

A relevant authority can apply to the county courts for a DBO against an individual if they and that individual are already party to proceedings (see section 4 of the VCR Act 2006). Alternatively, they can apply to be joined to proceedings in which the individual is a party if they consider it would then be reasonable to make a DBO application in respect of that individual. A further alternative, where the relevant authority is already party to proceedings in relation to which a person's conduct is material, is for the relevant authority to make an application for that person to be joined to the proceedings and to proceed to apply for a DBO when that individual is so joined. Stand-alone applications for DBOs cannot be sought through the county court – they must be attached to existing proceedings. The detailed procedures for DBOs in the county court proceedings are available in the updated Civil Procedure Rules. The forms for an authority to use when making an application to join proceedings can be found at www.justice.gov.uk/civil/procrules_fin/menus/forms.htm. These applications will require the form N244.

An example of where an application to join proceedings might be sought is where a local authority uses section 222 of the Local Government Act 1972 to bring injunction proceedings. This could be appropriate where a person has caused a public nuisance and there is a need to put a stop to such alcohol misuse behaviour. The local authority could make an application for a DBO against that individual if it is reasonable to do so, or the police could apply to be joined to those proceedings for the purposes of seeking a DBO, if it is reasonable to do so. Where local authorities issue possession proceedings in the county court to evict a family on grounds of anti-social behaviour, they can also attach an ASBO application against family members. This is another example of where an application for a DBO could be made if appropriate.

As explained earlier in this guidance, it is rarely going to be appropriate to seek a DBO in family proceedings and non-molestation cases. Domestic violence cases, for example, should be addressed through existing domestic-violence tailored measures such as restraining orders and non-molestation orders which should be tried first and enforced if breached. DBOs might then only be appropriate if, having tried these interventions, there is no other option to provide protection.

Consultation requirements

Before making an application to the county court for a DBO against an individual when the relevant authority is party to the proceedings, applying to be joined to proceedings, or making an application to join an individual to proceedings, the relevant authority must (see section 4(6) of the VCR Act 2006) consult with the relevant 'appropriate persons' for their application. For this purpose 'appropriate persons' are such of the following who are not party to the proceedings:

(a)   the chief officer of police for the police area in which the conduct in question took place;

(b)   the chief officer of police for the police area in which the subject usually resides;

(c)   every local authority in whose area the subject usually resides; and

(d)   the Chief Constable of the British Transport Police.

A district or county council and police division/basic command unit may wish to establish a nominated contact to undertake this process.

As for DBOs made on application to the magistrates' court referred to earlier in this guidance, consultation is required to inform the appropriate agency or agencies of the intended application for the DBO and to check whether they have any relevant information.

Interim DBOs made in the county court

A person who can apply for a DBO under section 4 of the VCA 2006 can also apply to the county court for an interim DBO in the county court once it is party to the proceedings (see section 5 of the VCR Act 2006). Any application for an interim DBO should be made early in the proceedings. The procedure for making applications for interim DBOs in the county court will be set out in the Civil Procedure Rules.

Varying or discharging DBOs made in the county court

An application can be made to vary or discharge a DBO to the county court that made the order. This can be made by the person subject to the DBO or by the relevant authority on whose application the DBO was made. The DBO, however, may not be varied so as to extend the period for which it has effect to more than two years. An order also should not be discharged before the end of the period which is half the duration of its length, unless consent is given by the relevant authority on whose application the DBO was made.

DBOs for 16 and 17-year-old persons

The role of the YOT needs to be clearly set out in terms of what it can offer in the prevention of alcohol misuse behaviour, and in the DBO process. Other agencies should therefore involve the YOT in any consideration of an order at an early stage as it is likely to have much information to share about that young person.

The YOT has a responsibility to prevent alcohol-related crime and anti-social behaviour by young people, and should help partners to obtain a DBO to stop the behaviour continuing where it is deemed appropriate. If there are any doubts about the option of obtaining a DBO, these should be explored at an early stage with the YOT and other partners, rather than in court. The YOT can also have a role in explaining the prohibitions of an order to the young person and their parents, explaining the impact of that person's behaviour on the community and making it clear that the order is the consequence of that behaviour. In addition, the YOT and other partners should offer support in order to aid compliance.

In cases of a breach of an order, the pre-sentence report (PSR) provided to the court by the YOT should outline the impact of the alcohol misuse behaviour. The PSR should also address the issue of parenting and further support to the young person.

Section 3: Other relevant information

Standard of proof

DBOs are civil orders, but the standard of proof that is applied to whether the past criminal or disorderly conduct alleged against the individual has occurred is ultimately a matter for the courts.

The inquiry as to whether the order is necessary to protect other persons does not itself involve a standard of proof but is an exercise of judgement of evaluation.

Although the imposition of a DBO is not a criminal penalty, a breach of a DBO without reasonable excuse is a criminal offence and therefore, in proceedings relating to the breach of a DBO, courts will apply the criminal standard of proof.

Disclosure

Before evidence is disclosed, the relevant authority making the application for the DBO should consult the local authority or police or other agencies to ensure that all reasonable steps have been taken to support witnesses and minimise any potential for witness intimidation.

The applicant should seek to maintain witness anonymity and ensure that it does not identify them by default (for example, through details of location, race, personal characteristics or age).

Use of hearsay and professional witness evidence

Hearsay and professional witness evidence allows for the identities of those too fearful to give evidence to be protected. Hearsay evidence cannot be excluded (at the request of defence lawyers) simply on the grounds that it is hearsay. It is a matter for the judge or magistrate to decide what weight they attach to hearsay evidence.

Hearsay allows the police officer (or other persons in receipt of second-hand information) to provide a statement on behalf of a witness or witnesses who may remain anonymous. Hearsay evidence must be relevant to the matters to be proved. It could include details such as dates, places, times, specific descriptions of actions, who was present and who said what.

Hearsay can include evidence from the person taking the statement. The person giving the hearsay evidence may attest to the observable conditions of the witness, for example that the witness appeared upset, and may give evidence based on their own judgement of the situation.

Where an applicant intends to rely on hearsay evidence in the county court, they must act in accordance with Part 33 of the Civil Procedure Rules.

Witness support

The principal purpose of the DBO is to protect other persons or their property from an individual's disorderly, or criminal, conduct while under the influence of alcohol. The protection provided should where necessary aim to protect those who are personally targeted by perpetrators, other witnesses who see this happen and the wider local community. Engaging, developing and supporting those persons whom it is sought to protect must be a primary concern of any relevant authority managing a case and seeking to use DBOs. Local strategies should indeed have the interests of the witnesses and the community at their centre. The welfare and safety of those who complain must be the first consideration.

Devolution

DBOs can be applied for by relevant authorities throughout England and Wales. The scheme does not apply to Scotland or Northern Ireland.

The scheme will be operated by the Home Office, with close liaison with the Welsh Assembly Government with regard to matters involving provision in Wales.

The Licensed Premises (Exclusion of Certain Persons) Act 1980

Section 65 and Schedule 5 of the VCR Act 2006 state that the Licensed Premises (Exclusion of Certain Persons) Act 1980 will be repealed when DBOs are commenced. We have not commenced this provision in the Act so the Licensed Premises (Exclusion of Certain Persons) Act 1980 remains in force and is a tool which can be used to exclude certain persons from licensed premises.

Contact details within the Home Office

Home Office contacts:

Joanne French
Tel: 020 7035 0066
Email: Joanne.French@homeoffice.gsi.gov.uk

Emma Lawrence
Tel: 020 7035 4671
Email: Emma.Lawrence8@homeoffice.gsi.gov.uk

Section 4: Drinking Banning Orders – after the order is made

Enforcement including the Police National Computer (PNC)

Recording of DBOs on the PNC will help police forces to enforce DBOs where a PNC enquiry is conducted on the subject. The force that made the successful DBO application should update the Wanted Missing section of the PNC names application using the orders category and the Drinking Banning Order qualifier. This facility allows the recording of any conditions imposed. PNC enquiries on subjects of DBOs will inform police officers of the existence of the order so that they can take appropriate action regarding breaches.

It would also be helpful to inform the neighbourhood policing team of any DBOs in their area as they may be better placed to observe if a recipient had breached their DBO. The neighbourhood policing team will also be able to reassure residents that action has been taken, and to inform licensed premises where individuals have been banned from entering them.

Licensed premises and the role of the alcohol industry

As previously explained in this guidance, relevant authorities should, as soon as is practically possible, ensure that the licensed premises from which an individual who is subject to a DBO is prohibited from entering are made aware of those individuals and the specific nature and duration of the prohibitions that apply to their DBOs. This is particularly important where the licensed premises have been specifically named in the order or where the geographical area of the ban is relatively small. That information could be shared through local Pubwatch schemes or other appropriate networks, but it would also be helpful for the relevant authority to inform the premises via a letter or through visits from licensing officers.

An individual who is subject to a DBO may already have a common law ban imposed by a Pubwatch scheme. A decision will have been taken under the Pubwatch scheme to ban the individual based on their own criteria. The ban may be as a result of a specific act unconnected with the behaviour that instigated the DBO and will be limited to the premises forming the watch scheme. However, even if the Pubwatch scheme has taken a decision to ban the individual based in whole or in part on the incident(s) that forms the basis of the DBO application, they will be entitled to take that independent action to protect staff and customers. This independence of decision making does not prevent individual Pubwatch members from supporting a DBO application by making statements etc as they would in any other criminal investigation.

Licensees should be encouraged to play their part in upholding DBOs as it is in their interest to do so. They should be made aware of their responsibilities and informed that if they are aware that an individual is the subject of a DBO that prevents the individual from entering their premises, then they should not allow them to enter, or if they have already entered, they should not serve that individual and should contact the police.

Monitoring and recording

Relevant authorities should agree common procedures for recording and monitoring both their successful and unsuccessful applications. Details of orders granted should be sent to the local Crime and Disorder Reduction Partnership and the local authority or police as appropriate as well as other agencies that may be involved with the subject (including the local YOT where the subject is an offender under 18 years old).

Promoting awareness of those individuals who have received a DBO

The effectiveness of a DBO will normally depend on its publicity. It is therefore essential that the public, support agencies and licensed premises know about the people who are subject to a DBO and know about the nature of the prohibitions. However, a case-by-case approach should be adopted by the relevant authority and each individual case should be judged on its merits as to whether or not the relevant authority wants to publicise the details of an individual who is subject to a DBO – but in most cases publicity should be expected. An individual who is subject to a DBO should also understand that the community is likely to learn about it. Publicity is not, however, intended to punish, shame or embarrass individuals. It is important to note that like ASBOs, a DBO is a civil order which restrains future alcohol misuse.

A court will not automatically impose restrictions on reporting cases concerning individuals who are subject to a DBO. Therefore the media can report on cases to inform local communities of action that is being taken against individuals to protect others from crime or disorder that is associated with alcohol misuse. The courts, however, retain the discretion to apply reporting restrictions if it considers it appropriate to do so.

Relevant authorities should ensure that Crime and Disorder Reduction Partnerships' media strategies take account of the need to publicise those who are subject to DBOs and promote the use of the orders to tackle alcohol misuse. This should help to increase community confidence that problems of alcohol misuse are being addressed as well as deter potential offenders from alcohol misuse behaviour.

Benefits of publicity

Publicising DBOs has the following benefits:

- Deterrent – deters the recipient of the order from breaching the order and deters others from behaviour that can result in a DBO.

- Breach – local people have the information needed to identify and report breaches.

- Confidence – victims and people within the community can see that action is being taken against those who commit alcohol-related crime and disorder.

Any decision to publicise details of recipients of DBOs should be recorded and an individual identified as being in charge of the process. The information recorded should include details on the need for publicity, consideration of the human rights of the public and the recipient of the DBO, and details on what the publicity should look like.

The content of the publicity should be carefully considered. Information should only be disclosed if deemed essential and should be factual and accurate. Publicity should be consistent with the characteristics of a DBO, ie that it is a civil order.

Particular consideration should be given when the recipient of a DBO is under 18, although this does not mean that their behaviour is any less distressing or frightening than that of an adult. Factual information should be obtained about whether an individual is particularly vulnerable. This should be done as early as possible, to avoid delays in informing the public once an order has been obtained. An order made against a child or young person in open court is in the public domain and newspapers are entitled to publish details. However, if reporting restrictions have been imposed, they must be scrupulously adhered to. In applications involving children or people where evidence has consisted of details of their past convictions, and reporting restrictions were not lifted for the proceedings leading to those convictions, the publicity should not make reference to those convictions.

If reporting restrictions were imposed at the original DBO hearing, then unless there has been a significant change in the intervening period, it is likely that the court will impose reporting restrictions at the hearing for the breach. If no reporting restrictions were imposed at the original DBO hearing, it is still open to the court to impose reporting restrictions at the hearing of the breach case. If reporting restrictions are not imposed, publicity can be considered, taking into account all the matters that are relevant when considering publicising the DBO itself.

Publicity of orders

The purpose of a DBO is to protect persons from further criminal or disorderly conduct by the individual. In order to ensure that DBOs are effective, the local community, in particular the staff of licensed premises to which the DBO relates, needs to be aware of the subject of the DBO and its conditions. However, DBOs are not intended to 'name and shame' and any decision to publish should be made on an individual basis, and only to the extent necessary in that case. However, once the decision has been made, the distribution of publicity through leaflet drops, newsletters or print and television media should be made as soon as the order has been made. This should be in the area where the disorder has occurred. If an order has been imposed to include a wider area, consideration should be given to how this information can be disseminated to members of the public. Publicity can be issued and re-issued if needed at any time.

Photographs

A recent photograph of the subject of a DBO will usually be required to assist in their identification in the situation of a breach. This is particularly helpful for older people or housebound witnesses who may not know the names of those who have caused trouble in their area. There is no restriction on the police sharing photographs of DBO recipients, as long as they are shared to assist in the enforcement of the order.

Police forces may already have a well-established system in place for the sharing of photographs with Pubwatch members where the watch scheme has decided to ban an individual using their own common law powers. The decision to share photographs in these circumstances will have been taken in order to reduce the likelihood of crime and disorder. Such an established system may provide an appropriate cost-effective means of sharing photographs of persons who are recipients of DBOs. When providing photographs, the police should take care to ensure that there is no confusion as to whether the person is the subject of a Pubwatch ban or a DBO.

Information sharing

Section 115 of the Crime and Disorder Act 1998 empowers any person to disclose information, where necessary or expedient for the purposes of the Act, to the following persons: a chief officer of police, a police force, a local authority, a probation area or a health authority, or to a person acting on their behalf. Where the agency requesting the information clearly needs it for the purposes of reducing criminal or disorderly conduct of those under the influence of alcohol, the presumption should be that it will be supplied.

In addition, as well as the power to share information under section 17A of the Crime and Disorder Act 1998 and regulations made under that section, there is now a **duty** for those persons listed in the above paragraph to share de-personalised data that are relevant for community safety purposes.

Section 5: Course providers

Applications for approval

The Secretary of State, on the recommendation of a steering group, has approved a number of course providers throughout England and Wales to provide DBO-approved courses under a national model. Details of the providers, including the areas that they cover, are available on the crime reduction website at www.crimereduction.homeoffice.gov.uk/dbo001.htm.

Any applications from prospective course providers are only to be submitted when a full tender process is launched.

Duration of approval

Course approval, once given to providers, has a maximum time limit of seven years, but can and will be withdrawn at any time if the Home Office is not satisfied that the terms and conditions of approval are being met. If the provision of the course is not satisfactory, the Home Office will outline in writing the changes that need to be made in order for the course to comply with the terms and conditions. Should improvement not be achieved, suspension or revocation of approval may occur. The Home Office reserves the right to update the course national model in the light of policy/legislative changes.

The Home Office should be notified as soon as possible if a provider is of the view that they may be unable to continue in the provision of courses in their given area. This should be done with as much notice as possible so that replacement provision can be organised if necessary.

A full review of approved courses will be held in two years' time, and is likely to result in some possible changes being made to the national model and terms and conditions. This review will take account of the effectiveness of the courses in driving behaviour change of the recipient of a DBO.

Funding

The Home Office does not support approved courses financially. Course providers will charge a fee for attendance on the course. The fee to be charged will be a matter for the individual providers to decide, but must be within the minimum (£120) and maximum (£250) limits set by the Home Office.

It is important for the cost of a course to be kept at a level that is affordable for the large majority of recipients; if fees are set too high there may be a low uptake. Course providers must notify the courts and the Home Office as to the level of fee they require to be paid by each recipient, including any concessionary rates.

Monitoring

Monitoring of courses will be carried out by the assessment of reports and other documentation received from course providers. The Home Office requires that each course provider notify the Home Office when they receive their first referral, confirming the court from which it was issued.

The Home Office also requires course providers to create a secure database to hold the following information fields in relation to each individual (to the extent applicable):

1. name (including initials);

2. date of birth;

3. unique identification number;

4. gender;

5. date of Drinking Banning Order;

6. date provider first contacted individual;

7. reason for refusal to attend a Drinking Banning Order course;

8. date notice of non-completion sent to applicant;

9. date on which the course began;

10. number of hours attended that involved individual sessions;

11. number of hours attended that involved group sessions;

12. date of completion;

13. date certificate sent to court; and

14. date certificate sent to applicant.

The Home Office requires each provider to submit the information in the list above that is recorded in each 3-month period within 28 days of the end of that 3-month period. This information is to be sent to the Home Office in the form of an Excel spreadsheet, and the Home Office can require any subset of the information to be sent in place of the full quarterly totals.

Course providers are also required to submit the annual totals for the list above at the end of every 12-month period and an annual report that provides a general progress summary evaluating the course(s) provided.

The 3-month and 12-month periods referred to above begin, in respect of each course provider, on the date the approval is granted in respect of that course provider.

In order to ensure that approved courses are being run in accordance with the terms and conditions and published guidance, Home Office officials or persons authorised on its behalf will carry out inspection visits when these are considered appropriate. These visits could be either pre-planned or unannounced. Investigations will also be carried out on receipt of any complaints about particular courses. Course organisers will be expected to co-operate fully with the Home Office or its agents when it carries out these functions.

Personnel

The way in which a course is presented will be vital to its success. Course providers must employ people with relevant teaching or training qualifications and/or experience, such as the Training and Development Lead Body (TDLB) competencies in training, which are the equivalent of National Vocational Qualifications. Tutors may also have TDLB: D32/33 (assessor awards) or D34 (internal verifier) or D36 (APL advisor). We suggest that the tutors/facilitators of the course should have two of the qualifications listed above or a recognised teaching qualification such as a certificate in teaching or training award from the Institute of Training and Development or equivalent. This is a preference and not a requirement, but providers should be satisfied that the qualifications and relevant experience of their facilitators meet those outlined above.

The tutors must have experience of working with offenders or of teaching in an adult environment. These people should be familiar with the latest teaching methods, as well as the available material on the effects of alcohol consumption and alcohol-related disorder. Experience of working with people who have a problem with excessive alcohol consumption is desirable.

Course providers should assess if a recipient of a DBO referred to them has other issues that require addressing such as mental health problems or drug dependency. In these instances, although the recipient should continue to attend the DBO course to which they have been referred by the court, the course provider should direct the individual towards appropriate support available in their area, which will assist in addressing their individual issues.

Freedom of Information implications

The Home Office is committed to meeting its responsibilities under the Freedom of Information Act 2000. Information submitted to a public authority may be subject to disclosure to a third party in response to a request for information under the Act. The Home Office may also decide to include certain information in the publication scheme that it maintains under the Act.

If a course provider considers any of the information held by the Home Office with regard to their organisation to be commercially sensitive and therefore exempt from disclosure under the Act, they should identify it and explain (in broad terms) what harm may result from disclosure if a request is received. Please also note that the receipt by the public authority of any information marked 'confidential' or equivalent should not be taken to mean that the public authority accepts any duty of confidence by virtue of that marking.

Section 6: Approved courses

Introduction

This section sets out the details of the content of approved courses, including which elements are considered to form the essential minimum national model requirements and standards for such courses.

The details are not, however, intended to be exhaustive. The Home Office welcomes different or new material, and courses that adopt different methods of working, provided it is satisfied that the course still meets the minimum national model requirements and objectives of the scheme.

The Home Office would particularly encourage providers to seek some form of accreditation for the course, which would allow participants to gain a qualification.

Participants on a DBO course will be referred by the court; however, the Home Office requires course providers to make provision so that voluntary referrals or participants referred from other areas can also be included on the courses if the course would be appropriate for them. Persons not referred by the courts would not have the opportunity to have the length of their DBO (should they have one) reduced.

Due to the nature of the behaviour for which a DBO is made, a recipient cannot be placed on an alternative course such as a drink drive rehabilitation course. They must attend a DBO-approved course.

Course providers must ensure that provision is made to protect against identity fraud such as another person attending a course in place of a recipient of a DBO.

Course objectives

A statement of the aims of the course should be provided. This should set out clearly and unambiguously the main objectives that the course is designed to achieve. The aims should be relevant to the overall objective, which is to protect people from alcohol-related crime and disorder.

Terms and conditions should be provided to the recipient on the first day of their attendance on a course. This will confirm what is expected of them in terms of behaviour and commitment and will make clear what they need to do to qualify for their completion certificate and so a reduction in their DBO.

Minimum requirements

The course must include the following essential elements:

- a knowledge check on alcohol issues and participants' attitudes towards their drinking habits at the beginning and end of each course;

- the use of the Alcohol Use Disorders Identification Test (AUDIT) to classify the type of drinker;

- information about alcohol and its effects on the body, including the concept of alcohol units, effects of alcohol consumption on different individuals, concepts of tolerance and dependence, alcohol-related disease, sensible drinking etc;

- effects of alcohol consumption on behaviour;

- information about the rates at which the body loses alcohol and the effects of 'topping up';

- the legal alcohol limit for drivers and what it represents;

- police enforcement of alcohol-related crime and disorder;

- the legal consequences of alcohol-related crime and disorder, eg PNDs, arrest for being drunk and disorderly etc;

- effects of alcohol-induced violence/criminality on victims and their families, and personal consequences for the participant such as employment, relationship with friends and relatives, victims and health;

- analysis of the participant's behaviour: what leads up to the offence, establishing patterns of drinking behaviour, examining results;

- alternatives to binge drinking and strategies for avoiding alcohol-related disorder, coping with pressures from peer groups, etc. The course should encourage the examination and discussion of personal drinking habits and promote a constructive change in attitudes towards alcohol consumption and related behaviours; and

- drug taking and its effect on behaviour when combined with alcohol.

Methods

The Home Office requires that at least one one-to-one session should be held with each individual participant at the beginning of the course before any other sessions are attended. This will include the assessment of the type of drinker using the AUDIT test, and the result of the test may then determine if following a one-to-one course or a group course would be more appropriate (if both are offered by the provider). This one-to-one session could also include an assessment of the participant's attitude to their drinking habits.

Some one-to-one sessions have been found to be particularly effective if family members or friends could also be present and the Home Office welcomes this participation where appropriate.

If deemed necessary, further referral should be made to a local GP or other treatment agency if a need is identified. Providers must take into account issues relating to drugs and mental health, and whether the participant requires referral to other experts in relation to these matters. Course providers should have close working relationships with local Drug and Alcohol Action Teams and other alcohol agencies in their areas to ensure that recipients receive all the additional support required. Leaflets and additional information should be available if required by the recipient.

Specific provision needs to be made for the delivery of courses to 16 to 17-year-olds with additional provision made to meet their requirements. It would not be acceptable to include a 16 to 17-year-old in a group course where adults were also present. Facilitators will need to have an enhanced CRB check before being able to deliver courses to this age group.

If interpreters are required for participants, the offer of the participant bringing a family member or friend should be made. Alternatively, a separate course should be considered if numbers requiring the individual language warranted it. Providers would be required to use facilitators or other staff who speak the language fluently. If an individual requires an interpreter an additional fee could be sought from the participant provided that the total amount charged is not more than £250.

Course providers should be fully aware of the requirements of the Disability Discrimination Act 1995 (as amended) that may apply to them so as to avoid discrimination against people with disabilities in the provision of DBO courses.

Course information must be presented using a variety of techniques that should be drawn from the following:

- short talks to convey essential information;

- group discussion – unless just one-to-one sessions are being used;

- self-observation forms/records of behaviour ('drink diaries');

- work sheets/exercises for individuals or group discussions including role-playing;

- audio/visual presentations;

- guest speakers, eg magistrates, police, other emergency services, victims of alcohol-induced offenders;

- information handouts to take away; and

- behaviour analysis, assessing performance and setting objectives.

Course providers/facilitators must closely monitor any talks by guest speakers to ensure that their tone and content are appropriate in every respect to the aims of the course.

Materials

The material, documentation and records developed and used for approved courses will remain the property of the organisers, but must be available to the Home Office if required. The Home Office will reimburse any reasonable costs incurred in reproducing material for its use. The Home Office expects course organisers to respect the confidentiality of course participants in making any public statements about the course.

If a course provider intends to use the Home Office logo in any of the materials they must submit a proof for approval by the Home Office prior to any publication.

Changes in content

Once a course has been approved, minor changes can be made to its organisation, methods and content provided that these still meet the minimum requirements. No major changes should be introduced without the prior approval of the Home Office. If there is any doubt as to the importance of a proposed change in the course, it is advisable to notify the Home Office in advance. Visits will be made from time to time by officials from the Home Office to monitor the operation of courses.

Course arrangements

The Home Office will specify which areas individual course providers have been approved to provide for. Provision should not be made outside these areas unless requested by the Home Office in situations of temporary provision if another provider is no longer able to provide courses.

The Home Office requires between 4 and 15 participants to be registered on each group course that is run unless solely one-to-one sessions are being provided.

The Home Office requires minimum hours of attendance by course participants. For solely one-to-one sessions there should be 6 hours' teaching time, and for group work 16 hours' teaching time, including the initial one-to-one session. However, there is not a limit on the number of sessions that can be provided.

Sessions should be flexible to provide the recipient with a choice of attendance such as morning/afternoon/evening/weekend. The Home Office requires a short reflection time to be available between sessions; therefore sessions should not be held on consecutive days.

Appropriate venues should be used in the delivery of courses. Venues should allow easy access on transport routes and should meet health and safety requirements etc.

The Home Office has set a fee of between £120 and £250, which must be adhered to. A number of payment options should be available for course fees such as cash, cheque, debit cards or credit cards, with instalment payments acceptable. If course providers offer concessions, the concessionary fee must not be below £120.

Course providers are required to provide a certificate of completion or notice of non-completion to each person in respect of whom their course is specified in a DBO. Copies must be provided to the court that made the DBO. Templates are available in Annex B.

On receipt of contact details from the court, the provider must make at least three attempts to contact each recipient of a DBO via two different methods (eg letter and telephone call) to invite them to attend an approved course and to offer at least two available dates.

Course providers are also required to make contact with the courts in their specified area to provide information/training on DBOs and their specific approved course. Providers should provide as much assistance and information as possible, which could include leaflets, holding regular liaison meetings or providing presentations to court representatives and administrative staff on DBOs.

Course providers must provide opportunities for course evaluation and client feedback. Internal quality assurance, including assessment of individual course content and trainers' performance, must also be carried out regularly.

Annex A

Step-by-step approach for applications to the magistrates' court for a Drinking Banning Order

Undertake statutory consultation
Documentary evidence of consultation (not agreement) is required by the court.

↓

Collect evidence
Relevant authorities focus on what is most relevant and necessary to provide evidence for the court to arrive at a clear understanding of the matter.

↓

Draw up prohibitions
The DBO must be drafted in full including its duration and take account of the licensed premises that the individual must be prohibited from entering along with any other necessary prohibitions.

↓

Make application to the magistrates' court
An application for a DBO is by complaint to the magistrates' court using the appropriate form at Annex C.
The complaint must be made within six months from the time when the matter of the complaint (the criminal or disorderly conduct while under the influence of alcohol) arose. A complaint may be made on the basis of one incident if sufficiently serious. Earlier incidents outside the six-month period may be used but it will be for the court to determine the weight to be given to them.
As a matter of good practice the application should primarily be made to the magistrates' court for the area in which the complaint arose or the individual resides.
A summons together with the application should be either given to the defendant in person or sent by post to the last known address.

↓

Applying for an interim DBO

Where there is an urgent need for a relevant authority to protect other persons or their property from an individual's criminal or disorderly conduct while under the influence of alcohol a court can make an interim DBO. Applications are likely to be appropriate where urgent protection is needed from the potential further conduct. Interim DBOs can be made at the outset of an application for a full DBO.

An interim DBO on application can be applied for without notice of proceedings being given to the defendant (ex parte) and can be heard in the absence of the individual. Such an application can only be made with the permission of the court and in the magistrates' court this means that the permission of the proper officer (justices' clerk) has to be given. Permission for such applications may only be given where the court or proper officer (justices' clerk) is satisfied that it is necessary for the application to made without the individual concerned receiving notice, and without it being heard in the individual's presence.

If an interim DBO is granted it should be served personally on the defendant together with the application for the full DBO and a summons giving a date for the defendant to attend court. The interim DBO will not take effect until it has been served on the defendant, who will then be aware of its terms. The interim order shall cease to have effect once the court has decided whether or not to make a full DBO.

The hearing

The lead officer in charge of the case should ensure that all the evidence and witnesses are available at the hearing, including any evidence in support for the court to make an immediate order. The lead officer should also seek to remind the court that they may refer the individual to an approved course and of the requirement under section 2(8) of the VCR Act 2006 to give its reasons in open court if not referring an individual to an approved course.

The defendant(s) should attend but a DBO can be made in their absence.

Immediate post-DBO procedure

Where a DBO is granted it is preferable for a copy of the order to be served on the defendant in person prior to their departure from the court. If it is not possible, personal service should be arranged as soon as possible thereafter. In the case of a juvenile the DBO should also be served on the parent, guardian or appropriate adult. In all cases service should be recorded.

If the original application is made by the local authority then it should ensure that a copy of the DBO is forwarded immediately to the police. Copies of the DBO should also be given to any other relevant agency and Crime and Disorder Reduction Partnership. Licensed premises should also be informed, where it is practical to do so, of those who have been prohibited from entering those premises.

A DBO comes into effect when the subject is made aware of its terms and in most cases this will be from the day it is made while the subject is in court. Alternatively, it will come into effect once served personally on the subject.

Other matters

An application can be made to vary or discharge a DBO. This can be made by the person subject to the DBO or by the relevant authority on whose application the DBO was made. A DBO made by a magistrates' court can be varied or discharged by any other magistrates' court acting for the local justice area in which the subject normally resides. Appeal from the making of a DBO in the magistrates' court is to the Crown Court. Breach of a DBO is a summary offence.

Guidance on Drinking Banning Orders on Application

Annex B

Home Office

Serial Number [   ]

Violent Crime Reduction Act 2006 – Courses for Drinking Banning Orders

Certificate of Completion

This certificate is issued under section 13 of the Violent Crime Reduction Act 2006

Details of Recipient of DBO

	Name	[ ]
Date of Birth [ ]	Address	[ ]
		[ ]
Sex (✓) M [ ] F [ ]		Postcode

Details of Supervising Court

Name of Court	[ ]
Address	[ ]
	[ ]
	Postcode
Case Number	[ ]

Details of Approved Course

Date on which order was made	[ ]
Name of course provider	[ ]
Contact telephone number	[ ]

Certification
The Person named above has successfully completed the approved course

Signed by, or on behalf of, course provider

Date

DBO1

Guidance on Drinking Banning Orders on Application

Home Office

Serial Number [ ]

Violent Crime Reduction Act 2006 – Courses for Drinking Banning Orders

Notice of Non-Completion

This certificate is issued under section 13 of the Violent Crime Reduction Act 2006

Details of Recipient of DBO

Name [ ]

Date of Birth [ ]   Address [ ]

Sex (✓)   M [ ]   F [ ]   Postcode

Details of Supervising Court

Name of Court [ ]

Address [ ]

Postcode

Case Number [ ]

Details of Approved Course

Date on which order was made [ ]

Name of course provider [ ]

Contact telephone number [ ]

DBO2

I am unable to issue a Certificate of Completion for the following reasons (✓)

Participant failed to make due payment of the fees ☐

Participant failed to attend the course as instructed by the course provider ☐

Participant failed to comply with any other reasonable requirements of the course provider ☐

Detailed statement of reasons:

Certification

Signed by, or on behalf of, course provider

Date

If you disagree with the course provider's decision not to issue a Certificate of Completion then you may contest this notice by applying to the court that made the Drinking Banning Order, or the court in the local justice area in which you normally reside, in accordance with section 13(6) of the Violent Crime Reduction Act 2006.

Guidance on Drinking Banning Orders on Application

Annex C

Application form for drinking banning order

Application by complaint for Drinking Banning Order (Violent Crime Reduction Act 2006, s. 3(1))

Magistrates' Court (Code) ....

Date: ....

Defendant: ....

Address: ....

....

....

Applicant Authority: ....

Relevant authorities consulted: ....

And it is alleged

(a)   that the defendant (aged 16 or over) has engaged (after commencement of these Rules) on
        .... [date(s)] at .... [place(s)] in criminal or disorderly conduct
        while under the influence of alcohol; and

(b)   that such an order is necessary to protect other persons (including the protection of their property from
        unlawful loss or damage) from further conduct by him of that kind while he is under the influence of alcohol.

Short description of conduct: ....

....

The complaint of: ....

Name of Applicant Authority: ....

Address of Applicant Authority: ....

....

....

Who [upon oath] states that the defendant was responsible for the conduct of which particulars are given above, in respect of which this complaint is made.

Taken [and sworn] before me

Justice of the Peace

[By order of the clerk of the court]

Application form for interim drinking banning order

Application by complaint for interim drinking banning order (Violent Crime Reduction Act 2006, s.9)

Magistrates' Court (Code) ....

Date: ....

Defendant: ....

Address: ....

....

....

Applicant Authority: ....

Relevant authorities consulted: ....

Reasons for applying for an interim order: ....

....

....

Do you wish this application to be heard:

☐ without notice being given to the defendant

☐ with notice being given to the defendant

If you wish the application to be heard without notice state reasons:

....

....

....

The complaint of: ....

Address of Applicant Authority: ....

....

....

Who [upon oath] states that the information given is correct.

Taken [and sworn] before me

Justice of the Peace

[By order of the clerk of the court]

NOTE: This application must be accompanied by an application for a drinking banning order under the Violent Crime Reduction Act 2006, s.3 (1).

APPENDIX 8

USEFUL CONTACTS

Home Office

www.homeoffice.gov.uk

The Together Actionline

tel: 0870 220 2000

www.respect.gov.uk

Information Commissioner

www.ico.gov.uk

Crime Reduction

www.crimereduction.gov.uk

The Social Landlords Crime and Nuisance Group

Sharon Mackley, SLCNG, c/o Whitefriars South, 42B New Union Street, Coventry CV1 2HN. Telephone: 024 7623 1748. www.slcng.org.uk

INDEX

References are to page numbers.

Acceptable behaviour contracts 1.36–1.41

Agreed paginated bundle 9.1

Anti-social behaviour

  Crime and Disorder Act

    solutions 1.20–1.23

  criminal proceedings 1.18, 1.19

  definition 1.2–1.5

  injunctions 1.14–1.17

  non-legal remedies to combat 1.6

  possession proceedings 1.7–1.12

  solutions, appropriate 1.46

Anti-social Behaviour Act 2003

  main changes 1.48–1.64

Anti-social behaviour order

  advantages 1.42

  applicant, practical considerations

    for 10.62–10.64

  criminal offences as terms 10.6–10.20

  defendant, practical considerations

    for 10.65–10.68

  disadvantages 1.43–1.45

  duration 10.69–10.71

  grounds for challenge 10.65

  Home Office Guidance 1.47

  terms. *See* Terms of order

  variation and discharge 11.22–11.41

Appeal by applicant body

  case stated 12.16

  from county court 12.17, 12.18

  from post-conviction orders 12.19

Appeal by defendant

  appropriate venue 12.11–12.15

  case stated 12.9

  Crown Court 12.6–12.8

  magistrates' court 12.1–12.4

  notice of appeal 12.5

  time-limits 12.5

Appeals from Variation of Orders 12.20

Application for ASBO

  aggregation 3.39–3.47, 3.66

  agreed paginated bundle 9.1

  burden of proof 3.48

  defences 3.57–3.60

  mental health/mental capacity 3.61–3.65

  necessity 3.55, 3.56

Application for ASBO—*continued*

  'not of the same household' 3.36–3.38

  relevant authority 3.4–3.7, 3.66

  standard of proof 3.49–3.54, 3.66

  subject of 3.8–3.24, 3.26–3.35, 3.66

  when 3.3

  where made 3.2

Assessment of needs and

  circumstances 14.2–14.13

Breach of ASBO

  challenging the order 13.5–13.9

  defence of reasonable excuse 13.16–13.18

  principles 13.1–13.4

  proving the order 13.10–13.15

Breach of discontinued term 8.3

Breach of interim order 13.19–13.25

Burden of proof 3.48

CCTV footage 4.29, 4.30, 4.34–4.36

Child curfew schemes 1.32–1.34, 10.47, 10.48, 14.39

Child safety orders 1.35, 14.39

Children in care of local authority *See*

  also Young persons 14.14–14.21

Communication aids 9.36

Consultation

  agencies 2.13–2.15

  Home Office guidance 2.16

  relations with other bodies 2.34–2.39

  statutory requirements 2.3–2.12

Costs

  county court 9.57

  Crown Court 9.58

  enforcement 9.59

  magistrates' court 9.54–9.56

County court

  application 6.1, 6.2, 9.39–9.43

  application to join a non-party 6.9, 6.10

  ASB Act 2003 amendments 6.3–6.5

  costs 9.57

  criminal conviction, orders on 6.16–6.69, 6.71–6.74

  interim orders 6.13, 6.14

  practice and procedure 6.6–6.8

County court—*continued*
service 6.15
variation and discharge of order 11.41
vulnerable witness 9.40–9.43
Criminal conviction, orders on
case-law 6.48–6.69, 6.71, 6.72
discharge 6.36–6.38
fairness guidelines on
post-conviction orders 6.73, 6.74
generally 6.16, 6.17, 6.43–6.47, 9.44
post-conviction orders, breach 6.42
practice and procedure 6.21–6.35
test 6.18–6.20
variation and discharge 6.36–6.38, 6.42
Crown court
costs 9.58
Crown Prosecution Service 2.34
Curfew 1.32–1.34, 10.47, 10.48, 14.39

Data protection 2.21–2.26
Designated Public Place Orders (DPPOs)
applicant 16.3
consultation 16.6–16.8
definition 16.1, 16.2
designated places 16.4, 16.5
enforcement 16.18
extension 16.16, 16.17
notification to the Government 16.15
publicity 16.10–16.12
revocation 16.16, 16.17
signs 16.13, 16.14
Disclosure 4.15–4.27
Drinking Banning Orders (DBOs) 15.1
age-limit 15.3
appeals 15.50
application
county court 15.25–15.28
criminal conviction, on 15.32–15.37
magistrates' court 15.22–15.24
approved courses 15.19–15.21
breach 15.51–15.54
civil or criminal in nature 15.8
completion certificates 15.19–15.21
definition 15.2
discharge 15.38–15.42
duration 15.14–15.18
interim orders 15.43–15.49
procedure 15.29–15.31
purposes 15.4
relevant authority 15.9
'relevant conduct' 15.7
statutory conditions 15.6
terms 15.10–15.13
variation 15.38–15.42

Drinking Banning Orders (DBOs)—*continued*
vulnerable individuals 15.5
Evidence
documentary 4.4–4.14
educational records 4.12
environmental services 4.11
hearsay 3.12, 3.66, 4.43–4.71, 6.30–6.32
Home Office Guidance 4.2, 4.3, 4.71
housing services 4.5, 4.6
police 4.13, 4.14
private, given in 9.31
social services 4.7–4.10
status 9.37
Exclusion zones 10.40, 10.41

Hearing
magistrates' court 9.2–9.38
special measures 9.9–9.38
Hearsay evidence 3.12, 3.66, 4.43–4.71, 6.30–6.32
Hearsay notices 4.47–4.61

Individual support order 11.60–11.68
Information
monitoring and recording 11.20
Information Commissioner 2.26
Information exchange 2.27–2.33
relevant authority 2.27, 2.28
Interim order 3.55, 3.56
application 8.1, 8.2
breach 13.19–13.25
breach of discontinued term 8.3
county court 6.13, 6.14, 8.22
post-conviction ASBOs 8.23
practice 8.18, 8.19
publicity 8.20
without notice 8.4–8.17
Intervention order 11.42–11.50

Lay witness 4.21, 4.22
Local authority
children in the care of 14.14–14.21

Magistrates' court
adjournments, directions on 7.4–7.7
costs 9.54–9.56
court forms 5.1–5.4
first appearances 7.1–7.3
main application 9.2–9.38
reporting restrictions 7.8
service of forms and evidence 5.5–5.8
variation and discharge of
order 11.37–11.39

Necessity 3.55, 3.56
Non-association 10.42, 10.43

Parental compensation orders 1.27–1.31
Parenting orders 1.25, 1.26, 11.51–11.59
Personal data 2.22–2.24
Post-conviction orders
  breach 6.42
  fairness guidelines 6.73, 6.74
  variation and discharge 11.40
Post-order procedure
  individual support orders 11.60–11.68
  intervention orders 11.42–11.50
  monitoring 11.11–11.21
  parenting orders 11.51–11.59
  service 11.1–11.10
Previous convictions 4.17–4.20
Problem-solving groups
  consultation 2.3–2.15
  court officials, meeting with 2.35, 2.36
  Crown Prosecution Service 2.34
  defendant, preventative work
    with 2.37–2.39
  generally 2.1, 2.2
  Home Office recommendations 2.16
  protocols 2.17–2.33
Professional witness 4.23–4.27
Proof
  burden 3.48
  standard 3.49–3.54
Protocols
  data protection and information
    exchange 2.21–2.33
  generally 2.17–2.20
Publicity 7.8, 8.20, 9.45–9.53

Rectification of mistakes 12.21–12.23
Relevant authorities 2.27, 2.28
Relevant persons 3.43
Reporting restrictions 7.8, 8.20, 9.38,
 9.45–9.53
RSLs (Registered Social Landlords) 1.50
  mutual exchange 1.13, 2.33
  relevant authority, as 2.28

Sentencing 13.26, 13.38
  case-law 13.39–13.53
  consecutive or concurrent 13.54, 13.55
  guidance 13.27–13.34
  young persons 14.37, 14.38
  youths 13.35–13.37
Service
  on defendant 11.1–11.5
  on police 11.6–11.10
  on witnesses 11.6–11.10

Service—*continued*
  on young persons 14.22
Sex offender orders 1.24
Social housing tenants 1.13
Special measures
  availability 9.10–9.14
  child witness 9.26, 9.27
  communication aids 9.36
  eligibility 9.15–9.17
  opposing application for 9.19–9.21
  procedure for application 9.18
  reporting restrictions 9.38
  screens 9.28
  status of evidence 9.37
  television link 9.29, 9.30
  wigs and gowns, removal 9.32
Special measures direction 9.22–9.25
Standard of proof 3.49–3.54
Surveillance 4.28–4.42

Television link 9.29, 9.30
Terms of order 10.1–10.5
  Boness case 10.21–10.26
  clothing 10.49, 10.50
  congregating in groups 10.46
  criminal offences, as 10.6–10.31
  curfew 10.47, 10.48
  drunkenness 10.59–10.61
  duration 10.69
  exclusion zones 10.40, 10.41
  general prohibition 10.51
  general prohibition as to anti-social
    behaviour 10.52–10.58
  improper 10.32–10.38
  Lamb case 10.27
  non-association 10.42, 10.43
  non-association clause 10.44, 10.45
  specific terms and considerations 10.39
  Stevens case 10.28–10.30

Variation and discharge of order
  ASBO 11.22–11.41
  intervention order 11.50
  parenting order 11.56
Video recording 4.29–4.33, 9.33, 9.34
Vulnerable witness, county court 9.40–9.43

Wigs and gowns 9.32
Witness
  child 9.26, 9.27
  examination through intermediary 9.35
  lay 4.21, 4.22
  professional 4.23–4.27
  special measures 9.9–9.38
  vulnerable 9.40–9.43

Young persons
assessment of needs and
circumstances   14.2–14.13
children in care of local
authority   14.14–14.21
court   14.25, 14.26
court procedure   14.23, 14.24
nature of review   14.33, 14.34

Young persons—*continued*
review of anti-social behaviour
orders   14.27–14.29
review periods   14.30–14.32
sentencing   14.37
service of summons   14.22
who reviews?   14.35, 14.36